JOURNAL FOR THE STUDY OF THE OLD TESTAMENT
SUPPLEMENT SERIES
152

JSOT Press
Sheffield

Juliet Pannett.
1977.

Understanding Poets and Prophets

Essays in Honour of
George Wishart Anderson

edited by
A. Graeme Auld

Journal for the Study of the Old Testament
Supplement Series 152

Published by JSOT Press
JSOT Press is an imprint of
Sheffield Academic Press Ltd
343 Fulwood Road
Sheffield S10 3BP
England

Typeset by Sheffield Academic Press
and
Printed on acid-free paper in Great Britain
by Biddles Ltd
Guildford

British Library Cataloguing in Publication Data

Understanding Poets and Prophets: Essays
in Honour of George Wishart Anderson.—
(JSOT Supplement Series, ISSN 0309-07887;
No. 152)
    I. Auld, A. Graeme II. Series
    224

    ISBN 1-85075-427-6

Contents

EDITOR'S PREFACE

A proper *Festschrift* in honour of George Anderson is long overdue.
The beginning of his seventieth year was marked with the dedication
to him in 1982 of the first fascicle of Volume 32 of *Vetus
Testamentum*—he had retired in 1975 after twenty-five years on its
editorial board. But, though essays by G. Gerleman, W. McKane and
E.W. Nicholson did accompany those by his journal collaborators,
that was largely an 'in house' affair. However, his retirement from the
Chair of Hebrew and Old Testament Studies in the University of
Edinburgh was not marked in any prominent fashion. And even this
celebration of his eightieth anniversary appears—*ipsius editoris
maxima culpa*—at the wrong end of 1993 for one born on 25th
January 1913. And yet, given my dilatory start to the planning, the
very fact that this volume is published at all within 1993 is witness not
just to the competence of a busy cohort of contributors and the skill of
an active press, but also to the affection and respect in which the
honorand is held by all those involved, which encouraged them to give
high priority in the last year to this collaborative effort.

The *Vetus Testamentum* fascicle in no way makes this volume
superfluous. However, at least its preface and closing select bibliography have rendered unnecessary either a full biographical sketch or a
complete listing of Professor Anderson's published works. He himself
has kindly supplied for this volume (p. 21) a record of his published
works of the last decade or so; and, for the other, suffice it to say that
he did retire in September 1982, that he and Anne continue to live in
Edinburgh at 51 Fountainhall Road, that he is a not-infrequent
attender at senior Hebrew seminars in the University, that he maintains a large correspondence—and, for the rest, his bibliography
speaks for itself.

The range and geographical spread of the essayists in the current
volume deliberately attempt to suggest something of the dedicatee.
The largest single group comes from Edinburgh where he taught for

more than twenty years and has lived for more than thirty. Then, to underscore his origins, there are articles also from Professors of the Hebrew Scriptures in all the three still more ancient universities of his native Scotland. Yet he is equally a European and international figure, and so contributions to his Festschrift link Ireland, via Italy, to Israel; mainland European tongues featured include French and German as well as Swedish, the language of his doctoral studies. And his wider role is sketched in by the presence of essays from a Professor teaching at Vanderbilt in the USA, and from two of Professor Anderson's former Chinese students from Hong Kong.

The honorand was one of the founders of *Vetus Testamentum* in a little pub, De Harmonie in Leiden. Its Editorial Board, past and present, is represented. He has had a close association with the Society for Old Testament Study, and served as Editor of the *Book List*, as President, and as Foreign Secretary. Appropriately, there are contributions from eight other past Presidents of the Society and from the President-elect. Long-standing commitment to closer under-standing between Christians and Jews finds answering echo in the participation of two Israeli colleagues and in the stuff of Robert Davidson's paper. The Edinburgh colleagues whose work is included not only represent each of the five teaching departments of the Faculty of Divinity, but have all shared in an interdisciplinary senior course in Biblical Interpretation in which joint teaching seeks to underscore the need for an open and 'catholic' approach.

'Understanding' and 'Biblical Interpretation' present themselves in many shapes and forms in this volume. All the essayists were given free choice of topic—they were invited so late and therefore so urgently that it could hardly be otherwise—and yet most have chosen topics appropriate to his interests and intersecting with each other. Bertil Albrektson's alphabetic priority gives happy prominence to Scandinavia and the Swedish language. And his subject too, the prob-lem of which text to make the starting-point of a national Bible trans-lation enterprise, is a basic one and close to George Anderson's heart. Translation is featured also by John Emerton, Stephen Lee and John Sawyer; while Hugh Williamson towards the end of the collection returns to text-critical matters. John Gibson offers a preview of his revision of the *Hebrew Syntax* by A.B. Davidson, one of our best-known New College predecessors. Henri Cazelles, John Rogerson and John Sawyer develop the themes of three of the most-respected of the honorand's essays: on Israel's tribal structure (1970), on enemies and evil-doers in the Psalms (1965), and on Isaiah 24–27 and apocalyptic (1963). Rudolf Smend salutes the author of *A Critical Introduction* (1959) with his biographical essay on the doyen of 'introduction'-writers. And *The History and Religion of Israel* (1966) is evoked in the essays by Henri Cazelles, Avraham Malamat, Andrew Mayes and Moshe Weinfeld.

GWA's three favourite 'Old Testament' books, at least the three on which he once admitted a hankering to write commentaries, all have their place in the Festschrift. The beginning of Genesis is handled by both Archie and Stephen Lee, and the Joseph stories at its end by Alberto Soggin. Psalms are treated by Edouard Nielsen and by John Rogerson. And different portions of Isaiah feature in the papers by Williamson, Sawyer and Stephen Lee. Yet I am sure that Exodus (William Johnstone), Judges (Moshe Weinfeld) and Lamentations (Magne Saebø) would all come high up his reserve list of challenging and engaging biblical books—not to speak of Jeremiah. Robert Carroll, Robert Davidson and William McKane all write about Jeremiah 31.31-34 and new covenant/testament. Were they aware how many second-year New College students had written on the same passage for the same Edinburgh Professor—and quite as differently, even if never as well? (Ronald Clements' essay on Jer. 1–25 and the Deuteronomists offers reassurance that Jeremiah is also studied outwith Scotland's universities.) The books of that newer 'testament' are represented by discussions of John's Gospel from David Mealand and Kevin Vanhoozer, and of the *Carmen Christi* in Philippians by Douglas Templeton; and each of these essays also explicitly addresses contemporary issues of interpretation. Topics in the history of interpretation are handled by Peter Hayman (early Jewish), David Wright (Calvin) and James Barr (earlier 20th century). And ethical issues come to the fore in the discussions by Ian McDonald and John Rogerson.

'Understanding Poets.' The phrase is deliberately ambiguous: our attempt to understand their words—the understanding their words disclose. There is a tension between the 'understanding' of our title and the 'interpretation' of our subtitle; and at least two rather different accounts can be given of this tension. One account would be troubled by any claim to 'understand' poetry: all that is possible is to offer 'readings' or 'interpretations' of the poetic text. The other account would say that 'understanding', the insight which the competent reader of a text may achieve, involves recognition of (the claims of) what is being studied; while 'interpreting', the account which that reader may offer (by translating and explaining) to others, implies a measure of distance and even of control—a control possibly vital to survival (Hayman). In these terms, if it is 'understanding' that Paul demonstrates of Jeremiah and in Jeremiah (Carroll), then it is 'interpretation' that the Cairo Wisdom text practises on Qohelet.

A definition of poetry should not too quickly exclude parts of the Gospel of John from its corpus—or the opening of Genesis, and not just because we are reminded that its keynote term *bara'* is found mostly in Hebrew poetry. The most interesting problems encountered in reading poetic texts are not for solving. But pondering them may lead to understanding. Their meaning may be clarified by commentary. And the poetic text may trigger an appropriate poetic response, as in Templeton's elegant Latin Georgic which both evokes Philippians 2 and celebrates the honorand.

By the end of the period of the Hebrew Bible—or just after the end, whenever that end was—some of its readers termed much if not all of the biblical material 'prophetic' *(meaning 'inspired'?)*. *Yet again,* according to 1 Corinthians 12–14, the prophets were people who understood all (sorts of) mysteries and knowledge—yet partially; and who spoke to the community clearly, and not 'in tongues'. Within the Hebrew Biblical books as preserved we find a discrete collection called 'Prophets', with two very different subsections. What meaning of 'prophecy' covers both Joshua–Judges–Samuel–Kings and Isaiah–Jeremiah–Ezekiel–The Twelve? And what definition of 'prophecy' includes all of these books while excluding Chronicles and Daniel—or, more important, Job (Fishbane 1989: 133)?

Auld (e.g. 1983) and Carroll (e.g. 1989) have already provoked vigorous response—both negative (Overholt 1990) and more sympathetic (Barstad 1993)—with their suggestion that many within even the inner circle of the 'Latter Prophets' are already 'interpreted' poets. Would Jeremiah have had to say of these texts too that the false pen of the scribes had made them a lie? What then about 'Understanding Prophets'? Comprehending why they may have been termed 'prophets' is of course a small part of the matter. Learning to interpret the words of these classical poets, coming to an understanding of them, learning to intuit the glimpses of understanding of which these give evidence, is the more important. As Templeton neatly puts it, 'To touch on the Jesus of history and turn to Hebrew song and story on the one hand and the God and the Christ of the poet's experience on the other is to turn not from the real to the imaginary, but to the imagined'.

BIBLIOGRAPHY

Anderson, G.W.
1959   *A Critical Introduction to the Old Testament* (London: Duckworth).
1963   'Isaiah XXIV–XXVII Reconsidered', in G.W. Anderson *et al.* (eds.), *Congress Volume, Bonn 1962* (VTSup, 9; Leiden: Brill): 118-26.
1965   'Enemies and Evildoers in the Book of Psalms', *BJRL* 48: 18-29.
1966   *The History and Religion of Israel* (Oxford: Clarendon Press).
1970   'Israel: Amphictyony; 'AM; KAHAL; 'EDAH', in H.T. Frank and W.L. Reed (eds.), *Translating and Understanding the Old Testament: Essays in Honor of Herbert Gordon May* (Nashville): 135-51.

Auld, A.G.
1983   'Prophets through the Looking Glass: Between Writings and Moses' (with responses by other contributors), *JSOT* 27: 3-44.

Barstad, H.M.
1993   'No Prophets? Recent Developments in Biblical Prophetic Research and Ancient Near Eastern Prophecy', *JSOT* 57: 39-60.

Carroll, R.P.
1989   'Prophecy and Society', in R.E. Clements (ed.), *The World of Ancient Israel: Sociological, Anthropological and Political Perspectives* (Cambridge: Cambridge University Press): 203-25.

Fishbane, M.
1989   'The Notion of a Sacred Text', in *The Garments of Torah: Essays in Biblical Hermeneutics* (Indiana Studies in Biblical Literature; Bloomington: Indiana University Press): 121-33.

Overholt, T.W.
1990   'Prophecy in History: The Social Reality of Intermediation' (with responses by other contributors), *JSOT* 48: 3-54.

ABBREVIATIONS

AB	Anchor Bible
ATD	Das Alte Testament Deutsch
AHw	W. von Soden, *Akkadisches Handwörterbuch*
AJSL	*American Journal of Semitic Languages and Literatures*
ANET	J.B. Pritchard (ed.), *Ancient Near Eastern Texts*
AOS	American Oriental Series
ARM	Archives royales de Mari
AuOr	*Aula Orientalis*
AUSS	*Andrews University Seminary Studies*
BA	*Biblical Archaeologist*
BARev	*Biblical Archaeology Review*
BDB	F. Brown, S.R. Driver and C.A. Briggs, *Hebrew and English Lexicon of the Old Testament*
BHK	R. Kittel (ed.), *Biblia hebraica*
BHS	*Biblia hebraica stuttgartensia*
BJ	Bible de Jérusalem
BJRL	*Bulletin of the John Rylands University Library of Manchester*
BKAT	Biblischer Kommentar: Altes Testament
BN	*Biblische Notizen*
BTB	*Biblical Theology Bulletin*
BWANT	Beiträge zur Wissenschaft vom Alten und Neuen Testament
BZ	*Biblische Zeitschrift*
BZAW	Beihefte zur *ZAW*
BZNW	Beihefte zur *ZNW*
CAD	*The Assyrian Dictionary of the Oriental Institute of the University of Chicago*
CB	*Cultura bíblica*
CBQ	*Catholic Biblical Quarterly*
CBQMS	*Catholic Biblical Quarterly*, Monograph Series
CO	*Calvini Opera* (ed. G. Baum *et al.*; 59 vols.; Brunswick: Schwetschke, 1863–1900) = *Corpus Reformatorum*, vols. XXIX–LXXXVII.
CH	*Church History*
CHB	*Cambridge Hisory of the Bible*
CTJ	*Calvin Theological Journal*

CTS	Calvin Translation Society: translations of Old Testament commentaries in 25 vols. by J. King *et al.* (Edinburgh, 1845–55).
DBSup	*Dictionnaire de la Bible, Supplément*
DTT	*Dansk teologisk tidsskrift*
EB	*Encyclopaedia Britannica* (ed. T.S. Traill; 21 vols.; Edinburgh: A. & C. Black, 8th edn, 1853–60; 11th edn, ed. H. Chisholm; 29 vols.; Cambridge: Cambridge University Press, 1910–11).
EstBíb	*Estudios bíblicos*
ETL	*Ephemerides theologicae lovanienses*
ExpTim	*Expository Times*
FC	*The Fathers of the Church* (Washington: Catholic University of America Press)
GTMMM	*Det gamle testament*, oversatt av S. Michelet, S. Mowinckel og N. Messel, I-V (Oslo, 1929–63).
HKAT	Handkommentar zum Alten Testament
HAL	W. Baumgartner, *Hebräisches und Aramäisches Lexikon zum Alten Testament*, 1967–.
Hen	*Henoch*
HSAO	Heidelberger Studien zum Alten Testament
HTR	*Harvard Theological Review*
HUCA	*Hebrew Union College Annual*
ICC	International Critical Commentary
IEJ	*Israel Exploration Journal*
Int	*Interpretation*
JAOS	*Journal of the American Oriental Society*
JBL	*Journal of Biblical Literature*
JCS	*Journal of Cuneiform Studies*
JNES	*Journal of Near Eastern Studies*
JQR	*Jewish Quarterly Review*
JSNTSup	*Journal for the Study of the New Testament*, Supplement Series
JSOT	*Journal for the Study of the Old Testament*
JSOTSup	*Journal for the Study of the Old Testament*, Supplement Series
JSS	*Journal of Semitic Studies*
JTS	*Journal of Theological Studies*
KAI	H. Donner and W. Röllig, *Kanaanäische und aramäische Inschriften*
KAT	Kommentar zum Alten Testament
KB	L. Koehler and W. Baumgartner, *Lexicon in Veteris Testamenti libros*
KHAT	*Kurzer Hand-Commentar zum Alten Testament*
LCL	Loeb Classical Library
LW	*Lutheran World*
MARI	*Mari: Annales de recherches interdisciplinaires*
NABU	*Nouvelles assyriologiques brèves et utilitaires*

NCB	New Century Bible
NEB	*New English Bible*
NJPSV	New Jewish Publication Society Version
NRSV	New Revised Standard Version
NTS	*New Testament Studies*
OrAnt	*Oriens antiquus*
OBO	Orbis biblicus et orientalis
OS	*Joannis Calvini Opera Selecta* (ed. P. Barth and W. Niesel; 5 vols.; Munich: Chr. Kaiser Verlag, 1926–36).
OTG	Old Testament Guides
OTL	Old Testament Library
PEQ	*Palestine Exploration Quarterly*
RA	*Revue d'assyriologie et d'archéologie orientale*
RAI	*Recontre Assyriologique Internationale*
RB	*Revue biblique*
REB	*Revista Eclesiástica Brasileira*
RGG	*Religion in Geschichte und Gegenwart*
RSV	*Revised Standard Version*
RTP	*Revue de théologie et de philosophie*
RV	*Revised Version*
SBLDS	SBL Dissertation Series
SEÅ	*Svensk exegetisk årsbok*
SEL	*Studo epigrafici e linguistici (sul vicino oriente antico)*
Sem	*Semitica*
SJOT	*Scandinavian Journal of the Old Testament*
ST	*Studia theologica*
TBl	*Theologische Blätter*
TDNT	G. Kittel and G. Friedrich (eds.), *Theological Dictionary of the New Testament*
THAT	*Theologisches Handwörterbuch zum Alten Testament*
ThWAT	G.J. Botterweck and H. Ringgren (eds.), *Theologisches Wörterbuch zum Alten Testament*
TLZ	*Theologischer Literaturzeitung*
TRE	*Theologische Realenzyklopädie*
UF	*Ugarit-Forschungen*
UTS	C.H. Gordon, *Ugaritic Textbook, Supplement*
VT	*Vetus Testamentum*
VTSup	*Vetus Testamentum*, Supplements
WBC	Word Biblical Commentary
WKG	Die Weisheitsschrift aus der Kairoer Geniza
WMANT	Wissenschaftliche Monographien zum Alten und Neuen Testament
WO	*Die Welt des Orients*
WZ	*Wissenschaftliche Zeitschrift der Karl-Marx-Universität, Leipzig*

ZAW	*Zeitschrift für die alttestamentliche Wissenschaft*
ZDMG	*Zeitschrift der deutschen morganländischen Gesellschaft*
ZDPV	*Zeitschrift des deutschen Palästina-Vereins*
ZTK	*Zeitschrift für Theologie und Kirche*

LIST OF CONTRIBUTORS

Bertil Albrektson is Professor and Member of the Swedish Bible Commission, Uppsala.

Graeme Auld is Senior Lecturer in Hebrew and Old Testament Studies and Dean of the Faculty of Divinity in the University of Edinburgh.

James Barr is Professor of Hebrew Bible in Vanderbilt University and Regius Professor of Hebrew, Emeritus, in the University of Oxford.

Robert Carroll is Professor in Biblical Studies (Hebrew Bible) and currently Dean of the Faculty of Divinity in the University of Glasgow.

Henri Cazelles is Professeur honoraire à l'Institut Catholique, Paris.

Ronald Clements is Professor Emeritus of Old Testament Studies, King's College, University of London.

Robert Davidson is Emeritus Professor of Old Testament Language and Literature in the University of Glasgow.

John Emerton is Regius Professor of Hebrew in the University of Cambridge and Fellow of St John's College.

John Gibson is Professor of Hebrew and Old Testament Studies in the University of Edinburgh.

Peter Hayman is Senior Lecturer and Head of the Department of Hebrew and Old Testament Studies in the University of Edinburgh.

William Johnstone is Professor of Hebrew and Semitic languages in the University of Aberdeen.

Archie Lee is Head of the Department of Religion and Senior Lecturer in Religious Studies, the Chinese University of Hong Kong.

Stephen Lee is taking up a Lectureship in Hebrew and Old Testament Studies at the China Graduate School of Theology, Hong Kong.

Ian McDonald is Reader in Christian Ethics and New Testament Studies in the University of Edinburgh.

William McKane is Professor Emeritus of Hebrew and Oriental Languages in the University of St Andrews.

Avraham Malamat is Professor of Biblical History in the Hebrew University, Jerusalem.

Andrew Mayes is Professor of Hebrew in the University of Dublin and Fellow of Trinity College.

David Mealand is Senior Lecturer in New Testament in the University of Edinburgh.

Edouard Nielsen was formerly Professor of Old Testament in the University of Copenhagen.

John Rogerson is Professor and Head of the Department of Biblical Studies, University of Sheffield.

Magne Saebø is Professor of Old Testament in the Free Faculty of Theology, Oslo.

John Sawyer is Professor of Religious Studies in the University of Newcastle-upon-Tyne.

Rudolf Smend is Professor of Old Testament in the University of Göttingen.

Alberto Soggin is Professor of Hebrew Language and Literature at the University of Rome, La Sapienzà.

Douglas Templeton is Senior Lecturer in New Testament in the University of Edinburgh.

Kevin Vanhoozer is Lecturer in Theology and Religious Studies in the University of Edinburgh.

Moshe Weinfeld is Professor of Bible in the Hebrew University, Jerusalem.

Hugh Williamson is Regius Professor of Hebrew in the University of Oxford and Student of Christ Church.

David Wright is Senior Lecturer in Ecclesiastical History in the University of Edinburgh.

Publications of George Wishart Anderson, 1983–1993

1982   'The Christian Use of the Psalms', in Elizabeth A. Livingstone (ed.), *Studia Evangelica*, VII (Berlin): 5-10.

1983   'Theology and Church: William Robertson Smith', *New College Bulletin* 14: 15-18.

1984   'Recent Commentaries on Exodus', *Epworth Review* 11.2: 99-104.

1985   'Wesley's Ordinations for Scotland', *Journal of the Scottish Branch of the Wesley Historical Society* 16: 3-6.

1986   'Aubrey Rodway Johnson, 1901–1985', *Proceedings of the British Academy* 72: 433-39.

1986   'Ministerial Training: Norman Henry Snaith', *Epworth Review* 13.1: 14-18.

1986   'Recent Ezekiel Studies', *Epworth Review* 13.1: 86-90.

1988   'Recent Books on the Psalms', *Epworth Review* 15.1: 90-95.

1990   'The History and Religion of Israel' (Chinese trans.; Hong Kong).

1991   'Characteristics of Hebrew Poetry', in B.M. Metzger and R.E. Murphy (eds.), *The New Oxford Annotated Bible* (New Revised Standard Version) (New York, revd.): 392-97.

1993   *The Translator's Old Testament. The Book of Psalms: Translation with Notes and Glossary* (in consultation with Dr Paul Ellingworth; Swindon: British and Foreign Bible Society).

GRUNDTEXT OCH URTEXT: OM UNDERLAGET FÖR SVENSKA ÖVERSÄTTNINGAR AV GAMLA TESTAMENTET

B. Albrektson

'En Bibeltolkning, icke gjord efter Urskriften, utan efter andra ofullkomliga Öfversättningar, i en mörk tid, i hast och utan tillbörlig granskning'—så karakteriserar Johan Adam Tingstadius i slutet av 1700-talet (Tingstadius 1794: 3) den svenska reformationsbibeln av år 1541, vars 450-årsminne vi nyss har firat. I jubileets sammanhang var det kanske naturligt att i första hand stanna vid Vasabibelns förtjänster. De är förvisso stora, och de har också fått tillbörlig uppmärksamhet. Samtidigt måste vi ju ge Tingstadius rätt: Gustav Vasas bibel var 'icke gjord efter Urskriften', och frågan om textunderlaget är onekligen en kardinalfråga när det gäller översättningar.

Gamla testamentet (GT) i Gustav Vasas bibel är alltså inte en översättning direkt från ett hebreiskt original utan bygger i första hand på Martin Luthers tyska översättning (se t.ex. Olsson 1968: 358). Johannes Lindblom har visserligen kunnat visa att åtminstone någon av de svenska översättarna har haft kunskaper i hebreiska; det finns drag i 1541 års GT som bäst förklaras som påverkan direkt från originalet (Lindblom 1941: 35). Men det gäller bara enstaka detaljer; i allt väsentligt är GT i Gustav Vasas bibel en dotteröversättning: dess grundtext är inte hebreisk utan tysk.

Det är naturligtvis inte särskilt förvånande att man i 1500-talets Sverige saknade möjligheter att åstadkomma en översättning av GT annat än via tyskan. Det är mera märkligt att det kom att dröja så länge, innan man fick en svensk översättning som verkligen byggde på det hebreiska originalet.

Insikten om behovet fanns där, och det gjordes försök att åtminstone revidera kyrkobibelns text och korrigera den med ledning av originalet. Redan de separatutgåvor av vissa gammaltestamentliga böcker som publicerades under 1500-talets senare del—t.ex. Psaltaren

1560—bär spår av sådana strävanden (Lindblom 1943: 13-22, 26-27).
År 1600 tillsatte Karl IX en kommitté som skulle gå igenom
bibeltexten och korrigera den, dels efter Luthers sista utgåva, men
dels också efter det hebreiska originalet. Arbetet resulterade i de s.k.
Observationes Strengnenses, en serie förslag till ändringar och
rättelser (Lindblom–Pleijel, 1943). Ständerna beslöt också att dessa
ändringar skulle föras in i en planerad nyutgåva. Men när Gustav II
Adolfs bibel trycktes 1618, var inga sådana ändringar införda, fastän
kungen själv liksom sin far ivrade för en ordentlig revision, som
verkligen gick tillbaka till grundtexten. I de riktlinjer för bibelarbetet
som han drog upp i mars 1615 står det att den nya editionen 'i thet
närmerste' skulle göras 'sin original effter ordasättet lijkformigh'
(Olsson 1968: 361).

Trots detta kungliga stöd och trots att kravet på en revision efter
originalet också omfattades av språkkunniga kyrkomän som de båda
Gezelierna och Jesper Svedberg, kunde dessa planer aldrig sättas i
verket. Alla sådana strävanden strandade till sist på det sega
motståndet hos majoriteten av prästerna, som framför allt var rädda
för att en förändrad bibeltext skulle skapa oro ute i församlingarna.
Också Karl XII:s bibel 1703 blev en seger för detta försiktiga
fasthållande vid reformationstidens text—den är som bekant inte
någon revision med ledning av originalet, än mindre någon
nyöversättning, utan i allt väsentligt ett omtryck av den gamla 1500-
talsbibeln. Man hade alla möjliga ursäkter för denna oförbätterliga
konservatism, och i företalet till Karl XII:s bibel tog man betäckning
bakom ett ståtligt citat från Augustinus: 'Uthi ett så beskaffat werck
hafwer ock then påminnelsen sitt rum: *Ipsa mutatio consvetudinis,
etiam quæ utilitate adjuvat, novitate perturbat*'—alltså ungefär: 'Om
det man vant sig vid blir ändrat, så hjälper det inte om det är bra och
nyttigt—det skapar förvirring därför att det är nytt'.

I samma förord står det också att 'et nogare Swenska textens
jämnförande medh original språken skal besparas til något annat
arbete/som efter tidernas omständigheter anbefallas kan'. Och det var
inte förrän mot slutet av 1700-talet som arbetet med en översättning
av GT från den hebreiska grundtexten kom i gång på allvar. Det var
då som Gustav III tillsatte den bibelkommission vars arbete till sist
resulterade i 1917 års översättning, den första svenska kyrkobibel som
har ett GT som är översatt från det hebreiska originalet.

Den kungliga instruktionen, utfärdad i maj 1773, har ett förträffligt avsnitt om textunderlaget (hela dokumentet är avtryckt i Olsson 1968: 371–75). Det heter i den första paragrafen: 'Fördenskull tillhörer det de af Hans Kongl. Maj:t til sådant vigtigt ärende utsedde Språkvittre Mäns första omsorg, at vid hvarje Bok, som företages, för sig stadga Grund-Textens rätta läsning, på det at de... däruti inkomne brister, måge på ricktige och aldeles osvikelige grunder varda utrönte, och en til sin rätta lydelse återstäld Text följas. Uti hvilket afseende ej mindre den uplysning nyttjas kan, som de med Ebræiskan närskylde Språken gifva, än de uti *Waltons* Bibliis Polyglottis införde äldre tolkningar; jämte andra Lärde Mäns, på fullgoda skjäl, i den delen gjorde anmärkningar, men förnämligast den berömde Engelsmannens Doctor *Kennicotts* Collation emellan et stort antal äldsta handskrefne Exemplar af Gamla Testamentet'.

Det kan vara värt att notera att instruktionen talar om Kennicotts variantsamling. Den började publiceras 1776; instruktionen är som sagt daterad tre år tidigare. Det visar att de gustavianska lärde hade livliga kontakter med sina kolleger ute i världen och väl visste vad som försiggick. Den frejdade orientalisten Carl Aurivillius i Uppsala, som var en av de ledande i Gustav III:s bibelkommission, hade t.ex. Kennicotts uppdrag att kollationera några hebreiska handskrifter i Uppsala universitetsbiblioteks samlingar.

Instruktionen, som troligen var författad av biskop Jacob Serenius i Strängnäs, den man som framom andra hade ivrat för tillsättandet av en bibelkommission, röjer som synes en klar insikt om de gamla översättningarnas betydelse för textkritiken. När det talas om 'de uti *Waltons* Bibliis Polyglottis införda äldre tolkningar', syftar det på den s.k. London-polyglotten, som biskop Brian Walton hade gett ut i sex band på 1650-talet. I den finner man förutom den masoretiska texten alla de gamla översättningarna: Septuaginta, Peshitta, Vulgata, Targumen och t.o.m. en arabisk version.

Under kommissionens första tid gjorde man verkligen allvar av instruktionens maning att utnyttja detta textmaterial. Birger Olsson har i sin stora översikt över svenskt bibelöversättningsarbete på goda grunder betecknat de gustavianska lärdes arbete som 'den modernare bibelforskningens förstlingsprodukt i den svenska bibelöversättningens historia' (Olsson 1968: 400). En ny översättning av hela bibeln utarbetades med berömvärd snabbhet och presenterades vid den stora jubelfesten i Uppsala 1793 till 200-årsminnet av Uppsala möte; den blev dock aldrig antagen som kyrkobibel. Det är en ytterst intressant version, inte bara därför att den är den första svenska översättning som utgår från grundtexten, utan också därför att man i den finner många tolkningar som förutsätter att den hebreiska standardtexten har blivit korrigerad med hjälp av de gamla översättningarna (Albrektson 1974: 36-38). Ett enda slumpvis valt exempel, som kanske just genom sin obetydlighet visar hur noggrant man granskade texterna: I Jes. 51.4 har den masoretiska standardtexten singularis, vilket troget återspeglas i kyrkobibeln 1917, 'Akta på mig, du mitt folk; lyssna till mig, du min menighet'. När den gustavianska provöversättningen i stället har 'Gifwer noga akt på mig, I folk, och hörer mig, I folkslag', så följer man en läsart som är representerad i den syriska översättningen och i några enstaka hebreiska handskrifter. Kommissionen har inte redovisat sitt textunderlag, men en av ledamöterna, J.A. Tingstadius—han efterträdde Aurivillius som professor i österländska språk i Uppsala och var sedan biskop i Strängnäs (se om honom Nyberg 1953)—gav 1805 ut en egen provöversättning av Jesaja-boken, och där motiverade han samma emendation med en textkritisk fotnot: 'Jfr. *Cod. Bodl.* och Syriska tolkningen' (Tingstadius 1805: 209).

Det här draget hänger säkert också samman med den internationella orienteringen. I företalet till Tingstadius' psaltarutgåva är det en enda utländsk forskare som nämns vid namn, 'framl. Hr. Just. Råd. och Ridd. J.D. Michaëlis' (Tingstadius 1794: 7). Det var en lärd och stingslig herre i Göttingen (Smend 1989: 13-24), som var känd för att späcka sina föreläsningar med vågade vitsar (till somliga teologistudenters förfäran och andras förtjusning). Men han ägde också mera substantiella meriter: han hade bl.a. gett ut en översättning till tyska av hela GT, och den var baserad på en hebreisk text som var korrigerad med stöd av Septuaginta och andra gamla översättningar. Denna översättning, som kom ut i häften mellan 1769 och 1783, tycks ha varit en av förebilderna för den gustavianska kommissionen. Just när det gäller textkritiken är inställningen mycket likartad. Tingstadius åberopar som sagt denna översättning i ett företal, och det fanns också personliga förbindelser mellan Aurivillius och Michaelis. I universitetsbiblioteket i Uppsala ligger det brev från den tyske filologen till den svenske (UUB: G4b); Michaelis frågar sin kollega till råds om arabiska växtnamn.

Det är mycket som förändras i kommissionens arbete under förra hälften av 1800-talet, men de textkritiska principerna är till att börja med oförändrade. Under 1830- och 1840-talen gav man häftesvis ut större delen av GT i en 'Ny Prof-Öfwersättning'. Stilistiskt är den mycket mera konservativ än den gustavianska (Olsson 1968: 405)— där ser man romantikens inflytande. Men textkritiskt går den i Aurivillius' och Tingstadius' fotspår, och man kan alltså hitta en del tolkningar som förutsätter att den masoretiska texten har rättats med ledning av versiones. Den som satte sin prägel på detta arbete var framför allt Per Sjöbring, även han professor i österländska språk i Uppsala. Men efter Sjöbrings död 1842 var det helt andra textkritiska principer som kom att prägla arbetet. En viktig roll spelade H.G. Lindgren, framstående orientalist, Tierps-prost och titulärprofessor. Han publicerade ganska många egna översättningar av gammaltestamentliga böcker, och i dem var han villig att fortsätta traditionen från Tingstadius och de andra. På åtskilliga ställen har han emenderat den masoretiska texten. Ofta hämtar han stöd av Septuaginta och andra gamla översättningar, någon gång tillåter han sig rentav en konjektur. Men dessa principer följde han bara i sina privata utgåvor; i en kyrkobibel ville han absolut inte se dem tillämpade. Över huvud behövde kyrkan enligt Lindgren inte någon ny översättning—man borde nöja sig med en mycket försiktig revision av den fäderneärvda texten. De textkritiska pärlor han skyltat med i sina nytolkningar skulle inte kastas för kyrkfolket. Det viktigaste är att inte oroa församlingarna—detta huvudargument i tidigare seklers sega motstånd mot en ny bibeltext plockas fram ur rustkammaren, och det är av Lindgren som det får den oförblommerade och ofta citerade formuleringen 'störom icke församlingens frid och den froma enfalldens lugn med våra lärda funderingar!' (Lindgren 1859: 38).

Lindgren var ingalunda ensam om denna inställning: den delades av hans kolleger i kommissionen, lundaprofessorn H.M. Melin och andra. Melin skrev t.ex. 1861: 'Huru en efter egna eller främmande åsigter, för att icke säga hugskott, reconstruerad grundtext skulle kunna hafva giltiga anspråk på större tillförlitlighet, än den gifna texten, är icke lätt att inse, och det dels oriktiga, dels onödiga i dessa textändringar har svårligen kunnat undgå någon bibelforskare' (cit. e. Nyberg 1966: 74).

I jämförelse med de nyanserade textkritiska principerna i den gustavianska instruktionen innebär detta vetenskapligt sett ett steg tillbaka. Men det var dessa riktlinjer som kom att följas, inte bara i provöversättningarna på 1860- och 1870-talen utan också i den version som utarbetades under 1800-talets båda sista decennier, antogs som normalupplaga 1903/4 och med obetydliga förändringar blev gillad och stadfäst av konungen 1917.

I mitten av 1880-talet fick bibelkommissionen nya medlemmar. Nu tillsattes de tre män som kom att bära huvudansvaret för 1917 års kyrkobibel: Esaias Tegnér d.y., professor i österländska språk i Lund, Waldemar Rudin, exegetikprofessor i Uppsala, och John Personne, till att börja med lektor i Stockholm, senare domprost och så småningom biskop i Linköping (Olsson 1968: 452-58). Med dem börjar en helt ny period i den gamla kommissionens historia. Men på en punkt innebar nyrekryteringen inte någon förändring. De principer för textunderlaget som nu kom att prägla översättningen av GT var just de som hade hävdats av Lindgren och andra några decennier tidigare: den masoretiska texten skall följas överallt, och man skall i princip inte ta hänsyn till avvikande läsarter i Septuaginta och de andra 'äldre tolkningar' som instruktionen 1773 anbefallde som hjälpmedel när det gällde att 'stadga Grund-Textens rätta läsning'.

Tyvärr har den tegnérska kommissionen ingenstans gett någon utförlig motivering för sina textkritiska grundsatser. Det enda man kan hitta är några ganska kortfattade uttalanden som slår fast själva huvudregeln och tämligen knapphändigt antyder skälen. Karakteristisk är en deklaration av Rudin, som 1898 inför kyrkomötets behandling av bibelöversättningsfrågan publicerade ett 'Yttrande med anledning af ingångna anmärkningar mot Bibelkommissionens öfversättning af Pentateuken'. Där heter det bl.a.: 'Visserligen har man, på grund af jämförelse med gamla öfversättningar och med hjälp af konjekturer försökt gifva oss en ny förbättrad text. Men dylika försök måste ännu betraktas blott såsom vågade och hafva ännu icke vunnit allmänt erkännande. Förslag till ändringar af enskilda ställen, många ganska sannolika, föreligga visserligen i rikt mått i lärda kommentarer, men komm., ehuru välbekant med dem, har icke vågat tillägna sig dem i en kyrkobibel, emedan den därigenom skulle hafva gifvit sig in på konjekturernas osäkra mark. Komm. har följaktligen, ehuruväl medveten om den masoretiska textens brister, nästan uteslutande hållit sig till denna, och i det stora hela till konsonanttexten. De små textänd-ringar, som framkallats af en alldeles tvingande nödvändighet, särskildt i Hesekiel, utgöra följaktligen ett ringa fåtal' (Rudin 1898: 9-10).

Att den masoretiska texten måste vara utgångspunkten för en översättning av GT bestrider väl ingen. Man kan också till en viss grad förstå den tegnérska kommissionens önskan att från början avgöra sig för en enda textform för att på det sättet slippa att på varje omstritt ställe väga varianterna mot varandra. Tanken att det är lämpligt med en viss textkritisk konservatism i en officiell bibelöversättning förefaller också rimlig. Men huvudprincipen blir trots allt tvivelaktig och deklarationerna om konsekvens blir en smula ihåliga, när den textform man har avgjort sig för faktiskt har brister som gör att det ibland inte *går* att följa den. Har man rättat den masoretiska texten på några ställen, så har man också gett upp principen att *alltid* följa den, och då är man ju, vare sig man vill det eller inte, i det läge som principen skulle rädda en ifrån: att behöva ta ställning i det enskilda fallet. Rudin nämner 'små textändringar, som framkallats av en alldeles tvingande nödvändighet"—vem avgör när en sådan nödvändighet skall anses föreligga? Personne talar på ett ställe litet förklenande om emendationer som 'en vetenskaplig privatmening' (Personne 1908: 2), men varje gång han och hans kolleger i kommissionen har avgjort, om ett besvärligt ställe nödtorftigt kunde tolkas som det stod eller om det hörde till det 'ringa fåtal' fall som krävde textändring, har de naturligtvis följt sin 'vetenskapliga privatmening'.

Den ende som på allvar nagelfor de textkritiska principerna i 1917 års översättning av GT—eller rättare sagt i normalupplagan 1904— var Erik Stave, exegetikprofessor i Uppsala och domprost där. Han publicerade i tidskriften Bibelforskaren en serie artiklar med detaljerade kommentarer och ändringsförslag till enskilda ställen i ordningsföljd med början i 1 Mos. Den första artikeln trycktes 1905, den sista 1907. Tyvärr fullbordade Stave aldrig serien: det sista bibelställe som granskas är 1 Sam. 30.21, och artikeln slutar med ett '(Forts.)', men detta löfte blev aldrig uppfyllt.

Innan Stave går in på enskilda ställen, ger han en ganska utförlig behandling av textkritiska principfrågor. Det är en i många avseenden klargörande kritik. Stave erkänner att den nya översättningen som helhet betraktad innebär ett stort framsteg. Men han har allvarliga invändningar mot valet av textunderlag. Han citerar en principdeklaration av Tegnér i kyrkomötet 1903, där Tegnér medgett att den masoretiska texten 'på flerfaldiga ställen är skadad, och att bemödandena att... bota skadan "i många fall otvifvelaktigt ledt till goda resultat"'. Och så frågar han: '*hvarför* har ändock Bibelkommissionen icke tagit någon hänsyn till dessa resultat på de många åsyftade ställena, utan äfven där följt "den af de judiske lärde sanktionerade massoretiska texten'?" (Stave 1905: 94). Stave vänder sig också mot att Tegnér motiverat detta med att översättningen 'icke är afsedd för mer eller mindre lärda kretsar, utan för folkkyrkan' och frågar 'Hvarför skulle vetenskapens *många otvifvelaktigt goda resultat* icke få komma till folkets kännedom'? (Stave 1905: 96).

Staves detaljerade genomgång av den textkritiska problematiken ställe för ställe innehåller en lång rad förslag till textförbättringar, men han kan också fastställa att kommissionen gång efter annan stillatigande *har* korrigerat den masoretiska texten med stöd av de gamla översättningarna. Det finns t.o.m. exempel på att man föredragit en konjektur av Wellhausen framför den traderade texten. Inte heller har ändringarna inskränkts till ställen där den masoretiska texten är obegriplig.

GT i 1917 års kyrkobibel har många och stora förtjänster, och ju mer jag arbetar med översättningsfrågorna, desto mer måste jag beundra den tegnérska kommissionens exegetiska prestation: som återgivning av den masoretiska textens innebörd fyller översättningen såvitt jag förstår högt ställda krav. Men det är svårt att komma ifrån att Stave hade rätt i sin kritik både av de textkritiska principerna och av deras delvis inkonsekventa tillämpning. Det är en smula överraskande, inte minst med tanke på att samma kommission när det gäller den nytestamentliga textkritiken har fått ett högt betyg: det brukar sägas att man där på ett föredömligt sätt tillämpade forskningens senaste resultat.

Den gamla kommissionens olyckliga låsning till den masoretiska texten i GT är bakgrunden till en passus i direktiven för den bibelkommission som nu arbetar. Där sägs det nämligen uttryckligen att 'den nya översättningen, i motsats till den nu gällande, skall baseras på en text som har fastställts enligt gängse textkritiska regler'. Det betyder att vi försöker göra allvar av de principer som var så väl formulerade redan i Gustav III:s instruktion men som inte tillämpades under den långa kommissionens sista halvsekel—och att vi också försöker dra lärdom av Staves kritik.

Direktivens formulering är ju kortfattad och allmän. Jag tror att det snarast är en fördel: man kan inte genom några utförliga och detaljerade direktiv s.a.s. förprogrammera översättningsarbetet. Det mesta hänger på hur de allmänna principerna tillämpas av forskarna i kommissionen. Alla tänkbara argument och synpunkter måste vägas in; varje enskilt ställe måste behandlas utifrån sina egna förutsättningar. Det hindrar naturligtvis inte att man ändå i stora drag kan ange de riktlinjer som bör gälla för det textkritiska arbetet när man översätter GT.

Huvudregeln måste självfallet vara att den masoretiska texten är grundvalen för översättningen. Den är helt enkelt den enda tillgängliga fullständiga versionen av GT:s hebreiska text och som sådan den givna utgångspunkten. Den är också en i många avseenden god och ofta väl bevarad text. Men den är långtifrån felfri, och framför allt är den av ganska olika kvalitet i olika böcker—Pentateuken är i mycket bättre skick än t.ex. Samuelsböckerna. Förtroendet för den har ju ökat, och den gammaltestamentliga textforskningen har vuxit ifrån det emendationsraseri som grasserade kring sekelskiftet. Men det är illa om reaktionen mot de ometodiska och lättvindiga textändringarna slår över i ett lika ometodiskt och lättvindigt fasthållande vid den masoretiska texten på punkter där andra textvittnen faktiskt erbjuder ursprungligare läsarter. Den semitiska filologins framsteg har möjliggjort en bättre förståelse av åtskilliga dunkla ställen i GT:s text, och det har minskat benägenheten att snabbt tillgripa emendationer, när texten är motspänstig. Men detta har naturligtvis inte alls gjort emendationer överflödiga.

Masoreternas text behöver alltså ibland rättas. Ett talande bevis för detta är att ingen översättning har lyckats följa den helt. Också tolkningar med den uttalade ambitionen att återge den masoretiska texten, t.ex. kyrkobibeln 1917 eller den judiska version som publicerades under 1970-talet i USA, tvingas att korrigera den här och var. Det rimliga måste då vara att utnyttja allt tillgängligt material, d.v.s. andra hebreiska texter än den masoretiska, framför allt naturligtvis Qumranmaterialet, och hela raden av gamla översättningar med Septuaginta i spetsen, i avsikt att återställa en så ursprunglig text som möjligt.

Denna allmänna princip kan kanske behöva preciseras på en punkt. Det är viktigt att undvika en tolkning av huvudregeln som inte sällan praktiseras men som jag tror är oförenlig med sund textkritisk metod. Många hävdar att bibelöversättaren bör hålla sig till den masoretiska texten så länge det är möjligt att avvinna den en begriplig mening; endast när den är oförståelig, har man rätt att ta andra textvittnen till hjälp. Men en klassisk filolog skulle med rätta betrakta det som en orimlig metod att följa en enda handskrift, så länge den inte erbjuder totalt meningslösa läsarter, och ta hänsyn till varianter bara när den bästa handskriften är oöversättlig. Det är ett alldeles elementärt konstaterande att skrivfel inte alltid ger upphov till meningslösa ord. Ofta kan det vara lärorikt att jämföra med vår egen tids misstag av samma typ, alltså tryckfelen.

I en antologi som heter Diktaren i dikten, utgiven som Bokvännens julbok 1954, lyder slutet på den sjätte strofen i Tegnérs Akademisång så här:

> Melanderhjelm beräknar himlafärden
> för månens skiva, för planetens ring,
> när Scheele skådar skapelsen i härden,
> och Bergman drar grundritningen till världen,
> och hävdernas mystär rannsakar Lagerbring.

Men när jag gick i gymnasiet, läste vi en förträfflig antologi som Josua Mjöberg hade gett ut, och där stod det inte att Scheele *skådar* skapelsen i härden utan att han *skedar* skapelsen. Två variantläsarter alltså. Vilken är den rätta? Ja, om Bokvännens julbok vore den masoretiska texten, så skulle vi enligt många inte ha lov att ställa den frågan. Vi borde bara konstatera att det går att få en rimlig mening ur 'skåda'. Får man inte ändra, om det alls är begripligt, måste 'skåda' stå kvar. Men en textkritiker med vetenskapliga anspråk bör i stället väga de båda läsarterna mot varandra. Då säger man sig att den svårare och ovanligare av två varianter förmodligen är ursprunglig. Att någon skulle ha ändrat det ganska vanliga 'skådar' till det utomordentligt sällsynta 'skedar' är inte särskilt troligt. Däremot är den motsatta ändringen mycket sannolik. Vår textkritiska slutsats skulle väl bli att 'skedar' just som *lectio difficilior* bör vara ursprungligt. Och går man till Svenska Akademiens Handlingar, sextonde delen, 1836, s. 245, så står där mycket riktigt 'skedar'. Det hjälper inte att 'skådar' ger mening. Det meningsfulla och begripliga kan visst vara fel, både i ett svenskt poesiurval och i den masoretiska texten.

I Jer. 48.4 står det enligt masoreterna ordagrant 'Moab är krossat, dess små låter höra klagorop'. Det är oneklign fullt förståeligt och även i textens sammanhang meningsfullt. Men den grekiske översättaren har läst צערה 'till Soar' i stället för masoreternas צעיריה 'dess små'. Då blir betydelsen att klagoropen hörs ända till Soar, och argument från kontexten och från ett parallellställe i Jes. 15 talar för att detta är den ursprungliga läsarten. Det är lättare att se den masoretiska texten som en förvanskning av Septuagintas förlaga än tvärtom. Jag tror att detta är ett fall där det är riktigt att följa den grekiska versionen, trots att masoreternas text ger god mening.

Alltså: allt material måste beaktas, alla läsarter vägas, både varianter i Qumran-handskrifter och läsarter som med rimlig säkerhet kan rekonstrueras med hjälp av de gamla översättningarna. Det är inte nog att den masoretiska texten ger mening; om en variant ger bättre mening, eller rättare sagt: om den kan antas företräda en ursprungligare text, bör den läggas till grund för översättningen i stället för masoreternas läsart. Det är ometodiskt att inskränka textkritiken till ställen där den masoretiska texten är svårförståelig eller obegriplig.

Naturligtvis kan det ibland vara svårt att definiera begreppet den ursprungliga texten, den vars återställande är textkritikens mål. Man kan använda uttrycket tämligen entydigt när det gäller ett litterärt verk av en enskild författare (sådana gammaltestamentliga texter finns ju). Men vad betyder det, när vi har att göra med t.ex. profetböcker med lång tillkomsthistoria, profetord som har tillämpats på nya lägen, omformats och kompletterats tills texten—kanske efter århundraden av tydningar och tillägg—fått sin slutgiltiga form?

Problemet är besvärligt men kanske inte alldeles hopplöst. Åtminstone i princip kan man dra en gräns mellan den process som utmynnar i den slutliga litterära produkten och den process som innebär att denna text traderas vidare och skrivs av, mellan det litterärt kreativa stadiet, då texten produceras, och kopieringsstadiet, då texten i princip bara reproduceras. Emanuel Tov vid det hebreiska universitetet i Jerusalem, framstående Septuaginta-specialist, har uttryckt det så här: 'Även om vi antar en mycket komplicerad litterär utveckling, upphör denna process vid en bestämd tidpunkt. Slutpunkt för denna process är ett avslutat litterärt verk, som samtidigt blir utgångspunkt för en ny process: kopiering, vidareförande av texten" (Tov 1991: 355-56). Det är denna punkt som är textkritikens mål; även om det aldrig helt kan uppnås, så är det dit man strävar. Det är texten på detta stadium som vi kallar 'den ursprungliga texten', eller rubrikens 'urtext', den som föreligger, när den litterära tillväxtprocessen är avslutad och avskrivarnas förvanskningar ännu inte har hunnit sätta in.

Det resonemanget tror jag också kan tillämpas på fall där vi har att

göra med olika utgåvor eller recensioner av bibelböcker. Vi vet ju
t.ex. att man i Qumran-samfundet har ägt både den kortare Jeremia-
texten, den som ligger bakom den grekiska versionen, och den längre,
som sedan blev masoreternas standardtext. Nu finns det goda skäl att
betrakta den kortare versionen som äldre, medan den längre texten
tycks utgöra andra utökade upplagan av profetboken. Då är ju Septuagintas kortare version egentligen mera ursprunglig—borde vi inte
översätta den i stället för den hebreiska?
Här måste vi då göra distinktionen mellan den litterära tillväxtprocessen och kopieringsprocessen. Den Jeremia-text som kom att bli
Septuagintas förlaga har så småningom utvidgats och kompletterats,
och denna bearbetning hör fortfarande till dess tillkomsthistoria, den
är det sista ledet i bokens litterära utveckling. Och det är först
slutprodukten av denna utveckling som vi skall översätta. Men det
betyder inte att Septuagintas kortare version blir oanvändbar för
textkritiska syften. Man kan mycket väl tänka sig att en bok i våra
dagar först kommer ut i en väl korrekturläst första upplaga och sedan
i en utvidgad andra upplaga som innehåller många tryckfel. Då kan
man naturligtvis ha hjälp av den första upplagan för att korrigera
tryckfel i den andra utan att göra första upplagans *omfång* till norm.
På samma sätt kan Septuagintas förlaga i Jeremia-boken leverera mera
ursprungliga läsarter utan att vi stryker allt som inte finns med i den
grekiska versionen. Självfallet kan det ibland i praktiken vara ganska
svårt att dra gränsen mellan bearbetares avsiktliga ändringar och
tillägg å ena sidan och avskrivares misstag å den andra, men det
upphäver inte den principiella skillnaden.
   Om begreppet 'urtext' kan vara en smula oklart, så gäller något
liknande om 'grundtext'. Det är ett ord som kan användas med litet
skiftande innebörd beroende på sammanhanget. 'Grundtext' brukar
ofta stå i motsats till 'översättning' och betecknar då den text från
vilken man översätter, översättarens förlaga. I så fall kan man säga att
Luthers tyska version tjänade som grundtext för 1500-talets svenska
översättare. Men det blir litet förvillande, när denna grundtext själv
är en översättning, för 'grundtext' kan ju också syfta på original-
versionen av en text. Använder man ordet så, blir det också
meningsfullt att påstå att Vasabibelns skapare inte gick till grundtexten
utan byggde på en översättning. I allmänhet framgår det nog av
sammanhanget vilket man menar.
   Kanske kunde man då sammanfatta den nuvarande bibelkom-

missionens praxis så att vi utgår från den masoretiska texten, den medeltida judiska standardtexten, men att vår grundtext, d.v.s. den hebreiska text vi översätter, är en korrigerad version av denna standardtext, rättad med hjälp av äldre handskrifter och gamla översättningar, och att vi därmed hoppas komma så nära urtexten som på forskningens nuvarande ståndpunkt är möjligt.

Mycket är naturligtvis provisoriskt och hypotetiskt och kommer att korrigeras av senare forskning. Det bekymrar och irriterar en del människor som kräver att allt som rör bibeln måste vara fast och visst och orubbligt säkert. Men det lönar sig inte att ställa sådana krav, när verkligheten vägrar att rätta sig efter dem. 'All mänsklig ting är bräcklighet' skrev Karlfeldt, och det gäller även sådana mänskliga ting som bibelhandskrifter, inklusive de masoretiska, det gäller textkritiska bedömningar, det gäller inte minst våra försök att tolka dessa gamla och svårtydda texter. Eller om jag en sista gång får citera företalet till 1703 års utgåva av reformationsbibeln: 'The feelachtigheter/som/kan skee/hafwa sigh inträngt/äro prof af menskliga swagheter. Rättsinnade menniskior warda them medh mildt och gunstigt omdöme anseende'.

*

Med ett sådant 'mildt och gunstigt omdöme' har mottagaren av denna festskrift betraktat våra strävanden att åstadkomma en ny svensk bibel, och det är en glädje att med dessa rader få hylla honom på hans högtidsdag. Hans behärskning av det svenska språket är lika beundransvärd som hans kännedom om vår historia och litteratur. Under sin tid i Lund, vår gemensamma Alma Mater, studerade han för Joh. Lindblom, i sin ungdom ledamot av den kommission som gav oss 1917 års kyrkobibel, livet igenom trogen vårdare av Tegnérs, Rudins och Personnes minne. Som Lindbloms lärjunge är George Anderson väl förtrogen också med detta vårt arv, och det är rätt och tillbörligt att den outtröttlige främjaren av förbindelserna mellan brittisk och svensk exegetik här hyllas av en ledamot av den nya bibelkommissionen, vars försök att skapa en översättning för vår tid han följer med eminent sakkunskap och kärleksfullt intresse.

LITTERATUR

Albrektson, B.
1974   'Textunderlag och textkritik', i *Att översätta Gamla testamentet.
            Texter, riktlinjer, kommentarer* (Statens offentliga utredningar 1974:
            33; Stockholm): 18-71.
Lindblom, J.
1941   *Till frågan om förlagorna för 1541 års översättning av Gamla
            testamentet* (LUÅ, NF 1.37.3; Lund).
1943   *Psaltaren 1560* (LUÅ, NF 1.38.6; Lund).
Lindblom, J., och Pleijel, H.
1943   *Observationes Strengnenses. Utgivna med inledning och kommentarer*
            (Samlingar och studier till svenska kyrkans historia, 5; Stockholm).
Lindgren, H.G.
1859   *Kyrkliga uppsatser* (Uppsala).
Nyberg, H.S.
1953   *Johan Adam Tingstadius. Orientalist och biskop* (Stockholm).
1966   *Esaias Tegnér den yngre som språkman och bibelöversättare*
            (Stockholm).
Olsson, B.
1968   'Svenskt bibelöversättningsarbete. En översikt främst med tanke på
            Nya testamentet', i *Nyöversättning av Nya testamentet. Behov och
            principer* (Statens offentliga utredningar 1968: 65; Stockholm): 349-
            500.
Personne, J.
1908   'Bibelkommissionens principer vid 1907 års öfversättning af Nya
            testamentet m.m.', i *Bibelforskaren*, 25: 1-16.
Pleijel, H.
1943   Se Lindblom, J.
Rudin, W.
1898   *Yttrande med anledning af ingångna anmärkningar mot
            Bibelkommissionens öfversättning af Pentateuken* (Stockholm).
Smend, R.
1989   *Deutsche Alttestamentler in drei Jahrhunderten* (Göttingen).
Stave, E.
1905   'Anmärkningar till Bibelkommissionens öfversättning af Gamla
            testamentet enligt Normalupplagan af år 1904', i *Bibelforskaren*, 22:
            89-122.
Tingstadius, J.A.
1794   *Psaltaren. Prof-Öfversättning*. Andra upplagan (Uppsala).
1805   *Profeten Esaia. Proföfversättning* (Uppsala).
Tov, E.
1991   'The Original Shape of the Biblical Text', *Congress Volume: Leuven
            1989* (ed. by J.A. Emerton; VTSup, 43; Leiden): 345-59.

Summary of B. Albrektson, Basic Text and Original Text:
On the Basis of Swedish Translations of the Old Testament

The first part deals with earlier Swedish Translations of the Old Testament. The first complete version was published in 1541 and was based mainly on Luther's German translation. The Royal Instruction for the translation committee set up in 1773 has an excellent paragraph on textual criticism. The Bible published in 1793 was based on the MT, emended with the aid of the ancient versions. It was, however, never authorized. These sound text-critical principles were abandoned during the 19th century. The version of 1917, the first official Swedish Bible based on the Hebrew original, was in all essentials a translation of the uncorrected MT.

The second part discusses the principles of the new translation now in progress, especially the concept of 'original text'. The errors in the MT should be corrected. It is important to realize that the MT may have to be emended in passages where it is intelligible: not all corruptions result in a meaningless text.

WILHELM VISCHER AND ALLEGORY

J. Barr

1. *Introduction*

Among George Anderson's many accomplishments has been his interest in the history of scholarship, and notably of Scottish scholarship in particular—see his study of the Robertson Smith episode (Anderson 1975: ix-xix). It may be appropriate to write in his honour a study of another case, not so famous and dramatic and not so peculiarly Scottish, but certainly one that excited discussion in Scotland.

When I was a student in Edinburgh the name of Wilhelm Vischer was often mentioned; his major book had recently appeared in English, and there was much interest in possible typological or otherwise not-purely-historical kinds of exegesis. Some mentioned his work with enthusiasm, many with deep reserve, and some with revulsion; to these last he was the classic example of how not to do it. And, as I will show, his name still comes up when matters of biblical interpretation are discussed.

It came up most recently as a link in the (seemingly endless) chain of disagreements between the writer and Professor Childs (Barr 1989; Childs 1990). My article argued—rather originally, as I thought—that there is not so complete a gulf of difference between critical scholarship and allegory as is commonly supposed. Part of Childs's reaction was to quote the case of Vischer. He thinks that scholars were dominated by the 'historical-critical method', and that they reacted against Vischer because they felt that his approach threatened this 'method'. Scholars far and wide, he points out, were horrified by his work, which they thought to involve 'a form of traditional allegory'. Norman Porteous is indignantly quoted as saying that Vischer in his book was not 'taking history seriously and *therefore not taking biblical revelation seriously*' (italicized by Childs to mark the outrageousness of this sentiment).[1] Childs wants us to believe that historicism and the historical-critical method governed everything and that theology was a secondary influence in comparison. And certainly one can find, here and there, statements in Vischer's writing that read like anticipations of Childs. Thus in the first paragraph of an early article (Vischer 1932: 22) he wrote that 'Historical-critical investigation, conservative just as much as liberal (*freisinnig*), has abandoned the real canonical claim of the Old Testament'.[2] Anyway, according to this point of view, Vischer was disapproved of because his work was allegory and allegory was contrary to the historical-critical method.

Clearly Childs thought that the reference to Vischer would damage my argument. Here, however, he is mistaken. On the contrary, the mention of his case was appropriate and welcome to me, for it had been much in my own mind throughout the course of my thinking on the matter. I had met Vischer personally, had talked with him, honoured him and was much influenced by him (in what way, I will mention later). I always hoped and intended to write a study of his thought and was pleased when this recent occasion provided the stimulus to do so.

Der Fall Vischer was a remarkable episode in the history of scholarship, and one that deserves to be further discussed while there remain those who experienced it and remember it. Professors put pressure on publishers not to publish an English translation of his main work[3] (in fact only the first volume appeared in English), librarians were told on no account to buy the book; if they did buy it they doubtless concealed it from students, keeping it under the counter as if it were *Lolita* or *Lady Chatterley's Lover*. Few works in these days have such honour paid to them. As Childs says, the book was widely 'rejected'. And yet this is not the end of the story.

For it is not so obvious exactly *why* the book was rejected. What was wrong with it? Why did it disturb people so much more than most other books? It is doubtful whether this has ever been properly explained. Childs's explanation is that the rejection 'rose from the fear

1.   Childs 1990 n. 6. For further remarks on Porteous's judgment, see below, pp. 11, 20-21.

2.   Vischer, 1932: 22-42. Cf. also the passage from the *Christuszeugnis* (1934: 34 = ET [1949]: 28-29), quoted by Rendtorff (1991: 88), which appears to put in question the entire tradition of critical scholarship.

3.   Vischer 1946, 1949. The German was first published in 1934 but the identical 1946 edition is the one generally used.

that historical critical scholarship was somehow being threatened by a form of traditional allegory'. Actually, as I remember it, few scholars went out of their way to analyse their objections or make them precise.[4] People used expressions like 'going too far' and 'much too extreme'. These were lacking in clarity; but even so they suggested that readers did not totally reject the approach, and would have been willing to go some small distance down the same road, but not so far. They wanted, they affirmed, some sort of connection between the Old Testament and Christ. They did not suppose that 'the historical-critical method' in itself provided such a connection, nor had it generally professed to do so. So the general purpose was cautiously agreed. But there was something quite appalling—and it was the *religious* consciousness that so felt—in the way Vischer had gone about it. And certainly, insofar as any more precise explanation was to be found, it was often one connected with allegory: allegory was what Vischer was introducing.

But was he? The one thing I hear from those who knew Vischer in those days, and who were close to him, is: 'he never really thought all those things that he was supposed to have thought'. And this is my own opinion, as I will show.

2. *Appreciation of Vischer*

In spite of the non-acceptance of the *Christuszeugnis*, Vischer remained throughout his life a fully accepted and honoured member of normal Old Testament scholarship.

In 1960 a Festschrift volume *Maqqél shâqédh* was presented to him. One of the striking things in it is the high proportion of the essays written by hard-headed philologists, historians, critical commentators, archaeologists and the like: John Bright, Caquot, Dhorme, Parrot, alongside persons more associated with Old Testament theology, such as Jacob, von Rad, Zimmerli. Moreover, even among the works by theologians, one notices the very limited amount, if anything at all, said about allegory, Christological interpretation and the like. The whole thing tastes like a representative selection of historical and

---

4. By far the best discussion is that of Reventlow 1979. I am in substantial agreement with his point of view, but approach the subject from a somewhat different angle. In addition, I think that a fresh consideration of the subject in English is needed.

philological studies mixed in with some biblical theology, just such as one would have found in a collection intended to honour any historical-critical scholar with theological interests. The only reference to allegory I can find within it comes from Samuel Amsler, a very central scholar, and he takes it as obvious that allegory is an erroneous approach: on pp. 18-19 he argues that there are two opposite errors in interpretation, allegory being one extreme, and historicist interpretation being the corresponding error at the other—and clearly Amsler thinks that this will be acceptable to Vischer.[5]

John Bright—not known as an allegorizer—begins his essay with greetings of esteem from himself and from his colleagues at Union Theological Seminary, Richmond, and thanks Vischer for his work on the Immanuel prophecy in Isaiah, which he has found to be of interest and profit—all of which suggests that the 'rejection' of Vischer's ideas was not so complete after all. Bright then goes on to write for him a paper on the date of Sennacherib's campaigns in Palestine, about as non-allegorical a subject as one can imagine. He shows (p. 30) that 2 Kings telescopes the reports of two distinct campaigns of the Assyrian monarch, and that Isaiah had no change of attitude during the crisis of 701 BC. No more 'historical-critical' approach can be thought of. Yet Bright obviously thought that this would be a welcome contribution and one agreeable to the spirit of Vischer's general approach to things. And rightly so, as we shall see. For so it goes on in the rest of the volume. Writer after writer, all admirers of Vischer and all confident that they are composing stuff that will please him and compliment him, produce historical, archaeological, philological, critical materials; not one of them seems to wish to overturn the tradition of biblical criticism and bring us into a Christological, allegorical world.

3. *Vischer against Allegory*

That is one side: what about the other, Vischer's own expressions of his purpose? Most striking of all aspects is his own complete lack of sympathy for allegory. Did he ever say a word in its favour? I have not seen any. On the contrary, he constantly repudiated it. In 1927 he

---

5.   Similarly, in the chapter on allegory and related matters of Amsler's general work on hermeneutics (1960: 164-77), he makes no mention of Vischer, although the latter is mentioned elsewhere in the volume and his works are fully listed in the bibliography.

wrote that 'Allegory makes one blind to the scandal, but does not overcome it, and therefore as a method it is to be rejected'.[6] Later in life he still rejected it. Reventlow thinks that allegory entered his work through the influence of early Barthian Christology around 1927–1931 but rightly adds the qualification that Vischer apparently never regarded his procedure in the *Christuszeugnis* as allegorical.[7]

I would go farther and say that, though it *looked* like allegory, Vischer had a rational case for denying that it was allegory. Throughout the many pages of his work I find no word of appreciation for the allegorical tradition: none for Philo, none for Origen, few if any for medieval allegory. Quite explicitly he denies the use of any 'pneumatic' method of exegesis.[8] He quotes extensively from Luther—well-known as an anti-allegorist, as my earlier article illustrated—somewhat from Calvin, often also from Hamann, sometimes from Kierkegaard; seldom or never from Philo or Origen, or from patristic sources of any kind. Vischer was, in the spirit of the Reformation, determinedly hostile to allegory. He did not belong—according to his own conception—to the allegorical tradition at all; like the Reformers, he thought of it as one of the sources of Roman Catholic corruptions of the truth, and therefore to be avoided like the plague. If the keynote of his book is 'Christological' interpretation—his own phrase—this is probably to be understood as in deliberate opposition to allegorical interpretation.

Allegory, one senses, would display relations of all kinds between the Old Testament and the entire system of Catholic truth and ritual. For example, it would be an easy and obvious piece of allegory to see the triple relation of high priest/priest/Levite as a similitude of the relation bishop/priest/deacon.[9] Leviticus doubtless makes this clear. But does Vischer thus interpret that book? Not a word of it. The term 'Christology' is used to imply relations exclusively between the text and Christ himself. Thus the keynote is *Protestantism*, and the reassertion of the Reformation is the dominant theme. In his famous

6.   *Zwischen den Zeiten* (1927), 387; cf. Reventlow 1979: 115 and note.
7.   Reventlow 1979: 116 and 115 n. On the relation to Barthian Christology, see further below, p. 52.
8.   Vischer 1946: I, 36. 'Pneumatic' was a term then in vogue for a possible 'spiritual' approach based upon faith perceptions and differing from critical exposition.
9.   Cf. the similar point made by H. Bornkamm, below, p. 55.

exposition of the judgment of Solomon, as displayed on the South façade of Strasbourg Cathedral, he emphasizes—contrary to the main allegorical tradition, which he describes—that it was not the 'legendary' death and rising of Mary, but the death and rising of her son, that was the primary event. 'It was not faith in Mary, but faith in the crucified and risen Christ of Israel, that distinguishes the church as the true Israel from the synagogue'.[10] Only one deeply concerned for the distinctively Protestant ideas—as distinct from the general allegorical tradition—could have thought it worthwhile to make this point with such emphasis.

The interpretation of the Solomonic judgment certainly *looks* very like allegory, more so than any other of Vischer's expositions. Yet, in consistency with his own principles and with his procedure elsewhere, it should be understood otherwise. Surely Vischer did not mean that there was a merely ordinary, historical tale of two women and a child, to which by allegory a further meaning of Christ, church and synagogue might be attached. He meant that the incident was an actual historical manifestation of the presence of Jesus in Solomon's time. What Vischer meant was that there was, as it were, a Christomorphic substance in the actual life and history of Israel, and this threw up verbal manifestations from time to time; see the further examples below.

In spite, then, of the similarity to allegory that many scholars detected in Vischer's approach, he was clearly opposed to allegorical interpretation. Thus in the essay quaintly entitled 'Everywhere the Scripture is about Christ alone',[11] he writes: 'We must not "apply" anything in the Old Testament by abstracting it from its original relation to the biblical history. Otherwise we would allegorize, that is, we would have it say something other than what it intends to say'.

Allegory, then, says something other than what the text intends to say.[12] Vischer's own interpretation, it is implied, does say what the text intends to say.

10. Vischer 1946: II, p. 297.

11. Anderson 1963: 90-101. The title is quaint because the article is not about that subject. It is in fact a resolute, if unclear, attack on Bultmann's ideas about the Old Testament, and ignores most of Vischer's own Christological approach. I have not been able to discover the original date of Vischer's article, nor whether an original text in German or French exists.

12. So again Vischer 1960: 120: 'Allegory is by definition the interpretation of a text in a sense that is not the proper sense of its words'.

Further confirmation of the literal and historical emphasis of Vischer's thinking is provided if we take into account the parallel of Bonhoeffer. Of the Song of Songs Bonhoeffer wrote,

> I must say I should prefer to read it as an ordinary love-song. That is probably the best 'christological' interpretation.[13]

'Christology' goes with literality, not with allegory. This fits so well with Vischer's approach that my argument seems scarcely to require further demonstration. In 1960 he wrote: 'Le sens qui répond à l'intention du Saint-Esprit est le sens littéral' (Vischer 1960: 121). The furthest he would go was to admit that he depended on 'deep' and metaphorical meanings, but these deep meanings were the actual meanings meant at the time, were historically and philologically observable, and were not a separate layer but were the true and only meanings and in that sense were literal. He may, of course, have slipped into allegory at times, against his own principles, but it was the literality that determined the general course of his exegesis and the reception of it. It was it that gave the special and distinctive flavour to his work.

4. *Vischer's Support for Historical Study*

Anyway, apart from his Christological interpretation, the other side of Vischer was his free and easy openness to the positions established by historical, philological and sociological study.

In this, however, there were apparent contradictions that ran across the texture of his work. I have already quoted an utterance that seemed very much to disparage the value of historical-critical work. This impression, however, is swiftly dissipated when we observe that the same article strongly affirms the necessity of that same study. In it he gave full approval to a statement of Hempel to the effect that 'historical critical work in all its branches does not stand in opposition to the theological comprehension of the Old Testament as a document of revelation, but rather forms the necessary and indispensable

13. See the helpful study of Kuske (1976), translated by my former student S.T. Kimbrough, Jr; quotation from p. 53. The footnote on the same page remarks that Vischer likewise thought that the Song should have its place in the canon 'as an ordinary love song, not allegory'. On Vischer's relation to Bonhoeffer, see pp. 16-17 and notes.

precondition for it'. In the same footnote he advised readers to be mindful of Eissfeldt's warning that the dialectical theologians should not neglect *religionsgeschichtlich* work on the Bible.[14] The approach clearly favours critical study.

The *Christuszeugnis* itself, however, seemed in some ways to go in the other direction. There Vischer sought to interpret the text 'as it stands'. His exposition tended to emphasize the unity of the existing text and to ignore questions of strata and sources; this is one of the aspects sharply criticized by von Rad. Beneath the surface, however, the presence in his mind of the customary critical analysis is often apparent. And not surprisingly, for later he returned to insist on its complete necessity—it is a real task of the exegete to distinguish the authentic message (for example, of Isaiah) from later accretions. One who refused this would be refusing to accept the writings in their concrete actuality. Critical analysis will help us to discover the different elements of a text, to estimate their weight, structure, function and value (1960: 115).

In the *Christuszeugnis*, though source criticism itself is muted, other historical aspects are freely admitted. Vischer cordially welcomed effects of modern research; see, for example, his integration of Alt's ideas about topography and archaeology into his chapter on Joshua.[15] Alt's studies are continually praised by him: his work on the formation of the Israelite state was, we are told, a powerful factor in demonstrating the essentially 'messianic' character of Samuel and Kings (Vischer 1932: 32 and n. 3). The sociological and socio-historical dimension was particularly prized.

> The exegete must diligently pursue every trace of Israelite history outside the biblical tradition and respect every discovery of historical science that can throw light on the Old Testament. It is archaeological and territorial-historical study that is most strongly advancing Old Testament scholarship at the present day [and helping it] to reach a more correct understanding of the historical reality. The exegete must pay attention to this (Vischer 1932: 26-27).

The *Christuszeugnis* is studded with favourable and respectful references to Stade, to Duhm, to Mowinckel. Particularly striking is Vischer's almost unreserved acceptance of the sociological ideas of Max Weber. His entire work provided a friendly, open and

14. Vischer 1960: 24 n. 1.
15. Vischer 1946: II, 23ff.

sympathetic entry into all sorts of ideas of modern research that might perhaps be fitted in (as Vischer thought they could be) with his theological point of view but which in any case were vastly enlightening and suggestive to the reader who had not known them beforehand. Such a reader might, at first sight, find the Christological connections appealing and attractive. They offered a quick and easy solution, and from the beginning it was noted (e.g. by von Rad) that it was the young, the beginners, who were most of all influenced by them. And so indeed it was. But in the end these interpretations led nowhere, and one soon came to filter them out from the interpretative consciousness. By contrast, the entries into historical scholarship which Vischer equally provided offered new vistas to be discovered and explored.

Thus Vischer's work, taken as a whole, never had the damaging effects that timorous people thought it might have. For a person like myself, coming from a rather extreme Barthian starting-point, Vischer actually provided a rather smooth, easy and friendly transition into the work of historical scholarship in the Bible, something that I would never have gained from the average critical 'Introduction'. If a scholar of such Reformational fervour and such Christological emphasis could so warmly recommend all these areas of scholarship, they must be really good!

This was also a major reason for the deep esteem that Vischer continued to enjoy among scholars of a wide variety of backgrounds and positions. If he represented a determined repristination of Reformation theology and interpretation, he also represented the open *polymathy* of the Reformation period, its readiness to consider and bring to bear all knowledge of any kind that might have a bearing upon the understanding of Scripture. There was, to Vischer, no sort of contradiction between the relevance of all this new research and the Protestant/ Christocentric theology that for him represented ultimate truth. Those who contributed to his Festschrift judged his mind well. Paradoxically, if Vischer's works had been more widely read, students might have become more sympathetic to 'historical-critical' scholarship than they in fact became.

There can be no doubt, I submit, that this friendliness to historical and critical scholarship, reiterated as it was both in his earliest writings and in his later work of the 1950s, was Vischer's own personal position. All his writings heavily stress the *humanity* of the

Bible;[16] if there is a question of balance between its divinity and its humanity, his emphasis falls markedly on the latter. 'Anyone who disputes the historical conditionedness and limitedness of the Old Testament', he declared in the same vein, 'has fallen victim to the same error as one who denies the Incarnation of the Word'.[17] If it should be that historical-critical study would discern a wide gap between the narratives as written and the realities of what had happened—and here he looked with equanimity, although not with acceptance, on the possibility that such criticism should have proved that Jesus had never existed at all!—this was only to be welcomed as a 'proof of the historical limitedness (*Gebundenheit*), the humanity, of the Old Testament documents'. He faced without worry the most extreme conceivable claims of historical criticism. Historical knowledge suffered from 'relativity' and would not provide all the final theological answers, but must nevertheless be taken positively and seriously.

The study on the Immanuel prophecy (1955) well exemplifies this. Far from upholding the basic unity of the book of Isaiah, it accepts from the beginning the critical separation of genuine Isaian sayings, the placing of them within the actual time of the prophet, the removal of later accretions, and the quite separate character of Deutero-Isaiah. It builds upon the reconstructed 'royal feast of Zion', which Vischer himself recognized to be a 'hypothesis' (1955: 7). In its starting point and approach it fully agrees with those affirmations of historical method which Vischer made clear as early as 1932 and as late as 1960.

We still have to explain, therefore: granted the friendliness towards historical study that Vischer showed, why did he in the *Christuszeugnis* remain so distant from that one particular historical-critical operation, the separation and dating of sources?

For the *Christuszeugnis* the Reformation was the key. The logic was: if you want a Reformational exposition written by a modern scholar, this is what you get. If you do not like it, then you stand outside the circle of the Reformation. Historical explanations and hypotheses, often fairly speculative, were accepted—the Reformation itself was full of such. For the Reformers, however, Scripture was basically unitary and source criticism of biblical texts scarcely existed. In that context Vischer could not use it either. The *Christuszeugnis* thus tried

16. Reventlow (1979: 113) thinks, doubtless rightly, that this is part of Vischer's inheritance from Hamann.

17. Vischer 1932: 22.

to treat the texts as unities and disliked or concealed source criticism.

The monograph on the Immanuel prophecy begins from the other end, from the author's position as a modern scholar. Historical criticism in the traditional sense is totally accepted from the beginning. In other respects, however, the basic conception is the same: textual details are made to correlate with the actual historical presence of Jesus.

5. Vischer a Historical Literalist?

Where does this take us with the question of literality and allegory? It must, I suggest, lead us to a surprising judgment: that Vischer's approach, far from being an allegorical one, was a literal/historical one. Those who reacted against his work on the grounds that it was 'allegorical' had not thought out very carefully what they were saying. Certainly, there were many features that *looked* like allegory—his reliance on word-associations, on the resonance of names, on situational similarities. It is understandable that people, seeking a simple concept ready to hand, thought of allegory. But further thought might have shown that this identification was a hasty one, and, as has been said, few took the time and trouble to analyse Vischer's thinking thoroughly and at length. Von Rad, who wrote one of the early and powerful counterblasts against Vischer's approach,[18] nowhere in that review called it allegorical; and von Rad was one of the most theologically-minded of biblical scholars of his time, and one who, as his later work was to show, was particularly interested in, and favourable to, a typological interpretation of Scripture. Though the term 'allegory' was indeed used at one point,[19] nowhere did Porteous in his careful and penetrating discussion of Vischer over three pages or more develop this diagnosis, and nowhere at all did he suggest that it was to be feared on the grounds of consequent danger to the 'historical-critical method'.

In particular, Vischer avoids one major characteristic feature of allegory, namely the idea that there are two or more levels of meaning. What critics mistakenly identified as excessive 'allegory' in Vischer would have been more correctly conceptualized as the opposite, namely Christological historical literalism. The priesthood of Melchizedek *is* the priesthood of Jesus. The bread and wine that he

18. Von Rad 1935.
19. Porteous 1951: 339, as quoted by Childs 1990: 9 n. 6.

brought forth indicate the Lord's Supper: that is the actual, intended, meaning. The 'man' who wrestled with Jacob *was* Jesus. There was no lower, literal meaning, to which the Christological understanding was added as a higher. It was Jesus who was historically there. Balaam's prophecy 'aims' in the first place at David, he sees no farther than that, but his words actually fly past to another figure, to Jesus the Messiah himself; this is the actual meaning to which the sayings 'testify'. Solomon's decision about dividing the child in two was not a literal event to which one might then add the allegorical interpretation of the difference between church and synagogue—his decision *was* that same difference. The attitudes of the two women to the disputed child were factually the same attitudes as those of Judaism and Christianity to the destiny of Jesus. As historical interpretation, indeed, such judgments call for a great deal of imagination of a very peculiar kind. To most people they were, in the long run if not immediately, totally unconvincing. They depended in part on the particular tradition that Vischer revered, and in part on the juxtaposition of all sorts of images, word associations and coincidences, in a manner that suggested allegorization and had been shared by it. But though these associations suggested allegory, Vischer used them in a mode that made them appear to be more like historical evidence. He handled them as if they established the literal sense. This better explains why people recoiled from his thinking.[20]

It was this historical literality in Vischer that allowed his strongly Christological interpretations to lie alongside materials based on highly modern historical and archaeological researches. For him they were, in a way, the same thing. His approach to the 'man' who wrestled with Jacob is not very different from the way in which a critical scholar approaches the identification of (say) the 'northern invader' in Jeremiah. The text mentions a personage, who is not explicitly identified. Certain features, however, are indicated. The northern invader is swift, he rides on horses, he is fierce, he speaks a barbarian language, he comes at a particular juncture, the direction at least is known. But who, precisely, is he? We look elsewhere for historical suggestions. Where else have we heard of something like this?

20. It also helps to explain the very serious point made by Rendtorff (1991: 92), that by Vischer's principles, and contrary to his own general opinion, the Christological exegesis in effect *denied* the possibility of a valid *Jewish* understanding of the Hebrew Bible.

Are not these conditions fulfilled by a Scythian invasion, for which there is some historical evidence? Similarly the 'man' wrestles with Jacob; 'wrestling' with God is something that surpasses the limits of all reason. This is evidence of an event of exceptional character. The 'man' says: thou hast fought with God and with man. Of whom is it true that 'with God and with man' refers to a struggle with the same one person? Why does the 'man' not tell his name when Jacob asks it? All these features point clearly to the right answer: he is Jesus Christ, no one else fulfils the conditions. The operation is not allegorical, but belongs to the naive realistic historicism of the Reformation.[21]

Vischer was not satisfied by any suggestion that Christological connections were a matter of faith; on the contrary, they work by normal processes of human examination of a text.[22] If Jesus was really hidden there in the letters of the Hebrew Bible, then an honest philological exegesis ought somehow to strike upon it (Vischer 1932: 40).[23] Here he comes close to claiming that his Christological interpretation *is* historical-critical exegesis. What Bornkamm says about Luther, that he, unlike the exegesis of the earlier church, refuses to look for types of Christ and of New Testament events in sacrifices, rites and persons of the Old Testament, and that he seeks 'real history... that is, universal Christ-history, in the Old Testament', seems to me to be exactly true of Vischer.[24] Vischer, after all, does not do much more to substantiate his exegesis than to quote Luther and Calvin. Moreover, though Vischer is doubtless more Calvinistic in his own outlook, this

21. For another example, cf. my article on Luther and biblical chronology (Barr 1990).

22. He only apparently contradicts this when he affirms (Vischer 1960: 117) that 'only faith can respond to the question of truth'. He there means questions such as whether it is really God who speaks to humanity through the Bible, or only human beings who were speaking about God.

23. Cf. for instance his treatment of the term *'ālmâ* at Isa. 7.14 (Vischer 1955: 49-50). He seems to treat this as simply a matter of normal Hebrew lexicography (in which, as it happened, Luther had been absolutely right!).

24. Bornkamm 1948: 211-19 (ET 1969: 249-58), also 76ff. (ET 89ff.). Bornkamm, incidentally, was acquainted with Vischer's approach, noted in the preface to his book (iv; ET viii) the frequent appeals made to Luther in the then current debate, and agreed with von Rad's judgment (von Rad 1935: col. 251) that it would be 'a blessing' if Old Testament exegetes would for the time being (*vorläufig*) impose upon themselves the greatest possible restriction in the use of citations from Luther and Calvin, however beautiful they might be.

helps us to see why he quotes Luther considerably more, for Calvin was distinctly more reserved about the historical actuality of Christ in the Old Testament.

Behind this there also stands the older belief, present in the New Testament itself, that the pre-existent incarnate Christ occasionally manifests himself in Old Testament times.[25] If Paul could say that the rock (apparently a mobile rock) that 'accompanied' the Israelites in the desert 'was' Christ, then it is quite easy to see Christ in the 'man' who wrestled with Jacob. Jesus Christ was a permanently existing historical figure, and actual historical manifestations of him appear from time to time. Thus Ussher, similarly on Calvinistic ground, noted it as an ordinary, straight, historical fact, to which a date could be given, that 'Jesus himself our Lord' appeared with drawn sword at Jericho, where the text (Joshua 5.13-15) specifies 'a man' with drawn sword claiming to be commander of the army of the Lord.[26] This is exactly the same sort of interpretation.

In the Immanuel prophecy (Vischer 1955: 49-54), straightforward lexical analysis, using especially Prov. 30.19, shows that there is some mystery here: the birth is not a normal one. The child cannot be simply identified, but he is, on purely historical grounds, certainly not a normal person like Hezekiah (p. 52). This does not mean that the child is *identical* with Jesus. Rather, he is a *sign*. Even taken as a sign, however, this means that Jesus is really present but in a hidden or disguised form, as with the 'man' who wrestled with Jacob. 'Jesus is already present in the eighth century. The living presence of the witness Immanuel testifies to the real and factual, even if still concealed, presence of Jesus' (p. 54).

6. *The Theology of History*

It may be more accurate, therefore, to think that the central characteristic of Vischer's thought is not an allegorical method, but a theology of history—something that should not be surprising, since an emphasis on exactly this was normal at the time and spread across large tracts of the biblical theology movement. Like Hamann, whom Vischer quoted so often and on whom he depended so much, he

25. This theme was studied especially by Hanson (1965). See note by F.F. Bruce in *SOTS Book List, 1966*, for an opinion on this work.

26. Barr 1985: 598.

emphasized historical events as the bearers of absolute truth. Hamann disclaimed any knowledge of 'eternal truths' and acknowledged only 'constantly temporal truths'—'facts which, through a confluence of causes and effects, became true at one point of time and in one place, and therefore can be conceived as true only from this point of time and space'.[27] But, Vischer explains, there is only one thing that makes real history, or that makes history real: the human life of Jesus, or indeed, more exactly, his death, for 'only with his death did he become fully historical'.[28] Dealing with real history and dealing with Christ are essentially the same thing. As Reventlow says, we see here the entry of a metaphysically conceived Christology on the model of the early Barth into the historical-theological understanding of the Bible.[29] Through Christ eternity becomes omnipresent in history. 'The history, which takes place in Jesus Christ as *temporal* history, is *eternal* history', and yet, surely as it has become temporal history, is not bound to the irreversible sequence of temporal history.[30] But historicity remains important and central. Thus, if I may suggest a paraphrase of his thought, all history, at least if it was real, had a connection with Christ, but at certain times and places this became more manifest and perceptible. Where highly historical-critical, archaeological or universal-historical insights could be seen to fit in in some way, therefore, they could just be lumped together with cases taken from the New Testament interpretation of prophecy or straight quotations from Luther. They were all really the same thing, in varying degrees of nearness. The whole thing is remarkably close to what is described for Luther by Bornkamm (1948: 216-17).

But a theology of history *of this kind* seemed to contain elements of severe self-contradiction. At places the Old Testament was a work of prophecy, looking forward to Christ. But at others Christ came to be so fully present and actual in the Old Testament that no real movement of preparation remained. Christ seemed to be transformed from the all-important category of temporal event into the opposite, that of an eternal principle—exactly what Vischer himself deplored. At many other places Vischer himself seemed unable to identify any 'witness to

27. Written against Moses Mendelssohn. See O'Flaherty 1979: 156-57.
28. 1934: II, 60.
29. Reventlow 1979: 116.
30. Reventlow 1979: 116-17; citation from *TBl* 1931, col. 7. The utterance is reinforced with a citation from Barth 1927: 239 = 1982: 319-20.

Christ' at all and contented himself with transcribing the Old Testament text; at others again he simply related the history of a period. Yet other large areas of the Old Testament he simply left ignored and uninterpreted.

There lies here a criticism which, in the circumstances of the time, was very naturally neglected. The universal opinion was that Vischer had gone much too far—one did not think of criticizing him for not having gone farther! But that would have been a very serious objection: what was the use of a Christological interpretation that left many pages, perhaps hundreds, of the Old Testament without a reference to Christ? Where the New Testament left a passage uninterpreted—and many, many pages of the Old Testament were thus left uncommented, especially if we proceed 'canonically' and stop short of Barnabas and the allegorists—Vischer often seemed unable to provide anything. 'Everywhere the Scripture is about Christ alone' was left as an empty slogan that Vischer himself could not succeed in filling with content. And it was precisely his non-allegorical approach that caused this failure: any competent allegorist could have interpreted a far larger proportion of the material, as Philo and medieval exegetes had done. It was his insistence on interpretation with reference to Christ—to him the reverse of allegory—that led to this failure.

It seemed then as if he did not have a *method*, but rather a mixture of quite contradictory methods, held together by the fact that they appeared to produce a Reformational Christ. *Theologically* this seemed to be incoherent. Porteous's judgment, 'This is very muddled theology',[31] was by no means an unfair one, even from the viewpoint of those who most respect Vischer's personality and achievement. Surprisingly, Vischer, seen in this way, turns out not to have been a serious *theological* thinker. He *was* muddled. He could put things together in a way that seemed suggestive, but he could not *explain* how or why they belonged together in this way. He was against allegory, but he did not succeed in explaining to people how he was against it. There was an appalling *occasionalism* in his exegesis. If Jesus Christ was 'the man' who wrestled with Jacob, why did this Jesus appear just at this point and why did he, who was so central and important, not appear a few other times and wrestle with a few other of the patriarchs? To such a question no answer was offered, indeed the question was not even asked. The ideas of history involved were in

31. Porteous 1951: 338.

no sense properly thought out. The warm acceptance of modern historical and social research fitted badly with his wavering between emphatic support and strong disparagement of *Quellenscheidung*. Imitations of Luther,[32] apophthegms cited from Hamann, ideas from Barth that Barth himself was soon to revise, religious slogans that might have sounded good in sermons, were compounded together in a blend that was supposed also to comprehend modern historical studies. It is as if he let modern knowledge lie in his mind alongside the revered older sources—the New Testament, Luther, Hamann—without it having any effect on them; the new knowledge was valid and valuable, but it presented no challenge to them, no suggestion that their validity must now be relativized. And, though generally open to historical ideas, Vischer—like many biblical scholars—hardly *thought* as a historian; he would pick up some suggestive hypothesis, but seldom faced all the arguments and possibilities, seldom worked out the full historical picture. Similarly, much of the idea of 'history' in his mind was a component of theology, rather than a consistent historical viewpoint.

And this in turn helps us to understand why people turned away in despair from Vischer's book. Suggestive and often fascinating as it was, it offered no sort of method, no set of criteria, by which these suggestions might be weighed and evaluated or compared with alternative possibilities, no sound explanation of how they had been reached in the first place or of why they should be accepted other than because the reader personally liked them. Often no argumentation was provided other than the mere juxtaposition of material from the New Testament or from Luther. Thus, one may suppose, the professors who spoke so strongly against the influence of the book upon the young probably feared, if we were to re-express their instincts more exactly, not so much allegory as sheer and simple chaos. Real allegory—and allegory had a tradition of reasoned philosophical principle behind it—would have been better.

As I have said, the *Christuszeugnis* certainly did not attack the historical-critical approach and was distinctly friendly towards it. Historical criticism was not an issue, at least not in the intentions of the participants. If it is a 'challenge' to combine the critical approach

---

32. Vischer gives the impression that he did not want to rethink Luther or follow out his ideas in a more modern intellectual setting; rather, he wanted to *be* Luther once again, to be able to say the same things, to repeat his thoughts and attitudes without any development.

with an understanding of Scripture as the Word of God (Childs's final sentence, 1990: 8), Vischer did not find it so: he found no challenge, problem or difficulty in combining them, and this was, of course, exactly the position that many in these early days thought to emerge from Barthianism and to be one of its achievements. But the *way in which* Vischer combined them was incoherent. There was no proper perception of the different modes and degrees in which different evidences might have to be evaluated. Opinions of Luther were treated as if they were direct historical evidence, as if they were equivalent to what the text actually says. If his work did make difficulties for historical criticism, this was not for the reason commonly alleged, namely that it was allegorical; it was rather for the opposite reason, that it was 'historical' in a totally undiscriminating way, the result of which was to make it quasi-historical. But this was little analysed or perceived.

Of course, in the long run, it was clear that the *Christuszeugnis* collided with historical-critical reading, and people saw this. But it does not mean that the approach was wrong simply because it was not historical-critical. Some may have said so, but if so it was a short-circuiting of a more complicated chain of reasoning. Vischer's own claims that his approach was historical, philological and literal made this conflict inevitable. The conflict between his exegesis and the textual reality thus inevitably cast doubt upon the theology of history through which he justified the whole. Critical investigation of that theology cast doubt on its claims to express the basic reality of the Old Testament within Christianity. These doubts provoked more serious criticisms of the detailed exegesis. The whole thing collapsed like a house of cards. But this was never purely and simply because it was not historical-critical; more likely, it failed because of its quasi-historical literality, which neither the text nor the theological assumptions could support.

7. *Opposition to Vischer was Theological*

The major opposition to Vischer was surely theologically motivated. It was theologically that his ideas produced difficulties.

Von Rad, one then already rising to be the leading Old Testament theologian of his generation, in his criticism of Vischer nowhere expresses fear that this new approach will do damage to the historical basis of historical-critical work. His criticisms are theological throughout, as one would expect. Thus he points out that Vischer's approach, by taking the Reformers' exegesis as totally authoritative for interpretation, makes it impossible for Scripture to exercise its function as authoritative critic of interpretations—a very genuine theological criticism. Von Rad does insist on the importance of the historical context of the text, but makes it clear that this emphasis does not arise out of antiquarian motives; rather, it is essential because it is only through its relation to the historical context that the text has a message to speak to later times. In particular, he insists, it is only through seeing how the text *in its own time* responded to older traditions that we may see how it leads towards fulfilment in Christ. All these are fully theological arguments. Still more, Vischer's approach reduced the scandal of the incarnation and operated a docetic Christology—a standard piece of theological polemic used by all parties, including Vischer himself, and, whatever the rights or wrongs of it, certainly a theological argument and not a historical-critical one.

Von Rad's opposition was highly important, for his early review set the tone for the later reception of Vischer in the English-speaking world. It was important not because of historical criticism, but for another very central reason: von Rad himself was already thinking along the lines that were to develop into his typological conception. In other words, although he fully affirmed the need for historical criticism (as Vischer also did), he wanted to go beyond it and produce something different or on a higher level. Precisely for this reason he found it essential to distance himself in a very drastic way from Vischer's approach. And though people accused Vischer of allegory, there is no doubt that he was against it; but von Rad not only used typology, he expressly affirmed and embraced it. And he had a quite well-formed theory to support this. 'Typological thinking', he tells us, 'is an elementary function of all human thought and interpretation'.[33] Von Rad must have thought, and no doubt rightly, that his kind of typology was clearly distinct from Vischer's sort of interpretation.[34]

33. Von Rad 1963: 17.
34. Vischer (1960: 120) rejects both allegory and typology at the same time, though he does not mention von Rad's typology and argues only that the so-called typological method has failed to understand the meaning of the words τύπος and τυπικῶς in the New Testament. He thinks it means the 'spiritualization' of texts which, when taken in their literal sense, are contrary to faith or morals.

And the difference might be this: that typology was truly analogical. There was one situation, and it related analogically to another situation at a later time. Vischer might also have appealed to an analogical principle at times, but in his practice he eliminated it, reducing the analogical element to little or nothing. If Christ was literally and historically there, then the other pole of the analogy disappeared. All this debate lay entirely on the plane of theology, and indeed on that of the relation of the Old Testament to Christ.

Norman Porteous similarly, in his review of Vischer's work, says nothing about the historical-critical method and argues entirely theologically. This is not surprising, for he was, among biblical scholars of high repute, recognized as one of the most theologically conscious and theologically informed of his time. In particular, among English-speaking scholars, he was one of the most in contact with the theological and philosophical currents in Germany out of which the dialectical theology had arisen. He knew Vischer's own sort of language and could express himself in it. Thus, to take the most obvious of the theological objections, Vischer's approach, by so accentuating the actual presence of Jesus Christ within ancient Israel, implied that nothing really new was effected by the Incarnation, by the coming of Christ into the world in the time of Herod and Pontius Pilate. Whether we call it allegory or not, his approach had the likeness to allegory that it turned temporal events into an unchanging eternal system.[35] This was contrary to Vischer's own dearly-held values; it is also what was meant by Porteous's phrase 'not taking history seriously': far from being a plea for the 'historical-critical method', it was a completely theological judgement and one that was shared by most theologians of all shades of opinion, and especially by the then rising currents of biblical theology.[36] Contrary to Childs's remark, which implies that Porteous's judgment was an improperly based one, that judgment used a criterion that Vischer himself would have regarded as proper and indeed decisive. That biblical revelation involved

35. I do not myself think that allegory necessarily has this effect; but it is commonly so believed, or was believed by all parties in the theological discussion of that time.

36. Thus Amsler (1970: 168-69) lists Cullmann, Goppelt, van Ruler, Lys, Eichrodt, Lampe and Woolcombe as representing a consensus that allegory is at fault (and this means *theologically* at fault) for its undervaluation of history, for its *confusion herméneutique du texte et de l'événement.*

'taking history seriously' was totally affirmed by Vischer himself. There was no question about the criterion or about its theological propriety; the question was only whether Vischer had fulfilled the requirements of that criterion. That Porteous was reasoning theologically is made clear also by his own phrasing of his judgment: 'and therefore not taking biblical revelation seriously'. He is talking about *revelation*. Revelation, as understood in the Bible, is of such a character that historical change and sequence is essential to it. Most theologians, indeed almost all, affirmed this. And Vischer agreed with them. Porteous, very correctly, fastened on Vischer's theology of history and pointed to its incoherence. The criticism that he published was entirely a theological criticism, as a moment's reading of it makes plain.

8. *Conclusion*

Thus, to conclude, the fact of the opposition to Wilhelm Vischer does not upset my argument about allegory at all; on the contrary, it enriches it, and indeed continued thought about the Vischer case over many years was a main factor in the development of my own ideas. Opposition to Vischer was as much an opposition to impossible literality as it was an opposition to allegory. At the most one might say: Vischer's way of avoiding allegory had the paradoxical result of producing something deceptively like allegory after all. If scholars sometimes blamed Vischer for producing allegory, that was no more than the result of momentary superficial judgment on their part. The fact of that criticism is no reason for questioning the affinities between critical scholarship and allegorical interpretation that I have discussed.

Vischer represented an openness and acceptance towards historical-critical scholarship that was a strength of the earlier Barthianism but was later, foolishly, thrown away; his interpretation, though often looking like allegory, is really a kind of quasi-historical literalism; his theology of history is filled with confusions over different kinds and levels within history and different methods of demonstration, which he never even attempted to sort out; and, if one is to think positively of allegory in relation to biblical scholarship, it is comforting to remember that Vischer was no allegorist, as he himself very clearly maintained.

BIBLIOGRAPHY

Amsler, S.
1960   *L'Ancien Testament dans l'église* (Neuchâtel: Delachaux & Niestlé).
Amsler, S. *et al.*
1960   *Maqqél Shâqédh* (Wilhelm Vischer Festschrift; Montpellier: Causse,
            Graille & Castelnau).
Anderson, B.W.
1963   *The Old Testament and Christian Faith* (New York: Harper & Row).
Anderson, G.W.
1975   'Two Scottish Semitists', *Congress Volume, Edinburgh 1974* (ed.
            J.A. Emerton et al.; VTSup, 28; Leiden: Brill): 9-19.
Barr, J.
1985   'Why the World was Created in 4004 BC: Archbishop Ussher and
            Biblical Chronology', *BJRL* 67: 575-608.
1989   'The Literal, the Allegorical, and Modern Biblical Scholarship', *JSOT*
            44: 3-17.
1990   'Luther and Biblical Chronology', *BJRL* 72: 51-67.
Barth, K.
1927   *Die Christliche Dogmatik im Entwurf.* I. *Die Lehre vom Worte Gottes:
            Prolegomena zur Christlichen Dogmatik* (Munich: Kaiser).
1982   Re-edition of the above (ed. G. Sauter; Zürich: Theologischer Verlag).
Bornkamm, H.
1948   *Luther und das Alte Testament* (Tübingen: Mohr).
1969   *Luther and the Old Testament* (Philadelphia: Fortress Press).
Bruce, F.F.
1966   Review of *Jesus Christ in the Old Testament*, by A.T. Hanson, in *SOTS
            Book List, 1966* (Leeds: Society for Old Testament Study, 1966).
Childs, B.S.
1990   'Critical Reflections on James Barr's Understanding of the Literal and
            the Allegorical', *JSOT* 46: 3-9.
Hanson, A.T.
1965   *Jesus Christ in the Old Testament* (London: SPCK).
Kuske, M.
1976   *The Old Testament as the Book of Christ: An Appraisal of
            Bonhoeffer's Interpretation* (trans. S.T. Kimbrough, Jr; Philadelphia:
            Westminster).
O'Flaherty, J.C.
1979   *Johann Georg Hamann* (Boston: Twayne).
Porteous, N.W.
1951   'Old Testament Theology', in H.H. Rowley (ed.), *The Old Testament
            and Modern Study* (Oxford: Clarendon): 311-45.
Rad, G. von
1935   Review of *Das Christuszeugnis des Alten Testaments*, by W. Vischer,
            TBl 14: cols. 249-54.

1963   'Typological Interpretation of the Old Testament', in C. Westermann
              (ed.), *Essays on Old Testament Hermeneutics* (Richmond, VA:
              John Knox): 17-39.

Rendtorff, R.
1989   'Christologische Auslegung als "Rettung" des Alten Testaments?
              Wilhelm Vischer und Gerhard von Rad', in R. Albertz (ed.),
              Schöpfung und Befreiung (Festschrift C. Westermann), (also in
              Rendtorff 1991): 81-93.

1991   *Kanon und Theologie* (Neukirchen: Neukirchener Verlag).

Reventlow, H. Graf
1979   'Der Konflikt zwischen Exegese und Dogmatik. Wilhelm Vischers
              Ringen um den "Christus im Alten Testament"', in *Textgemäss*
              (Festschrift Würthwein; ed. Gunneweg and Kaiser; Göttingen:
              Vandenhoeck & Ruprecht): 110-22.

Vischer, W.
1932   'Das Alte Testament und die Geschichte', *Zwischen den Zeiten*, 10:
              22-42.

1934   *Das Christuszeugnis des Alten Testaments* (2 vols.; Munich: Kaiser).

1946   New identical edition of Vischer 1934 (Zollikon: Evangelischer
              Verlag).

1949   *The Witness of the Old Testament to Christ* (London: Lutterworth).

1955   *Die Immanuel-Botschaft im Rahmen des Königlichen Zionsfestes*
              (Theologische Studien, 45; Zürich: Evangelischer Verlag).

1960   'La Méthode de l'Exégèse Biblique', *RTP* 3.10: 109-23.

1963   'Everywhere the Scripture is about Christ Alone', in Anderson 1963:
              90-101.

1985   'Das Christuszeugnis des Propheten Jeremia', *Bethel* 30: 5-61
              (contains bibliography of Vischer's works).

INSCRIBING THE COVENANT:
WRITING AND THE WRITTEN IN JEREMIAH

R.P. Carroll

Clay tablets wail:
These are bad times, the gods are mad,
children misbehave and
everybody wants to write a book.
                          —Miroslav Holub

Writing in the common sense is the dead letter,
it is the carrier of death. It exhausts life.
On the other hand, on the other face of the same
proposition, writing in the metaphoric sense,
natural, divine, and living writing, is venerated;
it is equal in dignity to the origin of value,
to the voice of conscience as divine law, to the
heart, to sentiment, and so forth.
…Death by writing also inaugurates life.
                          —Jacques Derrida

The book is the Book. Still to be read, still to
be written, always already written, always already
paralyzed by reading, the book constitutes the
condition for every possibility of reading and
writing.
                          —Maurice Blanchot

The prophetic collections which we know as Isaiah, Jeremiah and
Ezekiel contain many references to writing and therefore reflect some
of the stages in the transformation of the oral phenomenon that we
call prophecy into the written forms that constitute biblical prophecy.
Jeremiah 36 presents the strongest evidence for this troping of the
prophetic word as written document, but throughout the book of
Jeremiah are to be found a number of allusions to writing. These
allusions in Jeremiah may not be as many nor as dominant as the ones

in Isaiah and Ezekiel, but they are still interestingly diverse and quite fascinating as an entry into the analysis of the book of Jeremiah. In this short paper I want to look at the way writing operates in Jeremiah and to focus in particular on the inscribing of the new covenant in Jer. 31.31-34. The brevity of my remarks indicates neither the importance of the topic of writing in the prophets nor the depth of my regards for George Anderson. I have nonetheless chosen to write on Jeremiah because it is one of my main interest areas and on 31.31-34 because in his brief treatment of Jeremiah George Anderson refers to this pericope as 'the great New Covenant passage' (Anderson 1963: 183). I hope with this paper to supplement the extreme brevity of my own treatment of that well-known passage elsewhere (Carroll 1986: 609-14).

In spite of the enormous emphasis on the spoken word in the book of Jeremiah and the use of many formulaic expressions to indicate Jeremiah's reception and utterance of the divine word, there is also a focus on the transformation of orality into writing in the book that deserves our particular attention. Jeremiah is represented as sending a letter to the deportees in Babylon (29.1, 3-9, 28), though the text does not indicate whether he had written it himself or had had it written for him by somebody else. In 30.2 he is commanded to write all the divine words in a book, but at no point in the subsequent material is there any indication of whether he did write such a book. Commanded to take a scroll and write on it all the divine words of the previous 23 years of preaching (36.2-3), Jeremiah is represented as summoning Baruch (the scribe) to do the writing for him (36.4). After the burning of that scroll Baruch wrote a second scroll for him (36.32). In 51.60 Jeremiah is represented as writing a book himself—without assistance from Baruch—and having the book conveyed to Babylon by Seraiah (Baruch's brother?). Like Baruch's first scroll, which was destroyed by fire (36.23), this scroll was also destroyed—but by water (51.63). The destruction of each scroll may have signified different things, but we should not completely ignore the fact that there is a tendency in the book of Jeremiah for written things to have a precarious existence. As for Baruch's second scroll (36.32), we never hear of it again.

In contrast to the general precariousness of writing in the book of Jeremiah is an image in 17.1 of the permanence of Judah's sin drawn from writing equipment. The nation's sin 'is written with a pen of iron; with a point of diamond it is engraved'. Whatever the precise meaning of the Hebrew words used here (cf. Holladay 1986: 486), the sense of the imagery is that Judah's sin is deep-seated and indelible (cf. McKane 1986: 387; Carroll 1986: 349). This is a very effective figure of permanence taken from the sphere of writing and engraving. The interiority of reference—'engraved on the tablet of their heart'— allows for connections to be made between 17.1 and the images of inscribing processes in 4.4 (the circumcising of the heart) and 31.33 (the divine writing of the torah on the people's heart). This focus on interiority is a very important element in Jeremiah, as is the notion of inscribing the body (metaphoric or otherwise) which is entailed in these allusions to writing on or inscribing the heart (cf. Scarry 1985: 235 on circumcision as the materialization of God in human bodies). There is a considerable amount of material in Jeremiah on body language and interiority (e.g. 4.19; 8.19, 21; 10.19; 20.9; 23.9, 16-17; 30.12-15), but to deal with it here would be to distract us from the central topic of writing and the written in the book of Jeremiah.

Apart from the allusion to Baruch's writing a scroll at Jeremiah's dictation (45.1 referring to 36) and an oblique reference to 'everything written in this book' (25.13, which may allude to 51.60 or to 36), most of the references to writing in Jeremiah have been covered briefly here. The two texts that constitute the core of this paper remain to be considered. Perhaps the most interesting statement about writing that appears in the book of Jeremiah is 8.8. The RSV represents the Hebrew text as follows: 'How can you say, "We are wise and the law of the LORD is with us"? But, behold, the false pen of the scribes has made it into a lie.' Slight variations in translation favoured by various commentators (cf. Holladay 1986: 274; McKane 1986: 185-86) do not materially affect the sense of the verse. To a claim that the wise possess the torah of YHWH and are therefore wise, a speaker (Jeremiah? YHWH?) asserts that on the contrary what they actually possess is a scroll that has been turned into a lie by means of the lying instrument of the scribes.

Argument and debate about the precise meaning of 8.8 are unlikely to produce any degree of agreement among commentators as to what the reference to 'the pen of the scribe'—whether lying (*šeqer* 'false') or otherwise—may signify. Like so much in the book of Jeremiah, the verse is tantalizingly brief and referentially oblique. It may represent an attack on scribal techniques of elaborating the scroll of YHWH's

torah by means of exegesis and commentary or on the scribal practice
of drafting new laws. On the other hand, it should not be ruled out of
the discussion that the simplicity of the charge may well be the point
of the charge. It is the *writtenness* of the divine torah that constitutes
its falseness. I still hold to this viewpoint as expressing best the force
of the attack on the written torah consonant with so much else in the
book that is directed against the falseness of the institutions of the
community (Carroll 1986: 228-30). This interpretation draws its
strength from the point made in 8.9b, 'they have rejected the *word* of
YHWH, and what wisdom is in them'? The prophet as preacher of that
word cannot be gainsaid by a written scroll of YHWH's torah because
the scribal activity in producing such a document—whether as
copying, elaborating, exegesis or writing it in the first place—is what
makes it false. The written word cannot countermand the spoken
word. Prophet is superior to writer. The immediacy of the spoken
word communicated by the living person—who represents the living
God—takes precedence over the scribally constructed scroll. Whether
we should then view the fate of Jeremiah's words when incorporated
into a scroll (36) as a falsification of those words is a matter for
reflection when reading the *book* of Jeremiah. The reader who has a
ready eye and ear for irony may well appreciate this aspect of the
production of the book. At the same time all readers of Jeremiah
should be reminded that the prophet's outburst against writing reflects
an ancient suspicion about writing in favour of the spoken word (cf.
Alexander 1990 for a convenient gathering together of some of the
relevant material on this ancient discussion).

Whatever the defects and problems of inscribing the words of
YHWH, there is one point in the book of Jeremiah where YHWH does
his own writing and, in conjunction with 8.8, it constitutes the core of
this paper. In 31.31-34 there is a further supplement to the 'book of
the restoration of the fortunes' (30.4–31.22) which focuses on a future
new covenant between YHWH and the houses of Israel and Judah. In
the course of contrasting this new covenant with the old covenant
which had been broken by the ancestors, the new covenant is defined
as something that YHWH himself will *write*. 'This is the covenant
which I will make with the house of Israel after those days, says
YHWH: I will put my *torah* within them, and *I will write it* upon their
hearts; and I will be their God, and they shall be my people' (31.33).
Unlike the torah of YHWH written by the scribes (8.8), this torah of

YHWH *written by YHWH himself* will not be false. It is, however, only something that will happen in the future. This inscribing of the covenant will be unlike the original covenant written by Moses—there is in the book of Jeremiah a profoundly anti-Moses strand that suggests an ongoing dialectical intertextual debate between the book and the Pentateuchal/Deuteronomistic presentations of Moses (cf. Alonso Schökel 1981)—a writing that was inscribed on tablets of stone. It will be an interiorized writing on the hearts (i.e. the minds) of the house of Israel. Such interior writing is necessarily metaphoric. As it also tropes the story of Moses at Sinai and the writing (literal) of the torah, the statement in 31.33 is also metonymic.

There are further interesting contrasts and similarities between the written in Jeremiah and the tablets of stone on which Moses wrote YHWH's torah. The original tablets of stone on which were inscribed the torah, testimony, or covenant—what exactly was written on those stones is open to considerable debate in the light of the various accounts to be found in Exodus and Deuteronomy—are represented in Exod. 32.16 as being 'the work of God, and the writing was the writing of God' and in Exod. 31.18 they are represented as being 'written with the finger of God' (also in Deut. 9.10). These inscribed-on-both-sides tablets were broken by Moses when he came down from the mountain and encountered the people dancing before the golden calf (Exod. 32.15-20). They were destroyed, just like Baruch's scroll of Jeremiah's words which king Jehoiakim had burned in his winter quarters' fire (Jer. 36.23). Where Baruch's scroll differs from the tablets of stone of Moses is that it was never written by God in the first place and when it was rewritten it was longer than the original scroll. The general presentation of the story of Moses gives the impression that the two inscribings of the tablets of stone were essentially the same. Given the lack of specific and close detail in the text, it is always possible to argue that the two occasions of writing on the tablets allowed for the opportunity of making changes in the rewriting of the tablets. Between the destruction of the tablets of Moses and the scroll of Baruch there is a commonality of that 'lost and found' phenomenon so characteristic of biblical narrative (cf. Schwartz 1990: 46). Baruch's scroll and the tablets of Moses have in common also the fact that they were both made of material substance: stone (natural) and scroll made from papyrus, leather, skin or wood (cultural production—the precise materiality of the scroll is debated by scholars, but for the purposes of my argument here it hardly matters what the material used was).

The materiality of scroll and tablets of stone provides a striking contrast with YHWH's inscribing of the new covenant on the hearts (minds) of the house of Israel. The people had been able to break the original covenant—the people's breaking (*hēp̄ērû*: *prr 'break, frustrate, violate', v. 32; cf. Jer. 11.10) of the old covenant symbolizes the externality and frangibility of that covenant, of which Moses's breaking of the tablets is but an all too human parable of the covenant's capacity to be broken. In the future envisaged by Jer. 31.31-34 ('the days are coming') YHWH's inscribing of his new covenant will be an interior act on the hearts (minds) of the people and will therefore avoid all external features and fragile materials. Divine writing of this calibre will overcome all the problems of exteriorized materiality and will make good whatever defects may be imagined to have inhered in the original covenant. Such interiority, with its metaphoric-metonymic features, will constitute a newness in the covenant and will effectively overcome all the old problems of the fracturing of the covenant (whether literally as in the breaking of the tablets of stone or metaphorically, symbolically in the breaches of the terms of the covenant). A new covenant written on the heart (mind) cannot be broken because it is in itself a symbol, metaphor, trope or figure of divine action inscribed (indelibly?) internally on the collective (and individual? cf. 31.34) interior of the people. There is nothing external to be broken. The discourse of covenant making and breaking comes to an end with Jer. 31.31-34.

The kind of covenant mooted in 31.31-34 is difficult to categorize. It is not a covenant that can be broken, so it is very different from all the old collective agreements between tribes, clans, groups and the symbol of a national agreement between people and deity. It is much more like the kind of covenant in 33.20, 25—33.14-26 is a further series of supplements added to 32–33, already itself a supplement to the 'book of the restoration of the fortunes'—which is said to exist between YHWH and night and day. In that sense the term 'covenant' (*bᵉrît*) is but a figure of speech, a popular trope to be found in deuteronomistically influenced literature and in post-deuteronomistic terminology. The force of 33.20, 25 is that such a covenant between YHWH and day and night *cannot* be broken and that therefore the divine covenant existing with David, YHWH's servant, and the divine covenant existing with the Levitical priests cannot be broken. These covenants share with the new covenant in being unbreakable and so are very different from the other sense of covenant in the book of Jeremiah. Heavily influenced and edited by deuteronomistic language and ideological values, it is hardly surprising that there should be a considerable discussion of covenant as a frangible entity in Jeremiah. Apart from the allusion to the broken covenant in 31.32, there is a serious focus on such covenants in 11.1-13 where covenant and idolatry are interwoven. Idolatry is one of the most distinctive and serious forms of covenant-*breaking* in deuteronomistically influenced literature in the Hebrew Bible. In 11.1-8 Jeremiah is represented as a preacher of the covenant in the cities of Judah and in the streets of Jerusalem. As a covenant preacher his role model is clearly Moses— 11.1-13 is not part of the anti-Moses strand in the book. But woven into the material making up 11.1-13 is a recognition that not only did the ancestors break the covenant (11.8 does not use the word 'break', but the charge of not obeying is equivalent to it), but the current generation (11.9 'the men of Judah and the inhabitants of Jerusalem') is in revolt against YHWH. This revolt constitutes the breaking of the covenant (v. 10). Thus the narrative is conscious of the performance of Jeremiah in the present as a mirroring of the past (vv. 8, 10), just as elsewhere in the book of Jeremiah the destruction of Jerusalem is seen as something that happened in the past (e.g. 'as at this day' in 25.18; cf. 44.23 for the same phrase, even though the prolix deuteronomistic sermon there only focuses on idolatry and not on covenant-breaking).

The book of Jeremiah contains one of the finest midrashes on the theme of the broken covenant to be found in the Hebrew Bible in its account of the covenant made between king Zedekiah and all the people in Jerusalem (34.8-22). The narrative does not use the language of 'breaking the covenant', but works with its equivalent when it describes the breach of that specific covenant in terms of the abrogation (*hāʿōbrîm*) and non-maintenance (*loʾ-hēqîmû*) of the covenant. What makes the narrative a midrash is its relation to the regulations of the covenant governing the period of servitude for bond- or debtor-slaves (cf. Exod. 21.1-11; Deut. 15.1-11, 12-18). It is commentary on the torah by means of midrash. It also allows the book of Jeremiah to offer yet one more explanation for and justification of the destruction of Jerusalem. In other words, it is a midrash on covenant-breaking specific to the book of Jeremiah because it deals with king Zedekiah, a king particularly associated with Jeremiah (cf. 31.1-10; 24.8-10; 27–28; 32.1-15; 37–39). It gives a concrete example of covenant-breaking, rather than using the more generalized deuteronomistic discourse about breaking covenants characteristic of 11.1-13.

In strong contrast to those covenants which can be broken is the covenant described as 'new' in 31.31-34 and also the 'everlasting covenant' of 32.37-41. These uses of the word 'covenant' reflect a notion of covenant as something that cannot be broken. It is therefore a very different kind of covenant from the traditional deuteronomistic regulative principle for describing relations between YHWH and the people in the past. If permanent, non-frangible relations may be described by the same word 'covenant', relations such as those between night and day (33.20, 25), then the term 'covenant' must be given a very wide-ranging set of connotations in order to include the very different uses of the word throughout the Hebrew Bible. Covenant as a word for describing agreements that can all too readily be broken or disregarded and covenant as a term for unbreakable relationships indicate not only a site of contested meanings but also a rather unhelpful use of language. It seems to me that the word 'covenant' has become overloaded with signification and that it cannot perform its tasks adequately in the Bible because it lacks serious differentiation when used to describe the frangible and also the unbreakable.

I make these observations in order to underline the difficulty of categorizing the use of 'covenant' in the phrase 'new covenant' in 31.31. It clearly owes something to deuteronomistic usage, otherwise it could not usefully contrast the 'new' with the 'old' covenant (31.32-33). But it is either a post-deuteronomistic usage, in which the word 'covenant' is all that the two groups have in common, or an anti-deuteronomistic troping of the common word, which maintains that in spite of the broken covenant(s) of the past there were still covenants to be made in the future. For the producers of 31.31-34 YHWH goes on inscribing the covenant in the future, and the broken covenants of the past do not militate against such a divine policy. The writers of Deuteronomy, on the other hand, do not appear to be able to bring themselves to state future prospects for the people in terms of a 'new' covenant. They can envisage a future when the fortunes of the people will be restored (Deut. 30.3), but they cannot imagine a future when the commandments of the covenant will be kept automatically and never broken (a scrutiny of Deut. 30–31 will demonstrate this point). So the writers of Jer. 31.31-34 and 32.36-41 must be regarded as having transcended (or rejected perhaps) the anxiety-laden cautiousness of the writers (or compilers) of Deuteronomy. They can assert (and therefore imagine) a 'new covenant' that will have built into it its own performance. Under the terms of this covenant every person in the community will know YHWH and none will turn from YHWH (31.34; 32.40). Now that is very effective writing on the heart (mind) and contrasts most strongly with all the externally written covenants of the past. What makes the new covenant unbreakable is the combined factors of divine inscribing on the collective heart (mind) of the community. When YHWH writes, he writes good, effective material (copy) designed to last forever. When human beings inscribe covenants, they write weak, ineffectual things on very frangible materials. Small wonder that the story of the covenant is the history of broken covenants. But YHWH's inscribing of the covenant in the future overcomes all the defects of human writing because it is effective writing interiorized in the heart (mind) of the people. The renewed people will possess one heart (mind) and that will make their fear of YHWH permanent (32.39).

YHWH's inscribing of the torah on the hearts of the people in 31.33 contrasts strikingly with the false inscribing of YHWH's torah by the scribes in 8.8. However we may categorize the notion of *covenant* used in chs. 31 and 32, and whatever content we may give to the word *torah* in 31.33, we will have to differentiate between these terms and the precise sense of *torah* in 8.8. The essential difference between these statements is clearly the fact that in one set of sayings YHWH is the actor, whereas in 8.8 the performers are human. It is the human that is permanently under suspicion—not to mention judgment—in the book of Jeremiah. The dismissal of the torah of YHWH as false because the inscribing of it by scribes has falsified it (8.8)—whatever may be meant by that statement is less important, because less accessible to the modern reader, than the fact that the text contains such a statement—identifies the problem of the divine torah in terms of the human production of it. There may be nothing wrong or false with YHWH's torah, but in the written version of it the speaker of 8.8 can discern the corrupting influences of the scribes. However we may wish to read 8.8-9—and there can be no denying that the simple expressions used in the verses are opaque enough to keep commentators busy forever without coming to any defendable interpretations—the strong contrast between the written and the spoken is obvious. The word of YHWH that the scribes (or wise men, if difference there be between these two descriptions) have rejected is not the written torah but the spoken word. Since this statement is appearing in the book of 'the words of Jeremiah' (1.1), I guess it is not unreasonable for a competent reader to read 8.8-9 as a statement contrasting some written torah of YHWH with the spoken utterance of Jeremiah. The word spoken by the prophet—for the sake of argument I shall read the book of Jeremiah as the representation of the words of the prophet Jeremiah—outranks the written torah of the scribes. If the two are in conflict, as appears to be the case in 8.8-9, then the utterance of the prophet takes precedence over whatever may be written. That is how I would read 8.8-9.

It would be unwise to elevate 8.8-9 to an eternal, unchangeable principle of the book of Jeremiah. Unwise because ch. 36 represents a combination of the two activities of speaking and writing. Baruch the scribe is represented as effectively translating the words of Jeremiah into the scroll that is read so many times in the course of the narrative. 36.6, 17-18 identify the relation of what is said to what is written in terms of dictation. Presumably the narrative of ch. 36 is intent on making the point that there is an exactitude of wording between what Jeremiah said over the twenty-three years and what Baruch wrote in the scroll. Hence the charge made in 8.8 need not be levelled against Baruch's scroll. Or should the wise reader keep 8.8 in mind when reading the narrative of 36? In a book such as Jeremiah, which contains the observation (accusation) made in 8.8, it is probably a good reading technique to remember 8.8 when reading ch. 36. If we trope 36 with 8.8 then the hermeneutics of suspicion will attend any reading of 36. I believe the hermeneutics of suspicion to be a very good principle (praxis, certainly) when reading the book of Jeremiah because the figure of Jeremiah is represented throughout that book as exercising a very strong hermeneutics of suspicion in the Jerusalem of his day. This approach to the book may be too much a case of internalizing the book's ideology on the part of the modern reader to be a wise reading policy—I readily acknowledge here my awareness of being in territory patrolled by David Clines's critique of metacommentary—yet I think it is very important that scholars should not conspire with texts to leave the obvious unstated. The text of ch. 36 provides us with no evidence of what Baruch actually wrote. Despite the fact that the narrative represents three (if not four, depending on how v. 8 is read) readings of the scroll in the course of the fast day's proceedings (vv. 10, 15, 21, not to mention the recital of all the words of the first reading which Micaiah in v. 13 gives the princes), it never gives the slightest indication of what anybody heard when the scroll was read. Only in the most oblique manner possible are we told in v. 29 of the king's summary of the scroll (or is it a citation of what is actually written in it?) as 'the king of Babylon will certainly come and destroy this land, and will cut off from it man and beast' (I term the report oblique because of the indirection of speech indicators in v. 29: '…you shall say…says YHWH…saying…'). What the king is reported as saying seems so unlikely to be a quotation from the scroll because there is nothing in the oracles of Jeremiah up to the year 605 (or 604/601 depending on the version of 36.9 followed) that indicates that 'the king of Babylon' is what Jeremiah was speaking about. A scrutiny of chs. 2–20 (the main source for the oracles of Jeremiah) will find no reference to Babylon or its king. For Jehoiakim to know enough to utter what is said about his utterance in 36.29 is for him to know too much!

What is said to have been said by Jehoiakim—how oblique can reported speech get?—in 36.29 presupposes a knowledge of the *edited* book of Jeremiah and therefore must represent the editor's (or writer's) knowledge of the tradition. Babylon as the enemy is only identified in the supplemental section of chs. 21–24 (set in periods after 605) and in the concluding summary to chs. 1–25 (in 25.8-14). Of course Jehoiakim can be held to have uttered 36.29 because by the time the reader has reached ch. 36 knowledge of chs. 1–35 may be readily assumed in the reader (and in the characters in the text). In my carefully considered opinion I would have to admit to reading 36 as evidence of an unreliable narrator and therefore would have to contemplate the possibility that what Jeremiah said may not have been what Baruch wrote in the scroll. That possibility is always present in any reading of a text. Professional scribes in an essentially oral culture are employed to write. They themselves supply the words as well as the writing of such words. Whatever evidence we may have for the practice of scribal activity in the ancient world is consonant with this judgment. Of course some scribes may have copied words supplied by others, but generally the function of scribes was to translate (or even transform) oral expressions into written forms. This being the case, any written document that purports to be the production of a professional scribe based on the words of a non-writer (non-literate speaker?) must always raise a suspicion about its composition. Whose words appear in the scroll? The words may well represent the *gist* of the speaker's utterance, but the words will be the scribe's not the speaker's. I will allow that in view of our ignorance about these matters of ancient practices it is an open question as to what the exact relationship might be between what is said and what is written. But even open questions ought at least to be asked—whatever the answer may be imagined to be.

In my reading of the book of Jeremiah I tend to read 8.8-9 as a statement undermining any confidence we may have in the reliability of the written word. I know most commentators on Jeremiah tend not to understand it quite like that, but the words will bear this interpretation. I think that 8.8 calls into question any writing that claims to represent YHWH's torah. Where there is a prophet to whom YHWH reveals his words, then any written torah comes under suspicion. The written torah cannot compete with the speaking person (who is a prophet). Persons are more important than texts. Prophets in particular outrank texts. The torah uttered by a prophet is superior to the torah inscribed by a scribe. The living voice is greater than the (dead) text. I do not want to push this reading of 8.8 too far, but I think that behind the quarrel in 8.8-9 is an important conflict about the superiority of the prophetically uttered word over the scribally inscribed torah. It may be a rather subtle distinction, but much in the ancient world supports such an understanding of the matter. Ancient cultures of orality retained their deep suspicions of literate cultures over a very long period. One intertextual example, owing much to the pericope on the new covenant in Jeremiah, will have to suffice here by way of justification for my reading of Jeremiah.

In a very well-known passage in the New Testament Paul takes up a number of elements from biblical sources bearing on the discussion I have outlined above and makes some very acute observations on the nature of living writing and the new covenant. 2 Cor. 3.1-6 is a magnificent piece of very subtle exposition in which Paul essentially writes—or Paul says and somebody else writes (the matter is far from simple)—that living persons constitute better 'letters of recommendation' than do real, written letters. The intertextuality of the passage is remarkable and subtly tropes a series of biblical figures. The members of Paul's church at Corinth are not only described as letters of recommendation but are also represented as 'a letter from Christ... written not with ink but with the spirit of the living God, not on tablets of stone but on tablets of human hearts' (vv. 1-3). Already echoes of Jer. 31.33 can be heard in those words. There are of course many more echoes and intertextual tropings there than are in the new covenant passage in Jeremiah, but it is an important contributor to Paul's thinking. To get the measure of 2 Cor. 3.1-6, especially as a dense piece of intertextual writing, would require a book-length treatment (cf. Hays 1989: 122-53), so my comments on it should be recognized as a brief glossing of elements in Jeremiah rather than as a serious engagement with Paul's thought. The Christians at Corinth who are described as a letter of Christ written by God on the human heart represent a fascinating understanding of the new covenant as a radical transformation of the old covenant in language partly derived from the book of Jeremiah.

2 Cor. 3.6 takes the matter further. Paul describes himself (and his disciples at Corinth) as 'ministers of a new covenant, *not in a written code* but in the spirit; *for the written code kills*, but the spirit gives life' (emphases added). The new covenant of Jer. 31.31 is clearly referred to here. It would require a further paper to deal with all the New Testament uses of Jer. 31.31-34 (see all the standard commentaries), but the powerful intertextual uses made of it by various New Testament writers should not be ignored in any reading of Jeremiah (or its *Rezeptionsgeschichte*). Paul's notion that 'the letter kills' whereas 'the spirit gives life' is not the point of Jer. 8.8, but in my opinion the way he develops his argument through a subtle intertextual troping of various elements in the biblical text offers a way of understanding what may be going on in the attack of Jeremiah on the written torah of the scribes. It is all too easy to point to the written text and to claim for such documents an authenticity and authority that bypasses the immediacy of the spoken word and the importance of living persons. Paul's reference to being 'ministers of the new covenant' and his allusion to writing, without ink, on human hearts captures something of what is envisaged in the Jeremiah text about a future when covenants (or torahs) will not be written on stone but on the hearts of living people. What is actually inscribed in the literal sense of writing ('the letter': *to gramma*) kills. The language is different

from Jeremiah's charge of 'the false pen of the scribes has made it into a lie', but I think both men would feel that they had something in common on this point. Both might even have felt that they shared a point of view with Jacques Derrida on this matter, though as Derrida has written so much more than either (or both) ancient worthies he has also been able to rescue the written from the realm of death. As we continue to *read the writings* associated with Jeremiah and Paul we are not in a position to rule out the written as being simply the carrier of death. We know writing as that which also inaugurates life (as so much of the work of Derrida tirelessly tells us).

Where I think Jeremiah's point and Paul's intertextual reflections intersect may be in the sense of Jer. 8.8-9 as a statement on behalf of the living voice, the importance of the speaking person, over against the written as the false. Authentic existence concerns all writers, including the writers about Jeremiah and of Paul, and yet writings can be manipulated and used to falsify and to shout down the personal voice of the poet. In this century of fundamentalistic religions the truth of that observation must be all too evident. It should also be a helpful voice from the past enshrined as it is in the sacred text of Jewish and Christian communities. If its insight is combined with the various interpretations of Jer. 31.31-34, then it can be a powerful reminder to us that there is writing *and writing*. What is humanly written on scrolls (or whatever material) can always be false, only what is written on the heart (mind)—and written by God, whatever that may mean—has any hope of avoiding the falseness which is so characteristic of human systems. The written word must always give way to what is written on the heart and living persons are always more valuable and important than any amount of scrolls, books or bibles.

This is a good point at which to stop because it puts me in mind of a very well-known and obvious point about George Anderson. He is remembered with respect and affection by all his many students for his capacities as a teacher much more than for his written works. I recall his postgraduate seminars, even though they took place more than thirty years ago (when I attended them). I also recall him in his garden and in his library (there in Fountainhall Road), especially in the latter where I remember him as an excellent listener as well as teacher. One other memory remains to this day whenever I reflect on the many years over which I have known George. I think it was in

1980 when he and I shared a radio studio one Sunday morning for a programme on biblical prophecy (it was just after I had published *When Prophecy Failed*). After the usual talking that goes on in these programmes there was a period of phone-ins when members of the public put questions to the two of us or irately told us what they thought of us and our work. I shall never forget George's chuckles after one punter phoned in angrily to inform us that as far as he was concerned 'there were no Christians in the studio' that morning. While I could see a little truth in that outburst, it still generated enormous amusement all round because, by whatever criteria may be used, George Anderson represents for so many of us what a Christian scholar is truly like. On the few occasions since that morning whenever we have met George has reminded me of that programme and we have chuckled together over the phone-in observation. The above reflections are here offered to George Anderson as a reading of a minor strand in the book of Jeremiah in keeping, I hope, with the spirit (if not the letter) of Jeremiah.

NOTE

The epigraphic material reflects quotations from Miroslav Holub's poem 'Nineveh' (Holub 1990: 37), Jacques Derrida's essays 'The End of the Book and the Beginning of Writing' and '...That Dangerous Supplement...' (Derrida 1976: 17, 143), and Maurice Blanchot's essay 'The Absence of the Book' (Blanchot 1981: 146).

BIBLIOGRAPHY

Alexander, L.
1990   'The Living Voice: Scepticism towards the Written Word in Early
            Christian and in Graeco-Roman Texts', in *The Bible in Three
            Dimensions: Essays in Celebration of Forty Years of Biblical Studies in
            the University of Sheffield* (ed. D.J.A. Clines, S.E. Fowl and S.E. Porter;
            JSOTSup, 87; Sheffield: JSOT Press): 221-47.
Alonso Schökel, L.
1981   'Jeremías como anti-Moisés', in *De la Tôrah au Messie: Etudes
            d'exégèse et d'herméneutique bibliques offertes à Henri Cazelles pour
            ses 25 années d'enseignement à l'Institut Catholique de Paris (Octobre
            1979)* (ed. M. Carrez, J. Doré and P. Grelot; Paris: Desclée): 245-54.
Anderson, G.W.
1963   'Old Testament Books: VII. Jeremiah', *The Preacher's Quarterly* 92-
            97: 178-83.

Blanchot, M.
  1981   *The Gaze of Orpheus and Other Literary Essays* (trans. L. Davis; Barrytown, NY: Station Mill): 145-60.
Carroll, R.P.
  1986   *Jeremiah: A Commentary* (OTL; London: SCM Press; Philadelphia: Westminster Press).
Derrida, J.
  1976   *Of Grammatology* (trans. G. Chakravorty Spivak; Baltimore: Johns Hopkins University Press).
Hays, R.B.
  1989   *Echoes of Scripture in the Letters of Paul* (New Haven: Yale University Press).
Holladay, W.L.
  1986   *Jeremiah. I. A Commentary on the Book of the Prophet Jeremiah Chapters 1–25* (ed. P.D. Hanson; Hermeneia; Philadelphia: Fortress Press).
Holub, M.
  1990   *Vanishing Lung Syndrome* (trans. D. Young and D. Habova; London: Faber & Faber).
McKane, W.
  1986   *A Critical and Exegetical Commentary on Jeremiah. I. Introduction and Commentary on Jeremiah I–XXV* (ICC; Edinburgh: T. & T. Clark).
Scarry, E.
  1985   *The Body in Pain: The Making and Unmaking of the World* (New York: Oxford University Press).
Schwartz, R.M.
  1990   'Joseph's Bones and the Resurrection of the Text: Remembering in the Bible', in *The Book and the Text: The Bible and Literary Theory* (ed. R.M. Schwartz; Oxford: Basil Blackwell).

CLANS, ETAT MONARCHIQUE, ET TRIBUS

H. Cazelles

En étudiant la structure d'Israël en fonction de l'évolution de ses traditions, M. Noth avait recouru à la notion grecque d'amphictyonie dans sa brillante synthèse. Chaque tribu, ayant à sa tête un *nasi'*, aurait assuré pendant un des 12 mois de l'année l'entretien d'un sanctuaire central. Après avoir séduit, cette thèse fut contestée par le regretté H. Orlinsky (1962: 375). Puis notre jubilaire orienta la recherche vers d'autres notions, celles de *'am*, *qâhâl* et *'édah* (Anderson 1970). La critique s'est poursuivie avec R. de Vaux (1971; 1973: 19-26), B.E. Celada (1981), U. von Arx (1990); et la thèse est maintenant abandonnée.[1] Reste que la structure des 12 préfectures de Salomon (1 R 4.12-19) est bien une structure amphictyonique, avec entretien mensuel de la maison royale, dépositaire de l'Arche d'Alliance en attendant que le Temple soit construit.

La recherche s'est alors portée sur l'emergence' d'Israël, en Cisjordanie surtout, et ceci par confrontation des données bibliques et archéologiques. Ansi R. Coote et K.W. Whitelam (1987) étudient la formation de l'Etat davidique à partir des établissements (*settlements*) israélites au cours des relations interrégionales de l'époque des Fer I (1200–1150) et II (1000–587). B. Halpern (1983) étudie successivement la croissance d'Israël en Canaan depuis l'époque d'El-Amarna, et la croissance de la *Tribal League* après Deborah.

Le valeureux archéologue I. Finkelstein joint à l'archéologie l'étude de l'environnement et de l'anthropologie (1990). Or l'anthropologie a un aspect sociologique. G.E. Mendenhall a vu dans la conquête une lutte entre paysans et les cités cananéennes. J. de Geus a analysé les unités primaires que sont la 'maison patriarcale', exogamique (*beyth-avoth*), et le clan, endogamique (*mishpaḥah*), pour conclure que la

---

1. H. Seebass (1978) accepte une union prémonarchique des 12 tribus par une cérémonie cultuelle à Sichem.

tribu (*shevet, matteh*) n'etait qu'une 'branche' du peuple déjà constitué (1976: 149s); G. Auld en a précisé le sens préxilique. N. Gottwald a repris l'analyse et vu dans le 'tribalisme israelite' une réaction de défense contre la societé cananéenne et le centralisme politique qui suivit (1980: 325). Pur lui la *mishpahah* n'est pas un clan exogamique, c'est déjà une entité sociale d'importance majeure qui protège l'intégrité socio-économique des 'maisons patriarcales' (1980: 315); enfin 'la societé tribale est caractéristique de societés agricoles' (1980: 296).

Autonomie des Tribus ou des Mishpahôt

Ceci dit, les traditions bibliques témoignent d'une vie autonome des tribus ou des *mishpahôt*, terme que nous traduirons par 'clan' comme de Geus, pour raison de commodité. Il peut y avoir des tribus composées d'un seul clan comme Dan; Shuham (Nb 25.42), par métathèse Hushim (Gn 46.23). Tout en rejetant le caractère exogamique du clan, le terme implique le sens de 'postérité' qu'il a à Ugarit (KTU 1.14.I.24; 1.14.III.40, 48; 1.16.I.21) mais d'une postérité assez particulière, distincte de la 'descendance-ascendance' *htk* de Keret, et celle du mortel Keret, 'fils' du dieu El (KTU I.16.I.10, 21). Comme la racine, tant en Sud-arabique[2] qu'en akkadien, implique 'sortie', effusion', en qu'en hébreu la *shiphah* est une concubine, la *mishpahah* paraît designer une unite plus large que la famille patriarcale et plus mobile qu'elle. C'est précisément comme 'clan' que des Danites quittent la region de Soreah et d'Eshtaol qui restera traditionellement la leur. C'est comme clan que l'Ephratéen Jesse vient s'établir à Bethléem (1 Sam. 20.6). C'est comme clan que Mâkir (Nb 26.29) 'descend' en ses chefs en quittant Galaad (Jd 5.14 cf. 17). Ruben est resté lui aussi au delà du Jourdain, mais c'est probablement comme clan (plutôt que Gad) que, à la différence des autres fils d'Israël, il est passé dans le désert à l'orient de Moab selon l'itinéraire Nb 20.10-13. L'itinéraire synthétique P (Nb 33.44) laissera tomber ce detail.

Ces clans vont être les noyaux des tribus qui intégreront leurs traditions prémonarchiques et 1 Chr. 4.40-43 ne sait plus très bien si c'est tout Siméon ou des clans Siméonites qui se déplacent, certains au temps d'Ezéchias. La *mishpahah* danite devient tribu (*shevet*) en Jd 18, 19.

---

2.   Biella (1982: 341). Beeston *et al.* (1981: 124)—'convoquer, placer sous les ordres de'. Comme en akkadien (AHw 116—'vergiessen, breit hinstreuen'), la racine ne signifie pas l'émission de semen, mais l'élargissement d'un territoire.

D'ailleurs les clans peuvent passer de tribu à tribu. Karmi est rubénite en 1 Chr. 5.3 mais judéen en 1 Chr. 4.1 et Jos. 7.1. Zérah est édomite en Gn 36.13, mais judéen en Gn 38.30. Huppam et Shuppam sont rattachés à Manassé en 2 Chr. 7.1, mais ils sont Benjaminites en Nb 26.39, ce qui peut expliquer les relations étroites entre Yabesh de Galaad et Benjamin (Jd 21.14; 1 S 11.1ss).

En Jd 1, nous avons un texte ancien (vv. 21-35) inséré dans une rédaction deutéronomiste à la gloire de Juda qui a pris Jérusalem (v. 8), ce que n'avait pu faire Benjamin. Ce texte concerne 7 tribus du Nord[3] qui n'ont pas pu prendre les villes adjacentes; elles ne sont pas appelées tribus et c'est une *mishpaḥah* qui, par ruse, doit passer de Bethel à Luz. Gottwald voit dans ce texte une réaction de defense contre la société cananéenne et la centralisation qui suivit (1980: 172-5). Pour Halpern, c'est une glorification des conquêtes davidiques (1983: 181). A un autre point de vue, nous y verrons un témoignage du dimorphisme de la société cananéo-israelite avant l'établissement de la monarchie. C'est ce que M.B. Rowton appelle 'enclosed nomadism' (1965; 1967; 1973)—cp. Rowton (1976); Fales (1976); Gnuse (1991). Comme on le constatait encore il y a quelques décennies, à côté des cités vivent des familles ou clans vivant sous la tente. Les nombreuses monographies consacrées récemment a l'histoire particulière à chaque tribu font souvent apparaître aux origines cette vie de clan en sédentarisation progressive,[4] en transhumance ou non.

Ces monographies sont plutôt préoccupées de l'établissement des tribus sur leurs territoires. Pour Halpern l'origine des tribus est géographique (1983: 109—'The tribes seem to have had their origins in the geography of the Canaanite ridge'), et pour de Geus l'État a précédé la structure tribale (1976: 130ss). En fait la distribution du territoire entre les 12 tribus avec leurs frontières n'est pas antérieure à la monarchie (Kallai 1986: 279). A mon avis il faut admettre une édition sacerdotale P pour les ch 14 à 19 qui soumet l'allotissement au prêtre Eléazar, et qui, en Nb 34, met la Transjordanie hors des

---

3. Il est significatif que manquent la tribu d'Issachar et la ville de Yizréel, siège de la dynastie de Saül (2 S 2.9) et lieu de naissance de la première femme de David, Ahinoam (1 S 25.43). L'absence de Dan, Ruben, Siméon et Juda l'est moins. Sur la vie indépendante des tribus: H. Cazelles (1990: 44-51). C'est Asher qui pose le plus de problèmes.

4. Ainsi sur Ruben, Oded (1970); Siméon, Naʻaman (1980); Benjamin, Sapin (1972) et McDonald (1974).

frontières en conformité avec le schema d'Ezéchiel (47.18).

Mais nous avons des traces de prises de possession sans delimitation territoriale. Ansi Ephraim a Tappuah en territoire manassite (Jos. 17.8). De même, selon P ('devant Eleazar'), 'fils de Ruben' et 'fils de Gad' reçoivent ensemble un certain nombre de villes propices à l'élevage (Nb 32.3); mais on retrouve ces villes aux vv 34-38, données séparément à ces fils de Ruben et fils de Gad. Or il ne s'agit pas de territoire continu. Ce sont de points d'eau isolés: Gad a Dibon au sud de Heshbon donné à Ruben, et Ruben a Nébo très au nord d'Aroer et d'Atarôt, donnés à Gad. Gad et Ruben ne sont pas appelés ici tribus, pas plus qu'Isaac en Gn 26 qui, lui aussi, acquiert des droits sur trois puits disputés à Abimelek de Gerar. Ce dimorphisme est facteur de conflits où les futures tribus agissent indépendamment comme dans un des récits de Gn 34: Siméon et Lévi font le sac de Sichem indépendamment des autres 'fils de Jacob'.

Unions de Clans

Il m'était arrivé de parler d'unions de 'tribus' (Cazelles 1982: 77); après les travaux ci-dessus énumérés, il conviendrait de parler d'unions de clans. L'expression 'fils de Jacob' désigne déjà un groupement d'unités préalables que A. Lemaire a distingué de l'expression 'fils d'Israël'. Or 'fils de...' peut désigner, soit un peuple (en Gn 19.38, mais pas 37; Ex. 3.10), soit des tribus (non ainsi désignées), comprenant des clans (Nb 26), soit des familles; mais je ne connais pas d'exemple où une *mishpahah* soit désignée comme 'fils de...' (même en Gn 36.11 ou pourtant les 'fils d'Eliphaz' ont la fonction de clan appelé *'alluph* (36.15s).[5]

'Fils de Jacob' et 'fils d'Israël' ne sont donc pas des termes techniques pour les groupements d'unités sociales prémonarchiques. Toutefois il importe de compléter les études demandées par de Geus (1976: 210) 'dans le champ de la sociologie, de l'économie, de la politique et des analyses littéraires par une étude de la terminologie juridique sémitique, surtout depuis les travaux faits sur les textes de Mari, en particulier par A. Malamat (1962; 1967).

Le terme de 'mère', *'ém* désigne une unité territorale antérieure à l'allotissement des tribus. C'est un groupement autour d'une ville (ou

---

5. A rapprocher du *eleph* non militaire (en Mi 5.2, équivalent du *mishpahah* de I S 20.29, cf. 23.23). Voir Gottwald (1980: 276-82). Ce serait un terme archaïque devenu militaire (Ex. 18.21, 25).

plutôt village) pourvue d'un point d'eau, puits à Sichem ou vaste citerne comme à Bethléem (2 S 20.19). Sous la forme *'ummah*, plus proche de l'arabe, elle qualifie des groupements ismaélites ou madianites (Gn 25.16; Nb 25.15) et correspond à l'*ummatum* des textes de Mari (Malamat 1989: 41-43). Des 4 groupes que constituent les 'mères' des 12 tribus, 2 au moins sont territoriaux: Dan et Nephtali selon Gn 30.5-8, et Ephraïm-Manassé-Benjamin, fils de Rachel, séparant les tribus de Lea au nord et au sud. Dans le cadre de dimorphisme les clans peuvent avoir une implantation territoriale.[6]

Qu'en est-il des deux termes qui en hebreu désignent la tribu, *shevet* et *matteh*? Notons d'abord que l'*English-Akkadian Analytical Index* (Sasson 1977) ne donne aucun équivalent akkadien pour 'tribe', que les termes égyptiens *why/wt* et *mhwt* ne viennent pas du sémite, mais ne sont qu'un élargissement du terme signifiant 'famille' aux tribus asiatiques, et enfin que *shevet* est ignoré de l'ugaritique.

a) *shevet* a deux sens en hebreu: 1. Le sens de 'bâton, rigide, sec', avec lequel on frappe (Ex. 21.20): c'est le sceptre d'autorité (Gn 49.16; Mi 4.14; Is. 10.15). 2. Le sens de tribu (Gn 49.28; Nb 24.2). Ces deux textes, qui pourraient être anciens, sont considérés comme rédactionnels (Westermann 1988: *in loco*; Jagersma 1988: 151—au v. 5 Jacob habite sous la tente). En fait, en akkadien comme en sud-arabe, la racine *šbt* signifie 'donner un coup' comme verbe, 'sceptre' comme nom (AHw 1169a; CAD 17, 1, 8b, 10a; Biella 1982: 325; Beeston 1981: 123). Les textes préprophétiques comme le Jahviste ne connaissent pas le sens de 'rameau verdoyant' pour un arbre ou un peuple, mais celui de bâton dur, de pouvoir et d'autorité (v.g. Gn 49.10; Jd 5.14).

b) Il en est de même de *matteh*. La terme est connu sous sa forme nominale, sinon de l'akkadien, du moins à Ebla (Groneberg 1988: 71-73)[7] et à Ugarit (Aisleitner WU no 1551; Caquot-Sznycer 1974: 159, 374, 453); il a le sens de 'bâton'. C'est le sens qu'il a dans les textes anciens de la Bible: le bâton de Juda (Gn 38.18, 25), le bâton de Dieu (Ex. 4.20; 17.3) donné à Moïse (Ex. 4.17 cf. 2) avant de l'être à Aaron (P), contre l'autorité du Pharaon et de ses magiciens, le sceptre redoutable du roi d'Assyrie (Is. 10.5, 26). Le sens de 'tribu'

6.   Mâkir habita en Transjordanie près de Sukkôt (Lemaire 1981). Les 'fils de Jacob' n'apparaissent qu'en Gn 34 lors d'un coup de main sur Sichem, et séjournent près de Bethel (Gn 35).

7.   L'équivalence est donnée de Madu = GIS.RU, en akkadien *tilpanu*, 'bâton de jet'. Voir aussi Waetzold & Hauptmann 1988: 207.

n'apparait qu'en 1 R 7.14 et Mi. 6.2, et celui de 'branche' d'un arbre avec Ezéchiel (19.11-14).

Les clans ne s'unissent donc pas comme 'tribus' avant la monarchie; ils s'unissent comme *'am*; ainsi l'avait indiqué G.W. Anderson.

Ce terme sémitique a deux sens: un sens individuel, 'l'oncle paternel', et un sens collectif que l'on traduit par 'peuple'[8] mais qui, en punique, ira jusqu'à qualifier l'assemblée populaire d'une cité (Sznycer 1975; Teixidor 1976: 407s). Comme *'m* devient *'mm* au pluriel ou devant suffixe, le terme doit être rapproché de la racine verbale *'mm* (*ḫamamu* en akkadien) qui signifie 'rassembler' dans un sens très général.

Dans les textes cuneiformes, sud-arabes et ugaritique, c'est le sens individuel qui est de beaucoup le mieux documenté, et ceci par l'onomastique;[9] le sens individuel s'impose, qu'il s'agisse d'un homme ou d'un dieu qualifié d''oncle' comme il peut être dit 'père' (*'Ab*) ou 'frère' (*'Aḥ*). C'est un qualificatif de protection et d'autorité. Le sens collectif est rare et discuté. Le *ztr 'm* d'Ugarit (KTU 17, 1, 28) reste douteux, et ce serait le seul cas d'un emploi collectif.[10] Si ce sens est admis, il s'agirait donc d'un rassemblement, plus large que la maison patriarcale, autour de l'oncle paternel.

Il semble bien que ce soit comme *'Amu* que les scribes égyptiens ont désigné les tribus asiatiques. On peut hésiter car le terme est écrit *'3m(w)*. R. Giveon et D. Redford hésitent car le grand égyptologue que fut G. Posener avait abandonné cette étymologie, le *3* (aleph égyptien) valant *l/r* au Moyen Empire. Mais W. Helck donne une série de cas où ce aleph indique simplement l'allongement de la voyelle en sémitique (1962: 89).[11] Les plus anciennes attestations remontent à l'Ancien Empire. Le terme est doublement déterminé: 'homme et femme' signifiant une population, le 'bâton de jet' (dit boomerang),

8.   Sur les acceptions du terme, consulter les importantes monographies du *THAT* II, 290-305 (Hulst) et du *ThWAT* VI, 177-86 (E. Lipiński avec sa riche documentation épigraphique).

9.   *AhW* 317b et 318a (*Familien Oberhaupt*); CAD H, 69 (*master head of the family*); Huffmon 1965: 196-198; Benz 1972: 319; Ryckmans 1934: 309s; Beeston 1981: 16 (*uncle*); Biella 1982: 371 (*paternal uncle*). Rien à Ebla (Archi 1988).

10.   Caquot-Sznycer proposent 'clan' et Gibson 'ancestor' (1978: 104). Pour Ribichini-Xella (1991: 166) c'est la '*zio divinizzato*'. On ne peut retenir le sens proposé en WU 2042, et en Ug V, 6, 2 c'est la préposition *'im*. Références dans Whitaker 1972: 490.

11.   Il est vrai que dans les exemples donnés la consonne suivant est un *r*. Albright (1934: 37) donne des cas où le aleph n'est pas écrit.

servant d'arme de guerre pour des peuples étrangers. Cela est à retiner pour l'adoption de *shevet* et *matteh* par les scribes israélites.

En hebreu, le sens individuel s'impose pour des expressions archaïque comme 'êtré réuni à ses *'mm'* (Gn 25.8, 17; 35.29; 49.33; Nb 20.24; Dt 32.50 et même Ezé 18.18...) lorsque l'on meurt (Alfrink; Noth 1928: 66-82). Etant donné les termes parallèles (chefs, princes, *shevet*) en Jd 5.14 (cantique de Déborah), le sens individuel d'autorité est le plus vraisemblable. Ce n'est pas pour rien que l'oncle de Saül s'inquiète d'une onction possible de Saül comme roi (1 S 10.14-16), et le nom tout à fait exceptionnel de David pourrait plutôt se rapporter à l'autorité de l'oncle paternel qu'à l'affection.[12]

Pour en revenir au terme de *'am* comme rassemblement de deux clans (appelés 'fils de...'), en 'un seul *'am'*, nous en avons un excellent exemple en Gn 34.16. Ce n'est ici qu'une proposition qui échoue. Mais elle rappelle une expression juridique arabe enregistrée par les voyageurs européens, encore au debut de ce siècle. Deux tribus peuvent s'unir par le lien de *Ben 'ameh*) qui constitue une tribu 'fils de l'oncle de l'autre'[13] par un rite particulier autour d'une épée plantée en terre. Le sens est encore ici individuel, mais il concerne un groupe, celui des *Beney* de N...

On peut se demander si le rite d'adoption 'sur les genoux' des fils de Dan et Nephtali par Rachel (Gn 30.3-8), celui du clan des *Beney Makir*, fils de Manassé, par son aïeul Joseph (50.23), enfin d'Ephraïm et Manassé par leur aïeul Jacob (Gn 48.5-20), n'est pas une interprétation d'un rite de *Ben 'Ameh*. Ces deux dernières tribus sont d'ailleurs considérées comme *'am* (48.18, tels les Danites en Gn 49.16), et non 'tribus'; le rite d'adoption se complète par un rite de bénediction (imposition de mains).[14] Or la descendance d'Ephraïm sera plénitude de *goyim* (48.19).

12. L'onomastique akkadienne et égyptienne connaît beaucoup de Dudu/Tutu. Les livres Samuel-Rois ne mettent jamais le *y* avant le *d*, ce que fera le Chroniste. Le *dwd* de la stèle de Mesha reste énigmatique: 'Perhaps related to David with the meaning "leader, chief", perhaps the city of Atarôt's deity' (Dearman 1989: 113).

13. L'institution a été étudiée par Musil et surtout par A. Jaussen (1908: 143-62). C'est 'une alliance offensive et défensive entre tribus voisines, pour les confédérés source de bonheur'.

14. 'Fils de Manassé' et 'fils d'Ephraïm' constitueront la 'maison de Joseph' (Jd 1.22 Dtr). La notion de 'genou' (*brk*) entraîne celle de bénédiction (*brk*). Les rites d'adoption sont peu bibliques, mais très utilisées en civilisation hurrite (plus rarement mésopotamienne) pour les transferts de biens.

Du Groupement en un 'am aux 12 Préfectures

Ce terme de *goy* est un ancien terme amorite, *gayu*, qui désigne des clans[15] Hanéens ou autres, en marge du royaume de Mari et souvent en difficulte avec lui. Dans la Table des Peuples de P (Gn 10.5, 31b-32), il désigne des nations sédentarisées dont les 'langues' et les '*mishpeḥôt*' sont des subdivisions. Mais J ne l'emploie que pour Abram (12.2), qui part se sédentariser dans un pays où toutes les *mishpeḥôt* se béniront en son nom (Gn 12.2-3), c'est dire Canaan (10.18).

Dans la Table des peuples, ni J ni P ne connaissent de '*am*'. Le Jahviste ne connait que des Eponymes et leurs descendances; mais dans la terre entière (*kol ha'areṣ*), il n'y avait qu'un seul '*am* et une seule langue. Après la dispersion, le Jahviste va utiliser le mot au singulier pour la population d'une ville (Gn 19.4), d'un pays (Gn 26.10; 34.11) ou d'un dieu (Ex. 3.7). Au pluriel ce sont les peuples qui doivent être soumis à Jacob (Gn 27:29) ou à Juda (49.10).

C'est à partir de l'Exode que le terme désigne Israël, le peuple de YHWH. Ce terme désigne alors un rassemblement, non plus seulement des fils d'Israël unis aux fils de Jacob depuis le passage du Jabbok (Gn 32.8; 33.15; 35.6), mais de l'ensemble du peuple de Moïse (Ex. 4.16).

Or, pour le Jahviste, les groupes réunis dans ce peuple ne sont pas des tribus, ce sont des Eponymes. Il reste dans la terminologie de sa liste des peuples en Gn 10. Son problème est celui de l'ancêtre dynastique, porteur de promesses divines, et il veut répondre a un problème de foi au début de l'époque royale: à quel dieu national les peuples doivent-ils obéir (Gn 49.10)? En quel 'dieu du père' peut-il avoir foi et confiance (Gn 28.13…)? C'est dans cette visée qu'il puise dans les traditions tribales et locales pour orienter tous les descendants des Eponymes vers la reconnaissance de la royauté judéenne, bénéficiaire des promesses du Dieu d'Abraham et soumise à l'alliance mosaïque du Sinaï.[16]

---

15. Après avoir hésité entre 'territoire, pays' (cf. Dossin 141) et 'clan, tribu, peuple', l'équipe de Mari penche pour le terme de 'clan'; sous la forme *gayisham* 'de clan en clan' (Durand 1988: 15, et n. 42). Le terme de 'clan' convient à A. Malamat 1989: 38 [note] (cf. Gn. 20.4).

16. L'historiographie jahviste me paraît beaucoup moins orientée vers la possession du sol que vers l'élection dynastique (Cazelles 1991: 501-506); mais l'une suppose l'autre, car il était promis au dynaste non seulement descendance, mais

Il est très probable qu'il connait déjà la répartition du peuple d'Israël comme groupement de 12 Eponymes: 2 de Rachel la brebis (Joseph Gn 30.24, plus Benjamin 35.18s), 6 de Leah, la vache,[17] en deux groupes (Ruben, Siméon, Juda, Levi au sud, Issachar et Zabulon au nord), 2 de Bilhah et 2 de Zilpah. Ce schéma se retrouve en effet dans la bénédiction de Jacob/Israël en Gn 49 qui commence par les 4 premiers fils de Leah, et termine par Benjamin.[18] Il reconnait une certaine primauté à Joseph, *nazir* des ses frères (Gn 49,22-26), mais le sceptre (*shevet*) est donné à Juda.

D'où lui vient ce schéma, encore ignoré du Cantique de Deborah et des regroupements guerriers avant la synthèse du Livre des Juges? Ne serait-ce pas de la répartition du royaume de Salomon en 12 prefectures pour l'entretien mensuel de la maison du roi (1 R 4.7-13)? Des 12 préfectures,[19] 7 sont rattachées à des Eponymes, avec affectation géographique: Ephraïm, Manassé, Nephtali, Asher, Issachar, Benjamin, Gad. Cette répartition géographique offre des singularités. Le territoire de Dan (v. 9) est à l'Ouest de Juda et non près de Nephtali. Le pays de Hepher[20] forme une entité (Lemaire 1972: 13-20) qui sera considérée comme Manassite (Nb 26.32); il en sera de même de la 4ème préfecture (Dor).[21] La 5ème couvre un vaste territoire de

sol et prosperité. Je partage l'avis de ceux qui n'admettent pas d''époque patriarcale'; mais le Jahviste a puisé dans les traditions des 'fils de Jacob' pouvant remonter à l'époque amorite, ou dans celles de 'fils d'Israël' qui n'apparaissent qu'en Gn 32.29, comme parents des Araméens dont on n'a pas trace avant les 13ème–12ème s. BC. Je les verrais bien unis par un traité de *Ben 'ameh*.

17.   Dhorme rapprochait Leah de l'akkadien *littu*. On pense avec raison au nom de *'Aleyn Ba'al* qui est décrit comme un taureau, de la racine *l'y* 'être puissant'. Le groupe Lea est plus anciennement sédentarisé que le groupe 'moutonnier' de Rachel—cf. DBS VII, c. 119, art. 'Patriarches'.

18.   Pour le détail des 12 bénédictions cf. H.-J. Zobel 1965.

19.   A. Caquot, Art. *'Préfets'* DBSup VIII, c. 273–286, où l'on trouvera les références aux études d'Albright, Alt, Yeivin, Malamat, G.E. Wright (problèmes économiques). Ajouter Rösel 1984: 84-90. Les vv. 13 et 19 ont certainement été remaniés par Dtr.

20.   Ce pays, où se trouvent les 5 villes 'filles de Salpahad', est à situer au Nord et Nord-Est de Mannassé, autour de Tirsah (même position chez Rösel). Absorbé par Manassé, il n'est pas mentionné dans les ostraca de Samarie.

21.   Dor est appelé *naphat Dor* et expliqué d'une manière trés intéressante par Ben Dov grâce au grec *napè*, 'vallée, plaine cotière' (heb. Sharon), apud Z. Kallai, *Historical Geography*...p. 62. La ville n'a pas été conquise par Manassé mais il y a eu là un prêtre de YHWH (N. Avigad, IEJ 1975, p. 101). L'écriture serait du 8ème s.

Yoqmeam et Megiddo, à Bethshean et Sartân, c'est à dire les vallées de Yizréel, de Bethshean et une partie du Jourdain; c'est aussi une région manassite selon Jos. 17.1-13 (avec peut-être enclaves d'Asher et d'Issachar, v. 11). La 7ème préfecture est également Manassite (Mahanaim) selon Jos. 13.30 (Dtr, car Moïse seul) quoique Gadite en Jos. 21.38 (P, car le partage se fait devant Eléazar). Ainsi, après le Manassé oriental, se constituera le Manassé occidental.

Il y a là un mode de taxation en nature pour l'entretien de la maison du roi qui n'est pas sans analogies dans l'Ancien Orient. Les Archives du Palais d'Ebla dans la Syrie du 3ème millénaire font connaître de multiples livraisons de céréales et autres denrées pour 'la maison du roi'[22]: ce sont des rations périodiques mensuelles (Milano 1990: 3-52, 264s). Malgré la 'fluidité des titres' (Astour 148), il est sûr que des gouverneurs de différentes cités, donc avec répartition territoriale, livrent de l'or au roi (*En*).[23] Vers 2000 à la fin de la IIIème dynastie d'Ur et au début de la période d'Isin (sémitique), il y a une rotation dans les cités Sumériennes pour des 'services religieux mensuels' (Hallo 1960: 88-116).[24] Enfin, au temps de Salomon et de Roboam, une stèle de Sheshonq Ier établit des prélèvements mensuels sur differents domaines en faveur de sanctuaires royaux (Redford 1972: 141-56; 1975: 157-61). A ma connaissance, les Archives d'Ugarit et d'Emar témoignent de rations et cycles mensuels d'offrandes, ainsi que de taxations, mais non mensuelles.[25]

Puisqu'avant la monarchie centralisée de David et Salomon, Eponymes, *shevet* et *matteh*, ne désignaient que sceptre et pouvoir sur des clans, tout indique que la répartition territoriale de 'maisons' et de 'clans', constituant un peuple, a été faite pour les besoins de l'administration royale. Les dîmes ont été royales (1 S 8.15) avant de devenir sacerdotales (P).

---

22. Sur les rois et gouverneurs: Pettinato 1987: 15-19.

23. Il y aurait 14 districts—Pettinato 1981: 122-29; Pomponio 1984: 127-35.

24. Ce texte BALA (rotation) a été reconnu par Landsberger comme relatant un 'monthly religious service'. Il tient compte des intercalations de mois, mais ces prestations ne viennent pas toujours des mêmes villes ni au même mois.

25. Pour Ugarit, Sznycer, DBSup IX, c. 1423–6; Heltzer 1962: 15-22. Pour Emar, Arnaud 1986: 263ss sur les livraisons cultuelles, 1986: 430-38 sur les ordos liturgiques mensuels.

Des 12 Préfectures aux 12 Tribus

Cette répartition du royaume en 12 préfectures est certainement antérieure à 733 puisqu'elle inclut Dor, Galilée et Galaad, et très probablement aux guerres araméennes du 9ème s. qui ravagent le Galaad. Elle paraît avoir été amorcée sous David puisque 5 préfets, anonymes, ne sont que des 'fils' d'un titulaire antérieur (Caquot 283s). Mais elle englobe moins de territoire que le recensement de David (2 Sam. 24.5-7). Elle supposerait les pertes de territoires de Salomon (1 R 11). La commission va en effet jusqu'à Qadesh, pays hittite, avant de revenir sur Dan, Sidon, Tyr et la côte (pays des Hivvites et Cananéens). Malgré l'introduction qui parle de 12 tribus, les seuls Eponymes nommés sont Gad et Dan.

La répartition territoriale des 12 préfectures ne coïncide pas avec la répartition traditionnelle des tribus telle qu'elle sera fixée dans les listes du Livre de Josué (Dtr et P). Dès la mort de Roboam, il y a rupture entre le Nord et le Sud. Le Jahviste garde le principe de la division en 12 parts, mais sans donner de précisions territoriales. Toutefois, au lieu d'hériter de la 2ème préfecture, restée tradition-nellement dans le sud (Jos. 19.41-46), Dan est situé au nord, près de Nephtali (Gn 30.6-8) ou d'Issachar-Gad-Asher-Nephtali (Gn 49.14-21). Il y a plus grave: le rattachement de la 1ère prefecture (Ephraïm) aux 2-3-4-5èmes préfectures en un seul Joseph (Gn 30.24; 49.22-26). Ce très vaste territoire dépasse celui d'une unité administrative. On sait que le problème du jahviste est dynastique[26]; pour lui *shevet* veut dire sceptre, autorité d'un Eponyme, et non tribu ou préfecture.

Ce schéma des 12 tribus va être recueilli par l'Elohiste dans les milieux du Nord et lui permettre de substituer l'autorité de Moïse à celle de la dynastie judéenne. Moïse est seul médiateur de l'Alliance entre YHWH et les 12 tribus. Aussi l'Alliance Jahviste d'Ex 34.10,27 fait-elle place à celle d'Ex. 24.4-6, 8. Le don de l'Esprit aux rois qui les fait gouverner au nom de YHWH (1 S 10.1-2; 11.6; 16.12) passe à Moïse (Nb 11.25), ainsi qu'aux 70 anciens qui l'aident à gouverner.

Certains 'Juges' reçoivent aussi l'Esprit (Otniel, Gédéon, Jephté, Samson). De même, un rédacteur prédeutéronomique du Livre des

---

26. Cf. p. 84 supra, note 16. Après des essais plus ou moins heureux, les études récentes datent à nouveau le Jahviste des débuts de la monarchie; cf. Berge 1990; Zwickel 1992.

juges transfère la fonction royale de 'sauveur' (yš', 1 S 9.16...) sur un 'juge' par tribu. Mais il n'arrive au chiffre de 12 que par des procédés rédactionnels: en représentant Juda par le Qenizzite Otniel, en faisant jouer à Shamgar le rôle de Shim'on près des Philistins, en faisant de Bethléem de Nephtali une ville de la voisine Asher, en unissant en Jephté le Gil'adite la fonction de Gad et celle de Ruben en Moab (avec le dieu Kamosh), et en faisant déjà de Lévi une tribu sacerdotale au service de Dan qui, avec Samson, a une position prééminente dans la narration. Le texte Elohiste Dt 33 consacrera ce schéma par des bénédictions de Moïse. Les 12 *shivṭey* sont les branches d'un seul peuple (Dt 33.5) (de Geus; Halpern) alors qu'il y avait un roi en Yeshurun.

C'est donc la strate Elohiste[27] qui a donné au sceptre *shevet* son sens juridique de 'branche' d'un peuple. Mais auparavant, avant de former un *'am*, les clans, qui furent à l'origine de ces tribus, s'étaient unis non seulement comme *Ben 'ameh* mais par des actions guerrières communes en *qâhâl* (Gn 49.6; Nb 22.4; 1 S 17.47) et, peut-être, par un culte régulier commun en *'edah*.[28]

REFERENCES

Albright, W.F.
1934   *Vocalization of the Egyptian Syllabic Orthography* (New Haven).
Alfrink, B.
              'L'expression *n'sp el 'mmyw*', *OTS* 5: 118-31.
Anderson, G.W.
1959   *A Critical Introduction to the Old Testament* (London).
1970   'Israel: Amphictyony, *'Am Ḳahal, 'Edah*', dans H.T. Frank and W.L. Reed (ed.), *Translating and Understanding the Old Testament. Essays... H.G. May* (Abingdon): 135-51.
Archi, A.
1988   *Eblaite Personal Names and Semitic Name-Giving*, ARE, I (Rome).

27. G.W. Anderson a résumé clairement les caractéristiques de la strate Elohiste (1959: 34-38), tenant compte des travaux de ses prédécesseurs, de l'apport de l'école scandinave et de ses propres récherches. L'Elohiste est périodiquement rémis en cause. Il l'avait été par Volz et Rudolph, qui n'avaient pas été suivis, et furent réfutés en particulier par O. Eissfeldt.

28. Nous ne pouvons ici étudier ces deux termes suggérés également par G.W. Anderson. On trouvera les éléments fondamenteaux: pour *qâhâl* dans *THAT* II, 609-19 (H.-P. Müller), *ThWAT* VI, 1204-22 (Fabry); pour *'edah* dans *ThWAT* V, 1079–92 (Levy/Milgrom) avec la note de H. Ringgren.

Arnaud, D.
1986   *Recherches au pays d'Ashtata*, VI, 3 (Paris).
von Arx, U.
1990   *Studien zur Geschichte des alttestamentlichen Zwölfersymbolismus. I. Fragen im Horizont der Amphictyoniehypothese von Martin Noth* (Europäische Hochschulschriften XXIII/397, Bern).
Astour, M.
1988   'The Geographical and Political Structure of the Ebla Empire' dans *Wirtschaft und Gesellschaft von Ebla*, HSAO 2 (Heidelberg).
Auld, A.G.
1987   'Tribal Terminology in Joshua and judges', dans *Le origini di Israele* (Rome).
Avigad, N.
1975   *IEJ*: 101.
Beeston, A.F.L. *et al.*
1981   *Sabaean Dictionary* (Beyrouth–Louvain).
Benz, F.
1972   *Personal Names in the Phoenician and Punic Inscriptions* (Rome).
Berge, K.
1990   *Die Zeit des Jahwisten*, BZAW 186 (Berlin: de Gruyter).
Biella, J.C.
1982   *A Dictionary of Old South-Arabic* (Harvard).
Caquot, A.
1968   'Préfets', *DBSup*, VIII, c. 273–86.
Caquot-Sznycer
1974   *Textes Ougaritiques. I. Mythes et légendes* (Paris).
Cazelles, H.
1961   'Patriarches', *DBSup*, VII, c. 119.
1982   *Histoire politique d'Israël des origines à Alexandre le grand* (Paris).
1990   dans (ed.) E.M. Laperrousaz, *La protohistoire d'Israël* (Paris): 44-51.
1991   'Historiographies bibliques et prébibliques', *RB* 98: 501-506.
Celada, B.E.
1981   'La anfictiona de los 12 tribu de Israele, un concepto tanto discutible como repetido', *Cult. Bibl*: 59-97.
Coote, R.B., and Whitelam, K.W.
1987   *The Emergence of Early Israel in Historical Perspective* (Sheffield).
de Geus, C.H.J.
1976   *The Tribes of Israel—An Investigation into Some of the Presuppositions of Martin Noth's Amphictyony Hypothesis* (Assen/Amsterdam).
Dearman, A.
1989   *Studies on the Mesha Inscription and Moab* (Atlanta).
Dossin, G.
1952   *ARM*, V, 141.
Durand, J.M.
1988   *Archives Epistolaires de Mari*, I (Paris).
Fabry, H.-J.
1989   *qàhàl*, dans *ThWAT*, VI: 1204–22.

Fales, M.
1976   dans (ed.) S. Moscati, *La alba della Civiltà*, I (Torino): 149-59.
Finkelstein, I.
1990   'The Emergence of Early Israel: Anthropology, Environment, Archeology', *JAOS* 110: 677-87.
Gardiner, A.
1950   *Egyptian Grammar*³ (Oxford).
Gibson
1978   *Canaanite Myths and Legends*² (Edinburh: Clark).
Giveon, R.
        Lexikon der Aegyptologie, I.
Gnuse, R.
1991   'Israel Settlement in Canaan: A Peaceful Internal Process', *BTB* 21/2: 56-66.
Gottwald, N.K.
1980   *The Tribes of Yahweh—A Sociology of the Religion of Liberated Israel 1250–1050 BCE* (London).
Groneberg, B.
1988   *RA*: 71-73.
Hallo, W.
1960   'A Sumerian Amphictyony', *JCS* 14: 88-116.
Halpern, B.
1983   *The Emergence of Israel in Canaan* (SBLDS, Chico).
Helck, W.
1962   *Die Beziehungen Aegyptens zu Vorderasien im 3d und 2d Jahrtausend* (Wiesbaden).
Heltzer, M.
1962   *The International Organization of the Kingdom of Ugarit* (Wiesbaden): 15-22.
Huffmon, H.B.
1965   *Amorite Personal Names in the Mari Texts* (Baltimore): 196-98.
Hulst, A.R.
1976   *THAT*, II, 290-325.
Jagersma, H.
1988   *Numeri* (Nijkerk).
Jaussen, A.
1908   *Coutumes des Arabes au pays de Moab* (Paris): 143-62.
Kallai, Z.
1986   *Historical Geography of the Bible—The Tribal Territories of Israel* (Jerusalem/Leiden).
Lefevre, G.
1940   *Grammaire de l'Egyptien classique* (Le Caire).
Lemaire, A.
1972   'Le pays de Hepher', *Sem* 22: 13-20.
1978   'Les "Beney Jacob"', *RB* 85: 321-37.
1981   'Galaad et Makir', *VT*: 31.
Levy/Milgrom, J.
1986   'édah, dans *ThWAT*, V, 1079–92.

Lipiński, E.
  1989   *ThWAT*, VI, 177-86.
McDonald, B.
  1974   *The Biblical Tribe of Benjamin: Its Origins and its History during the Period of the Judges in Israel* (Diss. Washington Catholic University).
Malamat, A.
  1962   'Mari and the Bible: Some Patterns of Tribal Organization and Institutions', *JAOS* 82: 143-50.
  1967   'Aspects of Tribal Society in Mari and in Israel', *XV RAI* (Liège: Paris): 121-38.
  1989   *Mari and the Israelite Experience* (The Schweich Lectures, 1984; Oxford).
Mendenhall, G.E.
  1962   'The Hebrew Conquest of Palestine', *BA* 25: 66-87.
Milano, E.
  1990   Assegnazioni di prodotti alimentari', *ARE*, IX (Rome): 3-52, 264.
Müller, H.-P.
  1976   *qàhàl* dans *THAT*, II, 609-19.
Na'aman, S.
  1980   'The Inheritances of the Sons of Simeon', *ZDPV* 96: 136-52.
Noth, M.
  1928   *Die Israelitschen Personennamen im Rahmen der Gemeinsemitischen Namengebung* (Stuttgart): 66-82.
Oded. B.
  1970   *Studies Avenari* (Haifa): 11-36.
Orlinsky, H.
  1962   'The Tribal System and Related groups in the Period of Judges', dans *Studies and Essays in Honour of A. Neuman* (Leiden).
Pettinato, G.
  1981   *The Archives of Ebla* (New York): 122-29.
  1987   dans L. Cagni (ed.), *Ebla 1975–1985* (Naples): 15-19.
Pomponio, F.
  1984   'I LUGAL dell' administrazione di Ebla', *AuOr* 2: 127-35.
Redford, D.
  1972   'The Taxation System of Solomon. Structure of the Ancient Palestinian World', *Studies...Winnet* (Toronto): 141-56.
  1986   *Journal of the American Research Center in Egypt* 23: 127, avec bibliographie.
Ribichini-Xella
  1991   *SEL* 8.
Rosel, N.A.
  1984   'Zu den "Gauen" Salomos', *ZDPV* 100: 84-90.
Rowton, M.B.
  1965   'The Topological Factor in the Hapiru Problem', *Studies Landsberger* (Chicago): 375-87.
  1967   'The Physical Environment and the Problem of the Nomads', *XV RAI* (Paris): 109-22.
  1973   'Urban Autonomy in a Nomadic Environment', *JNES* 33: 201-15.

1976   'Dimorphic Structure and the Tribal Elite', *Al-Bahit* (Fest. Henninger; St. Augustin bei Bonn): 219-58.

Ryckmans, G.
1934   *Les noms propres sud-semitiques*, I (Louvain).

Sapin, J.
1972   La formation de la tribu de Benjamin sur von territoire (thèse, Strasbourg).

Sasson, J.
1977   *English–Akkadian Analytical Index* (Chapel Hill, NC).

Seebass, H
1978   *ZAW* 90: 196-220.

Sznycer, M.
1975   'L'assemblée du peuple dans les cités puniques d'après les temoignages épigraphiques', *Sem* 25: 47-68.
1980   *DBSup*, IX, c. 1423-26.

Teixidor, J.
1976   *Syria*: 407s.

de Vaux R.
1971   'La thèse de l'"amphictyonie Israelites"', *HTR* 64: 415-36.
1973   *Histoire ancienne d'Israël*, II (Paris): 19-26.

Waetzold, H., and Hauptmann, H.
1988   *Wirtschaft und Gesellschaft in Ebla* (Heidelberg).

Westermann, C.
1988   *Genesis* (BK, I).

Whitaker
1972   *A Concordance of the Ugaritic Literature* (Harvard).

Zobel, H.-J.
1965   *Stammesspruch und Geschichte* (Berlin: de Gruyter).

Zwickel, W.
1992   'Der Altarbau Abrahams zwischen Bethel und Ai (Gn. 12-13)—Ein Beitrag zur Datierung des Jahwisten', *BZ* 36: 207-19.

JEREMIAH 1–25 AND THE DEUTERONOMISTIC HISTORY

R.E. Clements

To a significant extent the prophetic books may be regarded as collections of collections in which the primary material consists of prophecies that were originally orally delivered and most of which were originally short in length. They have been preserved in writing by unknown editors, and in this process of written preservation some degree of grouping and structuring of the prophecies has certainly taken place. By what principles this structuring occurred is far from clear. The inclusion of short superscriptions (as in Jer. 1.1-3; 2.1; 3.1; 7.1; 11.1; 21.11; 25.1-2) has served to offer some brief contextual setting for the prophecies, and there appear also to be appropriate closures (so Jer. 5.18-19; 9.12-16). It is possible that other units were intended to mark transition points in the collection. Since we do not know in what context the prophecies were read, whether by small groups of trained scribes, or by larger communities in more formal acts of public confession and worship, the role of these beginnings and endings is not clear. They do little more than provide a bare minimum of historical information for the elucidation of the prophecy. They are, however, sufficient to indicate that we cannot be altogether dismissive of the role of the book's editors.

Alongside this we can note that there sometimes appear to be signs of a chronological sequencing of material, although this is not consistently carried through and the context of many prophecies remains obscure. Such a chronological scheme, even though very incompletely maintained, seems likely to reflect the processes of transmission. Further to this we may note that the classification of material on formal grounds, best linked with the name and work of S. Mowinckel, contains some implications for the editorial shaping of the book (Mowinckel 1914; cf. Hobbs 1972: 258). Mowinckel himself appears strongly to have hinted in the direction of assuming that the different classes of material were preserved in different transmission strata, although he later modified this conclusion substantially (Mowinckel 1946: 61ff.). Yet the nature and content of the so-called 'Source C' material fails to support the conclusion that it derives from a separate transmission 'source' as such. It appears rather to have been intended to be read in conjunction with other material in the book, on which it is partly dependent.

All of this suggests that we are faced either with assuming (1) that there is no very clear structure at all to the grouping of prophecies in Jeremiah 1–25, other than a very loose one, or (2) that whatever structure there may originally have been has undergone significant disturbance in the course of the book's further preservation and transmission.

What I wish to do in this short paper is to suggest one avenue of investigation, which appears to me to be sufficiently defensible to be worth serious consideration, and which does have some bearing upon the historical and literary context in which the book was formed.

Prophecy in the Deuteronomistic History

There exists in 2 Kgs 17.7-23 a very noteworthy reflection upon the final collapse of the Northern Kingdom, under Hoshea, before the power of King Shalmaneser of Assyria. It is listed by Martin Noth as one of the key passages, otherwise set out in the form of speeches or prayers, by which the Deuteronomist directly injects an element of meaning and explanation into the events narrated concerning Israel's rise and fall (Noth 1981: 6). We may summarize the main contents relatively concisely:

1. The people of Israel had sinned against Yahweh their God... They had worshipped other gods... They set up for themselves pillars and sacred poles... They served idols, of which Yahweh had said to them, 'You shall not do this' (vv. 7-12).
2. Yet Yahweh warned Israel and Judah by every prophet and every seer, saying, 'Turn from your evil ways and keep my commandments and my statutes, in accordance with all the law that I commanded your ancestors and that I sent to you by my servants the prophets'. They would not listen but were stubborn, as their ancestors had been. They went after idols

and became false... They rejected all the commandments of
Yahweh their God...(vv. 13-17).

3.   Judah also did not keep the commandments of Yahweh their
       God, but walked in the customs that Israel had introduced...
       (vv. 19-20).

4.   When he had torn Israel from the house of David, they made
       Jeroboam son of Nebat king. Jeroboam drove Israel from
       following Yahweh and made them commit great sins. The
       people of Israel continued in all the sins that Jeroboam com-
       mitted; they did not depart from them... So Israel was exiled
       from their own land to Assyria until this day (vv. 21-23).

The four central themes are the following: 1. The Northern
Kingdom of Israel had been disloyal to God, and this is proven by its
idolatry. 2. Yahweh had warned of God's anger through prophets, but
the people rejected the prophetic warnings. 3. Israel was punished by
being sent into exile, but Judah also has disobeyed God. 4. Disloyal
kings, who followed the path of Jeroboam and disobeyed God's law,
were primary causes of Israel's downfall.

What is worthy of note is that this reflects very closely indeed the
central themes of the structure of Jeremiah 1–25. We can outline these
as follows and note the correspondences. It is evident that this overall
structural pattern is introduced by the opening call and commissioning
narrative of Jer. 1.1-19 and is provided with a summarizing conclusion in Jer. 25.1-14. These two units provide an outer framework for
the whole larger structure. The call narrative, with its appended
visions, reflects a certain stylizing, but almost certainly draws on
authentic elements of the Jeremiah tradition. It serves both as an
affirmation of the divine origin and authority of the message that is
given in the book that follows, and also as a key to its central message.
This latter is then the subject of Jer. 25.1-14, which is unusual in that
it makes reference to the written scroll of the prophecies (25.13), but,
by doing so, clearly betrays its role as a formal ending to a literary
collection. It must undoubtedly have been composed to perform this
function.

The recognition that the material characterized by S. Mowinckel as
'Source C' had its origins in a Deuteronomistic circle of authors has
gained convincing recognition among recent scholars (so Nicholson
1970: 38ff.; Thiel 1973: *passim*; Stulman 1986: 49ff.). The purpose of
the present study is to extend this towards a recognition that the

structural shape accorded to Jeremiah 1–25 also betrays a strongly Deuteronomistic origin. By demonstrating this, it is hoped to suggest ways in which the use of the Jeremiah prophetic tradition contributed a major, and final, component of the Deuteronomistic theological development of the exilic era.

Both the opening and concluding sections of Jeremiah 1–25 contain explicit summaries of the purport of Jeremiah's prophecies (so especially 1.14-19 and 25.8-14). Such summaries reveal their purpose of serving as editorial guides to the comprehensive written collection of Jeremiah's sayings referred to in 25.13. They have been designed from the outset to introduce, explain the historical relevance of, and to summarize the message of the prophet Jeremiah. Their message, put briefly, is that God has called for hostile nations to come from the north to threaten and punish Judah for its many and grievous sins. These nations will set their thrones against Jerusalem to accomplish God's judgment upon the city (Jer. 1.14-16). This enemy from the north has materialized in the person of Nebuchadrezzar, who is Yahweh's 'servant' to punish Judah (25.9), so that the whole land will be left a ruin (25.11; cf. Overholt 1968: 39-48). While this enemy comes to inflict God's punishment, the faithful prophet, within the walls of Jerusalem, will be threatened but not overwhelmed (1.17-19).

Judah and Israel

Jeremiah 2.1–3.5 follows the call narrative with a long, and broadly based, indictment of Israel as a whole, but specifically addressed to the citizens of Jerusalem (Jer. 2.2). The nature of the indictment, and the appeal back to the national origins in the wilderness, make it clear that it is still 'all Israel' that is the subject of this prophetic condemnation. However, the immediate sequel in 3.6-11, which is, unexpectedly, specifically ascribed to 'the days of King Josiah' (3.6), affirms that the punitive lesson meted out to the Northern Kingdom had not been learned by Judah: 'Yet for all this her false sister Judah did not return to me with her whole heart, but only in pretense, says Yahweh' (Jer. 3.10). On the contrary, Israel's disobedience was not as bad as that of Judah: 'Faithless Israel has shown herself less guilty than false Judah' (3.11). The central features here are consistent with a Deuteronomistic origin (Thiel 1973: 83ff.; Stulman 1986: 56ff.). The appeal to Israel to return to Yahweh, which follows in 3.12–4.2 (interrupted by the reassuring insertion of 3.15-18) then establishes the possibility of repentance and renewal. What follows this in 4.3–6.30 is then very explicitly addressed to 'the people of Judah and the inhabitants of Jerusalem' (Jer. 4.3; cf. also 4.5, 11; 5.1, 20).

All of this suggests that there is an overall structure extending from 2.1 to 6.30 which pivots upon the basic assertion of 3.10-11 that Judah was more guilty of disobedience to God than its sister kingdom in the north. This links up closely with the Deuteronomistic assertion of 2 Kgs 17.7-23 that the Northern Kingdom's downfall was an act of Yahweh's punishment upon her. Although it is true that this concerns what happened to the Northern Kingdom in the eighth century, the lesson that it teaches was evidently intended to be a lesson learned by Judah. If Yahweh punished Israel so harshly, how much more did Judah and Jerusalem deserve to be punished since their sins were greater than those of the sister kingdom in the north! Jeremiah's prophecies were addressed to a specific community in a particular crisis situation. The structural setting has provided this warning with a larger context by establishing that the threat to Judah was fully justified and vindicated by comparison with the fate of its sister kingdom in the north. When the Northern Kingdom had suffered at the hands of the Assyrians, Judah had failed to heed the implicit warning this had provided.

That the overall structure of Jer. 2.1–4.2 endeavours to make this the lesson to be learned from the fate of the Northern Kingdom in the eighth century BCE can then be better understood if precisely the opposite conclusion was the one widely held. Study of the presuppositions of Josiah's cultic reform, of the rise and development of the Deuteronomic reform movement as a whole, and of the kind of hot-headed counsel that appears ultimately to have swayed Zedekiah into rebellion against Babylon—all these point to the conclusion that this was indeed the case in Judah (cf. Hardmeier 1990: 161ff.). Judah's survival in the eighth century, which contrasted with the ruination of the Northern Kingdom, had been widely interpreted as a mark of Judah's loyalty to Yahweh, in contrast to Ephraim's faithlessness. It is possible to go on from this to suggest that, at the heart of the reform movement which motivated Josiah, there lay such an interpretation of the events of the eighth century. It has left an imposing legacy in the collection and redaction of Isaiah's prophecies, and not least in the elaborated accounts of what had happened when Sennacherib confronted Hezekiah in 701 BCE. Judah's reprieve from Sennacherib's threat was understood as a consequence of her faithful allegiance to the Davidic dynasty (cf. 2 Kgs 19.34). Therefore, a primary problem of theodicy lay before the Deuteronomic movement—that of showing why the 'favoured' deliverance of Judah at the time of Ephraim's near destruction should have turned out merely to have been a temporary reprieve. What was thus necessary was to demonstrate that Judah's sins were as great as, and indeed even worse than, those of its sister kingdom in the north. This is precisely the central point of the section that follows in Jer. 7.1–10.25.

Idolatry—The Worst of Sins

If we turn next to consider the question, 'What was the evidence that the Northern Kingdom's downfall was an act of punishment from God?', we have a clear answer set out in 2 Kgs 17.7-12, with its decisive summarizing conclusion: 'they served idols, concerning which Yahweh had said to them, "You shall not do this"' (v. 12). This is then precisely the controlling theme which holds together the larger unit of Jeremianic prophecies in Jer. 7.1–10.16. It is introduced by the Deuteronomistic prose address concerning the Jerusalem temple in 7.1–15 (W. Thiel 1973: 103ff.; Stulman 1986: 58ff.), an affirmation regarding the uselessness of animal sacrifice as a means for removing sin (7.16-26), and a denunciation of the evil nature of the child-burning cult on the high-place of Topheth, which defiled the very temple area itself (7.30-34). The Jerusalem cultus had become no better than a form of idolatry, alongside which the overt practice of idolatry was widespread among the people (Jer. 10.10-16). The final unit of Jer. 10.12-16, which is didactic in character, reasserts the folly of idolatry as a form of human delusion. It would certainly appear that this admonition, with its psalm-like formulation, was originally of independent origin. Nevertheless the theme that it expresses, that idols are a delusion, that they characterize the worship of Gentile nations, but Yahweh is the true God, is a significant summing up.

The accusation of idolatry and its inevitable punishment holds together overall the unit of Jer. 7.1–10.16 and points directly to the central Deuteronomistic polemic regarding the downfall of the Northern Kingdom in 2 Kgs 17.7-12. Not only are Judah's sins worse than those perpetrated by its sister kingdom in the north, but they are essentially of the same character, namely idolatry. The detailed evidence given in support of this argues, as in Ezek. 8.1-18, that the temple of Jerusalem had become the setting for such idolatrous acts (Jer. 7.30-34). Even worse, this temple of Yahweh had been made into an idol (Jer. 7.4), for the people had trusted in its physical actuality rather than in the God who was worshipped there (Jer. 7.8-11).

The short unit of Jer. 10.17-25, which follows this extended affirmation concerning the idolatrous character of Judah's religion, concludes the section by offering a summary concerning the prophet's message and the divine judgment that it foretold. That there is an overall structure to the section of Jer. 7.1–10.25, which has been loosely built around the theme of idolatry, appears certain. So also does the fact that it is markedly Deuteronomistic in character. Where the reformist tendencies on which this movement was built had adopted a progressively more restrictive attitude towards the temple cultus, now the Deuteronomistic editors have affirmed that the entire cultus of Jerusalem had become unacceptable to God. First Hezekiah's age had witnessed the rejection of the Nehushtan image (2 Kgs 18.4). Then later the Asherah symbol within the temple had needed to be condemned (2 Kgs 21.7). The line of polemic was now drawn to an end-point, by the comprehensive condemnation of the temple cultus as idolatrous because of the way in which worshippers trusted in it falsely. Certainly much of this must be regarded as reflective apologetic made in the wake of the catastrophe of 587 BCE, but no doubt authentic Jeremianic material can be found in it. The important point is that the accusation of idolatrous practices has been built up to provide an explanation for a religious disaster of immense proportions. God had to destroy the sanctuary where the name of Yahweh was invoked, because of the manner in which it had been abused. In defence of such a claim the earlier example of the fate of Shiloh is cited (Jer. 7.14).

The Prophet as Covenant Mediator

The lengthy section, extending from Jer. 11.1–20.18, begins with a general introduction concerning the covenant nature of Israel's relationship to Yahweh and evidences a strongly Deuteronomistic character (Jer. 11.1-8; so Thiel 1973: 139ff.; Stulman 1986: 63ff.). This feature has been widely recognized, not least on account of its forthright covenant language and ideology. However, it is not simply the Deuteronomistic nature of this piece by itself, but the fact that it appears clearly to have been designed in order to establish a covenant framework for the larger unit it introduces. It is followed directly by a presentation of the prophet's role as a mediator of this covenant. The painful nature of this mediatorial role is illustrated by the first of Jeremiah's 'confessions', which immediately follows it (Jer. 11.18-20). This appears as a response to the threat upon his life made by the people of Anathoth (Jer. 11.21-23). At the beginning of the larger unit, therefore, a certain structural pattern is established: the prophet of God is a mediator of the covenant between Yahweh and Israel, but this mediatorial role is threatened by popular rejection.

Jeremiah is presented as the intermediary established by God to summon the people back to obedience to the covenant. However, not only had the people broken this covenant (Jer. 11.10), but their actions in threatening Jeremiah's life now served as proof of their rejection of the prophetic mediator. As the larger unit unfolds, punctuated by the further pain expressed through Jeremiah's confessions, we find that the experiences of the prophet parallel closely those of the 'founder' of the covenant—Moses. Yet, whereas Moses's intercession had availed to avert final disaster for Israel's ancestors in the wilderness before their entry into the land (Deut. 9.8-29), this could not now be repeated. Jeremiah's prayers could not avail to avert the inevitable consequences of the people's total rejection of Yahweh as Israel's God (Jer. 11.14-15). Israel's refusal to hearken to the prophet's words is demonstrated by the rejection of the message-bearer.

The theme of mediation, which provides a structure to the whole unit, is then further exemplified by additional signs of the people's rejection of the prophet (Jer. 15.15-21; 17.14-18; 18.19-23) and intensified warnings of the judgment that must follow. The entire sequence of Jeremiah's so-called 'confessions' finds its theological context in the understanding that the prophet is, like Moses, a mediator of the covenant. His likeness to Moses is spelled out for all to recognize in that he suffers pain and rejection as Israel's founding leader had done.

In case this point might be overlooked it is given explicit declaration in the brief introductory unit of Jer. 15.1-4. The Deuteronomistic character of this is clear (Thiel 1973: 178ff.), and is strikingly reinforced by the cross-linkage to 2 Kgs 21.10-15, which refers to the period of Manasseh's reign, with all its fearful brutalities, as explanation for the fact that even Josiah's reforms could not avert the final downfall of Jerusalem and Judah. If we follow the suggestion of F.M. Cross (Cross 1973: 285-86; cf. Nelson 1987: 247ff.), then this use of Manasseh's reign as explanation of the final catastrophe was a late feature introduced into the Deuteronomistic history. It helped to turn the original more hopeful narrative composed in Josiah's reign into one coloured by awareness of ultimate disaster at the hands of the Babylonians.

This covenant theology has an oddly dual character. On the one hand it makes clear that judgment is not a predetermined and fixed fate, but affirms that room for mediation and reconciliation exists. On the other hand it introduces a conditional factor that does not shrink from envisaging that Israel might finally be destroyed. The story of Moses's intercession in the wilderness serves to demonstrate this point. That prophets served Israel's needs as intercessors, in the manner of Moses and Samuel, is expressly made clear in Jer. 15.1:

> Then Yahweh said to me: 'Though Moses and Samuel stood before me,
> yet my heart would not relent concerning this people' (Jer. 15.1).

Overall it is clear that the historical figure of Moses has exercised a powerful role on the part of the editors of Jeremiah 1–25 in shaping a portrait of the office and role of Jeremiah as a prophet (Seitz 1989: 3-27). At the same time a reverse influence is also evident on the part of the Deuteronomists in which the portrait of Moses has been shaped according to Judah's encounter with prophets such as Jeremiah. 'Deuteronomy saw Moses as the first of the prophets. Intercession was an integral part of his prophetic vocation' (Seitz 1989: 7).

The conclusion of the entire larger unit comprising Jeremiah 11–20 finds its climax with a violent outburst from Jeremiah in which the prophet complains against the total rejection of his message by the people (Jer. 20.7-12). The full extent of this rejection, and the ultimate cry of pain with the prophet's recognition of its irreversible nature, are revealed in Jeremiah's curse upon the day of his birth (Jer. 20.14-18).

All of this parallels very closely indeed the highly distinctive Deuteronomistic presentation of the prophets as the rejected mediators of God's covenant set out in 2 Kgs 17.13-14:

> Yet Yahweh warned Israel and Judah by every prophet and every seer,
> saying, 'Turn from your evil ways and keep my commandments and my
> statutes, in accordance with all the law that I commanded your ancestors

and that I sent to you by my servants the prophets'. They would not listen
but were stubborn, as their ancestors had been, who did not believe in
Yahweh their God (2 Kgs 17.13-14).

What is especially significant in this, and what links it so closely
with the Jeremianic material, is that it not only presents the work of
prophets as that of covenant mediators, but it presents the rejection of
such prophets as an accomplished reality. This marriage between the
idea of popular rejection and of the 'true' prophet marks a formative
stage in the development of the notion that God's faithful prophet is a
martyr figure (Steck 1967: 199ff.). Such a development has provided
a central feature of the Deuteronomistic interpretation of prophecy in
the divine economy of Israel (Clements 1975: 41ff.). Admittedly such
earlier figures as Amos and Hosea were 'rejected' prophets of this
kind, but not until the time of Jeremiah could it be fully recognized
that prophecy had 'failed' in the sense that it had been unable to avert
the final collapse of the surviving part of Israel as Yahweh's people.
Until that time the hope could still be entertained that God's appointed
prophets would summon the people back to their ancestral loyalty.

Jeremiah is, in fact, the paradigmatic illustration of the degree of
total national rejection of the message of the prophets which is described in this Deuteronomistic reflection. The theology of covenant
shows the conditional nature of Israel's continuance before God; the
prophets are portrayed as reaffirming the terms of this covenant. Now
the figure of Jeremiah, typified in his rejection, serves to make plain
that Israel has not kept the covenant and must suffer the inevitable
curse spelled out in Jer. 11.1-8. More than any other prophetic figure
he is presented as the classic exemplar of 'the prophet like Moses' who
is ascribed an ongoing place in the life of the nation in Deut. 18.15-22
(Clements 1975: 41ff.; Seitz 1989: 3ff.).

If these observations are correct, to the effect that there is a close
correlation between the structure of Jer. 11.1–20.18 and the portrayal
of Jeremiah as an outstanding exemplar of the Deuteronomistic conception of a prophet 'like Moses', then some significant features must
be related to them. Not only are there passages of an undoubtedly
Deuteronomistic flavour within the larger unit as a whole, as has been
widely recognized, but the overall framework bears a Deuteronomistic
character. The individual 'confessions' of the prophet are located so as
to highlight this covenant-mediatorial role. Kathleen O'Connor notes

this vital structuring role of the so-called 'confession' passages within their larger setting:

> The arrangement and distribution of materials, the development of the theological argument, the placement of the confessions and the unifying function of both the call account and closing summary show that the final form of cc. 1–25 came from a writer (O'Connor 1988: 155; cf. Diamond 1987: 149ff.).

Overall the structure of Jeremiah 11–20 demonstrates, in a comprehensive fashion, an important presupposition of the covenant theology that the Deuteronomists had come to embrace. Disobedience could push Israel beyond the brink of disaster. Whereas Moses had interceded successfully with Yahweh on Israel's behalf (Aurelius 1988: 18ff.; 88ff.), such intercession could now no longer hold back the nation from catastrophe.

Undoubtedly all of this has been given its final shape in the aftermath of 587 BCE, as we should expect. It uses fundamental elements of the Deuteronomistic theology to develop a theodicy. The confessions attributed to Jeremiah have been incorporated by the prose writer in order to illustrate the indictment of Israel and to explain the disaster that finally overtook the nation (O'Connor 1988: 113; cf. Diamond 1987: 182). Nevertheless it is not simply a backwards-looking review, justifying an irremediable situation of the past. Rather it is forward-looking in that it ties the explanation of past tragedy to concepts of covenant, and to the realities of prophecy and *tōrâ*, which were to carry the remnants of the nation into a new future.

The Faithless Shepherds

We can move on then to a further observation in respect of the concluding part of the structure of Jeremiah 1–25. The final section in Jer. 21.1–24.10 has, as its central core, a series of prophecies concerning the fate of the various kings of Judah who ruled, sometimes only briefly, during Jeremiah's ministry. These prophecies are introduced in 21.1-10 by a prose section, with a broadly based announcement to Zedekiah, the last of the Davidic kings to rule in Jerusalem, that the city will fall to the king of Babylon. The collection of prophecies that deal with the Davidic kingship therefore begins chronologically at the end with the last of such rulers, but in a way that is thematically appropriate since it draws attention to the fact that it is the fate of the dynasty as a whole that is at issue. That this was an issue that lay close to the centre of the Deuteronomic movement as a whole is shown by the fact that the notion of a dynastic promise to the royal house of David provides the Deuteronomistic History with a pivotal centre (2 Sam. 7.1-17).

The sequel to the introduction in Jer. 21.1-10 concerning the fate of Judah's royal house is a sharp condemnation of an unnamed 'king of Judah' in Jer. 21.11-14. This monarch is addressed in 21.13 as 'You who are enthroned above the valley'. It is likely that one specific ruler was originally intended (Jehoiakim?), but, as it now stands, a larger framework has been accorded to it showing that it is the entire 'house of David' that is threatened (cf. the address in v. 12). As it now reads, the threat serves to draw out the important feature that the reproof, raised against an individual ruler in Jerusalem, places in jeopardy the future of the entire Davidic dynasty.

This feature is even more fully brought out in the passage that follows, which has served as something of an exemplary illustration of the manner in which the prophet's Deuteronomistic editors have developed the message of his prophecies. There stands in vv. 6-7 a short poetic threat, addressed to an unnamed king of Judah:

> For thus says Yahweh concerning the house of the king of Judah:
>> You are like Gilead to me,
>>> like the summit of Lebanon;
>> but I swear that I will make you a desert,
>>> —cities without inhabitants.
>> I will prepare destroyers against you;
>>> all of them with their weapons,
>> will cut down your prime cedars
>>> and hurl them into the fire.
>>>> Jer. 22.6-7

The authentic Jeremianic origin of this unit can be reasonably defended, with its poetic play on the imagery suggested by the impressive House of the Forest of Lebanon (cf. 1 Kgs 7.2; 10.17, 21). The link with 21.13-14 through the imagery of 'forest' and 'fire' is clear (Holladay 1986: 583). However, the threats of 21.11-14 and 22.6-7 addressed to the contemporary Davidic ruler have been given a Deuteronomistic elaborative interpretation in 22.1-5 that reinforces the threat and provides it with a fuller explanation (Thiel 1973: 230ff.; Stulman 1986: 81-82). W.L. Holladay opposes the Deuteronomistic ascription of this material, while largely conceding the strength of the arguments for it (Holladay 1986: 580-81). The kingship, even that of so august a dynasty as that of David, is to serve the welfare of the people by upholding justice (v. 3). It must operate within the requirements of the divine covenant made at Horeb between Yahweh and Israel.

This point is then spelled out further, and quite explicitly, by the Deuteronomistic editors in 22.8-9:

> When many nations pass by this city and say among themselves, 'Why has Yahweh treated this great city like this?' Then they shall answer, 'Because they abandoned the covenant of Yahweh their God and worshipped other gods and served them' (Jer 22.8-9).

In this manner the threat directed against a specific ruler in Jerusalem, most probably Jehoiakim, is broadened by the book's editors into a condemnation of the dynasty which he represented. The behaviour of one individual king is drawn upon to demonstrate that the future of the entire dynasty had been put in jeopardy. The God-given grace of a royal house could not override the necessity for each king to rule with justice and fairness. Where, in the past, such failure of individual kings had brought condemnation upon themselves, the message is now extended to threaten the continuance of the Davidic dynasty.

That the monarchy was a conditional institution in Israel, is a point explicitly made by the Deuteronomistic Historian (cf. 1 Sam. 12.25) and this is fully in line with the concessionary nature of the institution of kingship in Israel set out in Deut. 17.14-20. Jer. 22.9 makes the same point by insisting that the royal throne of David was subordinate to the covenant that Yahweh had made with his people. So we come to see that the editorial framework which has been given to Jeremiah's royal prophecies displays a strongly Deuteronomistic character. The Davidic kings were to be regarded as mediators of Yahweh's covenant with Israel, but only if they themselves obeyed the conditions of this covenant (cf. especially vv. 4-5).

Following on these primary oracles dealing with the Davidic kingship we have pronouncements concerning the fate of Shallum-Jehoahaz (Jer. 22.10-12), Jehoiakim (Jer. 22.18-19, preceded by sharp invective in vv. 13-17), and Jehoiachin (Jer. 22.24-30).

We can then relate this point to the observation that the structure of Jer. 21.1–24.10 appears to display a distinct interest in the fate of the Davidic dynasty in general, over and above the question of the

Understanding Poets and Prophets

personal fates of the last individual rulers of Judah. This more comprehensive concern with the final collapse of what had survived as a remnant kingdom of Judah, epitomized in the fate of its royal rulers, is further shown by the placing of 24.1-10 as a concluding element. Whether or not this unit, with its lessons from the good and bad figs, really goes back to a saying from Jeremiah has been disputed. Unterman summarizes a very probable conclusion thus: 'It cannot be denied that 24.4-7 has all the signs of an authentic Jeremianic prophecy' (Unterman 1987: 56; cf. also Holladay 1986: 656-57). Holladay would locate the saying in 594 BCE. Yet this is not to deny that there has been some Deuteronomistic elaboration of Jeremiah's words and the placing of the unit in its present position appears to fulfil a particular editorial role (W. Thiel 1973: 253ff.).

The symbolic fate of the good and bad figs comes to a meaningful end with a warning that king Zedekiah of Judah, together with those who had remained with him in Jerusalem, were all doomed (vv. 8-10). The significant point for the overall structure of Jeremiah 1–25 is that the characterization of the Judaean community as 'bad figs' has been given a larger significance in the wake of subsequent events and thereby has served to orient the hope expressed in the book towards the community exiled in Babylon. The threefold agents of death—sword, famine and disease—link together the opening and closing sections concerning the disastrous nature of Zedekiah's reign from its beginning to its end (so especially 21.9 and 24.10; cf. also 29.18).

By the use of such opening and closing declarations, the prophecy of 24.4-7 concerning the fate of the 'bad figs' who remained in Judah after 598 BCE is related to an awareness of the tragic events of 587 BCE, which brought the kingdom of Judah, and the royal dynasty which had given it a divine foundation, to an end. This is then repeated in 29.17. The final rounding off of the whole collection in Jeremiah 1–25 is then given in 25.1-38, with a remarkable summary statement of what was regarded as the divine plan determining the world events relating to Jeremiah's ministry in 25.8-13.

Clearly it cannot occasion surprise that a prophet such as Jeremiah should have made forceful pronouncements concerning the various kings who ruled Judah after Josiah's death in 609 BCE. Undoubtedly these rulers carried a primary level of responsibility for Judah's ultimate downfall. What is surprising is the extent to which the Deuteronomistic framework that is given to these royal prophecies invests them with a larger theological and political significance. Not only is the Davidic monarchy, as a primary institution of Israel, accorded only conditional approval, but the fate of the Davidic dynasty as a whole is placed in question. We cannot be in doubt that it is the Deuteronomistic editors of the book who have imposed this broadened layer of meaning onto Jeremiah's prophecies, and that they have done so in the light of what they knew had taken place in 587 BCE, with as much help as they could obtain from Jeremiah's authentic prophecies. At the same time they have used these prophecies to address issues that lay open, and unresolved, in the major history-work they had compiled.

The conditional interpretation of the kingly office compares closely with the Deuteronomistic Historian's explanation of the role of the monarchy in contributing to the downfall of the Northern Kingdom:

> When he (Yahweh) had torn Israel from the house of David, they made Jeroboam son of Nebat king. Jeroboam drove Israel from following Yahweh and made them commit great sin. The people of Israel continued in all the sins that Jeroboam committed; they did not depart from them until Yahweh had removed Israel out of his sight...' (2 Kgs 17.21-23).

In this evaluation the importance of the kingship as an institution is affirmed, its role in the downfall of the Northern Kingdom recognized, and the central significance of the Davidic dynasty implied. Defection from allegiance to the Davidic dynasty is presented as the beginning of Ephraim's misfortunes. These assertions fit smoothly with the points which the editorial framework of Jeremiah's prophecies to Judah's kings seek to bring out. Kingship only existed within Israel in order to serve the needs of the Mosaic covenant.

Conclusion

It remains to draw some basic conclusions from this examination of the structures of Jeremiah 1–25. First of all we may note again the primary point that there is a broad structural shape to these chapters, which fall into four major sections. These deal respectively with the coming downfall of Judah, rendered inevitable because it had failed to heed the warning implicit in the fate of the sister kingdom of Ephraim more than a century earlier. Secondly, the question of the temple of Jerusalem is focused upon, and the necessity for its destruction is explained in terms of the idolatry practised there. The historical sanctuary had served as a cover for idolatrous practises, but worst of all, the temple itself had been made into an idol because it had been treated as a false basis of security. The belief that human beings could 'possess' the presence and power of deity, and could thereby be assured of divine protection, was precisely what made an image of God an offence and an illusion. The house of Yahweh in Jerusalem had been regarded by the people of Judah in the same manner that worshippers of an idol believed that it gave them assurance of divine protection.

The third and fourth sections of the prophetic collection of Jeremiah 1–25 focus respectively upon two types of divine mediation. The first is that of Israel's prophets whose task had been to warn Yahweh's people of the divine anger when they departed from obedience to the divine order. The second was that of kingship, and more particularly that of the dynasty of the royal house of David, which had ruled in Jerusalem for almost four hundred years.

These are all issues of prime significance for the Deuteronomistic movement, the origins of which are to be traced back to Josiah's reign, and perhaps even earlier still to the time of Hezekiah. It is a well-nigh classic expression of the situation outlined by M. Weber that the words of a 'charismatic' prophetic leader have led to a process of 'routinization' in order to make his words accessible and adaptable to a larger community and their ongoing needs (Clements 1986: 56-76; Clements 1990: 203-20). However, in the structure given to Jeremiah 1–25 the shaping of the units does not simply reassert familiar, and firmly established, features of Deuteronomistic theology. Instead it uses these central themes as a tool for accommodating, interpreting and applying Jeremiah's prophecies. This literary process illustrates very clearly the way in which a prophet's editors provide the record of his sayings with a context of historical, theological and institutional references by which the enduring meaning of his prophecies is to be grasped. It illustrates the aims of such a work of 'routinization' by which the unique and extraordinary elements of the prophet's preaching are set within a larger context in which they are to be applied and understood.

The Final Days of the Deuteronomistic Movement

If these observations are correct regarding the structural shape that has been accorded to Jeremiah 1–25, then they provide us with an important clue to the origin and purpose of many of the Deuteronomistic elements to be found within this impressive collection. From the outset this material was written, and was designed to serve a literary and theological purpose. Its intention is to be seen in the literary and structuring role which it serves in its surviving location in the Jeremiah scroll. This at least would appear to be the case for such passages as Jer. 3.6-12, 15-18; 7.1-15; 11.1-8; 21.1-10; 22.1-9; 24.1-10; 25.1-14. There is therefore no need to posit a separate stratum of supposed Deuteronomistic homilies, composed independently and subsequently incorporated into the scroll of Jeremiah's sayings. The aim rather has been to elucidate and elaborate the meaning of Jeremiah's prophecies, seen in the painful retrospect of the events of 587 BCE. The Deuteronomistic authors were writers, not preachers, a characteristic which is wholly in line with the observations of M. Weinfeld regarding the wisdom–scribal aspects of the Deuteronomistic literature (Weinfeld 1972: 158ff.).

A further conclusion deserves serious consideration. If, as is argued here, Jeremiah 1–25 displays a clear structure, a coherent attachment to central Deuteronomistic themes, and an overall conformity in its theological ideas, then it is this work which constitutes the original 'Deuteronomistic' scroll of Jeremiah's prophecies (cf. Rietzschel 1966: 91ff.). Admittedly some subsequent additions have been made to this, but these are not extensive, and essentially the work has survived as a coherent and consistent unity. When we turn to Jeremiah 26–52, however, the situation is substantially changed. Not only are the literary forms significantly different, with so much narrative reportage (Mowinckel's 'Source B'), but the theology and political outlook is very much modified. Most notably this is evident on three key issues: kingship, covenant and Israel's future hope. It would extend the present study too far to explore these in detail, but we may note some basic points.

In the first instance the hope of a restoration of the Davidic dynasty has been accorded a major role (Jer. 33.14-26), whereas the original 'Deuteronomistic' edition of Jeremiah's prophecies was indifferent to this, and even basically negative in its attitude to such an expectation. Secondly, the covenant theology of Jeremiah 1–25 has been wholly changed and recast with the introduction of the hope of a 'new' covenant in Jer. 31.31-37. Thirdly, and perhaps most remarkably, the original hope of Jeremiah 1–25, which looked for a survival and renewal within Judah of a chastened and penitent community, has been abandoned. All hope for the future now rests with a return from Babylonian exile of those who had been taken there in 598 BCE, and later (Jer. 29.1–31.26).

Clearly much authentic reminiscence of Jeremiah's part in the events of Judah's final collapse has been preserved and much echoing of 'Deuteronomistic' language and theology is still to be found. Nevertheless the move beyond the central ideas and themes found in the Deuteronomistic History and Jeremiah 1–25 is very marked. The original Deuteronomic movement has clearly collapsed, and new expectations and ideas have taken over the centre stage in the light of new events!

What we have are essentially an original book of Jeremiah's prophecies, edited by the Deuteronomic circle most probably at a time close to the completion of the History (c. 550 BCE?) and an extensive addendum to this in Jeremiah 26–52. This was forced upon the Deuteronomic traditionists in the wake of major upheavals that took place in Judah after 550 BCE, and Part II of the present Jeremiah book undoubtedly reflects this. We may go on to speculate that the original editorial composition of Jeremiah 1–25 took place in Judah, where all the Deuteronomistic literary ventures had their home. The location where the revised book (Jeremiah 1–25 + 26–52) was completed is no longer clear, although a Babylonian setting would seem to be most plausible.

If these conclusions regarding the origin of Jeremiah 1–25 and its connections with the Deuteronomic movement are valid, then we may venture a further comment. Since the study by Martin Noth of the overall shape and composition of the Deuteronomistic History, scholars have noted the seeming abruptness and enigmatic nature of its conclusion in 2 Kgs 25.27-30 (von Rad 1962: 342ff.). If our conclusions regarding the involvement of the Deuteronomic circle in the editing of Jeremiah's prophecies are correct, then we can see in the major shift between the shape of Jeremiah 1–25 and that of Jeremiah 25–52 some important clues as to how this enigma came to be resolved.

There is also an unresolved question concerning the strange pessimism of the work, if it held out no clear line of hope for Israel's restoration in the future (Wolff 1982: 99). The awkwardness and seeming unlikelihood of such perceptions are considerably reduced, once we recognize the closeness of the connections between the History and the Deuteronomistic edition of Jeremiah's prophecies. They were both products of the same scribal-theological circle. Positions left unresolved in the History, particularly those regarding the uncertain future of the kingship, and the restoration of national life in Judah as God's people (cf. Diepold 1972: 193ff.) are much clarified by the original Deuteronomistic book of Jeremiah (Jer. 1–25). At the time when this was made there was still room to hope that the Judaean community, penitent and spiritually furnished with the Mosaic *tōrâ*, would lift itself up from amidst the ruins of Jerusalem and rebuild the city and surrounding countryside. This was a hope that Jeremiah personally clearly shared (Jer. 40.1-12). By the time that the revised scroll of Jeremiah appeared (Jer. 1–52), all such expectation had been abandoned and the idea of 'Return' (Heb. *šûb*), both spiritually and physically to the land of Judah, and to its cultic centre Jerusalem, remained the only effective line of hope that appeared practicable.

If the claim is correct, therefore, that the original Deuteronomistic edition of Jeremiah is to be found in Jeremiah 1–25, then we are able to shed considerable fresh light upon the contrasting patterns of future hope which took time to achieve resolution after the catastrophe of 587 BCE.

BIBLIOGRAPHY

Clements, R.E.
   1975   *Prophecy and Tradition* (Oxford: Basil Blackwell).
   1986   'Prophecy as Literature: A Re-Appraisal', in D.G. Miller (ed.), *The Hermeneutical Quest: Essays in Honor of James Luther Mays on his Sixty-Fifth Birthday* (Allison Park, PA: Pickwick Press): 56-76.
   1990   'The Prophet and His Editors', in D.J.A. Clines, S.E. Fowl and S.E. Porter (eds.), *The Bible in Three Dimensions: Essays in Celebration of Forty Years of Biblical Studies in the University of Sheffield* (JSOTSup 87; Sheffield: JSOT Press): 203-20.
Cross, F.M., Jr
   1973   *Canaanite Myth and Hebrew Epic* (Cambridge, MA: Harvard University Press).
Diamond, A.R.
   1987   *Jeremiah's Confessions in Context: Scenes of Prophetic Drama* (JSOTSup 25; Sheffield: JSOT Press).
Diepold, P.
   1972   *Israel's Land* (BWANT, 95; Stuttgart: Kohlhammer).
Hardmeier, C.
   1990   *Prophetie im Streit vor dem Untergang Judas* (BZAW, 187; Berlin: de Gruyter).

Hobbs, T.R.
1972 'Some Remarks on the Composition and Structure of the Book of Jeremiah', *CBQ* 34: 257-75 (repr. in L.G. Perdue and B.W. Kovacs [eds.], *A Prophet to the Nations: Essays in Jeremiah Studies* [Winona Lake, IN: Eisenbrauns, 1984]): 175-92.

Holladay, W.L.
1986 *Jeremiah 1–25* (Hermeneia; Philadelphia: Fortress Press).

Mowinckel, S.
1914 *Zur Komposition des Buches Jeremia* (Kristiania: Dybwad).
1946 *Prophecy and Tradition: The Prophetic Books in the Light of the Study of the Growth and History of the Tradition* (Oslo: Dybwad).

Nelson, R.D.
1981 *The Double Redaction of the Deuteronomistic History* (JSOTSup, 18; Sheffield: JSOT Press).
1987 *First and Second Kings* (Interpretation Commentaries; Atlanta: John Knox, 1987).

Nicholson, E.W.
1970 *Preaching to the Exiles: A Study of the Prose Tradition in the Book of Jeremiah* (Oxford: Basil Blackwell).

Noth, M.
1957 *Überlieferungsgeschichtliche Studien* (Tübingen: Max Niemeyer).
1981 *The Deuteronomistic History* (ET J. Doull *et al*; JSOTSup, 15; Sheffield: JSOT Press).

O'Connor, K.
1988 *The Confessions of Jeremiah: Their Interpretation and Role in Chapters 1–25* (SBLDS, 94; Atlanta: Scholars Press, 1988).

Overholt, T.W.
1968 'King Nebuchadrezzar in the Jeremiah Tradition', *CBQ* 30: 39-48.

Rad, G. von
1962 *Old Testament Theology. II. The Theology of Israel's Prophetic Traditions* (ET D.M.G. Stalker; Edinburgh: Oliver & Boyd).

Rietzschel, C.
1966 *Das Problem der Urrolle: Ein Beitrag zur Redaktionsgeschichte des Jeremiabuches* (Gutersloh: Gerd Mohn).

Seitz, C.R.
1989 'The Prophet Moses and the Canonical Shape of Jeremiah', *ZAW* 101: 3-27.

Steck, O.H.
1967 *Israel und das gewaltsame Geschick der Propheten: Untersuchungen zur Überlieferung des deuteronomistischen Geschichtsbildes im Alten Testament, Spätjudentum und Urchristentum* (WMANT, 23; Neukirchen–Vluyn: Neukirchener Verlag).

Stulman, L.
1986 *The Prose Sermons of the Book of Jeremiah: A Redescription of the Correspondences with the Deuteronomistic Literature in the Light of Recent Text-Critical Research* (SBLDS, 83; Atlanta: Scholars Press).

Thiel, W.
 1973 *Die deuteronomistische Redaktion von Jeremia 1–25* (WMANT, 41; Neukirchen–Vluyn: Neukirchener Verlag).
Unterman, J.
 1987 *From Repentance to Redemption: Jeremiah's Thought in Transition* (JSOTSup, 54; Sheffield: JSOT Press).
Weinfeld, M.
 1972 *Deuteronomy and the Deuteronomic School* (Oxford: Clarendon Press).
Wolff, H.W.
 1982 'The Kerygma of the Deuteronomistic Historical Work', in W. Brueggemann (ed.), *The Vitality of Old Testament Traditions* (Atlanta: John Knox Press, 2nd edn): 83-100.

THE OLD TESTAMENT IN THE CHURCH?

R. Davidson

Round about the year 160 CE Ptolomaeus the Valentinian wrote a letter to a lady of his acquaintance, Flora. In it he tried to deal with a situation in the church where 'many do not understand the law given through Moses, and have got accurate knowledge neither of who gave it nor of its commandments' (Stevenson 1957: 91; cf. Grant 1957: 30). In an attempt to clear up such misunderstandings Ptolomaeus appeals to the gospel tradition to justify a three-fold distinction in the material within Torah. In its entirety Torah does not come from God alone. A clear distinction must be made between:

a.   what is to be ascribed to God himself and his legislation,
b.   what is to be ascribed to Moses, and
c.   what is ascribed to the elders of the people.

The distinction between a. and b. is illustrated from Mt. 19.3-8, where Moses ordains a law contrary to God's law since divorce is contrary to no divorce; and Mt. 15.4-9 illustrates the distinction between the tradition of the elders and the law of God. Since his Valentinian theology leads him to attribute the law of God not to 'the perfect God' but to the 'Demiurge', the creator of the world, he argues for a further three-fold distinction within the material attributed to God:

a.   pure legislation, the legislation which Jesus came 'not to destroy but to fulfil'. This he identifies with the Decalogue.
b.   rules about retribution, an eye for an eye, tooth for a tooth, necessary because of the weakness of those for whom the legislation was made, but 'alien to the nature and goodness of the Father of all'.
c.   material such as circumcision, sabbath, sacrifice, and so forth, which must be regarded as images or symbols, 'good as long as the truth had not yet appeared, but as the truth is now present one must do the deeds of the truth, not those of the image'.

Strip away the Valentinian theology and there is a contemporary ring about some of the issues Ptolomaeus is seeking to tackle. He is dipping his toe into the muddy waters of hermeneutics, attempting to assign different levels of validity to material within Scripture, and from a Christian standpoint using the Jesus tradition as the controlling factor in assessing validity.

Ptolomaeus is but a minor actor on a stage dominated by Marcion, against whom 'Almost every prominent Christian writer in the second half of the second century from Justin to Tertullian felt obliged to publish a book...' (Blackman 1948: 3). It is hardly surprising therefore that F.C. Burkitt could declare 'the real battle of the second century centres round the Old Testament' (Blackman 1948: 119). To state the issue in these terms, however, is to introduce what is historically an alien concept into the discussion. The same comment may be made concerning C.K. Barrett's otherwise valid insight when he writes,

> It is doubtful whether any New Testament writer ever formulated for himself the question 'What is the authority of the Old Testament?' So far as they were Jews, the question was one which could take care of itself. Of course the Old Testament had the authority of the voice of God (Barrett 1970: 411).

But insofar as they were Jews the very idea of 'the Old Testament' is totally alien and within early Christian tradition it took a significantly long time before that idea became common currency.

Christians today speak naturally, as Christians for many centuries have spoken naturally, about the Old Testament, seldom stopping to think that this is arguably an apologetic, highly emotive and perhaps questionably necessary description of a collection of books which may with greater reason be called simply the Hebrew Scriptures or in Jewish terms Tanak. I deliberately use the phrase 'a collection of books' because it is not my intention to get involved in questions concerning the canon as such, whether in Jewish or in Christian terms. But why and when did such a collection of books first attract to itself the title 'Old Testament'?

The phrase παλαιὰ διαθήκη is found in the New Testament only once, in 2 Cor. 3.14, where Paul is using for his own purposes the Exodus 34 tradition concerning the veil on Moses' face:

> Since, then, we have such a hope, we act with great boldness, not like Moses, who put a veil over his face to keep the people of Israel from gazing at the end of the glory that was being set aside. But their minds

were hardened. Indeed, to this very day, when they hear the reading of the *old covenant*, that veil is still there, since only in Christ is it set aside. Indeed, to this very day whenever Moses is read, a veil lies over their minds; but when one turns to the Lord the veil is removed (2 Cor. 3.12-15).

Whatever the meaning of the veil motif in Exodus 34 and whatever the overall argument of 2 Corinthians 3, it is important for the interpretation of παλαιὰ διαθήκη in v. 14 to note that Paul moves in the course of his argument from the ancient Israelite story to the synagogue of his own day, 'and from an episode in the history of the old covenant to the record of that episode as it is read in scripture' (Childs 1974: 622). C.K. Barrett makes the general comment that παλαιὰ διαθήκη in this passage 'implies what we call the Old Testament and could be so translated'. It is wiser to stick to his more specific comment that Paul is 'writing with special reference to the covenant that was made at Sinai in terms of the commandments given to Moses on the tablets of stone' (Barrett 1973: *ad loc.*). If the parallel with 'whenever Moses is read' in v. 15 is stressed, then the reference at most is to Torah and more probably simply to the reading of that section of Torah which refers to the Sinai covenant tradition. (Bruce 1971: *ad loc.*). Elsewhere Paul introduces quotations from the Hebrew Bible with standard formulae. He will refer to ἡ γραφή, αἱ γραφαί (ἱεραί), γράμματα (ἱερά) but never does he refer to παλαιὰ διαθήκη. The theological contrast between 'old' and 'new' of course appears in a variety of different contexts in the New Testament documents, but it is a theological not a bibliographical contrast. The author of the Epistle to the Hebrews, among the many illustrations he uses of his claim concerning the superiority and finality of Jesus, appeals twice to the Jeremiah new covenant passage (8.8-13 and 10.16-17). The theological contrast is underlined: 'In speaking of a "new covenant", he has made the first one obsolete. And what is obsolete (τὸ δὲ παλαιούμενον) and growing old will soon disappear' (8.13). Nowhere, however, does he ever describe the scriptures to which he appeals as authoritative as παλαιὰ διαθήκη.

Hebrews is an interesting case study, because while it refers to or quotes from the Hebrew Scriptures more extensively than any other New Testament document it remains remarkably flexible in the way in which it introduces such references and quotations:

'For to which of the angels did God ever say' (1.5), introducing a
quotation from Psalm 2 (cf. 1.13);
'he says' (1.6); 'just as he has said' (4.3); 'as he says also in another
place' (5.6); 'when he says' (8.8); in each case the 'he' referring to God;
'Therefore as the Holy Spirit says' (3.7; cf. 10.15);
'As it is said…' (3.15);
'But someone has testified somewhere' (2.6)—a comfortably modest
way of introducing a quotation from Psalm 8;
'saying through David much later, in the words already quoted' (4.7);
'And you have forgotten the exhortation that addresses you as
children' (12.5);
'So we can say with confidence' (13.6).

The author of Hebrews assumes throughout that he shares with his
readers the common acceptance of the unquestionable authority of the
Hebrew Bible and that no apologetic formulae are needed to substantiate this. He draws quotations and allusions from all sections of
Hebrew Scripture, from Torah, from the prophets, former and latter,
and from Psalms, Proverbs and Daniel. All of this is Scripture but not
παλαιὰ διαθήκη.

The same fluidity in introducing quotations from and appealing to
the authority of what is regarded as Scripture continues up to the last
quarter of the second century of the Christian era. We can do no more
than give a few representative samples (Greenslade 1956: *ad loc.*).

1 Clement (c. 96 CE), although familiar with the teaching of Jesus
and 'the letter of the blessed apostle Paul' (47.1), refers to the Hebrew
Bible as 'sacred scripture' (ἱερὰ γραφή 23.3; 34.6), 'the oracles of
God's teaching', and speaks of Moses recording 'in the sacred books
all the ordinances given to him' (43.1).

In the sermon based on Isa. 54.1 which we know as *2 Clement*
(c. 150 CE) we find quotations from the Hebrew Scriptures introduced
as follows:

'Further the scripture also says in Ezekiel', introducing a brief summary
of material drawn from Ezek. 14.14-20 (6.8);
'For scripture says, God made them male and female' (14.2);
'It says' introducing a quotation from Isa. 66.24 (7.6);
'For the LORD says', introducing a quotation from Isa. 52.5 (31.2; cf.
17.4).

Side by side with this last quotation from Isa. 52.5 and governed by
the same introductory formula there is a quotation from the *Gospel of
the Egyptians*, and there are at least two other quotations from the

same book similarly introduced (4.5; 12.2). In *2 Clem.* 11.2 the formula 'For the word of the prophet says' introduces a quotation which also appears in *1 Clem.* 23.3 but whose source is uncertain. Quotations from material now in the New Testament are introduced in the same way. Thus in 2.4 'And another scripture (γραφή) says, I did not come to call the righteous but sinners'; while 18.5 introduces a variant on Lk. 16.10-12 with the words 'The LORD says in the Gospel'. In 14.2 there is a reference to 'what the books and the apostles say'. Thus in *2 Clement* we find a situation where the writer accepts as authoritative, and as having relevance to the beliefs and practices of the Christian community, passages from the Hebrew Scriptures, passages from the Gospels and passages from sources which were not to achieve canonical status—and introduces them with common formulae.

Although Ignatius, early in the second century, in his attempt to refute a Jewish-based gnosticism, asserts that 'it is Jesus Christ who is the original documents. The inviolable archives are his death and resurrection and the faith that came by him' (*Letter to Philoctes* 8.2), elsewhere he repeatedly appeals to the prophets, to passages from the Hebrew Bible introduced by 'It is written' or 'Scripture says' or simply goes directly into quotation without any introductory words (cf. *Trall.* 8.2 where a quotation from Isa. 52.2 is introduced by nothing more than 'For...'

Justin Martyr in his first Apology, written c. 155 CE, makes great play with the argument from prophecy as confirming the truth of the Christian faith. 'There were among the Jews certain men who were prophets of God, through whom the prophetic Spirit announced in advance events that were to come' (31). Thus almost every event in the gospel tradition from the virgin birth, through the ministry of Jesus to his death and resurrection and on into the mission of the apostles, is seen to have been announced in advance in such prophetic passages. Many of the passages are based on the citations in Matthew's Gospel, e.g. Isa. 7.14 with the reference to the virgin birth, Mic. 5.2 for the place of birth as Bethlehem. For the entry into Jerusalem, 'we will quote the words of another prophet Zephaniah' (35.3), an interesting lapse of memory since he quotes Zech. 9.9. He gets the quotation right in the *Dialogue with Trypho*! Many other passages, however, not in the Matthean tradition are similarly used. The passage from the Blessing of Jacob in Gen. 49.10-11, beginning, 'The sceptre shall not depart from Judah' is attributed to 'Moses who was the first of the prophets', and is lengthily interpreted in all its detail as applying to Jesus. The mission of the twelve is substantiated by an appeal to the prophetic oracle common to Isaiah 2 and Micah 4 and introduced by the words, 'when the prophetic spirit speaks as prophesying things to come...' The mission to the Gentiles is found in several passages in Isaiah, notably 52.13-53 and 65.1-3. A series of first-person passages from Psalms 22 and 35 and Isaiah 50 and 65 are introduced by 'When the prophetic spirit speaks in the character of Christ...' What is taken to be the palpable fulfilment of such prophetic passages in the Christian revelation is then used as the basis for believing that other elements in Christian belief which still lie in the future, such as the second coming, are equally prophesied, Ezekiel 37 and Isa. 45.23 being appealed to in this context. Thus for Justin Martyr it is the Hebrew Bible which is fundamentally Scripture, and its significance is seen to lie above all in its prophetic function.

In none of these, or in any other writings from main stream Christianity up to the middle of the second century, is there any evidence of Scripture being regarded as a collection of books, one part of which may be referred to as the Old Testament. The boundary as to what constituted Scripture might be vague but no one doubted that the Hebrew Bible was of its essence. There were problems enough to be faced in the interpretation of Scripture, with not all Christians claiming equal facility. Polycarp, with becoming modesty and doubtless a certain degree of realism, in writing to the Philippians c. 110 CE, says, 'I am confident indeed that you are well versed in the Sacred Scriptures and that nothing escapes you—something not granted to me' (12.1).

But what of Marcion? It is often claimed that Marcion rejected the Old Testament; but did he? The cautious comment of E.C. Blackman is worth recalling:

> Both our reconstruction of Marcion's text and our information about his methods are after all fragmentary and therefore not capable of becoming too solid a superstructure of deduction and theory. They are sufficient foundation for a modest house, but not for a skyscraper (Blackman 1948: 4).

Not only is the information fragmentary, but it comes in the main from highly hostile sources; and as anyone involved in political or ecclesiastical debate well knows, hostile sources can distort, even when quoting.

While Tertullian in *De Praescriptione Haereticorum* is later to accuse Marcion of separating the New Testament from the Old (ch. 30), he perhaps puts it more accurately when he says, 'Corruption of Scriptures and their interpretation is to be expected whenever difference in doctrine is discovered... Marcion openly and nakedly used the knife, not the pen, massacring Scripture to suit his own material' (Greenslade 1956: 58–59). Marcion's starting point is theological. The only true God is the God of love, his sole work the work of redemption. The visible world is not the revelation of this God, but of the creator demiurge. Whether this creator god is to be regarded as evil (κακός) or whether he has elements of what is just (δίκαιος) is not clear; but even if he is in some sense δίκαιος he is not the God of love and redemption and is therefore to be rejected. The function of Marcion's knife was to excise the false from Scripture and leave only the true as his theology defined it, rather than to excise something called the Old in the interests of the New. Thus in the text of Lk. 22.20, which speaks of 'the new covenant in my blood', Marcion eliminated the word new (καινός) because there could only be one covenant, the work of the one true God. From the Pauline Epistles he retained, he eliminated many quotations from Scripture, that is, from the Hebrew Bible, but by no means all. Rom. 13.8-10, for example, with its citation of the commandments, summed up in the statement, 'you shall love your neighbour as yourself', is retained in its entirety, because it contains an obvious expression of the will of the true God. On other occasions he can appeal to Torah as providing guidance on ethical issues and on matters of order within the Christian community.

To his credit, Marcion refused to solve his theological problem by resorting, as many of his Christian contemporaries did, to a highly fanciful allegorical interpretation of much material in Scripture which might otherwise have been regarded as offensive or irrelevant. There is no evidence, as far as I am aware, that he himself ever referred to the Scriptures he found theologically objectionable as the Old Testament in contrast with an emerging New Testament. Nor is such a contrast characteristic of other gnostic documents of the early centuries. Among the documents discovered at Nag Hammadi there is an exhortation to otherworldliness entitled by its editor 'The Expository Treatise on the Soul' (Mayer 1977: 180-87). Dated c. 200 CE, it appeals to a wide variety of proof texts. Early on in the treatise there is a catena of passages from the Hebrew prophets introduced by the words, 'Now concerning the prostitution of the soul, the Holy Spirit prophesies in many places... For he said in the prophet Jeremiah [quoting 3.1-40]... Again it is written in the prophet Hosea [quoting 2.2-7]... Again he said in Ezekiel [quoting 16.23-26]...' Passages from the Psalms are later introduced by 'Therefore the prophet said', quoting Psalm 45.10-11 and Psalm 103.1-5. Likewise Gen. 2.24 is cited under the rubric 'Wherefore the prophet said...' There are quotations from the Gospels introduced by 'the Saviour cries out' or 'the Saviour said'; Paul is also cited. The document ends on the theme that God, 'he who is long suffering and abundantly merciful', hears and heeds the sighs of those who are truly penitent. This theme is illustrated by quotations

from *1 Clem.* 8.3 introduced by 'Therefore he said through the Spirit to the prophet';
from Isa. 30.15, 19-20 introduced by 'Again he said in another place';
from Ps. 6.6-9 introduced by 'Again it is written in the Psalms';
from the *Odyssey* 1.48-59 introduced by 'Therefore it is written in the poet';
from *Odyssey* 4.261-64 introduced by 'Again Helen saying...'

This treatise is a very good example of the flexible gnostic approach to Scripture, with citations from the three sections of the Hebrew Bible, from Gospels and epistles, from *1 Clement* and from Homer without implying different levels of authority to the sources and without any hint of a Bible divided into Old and New.

By the time this document was written, however, there are signs of a change in terminology within mainstream Christianity, even while the traditional ways of referring to Scripture remain. According to Eusebius, Melito of Sardis sought to gratify the request of one Onesimus

to have selections from the Law and the Prophets concerning the Saviour and our faith as a whole; and moreover you wanted to learn the exact truth concerning the ancient books, in regard to their number and their order (Lawlor 1927: 133).

Melito claims to have learned in the East 'which the books of the Old Covenant are' and he appends a list which coincides with what was to be the standard Hebrew Bible. Clement of Alexandria, early in the third century, claims that 'God is the cause of all good things, but especially of some, as of the Old and New Covenants' (Roberts 1867: 316), and context makes it clear that he is talking about Scripture. Tertullian asserts that the Roman church 'mingles the law and the prophets in one volume with the writings of the evangelists and apostles from whom she imbibes her faith' (Greenslade 1956: 57).

Translating διαθήκη by *testamentum*, he declares in his later Montanist period, 'If I fail to settle this article of our faith by passages out of the Old Testament, I will take out of the New Testament a confirmation of our view' (Holmes 1870: 53).

Increasingly from this time onwards we find in Christian writings 'Old Testament' being used as a description of the Hebrew Bible in contrast to the Gospel or the New Testament, until the usage is officially adopted by the church at the Council of Laodicea (c. 350), Canon 59 stipulating that there should be read in the church 'only the canonical books of the new and old covenant' (μόνα τὰ κανονικὰ τῆς καινῆς καὶ παλαιᾶς διαθήκης). What prompted the vocabulary change and its increasing acceptance? Several general factors were probably influential.

1. There was the gradual emergence and recognition of a definable body of Christian literature, Gospels and letters, regarded as encapsulating the essence of the Christian faith. This led to the need to differentiate this literature from Scripture in the sense of the Hebrew Bible. Arguably Paul's use of the term παλαιὰ διαθήκη in 2 Cor. 3.14, to refer to what was being read in the synagogue, provided Christian warrant for the acceptance of Old Testament and correspondingly New Testament, even if that was not the original Pauline intention. The original meaning of not a few Pauline passages has suffered in this way across the centuries!

2. Changing historical circumstances must have challenged the church to take a new look at its scriptural foundations. The church began life discussing the relationship between Law and Gospel in terms of the conditions on which Gentiles should be admitted to what was in origin predominantly a Jewish sect. By the middle of the second century, although it had a continuing significant Jewish-Christian element, it was predominantly a Gentile church seeking, *inter alia*, to define its position over against a Jewish community that based its continuing life and identity on the Hebrew Bible. The dialectic of that relationship Christians often found exceedingly difficult to handle. Witness, at the end of the second century, the *Letter to Diognetus*. This apology for the Christian faith begins with a scathing attack on pagan religion, then turns to the Jews. They are ridiculed for the sacrificial cult, for food taboos, for circumcision. In this context it is highly unlikely that we should find a positive evaluation of Hebrew Scripture. The inevitably negative attitude is voiced in 8.1: 'as a matter

of fact before Christ came, what man had any knowledge of God at all'? On this view the Hebrew Bible must be theologically irrelevant and of little or no value to the Christian. Not many Christian apologists, however, were prepared to go this far. In the homily concerning the Mystery of the Faith attached to this letter, we find in ch. 11 a different attitude much more concerned to stress an element of continuity between the Hebrew Bible and Christian relevation. With the coming of the Logos into the world, claims the homily, 'the reverence taught by the Law is celebrated, the grace given to the prophets is recognised, the faith of the Gospel is made secure, and the tradition of the Apostles is maintained'.

3. Is it possible to be more specific? Although the extent of his influence has been varingly assessed, it is generally recognized that Marcion with his limited canon of Scripture was one factor in the emergence of the catholic canon. May it not be that Marcion, although he himself did not use the expression 'the Old Testament', may have been to some extent responsible for its emergence in more orthodox circles towards the end of the second century? The theological problem which Marcion posed to the church was how to hold on to the theological newness that was in the gospel, a newness which he stressed to the fault of exaggeration, while at the same time retaining the essential continuity of its faith with what was already there in the Hebrew Scriptures. Whatever conclusions scholars may reach concerning the history and provenance of the word covenant (ברית; see Davidson 1989: 323-48), it is a word that seems conveniently to straddle much of the Hebrew Bible, and it is an important word in many early Christian writings. It was therefore capable of providing the essential element of continuity between the two traditions which many considered to be significantly lacking in Marcion's approach. While the epithets 'old' and 'new' served conveniently to point to contrasts, I suspect that initially the expressions 'the Old Testament' and 'the New Testament' were used by orthodox Christians primarily to stress the element of continuity that held together Hebrew Scripture and the Christian tradition.

The vocabulary of religion, however, tends too easily to degenerate into religious slogans which either become devoid of their original significance or become filled with a negative or pejorative meaning. The use of the term 'the Old Testament' with connotations which, not surprisingly, it evoked when placed side by side with 'the New

Testament', gave added impetus to and set the seal on certain trends in Christian thinking, trends present before the terms were used in a bibliographic sense. For example,

a. It encouraged a highly selective approach to material within the Hebrew Bible, an approach which it may rightly be claimed has its roots in the earliest documents in the New Testament. The implications of this are clearly visible in Justin Martyr with his concentration upon the prophetic character of Scripture. Thus it was only those passages in Hebrew Scripture which could be demonstrated to be prophetic announcements of the Christ event, or aspects of the Christian mission in the world, which could be regarded as of lasting significance for the Christian. Even the remarkable allegorical ingenuity with which this search was pursued had its limitations. Increasingly the parameters of relevance for material in the Hebrew Scriptures would be decided by what was considered the central content of the Christian revelation. Thus Melito of Sardis's response to Onesimus. A Christian *Readers Digest* approach to Tanak was being encouraged. Indeed a collection of Christological proof texts was all that was considered necessary for the ordinary Christian to extract from Tanak. That has continued down the centuries, and is still with us today. There are many Christians today whose knowledge of the Hebrew Scriptures does not extend much beyond the traditional lectionary passages considered appropriate for the festivals of the Christian year or used in the Eucharist.

b. The Old–New Testament contrast has often made it difficult for the Christian Church to take seriously, or indeed make *any* attempt to understand, Judaism as a living faith with its roots in Hebrew Scripture. Caricatures of Judaism and of its biblical basis abounded in the early church, have flourished across the centuries and continue down to the present day, even among those who ought to know better. Thus in a book discussing how the Bible, and in particular the Old Testament, should be taught in the context of Christian education today, one author talks about the burden of Old Testament history as being that of

> a people... in the perils and bleakness of luxury and greed, and involved in the shifts and schemes of politics... they were broken by the powers they sought to exploit, and struggled back from exile, aware that the God of history demanded their complete allegiance. In their corporate guilt and fear they refined their laws and regulations in the vain hope of manufacturing a system which would keep them morally and ritually pure; and

they were held in it and lost their vitality. Jesus born into that freezing tradition took hold of it, illuminated it and released the spirit of liberty in which obedience to the will of God became vitalising and creative, instead of negative and oppressive. The forces of fear gathered themselves to destroy him but they failed, for the love of God broke out through his death, swept out through his risen life into the lives of men and spread through the world (Loukes 1962: 151).

But is this the story of the Hebrew Bible? I do not recognize in this the burden of Hebrew history, nor the faith of the Psalmists, nor of the post-exilic community, nor that of the Jewish Rabbis at the time of Jesus. If this is the consequence of viewing the Hebrew Bible through what has been termed 'Christian spectacles', then I wish to change my optician, preferably to one with a Jewish name.

Samuel Sandmel, commenting on the place of the Hebrew Scriptures in both Judaism and Christianity, says,

> It is, of course, quite as legitimate for Christians to view the Tanak through the prism of the New Testament, as it is for Jews to view it through that of rabbinic literature. But it is necessary to distinguish between the pristine sense of Tanak and what Tanak came to mean in rabbinic and New Testament literature (Sandmel 1978: 546).

It is possible to be somewhat less sanguine than Sandmel seems to be about our ability to get back to the pristine sense of Tanak, but most Christians would receive new insights into the Hebrew Bible if they stopped viewing it solely through the prism of the New Testament, forgot about its Old Testament label and listened to others who share with them a common heritage in the Hebrew Bible. No one who had the privilege of being a student or a colleague of George Wishart Anderson ever failed to get that message.

BIBLIOGRAPHY

Barrett, C.K.
1970   *The Cambridge History of the Bible* (Cambridge: Cambridge University Press).
1973   *A Commentary on Second Corinthians* (London: A. & C. Black).
Blackman, E.C.
1948   *Marcion and his Influence* (London: SPCK).
Bruce, F.F.
1971   *1 and 2 Corinthians* (NCB; London: Oliphant).
Childs, B.S.
1974   *Exodus* (OTL; London: SCM Press).

Davidson, R.
  1989   'Covenant Ideology in Ancient Israel', in R.E. Clements (ed.), *The World of Ancient Israel* (Cambridge: Cambridge University Press): 323-48.

Grant, R.M.
  1957   *Second Century Christianity* (London: SPCK).

Greenslade, S.L.
  1956   *Early Latin Theology* (London: SCM Press).

Holmes, P.
  1870   *The Writings of Tertullian*, II (Edinburgh: T. & T. Clark).

Lawlor, H.J.
  1927   *Eusebius: Ecclesiastical History* (London: SPCK).

Loukes, H.
  1962   *Teenage Religion* (London: SCM Press).

Mayer, M.W. (ed.)
  1977   *The Nag Hammadi Library in English* (Leiden: Brill).

Roberts, A. (ed.)
  1867   *Clement of Alexandria* (Edinburgh: T. & T. Clark).

Sandmel, S.
  1978   *The Hebrew Scriptures: An Introduction* (New York: Oxford University Press).

Stevenson, W.
  1957   *A New Eusebius* (London: SPCK).

LICE OR A VEIL IN THE SONG OF SONGS 1.7?

J.A. Emerton

One of the controversial renderings in the NEB that have attracted
attention and criticism is Song 1.7:

> Tell me, my true love,
>> where you mind your flocks,
>> where you rest them at midday,
>> that I may not be left picking lice
>>> as I sit among your companions' herds.

The disputed fourth line, which refers in the NEB to picking lice,
corresponds to the following words: שׁלמה אהיה כְּעֹטְיָה. The third word,
whose meaning has been questioned, is the feminine singular active
participle qal of עטה preceded by the preposition כ, 'like'. It is unnecessary for the present purpose to weigh the merits of the traditional
vocalization against those of כְּעֹטְיָה, which some favour. The question
to be considered here is, rather, the meaning of the verb in this
context, and whether the rendering of the NEB is to be rejected,
regarded as at least a possibility, or even preferred.

I

BDB distinguishes between two verbs עטה. The first is given the
following meaning in the qal: 'wrap oneself, enwrap, envelop oneself';
and the hiphil is given a corresponding transitive sense. Such a
meaning certainly exists. In Ps. 104.2, for example, עטה־אור כשׂלמה
refers to Yahweh clothing himself in light as with a garment. The
LXX's περιβαλλομένη in Song 1.7 appears to understand the word in
the same sense.

The verb עטה is used with על־שׂפם of a rite of mourning in Ezek.
24.17, 22, and of what הצרוע (whatever his skin disease may have
been) is to do in Lev. 13.45. Rashi suggests that Song 1.7 refers to a

shepherd of whom it might be said כאבילה עוטה על שׂפה בוכיה על צאנו
(although שׂפה is used, rather than שׂפם, there is probably an allusion to
the passages mentioned above). It has therefore been thought that כעטיה
denotes someone who mourns: if the woman cannot find her lover, she
will be like a mourner. In Mic. 3.7 the clause ועטו על־שׂפם appears to
refer to shame, rather than grief, and it has been suggested that the
woman in Song 1.7 will feel shame.[1] On such a theory, whether the
reference is to grief or shame or to both, there is presumably an
ellipse of על־שׂפם in the Song of Songs.

In seeking to evaluate the suggestion that there is a reference to
grief or shame in Song 1.7, it must be asked what is meant by שׂפם. It
has usually been thought to denote a moustache (e.g. BDB, Ges.-B.,
KB, *HAL*). In 2 Sam. 19.25 we are told that Mephibosheth had
neglected himself and his appearance until David returned safely, and
that ולא־עשׂה שׂפמו. The LXX translates the noun by τὸν μύστακα αὐτοῦ
which can mean either 'his moustache' or 'his upper lip' (and both the
Vulgate and the Peshitta understand the word to mean 'his beard').
Since the clause must refer to some lack of care for himself by
Mephibosheth, and the upper lip itself needs no special attention, the
rendering 'his moustache' is the more probable of the two. Further,
since the expression presumably refers to the covering of something
that is not normally covered, and since it may be suspected that שׂפם is
related to שׂפה, 'lip', it is not surprising that the rendering 'moustache'

---

1. It has also been held (e.g. by Rudolph) that covering the head was a sign of
shame or grief. Thus, in Jer. 14.3 people who are ashamed are said to cover their
heads (וחפו ראשׁם), and 2 Sam. 15.30 speaks of David weeping with his head covered
(וראשׁ לו חפוי). Neither of these verses, however, uses the verb עטה. Further, Gordis
draws attention to the difficulty that 'Mourning rites usually arise as a striking change
from normal practice', and that men's heads were normally covered. Moreover, Lev.
10.6, 21.10 and Ezek. 24.17 imply that the head was normally uncovered in
mourning. In Lev. 13.45 it is said of the man with a skin disease, who is considered
above, not only ועל־שׂפם יעטה but also וראשׁו יהיה פרוע. It is interesting that in this
verse, as well as in Ezek. 24.17, uncovering the head is mentioned alongside the use
of עטה with על־שׂפם. Gordis seeks to avoid the contradiction between passages that
imply that a mourner's head was uncovered and apparent references to its being
covered by postulating two homonyms in Hebrew: חפה I = Arabic *ḥafā*, 'hide, be
hidden', and חפה II = Arabic *ḥafā*, 'uncover, reveal'. His suggestion, which has been
accepted by Driver (1950: 342-43) and appears in the NEB and REB at 2 Sam. 15.30
('bareheaded') and Jer. 14.3 ('they uncover their heads'), may be the best solution to
the problem.

has won general support. Rashi and Qimhi understand the word to denote the hair that is on the lip, and the former explicitly identifies its meaning with that of an Old French word for moustache. While it is conceivable that 2 Sam. 19.25 uses a word meaning 'upper lip' to denote what was on the lip, i.e. a moustache, there seems no reason to prefer that understanding to the more directly obvious meaning 'moustache'. Such a meaning, however, scarcely fits כעטיה, which is a feminine participle referring to a young woman who is unlikely to have had a moustache.

Another view, which has been widely accepted, is that כעטיה means 'like one who is veiled' (so the NRSV). The verb עטה is nowhere else clearly used of wearing a veil, but such an understanding of it is worthy of consideration. The passage has been understood in the light of Gen. 38.14-15, where Tamar puts on a veil (צעיף) and waits for Judah, who supposes her to be a prostitute 'because she had covered her face'. Perhaps 'one who is veiled' denotes a prostitute, and the young woman in Song 1.7 fears that if she wanders around among the shepherds, she will be thought to be a prostitute looking for business.

The theory is open to objection. If it was the practice of prostitutes to wear veils, then presumably the woman in Song 1.7 was not wearing a veil. It would be strange to say that she, though unveiled, would be 'like one who is veiled'. Further, it would be self-contradictory to suppose both that prostitutes wore veils as a badge of office and that the woman would be taken for a prostitute when she was not appropriately dressed.

Murphy suggests a different explanation: 'she seems rather to refer to some kind of covering she will be forced to use unless she knows where to find him'. He infers that she does not wish to be 'identified by his "companions," but no reason is given (perhaps she does not want them to know about the rendezvous?)' (1990: 131; cp. p. 134). This view, however, is difficult to reconcile with the answer given to the woman in the following verse. She is told to follow the tracks of the sheep and to pasture her kids precisely 'by the dwellings of the shepherds (על משכנות הרעים)', and so it seems that the meeting between the woman and her lover is not to be secret.

It is thus difficult to make sense of כעטיה if it refers to mourning, the veiling of prostitutes, or the desire to keep a meeting secret. Another way of understanding the word must be sought.

II

Several of the ancient versions understand כעטיה, or whatever they read in the Hebrew text before them, to refer to wandering. Symmachus has ῥεμβομένη, the Vulgate *ne vagari incipiam*, and the Peshitta *'a(y)k ṭā'îtā'*. The same understanding probably lies behind the Targum's free interpretation of the last six words in the verse: 'why should they [*sc.* the Israelites] be exiled (מטלטלין)[2] among the herds of the sons of Esau and of Ishmael who attach their idols [literally 'their errors', טעוותהון) to thee as companions?' These versions depend on either a Hebrew text with כטעיה instead of כעטיה or on understanding עטה as equivalent to טעה. The verb טעה, 'wander, stray', is found in Mishnaic Hebrew and is cognate with Aramaic טעא. The usual Biblical Hebrew verb is תעה, but in Ezek. 13.10 there is an example of the hiphil of טעה with an emphatic *teth* in place of the normal non-emphatic *taw* as the first radical. There are examples of metathesis in Biblical Hebrew (e.g. שמלה and שלמה, and כבש and כשב), but it may be doubted whether there was an otherwise unattested עטה synonymous with טעה, whatever the ancient translators may have thought. Anyhow, whether or not these versions were dependent on a Hebrew *Vorlage* different from the MT, some scholars have appealed to them in support of an emendation to כטעיה. The RSV, for instance has: 'why should I be like one who wanders...?' The resulting sense is good: if the woman does not know where to find her lover, she will wander about looking for him. There is much to be said for this emendation, which involves only changing the order of two consonants. Nevertheless, even so small a change is still an emendation; before the change is accepted, it must be asked whether there is yet another way of understanding the MT as it has been transmitted to us that yields good sense in the context.

III

It was mentioned above that BDB recognizes two Hebrew verbs עטה. The first of the homonyms, עטה I, which has already been considered,

---

2.   Dr G.I. Davies, who has kindly read a draft of the present article and offered some helpful comments on it, suggests that the Targum's choice of מטלטלין may have been influenced by the fact that Isa. 22.17 has מטלטלך in a sentence in which the verb עטה also appears.

is thought to be cognate with Arabic *ġāṭâ*, 'cover, conceal'. The other Hebrew verb, עטה II, is regarded as cognate with Arabic *'āṭā*, which is used in the I and VI themes to mean 'take with the hands'. BDB finds this verb in Isa. 22.17, where עטך עטה is to be translated 'he shall grasp thee forcibly'. I do not know who first distinguished between two Hebrew verbs and their Arabic cognates, but the distinction was already made by Michaelis two centuries ago.

Isa. 22.15-19 is part of an oracle against Shebna the steward. Verse 18 contains the words 'to a broad land', and goes on to say that Shebna will die there. This is usually, and no doubt rightly, understood to mean that he will be taken to Mesopotamia and will never return. That is the context in which the details of vv. 17-18 must be interpreted.

Verse 17 begins: הנה יהוה מטלטלך. The verb טול occurs only here in the pilpel in the Old Testament, and there are two principal ways of understanding it. First the hiphil means 'throw, hurl', and it has sometimes been supposed that the first clause should be translated 'Behold, Yahweh will hurl thee'. If that is how the verb is to be understood, it is linked in sense with the reference in v. 18 to Shebna's deportation to Mesopotamia. Secondly, the pilpel here may be given the meaning that it has in post-biblical Hebrew: 'be moved, handled; be made restless'; similarly, טלטל in Aramaic can mean 'move, shake' (Jastrow 1904: *in loc.*). It is therefore possible that Isa. 22.17 says that Shebna will be shaken (Eitan 1937–38: 68; Ginsberg 1950: 55; Driver 1968: 49). Ginsberg has an alternative suggestion, which must be recorded but should not be accepted, namely, that מטלטלך is related to the post-biblical verb טלי, 'patch, cover up', and the nouns טְלִי, 'patch', טלית, 'sheet', and מטלית, 'cloth, rag'. The meaning would then be: 'Behold YHWH is going to *fold* you as one *folds* a garment and is going to *wrap* you *up*' (ועטך עטה). This alternative theory is to be rejected. The form of מטלטלך shows that it is not derived from a root with י as the third radical.

Of the remaining four words in v. 17, it is unnecessary for the present purpose to discuss the minor problem of the first two, טלטלה גבר; and consideration of ועטך עטה, which are the centre of the present discussion, will be postponed until the rest of the context has been examined.

Verse 18a contains some difficulties: צנוף יצנפך צנפה כדור אל־ארץ רחבת ידים. In post-biblical Hebrew and Aramaic כדור is a noun meaning 'ball', and most commentators believe that to be the meaning here. It is also possible to suppose that the word consists of the preposition meaning 'like' and a noun דור, whatever that might mean in the context.

Words from the root צנף are found elsewhere in the Old Testament. The nouns צניף and מצנפת are used of something worn by the high priest and are usually thought to denote his turban. The verb appears only in Lev. 16.4, where it is used of Aaron's wearing the high-priestly turban. Since turbans are wound round the head, it has been thought that in Leviticus it means '*he shall wind* (his head) with (ב) the turban' (BDB). Consequently, some kind of circular motion has been postulated in Isa. 22.18, and it has been understood in two ways. First the RV has 'He will surely turn and toss thee like a ball', a meaning that is expressed more vigorously in the RSV: 'whirl you round and round, and throw you like a ball'. The words 'and toss' or 'throw' have presumably been added from the context (both translations understand מטלטלך in v. 17 to mean 'hurl') and are intended to give a smooth sentence in English which links what has been said before with the words 'to a broad land'. Secondly, the RV margin has 'wind thee round and round like a ball', and the NEB 'then he will bundle you tightly and throw you like a ball'. This second kind of translation follows BDB: '*he will wind thee entirely up* (with) *a winding* (under fig. of ball, to be driven far off, in exile)'.

A different form of the second interpretation of צנף is found in the NJPSV, which has understood מטלטלך in v. 17 to mean 'about to shake you'. Although I shall leave a fuller discussion of ועטך עטה until later, it is necessary to note here that the NJPSV understands the words to mean 'and then wrap you around Himself'. These words lead up to v. 18a: 'Indeed, He will wind you about Him as a headdress, a turban. Off to a broad land!' It is unnecessary for the present purpose to discuss precisely how כדור has been understood. The phrase אל־ארץ רחבת ידים, which is difficult to fit into the same sentence as the previous words in this translation, is regarded as an exclamation. This rendering of v. 18a is open to question for several reasons. First, the idea of Yahweh wrapping Shebna round himself is bizarre. A footnote explains: 'I.e. and walk off with you; cf. Jer. 43.12'. We shall look at Jer. 43.12 below and see that the NJPSV's understanding of it is questionable. It is enough now to note that the gloss 'and walk off with you' has to be supplied without any clear basis in the Hebrew, and that no other parallel for God 'putting on' a person is given. Secondly, the idea of Yahweh wrapping Shebna round himself, which implies wearing a garment, is scarcely compatible with the figure of winding him round his head as a turban. Thirdly עטה I, 'wrap oneself', is elsewhere intransitive, apart from Jer. 43.12, whose interpretation is itself disputed.

Attempts have also been made to interpret Isa. 22.17-18 by suggesting a different root for צנף from the one associated with a turban. Eitan (1937–38: 68) advances the hypothesis that it may be related to Arabic *dafana*, 'kick', and for good measure he links Hebrew עטה in this verse with Arabic *'atta*, 'fell a.o. (on the ground)'. He comments: 'Thus the three verbs—to shake, to fell (throw) on the ground, and to *kick* off—constitute the three *successive* moments of a simile graphically depicting the way in which the LORD will rid the country of the hated Shebna'. Wildberger seeks to improve on the former suggestion by comparing Arabic *safana*, 'fly'. While the meaning suggested by Wildberger fits the context (Yahweh will fling Shebna to a foreign land), the theory runs the familiar danger of appealing to the vast resources of Arabic vocabulary to explain a supposed *hapax legomenon* which is homonymous with an attested Hebrew verb. The hypothesis lacks support in the versions, and is not strengthened by the fact that it has to postulate metathesis. Further, it has been seen that it is possible to make sense of צנף by supposing a meaning close to its meaning elsewhere, and it is better to accept such a meaning than to appeal to an Arabic root. If that is true of Wildberger, how much stronger is the case against Eitan who postulates new meanings for two verbs!

Now that the other main problems of Isa. 22.17-18a have been considered, it is time to examine ועטך עטה in v. 17. It must be asked whether it can be more satisfactorily explained by postulating the presence of עטה I or II, or whether either root makes equally good sense. We begin with עטה I. We have already seen that the presence of a pronominal suffix raises a problem, since the verb 'wrap oneself' is normally intransitive in the qal; and the hiphil is expected for a transitive sense. We have also seen that the idea of Yahweh wrapping himself in Shebna is not an easy one. Further, it must be asked how much an understanding of עטה would be related to that of צנף in v. 18. If עטה means 'wrap oneself', then the garment in which one is wrapped cannot at the same time be whirled round or wound up. It has been suggested, however, that there has been a semantic development from 'wrap oneself' to 'wrap or roll up'. The text of the RV, as distinct from the margin, has 'yea, he will wrap thee up closely'; and BDB notes the theory that it means 'he shall wrap thee up, roll thee tight together'. This follows Gesenius, who suggests: '*convolvit, quod proficiscitur ab induendo et velando*'. This theory is not easy to reconcile with the view that צנף means 'wind up', since it seems to be saying essentially the same thing, and the distinction between the two statements is not clear. It is, however, compatible with the view that צנף means 'whirl round', since the whirling would come after the rolling up was complete. But the theory of such a semantic development is no more than a theory, and it is not self-evident that it is a natural development from 'wrap oneself'.

On the other hand, the theory that עטה II is used in this verse fits the context well. Whatever the significance of צנף may be, it makes sense to say that first Yahweh will grasp Shebna forcibly. It seems more likely that the verb is עטה II than עטה I.

Some scholars go farther and suggest that there is a reference to picking lice in Isa. 22.17. A consideration of their opinion must wait until after Jer. 43.12 has been examined.

IV

It has been suggested that עטה II is also to be found in Jer. 43.12. The context concerns Nebuchadrezzar's coming invasion of Egypt. The RV, which presupposes that the verb is עטה I, translates the verse as follows:

> And I will kindle a fire in the houses of the gods of Egypt; and he shall burn them, and carry them away captives: and he shall array himself with (ועטה) the land of Egypt, as a shepherd putteth on (יעטה) his garment; and he shall go forth from thence in peace.

It is unnecessary here to discuss whether the verb והצתי, which is in the first-person singular, should be emended to the third-person והצית (after the LXX, Vulgate and Peshitta) so as to make Nebuchadrezzar the person who kindles the fire. For the present purpose, the important words in the Hebrew are ועטה את־ארץ מצרים כאשר יעטה הרעה את־בגדו. The LXX (in which the verse is 50.12) does not make Nebuchadrezzar put on the land of Egypt as a shepherd puts on his garment, but translates as follows: 'and he will pick lice off (φθειριεῖ) the land of Egypt as a shepherd picks lice off (φθειρίζει) his garment'. This way of understanding the verbs makes sense. According to von Gall, it means that, as a shepherd removes vermin from his cloak, 'so wird Nebukadnezar das Land Ägypten ablausen, seine Bewohner heraus-holen und vernichten' (1904: 107)—'picking off the objectionable inmates one by one', as Peake puts it. Alternatively, Holladay under-stands it to mean 'pillage it'.

The text of the LXX has been questioned. Bochart (1692: col. 456) suspected that φθειριεῖ and φθειρίζει were corruptions of φθερεῖ and φθειρεῖ, respectively, forms of φθείρω, 'destroy, corrupt' (cf. the Arabic version). We should then have the comparison: '*ut pastor corrumpit*, seu *deterit*, vestem suam'. Bochart suggested that the Hebrew was understood in the light of Syriac *'āṭā'*, 'blot out, efface'. Gesenius and von Gall (1904: 107-108) have noted that there are variant readings in the Greek manuscripts, some of which might appear to offer some support to Bochart. But von Gall points out that the majority of Greek manuscripts have φθειριεῖ and φθειρίζει, and that those readings are supported by the Syro-Hexaplar and Bohairic versions. It may be added that it is also inherently more likely that the rarer verb φθειρίζω should be corrupted to the more common φθείρω than vice versa. Further, if Bochart's suggestion about the original Greek rendering were correct, it would imply that the LXX contained the improbable idea of a shepherd deliberately destroying his own clothes, unless it referred to a shepherd gradually wearing out his clothes, neither of which would be an apt comparison to Nebuchadrezzar's invasion of Egypt. The usual readings, however, ascribe to the translator a rendering that makes sense in the context. If Bochart thought that there was a Hebrew verb עטה, 'blot out, efface', then the meaning would have been no more appropriate in the Hebrew than in the LXX. If, on the other hand, the LXX translator misunder-stood the Hebrew under the influence of the Syriac verb, it must be asked whether a Syriacism is likely in the LXX. It seems best to accept the majority readings in the Greek manuscripts, to give the translator credit for producing a rendering that fits the context, and to reject as improbable the idea (which is not, in fact, stated by Bochart) that the Hebrew refers to a shepherd destroying, or wearing out, his own garment.

Although the LXX's understanding of the verse makes good sense, it would be premature to accept it without asking whether the Hebrew can also be translated intelligibly if explained in terms עטה I, 'wrap oneself', as in the RV, which was quoted above. The view that the verb is עטה I underlies the NJPSV: 'He shall wrap himself up in the land of Egypt, as a shepherd wraps himself up in his garment'. An obvious objection to this understanding of the verse is that it goes on immediately to say that Nebuchadrezzar will 'depart from there' (NJPSV). Nebuchadrezzar could not at once both wear the land of Egypt as a garment and leave the land of Egypt, and so the NJPSV would make sense only at the cost of attributing clumsiness of expression to the prophet. Further, if such a translation is to be defended, there should be some point in the specific mention of a shepherd, as a number of commentators have stressed. This tells against the theory (e.g. of Gesenius) that the figure of speech refers to the speed and ease of Nebuchadrezzar's conquest of Egypt, which he will achieve as quickly and easily as a shepherd takes off his cloak; but a shepherd does not take off his cloak faster or more easily than someone who is not a shepherd. Nor does the reference to a shepherd seem especially appropriate to Jones's view that the verse 'suggests a picture of the Babylonian king claiming Egypt as his personal possession' (1992: 480). Why speak of a shepherd putting on his garment rather than of anyone else doing so?

An attempt to make the reference to a shepherd meaningful has been made by Hitzig, who thinks of a sheepskin cloak worn by a shepherd. When the weather is cold, the shepherd turns it so that the woolly side is next to his body; so Nebuchadrezzar will turn the land of Egypt upside down. But as Böttcher pointed out long ago (1849: 36), Hitzig's understanding of the verse leads one to expect הפך rather than עטה; the verse says nothing about a shepherd turning his cloak inside out.

An ingenious explanation is advanced by Giesebrecht: a shepherd wrapped his belongings in his cloak, and here Nebuchadrezzar rolls or wraps together ('zusammenwickeln') his plunder ('Beute'). He thinks that this understanding is justified by Isa. 22.17, where he gives to עטה the meaning 'er wickelt zusammen'. The suggestion makes sense of the mention of a shepherd (though we do not know whether ancient Israelite shepherds carried their possessions rolled up in their cloaks), but it is open to objection. It is not certain that עטה had the meaning that he ascribes to it in Isa. 22.17, and it is questionable whether 'the land of Egypt' can be identified with the spoil taken from it, especially since משם in v. 18 implies that it is to be understood in a geographical sense.

Attempts to interpret Jer. 43.12 on the hypothesis that the relevant verb is עטה I are thus unsatisfactory, whereas the LXX's understanding of it makes sense. If the LXX was right and the verb here means 'pick lice off', it has plausibly been suggested that it is the same verb as עטה II in Hebrew and related to Arabic *'aṭā*: the shepherd 'takes, picks' lice with his hand. The connection is made by von Gall (1904: 121) in his article on עטה (cf. the earlier discussion by Böttcher [1849: 36], who mentions the meaning 'prehendit'). Michaelis, however, sought to explain the verse on the basis of עטה II without seeing a connection with the LXX's rendering. He understood the Hebrew to mean *'prehendit terram Aegypti, ut pastor prehendit*, (manu capit), *vestem suam et exibit'*. But his rendering fails to meet the objection that a shepherd takes his cloak with him when he leaves a place, whereas Nebuchadrezzar leaves the land of Egypt behind when he departs from it.

There is thus a strong case for supposing that the LXX is correct in understanding Jer. 43.12 to refer to removing lice from a cloak, and that the verb is עטה II, which is cognate with Arabic *'aṭā*. Since the publication of von Gall's article in 1904, his explanation of the verb in this tense has been accepted in a number of commentaries (e.g. Cornill 1905; Volz 1928; Rudolph 1962; Holladay 1989), in three standard dictionaries—Ges.-B., KB and *HAL*—and in several translations of the Bible (RSV, NRSV, NEB, REB).

Jer. 43.12 was not, however, the only verse in which von Gall claimed to find the meaning 'pick lice'. He suggested (1904: 117-18) that it is also present in Isa. 22.17, which he translated 'siehe Jahve wird dich zausen, ja zausen, jausen, ja lausen'. The suggestion was adopted by Rothstein (1922: 627), and later by Ginsberg (1950: 56). Driver (1968: 48-49) went farther and emended גבר to בגד: 'the Lord will shake thee out as one shakes a garment (הבגד טלטל) and rid you of lice'. He comments: 'the Lord will shake out Shebna like a lousy garment, then roll him up into a ball and fling him into a far land'. Driver's suggestion has been adopted in the NEB and REB. This understanding of the verb עטה fits the context if Driver's conjectural emendation is accepted. But the emendation presupposes that understanding, and one wonders why delousing was added to Shebna's punishment. If the word 'garment' is not introduced into the verse by emendation, delousing has no special relevance to the context, and there is no advantage in seeing in the verb a reference to it rather than to seizing

violently. It now remains to ask what relevance Jer. 43.12 has to
Song 1.7.

V

Von Gall's article works through different verses in the Old
Testament in which עטה appears, and comes finally to Song 1.7 (1904:
118-20), where he thinks that the relevant words mean 'warum soll
ich sein wie eine lausende bei den Herden deiner Gefährten?' As far as
I am aware, he was the first scholar to go on from Jer. 43.12 and
apply this understanding of עטה to Song 1.7. His interpretation of the
verse has been accepted by Driver (1950: 346; 1968: 49; 1974: 159-
60), and it appears in the NEB and REB. The original edition of BDB
finds עטה II only in Jer. 43.12, as does the 1952 reprint in my possession. It was presumably Driver who added the references to Isa. 22.17
and Song 1.7, which appear in my copy of the reprint of 1977. It is
far, however, from having won general acceptance, as was noted at
the beginning of the present article.

If von Gall's interpretation of Song 1.7 is accepted, what does it
mean? What is the point of the reference to picking lice? Driver
(1974: 160) explains: 'it was, and indeed still is, a way of whiling
away time', and he gives examples, ancient and modern, of the need in
the world of the eastern Mediterranean to deal with lice. It is as if—to
use a different figure—she were to say, 'Why should I be left with
nothing better to do than twiddle my thumbs if I can't find you?' And
her choice of a reference to picking lice may indicate how annoyed
she will be if her lover does not tell her where he may be found.

What conclusion is to be drawn from the above discussion of the
evidence? It seems to me that the case for understanding עטה in Isa.
22.17 to mean 'take, seize' or the like is convincing and is to be preferred to the view that it is עטה I. Jer. 43.12 makes best sense if the
LXX's understanding of the verse is accepted, and picking lice may be
understood as an example of עטה II with an ellipsis of the object. In
Song 1.7 it is difficult to make sense of כעטיה on the supposition that it
is a form of עטה I, whereas it is intelligible if it refers to picking lice.
Alternatively, the text may be emended to כטעיה on the basis of
Symmachus, the Vulgate, the Peshitta, and probably the Targum. Is it
better to emend the text with the support of three versions (though not
the LXX, which confirms the MT), or to postulate the use of עטה II in

the sense of picking lice as in Jer. 43.12? It may be claimed that there is a good case for the latter option, and that the NEB and the REB are right to understand כעטיה to mean that if she cannot find her lover she will be like someone picking lice.

Some forty years ago, when I was in my first academic post, George Anderson was kind and helpful to a younger colleague, and it is a pleasure now to dedicate this essay to someone who has been a friend for so long.

BIBLIOGRAPHY

Böttcher, F.[3]
  1849   *Exegetisch-kritische Aehrenlese zum Alten Testament* (Leipzig).
  1864   *Neue exegetisch-kritische Aehrenlese zum Alten Testament* I.
Bochart, S.
  1692   *Hierozoicon*, I (Leiden, 3rd edn): 455-56.
Cornill, C.H.
  1905   *Das Buch Jeremia* (Leipzig).
Driver, G.R.
  1950   'L'interprétation du texte masorétique à la lumière de la lexicographie hébraïque', *ETL* 26: 337-53.
  1968   'Isaiah i–xxxix: Textual and Linguistic Problems', *JSS* 13: 36-57.
  1974   'Lice in the Bible', *PEQ*: 159-60.
Eitan, I.
  1937–38   'A Contribution to Isaiah Exegesis', *HUCA* 12–13: 55-88.
Gall, A. von
  1904   'Jeremias 43,12 und das Zeitwort 'ṭh', *ZAW* 24: 105-21.
Gesenius, W.
  1839   *Thesaurus philologicus criticus linguae hebraeae et chaldaeae Veteris Testamenti*, II (Leipzig, 2nd edn): 1014-15.
Giesebrecht, F.
  1903   *Das Buch Jeremia* (Göttingen, 2nd edn).
Ginsberg, H.L.
  1950   'Some Emendations in Isaiah', *JBL* 59: 51-60.
Gordis, R.
  1936–37   'Studies in Hebrew Roots of Contrasted Meanings', *JQR* NS 27: 33-53; ḥāpâ is discussed on pp. 41-43.
Hitzig, F.
  1841   *Der Prophet Jeremia erklärt* (Leipzig).

---

3.   Böttcher (1849: 36; 1864: 163) refers to an earlier article of his, 'Versuche', which was published in Winer's *Zeitschrift für Systematische Theologie* 2 (1832): 97ff. Unfortunately, I do not have access to this periodical.

Holladay, W.L.
    1989   *Jeremiah*, II (Minneapolis).
Jastrow, M.
    1904   *A Dictionary of the Targumim, the Talmud Babli and Yerushalmi, and the Midrashic Literature* (London and New York).
Jones, D.R.
    1992   *Jeremiah* (London and Grand Rapids).
Michaelis, J.D.
    1792   *Supplementa ad lexica hebraica* (Göttingen): 1882-83.
Murphy, R.E.
    1990   *The Song of Songs* (Minneapolis).
Peake, A.S.
    n.d.   *Jeremiah and Lamentations*, II (Edinburgh and London).
Rothstein, J.W.
    1922   'Der Prophet Jeremia', in E. Kautzsch and A. Bertholet (eds.), *Die heilige Schrift des Alten Testaments*, I (Tübingen, 4th edn).
Rudolph, W.
    1962   *Das Buch Ruth. Das Hohe Lied. Die Klagelieder* (Gütersloh).
Volz, P.
    1928   *Der Prophet Jeremia* (Leipzig, 2nd edn).
Wildberger, H.
    1978   *Jesaja*. II. *Jesaja 13–27* (Neukirchen–Vluyn).

THE ANATOMY OF HEBREW NARRATIVE POETRY

J.C.L. Gibson

Compared with the syntax of classical Hebrew prose, which has down the years been the dominant concern of student's textbooks and attracted a plethora of scholarly studies and monographs, the syntax of classical Hebrew poetry has been seriously neglected. I cannot hope to redress this imbalance in one small article, even if I knew all the answers; but perhaps I can set out some guidelines for how I believe the matter should be approached. In my forthcoming revision of A.B. Davidson's *Hebrew Syntax* (Edinburgh: T. & T. Clark, 3rd edn, 1901), I will be trying to give the syntax of Hebrew poetry a larger profile than it received in the original editions or indeed than it has received in any of Davidson's competitors, including the recent volume by Waltke and O'Connor (see *Bibliographical Note*). This article deals in a little more detail than in my new *Syntax* with narrative poetry which is, compared with lyric or prophetic or wisdom poetry, a relatively minor subdivision of the field. It concentrates in particular on the incidence within that genre of the two main verbal conjugations which, for reasons which should become apparent in the body of the article, I content myself with identifying by the non-committal labels qatal and yiqtol. It is a pleasure to dedicate the article to a distinguished successor of A.B. Davidson in the Chair of Old Testament at New College.

The feature more than any other which sets poetry apart from prose in Hebrew is parallelism, and narrative poetry is, like other kinds of poetry, structured around that feature. Each succeeding statement has to be repeated at least once and each couplet or triplet so formed has, even in long passages, an independence of sorts. It is not surprising, therefore, that the *waw* consecutive construction, the workhorse of narrative prose and what above all gives it continuity and coherence, should be frugally used, at any rate in the earlier of our narrative poetic texts, nor that ויהי, narrative prose's chief means of effecting changes of scene or episode, should be even less prominent. Neither is at home in such a staccato environment. As a free standing form that can occupy any position in a clause, the yiqtol which appears in the *waw* consecutive construction is, however, very much at home in narrative poetry. It is a pity that this yiqtol, whether attached to *waw* consecutive or on its own, is only distinguishable from other yiqtols in a few paradigms, notably in the hiphil of the regular verb and in a number of weak verbs, where it has shorter forms (cf. יגל over against יגלה) and that even in these paradigms it is sometimes replaced by a longer form. Nevertheless, let us call the two yiqtols for functional purposes short and long.

In accordance with this nomenclature all yiqtols in the consecutive construction will of necessity be short, whether they are formally so or not. It is, however, not so easy to be sure in the case of free standing yiqtols, though we may reasonably assume that in narrative poetry most will be functionally short. But it cannot be excluded that some will be long and have a frequentative function. In prose narrative these long yiqtols are generally recognized by their avoidance of the first position in a clause and by their collocation with *waw* consecutive qatals, as in Gen. 2.6 ועד יעלה...והקשה 'now a mist used to go up...and water'; or v. 25, ולא יתבששו 'but they were not ashamed'. In the view of S.R. Driver and many others we encounter not a few examples of this functionally long yiqtol in narrative poetry; but I will be arguing below that these should properly be regarded as functionally short. Indeed, the only clear instance of a frequentative yiqtol in past time that I have been able to find in poetry occurs not in a story but in a backward reminiscence within a poem set mostly in present time, Ps. 42.5: 'these things I remember כי אעבר בסך אדדם how I used to go with the crowd, lead them in procession...'

That the free standing short yiqtol of narrative poetry is the same form as *waw* consecutive yiqtol is shown not only by the fact that both are most naturally translated into English by a past tense, but by a number of significant equations between the narrative portions of two versions of the same poem preserved in 2 Samuel 22 and Psalm 18. Compare, e.g. v. 12 in the Samuel passage וישת 'and he made darkness his covering', with v. 12 in the Psalm: ישת 'he made'; or v. 14 in the Samuel passage: ירעֵם 'he thundered', with v. 14 in the Psalm: וירעם 'and he thundered'. In this particular poem there are, in both versions, about the same number of *waw* consecutive and free standing yiqtol forms, and about half that number of qatals, also translated by a past tense in English. There are similar series of short yiqtols and qatals in other longer poems with narrative sections. Thus Exod. 15.4-10 (note v. 5: יכסימו 'the deeps covered them', v. 10: כסמו 'the sea covered them'); Deut. 32.8-20 (note v. 8: יצב 'he fixed', v. 18: 'the rock which bore you תשׁי you forgot'); Pss. 44.10-15; 68.8-15 (note v. 15 תשׁלֵג 'it snowed'); 74.3-8, 12-15; 78 *passim* (note v. 26 יסע, v. 52 ויסע '[and] he led out'); 104.6-9; 107 *passim* (note v. 29 יקֵם 'he turned storm into silence'). We should presumably regard in the same light the (formally) long yiqtols in other narrative passages like Hab. 3.3ff.; Pss. 80.9-13; 116.3-4; Job 4.12-16, etc.; and indeed in other past contexts, e.g. Job 3.3: 'cursed be the day אולד בו on which I was born'; 15.7, 8; Isa. 51.2, etc.

There has been, as I have already hinted, not a little reluctance among scholars to admit that these yiqtols in narrative poetry, or indeed the *waw* consecutive yiqtol in general, are other than imperfects, or, as linguists nowadays prefer to say, imperfectives. I suspect that many of us assume, without giving it much thought, that the shortened forms in the *waw* consecutive construction are only stylistic variants, doublets as in Jer. 10.13 ויעלה and 51.16 ויעל, that the unbound shortened forms in narrative poetry are somehow connected, perhaps by being allowed to become detached from *waw*, and that the past meaning assigned to them has something to do with the 'conversive' nature of the *waw* consecutive construction. We have dropped conversive in favour of consecutive, but in our thinking we are still constrained by the conversive theory. I do not think we can take this assumption, however widespread, seriously, especially when we do not let the quite common substitution in present and future contexts of a long yiqtol for a jussive (e.g. Gen. 1.9: ותראה 'and let the dry ground appear') tempt us into arguing for a conflation of these two forms. The suggestion sometimes made that many of the yiqtols in narrative poetry are what we call in English 'historical presents' seems to me equally unconvincing. How can you have a 'historical', or for that matter any other kind of present, in a language which does not possess tense? The view of S.R. Driver that many of these yiqtols are frequentatives is more plausible; but it is not enough to argue this on logical grounds, on our feeling that such and such an action is being extended or even repeated over a considerable time. We want more evidence than that, for instance a collocation with *waw* consecutive qatal as in prose narrative. Thus a good candidate might seem to be Ps. 78.14, which speaks of God leading the people in daytime by cloud and at night by fire; but the verb is *waw* consecutive, וינחם. I cannot see that the case is any different in v. 38 where the verb is free standing yiqtol, יכפר עון 'he forgave (their) iniquity'; in the context it is clear that this is being done often.

There is in fact no reason to doubt that the actions described by yiqtol in narrative poetry are normal narrative actions and that the time they last is not in these contexts relevant—cf. in prose 1 Kgs 15.25 וימלך 'and he reigned over Israel two years'. Nor furthermore is it possible to see them as other than perfective in aspect, describing whole or completed actions, whether punctual or lasting some time or even, in the latter case, involving repetition of the action. We ought to have the courage to come clean and admit that 'imperfect(ive)' is a misnomer for the yiqtol conjugation as a whole. Its primary role in narrative seems to be to describe actions, either simple and perfective (short yiqtol) or iterative, frequentative and imperfective (long yiqtol), prose and poetry differing only in the uses they make of these two forms.

A different kind of claim has been made by scholars with an interest in comparative Semitics, namely that short yiqtol is a preterite (cf. *iqtul* in Akkadian and *yqtl*, presumably *yaqtul*, in Ugaritic epic). But this view comes up against the same objection as the suggestion that some yiqtols in narrative poetry are 'historical presents', namely the intrusion of a tense form into an aspectual system; and it is further gainsaid by the existence in other than narrative contexts of a considerable number of short yiqtols. Thus in present time settings, Ps. 90.3 תשב 'you turn men back to destruction'; Job 18.9 a snare יחזק seizes hold of him. In future time settings, Gen. 49.17 יהי־דן נחש 'Dan shall be a serpent in the way'; Isa. 27.6 ישרש יעקב 'Jacob shall take root'. Perhaps these forms hint at a once more widespread distinction in present contexts between a short yiqtol expressing simple action and a long yiqtol expressing extended action, and in future contexts between an indicative short yiqtol (i.e. with non-jussive meaning) and an indicative long yiqtol. The matter requires further investigation.

The qatal conjugation also occurs in narrative poetry. It is, as we have seen, translated into English by a past tense in the same way as *waw* consecutive and free standing yiqtol, as though it were a mere alternative to these. I do not believe this to be so. In making out this case, I would like first to examine qatal's role in narrative prose.

Qatal in narrative prose is, in fact, not a true narrative form. It cannot begin a narrative nor, within a narrative, should it be regarded, in spite of the oft quoted rule in the Grammars, as an alternative to wayyiqtol used when, due to the vagaries of word order, another word or phrase happens to come between *waw* and the verb. Rather, *waw* consecutive yiqtol carries forward the story line while qatal marks a pause at any point along that line to enable a different kind of statement to be made; and the changed word order is an integral element of such different kinds of statement.

The pause in the sequence of events may be small, as with a negative clause, which denies that some action took place, Gen. 31.33 ולא מצא 'but he did not find (them)'. Or it may be more significant, as in the use of circumstantial clauses, which begin with the subject, usually with, sometimes without *waw* and which, by their nature, supply background or tangential information, moving therefore off the narrative line. Thus, opening a story, Job 1.1 איש היה 'there was a man'; within a story, Gen. 20.4 ואבימלך לא קרב אליה 'now Abimelech had not (yet) approached her'. Subject–qatal order may also be used non-circumstantially, for example, to round off a story or episode, 2 Sam. 18.17 וכל־ישראל נסו 'and (so) all Israel fled'; or, within a story, to re-identify a participant after an absence, 2 Kgs 9.1 ואלישע הנביא קרא 'then Elisha the prophet summoned'. In each case a pause is felt. Other clauses beginning with the subject or the object occur in constructions which have as their purpose the expression of non-sequential situations, either simultaneous or contrastive. Thus in a well-formed conjunctive sentence, Gen. 13.12 אברם ישב...ולוט ישב 'Abram dwelt in the land of Canaan, while Lot dwelt among the cities of the valley'. Or in a sentence with chiasmus, Gen. 4.4 וישע יהוה אל־הבל...ואל־קין...לא שעה 'and Yahweh had regard to Abel...but to Cain...he had no regard'. It is worth noting that in this last example לא שעה is not continued by ויחר לקין מאד 'and Cain was very angry', though it is often cited by the Grammars as an instance of *waw* consecutive yiqtol succeeding qatal; rather ויחר etc. continues the whole sequence beginning with וישע, and the clause beginning with ואל־קין is, as in their different ways are all the examples quoted in this paragraph, 'off-line'. The same is, of course, true of subordinate clauses with qatal; these have the function of qualifying or giving an explanation of a previous statement, and the narrative is again perceptibly halted.

Qatal may not begin a prose narrative, but occasionally it may begin a clause within it, though only when such a clause is in apposition to the previous one. This does not, however, materially affect the role of qatal in prose narrative, since apposition is a device of restatement or amplification, and there is normally no advance in the narrative. Gen. 21.14 ויתן אל־הגר שׂם על־שׁכמה 'and he gave (it) to Hagar, he put (it) (putting it) upon her shoulder'.

But what aspectually is the value of this qatal? A good case can be made out that it is essentially stative in function, as are most qatals in present-time settings. It is well known that there qatal usually denotes a physical or mental condition (as in stative verbs proper) or describes a present state arising out of a past action (like the English perfect with *have*). Gen. 4.6 למה נפלו פניך 'why has your face fallen?' Sometimes English, concentrating on the past action, may render this qatal with a past tense, Gen. 3.11 מי הגיד לך 'who told you that you were naked?'; and sometimes, concentrating on the result, with a present tense, Isa. 53.6 'and by his stripes נרפא־לנו we are healed'. Or it may use two different renderings within the same verse, Job 1.21 יהוה נתן ויהוה לקח 'Yahweh gave and Yahweh has taken away'. But these are matters of English, not Hebrew, usage. It is also well known that, largely in poetry, qatal may be used to describe a number of actions which are tantamount to states in that they occur in non-specific, i.e. typical or recurrent situations. Ps. 84.4 גם־צפור מצאה 'even the sparrow finds a house'. The usage of qatal in narrative prose does not seem to me to be greatly different from these present time usages. The context is past and therefore necessitates a translation by a past tense in English; but its role is, if not exactly stative, at least static. We can see how it eventually became, as in Mishnaic Hebrew, a straightforward past tense, but in classical Hebrew it still denotes aspect, the time reference being given by the context. Qatal must therefore still be an aspectual category in narrative poetry also.

Let us examine how it fulfils this role. The first difference from narrative prose is that narratives or episodes within them may begin with qatal, Ps. 107.4 תעו במדבר 'they (some) wandered in the desert', cf. v. 10; or should I say formal narrative prose? For qatal may also begin a narrative report in direct speech in prose, as in Gen. 42.30 דבר האישׁ אתנו קשׁות ויתן 'the man...spoke roughly to us and gave us out to be spies'. Qatal can also occur at the start of a verse, Ps. 68.19 עלית למרום

'you ascended on high'; Ps. 78.13 בקע ים 'he divided the sea'. Or at the start of a clause, Ps. 68.19 שבית שבי לקחת מתנות 'you led captives, you took gifts'. In both these cases, the verbs are in apposition with those in a previous clause, repeating or amplifying its meaning. Incidentally, apposition is much commoner in narrative poetry than in narrative prose, fitting in well with the parallelistic structure (for examples with short yiqtol see Judg. 5.8, 2 Sam. 22.17-18, etc.). Or qatal can occur anywhere within a clause and be regarded as contributing to what is, by the nature of parallelism, a static situation, Ps. 68.19 לקחת; Ps. 78.25 לחם אבירים אכל איש 'the bread of angels each ate', cf. שלח; v. 24 נתן. In other words, nothing in the use of qatal in narrative poetry removes from it its essentially stative character. If difficulties arise from its collocation in such passages with the short yiqtol, these are difficulties for the English translator rather than the Hebrew audience. English is forced to use a past tense for both and so obscures the aspectual patterning which a Hebrew ear would appreciate. The qatal catches well the episodic and staccato feel of narrative poetry while, in the (relative) absence of *waw* consecutive forms, the short yiqtol serves to supply it with movement. This patterning, differing from poem to poem, may be studied passim in Psalms 68, 78, 105, 106, 107, etc.

At this point I rest my case. I have restricted myself more or less to narrative poetry and my brush has been broad. But I hope that I have demonstrated the importance of two matters. The first is that in poetry even more than in prose it is vital to respect the aspectual nature of the Hebrew verb and not to let translation into English, a language in which, although it has aspect, tense dominates, interfere with our investigations. I have suggested that the opposition between the verbal conjugations in Hebrew is more satisfactorily seen as one of stative versus active than, as is usual nowadays, as one of perfective versus imperfective. But secondly and chiefly I have taken the feature of parallelism as the key to poetic syntax. It is this feature above all which differentiates poetry syntactically from prose. Poetry, narrative or otherwise, shares the same aspectual verbal system with prose but, because of parallelism, disposes it quite differently.

BIBLIOGRAPHICAL NOTE

There are useful accounts of the history of tense and aspect theories of the Hebrew verb in L. McFall, *The Enigma of the Hebrew Verbal System* (Sheffield: Almond

Press, 1982) and B.K. Waltke and M. O'Connor, *An Introduction to Biblical Hebrew Syntax* (Winona Lake, IN: Eisenbrauns, 1990), pp. 343-50. S.R. Driver's classic study of a century ago, *A Treatise on the Use of the Tenses in Hebrew* (Oxford: Clarendon Press, 3rd edn, 1892), is still indispensable for any serious research in the subject, but naturally has little help to give on modern aspectual theory. For a different reason the same is true of the only modern book on the verb in poetry, D. Michel's *Tempora und Satzstellung in den Psalmen* (Bonn: Bouvier, 1960); it analyses usage, often acutely, but intentionally eschews theoretical conclusions. For recent studies of the syntax in prose narrative, see, in addition to Waltke and O'Connor, M. Eskhult, *Studies in Verbal Aspect and Narrative Technique in Biblical Hebrew Prose* (Studia Semitica Upsaliensia, 1990); A. Niccacci, *The Syntax of the Verb in Classical Hebrew Prose* (trans. W.G.E. Watson; Sheffield: JSOT Press, 1990). On the conjunctive and chiastic sentence types mentioned on p. 145 see F.I. Andersen, *The Sentence in Biblical Hebrew* (The Hague: Mouton, 1974), chs. 8, 9; and on the syntactical role of subject-qatal order see G. Khan, *Studies in Semitic Syntax* (Oxford: Oxford University Press, 1988), pp. 86ff. Waltke and O'Connor provide a good up-to-date bibliography on all areas of Hebrew syntax, including a short section of books on General Linguistic Theory.

QOHELET, THE RABBIS AND THE WISDOM TEXT
FROM THE CAIRO GENIZA[*]

A.P. Hayman

1. *The Cairo Geniza*

Prior to the discovery of the Dead Sea Scrolls the most important find
of Hebrew manuscripts in the modern period was from the Cairo
Geniza. Like many ancient synagogues the Ezra Synagogue in Old
Cairo had a closed off room at the back where old books, documents,
and manuscripts were deposited mainly out of a reluctance to destroy
texts that contained the divine name, the tetragrammaton. Usually,
after a decent interval, these were taken out and buried, but for some
reason, the congregation simply forgot that the Cairo Geniza existed
and its contents lay forgotten for many centuries until discovered by
travellers in the late nineteenth century. The first scholar to recognize
the immense value of the material in the Geniza was Abraham
Firkowitch, a Karaite Jew from the Crimea. Sometime in the late
1860s he carried away a lot of the material which now forms the basis
of the Firkowitch Collections in the Russian Public Library in St
Petersburg. These collections contain some of the most valuable MSS
we have of the Hebrew Bible with much else besides.

In 1896 Elkan Nathan Adler was allowed to take away from the
Geniza as much material as he could carry in an old Torah mantle.
This material now forms the basis of the collection of Geniza material

---

[*]   It gives me great pleasure to dedicate this paper to Professor George
Anderson, my colleague for fourteen years in the Department of Hebrew and Old
Testament Studies at the University of Edinburgh. I am grateful for his wise advice
and guidance over the years but particularly in the early years when I was a young
and inexperienced scholar. This paper was first presented to the Department's Staff
and Postgraduate Seminar at New College in October 1991. This seminar attempts to
continue the great tradition of scholarly discussion established by Professor
Anderson at his regular Saturday morning Psalms Seminar.

in the Library of the Jewish Theological Seminary in New York. In December 1896 Solomon Schechter, Reader in Rabbinic Studies at the University of Cambridge, was sent by Charles Taylor, the master of St John's College, Cambridge to get as much of the Geniza material as he could for the Cambridge University Library. Schechter took all the manuscript material that was left in the Geniza; and that now forms the Taylor–Schechter collection of Cambridge University Library. Under the vigorous leadership of Stefan Reif, the current curator of this collection, more and more of its riches have been made available to scholars in recent years. Paul Kahle estimates the total number of manuscript fragments from the Geniza as around 200,000, of which Cambridge has about half (Kahle 1959: 13).

The Geniza collections are especially valuable because they give us access to the material that had been discarded by medieval Jews as out-of-date, no longer relevant especially to orthodox Judaism, so it is no surprise that among these MSS were discovered the Hebrew text of the Book of Ecclesiasticus (Ben Sira) and the Damascus Document (CD) subsequently found to be one of the most important texts among the Dead Sea Scrolls. Also discovered were many texts produced by the Karaites who broke away from Rabbinic Judaism in the eighth century. The Geniza produced the oldest scroll of Sefer Yeṣira (the Book of Creation), a foundation document for the Kabbala. The rabbinic technique for dealing with material that was incompatible with their version of Judaism was simply to ignore it, make sure that it was not copied and preserved and, in the course of time, it just disappeared from the tradition. Hence the crucial importance of the Geniza material for scholars who are interested precisely in the sort of material that does not fit into rabbinic Judaism but yet, from all the evidence, was widely popular among many Jews.

2. *The Wisdom Text from the Cairo Geniza*

Among the first of the Geniza texts to be published by Schechter were seven leaves of a text which he simply labelled as 'Gnomic' (1904: 425). Schechter made only a few brief remarks about it, mentioning that it drew on the Bible and the Talmud but was also 'acquainted with Greek philosophy'. He was unable to place it at all, feeling that it contained 'strange words and unusual expressions'. He thought that the polemic it contained against those who forget Jerusalem pointed in some way to Karaite authorship. At about the same time, Abraham Harkavy published two leaves of a MS from the St Petersburg Geniza collection. Schechter suggests in an appendix to his article that these pages belong to his gnomic text. Harkavy wrote mainly in Hebrew and Schechter's comments seem to have written off the 'gnomic' text as uninteresting, so the scholarly world just forgot that this text existed. I must confess that I did not myself know of its existence until after I had delivered a paper on Sefer Yeṣira at the European Congress for Jewish Studies in Troyes in 1990. My attention was then drawn to a recent republication of this text in Germany in 1989 and I was advised that anybody interested, as I am, in what happened to the Jewish wisdom movement after Qohelet so comprehensively mauled it, ought to have a look at this Geniza text.

Klaus Berger, Professor of New Testament Theology at the University of Heidelburg, has provided us with the first complete edition and translation of what he calls 'Die Weisheitsschrift aus der Kairoer Geniza' or WKG for short (Berger 1989). The edition, on which he worked for twenty years, reunites the leaves published separately by Schechter and Harkavy and is accompanied with photographs and a very extensive commentary. But Berger's view of this text is very different from Schechter's. He dates it to c. 100 CE at the end of the New Testament period and he sets its place of origin within the Jewish community in Egypt. He relates it to the kind of dualistic, ascetic, philosophically inclined Judaism about which Philo writes when he discusses the Essenes and the Therapeutae. He also traces many connections with the Dead Sea Scrolls, and material that came out of the early Jewish Christian groups such as the apocryphal Gospels and the Pseudo-Clementine literature. He claims that it used a pre-masoretic version of the Hebrew Bible. It is the work of an ascetic, pious, pacifistic and elite group who wished to renew Jewish spirituality after the debacle of the destruction of Jerusalem in 70 CE. He thinks that it is extremely important for understanding the Jewish background to the New Testament, especially the 'other-worldly' fiercely eschatological elements in Christianity which are notably lacking in rabbinic Judaism. Any New Testament scholar's ears would prick up upon hearing WKG 4.7-8:

> Do not hurt any brother who believes in the God of Israel,
> Even though he has no knowledge, for a little faith is righteousness.

According to Berger, WKG represents the last attempt to bind together the dualistic approach of hellenistic philosophy with the traditional dualism of the Jewish wisdom literature. Thereafter people who thought like this became gnostics.

If Berger is correct this is a sensational discovery and the text would have to rank along with 4 Ezra and 2 Baruch as among the very few texts we have left that witness to non-rabbinic forms of Judaism after 70 CE. It is indeed a strange text. It presents itself very much in the style of the Book of Proverbs or the more proverbial type material in Qohelet. From the point of view of genre it is closer to the Book of Proverbs than either Qohelet or Ben Sira. It also closely mimics biblical style. It is laid out in rythmic, one line couplets displaying the full range of biblical-style parallelism. The MS preserves this structure by setting the text out in two columns, each line in a column containing one bicolon.[1] This text speaks with authority. It assumes that what it has to say is self-evidently true. It does not use the device of pseudonymity nor appeal to any biblical or rabbinic text to authenticate what it has to say. There are no attributed statements at all. It has none of the characteristic features of texts produced by the rabbis. This is not to say that it does not use material coming from the Bible or possibly rabbinic Judaism. Indeed, its primary method of composition is to weave together seamlessly biblical texts (usually no more than a phrase in length) with other traditional Jewish material along with the author's own contribution. But nothing marks the division between these types of material, unlike the midrashim where the biblical text is clearly marked off, even lemmatized, so that the division between sacred text and interpretation is always clear. Either, like the similarly constructed Wisdom of Ben Sira, this text precedes the canonisation of the Bible as Berger claims, or it ignores it.

Here are two examples of the way in which WKG uses the text of the Bible:[2]

1. The quotation below from WKG 1.1-7 preserves the layout of the manuscript. 1.3-4 is a good example of antithetic parallelism in the text.

2. In the following quotations from WKG the vocalization is taken from the manuscript and does not, therefore, in biblical texts always agree with that of MT. The text is transcribed from the photographs provided by Rüger. The translations are my own.

(1) WKG 4.13-14:

13 For those who fear the Lord do not love this world	כִּי יִרְאֵי יְיָ אֵינָם אֹהֲבִים עוֹלָם הַזֶּה
And they do not love with their eyes	וְאֵינָם אֹהֲבִים בְּעֵינֵיהֶם
14 But they take pleasure in the world to come	וַחֲפֵצִים בְּחַיֵּי עוֹלָם הַבָּא
Therefore *the righteous is protected when he dies* (Prov. 14.32)	לְכָךְ חֹסֶה בְּמוֹתוֹ צַדִּיק

Here WKG smoothly incorporates Prov. 14.32 and may well read it correctly, unlike the RSV which chooses to follow the LXX presumably because Jews were not supposed to believe in a worthwhile life after death before the Maccabean period.

(2) WKG 1.17-18a:

17 And he who honours the Torah and works at it will certainly attain the World to come,	וּמְכַבֵּד תּוֹרָה וְעוֹסְקָהּ בְּוַדַּאי יַשִּׂיג לְעוֹלָם הַבָּא
18 And will walk among *the Standing Ones* to acquire understanding and what is best of all.	וְיִתְהַלֵּךְ בֵּין הָעֹמְדִים קְנֹה בִּינָה וּבָחוֹר מִכֹּל

Here only the word העמדים and the use of the verb הלך hint at Zech. 3.7, but the author builds on the traditional view that the angels are the 'standing ones' and is saying that, like the high priest Joshua, the righteous will become members of the heavenly court when they die.

Like the Book of Proverbs, Qohelet and some wisdom psalms, e.g. Ps. 119, WKG seems to ignore the Pentateuch, Moses and the whole 'salvation-history' element of Judaism. In this respect it is similar to Sefer Yeṣira and I have discussed this phenomenon at some length in various articles, most recently in 'Qohelet and the Book of Creation' (Hayman 1991). WKG talks a lot about the Torah but, just like Ps. 119, or the Wisdom of Solomon, this never has any hard content that would relate it to the Pentateuchal laws and rabbinic Halakhah. Like Proverbs 8 and related passages, one suspects that this Torah is much more closely related to what the Greeks would call 'the law of nature'. What 'Torah/Law' means in Jewish wisdom texts is one of those areas that still awaits satisfactory clarification by scholars. Even Ben Sira, who explicitly identifies Wisdom and the Law of Moses, seems to show no interest in the precise details of the Torah.

The most prominent theological trait of this text is an enhanced dualism and stress on the abiding value only of the World to Come. Its two-age dualism is very similar to that of 4 Ezra and, indeed, its use of the terminology 'This World' and 'The World to Come' means that it cannot be earlier than the first century CE when this terminology is first attested. As it says in an image that is attributed to Jesus in the Islamic tradition of the Apocryphal sayings: 'like a bridge which travellers cross, so is this world to human beings' (2.18). There is a sustained polemic against what it calls תאות עולם (desire for the world), concretized in objections to all worldly pleasures such as eating, drinking and sleeping (sex?). This does not sound at all like rabbinic Judaism, but very much like Philo's Therapeutae and the early Christian ascetics.

So do we have here one of the long lost bridges between Judaism and Christianity for which Professors of New Testament at German universities (and elsewhere) are always searching? Unfortunately not. Two years after Berger published his edition of WKG, Hans Peter Rüger, of the Evangelical-Theological Faculty at Tübingen, published his edition of the text with exactly the same title (Rüger 1991). Reading between the lines it is not difficult to see that he did so basically because he thinks Berger's book is both misleading and inaccurate. He accuses Berger of misreading both the consonantal text of the manuscript and its Babylonian supralinear vocalization. So far as I can judge from the photographs of the manuscript that both Berger and Rüger provide, Rüger's readings are invariably correct. As for the date, Rüger puts it 1000 years later than Berger—into the 12th century, very close to the probable date of the manuscript. He argues that it draws on the completed Talmud and on Sefer Yeṣira but above all on Baḥya ibn Pakuda's *Sefer Ḥovot ha-Levavot*, which was composed around 1080. He locates it in the group known as the 'Mourners for Zion' who appeared after the Muslim conquest of Palestine and lived in Jerusalem until well into the Middle Ages. They were ascetics supported by diaspora Jews in order to maintain the Jewish presence in Jerusalem and to 'weep for Zion' (Baron: 185, 257-58, 376 n. 48). This group was often dominated by the Karaites who established a non-rabbinic identity for themselves by adopting a rigorously ascetic interpretation of Judaism especially in the area of Sabbath observance. The rabbinic Sabbath was an occasion of joy, dominated by eating and drinking and sleeping (sex with one's wife was enjoined on the eve of the sabbath). So the Karaites did the opposite. This looks like a very credible 'Sitz im Leben' for our text.

Who is right—Berger or Rüger? What we have here is a very

interesting test for our discipline: two highly respected and competent scholars differing by 1000 years in their dating of a Hebrew text. If this can happen in a period for which we have so much information, manuscripts, inscriptions, etc., what does it do for our confidence in the datings given by scholars to biblical texts?

There is one criterion for dating that I have not yet mentioned, indeed have deliberately kept to the last, namely, the language of the text, the type of Hebrew it contains. This is the point at which Rüger's book is so superior to Berger's. Berger devotes nine lines in his introduction to the type of Hebrew in which his text is written and there are hardly any philological remarks in his commentary. Rüger, on the other hand, subtitles his book: 'Text, Übersetzung und philologischer Kommentar'. Berger claims the text is written in Mishnaic Hebrew; Rüger says it is Medieval Rabbinic Hebrew. He points to words like הצלחה 'success' which are not attested before the Middle Ages or קָצִיר 'short' instead of Hebrew קָצָר. He says קָצִיר is a loan word from Arabic. There are quite a lot of other words and expressions that make it quite clear that this text cannot go back to 100 CE. On the other hand, how secure a criterion is this sort of linguistic analysis for dating texts? Often in biblical texts it is all we have to go on—a good example is the dating of Qohelet. But often it involves circular reasoning since our presumed ordering of the phases of the Hebrew language is based on our dating of the texts. Take the word חצלהה for example. The verb הצליח is attested in the Bible while the hiphil verbal noun pattern based on the Aramaic haphel infinitive also goes back to biblical times (GK §85c and Kutscher 1982: §103). At any time, someone could have used the natural word-forming patterns of the Hebrew language to create הצלחה from הצליח. The step from the well-known Biblical Aramaic הַצְלָח (he prospered, succeeded) to the Hebrew noun הַצְלָחָה (success) is very short. Maybe WKG is the first to attest it! The transition from Mishnaic to Medieval Rabbinic Hebrew is so gradual that on linguistic grounds all we can say is that WKG is likely to belong to the second half of the first millenium CE.

But there is another problem of which we need to be aware. Most Jewish texts from the Pentateuch and the Prophets, to the Mishnah and the Talmud, grew by a process of accretion over many centuries. They contain, therefore, the Hebrew of many different stages in the development of the language. In the case of Sefer Yeṣira I was able to show in a paper that I gave at the European Association for Jewish

Studies in Berlin in 1987 (Hayman 1987) that the linguistic data which some scholars had used to date it to the seventh or eighth centuries CE were all clustered in those parts of the text which the text-critical data demonstrated to be among the latest to get added to it. In the case of SY we have over 120 MSS to work with and three main recensions. I can discern three stages of the developing Hebrew language within it—pure Mishnaic Hebrew, talmudic and post-talmudic Hebrew. In the case of WKG we have one MS only. If we had more than one manuscript we might well discover that it too had a history and that we were trying to date a tradition and not a fixed text. All too frequently with texts from the rabbinic period we find that two manuscripts of a work give us two texts, not two witnesses to one text. This should make us cautious about dating by linguistic criteria on a very thin manuscript base.

3. *WKG and the Book of Ecclesiastes*

One of the most striking features of WKG is its subtle but sustained critique of the Book of Ecclesiastes. As we have noticed earlier, biblical texts are seamlessly woven into the fabric of the text. The same goes for the use of Qohelet but with one striking difference. Whereas with other texts their substance is affirmed (see, e.g., the use of Prov. 14.32 in 4.14), in almost every case Qohelet's words are used to negate the substance of his text.

Examples:
(1) WKG 1.1-7:

1	דְּרוֹשׁ חָכְמָה וְדֶרֶךְ טוֹבָה	לְהִתְגַּדֵּל בְּעֵינֵי יְיָ [וְאָדָם]
2	מַרְחִיק סַכְלוּת וְנַבְהוּת מִנַּפְשׁוֹ	לְהִתְחַכֵּם וְלִתְגַּבֵּר לִמְאֹד
3	טוֹב לְבָחוּר בְּיִתְרוֹן מִכֹּל	מִלְהַרְחִיק מִלֵּב כֹּל הֲבָלִים
4	עוֹלָם הַזֶּה הֶבֶל הוּא	וְעוֹלָם הַבָּא יִתְרוֹן הוּא
5	לֹא רָאוּי לְהִתְעַסֵּק בְּאֵין יִתְרוֹן	כִּי יֵאָשֵׁם הֶעָמֵל בּוֹ
6	מְעַט עָסָק בְּטֶרֶף חָקוֹ	כִּי אֵין וְגוֹי מִלֶּחֶם חֹק
7	עֲסָק מְעַט וְלַהַג הַרְבֵּה	יֵאוֹשַׁר לִפְנֵי יְיָ

1.1   Seek wisdom and the good way in order to become great in the eyes of God [and human beings].

2   He who distances himself from folly (סכלוּת—in OT only in Qoh.) and pride will show himself to be wise and exceedingly strong.

3   It is good to choose what is best of all (יתרון - ביתרון מכל in OT only in Qoh) and to put[3] all futile things (pl. of הבל, Qohelet's leitmotif) out of one's heart.

4   This world is futile, but the world to come is real profit (יתרון again).

5   It is not fitting to be occupied with things that bring no profit, for the one who labours at them is guilty.[4]

6   Only work a little for your food ration, for there is no light[5] from a bread ration.

7   Little work (עסק again) and much study (להג הרבה from Qoh. 12.12) will bring blessing from God.

Here the characteristic vocabulary of Qoholet is interwoven into the text but in such a way as to reverse its meaning. Qohelet spends a lot of time proving that there is no 'profit or advantage' (יתרון) in any human activity. For him אין יתרון is the first example of הבל הבלים (1.2). By contrast our author neatly uses the two-ages doctrine to reverse Qohelet's position. הבל and יתרון are distinguished (1.4). This world is הבל, but the World to Come is יתרון. If Qoholet had thought this, he would not have had a problem! Again, note how Qoh. 12.12 is reversed in WKG 1.7 by judicious selective quotation. The author cites only להג הרבה from Qoh. 12.12c and leaves out the following יגעת בשׂר (is a weariness of the flesh), since for him 'much study' is what life on earth is for. But he does know the missing words. Look at what he does with them in 7.17:

Wisdom loves those who seek her[6]	חָכְמָה יֶאֱהַב לְדֹרְשֶׁיהָ
with much study *and* weariness of the flesh	בְּלַהַג הַרְבֵּה וִיגִיעַת בָּשָׂר

Here the insertion of a waw before יגעת is sufficient to reverse the meaning of Qoh. 12.12 and to support the ascetic teaching of our text that wisdom can only be obtained by a lot of study and fleshly abstinence.

3.   Reading ולהרחיק with Harkavy and Berger.

4.   Words formed from the root עסק and the use of the verb עמל are very frequent in Qoh.

5.   Reading נֻה with Berger (1989: 12). וני in the MS is meaningless. The fact that the scribe left it unvocalized suggests that he too could not make sense of it. Rüger (1991: 81) suggests the reading יגון (grief, sorrow) but that leaves us with a bland, almost meaningless statement. We cannot be sure what this line means.

6.   In translating thus, I am following the two eidtors of WKG, who note a link with Prov. 8.17.

(2) WKG: 2.3-5

3	He who honours Wisdom will be honoured	מְכַבֵּד חָכְמָה יְכֻבָּד
	and his memory will be exalted for ever.	וְיִתְעַלֶּה זִכְרוֹ לְעוֹלָם
4	Seek Wisdom and the fear of the Lord.	חַפְּשׂוּ חָכְמָה וְיִרְאַת יְיָ
	for then it will be well with you.	כִּי אָז טוֹב לָכֶם
5	Do not choose worldly success,	אַל תִּבְחֲרוּ בְּהַצְלָחַת הָעוֹלָם
	for there is one fate[7] for all.	כִּי מִקְרַת אֶחָד לַכֹּל

In line 3 the author takes the word זֵכֶר and לְעוֹלָם from Qoh. 2.16 in order to reverse precisely what Qohelet says in this verse, namely, 'There is no memory ever of the wise man along with the fool, since in the days to come all will be forgotten, and how the wise man dies along with the fool!' In line 5 he takes the phrase כִּי מִקְרֶה אֶחָד לַכֹּל from Qoh. 9.3 (cf. 2.14) and uses it to show the folly of aiming at worldly success. But Qohelet uses the phrase to negate the value of the life of wisdom and goodness. For him death makes everything futile. However, he is quite clear on the fact that, although everything is futile, a full stomach and a good woman in your bed are highly preferable to hunger and loneliness. Even the clever hermeneutics of the author of WKG seem to have given him insufficient confidence to tackle Qoh. 9.7-9! He ignores most of the so-called 'positive' passages in the Book of Ecclesiastes and tackles Qohelet's view that worldly success is a gift from God by carefully wedging an allusion to Qoh. 5.18 between his revamping of הבל and יתרון and his perversion of Qoh. 12.12, as seen in the next example.

(3) WKG 7.15-18:

15	For all the world is futile	כִּי כָל הָעוֹלָם הֶבֶל הוּא
	and there is no profit apart[8] from Wisdom	וְאֵין יִתְרוֹן לב חכמה
16	Kingship and wealth and worldly honour	מְלוּכָה וְעֹשֶׁר וּכְבוֹד עוֹלָם
	are the gift of God.	מַתַּת אֱלֹהִים הֵם
17	Wisdom loves those who seek her	חָכְמָה יֶאֱהַב לְדֹרְשֶׁיהָ
	with much study *and* weariness of the flesh	בְּלַהַג הַרְבֵּה וִיגִיעַת בָּשָׂר
18	(The right to exercise) authority comes by inheritance,	שִׁלְטוֹן מוֹרְשֵׁי אָבוֹת
	but Wisdom by a lot of hard work.	וְחָכְמָה בְּרֹב עָמָל

---

7. Read מִקְרֶה with Berger (1989: 14).
8. Read לְבַד with Rüger (1991: 113).

In this passage, apart from the reversal of Qoh. 12.12 which we have already dealt with, the words מתת אלהים in line 16 come from Qoh. 5.18 as does עשר, while שלטן in line 18 was probably suggested by Qohelet's השליטו. The author has to concede what has been a commonplace of all Jewish wisdom teaching (namely, that worldly authority and success come from God), but the context takes away most of the value of his concession since, for him, worldly goods and prosperity have no value in contrast with wisdom. The second half of line 18 may be quite literally a reversal of Qoh. 1.18 where Qohelet says that basically wisdom is a pain in the neck: כי ברב חכמה רב־כעס.

In 12.10-12 and 13.16 the author makes his view of kingship, wealth, and the like quite explicit while weaving more webs out of the words of Qohelet:

(4) WKG 12.10-12:

10	Does not all the world experience futility?	הֲלוֹא כּוֹל הָעוֹלָם רֹאִים הֲבָלִים
	For there is no profit in anyone's work.	כִּי אֵין יִתְרוֹן בְּכֹל עָמָל
11	Life and kingship, wealth and ability	חַיִּים וּמְלוּכָה עֹשֶׁר וִיכוּלָה
	physical appearance, pomp and glory—	וְחֵן וְתִפְאָרֶת וְכָבוֹד
12	They are worthless and futile	כּוּלָם נִפְסָדִים וַהֲבָלִים
	(but) wisdom is better than all this.	חָכְמָה יְתִירָה עַל כָּלֹה

(5) WKG 13.16:

17	Wisdom and joy[9] are God's gifts to the good	מַתַּת אֵל לַטּוֹבִים חָכְמָה
	To the sinners he has assigned worldly tasks.	וְשִׂמְחָה לַחַטָּאִים נָתַן עִסְקֵי עוֹלָם

Qohelet and the Rabbis

In arguing that the author of WKG was cleverly using Qohelet's words in order to reverse his views I am not, of course, assuming that he was conscious of what he was doing. From his perspective he would be bringing out the meaning Qohelet had all along intended. However, there were in Jewish society people who could read Qohelet as we do and who, therefore, had a big problem. What to do with a text that had somehow acquired the same authority within Jewish society as the other 'canonical' wisdom texts but yet which set out to deliberately undermine them. What the rabbis had to say about

---

9.   Redividing the line with Berger (1989: 35). The photograph of the MS shows clearly that 13.16b is overloaded and runs beyond the margin.

Qohelet and how they tackled the problem he presented them with is a fascinating example of the primacy of hermeneutics as *the* device that ensured Jewish survival.[10]

Along with some other books (mainly from the Writings section of the canon) we know that the canonicity of Qohelet was a matter of dispute between the rabbis:

> All the Holy Scriptures defile the hands. The Song of Songs and Ecclesiastes defile the hands. R. Judah [135–170] says: The Song of Songs defiles the hands but there is a dispute concerning Ecclesiastes. R. Jose [135–170] says: Ecclesiastes does not defile the hands but there is a dispute concerning the Song of Songs. R. Simeon [135–170] says: Ecclesiastes is among the lenient decisions of the School of Shammai and among the stringent decisions of the School of Hillel. R. Simeon b. Azzai [110–135] said: I have heard a tradition from the 72 elders on the day that R. Eleazar ben Azariah [110–135] was appointed head of the academy, that the Song of Songs and Ecclesiastes defile the hands. R. Akiba [110–135] said: God forbid: No man in Israel ever disputed the status of the Song of Songs saying that it does not defile the hands, for the whole world is not worth the day on which the Song of Songs was given to Israel: for all the Writings [= the Hagiographa] are holy, but the Song of Songs is the holiest of the holy. If there was a dispute, it conerned Ecclesiastes. R. Johanan b. Joshua [135–170], the son of R. Akiba's father-in-law, said: Ben Azzai's version of what they disputed and decided is the correct one (*m. Yad.* 3.5).

This is our oldest testimony to the dispute, coming from towards the end of the second century CE. Our next oldest text, *t. Yad.* 2.14, directly addresses the issue of Qohelet's inspiration:

> R. Simeon b. Menasia [170–200] says: The Song of Songs defiles the hands because it was composed under divine inspiration. Ecclesiastes does not defile the hands because it is only the wisdom of Solomon[11] (*t. Yad.* 2.14).

The midrash to Qohelet (*Qoh. R.* 1.3) goes even further: 'the sages sought to suppress the Book of Qohelet because they discovered therein words which savour of heresy'.

---

10. For this way of viewing the history of Judaism see Shmueli 1990.

11. Cf. Theodore of Mopsuestia, 360–428, who attributed to it a low degree of inspiration 'for Solomon had not received the grace of prophecy, but only the grace of prudence'.

What these texts do not tell us is precisely why the status of Qohelet was disputed. Some, mainly later, texts are more forthcoming:

> R. Judah [260–300] son of R. Samuel B. Shilath said in Rab's [220–250] name: The Sages wished to withdraw the book of Ecclesiastes because its words are self-contradictory (*b. Šab.* 30b).

Less specific is Abba Saul (120–150) in *ARN* 1.4—'Originally they used to say: Proverbs, Song of Songs, and Qohelet were withdrawn, for they presented mere parables and were not part of the Writings'. Most informative of all is Jerome in his commentary on the book:

> The Hebrews say that although it would seem that among other writings of Solomon which have become obsolete, and the memory of which has perished, this book also ought to be destroyed, for the reason that it affirms that the creatures of God are 'vain', and considers the whole [universe] to be as nothing, and prefers food and drink and passing pleasure to all else, yet it has from this one chapter [ch. 12] acquired the merit of being received as authoritative, so that it should be included in the number of the divine volumes. The reason is that it combines its whole argument, and the whole list of its contents, in this brief recapitulation, and says that the end of its words is very readily heard, and has nothing difficult about it, namely, that we should fear God, and keep his commandments (Jerome 1959: 360).

Here Jerome tells us how the rabbis dealt with the problem Qohelet posed to them. But the rabbis are equally forthcoming:

> R. Judah [260–300] son of R. Samuel B. Shilath said in Rab's [220–250] name: The Sages wished to withdraw the book of Ecclesiastes because its words are self-contradictory; yet why did they not withdraw it? Because it begins with words of Torah and it ends with words of Torah... The Book of Proverbs too they wished to withdraw, because its statements are self-contradictory. Yet why did they not withdraw it? They said: Did we not examine the book of Ecclesiastes and find a reconciliation? So here too let us make search (*b. Šab.* 30b).

> Abba Saul [120–150] says:...Originally they used to say: Proverbs, Song of Songs, and Ecclesiastes were withdrawn, for they presented mere parables and were not part of the Writings. So they arose and withdrew them, until the Men of the Great Assembly came and *interpreted* them (*ARN* ch. 1, cit. Schechter 1904: 2-3).

B. Šab. 30b and Jerome make clear the crucial role of the conclusion of the Book for keeping it in the canon. Obviously, the rabbis used these last few verses (now universally ascribed to a later editor) as the hermeneutic key to the book. Many scholars have argued that these verses were added to Qohelet's own work precisely to achieve this object. What the rabbis did with the rest of the book is difficult to reconstruct. Unfortunately, the midrash on Qohelet (*Qohelet Rabba*) is quite a late text (no earlier than the seventh century) and may not even have been composed until the practice arose of reading the book at the feast of Succot (Tabernacles) and this is not attested before the end of the first millennium. The midrash is hardly a unified or well-constructed work and consists mainly of a mosaic of quotations from earlier rabbinic texts arranged loosely around selected parts of Qohelet. Most of the time the technique used to neutralize Qohelet seems to be the time-honoured one of simply ignoring what he says and using his words as a peg to make points quite unrelated to the text at hand. However, just occasionally, the Midrash does actually engage with the text and then, the technique is quite similar to that of WKG: the message is neutralized by means of the doctrine of the two worlds:

> R. Huna and R. Aḥa said in the name of R. Ḥilfai: a man's labour is *under the sun*, but his treasury of reward is above the sun. R. Judan said: *under the sun* he has no profit, but he has it above the sun (*Qoh. R.* 1.3).[12]

Commenting on Qohelet 2.1, 'Come now, I will make a test of pleasure; enjoy yourself', the Midrash says that this refers to the 'pleasure of the World to Come. R. Jonah said in the name of R. Simon b. Zabdi: All the prosperity which a man experiences in this world is "vanity" in comparison with the prosperity of the World to Come.' The Midrash's version of Qoh. 1.14 is as follows: 'I have seen all the works that are done under the sun; and behold, all is vanity and a striving after the wind, *except repentance and good deeds*'. And so the Midrash goes on, taking as its key precisely what Qohelet does not say, rather than what he does say. No opportunity is lost to supplement his words by placing them in the context of the belief in a worthwhile life after death. Perhaps the overkill was designed to prevent people from noticing that the text actually says nothing at all about this!

An important clue to the original context in which this reinterpretation of Qohelet should be set is the fact that the Midrash incorporates

---

12. It is interesting to note that this 'under the sun/above the sun' distinction is precisely the hermeneutical key used by the modern evangelical commentator Michael Eaton (drawing on an earlier work by Derek Kidner [1976] to present us with an 'orthodox' Qohelet). See Eaton 1983.

whole a large chunk of material from the Jerusalem Talmud, *Ḥag.* 2.1. This is the material that deals with the apostasy of Elisha ben Abuyah from Judaism during the course of the persecution following the Bar Kokhba war and the subsequent attempts of Elisha's most famous pupil, Rabbi Meir, to reconvert his teacher to Judaism. Ostensibly the material is incorporated in *Qohelet Rabba* because it offers an illustration of Qoh. 7.8, 'Better is the end of thing than its beginning'. But as Rashi on Qoh. 7.8a rather acutely comments, 'When they began (interpreting) it R. Meir would expound every word in Midrash Qohelet in relation to Elisha ben Abuyah'. Why should this be? Let us look at the relevant section of *j. Ḥag.* 2.1:

> Elisha said, 'Once as I was passing before the Holy of Holies riding upon my horse on the Day of Atonement which happened to fall upon a Sabbath, I heard a *Bath Qol* coming out of the Holy of Holies saying, "Repent children, except for Elisha ben Abuyah, for he knew my power yet rebelled against me!"'

> Why did all this happen to him? Once Elisha was sitting and studying in the plain of Gennesaret, and he saw a man climb to the top of a palm tree, take the mother bird with her young, and descend safely. The following day he saw another man climbing to the top of the palm tree; he took the young birds but released the mother. When he descended a snake bit him and he died. Elisha thought, 'It is written, [If you chance to come upon a bird's nest, in any tree or on the ground, with young ones or eggs, you shall not take the mother with the young;] you shall let the mother go, but the young you may take to yourself; that it may go well with you, and that you may live long' [Deut. 22.6-7]. Where is the welfare of this man, and where his length of days?

> He did not know that R. Jacob had explained it before him: 'That it may go well with you'—in the World to Come which is wholly good. 'And that you may live long', in the time which is wholly long.

> Some say [he defected] because he saw the tongue of Rabbi Judah the Baker, dripping blood, in the mouth of a dog. He said, 'This is the Torah, and this its reward! This is the tongue that was bringing forth the words of the Torah as befits them. This is the tongue that laboured in the Torah all its days. This is the Torah, and this its reward! It seems as though there is no reward [for righteousness] and no resurrection of the dead.'

In the depressing circumstances of the War in which the Jews finally lost all hope of restoring their national independence and rebuilding the Temple, Elisha posed an acute theological challenge to his erstwhile colleagues (see Hayman 1975–76). The rabbis were acutely aware that in posing this challenge Elisha had an illustrious forebear in Qohelet (*Qoh. R.* 1.3 [p. 7]):

> R. Samuel b. Isaac said: The Sages sought to suppress the Book of Qoheleth because they discovered therein words which savour of heresy. They declared: All the wisdom of Solomon is contained in the statement, *Rejoice, O young man, in thy youth, and let thy heart cheer thee in the days of thy youth, and walk in the ways of thy heart, and in the sight of thine eyes* (Eccl. xi, 9). Now Moses said, *That ye go not about after your own heart and your own eyes* (Num. xv, 39), whereas Solomon said, '*Walk in the ways of thy heart, and in the sight of thine eyes!*' Is restraint to be abolished? Is there no judgment and no Judge?

If the rabbis were to deal with the tremendous challenges posed to Judaism by the loss of national independence and the apparent disconfirmation of fundamental Jewish beliefs such as God's providence, his justice, and his election of the Jewish people, they had to neutralize Qohelet along with Elisha ben Abuyah. Is it then any surprise that the rabbis who expressed doubts about Qohelet in the texts I quoted earlier belong precisely to the generation during and after Bar Kokhba, namely, Akiba, R. Judah, R. Simeon, Abba Saul, Simeon Ben Azzai and Simeon ben Menasia?

5. Conclusion

We can see now that WKG fits into a well-established tradition of reinterpreting Qohelet, a tradition that can be traced back to the crisis faced by the Jews in the aftermath of the Bar Kokhba war. The rabbis enabled the Jewish people to survive this crisis by completely refocusing their attention away from the political issues of Land, Temple and freedom from foreign rule, to other-worldly occupation with the Torah. Hence was inaugurated the second of Israel's seven cultures described by Efraim Shmueli in his important work *Seven Jewish Cultures*. In this book Shmueli argues that the crucial device that greased the transition from one Jewish culture to the next was hermeneutics, the technique by which one Jewish culture appropriated the heritage of an earlier one, while almost invariably transforming and, very often, reversing the meanings given to the texts by the earlier culture. And so the treatment of Qohelet in the Wisdom Text from the Cairo Geniza does not seem so out of place after all.

BIBLIOGRAPHY

Baron, S.
 1957   *A Social and Religious History of the Jews*, V (New York: Columbia University Press).
Berger, K.
 1989   *Die Weisheitsschrift aus der Kairoer Geniza* (Tübingen: Francke Verlag).
Eaton, M.
 1983   *Ecclesiastes: An Introduction and Commentary* (Leicester: IVP).
Hayman, A.P.
 1975–76   'Theodicy in Rabbinic Judaism', *Transactions of the Glasgow University Oriental Society*, XXVI: 28-43.
 1987   The Vocabulary and Date of Sefer Yeṣira.
 1991   'Qohelet and the Book of Creation', *JSOT* 50: 93-111.
Jerome
 1959   *Commentarius in Ecclesiasten, S. Hieronymi Presbyteri Opera, Corpus Christianorum* (Turnholti).
Kahle, P.
 1959   *The Cairo Geniza* (Oxford: Basil Blackwell).
Kidner, D.
 1976   *The Message of Ecclesiastes* (Leicester: IVP).
Kutscher, E.Y.
 1982   *A History of the Hebrew Language* (Jerusalem: Magnes; Leiden: Brill).
Rüger, H.P.
 1991   *Die Weisheitsschrift aus der Kairoer Geniza* (Tübingen: J.C.B. Mohr).
Schechter, S.
 1904   'Geniza Fragments I: Gnomic', *JQR* 16: 425-42.
Shmueli, S.
 1990   *Seven Jewish Cultures* (Cambridge: Cambridge University Press).

THE DEUTERONOMISTIC CYCLES OF 'SIGNS' AND 'WONDERS' IN EXODUS 1–13*

W. Johnstone

I. *Posing the Question*

A series of observations suggests that interconnections exist between some of the later chapters of the book of Exodus and the Deuteronomistic corpus.[1] If such interconnections exist elsewhere in Exodus, then may there not be a relationship between Exodus 1–13, in particular the so-called plague-cycle in chs. 7–12, and appropriate texts in the Deuteronomistic corpus?

Interconnections that may be observed between Exodus and the Deuteronomistic corpus include the following:

(1) There are cross-references between Exodus and the Deuteronomistic History. The best recognized cross-reference is, perhaps, that between the golden calf incident (Exod. 32.4) and Jeroboam's golden calves at Bethel and Dan (1 Kgs 12.28; 2 Kgs 17.16)[2]. But there are, I believe, others: in particular, the coda to the Book of the Covenant in Exod. 23.20-33 and the coda to the conquest narrative in Judg. 2.1-5; the מסכנות which Pharaoh built (Exod. 1.11) and those

---

* Earlier drafts of this paper were read at the Old Testament Seminar, University of Cambridge, in January 1991 and at the Fourteenth Congress of the International Organization for the Study of the Old Testament, Paris, July 1992. It is a happy coincidence that the scholar to whom these pages are dedicated in gratitude, both for his own distinction and because he has been a great encourager of the succeeding generation, should have been such an eminent associate of each of these institutions.

1. I have explored some of these already in Johnstone 1987 and, most recently, 1992a, b.

2. For a guarded discussion (not, I think, including 2 Kgs 17.16) one might refer to Moberly 1983: 162-71.

which Solomon built (1 Kgs 9.19),[3] especially in the light of the anti-Solomon polemic of the Deuteronomic legislation on the monarchy (Deut. 17.14-20). Long ago, de Vaux argued that one of the narratives of the crossing of the Sea in Exodus 14 was modelled on that of the crossing of the Jordan (Josh. 3-4).[4]

These cross-references are too significant to be regarded as merely sporadic glosses: they suggest deliberate editorial work. Indeed, they suggest joint-editorial work: DtrH is not simply quoting a pre-existing source, for the plural reference in the golden calf incident ('These are your gods, O Israel, who brought you up out of the land of Egypt') suggests that the primary focus lies with the Kings passage in the light of which the Exodus passage is being written up, just as, on de Vaux's argument, priority lies with the narrative of the crossing of the Jordan rather than with that of the crossing of the Sea.

(2) There are parallels between Exodus and the Book of Deuteronomy itself. These parallels in language and phraseology, many of which have long been noted,[5] again suggest that the phenomenon is not simply a matter of sporadic glosses but of deliberate editorial design. In particular:

(a) Deuteronomy provides material that enables the reconstruction of a pre-final edition text (I should call it 'pre-P') in Exodus (for example, Exod. 13.3-8* // Deut. 16.1-8; Exod. 34.1-4*, 27-28* // Deut. 10.1-4,[6] not to mention the Decalogue, Exod. 20.2-17* // Deut. 5.6-21).[7]

(b) Material in Exodus is the narrative counterpart to reminiscence in Deuteronomy (e.g. in the making and, especially, the renewal of the covenant in Exod. 24.12-18*; 31.18–34.28* // Deut. 9.7–10.11)[8] and is occasionally referred to as such, as in connection with the revelation of the Decalogue, where the cross-reference is specific ('as the Lord

---

3.   Apart from five passages in Chronicles, including the parallels to the Kings passage, מסכנות occurs nowhere else in the Hebrew Bible. The root סבל is also of significance between the two passages (Exod. 1.11; cf. 1 Kgs 5.29; 11.28).

4.   De Vaux 1971: 361-64.

5.   See, e.g., Hyatt 1971.

6.   Johnstone 1992a: 161-62, 166-170.

7.   Johnstone 1988: 361-85.

8.   Johnstone 1987: 26.

your God commanded you', Deut. 5.12, 16, referring to Exod. 20.8*, 12; cf. Deut. 4.23).[9]

(c) Perhaps even more significantly, material in Exodus provides the narrative counterpart to legislation in D. This is particularly the case with the Passover: the 'octave' of the revolutionary D Passover of Deut. 16.1-8 can be found in Exodus in the night of expulsion, the three days' pilgrimage into the wilderness 'to sacrifice' (Exod. 3.18, etc.) and the three days' preparation at Horeb (Exod. 19.10-16*),[10] culminating in the solemn covenantal assembly on the seventh day (Exod. 24.3-8). Indeed, the narrative sequence in the penultimate edition of Exodus 1–24 matches the sequence of the legislation in Deut. 15.12–16.8 as a whole (release of Hebrew slaves, offering of first-born, Passover).[11] Deduction: if a Passover narrative can be reconstructed in Exodus that matches the unique Passover of D, then that narrative must be specifically Deuteronomic not only in content but also in date.

All of this raises the question whether a Dtr version of the 'plague-cycle' can be reconstructed in Exodus 7–12. Is there reminiscence of the plagues in Deuteronomy, and is there a narrative in Exodus that corresponds to that reminiscence?

II. *A Disclaimer*

Lest it be thought that one is merely trying to find what one is looking for, it should first be said that there is little *ex hypothesi* pressure to recover a Dtr plague-cycle in Exodus. On the argument alluded to above that the pre-final edition of Exodus 1–24 contains the narrative counterpart of the D-legislation on the release of the Hebrew slave, the first-born and the Passover, the only absolutely essential element of the plague-cycle in Exodus for Dtr would be Plague X, the death of the Egyptian first-born and the spoiling of the Egyptians.

---

9.   Johnstone 1988: 369-70.

10.   Renaud (1991: 92-93) helpfully draws attention to the parallel in the motif of 'sanctification' in Josh. 3.5; 7.13-14 [i.e. DtrH].

11.   Johnstone 1992a: 173-77.

III. *The Deuteronomistic Model of the Conditions of Israel's Life in Egypt*

In order to establish whether there *was* a Dtr version of the plague-cycle in the penultimate edition of Exodus one must first construct the model of the D/Dtr view of the conditions of Israel's life in Egypt and of the means of their deliverance from it and then apply that model to Exodus. Three stages of this process are represented by the tables: Table 1 lists references in Deuteronomy to Israel's experience of life in Egypt; Table 2 constructs the model from these references taking Deut. 4.34 as focus and adding in the further D and Dtr material; Table 3 applies the data in Tables 1 and 2 heuristically to the text of Exodus.[12] But detailed argumentation is required beyond that. Table 3 is an undifferentiated list of raw data—the occurrences in Exodus of the key terms listed from Deuteronomy are compiled purely mechanically using a computerized concordance. It is unable to distinguish between original use and reuse by a subsequent editor or editors. To establish the extent of any Dtr version one would have to consider two additional factors: (1) passages already identified in Exodus 1–13 as the narrative counterpart to the D legislation on slaves, first-born and Passover; (2) any further vocabulary and thematic connections required for the sake of narrative coherence.

Table 1. *References in Deuteronomy to the Conditions of Israel's Life in Egypt*

1.30; 3.24; 4.20, 34, 37, 45, 46; 5.6, 15; 6.12, 21, 22; 7.8, 15, 18, 19; 8.14; 9.7, 12, 26, 29; 10.19, 21, 22; 11.2, 3, 4, 10; 13.6, 11; 15.15; 16.1, 3, 6, 12; 20.1; 23.5; 24.9, 18, 22; 25.17; 26.5, 6, 7, 8; 28.27, 60; 29.1, 2, 24; 34.11, 12.

12. Tables compiled by I. McCafferty, part-time research assistant in my Department in 1990–91 (Table 2 simplified). I am aware of the distinct possibility of the composite nature of Deuteronomy and that a diachronic factor has to be taken into consideration, as discussed in, e.g., Mayes 1979: 29-55. But the wide range of material in Tables 1–3 may justify holding that the Deuteronomic view of the plagues is relatively consistent across any layers the book may contain.

Table 2. *The Deuteronomistic View of YHWH's Deliverance of Israel from Egypt*

1. Deuteronomy 4.34 provides the focal statement:

I. General characterization of the act of God (by means of a rhetorical question) הנסה אלהים לבוא לקחת לו גוי מקרב גוי במסת
IIa. The means. The 'signs' and 'wonders': באתת ובמופתים
IIb. The means. The engagement at the Sea: ובמלחמה וביד חזקה ובזרוע נטיה ובמוראים נדלים
III. The corresponding general affirmation and statement of immediacy of experience: ככל אשר־עשה לכם יהוה אלהיכם במצרים לעיניך

2. These elements are repeated and variously elaborated in other verses in Deuteronomy. The supplementary materials are:

I. Alternative rhetorical question, 3.24 (עשה). Alternative general term, 11.2 (מוסר). Alternative verbs, 4.20, 45 (הוציא, יצא); 20.1 (העלה). Conditions in Egypt described, 4.20; 6.21 (עבדים); 7.8, 15; 10.19; 11.10; 26.6, 7 (לחץ, עמל, עני, צעק); 28.27, 60.
IIa. Variations in the 'signs' and 'wonders':[13] 34.11 מעשיו; 11.3 הגדלת; 10.21 ויפדך; 7.8 מפתים נדלים ורעים; 6.22 נדלך, מעשיך; 3.24 לכל־האתות והמופתים אשר שלחו יהוה לעשות בארץ מצרים לפרעה ולכל־עבדיו ולכל־ארצו
IIb. Variations in the engagement at the Sea: מורא; 34.12; 26.8; 10.21 הנוראת; 4.37 כחו הגדל; נבורתך 3.24 11.4 The event is explained ואשר עשה לחיל מצרים לסוסיו ולרכבו אשר הציף את־מי ים־סוף על־פניהם ברדפם אחריכם ויאבדם
III. The variants from and additions to the general affirmation and statement of immediacy of experience: variants—1.30; 3.24; 10.21; 29.2; additions—4.20; 11.4. The consequences for Israel/Israel's status: 4.20, 37; 7.8; 10.22; 26.5.

3. These elements are repeated and variously elaborated in DtrH and DtrJer. The supplementary materials are:

I. General characterization: Judg. 6.13 נפלאת. Alternative verbs: Judg. 6.9 (הציל); 11.13; Jer. 31.32. Conditions in Egypt: Josh. 24.14; 1 Sam. 12.8; 2 Kgs 17.7.
IIa. Variations in the 'signs' and 'wonders': ואשלח את־משה ואת־אהרן ואנף את־מצרים 24.5 Josh. למה תכבדו את־לבבכם כאשר כבדו מצרים ופרעה את־לבם הלוא כאשר 6.6 Sam. 1 התעלל בהם
IIb. Variations in the engagement at the Sea: הוביש יהוה את־מי ים־סוף מפניכם 2.10 Josh. וירדפו מצרים אחרי אבותיכם ברכב ובפרשים 24.6 Josh. ויצעקו אל־יהוה וישם מאפל ביניכם ובין המצרים ויבא עליו את־הים ויכסהו 24.7 Josh. האלהים המכים את־מצרים בכל־מכה במדבר 4.8 Sam. 1
III. The variants from and additions to the general affirmation and statement of immediacy of experience: Josh. 5.5-6.

13. IIa and IIb are transposed in 11.2-3 and 26.8.

Table 3. *A Deuteronomistic Edition of Exodus 1–13?*

The key vocabulary terms are:

אות, מופת, גדל, שלח, עלה, עבד, בית עבדים, לקח לו, נצל, אברהם יצחק יעקב, נגף, נחלה, שבע, לי לעם, עד היום הזה, יצא, יד פרעה, זעק, נפלאת, יד חזקה, עין, ראה, עשה.

1.10, 13, 14, 16, 21; 2.2, 5, 6, 11, 12, 23, 24, 25; 3.2, 3, 4, 6, 7, 8, 9, 10, 11, 12, 13, 14, 15, 16, 17, 19, 20, 21; 4.1, 4, 5, 9, 10, 13, 14, 15, 17, 18, 21, 23, 28, 30, 31; 5.1, 2, 9, 11, 15, 16, 18, 19, 21, 22; 6.1, 3, 5, 6, 7, 8, 9, 11, 13, 26, 27; 7.1, 2, 3, 4, 5, 6, 9, 10, 11, 14, 16, 20, 22, 26, 27, 28, 29; 8.1, 2, 3, 4, 5, 7, 9, 11, 13, 14, 16, 17, 19, 20, 22, 24, 25, 27, 28; 9.1, 2, 5, 6, 7, 8, 13, 14, 15, 16, 17, 19, 20, 21, 27, 30, 34, 35; 10.1, 2, 3, 4, 5, 6, 7, 8, 10, 11, 12, 14, 15, 20, 23, 24, 26, 27, 28, 29; 11.1, 3, 6, 8, 9, 10; 12.12, 13, 17, 23, 25, 26, 28, 30, 31, 33, 35, 36, 38, 39, 41, 42, 50, 51; 13.3, 4, 5, 7, 8, 9, 11, 13, 14, 15, 16, 17, 18, 19.

What, then, if any, is the Dtr model of Israel's experience in Egypt, which would be the counterpart of the material narrated in Exodus 1–13? If it exists at all, that Dtr model must be contained within Part II of Table 2, specifically Part IIa. The focal statement is Deut. 4.34:

I   הנסה אלהים לבוא לקחת לו גוי מקרב גוי במסת

IIa   באתת ובמופתים IIb   ובמלחמה וביד חזקה ובזרוע נטויה ובמוראים גדלים

III   ככל אשר־עשה לכם יהוה אלהיכם במצרים לעיניך:

One has to face the possibility that in Deut. 4.34 Part IIa, אתת ומופתים, has nothing to do with the material in Exodus 1–13 but is simply part of the D version of Exod. 14, God's deliverance of his people at the Sea.[14] However, the amplifications of Deut. 4.34 in other parts of Deuteronomy (Table 2, Section 2.IIa) suggest that there is indeed a certain specialization in Deuteronomy's vocabulary: אתות ומופתים allude specifically to the pre-Sea actions of God, יד חזקה וזרוע נטויה to his actions at the Sea. Deut. 34.11 is relatively clear: כל האתות והמופתים אשר שלחו...לעשות בארץ מצרים. So too is Deut. 11.3, where the אתות ומופתים 'in the midst* of Egypt' are separated from the action at the Sea by the conjunction at the beginning of v. 4.[15] The material from DtrH

14. Cf. Childs 1967: 32, 'Nowhere in Deuteronomy is there a specific identification of the signs and wonders with the plagues'.

15. Deut. 29.2 could also be discussed: 29.2a is in apposition to את כל אשר עשה יהוה in 29.1bβ; 29.2b is a specification—'viz., האתת והמפתים'. That אתת ומופתים in 4.34 is a similar specification is clear from that fact that it is not connected by 'ו' to

(Section 3) supplies further supportive evidence. Can this model then be applied to Exodus 1–13? Does there occur there material that corresponds to D's אתות ומופתים?[16]

IV. *The Distribution and Use of* אתות *and* מופתים *in Exodus 3–13*

It is indeed clear from the material in Table 3 that there is a concentration of אתות material in chs. 3–4 concerning Israel and Moses (3.12; 4.8, 9, 17, 28, 30) and of מופתים material announced in 4.21 concerning Egypt. But whereas in the earlier chapters there is a clear distinction between the two—that is, the אות (3.12–4.30) is a sign of reassurance to Israel and the מופת (4.21) is a portent publicly worked in Egypt, a 'plague' (so 11.9 [and10?])—in later chapters the two are indiscriminately used: in 7.3 they are combined to describe the action of Yahweh in Egypt; in 7.9 מופת no longer refers to a plague proper but to a public demonstration, a 'sign' worked to convince the Egyptians; in 8.19 (Plague IV) and 10.1-2 (Plague VIII) אות is used of the plagues. How is one to account for this strict use of אתות and מופתים as virtual technical terms in chs. 3, 4 and 11 and this more indiscriminate use in chs. 7–10? The next step must be to establish the affiliation of these blocks of material.

V. *The Affiliation of the Distinctive and of the Indiscriminate Uses of* אתות *and* מופתים *in Exodus 3–13*

It seems to me that good grounds can be adduced for regarding Exod. 2.23–6.1,[17] where אתות and מופתים are distinctively used respectively of

the immediately preceding general term מסות. The 'ו' in 7.19 is textually uncertain (see apparatus in *BHS*).

16. This is expressly denied by, e.g., Van Seters (1986: 35): 'Deuteronomy does not know of any plagues tradition but makes reference to the "signs and wonders" that God did in Egypt in a very general way. Only in the latest development of the exodus tradition are "signs and wonders" restricted to the plagues.' For Van Seters the plagues were developed by his exilic J from the curses in Deuteronomy.

17. To go no further back. It could be argued on grounds of narrative coherence that much of the remaining material in Exod. 1–2 is Dtr, since it provides the necessary background for what follows; e.g., Pharaoh's command to slay the sons of the Israelites—and that would include the first-born—sets the scene for the theme of the offering of the first-born which dominates the presentation down to ch. 13. The argument from narrative coherence can be backed up by the use of stock Dtr

'signs' as regards Israel and 'wonders' as regards Egypt, as a consistently Dtr redaction. For example:

a. 2.23 conveniently begins a new section. 'Work' (2×), 'cry' are D (cf. Deut. 26.7 Table 2, 2.I). 'Cry' again in 3.7, 9; play on the root עבד again in 3.12.

b. 2.24 'covenant', Deut. 4.13, etc.

c. 2.24 'Abraham, Isaac and Jacob', Deut. 1.8, etc.; so 3.6.

d. 3.1 'Horeb', Deut. 1.2, etc.

e. 3.6-7 Yahweh, the God of the fathers, seeing affliction and hearing the cry, Table 2, 2.I and 3.I. 'Taskmasters' only again in 5.6, 10, 13-14. Finite verb from the root נגש in Pentateuch only Deut. 15.2-3, in connection with the sabbatical year of release of debts, a suggestive location, given the use of the pattern of Deut. 15.12–16.8 in Exodus 1–24 as a whole.

f. 3.8 'to deliver from the hand of the Egyptians', Table 2, 3.I; 'to bring up', Table 2, 2.I; the 'good land', Deut. 1.25; 8.7; 'flowing with milk and honey', e.g. Deut. 26.9, with the list of indigenous population, e.g. Deut. 7.1.

g. 3.9 'seen the oppression', Table 2, 2.I.

h. 3.10 'bring out', Table 2, 2.I; so vv. 11, 12.

i. 3.12 אות, the twin focus of this argument, Table 2, 1.IIa; so 4.8, 9, 17, 28, 30; 'send', Table 2, 3.IIa; so again 3.13,14; cf. 3.20.

j. 3.13-14 'Name' theology, highly characteristic of D/DtrH, e.g. Deut. 12.11; 1 Kgs 8.43.

k. 3.14-17 repeats in large measure the vocabulary of 3.6-10.

l. 3.18 presupposes the chronology of the seven-day D Passover and uses זבח, the sacrificial terminology of the centralized cultus, for it.

m. 3.19 יד חזקה, see Table 2, 1.IIb. Cf. 'my hand', v. 20.

n. 3.20 נפלאתי, Table 2, 3.I; שלח begins the key thematic series of 'freeing of the Hebrew slaves', which casts the legislation of Deut. 15.12-13 into narrative form.

o. 3.21-22, 'not empty-handed', has its fulfilment in the Plague X narrative (11.2-3; 12.35-36).

p. 4.1-17 contains the series of three further אתת and, besides

expressions: the descendants of Jacob as 'seventy souls' (1.4; cf. Deut. 10.22); in 1.11-14 the repeated use of the verb ענה (cf. Table 2, 2.I) and of the root עבד. 'Hebrew' in 1.15 is to be a consistent theme (e.g. 7.16; 9.1) and echoes the D legislation on the release of Hebrew slaves in Deut. 15.12 (cf. Jer. 34.9). The 'storehouses' for Pharaoh (1.11) have already been mentioned in the text above.

continuing the thematic vocabulary introduced in ch. 3 ('send' vv. 4 [2×], 13 [2×], 'God of the fathers' v. 5, play on root עבד v. 10), introduces new thematic terms: 'believe' (vv. 1, 5, 8, 9; so again v. 31, 14.31; cf. 19.9 and 2 Kgs 17.14), שמע בקול (v. 1, so again 5.2; cf. 19.5; 23.21-22, Deut. 1.45 etc.; cf. שמע לקול vv. 8-9 [already in 3.18]), Moses' staff (v. 2, so again vv. 4, 17, 20; 7.12, 15, 20 [Plague I]; 9.23 [Plague VII]; 10.13 [Plague VIII]; 17.9), which will be instrumental in working the אתת (v. 17), 'mouth' (vv. 10, 11, 12, 15, 16), 'teach' (vv. 12, 15, while it is typically a P word, it is found in Deut. 17.10-11; 24.8; 33.10). Aaron enters the narrative for the first time at v. 14 and is required for the sequel in vv. 27-31 (not to mention the 'Golden Calf' incident in Exod. 32; cf. Deut. 9.20; 10.6; 32.50).[18] Verse 15 picks up the Divine Name of 3.14.

q. 4.18-20: the reference to Moses' staff as 'the staff of God' is a novelty, but emphasizes the link between Moses as agent and God as sender (cf. 10.12-13, where Moses' deeds shade into Yahweh's deeds, just as Yahweh's words shade into Moses' words in 7.17; 9.3; 11.7-8, and as the acts of Moses and Yahweh are equated in 10.12-13). This lack of distinction between God's instrumentality and word and Moses' instrumentality and word fits with the D understanding of Moses as prophet, indeed as prophet *par excellence* (Deut. 18.15-18; 34.10-12). Cf. also Moses' role as intercessor (8.4-5, 24-25; 9.28; 10.17).

r. 4.21-23 introduces the series of מופתים, the cycle of 'wonders' which is the joint topic of this discussion. Again all the indications are that this passage belongs to the D-version. The verses are replete with D terms, especially שלח, vv. 21, 23 [2×], בכור, vv. 22, 23, which anticipate precisely Plague X, the crucial plague for the D presentation, as noted above. The plural מופתים signals that, however, more than one plague is now to be expected in the D cycle of wonders.[19]

18. The role of Aaron has to be carefully evaluated: in ch. 4 he appears merely as spokesman for Moses to the Israelites. In ch. 5 he appears in vv. 1-5, 20-21 as joint-spokesman with Moses to Pharaoh (though it is clear by the reversion to the singular in 5.22–6.1 that, essentially, it is Moses alone who is God's spokesman). In 7.2 it is Aaron alone who is to speak to Pharaoh. It will be argued below (in common with many commentators) that 7.2 is P material. While it would be neat to argue that the role of Aaron as joint-spokesman to Pharaoh in ch. 5 is also to be attributed to P, this would involve a fairly extensive excision or modification of text and seems to me, on balance, too complex an operation to be convincing.

19. The sole instrumentality of Moses here contrasts with the role of Aaron as wonder-worker in 7.1-13 (P, as will be argued below).

The passage resumes the thematic root עבד (v. 23; cf. 2.23) and introduces new thematic terms 'harden the heart' (v. 21)[20] and 'refuse' (v. 23; cf. 7.14, 27; 9.2; 10.3,4).

s. 4.24-26, the redeemer redeemed, fits, as I have argued elsewhere,[21] appropriately into the Dtr version of Exodus since it involves the sparing, by the dedication of his own first-born through circumcision, of the leader of the Hebrew slaves who are released at the cost of the first-born of Egypt, and who are themselves about to be dedicated

20. In my view, the three terms used for 'hardening the heart' are not to be ascribed to different sources: they are all D terms, which may be reused by P (for difference of language not necessarily implying difference of source, precisely in this connection but following a rather different argument, see Kegler 1990: 58 n. 8). The evidence is as follows:

1. (a) חזק, the verb used here in the piel, of Yahweh as subject hardening the heart of Pharaoh, recurs in Plague VIII (10.20) (D) but also in Plagues VI (9.12) and IX (10.27) (P) and in the summary on the 'plagues' in 11.10 (P reusing D, as will be argued in the text below).

(b) The qal of the same root, with the heart of Pharaoh as subject, occurs in P passages (7.13, 22; 8.15; 9.35). But the qal is used in a D passage of the hand of the Egyptians urging the Israelites to leave their country (12.33), which picks up the expression יד חזקה in the D passages 3.19; 6.1. (This יד חזקה is to be distinguished from the use in parallel to זרע נטייה of Yahweh's hand in the action at the Sea, Table 2, 1.IIb.) Cf. hiphil of Pharaoh maltreating Israel (9.2 [D]).

2. כבד is the other major root used in connection with 'hardening of the heart': 1. the qal (subject 'Pharaoh's heart') is used in 9.7 (cf. the adj. also of Pharaoh's heart in 7.14; both D); 2. the hiphil (subject 'Pharaoh', object 'his own heart') occurs in 8.11 (P), 28 (D); 9.34 (D); 3. the hiphil (subject 'Yahweh', object 'Pharaoh's heart') occurs in 10.1 (discussed in text below).

3. The verb הקשה (subject 'Yahweh', object 'Pharaoh's heart') is used in 7.3 (P, though it is a perfectly good D term—cf. Deut. 2.30; cf. Exod. 13.15 [D], where the subject is 'Pharaoh', object 'his own heart').

If one were to insist on these uses being diagnostic of different sources, as in traditional literary criticism, then one might be forced to some such conclusion as that of Friebe 1967: 75. While correctly, in my view, detaching the plague-cycle in origin from the Passover, she also refuses to relate it to the First-born, interpreting it, rather, as arising from the confession of God's intervention to deliver Israel from Egypt and the answer to the associated question, 'how?'. In her view, then, 4.21-23 is to be attributed to the final Redactor who has combined materials from the two major sources, J and P (p. 109).

21. Johnstone 1990: 109.

through the dedication of their first-born.

t. 4.27-31 fulfils 4.14-17, using the appropriate vocabulary; it resumes thematic terms ('mountain of God', v. 27, cf. 3.1; 'elders of Israel', v. 29, cf. 3.16; 'believe', v. 30, cf. v. 1; 'visit', v. 30, cf. 3.16; 13.19; 20.5; 'see the oppression' v. 31, cf. 3.7) and introduces a new one ('fell down and worshipped', v. 31, cf. 12.27 [D reused by P]; 34.8).

u. 5.1–6.1 recounts the initial attempt of Moses and Aaron to secure the release of the Hebrew slaves (cf. the thematic verb שלח in vv. 5.1-2 [3×] and 6.1). It alludes to Passover according to D conceptions (a pilgrimage feast, 5.1; cf. the 'three days' in 5.3 as in 3.18; the sacrificial terminology, 5.3, 8, 17). Thematic terms are resumed: שמע בקול (5.2), 'cry' (5.8, 15), play on the root עבד (5.9, 11, 15, 16 [2×], 18, 21), 'deliver' (5.23), יד חזקה (6.1 [2×], where it is used with the omission of the parallel זרוע נטויה, as in Deut. 3.24; 6.21; 7.8; 9.26; 34.12). It introduces the new thematic term 'drive out' (6.1), which is to be resumed in the introduction to Plague X in 11.1.

v. In 5.1–6.1 there are other anticipations of the plague-cycle. As there, so here, Moses functions as archetypal prophet, introducing the command to release Israel with the 'messenger formula'. Pharaoh's response, 'I do not know Yahweh', anticipates the purpose of the מופתים—the demonstration and acknowledgement that Yahweh is God (7.17 [Plague I]; 8.6 [Plague II],18 [Plague IV]; 9.14, 29 [Plague VII]; 11.7 [Plague X]; cf. 10.7). The title, 'the God of the Hebrews' (5.3), suits well the nature of Exodus 1–13 as the narrative counterpart of the D legislation on the release of Hebrew slaves.

w. The remainder of ch. 5 is prolix. But interpreted as anticipation of the plague narratives to come, the passage contains some significant features, pre-eminently a burlesque on the commissioning of the agent to carry out the lord's bidding, in this case the overseers on behalf of the Pharaoh. As the plague narratives contain in principle five scenes— the commissioning of Moses by Yahweh, the delivery of the message, including the messenger formula followed by an inceptive participle, the execution of the message, the reaction to the execution and the outcome, prefaced by Moses' intercession—so it is here: vv. 6-9 are the commissioning; vv. 10-11 the delivery of the message including the messenger formula and inceptive participle; vv. 12-14 the execution; vv. 15-21 the reaction; vv. 22–6.1 the outcome, prefaced by Moses' intercession. Two points in particular mark the foreshadowing of the plague narratives: Pharaoh's words in v. 18, לכו עבדו, anticipate precisely his command in Plagues IX (10.24; but this is P reuse of D, as will be argued below) and X (12.31); the bitter words of the despairing Israelite marshalls, הבאשתם את ריחנו בעיני פרעה ובעיני עבדיו (v. 21), are the counterpart to the action of Yahweh in 11.3: ויתן יהוה את חן העם בעיני מצרים (cf. 12.36).[22]

While, thus, I regard 2.23–6.1 as a largely uninterrupted Dtr composition, 6.2–7.13, on the other hand, where the very specific purposes of the אתות and מופתים are confused, seems to me to represent a P composition, reusing, in part at least, D/Dtr elements. But on quite other grounds than this confusion in the use of אתות and מופתים, 6.2–7.13 is widely recognized by the commentators as a P composition. One may append the following observations:

a. There is non-continuity: 7.14 resumes 6.1.

b. As conventionally in literary criticism, 6.2-13 can be regarded as offering an alternative resumption of 2.25, parallel to 3.1–6.1 (v. 5, for example, picks up 2.24).

c. 6.29–7.7 is represented as Moses and Aaron's first interview with Pharaoh in contrast to ch. 5.

d. 6.30 introduces the role of Aaron as 'prophet' for Moses and miracle-worker, which stands in contradiction to 4.13-17, 27-30. In ch. 4, Aaron is to be spokesman for Moses to the people (a role that fits with Aaron's presumptuous arrogation to himself of that role in Exod. 32), while Moses speaks directly to Pharaoh and performs the מופתים; in 7.1-13, by contrast, Aaron is spokesman for Moses to Pharaoh, is endowed with a hitherto unheard-of miracle-working staff like Moses' (v. 9), and performs the מופת in competition with the Egyptian magicians (vv. 9-12); vv. 7, 9 and 12, in particular, with their statement that Israel is yet to acknowledge and obey, stand in tension with 4.31, which speaks of the believing submission of the Israelites.

e. There is distinctive language, e.g. אני יהוה (6.2, 6, 7, 8, 29; 7.5, cf.

---

22. Vocabulary items are compatible with, or diagnostic of, D/Dtr provenance: the potential threats from plague or sword (v. 3) are particularly characteristic of (the Dtr editing of) Jeremiah (14.12; 21.9; 27.8, 13, etc.); the thematic terms 'burdens' (vv. 4, 5; cf. related terms in 1 Kgs 5.29; 11.28); 'taskmasters' (vv. 6, 10, 13-14; so already 3.7); 'each day's assignment daily accomplished' (vv. 13, 19; 1 Kgs 8.59; 2 Kgs 25.30) and the highly characteristic D word 'marshalls' (Deut. 1.15; 16.18, etc.). 'Standing ready to encounter them' (v. 20) anticipates 7.15; cf. 9.13.

7.17; 8.18; 10.2; 12.12; 29.46; 31.13 and some 52× in Leviticus; the phrase does not occur in D, except 1× in conjunction with ידע [Deut. 29.5]; the phrase is especially characteristic of Ezekiel [some 87×]); הקים ברית (6.4; cf. e.g., Lev. 26.9); perhaps עבד in the hiphil (6.5, used already in 1.13-14 in association with פרך, which recurs in the Pentateuch only in Lev. 25.43, 46, 53); גאל (6.6) is used of the human avenger of blood in Deut. 19.6, 12—the metaphorical use for Yahweh is typical of Second-Isaiah; the זרע נטויה (6.6) is always coupled in Deuteronomy with יד חזקה, except once, where כח גדול is used (Table 2, 1.IIb, 2.IIb); שפטים (6.6) recurs in 7.14; 12.12 and Num. 33.4 in the Pentateuch (probably all P passages) and is characteristic of Ezekiel (10×); the idiom נשא יד (6.8) is found seven times in Ezekiel (though once in poetry in Deut. [32.40]); מורשה (6.8), though occurring in Deut. 33.4, is typical of Ezekiel (7×); the genealogical material in 6.14-25; the usage, 'hosts' for Israel as a whole (6.26, as opposed to Israel as an army, e.g. Deut. 20.9), seems, again, to be typical of P (so again 7.4; 12.17, 41, 51 and, especially, Numbers, e.g. 33.1). The chronological data in 7.7 too are likely to stem from P.

The contours of a hypothesis are beginning to emerge: where אתות and מפתים are used as technical terms, the D-version is in evidence; where they are indiscriminately used, it is the P-edition. Does this hold true for the narrower plague-cycle beginning in 7.14? The first step must be the identification of P-passages by means of the themes and vocabulary of 6.2–7.13, for example, those referring to Aaron as agent of מופת, to his wonder-working staff and to his competition with the Egyptian magicians.

On this basis it is likely that the short Plagues III (8.12-15) and VI (9.8-12) should be identified as P (for ויחזק לב פרעה [8.15; cf. 9.12], cf. 7.13; for שמע אל [8.15; 9.12], cf. 6.9; for כאשר דבר יהוה [8.15; 9.12], cf. 7.13). This is confirmed by the striking formal point that in both there is a bare plague, with neither the commissioning of Moses to deliver a message of command, accusation and announcement of the impending act by God nor the delivery of such a message (one or other of these elements invariably occurs in plague narratives I–II, IV–V, VII–VIII, X). In the retrospect in 9.15 in Plague VII, it is not Plague VI that is being referred to but V.

On similar grounds, Plague IX must fall under suspicion (cf. the formulation נטה יד על [10:21-22], which echoes 7.6, and has recurred in 7.19; 8.2 [also, however, 9.22; 10.12]). Most significant is the vocabulary for Israel's rite in the desert in 10.26: whereas the D/Dtr material has been using the D Passover terminology of חג and זבח (e.g. 3.18; 10.9), here it is the priestly terminology עבד, that is being used (cf. e.g. 12.25-26; 13.5). That observation may then clear Moses of disingenuousness when, in the same verse, he says to Pharaoh, 'For our part, we do not know how we shall serve Yahweh until we get there'. On the P scenario the legislation on sacrifice and festival is given on Sinai and has not yet, therefore, been revealed. Cf., too, Moses' request to Pharaoh that *he* furnish him with the necessary sacrifices (9.25). In addition, Pharaoh's prohibition in 10.28 on Moses' seeing him again contradicts 11.4-8, where Moses is once more in Pharaoh's presence (so, explicitly, 11.8b).[23]

The remaining seven-plague cycle (I–II, IV–V, VII–VIII, X) can be defended as belonging to the D-version (retouches by P will be noted below). Many of the thematic terms already recognized in chs. 3–4 are now resumed. For example:

a. שׁלח of freeing slaves (3.20) in Plagues I (7.14, 16), II (7.26, 27; 8.4), IV (8.16, 17, 24, 25, 28), V (9.1, 2, 7), VII (9.13, 17, 28, 35), VIII (10.3, 4, 7, 10, 20) and X (11.1[2×],10; 12.33; reused also in IX [10.27]).

b. 'Not empty-handed' (3.21-22) is fulfilled in Plague X (11.2-3; 12.35-36).

c. Moses' staff (4.2, 4, 17, 20) recurs in Plagues I (7.20), VII (9.23) and VIII (10.13).

d. Pharaoh's 'I do not know Yahweh' (5.2) is made the reason for Plagues I (7.17), II (8.6), IV (8.18), VII (9.14, 29) and X (11.7).

e. 'God of the Hebrews' (3.18; 5.3) is picked up as a thematic term in Plague I (7.16) and Plague V (9.1).

f. מאן is picked up as a thematic term from 4.23 in 7.14, 27; 9.2; 10.3, 4 in Plagues I, II, V and VIII.

Further characteristics that suggest Dtr affiliation can be noted in the individual Plagues:

a. I: For D associations of ידע with Yahweh (7.17) cf. Deut. 29.5; for שׂית לב (7.23) cf. Deut. 11.18.

b. II: For the root נגף (7.27), cf. Table 2, 3.IIa; משׁארת (7.28) occurs in the Hebrew Bible only in 12.34; Deut. 28.5, 17; העתיר (8.4-5) is

---

23. In Ps. 78.43-51 it is precisely these three Plagues, III, VI and IX, which are missing, though the material on the remainder is somewhat rearranged and re-expressed.

now introduced as a thematic term, recurring in 8.24-26 (IV) 9.28 (VII) and 10.17-18 (VIII); for 'he hardened his heart' (8.11), cf. Table 2, 3.IIa.

c. IV: For the new thematic term הפלה (8.18 [IV]; 9.4 [V]: 11.7 [X]), cf. 33.16.

d. V must also, I think, be regarded as Dtr, being replete with now familiar thematic terms.

e. VII: While there are several parenthetical sections that interrupt the standard pattern of the plague narratives (the retrospect in vv. 14-16, the instruction to the Egyptians and response of many of them in vv. 19-21 and the definition of the season of the year in vv. 31-32, which provides the necessary explanation, however, for the vegetation about to be destroyed in Plague VIII), none of the vocabulary need be denied to a Dtr version.

f. VIII: Once again, the vocabulary may be regarded as, in the main, fully compatible with a Dtr version (cf. the frequent references back to Plague VII; vv. 5, 12, 15, link Plagues VII and VIII closely together).

g. X, as already mentioned above, is the essential plague in a Dtr plague-cycle, reflecting the sequence of Deut. 15.12–16.8 concerning the freeing of the Hebrew slave 'not empty-handed' in association with the offering of the first-born and the celebration of the Passover. The key term בכור, already announced in 4.22-23 recurs in 11.5 (4×); 12.29 (4×).[24] But even in this plague, relatively replete with D/Dtr phraseology though it is, things may not be all that they appear. I have reservations about 11.9-10 in particular. 12.29 joins happily enough with 11.8. One could well see how P, having once introduced the heavily polemical correction of D's concept of the Passover into 12.1-28, linking Plague X now with Passover rather than, as in D, with the Offering of the First-born, draws, so to speak, a line under the plague-cycle by introducing a summary. If so, he has done his work rather subtly, for he correctly uses the D word מופת (and עשׂה and שׁלח). There are, however, some disturbing elements: the inclusion of Aaron as an agent of מופת with the use of a plural verb (v. 10), the use of the

---

24. Other typical D/Dtr expressions are the stress on eyewitness/personal experience ('eyes' 11.3 [4×]; 12.36; cf. Table 2, 1.III, 2.III); 'great' (11.3, 6; 12.30; cf. Table 2, 2.IIa); זעקה/צעקה (11.6; 12.30; cf. Table 2, 2.I); variations of the root עבד (11.3, 8; 12.30, 31; cf. Table 2, 2.I); the verbs יצא (11.8; 12.31) and עשׂה (11.10; 12.35; cf. Table 2, 2.I).

idiom שמע אל (v. 9), which, while it is abundantly attested in D (Deut. 3.26; 4.1; 9.19, etc.), occurs in Exodus 1–15 again only in 6.9 (the idiom is otherwise שמע ב/לקול [4.1, 8-9, etc.]) and the terminology for the hardening of the heart in v. 10bα is characteristic rather of P (cf. n. 20). Perhaps the safest conclusion would be that 11.9-10 represents the reuse by P of largely D material.

The confusions that remain within the plague-cycle, in particular for the present purpose in 8.19 and 10.1-2, can be attributed to P:

a. I. 7.19: cf. the further opening formula and how the 'waters of the Nile' (v. 17) have become all the waters throughout all the land of Egypt, including those in every container (so v. 21b)—which contradicts v. 24; the pl. verb and 'and Aaron' in 7.20aα (cf. sg. verb in 20aβ); 7.22 (cf. 7.13; in addition, v. 23 would be redundant after v. 22).

b. II. 8.1-3 the role of Aaron and the parallel to 'all the waters of Egypt' in 7.19; perhaps the last phrase of 8.11a and 11b (cf. 6.9; 7.13).

c. IV. 8.19, where אות is used as a portent to Egypt as in 7.3 thus diverging from the regularity of the D usage. Assuming the soundness of the text,[25] there are reasonable grounds for holding that the verse belongs to the P-edition: it repeats 8.18; it uses the word פדות, the termination of which is conventionally regarded as a mark of late Hebrew[26] (though it mirrors the use of the verb פדה in 13.13, 15; Deut. 7.8; 9.26, etc.).

d. VII. 9.35aαb (cf. 7.13 and the repetition of 9.34b). 9.25bβ, which contradicts 10.5bβ, may be a secondary heightening.

e. VIII. In 10.1, 2 there are two divergences (vv. 1bβ, 2aγb) from the regularity of the pattern laid down in chs. 4–5: אתות not מפתים, is used of the plagues; the point of the plagues is that Israel, not Egypt, may believe (cf. 6.12 contrasted with 4.31). These divergences are shared precisely with the P material in 7.1-13. There is no overwhelming reason to deny the rest of the passage to D (e.g. for התעלל cf. Table 2, 3.IIa), even if one were to suspect that the hand of P is considerably more influential, reusing as in 11.9-10 elements of D. Factors that suggest the wider presence of the hand of P include the use of the shorter form of the first person singular personal pronoun

---

25. See apparatus in *BHS*.
26. Again assuming the text is in order; see, e.g., Davies 1974.

'I'[27] and the instruction of the children in 2a (cf. 12.26-27, where it is secondary).[28] All of these materials are contained within an explanation to Moses of why he is being sent (vv. 1b-2) which is unique in the plague-cycle. The D-version may then have run from 1a to 3aαii (reading ואמרתם; cf., e.g., the opening of II in 7.26). In v. 20a there is again P formulation.

In sum, the identification of 7.1-13 as P, backed up by less direct indications, requires the identification of 8.19 and 10.1b-3aαi as P. With the exclusion of Plagues III, VI and IX and 8.19 and 10.1b-3aαi as P, a coherent picture emerges of Dtr cycles of 'signs' and 'wonders' in the penultimate version of Exodus 1–13.

VI. *The Reason for the Difference between the D-Version and the P-Edition in the Matter of 'Signs' and 'Wonders'*

The isolation of the D/Dtr material throws into relief certain thematic elements.[29] Already in the D-version, there are clear interconnections between the plagues and preceding materials, making it clear that the 'plague-cycle' should not be separated off as an independent composition but is integral to a much larger whole.[30] For the present

27. The statistics for Exodus are אני 36× (2.9; 3.19; 4.21; 6.2, 5, 6, 7, 8, 12, 29, 30; 7.3, 5, 17; 8.18; 9.14, 27; 10.1, 2; 11.4; 12.12; 13.15; 14.4, 17, 18; 15.26; 16.12; 18.6; 22.26; 25.9; 29.46; 31.6, 13; 33.16, 19; 34.10), 15× in definitely P contexts. The longer form אנכי, conventionally regarded as earlier, 21× (3.6, 11, 12, 13; 4.10, 11, 12, 15, 23; 7.17, 27; 8.24, 25; 17.9; 19.9; 20.2, 5; 23.20; 32.18; 34.10, 11), none in a definitely P context. But אני with the perfect of the verb, as here, is paralleled in D contexts, e.g. 3.19. The perfect hiphil of כבד may well be D, as in 8.11aγ (cf. n. 20); 10.1bα seems deliberately to resume 9.34b (D).

28. Johnstone 1992a: 169.

29. Many excellent observations on the contributions of the two main editions of the plague-cycle (though attributed to 'two main tradition-complexes...corresponding roughly to *JE* and *P*') are made by Greenberg (1971).

30. It may be instructive to contrast at this point a recent account of the 'plague-cycle' along more traditional literary critical lines—that of Schmidt (1990). In the plague-cycle as delimited in the main in the title of his work, Schmidt finds there is no E document, only J, JE, P and R[Pch]. J describes 4 *Erzwingungswunder* (I, II, IV, VIII, the latter including 11.8b). JE expands these to 6 *Schauwunder* (7 with death of First-born; I, II, IV, V, VII, VIII, X). P recounts 5 *Schauwunder* (including Aaron's staff, 7.8-13, plus I, II, III, VI, concluding with 11.9-10). R[Pch] begins again at 7.14—he describes 10 plagues (including the death of the First-born): to reach this figure, he constructs the IXth plague. Quite apart from the, to my mind, questionable

purpose, there is an אתות section in 3.11–4.17, where the word is used for a number of signs given to Moses to show to Israel in order to overcome all doubts both in himself and in his people. Equally, in 4.21-23 מופתים is used of the plagues, terminology which is accurately picked up in the summary in 11.9-10. These two series of אתות and מופתים are locked together by the demonstration of the אתות to Israel in 4.27-31. In the D-version, Israel is already responsive to the אתות in 4.31, as Yahweh's potential covenant partners; the מופתים are reserved for the Egyptians. By contrast, the P-edition, as in its version of the Passover and in its insertion of the cycle of 'murmuring in the wilderness' *between* exodus and Sinai,[31] is much more pessimistic about Israel: the people are not immediately responsive but still require to be convinced (6.7, 12). They even require a מופת as an אות to persuade them (10.2). They are spared from the climactic plague, not because they are already set apart in Goshen as God's people long poised ready for freedom, but because they have participated in the rescuing rite of the Passover.

Summary

As in connection with other parts of Exodus (especially the 'octave' of the Passover, the Decalogue and the making and renewal of the

procedure of beginning with the hypothetical earliest document, 'J' (no-one knows who 'J' or 'E' or 'JE' were, but Deuteronomy certainly exists and provides the starting-point for proceeding from the known to the unknown), the following are the principal weaknesses of Schmidt's reconstruction, in my view: the inclusion of Aaron's wonder in 7.8-13 within the plague-cycle proper in P (it is merely reusing D's technical term מופת loosely in 7.9 as it has loosely used D's technical term אות in 7.3); the separation across two versions between the word and act of God and those of Moses in 7.16; the quite arbitrary separation off of 11.8b and attachment of it to Plague VIII and the equally arbitrary separating off of 11.9-10 and attachment of it as the conclusion of P's cycle to the end of VI in 9.12; the slicing in half of Plague X by the omission of 12.29-36; above all, the admission of uncertainty over the attribution of 11.2-3, which precisely leads the discussion beyond Schmidt's separation of the 'plague-narrative' from the wider context of Exodus and links it to the whole cycle of the narrative presentation of D's legislation on the release of Hebrew slaves, Israel's offering of the firstborn and celebration of the Passover. Even if such analytical scholars as L. Schmidt are right—and there is, I submit, no way of knowing that—it would affect the completeness but not necessarily the at least partial correctness of my conclusion.

31. Johnstone (1992a: 177-78).

Covenant), so with regard to the so-called 'plague-cycle' in Exodus 7–12, materials in Deuteronomy and, more widely, the Deuteronomistic corpus provide a reminiscence that enables the reconstruction in Exodus of a corresponding narrative. These materials gathered from the D model of Israel's experience of life in Egypt, coupled with the reconstruction of the Dtr Passover 'octave' in Exodus and considerations of narrative coherence, suggest that there is a Dtr cycle of 'signs (אתות)' in Exodus which refers specifically to the attestation of Yahweh's beneficent purpose towards his people and the authentication of Moses' status (2.23–4.31[6.1]). A further Dtr cycle of 'wonders (מופתים)' refers to the seven punitive acts (so-called 'Plagues' I, II, IV, V, VII, VIII and X) by which the Pharaoh is coerced into releasing Israel (7.14–11.8*; 12.29-36). These two cycles are connected by motifs such as Moses' staff, which figures in 'Plagues' I, VII and VIII and links back to Exodus 4, and are interlocked by Exod. 4.21-23, which introduces the מופתים, and Exod. 4.27-31, which records the execution of the אתות. Together these are only part of a still wider whole: the demonstration of Yahweh's מסות, מוסר, נפלאות, by which he is to bring Israel into being as the chosen, loved and covenanted people of his own possession. This penultimate version (the 'D-version') was subsequently modified in the final edition (the 'P-edition'). It is only in the P-edition, with the insertion of the Aaron narrative in 6.2–7.13 and the reuse there and in 8.19 and 10.1b-3aαi of D's technical terms אתות and מופתים in less precise fashion (not to mention the long insertion in 11.9–12.28 which bisects the final Dtr מופת) that Israel ceases to be the immediately believing, responsive potential covenant-partner and becomes the less readily impressed, potentially recalcitrant object of Yahweh's redeeming purpose.

BIBLIOGRAPHY

Childs, B.S.
1967   'Deuteronomic Formulae of the Exodus Traditions', in B. Hartmann *et al.* (eds.), *Hebräische Wortforschung* (Festschrift W. Baumgartner; VTSup, 16; Leiden: Brill): 30-39.

Davies, G.I.
1974   'The Hebrew Text of Exodus viii 19—An Emendation', *VT* 24: 489-92.

Friebe, R.
1967   *Form und Entstehungsgeschichte des Plagenzyklus Exodus 7, 8—13, 16* (ThD Dissertation, Halle-Wittenberg).

Greenberg, M.
1971   'The Redaction of the Plague Narrative in Exodus', in H. Goedicke
               (ed.), *Near Eastern Studies in Honor of William Foxwell Albright*
               (Baltimore: Johns Hopkins University Press): 243-52.
Hyatt, J.P.
1971   *Exodus* (NCB, London: Oliphants.)
Johnstone, W.
1987   'Reactivating the Chronicles Analogy in Pentateuchal Studies', *ZAW*
               99: 16-37.
1988   'The Decalogue and the Redaction of the Sinai Pericope in Exodus',
               ZAW 100: 361-85.
1990   *Exodus* (OTG; Sheffield: JSOT Press).
1992a   'The Two Theological Versions of the Passover Pericope in Exodus',
               in R.P. Carroll (ed.), *Text as Pretext* (Festschrift R. Davidson;
               JSOTSup, 138; Sheffield: JSOT Press): 160-78.
1992b   Review of *La Théophanie du Sinaï*, by B. Renaud, *JTS* NS 43: 550-55.
Kegler, J.
1990   'Zu Komposition und Theologie der Plagenerzählungen' in E. Blum
               et al. (eds.), *Die hebräische Bibel und ihre zweifache Nachgeschichte*
               (Festschrift R. Rendtorff; Neukirchen: Neukirchener Verlag): 55-74.
Mayes, A.D.H.
1979   *Deuteronomy* (NCB; London: Oliphants).
Moberly, R.W.L.
1983   *At the Mountain of God* (JSOTSup, 22; Sheffield: JSOT Press).
Renaud, B.
1991   *La théophanie du Sinaï* (Cahiers de la Revue Biblique, 30; Paris:
               Gabalda).
Schmidt, L.
1990   *Beobachtungen zu der Plagenerzählung in Exodus VII 14—XI 10*
               (Studia Biblica, 4; Leiden: Brill).
Van Seters, J.
1986   'The Plagues of Egypt: Ancient Tradition or Literary Invention?',
               ZAW 98: 31-39.
Vaux, R. de
1971   *Histoire ancienne d'Israël* (Paris: Gabalda).

GENESIS 1 FROM THE PERSPECTIVE OF A CHINESE CREATION MYTH

A.C.C. Lee

I. Cross-Textual Hermeneutics

Before there were heaven and earth [the universe] was in Chaos (*hun-tun*)[1] like a chicken's egg. At the time of dawn, when the darkness was about to dawn, P'an-ku was engendered within it. After 18,000 years Chaos split apart, what was bright and light formed the heaven, and what was dark and heavy[2] formed the earth. P'an-ku had daily transformed nine times within the Chaos.[3] He was more divine than the heaven and holier than the earth. Thereafter, during another 18,000 years, the heaven daily increased ten feet in height, the earth daily increased ten feet in thickness, and P'an-ku, between the two, also daily increased ten feet in size.[4] This is how the heaven and earth came to be separated by their present distance of 90,000 li [roughly 30,000 miles] (Chiu 1984: 123).

This myth of P'an-ku is one of the ancient Chinese creation myths I have in mind when I approach the sacred text of the Judeo-Christian

---

1. Or, translated differently, 'blurred entity' (Ding 1988: 3). The meaning of *hun-tun* will be examined in Section II.
2. The phrase 'bright and light' represents an important word *yang* which is the male element of matter and the phrase 'dark and heavy' has the word *yin*, the female element. These two characters should be left untranslated because they express complicated concepts and ideas basic to Chinese cosmology. Ding's rendering is 'the *yang* which was light and pure' and 'the *yin* which was heavy and murky' (Ding 1988: 3).
3. 'Within the Chaos' is better understood as in between the *yang* and *yin* or heaven and earth.
4. According to the original text of *Yi wen lei ju* (*Classified Anthology of Literary Works*) there are a few more sentences here: 'Then came the Three Emperors. The number begins with one, becomes established at three, is completed at five, prospers at seven and ends in nine'. Further research should be done on the meanings of these numbers in Chinese numerology and religious concepts. Comparison can also be made in this respect between Chinese and Hebrew.

tradition. It is hard to imagine that I, as a Chinese brought up and nurtured by this story of creation, could unlearn the Chinese notion of separation of heaven and earth or pretend that it just did not exist at all when reading the creation narrative of Genesis. For Asian Christians, the key issue of biblical hermeneutics is the question of having two texts, the cultural text and the biblical text.

Asian Christians are faced with the challenge of whether it is legitimate to bring our cultural-religious texts to the reading and under-standing of biblical texts. We were told and educated by missionaries that we had to cut ourselves off completely from the pagan world and non-Christian culture. We should leave aside our own text in the interpretation of the Bible. But could we even do it, knowing that the interpreter's social location and religious-ideological conviction will have some bearing on our exegetical endeavour? The interpreter will never pretend to be completely neutral, or to aim to do 'objective' biblical interpretation.

As was suggested in my article on 'Biblical Interpretation in Asian Perspectives' (Lee 1993), a cross-textual approach could be adopted in Asia to deal with the situation of two texts. It is an approach that takes both the cultural text and the biblical text seriously and lets them interact one with the other in a creative and meaningful way so that both can be mutually enriched for theological reflection. Cross-textual hermeneutics in Asia tries to interpret the biblical text (text A) in the Asian context in constant mutual interpretation and interaction with the Asian cultural-religious text (text B).

This article attempts to apply this approach in the area of creation narrative. The P'an-ku myth of the Chinese tradition is studied in the light of Genesis and the latter is read with the former in mind. The other Chinese creation stories, such as the fashioning of human beings with yellow earth by Nu Wa, the female deity of creation, and numerous creation stories of minority nationals in China, will be studied in separate articles.

II. תהו ובהו *and the Chaos* (hun-tun)

'Chaos' was represented by two Chinese characters, *hun-tun*, which are used in the Chinese translation of the Hebrew בהו in Gen. 1.2. *Hun-tun* describes the original primeval state of the universe before the coming into existence of the heaven and the earth. It also carries some of the basic concepts denoted by the English word 'chaos' which, according to Webster's New International Dictionary, conveys the meaning of 'unorganized state of primordial matter before the creation of orderly forms in the universe'. It refers to the undifferentiated and unseparated state of matter which commingles in a confused mixture and fused enclosure.

The first of the two characters, *hun*, individually means 'confusion' and 'conglomeration' and the second has the meaning of 'abyss' and 'deep' (Chiu 1984: 124). The two words are used together to refer to the original uncreated and unformed primordial condition from which heaven and the earth have their origin. This pre-existent *hun-tun* is represented by the symbolism of a cosmic egg or 'egg-like enclosure' which represents perfection, undifferentiation and potentiality (Yu 1981: 481).

By reading the biblical creation narrative from the perspective of the Chinese perception of *hun-tun*, one will not arrive at the Christian theological position of *creatio ex nihilo*. In the Chinese myth, heaven and earth are not created out of nothing, neither was P'an-ku, the cosmic being who separated heaven and earth from the undifferentiated matter. Contrary to the biblical affirmation, there is no suggestion that the universe is created by an external divine 'creator'. P'an-ku was only the first-born who was engendered within the chaotic cosmic egg.

It has often been asserted that the Chinese case is an exception among the major ancient civilizations in that it does not have a creation myth which portrays the involvement of an external personal creator independent of the universe.[5] Several scholars have outlined the problem and discussed the issues of Chinese mythology (Girardot 1976: 298-304; Allan 1991: 19-20). John S. Major affirms that 'the Chinese did have an important cosmogonic myth (the *locus classicus* for which is *Chuang-tzu* 7), namely the differentiation of the phenomenal world from primordial chaos, *hun-tun*' (Major 1978: 9).

Hun-tun is depicted in *Chuang-tzu* (ch. 7), composed between 350 and 222 BCE, as Emperor of the Central Region in a fragment of a supposedly ancient myth:

5. Derek Bodde suggests that the idea of a personal creator of the universe is 'wholly absent from Chinese philosophy and yet occurs in Chinese popular religion' (1953: 19). There are creation myths with Lao Tzu as the creator in the Taoist Canon.

> The Emperor of the South Sea was called *Shu* (Swift), the Emperor of the
> North Sea was called *Hu* (Sudden), and the Emperor of the Central
> Region was called *Hun-tun* (Chaos). Shu and Hu from time to time came
> together for a meeting in the land of *Hun-tun*, and *Hun-tun* treated them
> generously. They said, 'All men have several openings so they can see,
> hear, eat, and breathe. But *Hun-tun* doesn't have any. Let's try to bore
> him some!' Every day they bored another hole, and on the seventh day
> *Hun-tun* died (Yu 1981: 481).

Within the context of the Taoist conceptual world which places a great
emphasis on the pursuit of simplicity and naturalness, there is a negative tone to the kindliness of *Shu* and *Hu's* intention. To Chuang Tzu,
when *Hun-tun* was destroyed by superficiality and artificiality, the
spirit of simplicity, spontaneity, freedom and creativity were lost. He
called for a return to the original naturalness of things. But presumably the idea of opening up *Hun-tun* signifies the beginning of creation. When *Hun-tun* dies, an ordered universe takes shape and comes
into existence.

There are numerous Chinese texts that adopt the same usage and
connotation of *Hun-tun* in the description of the pre-creation condition
of the cosmos—formless, shapeless, void and empty. Two passages
from ancient texts are cited as examples, *Lao Tzu* (ch. 25) from the
third century and *Huai Nan Tzu* (ch. 7) from the second century
BCE. Both assume Chaos as the origin of creation. The first passage by
Lao Tzu (4th–3rd cent. BCE) refers to the chaotic origin by *Tao*, the
way.

> There is a thing confusedly formed;
> Born before the Heaven and Earth
> Silent and void
> It stands alone and does not change,
> Goes around and does not weary.
> It is capable of being the mother of the world
> I know not its name,
> So I style it 'the way'.
> I give it the makeshift name 'the great'.
> (Lau 1982: 37)

> Of old before Heaven and Earth even existed,
> there were only images and no physical shapes.
> It was dark, shapeless and abysmally still:
> so undifferentiated it was that no one knew its door.
> Then two divinities were born commingledly

who were to supervise Heaven and regulate Earth...
They were divided into *yin* and *yang*
and separated into the eight extremes (of the compass).
(Fung 1952: 398)

The emphasis on the chaotic pre-creation condition in Chinese tradition will certainly give us a great impetus to focus attention on the search for the meaning of תהו ובהו in the biblical text when Chinese Christians come to interpret and understand the Genesis account of creation. The conception of undifferentiation of form and shape must then be underlined for the Chinese mind. It is not easy to reconcile the formulation in terms of *creatio ex nihilo* with the idea of *Hun-tun*. Creation can be grasped more readily as ordering and managing the chaos (Lee 1989: 110-23).

III. *Separation of Heaven and Earth*

The motif of separation is common in myths of creation (Long 1963: 64-80). In *Enuma Elish*, Marduk's splitting up of the defeated Tiamat into two parts out of which heaven and earth are created is the major act of separation. Putting the Priestly creation account of Gen. 1.1–2.4a side by side with *Enuma Elish*, the parallels are crystal clear (Heidel 1951: 82-140). It helps to underline the importance of the act of separation in Genesis: light from darkness (v. 3), waters above from waters below (vv. 6-7), dry land from the seas (v. 9). There results the division of space (heaven and earth) as well as time (day and night). Creation is therefore rightly conceived in Genesis as separation.

The Chinese narrative also presents a similar cosmogony in terms of an act of separation, the basic division of *yin* and *yang*, female and male, and therefore earth and heaven, darkness and light, etc. The technical terms *yin* and *yang* are among the most important pair-words in Chinese cosmology, used to denote a dualistic concept of opposition as well as complementarity. *Yin* symbolizes femaleness, earth, darkness, coolness and a lot of other qualities, while *yang* embraces their opposites: maleness, heaven, brightness, warmth, etc. *Yin* and *yang* are found as an integral part of the chaos.

The act of creation begins when P'an-ku is engendered within the chaos. After 18,000 years chaos splits and P'an- ku, standing between the *yin* and *yang*, pushes the two sides apart. The book *Huai Nan Tzu* further confirms the understanding that the separation of the *yin* and *yang* forms the heaven above and the earth below:

> Before heaven and earth had taken form all was vague and amorphous.
> Therefore it was called the Great Beginning.
> The Great Beginning produced emptiness and emptiness produced
> the universe.[6]
> The universe produced material-force which had limits.[7]
> That which was clear and light drifted up to become heaven,
> while that which was heavy and turbid solidified to become earth.
> It was very easy for the pure, fine material to come together but extremely
> difficult for the heavy, turbid material to solidify.
> Therefore heaven was completed first and earth assumed shape after.
> The combined essences of heaven and earth became the *yin* and *yang*...
> (de Bary 1960: 192-93)

The separation of *yin* and *yang* form earth and heaven, which in turn embrace *yin* and *yang* respectively in Chinese tradition as the archetype of cosmological speculation (Yu 1981: 480). Heaven (*yang*) and earth (*yin*) are opposites but at the same time are complementary and interdependent. The eternal interplay of these two cosmic forces, the *yang* and the *yin*, results in a universe which is in a constant state of flux and change (Bodde 1953: 21). The cosmos is not governed by a superior authority external to and independent of it. Rather it is a self-operating, self-sufficient and self-creating harmonious entity within which is embedded the *Tao*, the 'unitary world-principle' (Major 1978:10) which, according to Lao Tzu (chs. 1 and 14), can neither be seen, touch, apprehended nor named.

David Yu, quoting from the supposedly fourth-century BCE document *Tao-yuan*, asserts that '*Tao* was viewed as being identical to chaos':

> In the beginning of the ancient past,
> All things were fused and were identical to the great vacuity
> Blended vacuously as one,
> It rests in the one eternally.

---

6. 'The word *ch'i* translated in our readings as material-force or vital force, in order to emphasize its dynamic character, plays an important part in Chinese cosmological and metaphysical thought. At times it means the spirit or breath of life in living creatures, at other times the air or ether filling the sky and surrounding the universe, while in some contexts it denotes the basic substance of all creation' (de Bary 1960: 192-93).

7. 'had limits' may better be rendered 'was extremely secure'.

> Moist and chaotic,
> There was no distinction of dark and light...
> From the ancient times it (*Tao*) had no shapes,
> Blended greatly, it had no names.
>
> (Yu 1981: 485)

It is understood by Taoism and P'an-ku myth that the cosmos and the myriad things came into existence through a process of separation and multiplication. This one, chaotic and greatly blended *Tao* or *huntun* separated into *yang* and *yin*, heaven and earth. Lao Tzu explains the process of creation in ch. 42 of *Tao Te Ching*:

> The Way (*Tao*) begets one;
> one begets two;
> two begets three,
> three begets the myriad creatures.
> The myriad creatures carry on their backs the *yin* and embrace in their arms the *yang*, taking the *ch'i* in between as harmony.
>
> (Lau 1982: 197)

'One', 'two' and 'three' are rendered by Bodde as 'oneness', 'duality' and 'trinity' (Bodde 1953: 23). He further interprets the oneness as referring to 'undifferentiated being' and duality as pointing to the separation into heaven and earth. With reference to the myth of P'an-ku, 'trinity' will then be represented as heaven, earth and P'an-ku through whom the myriad creatures are formed and produced. *Yin* and *Yang* can be found in the myriad creatures in whom the *ch'i* ('wind', 'breath' or 'energy') operates in harmony.

It is clear from these analyses that creation as an act of separation implies a process of polarity and multiplicity. Such an understanding of creation may help us to grasp the same conception presented in Genesis 1, from oneness to polarity to plurality: heaven/earth, light/darkness, day/night, land/sea and 'according to its kind'. It will be enlightening if we read Genesis 1 from this Chinese understanding of creation in terms of separation and multiplication.

IV. *The Transformation of P'an-ku: from Death to Life*

According to Claus Westermann there are four types of creation (Westermann 1984: 26-40): (1) creation by birth or by a succession of births; (2) creation as a result of a struggle or victory; (3) creation by an action or activity; and (4) creation through word. Type 1 is more prominent in the Chinese story, whereas type 4 predominates in the Hebrew creation story. Type 3 is found in both, while type 2 is in neither. In order to uphold the supremacy of the divine sovereignty of Yahweh (Brooke 1987: 245), this Hebrew writer has tried consistently to eliminate and exclude the element of struggle and the battle of the gods from his composition. It is evident that the theogonic account of the birth of the gods or genealogy of the gods does not find its way into the Genesis narrative at all. It has also been noted that even the great sea monsters, enemies of God in other contexts, are created by God in Gen. 1.21. The P'an-ku myth, too, does not have any theogony and therefore no presentation of struggle between the gods. Harmony seems to be the frame of mind in both the Hebrew and the Chinese narratives.

Regarding the use of the theme of creation by birth to describe the origin of the universe, it is clearly laid out in the Chinese myth. Before the separation of heaven and earth takes place, the birth of P'an-ku in the midst of chaos triggers off the process of creation. Not only was P'an-ku born, he was also transformed and grew in size as heaven and earth grew in height and thickness respectively during a long period of 18,000 years. This conception of birth goes beyond the presumably implied recollection of birth by the summing up word תולדות in Gen. 2.4a (Westermann 1984: 26). Birth, separation and transformation are motifs found in the origin account of P'an-ku. The last of these motifs has become predominant in some other stories of P'an-ku.

The Chinese myth mentions the daily transformation of P'an-ku in the process of separation of heaven and earth. There is another written document, *Ssu-i Chi* (Record of Strange Events) edited in the sixth century CE by Jen Fan, which relates several additional ancient traditions associated with P'an-ku:

> Long time ago when P'an-ku died, his head became four mountains, his eyes the sun and the moon, his blood the rivers, and his hairs the plants and trees.

> In the folklore of Ch'in Han time [third cent. BCE to third cent. CE], it said that P'an-ku's head became the eastern mountain, his belly the central mountain, his left arm the southern mountain, his right arm the northern mountain, and his legs the western mountain.

> According to the ancient scholars, P'an-ku's tears became the rivers, his breath the wind, his voice the thunder, and his eye-sight the lightning. An

ancient story also said that when P'an-ku was happy, the weather would be clear, and when he was angry, the weather turned cloudy and dark...

In the South Sea, there is a country called the P'an-ku Kuo, and all the people living there have P'an-ku as their family name. I think it is natural since P'an-ku is the primordial ancestor of all things, and all living beings came from P'an-ku.

The self-transformation of the cosmic giant P'an-ku into the universe and all things there within is a basic theme in these Chinese Creation traditions. P'an-ku's death, which is a destruction in itself, a sacrifice, is understood to have a creative force and a constructive power. Everything in the world comes from the decomposition of his body. It is proper to say that the cosmos is the body of P'an-ku, whose death gives birth to all life and whose sacrifice brings about an ordered creation.

P'an-ku is conceived as the first-born among all creatures and the first who died to make the creation complete (Ding 1988: 5).

Pangu (P'an-ku), who was born before anything else, underwent great bodily changes when he was dying. His breath became winds and clouds, his voice thunder, his left eye the sun and his right eye the moon; his arms and legs the four poles of the earth and the five parts of his body the five mountains;[8] his blood formed the rivers and his veins the roads; his flesh and skin became the soil of the fields and his hair and moustache the stars; the fine hair on his skin turned into grass and trees, his teeth and bones metals and rocks; his marrow changed to pearls and jade, and his sweat fell as rain that nourished all things; the insects on his body, caressed by the winds, took the shape[9] of men and women.

Human beings are 'transformed' from the impregnation of the insects or parasites on P'an-ku's body with the wind of nature. In reality, the wind is also from P'an-ku since it is his breath. There are two aspects of human life, the physical form and the breath of life. *Huai Nan Tzu* spells it out that human beings are transformed from the finest essence of breath which becomes the human spirit. 'Hence,

8.   The five mountains: Mount Taishan in the east; Mount Huashan in the West; Mount Hengshan in the north; Mount Hengshan (a different Chinese character from the one used for the north mountain) in the south; and Mount Songshan in the central region (Ding 1988: 5).

9.   The Chinese character is 'transformed', the same word for P'an-ku's daily nine times transformation used in the narrative quoted from *Yi wen lei ju* at the beginning of this article.

spirit belongs to heaven and the physical belongs to earth. When the spirit returns to the gate of heaven and the body returns to its origin, how can I exist?' (*Huainan Honglie Jijie*, 218-19). This reminds us of רוח in Gen. 1.2 and the breath of God in 2.7. Further discussion on the 'wind' and 'spirit' will certainly help us to clarify their ambiguous meanings in both texts (Luyster 1981: 1-10).

It must be noted that the Chinese myth places greater emphasis on the dependence of humanity on the cosmos. Heaven and earth together with humanity form the triad of the universe. Therefore, on the one hand, human beings have a humble origin as they are transformed from the parasites on P'an-ku's body, but on the other hand, they are invited to unite with heaven and earth.

Human being shares with the universe the same organic unity and substance. Since P'an-ku's human body exists in the cosmos, there is a set of homologies between parts of the human body (microcosm) and corresponding parts of the cosmos (macrocosm). In this respect, the myth of P'an-ku is not unique, and there are similar myths from Indo-European cultures (Lincoln 1986: 1-39).

Furthermore, transformation of P'an-ku suggests a basic continuity between the cosmic giant and the creatures. This motif of the continuity of being has a profound implication for Chinese philosophy, religion and ethics. Tu Wei-ming comments:

> Forming a trinity with heaven and earth, which is tantamount to forming one body with the myriad things, enjoins us from applying the subject–object dichotomy to nature. To see nature as an external object out there is to create an artificial barrier which obstructs our true vision and undermines our human capacity to experience nature from within (Tu 1989: 77).

V. *Concluding Remarks*

This is an initial survey of the traditions of the P'an-ku creation narrative which aims at illustrating the apparent parallels and essential differences between a cultural text of the Chinese and the biblical text of the Judeo-Christian faith. Further research has to be done in studying both texts together critically. The differences in world-views need to be examined in greater detail. Chinese Christians have two identities and have inherited two world-views. In order to uphold our integrity as both Christian and Chinese, we have to embrace the two texts. Biblical interpretation, therefore, needs to take into account the other text which forms the interpreter's perspective with which he or she approaches the Scripture.

Over the past twelve years I have been privileged to teach the Hebrew Scripture to the Chinese University students in Hong Kong. I have become more and more convinced that it is very fruitful to biblical scholarship to let the Chinese cultural texts shed light on the interpretation of the Scripture and vice versa. I am very grateful to Professor George W. Anderson for his profound wisdom and under-standing of the Hebrew Scripture and his interest in training graduate students from Asia. Professor Anderson's dedication and openness to innovation in biblical interpretation have motivated me greatly in my own research for the Asian ways of interpreting the Scripture.

BIBLIOGRAPHY

Allan, S.
1991   *The Shape of the Turtle. Myth, Art and Cosmos in Early China* (New York: State University of New York Press).
Anderson, B.W.
1967   *Creation versus Chaos* (New York: Association Press).
Bodde, D.
1953   'Harmony and Conflict in Chinese Philosophy', in A.F. Wright (ed.), *Studies in Chinese Thought* (Chicago: University of Chicago Press: 19-80).
1961   'Myth of Ancient China', in S.N. Kramer (ed.), *Mythologies of the Ancient World* (New York: Doubleday): 369-408.
Bary, W.T. de, W.T. Chan and B. Watson (eds.)
1960   *Sources of Chinese Tradition* (New York: Columbia University).
Brooke, G.J.
1987   'Creation in the Biblical Tradition', *Zygon* 22: 227-48.
Chang, K.C.
1959   'The Chinese Creation Myth: A Study in Method', *Bulletin of the Institute of Ethnology, Academica Sinica* 8: 47-79.
1976   *Early Chinese Civilization: Anthropological Perspectives* (Cambridge, MA: Harvard University Press): 149-73.
Chiu, M.M.
1984   *The Tao of Chinese Religion* (Lanham, MD: University Press of America).
Christie, A.
1968   Chinese Mythology (New York: Hamlyn Publishing).
DeRoche, M.
1988   'The *ruah 'elohim* in Genesis 1.2c: Creation or Chaos?' in L. Eslinger

and G. Taylor (eds.), *Ascribe to the Lord: Biblical and Other Studies* (JSOTSup, 67; Sheffield: JSOT Press): 303-18.

Ding, W.D.
1988   *100 Chinese Myths and Fantasies* (Hong Kong: The Commercial Press).

Frymer-Kensky, T.
1987   'Biblical Cosmology', in M.P. O'Connor and D.N. Freedman (eds.), *Backgrounds for the Bible* (Winona Lake, IN: Eisenbrauns).

Fung, Yu-lan
1952   *A History of Chinese Philosophy*, I (trans. D. Bodde; Princeton, NJ: Princeton University Press).

Girardot, N.J.
1976   'The Problem of Creation Mythology in the Study of Chinese Religion', *History of Religions* 15: 289-318.
1983   *Myth and Meaning in Early Taoism* (Berkeley: University of California Press).
1985   'Behaving Cosmogonically in Early Taoism', in R. Lovin and F. Reynolds (eds.), *Cosmogony and Ethical Order* (Chicago: The University of Chicago Press).

Hasel, G.F.
1972   'The Significance of the Cosmology in Genesis 1 in Relation to Ancient Near Eastern Parallels', *AUSS* 10: 1-20.

Lau, D.C.
1982   *Chinese Classics, Tao Te Ching* (Hong Kong: The Chinese University Press).

Le Blanc, C.
1985   *Huai Nan Tzu, Philosophical Synthesis in Early Han Thought* (Hong Kong: Hong Kong University Press).

Lee, A.C.C.
1989   'The Dragon, the Deluge and Creation Theology', *Association for Theological Education in South East Asia Occasional Papers* (Singapore: ATESEA) 8: 110-23.
1993   'Biblical Interpretation in Asian Perspective', *Asia Journal of Theology* 7: 35-39.

Lincoln, B.
1986   *Myth, Cosmos and Society: Indo-European Themes of Creation and Destruction* (Cambridge, MA: Harvard University Press).

Long, C.H.
1963   *Alpha: the Myths of Creation* (Chico, CA: Scholars Press).

Lui, M.D.
1989   *Huainan Honglie Jijie* (Beijing: Chung Hua).

Luyster, R.
1981   'Wind and Water: Cosmogonic Symbolism in the Old Testament', *ZAW* 93: 1-10.

Major, J.S.
1978   'Myth, Cosmology and the Origins of Chinese Science', *Journal of Chinese Philosophy* 5: 1-20.

Numazawa, K.
1984   'The Cultural-Historical Background of Myths on the Separation of Sky and Earth', in A. Dundes (ed.), *Sacred Narrative: Readings in the Theory of Myth* (Berkeley: University of California Press): 182-92.

Rad, G. von
1966   'Some Aspects of the Old Testament Worldview', *The Problem of the Hexateuch and Other Essays* (London: SCM Press).

Tu, Wei-ming
1989   'The Continuity of Being: Chinese Visions of Nature', in J.B. Callicott and R.T. Ames (eds.), *Nature in Asian Traditions of Thought: Essays in Environmental Philosophy* (New York: State University of New York Press): 67-78.

Westermann, C.
1984   *Genesis 1–11: A Commentary* (Minneapolis: Augsburg Publishing House).

Yu, David
1981   'The Creation Myth and its Symbolism in Classical Taoism', *Philosophy East and West* 31: 479-500.

POWER NOT NOVELTY:
THE CONNOTATIONS OF ברא IN THE HEBREW BIBLE

S. Lee

Introduction

It almost sounds theologically commonplace to repeat the unanimous
observation that as a verb used exclusively of God, ברא ('to create')
expresses the uniquely divine act of bringing into existence something
miraculous, wonderful and new.[1] However, when YHWH declares to
his people in Isa. 54.16 that he himself has created their enemies, it
seems that a consistent understanding of the verb ברא may be more
inclined towards the nuance of sovereign power and control than that
of novelty or election. The intention here is to ascertain how such an
interpretation correlates with all the other occurrences of ברא within
the Hebrew Bible.

Well rehearsed are the facts that the verb ברא appears predominantly (38×) in its qal form and less frequently (10×) in its niphal
form,[2] with the majority of its usage found in Isaiah 40–55 (16×) and
the beginning of Genesis (11×). In addition, it appears another eleven
times within the prophetic literature, of which five are from the rest
of the book of Isaiah. It also occurs six times in the Psalter, and is
found once in each of the remaining books of the Pentateuch except
Leviticus. Finally, apart from appearing once in Ecclesiastes, it is
almost entirely absent in the wisdom writings. Judging from such a
pattern of distribution, we may be justified to begin our survey on the
meaning of ברא from Isaiah 40–55.

---

1.   For literature on the meaning of ברא, see Botterweck and Ringgren 1977: 242,
to which the studies of Miguens (1974) and Angerstorfer (1979) should be added.

2.   Because of their non-theological usage, the five occurrences of the piel form
(בֵּרֵא) together with the single appearance of the hiphil infinitive (הבריא) will not be
discussed. Moreover, the adjective בריא (14×), the Aramaic noun ברא (8×), and the
proper name בראיה may also be left safely outside our consideration.

Isaiah 40–55

Right in the middle of a prophetic disputation, YHWH is depicted as 'creator of the ends of the earth' (Isa. 40.28). In fact, the focus of refutation begins precisely at this verse, arguing for YHWH's abundant power through the thrice-repeated pair of key words, יעף and ייגל: he 'does not faint nor grow weary' (v. 28a), but empowers those who 'faint and grow weary' (v. 30a), so that those waiting for him 'will not faint nor grow weary' (v. 31b). The same emphasis has also been crystallized in the dual epithets given to YHWH, since the implications of YHWH as creator have already been so fully explored in the previous parallel sections (vv. 12-20 and vv. 21-26) that now the divine title can afford a simple allusion without further elaboration. The earlier statement in v. 26 clearly illustrates such a close link between the verb ברא and divine power, for YHWH, who has created the heavenly hosts, is capable of commanding them 'because of abundant strength and mighty power'.

Similar conclusions may be drawn in two other instances where YHWH is referred to as the one 'creating the heavens', albeit at first sight they seem to be less straightforward. Isa. 42.5 introduces YHWH as creator in the expanded messenger formula, while the divine speech closes subsequently with the mentioning of 'the former things' and 'the new things' (v. 9), just as the adjoining pericope starts immediately with an appeal to sing to YHWH 'a new song' (v. 10). Does the reference to YHWH's creating activities constitute thereby a preamble to this concluding motif of 'newness'? Such a likelihood diminishes as we consider carefully the core of the divine speech, where YHWH is declared as 'calling' his servant 'with victory', 'upholding' his hand, 'guarding' him, and 'setting' him for a special task to the nations. We observe that all four verbs point undoubtedly to YHWH's sovereign power, and that these declarations are joined closely with the preceding descriptions of creating acts of YHWH by the self-identification phrase, 'I am YHWH' (v. 6a). The same phrase reappears in v. 8, with the emphasis being unmistakably on YHWH's 'glory' and 'praise', which are attested to by both 'former things' and 'new things'.

The second reference to YHWH as 'creating the heavens' appears in Isa. 45.18-19, again with YHWH's sovereign power as the central theme. To begin with, the expanded messenger formula explains: 'Not a chaos he created it'. In all the other five occurrences of 'chaos' in

Isa. 40.17, 23; 41.29; 44.9; and 49.4, the nuance of powerlessness can be distinctly identified from its context. The verse then continues to declare: לשבת יצרה. Now לשבת is commonly rendered 'for habitation', yet again a glance at the other three appearances of the word in Isa. 40.22; 44.13; and 47.14 suggests that perhaps a more accurate understanding should be 'to sit'—with the added nuance of being in control. As a result, the proclamation of YHWH as creator is elaborated with an affirmation highlighting his sovereignty rather than the novelty of his creation: 'Not a weakling he created it—[but] for dominion he fashioned it' (v. 18aβ). This is further substantiated by the conclusion of v. 19b, where YHWH is portrayed as a supreme ruler bringing law and order after his victory and success. Finally, the appearing together of the three creation vocables (ברא, יצר, and עשׂה) at the start of v. 18 reminds us of two other similar occasions where the motif of YHWH's power is equally dominant, and to them we shall now direct our attention.

Isa. 45.6b-8 brings the pericope of YHWH's commissioning Cyrus to its climax. The main thrust of the announcement lies unequivocally in the very last clause of v. 7: YHWH, who 'creates', 'fashions' and 'makes', is the one God 'making all these'. Since there is no other deity beside him, YHWH is in control of both darkness and woe on the one hand, and victory and salvation on the other. Lindström (1983: 198) is probably correct in arguing

> that the action ascribed to YHWH in Isa. 45, 7 refers solely to the imminent liberation of Israel from her Babylonian captivity. The *positive* phrases 'who forms light' and 'who makes weal' have to do with YHWH's saving intervention on behalf of his people, while the negative phrases 'who creates darkness' and 'who creates woe' refer to YHWH's destruction of the Babylonian empire.

The metaphysical origin of evil does not come into consideration if the verb ברא carries the meaning of control and not that of *creatio ex nihilo*.

Similarly, the conclusion of the salvation oracle in Isa. 43.1-7 emphatically declares that YHWH has 'created', 'fashioned' and 'made' Israel, echoing the opening address where YHWH is for the first time described as the creator of his people. While Westermann (1969: 117) is certain that '[t]he creating and forming would then refer to an actual historical act of God, the saving act by which he brought Israel into being', Elliger (1978: 293) is equally sure that creation here means a repeated intervention, like the present liberation of Israel from foreign control. Nevertheless, if we compare Isa. 43.7 with 45.7, YHWH's concluding declaration may well imply that he alone is responsible for everything good or bad happening to his people. Such a self-affirmation reminds us of the rhetorical question raised in Isa. 42.24 of the preceding pericope: 'Who has given Jacob to be plundered, and Israel to robbers? Was it not YHWH?' Moreover, the phrase 'and for my glory' (Isa. 43.7a; cf. 42.8 and 48.11) also refers clearly to the polemics against the idols, which must be 'made' and 'fashioned' by human hands in contrast to YHWH, who 'makes' and 'fashions' Israel. The depiction of YHWH as Israel's creator therefore points once again to his unique supremacy and sovereign control over Israel.

Another reference to YHWH as the creator of Israel appears in Isa. 43.15. We must be very cautious here because of the corrupt state of v. 14, but the two other instances where YHWH is described as king (Isa. 41.21 and 44.6) both suggest the nuance of absolute power and sovereignty, and this idea fits well with the motif of YHWH acting on behalf of Israel against Babylon. The same context of YHWH's sovereign power may be located in Isa. 45.12, where YHWH proclaims himself to be the creator of both the cosmos and humanity. Hermisson (1987: 16) flirts with the idea that the pericope may be constructed originally as YHWH's solemn proclamation before the heavenly court, but we should pay more attention to the parallel use of the three verbs of creation (עשׂה, ברא, and נטה) with the fourth, צוה ('to command'), which distinctly carries the nuance of supreme authority. To be fair, we must concede the possibility of a 'personal relationship' being expressed here between the creator and his creatures, but such an opinion would shipwreck when confronted by the most salient use of ברא in Isa. 54.16, which Stuhlmueller (1970: 211) considers to be 'out of step with the others, in that its scope is very limited to God's control of enemy forces'. Nonetheless, the tables ought to be turned as I see it, for the verse is no less than the kingpin for a correct perception of the basic meaning of ברא and the wide-ranging spectrum of YHWH's incomparable sovereignty.

There remain two examples that may lend some support to the long accepted view that ברא is often connected with the notion of newness. Isa. 41.20 concludes what Westermann calls a salvation proclamation describing the transformation of nature, which is a well-recognized motif for representing the powerful impact of YHWH's theophany (cf. Pss. 104.27-30 and 107.33-35). At the same time, the point of confession that YHWH has created these changes is also focused squarely upon YHWH's supremacy. The emphasis on any sense of novelty must not be assumed, unless we insist on reading it *a priori* in every use of the verb ברא. Having said that, we must now examine Isa. 48.6-7, where YHWH announces that the 'new things' (חדשׁוֹת) have been created now. It looks like the unique case among all the sixteen occurrences of ברא within Isaiah 40–55 where one may justifiably argue for the primary notion of newness in the verb 'to create'. However, we must pay careful attention as well to the fact that here נבראו ('they have been created') is used in parallel to השׁמעתיך ('I have announced to you'), which is applied not only to 'new things' but to 'former things' in v. 3a as well. Since YHWH's declaration of both 'former things' and 'new things' represents not so much his ability to predict but his absolute control over all historical events, it is not without ground that we understand the use of ברא here as a reiteration of YHWH's sovereignty in his decision of the timing of the announcement.

As an initial conclusion, this examination of all the sixteen cases of the use of ברא in Isaiah 40–55 has indicated that, among a wide range of its direct objects, the verb consistently conveys the basic nuance of YHWH's supreme power and sovereign control over all of his creation.

The Prophetic Literature

In addition to the sixteen occurrences in Isaiah 40–55, the verb ברא appears another five times in the rest of the book of Isaiah, and three of them are found in Isa. 65.17-18. Here YHWH declares his creating 'new heavens and a new earth', which are set in sharp contrast with 'the former things'. Westermann (1969: 408) is correct to note that הראשׁנות in v. 17b is identical in meaning with הצרות הראשׁנות ('the former troubles') in v. 16b, hence the contrast lies between the past oppressions and sufferings and the future peace and tranquillity, which is precisely what the picture of the new Jerusalem in vv. 19-25 endeavours to convey. The deliberate repetition of 'for look at me creating' in v. 17a and v. 18b confirms the parallelism between YHWH's creation of the new heavens and the new earth on the one hand and his creation of Jerusalem on the other. In the latter case, the focus of attention progresses from the sense of newness to that of joy and delight. The picture of an idyllic lifestyle is nothing innovative or unprecedented, granted that we accept some of its exaggerations as poetic hyperbole, but YHWH's power and sovereign control must remain the sole reason for this dramatic deliverance and drastic change from dereliction to prosperity. Such a significant fact is indeed forcefully expressed through the careful choice of the verb ברא.

A similar understanding of the use of ברא is also found in Isa. 57.18-19, where YHWH is said to be creating fruit of lips for Israel's mourners.[3] Although the Masoretic reading of these two verses is unsatisfactory, I shall still attempt to offer an observation. It seems that v. 19bα constitutes the content of YHWH's saying and not that of the 'fruit of lips', because its syntax is closely mirrored in v. 21.[4] Consequently, the 'fruit of lips' may be taken as a response to YHWH's saving acts described in v. 18. The turning from lament to praise again rests upon the sovereign power of YHWH bringing into effect divine deliverance, expressed here in an abridged manner once more by the verb ברא.

A final text from the book of Isaiah is Isa. 4.5-6, which announces that YHWH will create over the assembly of Zion a cloud by day and smoke and fire by night. The *Septuagint*'s καὶ ἥξει at the beginning of v. 5 seems to suggest a reading of ובא ('and he will come') instead of וברא. However, the Masoretic text is preferable, for it is the more difficult reading and is supported by 1QIsa[a] and other ancient Versions. Furthermore, as Wildberger (1991: 163) aptly puts it, 'the present passage apparently does not intend to speak of an appearance by Yahweh, but about the protection which Yahweh will bestow upon Zion after the judgment'.[5] Once again, YHWH's absolute power provides the basis for his secure protection over Zion, and it is in the context of divine sovereignty rather than creative novelty that the verb ברא is employed.

Outside the book of Isaiah, the one example that most clearly

---

3. Since v. 18b seems to be overloaded, I agree with most commentators to move ולאבליו to v. 19a against the Masoretic tradition. I have also chosen to follow the *Qere* ניב, which has the support of 1QIsa[a], and not the *Ketiv* נוב, which is a *hapax*.

4. *Pace* Rashi and Redak (in Rosenberg 1983: 454), both of whom consider the שלום to be the new speech created by YHWH in human mouths.

5. Wildberger (1991: 171) also cites the opinion of Hertzberg, 'who considers the Septuagint text to be more original'.

represents the use of ברא again in the context of YHWH's sovereignty and power comes from Amos 4.13. The absolute power of YHWH is portrayed through successive sketches of him 'fashioning mountain', 'creating wind', 'making the morning darkness', and what Andersen and Freedman (1989: 455) describe as 'an echo of YHWH's trampling the primordial dragon, whose humps are the ridges'. The reference to YHWH's acts of creation does not indicate any new beginning or special relationship for Israel, who have been warned that they should prepare to meet their God (v. 12), but rather points unmistakably to the creator as the supreme judge.

A similar context of judgment is apparently reflected in Ezek. 21.35 (30), where the sword of judgment has come under judgment itself. Miguens (1974: 43-44) thinks that the verb נבראת ('you are created') indicates 'an activity which brings about something new', but the polemical context of power and control must not be overlooked, and I agree with Zimmerli (1979: 449) that it is 'the createdness of those addressed' which is being emphasized here. The same conclusion may be drawn in relation to the two mentionings of 'the day you have been created' in the taunt song against the king of Tyre (Ezek. 28.13 and 15). In view of the predominant motif of pride running through the divine speech, the repeated remark looks more pregnant than an innocent temporal reference.

Our last two cases from the prophetic literature are more ambiguous concerning the meaning of ברא. Mal. 2.10 presents a situation where we must decide what exactly is the premise of the discussion when the prophet asks rhetorically, 'Has not one El created us?' Bearing in mind similar arguments in Prov. 14.31, 17.5, and 22.2, we may insist that here both ideas of origin and superior authority are present in the reference to YHWH as father and creator, whereas any notion of newness is definitely at odds with the context of the prophetic disputation.

Finally, Jer. 31.22 announces that 'YHWH has created a new thing (חדשה) on earth'. The crux of the matter is of course the accurate translation of תסובב, and hence the precise meaning of the phrase 'a female "encompassing" a male'. Granted that we plead ignorance over this baffling verb, there remains some room for exploration of the use of ברא here. If the 'new thing' created by YHWH is meant to overcome the wavering of faithless Israel in their decision to return, we may want to ask if it is simply the novelty of YHWH's creation that will provide the absent conviction. Is it not more important for the

people to witness the power and sovereignty of YHWH coming to
their aid before responding to the prophetic exhortation, hence the
careful choice of ברא in this present context? Nonetheless, we must
concede the fact that because of its obscurity this present text offers
dangerous ground upon which to base any conclusion.

Our examination of the additional eleven appearances of ברא within
the prophetic literature has enabled us to draw the interim conclusion
that, despite the two cases of Isa. 65.17 and Jer. 31.22, where the verb
is explicitly linked to the notion of חדשה, the meaning of ברא remains
inextricably tied to the sovereign power of YHWH. It is now necessary to test our thesis further with the fourteen texts of the Pentateuch,
particularly in the beginning chapters of the book of Genesis.

The Pentateuch

Eleven of the fourteen occurrences of ברא in the Pentateuch are found
at the beginning of the book of Genesis, and out of these eleven occurrences six appear right within the very first section of Gen. 1.1–2.3.

On closer examination, we further observe the fact that, apart from
its use in the opening and closing sentences (Gen. 1.1 and 2.3b), ברא
appears only in vv. 21 and 27. It is therefore not justifiable for
Westermann (1984: 86) to remark that '[t]he verbs "make" and
"create" predominate'. On the contrary, ברא appears to be utilized
very sparingly in the narrative of the course of creation. Westermann
is also of the opinion that there is hardly any distinction in meaning
between ברא and עשה in this text, for both verbs are sometimes used to
describe the same act of creation (e.g. Gen. 1.26-27). When ברא is
used instead of עשה, it is no more than a preference of the Priestly
redactor, who has nevertheless chosen not to replace עשה in the source
materials with ברא on each and every occasion. However, the way ברא
has been employed looks far from being arbitrarily synonymous with
עשה. Even Westermann (1984: 137) himself has to admit later on that
ברא 'may have been chosen deliberately at the beginning of the
creation of living beings' in Gen. 1.21. It is particularly interesting
here to find the notorious 'giant serpents'[6] topping the list of the living

---

6.   התנינם הגדלים undoubtedly allude to the mythical sea monsters representing
the evil force in opposition to YHWH. Cf. Pss. 74.13; 148.7; Isa. 27.1; 51.9; and Job
7.12. The noun is also used to refer to snakes in Exod. 7.9-12; hence our choice of
'serpents' instead of 'dragons' or 'monsters'.

creatures. While it is possible to argue that the use of ברא here may signify a new stage of the emergence of animate beings, I tend to agree more with Wenham's (1987: 24) suggestion that 'it may well be that this verse mentions that the great sea monsters were created by God precisely to insist on his sovereignty over them'. There is a subtle but familiar nuance of power struggle when ברא is applied to God's archenemy; it certainly reminds us of the similar use of the verb in Isa. 54.16.

The triple application of ברא to God's creation of humanity in Gen. 1.27 may now be approached from this perspective of divine sovereignty as well. Humanity has been singled out from the entire creation by God's command to 'subdue' and 'dominate' the earth and its creatures (vv. 26 and 28). Whereas the royal implication and imperialistic flavour are recognizable, they are also readily open to hubristic misinterpretations. Thus there is a need for reminding each and every member of the human race that they are nonetheless being held accountable to the supreme authority of their creator. The three-fold repetition of ברא serves to drive home the truth of responsible stewardship, which is also expressed in the concept of *Imago Dei*.

The use of ברא at Gen. 1.1 and 2.3 refers also to God's sovereign control over his entire creation. This significant motif of God's absolute power underlies at the beginning the intriguing description of the divine רוח 'swooping down'[7] upon the surface of the primaeval ocean, brings about the divine fiat ('and God said') as the prevalent formulation of God's mode of creativity,[8] and anticipates the confidently triumphal rest of God on the seventh day.[9] Moreover, Wenham (1987: 126) is right to observe that both summary sentences of Gen. 2.4 and 5.1-2 are heavily dependent on Gen. 1.1–2.3, and so the nuances of ברא are being carried over into these verses. The same is also true with Gen. 6.7, where the use of ברא may have hinted at the sovereignty of

7. The piel form of רחף appears only in Gen. 1.2 and Deut. 32.11, where it describes how eagles teach their young to fly by 'swooping down' at them in order to get them jump out from the nest (Peters 1914). The imagery is therefore one of violent attack rather than of gentle incubation. Cf. Ps. 93.3-4.

8. Cf. Ps. 33.6 and 9. The implications of supreme authority behind the apparently simple act of speaking are also amply illustrated in an incident recorded in Mt. 8.5-10 (= Lk. 7.2-10).

9. As Levenson (1988: 111) wittily puts it, 'the order that he brings into existence through creation is so secure and self-sustaining that it can survive a day without his maintenance'.

YHWH as the supreme judge of all humankind. In fact, that the Deluge comes under the very command of YHWH and not from the hostile forces of evil reiterates the absolute power of YHWH.

Outside the first chapters of Genesis, ברא appears in Exod. 34.10, although none of the more recent English translations has chosen to render it with 'created'. Now one of these 'wonders' which has not been 'created' but will be 'made' by YHWH is the driving out of Israel's enemies who are inhabitants of the promised land (v. 11), and such a 'making of YHWH' will induce fear among the people who see it. In my opinion, the use of ברא in this context refers ultimately to YHWH's sovereignty. Displacement of tribes is nothing new or miraculous in the history of the ancient Near East, and reverence is only caused by the manifestation of YHWH's absolute power. The verb ברא has its own unique nuances and should not be toned down to become synonymous with עשׂה.

A similar conclusion may be drawn in relation to Num. 16.30, although we must first consider the possibility of repointing the Masoretic text. The verbal noun בריאה is a *hapax*, and, quoting Ibn Ezra, Milgrom (1990: 137) suggests repointing the verb from יִבְרָא (qal) to יְבָרֵא (piel), hence the translation: 'if YHWH cuts open a chasm', which is corroborated by the use of בקע ('to burst open') in the fulfilment passage of v. 31. The Septuagint's ἐν φάσματι δείξει ('if he shows in a portent') reflects a reading of בראי יראה, and thus suggests a possible confusion about the original text, though admittedly it falls short of lending a clear support to the proposed repointing. However, if the Masoretic tradition is to be followed, we must then decide what is the purpose of the use of ברא in the present context. Rashi (in Isaiah and Sharfman 1950: 174) does not hesitate to equate בריאה with חדשׁה ('a new thing'), but granted that the bursting open of the ground is something unprecedented, there is also a strong sense of YHWH's power which causes such a terrifying incident to happen. After all, it must be precisely this clear manifestation of YHWH's absolute power, and not just his ability to perform a new miracle, that will show beyond any doubt that 'these men have despised YHWH'.

The final example from Deut. 4.32 appears to be a relatively neutral one. The mentioning of God creating humanity seems *prima facie* no more than a temporal reference to the beginning of history, but if the creation of humanity is seen among the great events (such as God's voice being heard out of a fire) where the supreme power of YHWH has clearly been revealed, then are we supposed to be reminded of the unique sovereignty of God in his great act of creating humanity as well?

Our further examination of all the fourteen occurrences of ברא within the Pentateuch has provided more evidence for the thesis that the verb should be understood to mean the absolute power and sovereign control of YHWH. This is especially the case in Gen. 1.1–2.3. In the few instances where the sense of newness may be legitimately present, there is always an equally strong, if not even stronger, motif of YHWH's power and authority underlying the passages. It remains for us now to extend our survey into the last major area of the Hebrew Bible, namely, the Writings.

The Writings

Among the six occurrences of ברא in the Psalter, Ps. 148.5 offers us a straightforward enough case for the verb to be interpreted in terms not of newness but of power. This verse and the one following bring to a climax the first half of the psalm, in which the heavenly powers named in vv. 2-4 are exhorted to praise YHWH who commands their creation and determines their activities. A similar allusion to YHWH's sovereignty may also be located in Ps. 89.13(12), where the motif of YHWH's power and might surrounding the verse (vv. 6-15[5-14]) helps to make its meaning obvious. ברא then reappears later on in v. 48(47). The reference to YHWH's creation of humanity is made in relation to the helplessness of one who is confronted by the conquering power of death, and thus the psalmist prays to YHWH for deliverance with a specific appeal to his absolute sovereignty as creator.

There are two cases where ברא is used parallel to the verb חדש ('to renew'). Here in Ps. 104.30 the notion of newness is indeed present in YHWH dispatching his Spirit, but the verb ותחדש seems to incline towards the sense of restoration more than that of unprecedented novelty. Moreover, the emphasis on YHWH's absolute control over life and death is certainly in tune with the dominant concern for YHWH's power throughout the entire psalm, while the presence of YHWH's Spirit and the mentioning of his creating authority are only two more telltale signs of this underlying theme. On the other hand, a more subtle case may be found in Ps. 51.12-14(10-12), where the fact that all three verses begin their second halves with ורוח suggests the identity of this 'spirit' throughout as YHWH's Spirit. Thus in v. 12(10) the psalmist is praying for the restoration of the divine Spirit and not the renewal of the human spirit. The profound realization of his sinful nature has prompted the psalmist to concede his own inability to change himself, hence his appeal to the divine power to help him. There is of course an inevitable sense of renewal in the language of penitence, but again the underlying theme remains clearly focused on YHWH's sovereign power.

Finally, the last example of ברא in the Psalter is found in Ps. 102.19(18), which is part of an appeal to praise YHWH. The context of this appeal (vv. 13-23 [12-22]) refers clearly to YHWH's power to save and consequently his sovereignty being recognized among the nations. Kraus (1989: 286) is right in pointing out that 'עם נברא applies to the "new creation" of the people of God after the exile', though it would be even more to the point to say that the people have been 'created' through the saving power of YHWH.

Our very last example of ברא in the entire Hebrew Bible comes from Eccl. 12.1. Fox (1989: 299) is keen to defend the integrity of the verse, showing that there is no textual ground for emendations of בוראיך ('your creator'). The argument that a reference to the creator is inconsistent with the encouragement to enjoy life prior to old age and death cannot be sustained either, for the preceding two paragraphs (11.7-8 and 9-10) both juxtapose a 'hedonistic' advice with an unpleasant reminder (Murphy 1992: 117). Furthermore, the fact that ברא appears only here in all the wisdom writings of the Hebrew canon is not an adequate reason for us to reject this text as a proper reference to the creator. In fact, the motif of divine judgment appears in Eccl. 3.16-17, 8.5-6, 11.9 and 12.14, and within this context, to remember one's creator is to think of the supreme judge of one's life and work. Once again there is strong evidence for us to understand the verb ברא as carrying precisely the nuance of divine sovereignty and power.

Conclusion

Our survey of the 48 occurrences of ברא in the Hebrew Bible shows that YHWH as the supreme creator not only manifests his mastery over the physical universe, for his absolute authority is equally efficacious over friends or foes. Moreover, when YHWH is portrayed as Israel's creator, it indicates not so much a special relationship but YHWH's sovereign control over everything happening to his people. Furthermore, the five examples where ברא is explicitly linked with the root חדשׁ do not necessarily imply a semantic identification between the two, for in every one of them the motif of YHWH's power is present as well. As a result, we may now draw the final conclusion that a consistent understanding of the verb ברא does point definitively to the connotations of YHWH's sovereign power and control. It is with a deep sense of gratitude and affection that I wish to dedicate the above study to my first mentor in Biblical Theology.

BIBLIOGRAPHY

Andersen, F.I. and D.N. Freedman
1989   *Amos* (AB; New York: Doubleday).
Angerstorfer, A.
1979   *Der Schöpfergott des Alten Testaments. Herkunft und Bedeutungsentwicklung des Hebräischen Terminus* ברא <*schaffen*> (Bern: Peter Lang).
Botterweck, G.J. and H. Ringgren (eds.)
1977   *Theological Dictionary of the Old Testament,* II (Grand Rapids, MI: Eerdmans).
Elliger, K.
1978   *Deuterojesaja 40,1–45,7* (BKAT, XI/1-6; Neukirchen–Vluyn: Neukirchener Verlag).
Fox, M.V.
1989   *Qohelet and his Contradictions* (Sheffield: Almond Press).
Hermisson, H.J.
1987   *Deuterojesaja 45,8–25* (BKAT, XI/7; Neukirchen–Vluyn: Neukirchener Verlag).
Isaiah, A. ben and B. Sharfman (eds.)
1950   *The Pentateuch and Rashi's Commentary. IV. Numbers* (Philadelphia: Jewish Publication Society).
Kraus, H.J.
1989   *Psalms 60–150: A Commentary* (Minneapolis: Augsburg Fortress).
Levenson, J.D.
1988   *Creation and the Persistence of Evil: The Jewish Drama of Divine Omnipotence* (San Francisco: Harper & Row).
Lindström, F.
1983   *God and the Origin of Evil: A Contextual Analysis of Alleged Monistic Evidence in the Old Testament* (Lund: CWK Gleerup).

Miguens, M.
 1974   'BR' and Creation in the Old Testament', *Studii Biblici Franciscani Liber Annuus* 24: 38-69.
Milgrom, J.
 1990   *Numbers* (The JPS Torah Commentary; New York: Jewish Publication Society).
Murphy, R.
 1992   *Ecclesiastes* (WBC; Dallas: Word Books).
Peters, J.P.
 1914   'The Wind of God', *JBL* 32: 81-86.
Rosenberg, A.J. (ed.)
 1989   *Isaiah: A New Translation of Text, Rashi and Commentary*, II (New York: Judaica Press).
Stuhlmueller, C.
 1970   *Creative Redemption in Deutero-Isaiah* (Rome: Biblical Institute Press).
Wenham, G.J.
 1987   *Genesis 1–15* (WBC; Waco, TX: Word Books).
Westermann, C.
 1969   *Isaiah 40–66: A Commentary* (OTL; London: SCM Press).
 1984   *Genesis 1–11: A Commentary* (Minneapolis: Augsburg).
Wildberger, H.
 1991   *Isaiah 1–12: A Commentary* (Minneapolis: Augsburg Fortress).
Zimmerli, W.
 1979   *Ezekiel 1* (Hermeneia; Philadelphia: Fortress).

THE GREAT COMMANDMENT AND THE GOLDEN RULE

J.I.H. McDonald

It is a pleasure for me to be associated with this *Festschrift* in honour of Professor George Anderson. While I can claim no special expertise in the field of Old Testament studies, I share an enthusiasm for all things biblical and ethical. I have chosen therefore to write briefly on the Great Commandment and the Golden Rule because they embody both interests. They also impinge upon areas which, I think, reflect some of Professor Anderson's own concerns: the relation of the Old Testament and the New; the context of biblical teaching; theological perspectives on ethics in the Bible; and cross-cultural factors, with at least a passing glance towards the important topic of dialogue between Jews and Christians.

The article itself considers Commandment and Rule under four headings. The first discusses their relation to Christian and Jewish paraenesis; the second to their community context; the third to cultural tradition; and the fourth to the complementarity of divine revelation and human awareness.

I. *Christian and Jewish Paraenesis*

'There are two ways, one of life and one of death; and between the two ways there is a great difference. Now, this is the way of life: "First, you must love God who made you, and second, your neighbour as yourself". And whatever you want people to refrain from doing to you, you must not do to them' (*Did.* 1.2).

The Didache's unequivocal statement of the fundamentals of the Christian life is the catechist's way of reading the tradition of Jesus's moral teaching. The great Commandment is taken as the positive pole, providing coherence for material such as love to enemies, non-violence, generosity and similar themes. The Golden Rule, in the form cited here,[1] is the negative pole which attracts a catalogue of prohibitions: 'Do not murder, do not commit adultery, do not corrupt boys, do not fornicate, do not steal, do not practice magic...'

The catechist's approach is *one* way of using the material. Its merit lies in its simple didactic structure, its communicability, its uncompromising prescription. But the anchoring of moral teaching in catechetics and eventually in penitential discourse impoverished moral theology. Even the Didache, which identifies some kind of interaction between Great Commandment and Golden Rule, places both in a straitjacket. To break out of it requires us to extend our discussion beyond the world of the Didache's catechist.

As is well known, Great Commandment and Golden Rule occur in Judaism as summative statements of the moral requirements of the Torah.[2] They occur as part of persuasive communication at the interface between the Jewish and Hellenistic worlds. Rabbinic attitudes to the Golden Rule are illustrated by the famous story of the divergent responses of R. Shammai and R. Hillel to a request by a Gentile to be taught the whole of the Law while standing on one foot.[3] Shammai drove him away with his rod. No such reductionist suggestion was acceptable to this militant traditionalist who regarded the multiplicity and equality of the commandments as the glory of Judaism. But when the same question was put to R. Hillel, he replied: 'What is hateful to yourself do not do to anyone else. This is the whole Law. The rest is commentary. Go and learn it.' There may be a danger in reading too much into this rhetorical exchange, which Hillel handled so effectively. The basic sentiment is not unusual in the Judaism of the period. One must not underestimate the importance of the commentary or interpretation, which translates general principle into specific requirement, nor can one miss the final punchline, which requires not merely academic learning but learning with a view to practice. It might be said that we have here no more than pedagogical devices which are neither fundamental nor exhaustive. But there may also be a danger of underestimating the daring step which Hillel took when he asserted, 'This is the whole Law!' He did not say, 'This is the meaning of the

---

1. There is little to choose between positive and negative forms. Both forms require supplementation. Both forms also pre-date Jesus; cf. Dihle 1962: 9-10.

2. Cf. *Sifra* on Leviticus 19.18; *b. Šab.* 31A.

3. That is, while the enquirer—not the rabbi—stood on one foot! See further Abrahams 1917.

Torah for beginners'. His unqualified statement, elicited in the course of the encounter, suggests that, even if one observes the whole Law to perfection, one never transcends the Golden Rule in terms of moral practice.

When we turn to the Synoptic Gospels, we find that the rhetorical settings vary. The ministry of Jesus raises real problems of moral priorities. Controversy centres not on the proverbial Golden Rule (which is integrated with paraenesis) but on the role of the 'double commandment'. On it the whole of the law and the prophets depends (a rabbinic turn of phrase congenial to a Christian scribe like Matthew). To observe it is 'much more than all whole burnt offerings and sacrifices' (Mk 12.33); indeed, it is to 'inherit eternal life' (Lk. 10.25, 28). Whatever differences there may be in the rhetorical situations, the Synoptic context is always that of debate. Deliberative rhetoric explores issues and sharpens perception. One may therefore ask: if Commandment and Rule regularly occur in the New Testament in dialogue and controversy, should our understanding of Christian ethics and moral teaching reflect this interrogative and critical mood? Does advance in ethics presuppose a questioning of moral priorities and their application, an interrogation of moral traditions, and an appraisal of the situation which gives rise to the questioning? Moral discourse, in other words, entails not only rationality and commitment but also dialogue—the reaching out to the other (Bartley 1984: 163-65). And may this be done, at least on occasion, as part of Jewish–Christian dialogue?

II. *Community Context*

The Great Commandment and the Golden Rule were widely used in the Christian communities. In the Synoptic Gospels, the Commandment is consistently ascribed to Jesus but in contexts governed by the interests of the evangelists and the communities they represent. Mk 12.28-34, for example, provides a scholastic dialogue which highlights the priority of the Commandment as against cultic requirements and seems to emphasize the moral and rational understanding of acknowledging the one God. The pericope is taken to reflect the Hellenistic mission setting and therefore to preserve pre-Markan tradition (Bornkamm 1957: 85-92). It emphasizes a fundamental accord between Jesus's perception of the meaning of the Torah and at least certain radical Jewish understandings of it. But Matt. 22.34-40 reflects, if not controversy about the interpretation of the Torah, then at least the desire to test Jesus's soundness as a teacher in Israel. Here, the double commandment is taken as the interpretative key to the Torah, supplying—so Christian exegetes have held—'the decisive word about its *meaning*' (Furnish 1973: 34). Lk. 10.25-37, containing elements of controversy and dialogue as well as the parable of the Good Samaritan, seems to reflect a considerable degree of editorial recasting—a safer hypothesis than that prompted by the kind of historicism advocated by T.W. Manson among others, which would attempt to trace this peri-cope to a separate occasion in the ministry of Jesus and even to claim a certain priority for it. The editing, it should be noted, is carried out with consummate interpretative skill, which effects the transformation of casuistry into action and hermeneutical discussion into inescapable involvement. The very fractures in the narrative challenge the reader. The setting would appear to be the Hellenistic Christian mission, with its universalistic protest against exclusivism and against all national, religious and racial prejudice. But in spite of the differences in ethos and the community interests reflected in these Synoptic passages, there is also a strong sense of a tradition received and applied in the community's life and witness.

Contextual factors governing the use of the Golden Rule are less distinctive, although it plays an important interpretative role in relation to the more radical moral teaching ascribed to Jesus. In Lk. 6.27-28, a highly structured passage, it occupies a cardinal position (6.31), inter-preting the preceding themes of love to enemies, non-resistance and community of goods in terms of reciprocity, and it thereafter reinter-prets the principle of reciprocity in the light of divine forgiveness rather than conventional morality. This would seem to represent a major tradition of early Christian catechesis, based on the teaching of Jesus. Matt. 7.12 uses the Golden Rule to interpret another passage of traditional teaching (cf. Lk. 11.9-13), relating to responsive action at the human and divine level and connecting with biblical interpretation (as some rabbis might do). The Golden Rule is therefore used as an interpretative device in ethical and hermeneutical debate, bridging the cultural divide represented by Luke and Matthew. In using it thus, both evangelists doubtless intended to interpret the procedure of Jesus himself.

By contrast, the 'new' commandment in John—'that you love one another; even as I have loved you, that you also love one another' (13.34; cf. 15.12, 17)—presents a reinterpretation of the Great Commandment and Golden Rule themes in a predominantly community setting. The reinterpretation focuses on the reciprocal relationship between disciple and master, embracing both friendship and dominical command, and on the definitive, self-giving act of the master as example and motivation. Here we are clearly involved in the 'christological ethics' of the Johannine communities, where the concept of *agapē* is simultaneously universalized and constricted. On the one hand, there is magnificent portrayal of the divine self-giving and humility, of which the washing of the disciples' feet is the leading expression; and this includes a sublime statement of discipleship. On the other hand, this close community defines itself over against the world which spurns the divine self-giving, and particularly over against 'the Jews'. Such developments were doubtless prompted by the particular context in which the community found itself (Käsemann 1968: 59). Nevertheless, there is a real tension in this Gospel between the love of God which reaches out through the Son to the cosmos, and the community ethos which embodies the Great Commandment and the Golden Rule but also in some sense domesticates and restricts them. The community has to be reminded: 'Other sheep I have who are not of this fold...'

In view of the Johannine scene in particular, one may well reflect on whether a health warning should be attached to all community or sect-type ethics—whether relating to churches, families, small groups, schools and clubs, or to social and sacramental practices. This is not intended to be frivolous; for some advocate (with much justification) that the Christian ethos presupposes the ethics of *koinonia*. The ethical dilemma of the Johannine tradition should serve as a danger signal. It is imperative that Christian obedience should be expressed within community, but equally that it should not be bounded nor distorted by it. Distortions can easily spread from primary to secondary groupings and lead to the exploitation of religious teaching for racist or sectarian ends. Clearly, something more is needed than community ethics *simpliciter*. Indeed, the New Testament traditions of the Great Commandment and the Golden Rule may be read as a radical critique of inward-looking morality.

III. *Socio-Historical Tradition*

The suggestion made in the last paragraph would be extremely paradoxical if the Great Commandment and the Golden Rule were themselves community products, embodying the higher aspirations of the group or a cultural ideal. To what extent might this be the case?

Adumbrations of the Great Commandment are certainly to be found amid the diversity of ancient Judaism, though usually as summary statements or in gnomic settings. In the Judaism of the Diaspora, for example, Philo commends the wisdom of the synagogue by suggesting that the vast range of rules and principles finds unity in two main heads: duty to God expressed in piety and holiness, and duty to humanity expressed in philanthropy and justice. In the *Testaments of the Twelve Patriarchs*, whose origins and milieu are much discussed, *T. Dan.* 5.3 counsels, 'Love the Lord all your life, and one another with a true heart'. As in other passages in the *Testaments*, the literary setting is the gnomic or wisdom saying, although overtones of the prophetic tradition may be detected. Thus *T. Iss.* 5.2 urges, 'Love the Lord and your neighbour, and have compassion on the poor and weak' (cf. also 7.2-7). The exhortation to 'speak truth each one with his neighbour' (5.2) is a reflection of Zech. 8.16. *T. Benj.* 3.1-5 exhorts the faithful to love the Lord and keep his commandments, following Joseph's good example. In this context, most MSS read at 3.3: 'Fear the Lord and love your neighbour'. *T. Zeb.* 5.1 adds a distinctive touch: 'And now, my children, I bid you to keep the commands of the Lord, and to show mercy to your neighbours, and to have compassion towards all, not towards men only, but also towards beasts'—a welcome hint that the interpersonal may be extended to the ecological. In rabbinic literature, the *Sifre* on Deut. 32.29 says: 'Take upon you the yoke of the kingdom of heaven' (as one does when reciting the Shema), 'excel one another in standing in awe of heaven, and conduct yourselves one toward another in love'. All of these represent the substance of the two-fold commandment, but in general terms and without the sharp focus found in the Gospels. While the Great Commandment is in tune with the spirituality of the Hellenistic Jewish age, the case for suggesting that it is purely a community product—that is, that it was generated in form and substance within the Jewish faith communities—is not strong. It remains true, as has often been remarked, that nowhere do we find Deut. 6.5 and

Lev. 19.18 coupled together precisely in the manner in which the Synoptic Gospels present them.

If the immediate socio-historical context does not provide the stimulus for the treatment of the Great Commandment ascribed to Jesus, a clue may be found in the scriptural orientation of the Gospel passages and in their sense of continuity with the prophetic tradition. Thus Mark cites the Shema, the basic confession of Israel (Deut. 6.4), as a preface to the commandment in Deut. 6.5 which specifies the response of the true Israelite to Yahweh. This response is total and involves not only what we might call today 'the whole person' but also all one's material resources or substance ('might'). It must be lived out in society, hence the appositeness of linking Deut. 6.5 with Lev. 19.18. To love your neighbour means not taking vengeance nor bearing grudges 'against the sons of your own people'—not hating but reasoning with your neighbour (19.17). It means making provision for the poor and the sojourner (19.10), dealing honourably with your employees (19.13), acting positively towards the disabled (19.14), safeguarding justice in the community (19.15), and refusing to discriminate against the stranger in your midst. 'The stranger who sojourns with you shall be to you as the native among you, and you shall love him as yourself' (19.34). If we care to reflect on events in Europe today (for example), the importance of this commandment cannot be underestimated. In short, neighbour love is grounded in the total life of the people. It ranges over their world—albeit a relatively static world in which only the occasional stranger comes to live in their midst. It does not, however, relate simply to individual or interpersonal ethics, important as that may be, but has a social, political and economic aspect. The refrain 'I am the Lord' emphasizes the divine command and the rootedness of this ethic in the divine purpose. It is into this realm of discourse that Jesus inducts his hearers, rather than into the commonplaces of Hellenistic Jewish morality and piety.

A real priority was thus given to love to God and neighbour in the Holiness Code in Leviticus. When imbalance or distortion occurred in Israel's practice, the prophets were constrained to reaffirm this priority over against false values, such as cultic punctiliousness divorced from moral obedience. It is interesting that the scribe in the Markan account expressly affirms that to observe the two-fold commandment 'is much more than whole burnt offerings and sacrifices' (12.33), and the two in the parable who failed to carry out their primary moral duty were the priest and the Levite (Lk. 10.31-32). When confusion abounded, the prophets were forced to raise the radical question, 'What does the Lord require of you?' and to answer: 'to act justly, to love mercy, and to walk humbly with your God' (Mic. 6.8). The question of the Great Commandment—like the question about eternal life—is radicalized when answered in terms of real priorities in interpreting the will of God. Love to God and neighbour—like righteousness, mercy and humility in God's sight—becomes the criterion of all right interpretation and practice. The Synoptic Gospels relate Jesus to this prophetic tradition, not least when they depict him in controversy with conventional piety and wisdom and requiring a higher righteousness.

If we turn now to the Golden Rule, we find something akin to a universal moral perception reflected both in cross-cultural developments and in cultural parallelism.

The Greek tradition from Homer onwards provides examples of most forms of the Golden Rule, presupposing the notions of fairness, mutuality and empathy. Mutuality may be an ambivalent moral concept. Xerxes was not Greek, but when he said that honour demands that we avenge ourselves for what has been done to us, he would have found few to disagree. As Plato put it in the Republic: 'What about enemies? Are we to render whatever is their due to them?' 'Yes, certainly what really is due to them; which means, I suppose, what is appropriate to an enemy—some sort of injury' (*Rep.* 1332E). This version of proportionate justice does not rule out magnanimity, but the notion that one should requite good with good and evil with evil occurs not infrequently in Plato's dialogues, in the orators and rhetoricians, and in a number of Latin writers. Isocrates, however, can personalize the positive Rule within his group of pupils: 'You should conduct yourselves in your dealings with others as you expect me to do in my dealings with you'. Here the teacher embodies the Rule and provides the model. At other times he states the Rule more generally: 'Do not do to others that which angers you when they do it to you'. Speaking in idealistic fashion of the leaders of Greece, he repeats the note of magnanimity: they thought it their duty 'to feel toward the weaker as they expected the stronger to feel towards themselves'.[4] The Golden Rule, however, is little more than popular, gnomic wisdom. As such it is used by orators in speeches and exercises, by

4. Isocrates anticipates the Golden Rule at several points: cf. *To Nicocles* 49.61; *To Demonicus* 14, *Panegyricus* 81.

philosophers in dialogue, and by politicians commending their policies.

Israel developed the notion of reciprocity in a distinctive way. A prime area in which it found expression was that of punishment.

'He who kills a man shall himself be put to death' (Lev. 24.17).
'When a man causes a disfigurement in his neighbour, as he has done it shall be done to him, fracture for fracture, eye for eye, tooth for tooth; as he has disfigured a man, he shall be disfigured' (Lev. 24.19-20).

Primitive though the *lex talionis* may be, it is a clear advance on tribal vengeance in its recognition that the punishment should fit, but not exceed, the crime, and in its implied principle of proportionate compensation. At the level of the interaction of individual and society, the notion of mutuality is encompassed by that of justice, and there are paeans of praise for the just person. Mutuality, however, presupposes a basic equality between the partners. What happens in relation to the weak and the dependent? The whole notion of justice in the Hebrew tradition becomes creative precisely when it is set in the context of Yahweh's generous dealings with his people. This strikes a note of superabundance which imparts not only an element of generosity but also of imaginative empathy into one's dealings with others, especially those in a dependent position. 'You shall remember that you were a servant in the land of Egypt, and the Lord your God brought you out thence with a mighty hand and an outstretched arm' (Deut. 5.15). The just are therefore merciful and compassionate, not vengeful nor oppressive. There is no need for surprise, therefore, that the Golden Rule was not native to Israel; Israel had its own way of expressing and even transcending its requirements.

The Golden Rule was naturalized in Jewish teaching during the Hellenistic period. The Letter of Aristeas adumbrates the positive form, and Tobit the negative: 'what you hate, do not do to anyone' (4.15). Sirach 31.15 evokes the imaginative empathy that the Golden Rule implies: 'Judge your neighbour's feelings by your own, and in every matter be thoughtful'. Philo, of course, is happy to use it, and its occurrence in the rabbinic tradition has already been noted.

In the Synoptic Gospels, the striking characteristic of the use of the Golden Rule in the Gospels is its interpretative role. In Matthew, it is used in a highly relational context which presupposes imagination and empathy. Imagine a father responding to his son's request for bread. Even fallible human beings know how to give abundant gifts to their children. When we think of God as Father, we recognize that his gifts are superabundant; therefore, ask, seek, knock—and reflect the divine generosity by putting the Golden Rule into practice. Matthew has in fact related the Golden Rule to God and neighbour. With a scribal flourish, he adds, 'for this is the law and the prophets'.

Luke's treatment of it is even more striking. Far from being the detached saying that some suggest, it is in fact the interpretive hinge in Lk. 6.27-36. On the one hand, it interprets the themes of love to enemy, non-retaliation and sharing of resources; reflecting as they do the Levitical neighbour-love, these themes also represent what we may call the elevated Golden Rule. On the other hand, it connects with a passage that demonstrates that when the Golden Rule is understood merely as reciprocation in kind, it is unworthy of the God who in his mercy is generous to the ungrateful and the selfish. The divine factor is the means of elevating the discourse.

Two reasons can be given for the propriety of conjoining the Great Commandment and the Golden Rule. One is their suitability for interpreting the divine action, whether in terms of command or of generosity of spirit; and the invoking of the divine action transforms and elevates human conduct. The second deserves special note. We have spoken of the imaginative empathy implied by the Golden Rule. The Great Commandment speaks of 'loving your neighbour as yourself'. What does 'as yourself' imply? Not 'self-love', as is sometimes suggested. Rather, it means 'act as if you were in the other's position'—that is, the victim at the receiving end of the transaction. Act as if you were the poor man scraping at the gleanings of the harvest. Here we return to the imaginative empathy that links neighbour-love so directly to the Golden Rule tradition.

IV. *The Complementarity of Divine Revelation and Human Awareness*

Questions abound. Does the concern with the divine, the God-talk in the ethics of the New Testament, detract from the autonomy of Christian ethics or enhance its validity? Does the popular Greek origin of the Golden Rule render it a weak partner to the Great Commandment in the priority area of New Testament ethics? Or does its cross-cultural nature add a further dimension to it? Three responses may be made in brief.

1. *Interpreting God and Discerning Moral Value*

In the above discussion we have tended to accept the Gospel claims that Jesus himself prioritized Commandment and Rule in the interpretation of Torah and in moral teaching. By the conventional criteria of *Leben-Jesu* research—coherence, multiple attestation, differentiation, contextuality, and the like—the case is reasonably cogent. However, a qualification is perhaps in order. The tradition of the Great Commandment comes to us in remarkably fluid form. It contains two constant elements: the citation of Deut. 6.5 and Lev. 19.18, and their priority for interpreting the Torah. All other elements—including the precise form of Deut. 6.5—are variable. This perhaps reflects the element of debate, whether in the milieu of Jesus or the first Christian communities. As research brings us closer to the historical Jesus, we discern not so much the *ipsissima verba* (in fact, scriptural quotation predominates) but Jesus' involvement in a hermeneutical process which gives specific direction to his moral teaching. His use of the Golden Rule is similarly directed. In itself, it is a commonplace. In Jesus's hands, it is a hermeneutical tool. To read this tradition is to be invited to join in the interpretative process and in moral discernment.

If time and space permitted, it would be possible to follow out this line in relation to parabolic teaching (as Luke does) or to the theme of the Kingdom of God (as Mark does). Instead, we shall consider a fundamental question about Jesus and ethics. There is a longstanding theological debate about whether something is right because God wills it or whether God wills it because it is right. Let us rephrase this in relation to Jesus and ourselves. Do we believe that something is right because Jesus commands it, or does Jesus command it because it is right?

It is evident that, in the tradition in which Jesus stood, to enquire about moral value was to enquire about the will of God. The God of Israel was righteous and merciful—and never morally capricious. 'Shall not the Judge of all the earth do right?' (Gen. 18.25). To interpret the Scripture is therefore to seek moral discernment. But moral discernment is also part of human experience; the parables and images Jesus used, as well as the Golden Rule, provide ample testimony. In combining Commandment and Rule, Jesus in effect recognized both streams of moral awareness and presented a highly persuasive understanding of moral reality.

2. *Theological Understanding*

The theoretical difficulty that arises in relation to the Great Commandment pertains to the language of command. Assuming that 'love' (*agapē*) has at least some emotional content, how can one be commanded to love? Emotions can only be evoked, not commanded. C.H. Dodd and others attempted to circumvent the difficulty by emphasizing the conative rather than the affective aspect: agapeistic love is a matter of the will! But no solution along these lines is possible, since love clearly involves 'the whole person'; and the emotions must be given a place alongside the cognitive and conative. The context in which the language of divine command occurs—predominantly that of covenant—points towards an answer. God both commands and evokes. The narrative of his relation to Israel (and the cosmos) provides the setting in which his will is known. In theological language, law operates only in the context of grace.[5]

The Golden Rule has fared less well at the hands of commentators. Bultmann observed that the saying in itself 'gives moral expression to a naive egoism' (Bultmann 1968: 103), and Tillich described it as projecting a 'calculating justice' which stands in need of transformation (Tillich 1955: 32). These negative comments, however, are no more than general reflection on a legalistic view of mutuality or equivalence. As is well known, this kind of logic can prompt the worst kind of committee manipulation: 'I'll scratch your back if you scratch mine!' Or we can imagine what the Rule might mean in the hands of a masochist! All this, however, represents non-contextual comment, for Matthew and Luke are concerned to specify clearly that it is the elevated Golden Rule that is to be used: clearly distinguished from the ways of the Gentiles and transformed by the operation of grace. Thus Paul Ricoeur speaks of the polarity between the logic of equivalence, which operates in everyday ethics, and the 'logic of superabundance' which characterizes 'the economy of gift' that is basic to the religious perspective on ethics (Ricoeur 1990: 392-97).

The ethics of the New Testament is oriented to two poles. One is the moral and historical experience of humankind, which transcends national and religious boundaries and is expressed *par excellence* in the Rule. Here if anywhere a concept of natural law operates in New Testament ethics. Moral perception springs from the relational and social nature of human existence, which presupposes the fundamental

5. Cf. Fairweather and McDonald 1984: 82-86.

necessity for fairness or equivalence and reciprocity in human interaction. New Testament ethics must remain true to this holistic view of
moral reality. At the same time, universal moral perceptions are
prone to manipulation and debasement at the hands of sinful humanity,
and human beings require to be moved to a love of action which transcends measured equivalence. The second pole now comes into play:
the notion of grace or gift, which elevates and transforms human perceptions of mutuality and thus the Rule itself. If loving God and
neighbour is the way to eternal life, it is because it presupposes such
responsiveness to grace, such acceptance of the logic of superabundance, as to make such love possible.[6]

3. *Sharing Religious and Moral Insight*
The Great Commandment and the Golden Rule present opportunity
for sharing insight. If the latter opens up the possibility of making
connections with at least the popular moral teaching of the ancient
world, the former invites dialogue between Christian and Jew.
Dialogue of this kind is as important as it is difficult. As Hilton and
Marshall make clear, both sides may have to abandon cherished positions: Christians must give some ground on the alleged uniqueness of
Jesus' teaching and Jews about the extent of his indebtedness to
rabbinic sources. As a Jewish teacher, Jesus both affirmed Jewish
religious and moral understanding and afforded surprising insights
into it. 'In the past much debate between Jews and Christians has
centred on each trying to prove to the other that their side came up
with better ideas first: that their side embraces wider ethical principles' (Hilton and Marshall 1988: 36). All such posturing requires
deconstruction. If self-knowledge is a precondition of dialogue, the
sharing of insights into a common tradition is the way forward in
understanding. Today we are challenged not merely to rise above
tendentious apologetics but also to go beyond the shibboleth of
'objectivity'—not least when studying and sharing moral understanding. To discuss ethics is to reach out to moral truth, to participate
in the quest for what is right. The spirit of the Golden Rule prompts
us to the deepest possible respect for our partners in dialogue. The

---

6.   Attempts have often been made to relate this kind of New Testament discourse to Kant's categorical imperative—cf. Manson 1931: 307. It is important, however, not to subordinate the ethics of the New Testament to such a totally cognitive
realm of discourse nor to employ wholly western assumptions in interpretation.

Great Commandment bids us respond to divine gift in loving acceptance of our fellow human beings.

BIBLIOGRAPHY

Abrahams, I.

1917   'The Greatest Commandment', *Studies in Pharisaism and the Gospels* (First Series; Cambridge: Cambridge University Press).

Bartley, W.W. III

1984   *The Retreat to Commitment* (La Salle; London: Open Court Publishing Company).

Bornkamm, G.

1957   'Das Dopplegebot der Liebe', *Neutestamentliche Studien für Rudolf Bultmann* (BZNW, 21; Berlin: Töpelmann, 2nd edn).

Bultmann, R.

1968   *History of the Synoptic Tradition* (Oxford: Basil Blackwell, 2nd edn).

Dihle, A.

1962   *Die Goldene Regel* (Göttingen: Vandenhoeck & Ruprecht).

Fairweather, I.C.M., and J.I.H. McDonald

1984   *The Quest of Christian Ethics* (Edinburgh: Handsel).

Furnish, V.P.

1973   *The Love Command in the New Testament* (London: SCM Press).

Hilton, M., and G. Marshall

1988   *The Gospels and Rabbinic Judaism* (London: SCM Press).

Käsemann, E.

1968   *The Testament of Jesus* (London: SCM Press).

Manson, T.W.

1931   *The Teaching of Jesus* (Cambridge: Cambridge University Press).

Ricoeur, P.

1990   'The Golden Rule: Exegetical and Theological Perplexities', *NTS* 36: 392-97.

Tillich, P.

1955   'The Golden Rule', *The New Being* (New York: Scribner's).

OLD AND NEW COVENANT (TESTAMENT):
A TERMINOLOGICAL ENQUIRY

W. McKane

The first use of the term ἡ παλαιὰ διαθήκη is made by Paul in the middle of the first century (2 Cor. 3.14). Its equivalent (הברית העתיקה) does not occur in the Hebrew Bible and ἡ παλαιὰ διαθήκη is not a Septuagintal usage. 2 Cor. 3.14 is made particularly significant by the fact that Paul is using ἡ παλαιὰ διαθήκη of a collection of books, alleging that when the Jews read them they lack discernment and do not fathom their profundity, from which their minds are veiled (ἡμέρας τὸ αὐτὸ κάλυμμα ἐπὶ τῇ ἀναγνώσει τῆς παλαιᾶς διαθήκης). Hence Paul is making the claim that the books to which he refers are Christian scriptures and he is charging the Jews with misinterpreting them. In the era of critical biblical scholarship his bulldozing exegetical methods will not pick up much support, but in the context of the first century they are understandable.

The Church's first Bible was the Septuagint and it was appropriated as Christian scripture, demanding Christian exegesis. It may be that Paul is not alluding to the entire collection of books in the Septuagint, but, more particularly, to the Torah and Haftarah of the regular synagogue readings. It should be borne in mind, in this connection, that doubt has been cast on whether the Jews ever advanced to any canonical definition of the books of the Septuagint and, if this is so, the determination of an authorized collection of Greek books would be Christian and subsequent to the appropriation of the Septuagint by the church.[1]

Whatever be the canonical scope of Paul's use of ἡ παλαιὰ διαθήκη, it is the first use of the term and inserts it into a context different from the theological one in which it is frequently used in the early literature of the Church. It may be mentioned incidentally that

1. McKane 1988: 12.

the Church valued those books which, though not part of the canon of the Hebrew Bible, were included in the Septuagintal collection of books. That Origen took pains to find a common scriptural basis for his dialogue with the Jews did not deter him from using such books for Christian edification.[2]

The point has been made by Grant[3] that for as long as the Church was predominantly Jewish in character and Jerusalem remained its heartland there was not great pressure to advance those books which had been generated by the Church to the status of scripture, the Septuagint being regarded as an entirely adequate scriptural basis. It is striking, however, that, given the Jerusalem *locus* and the Jewishness of earliest Christianity, that it was the Septuagint and not the Hebrew Bible which was taken over as Christian scripture. It should perhaps be supposed that Greek-speaking Jews, who had returned to Jerusalem from the diaspora, played a prominent part in the founding of the Church and that Greek-speaking synagogues were the institutions out of which they emerged as the first Christians. This is not a problem which will be pursued on the present occasion.[4]

Grant[5] has remarked that once the Christian Church broke out of Jerusalem into the Hellenistic world more interest and attention were directed to those books which had been generated by Christianity and that some doubt arose whether the Septuagint was an adequate foundation for Christian theology. This is illustrated by the attitudes of Polycarp at Smyrna and Ignatius at Antioch early in the second century, though both stay with the assumption that the Septuagint only is the Church's scripture. Powerful influences are abroad in this historical context and they do not all pull in the same direction. The demands of Jewish–Christian dialogue counsel against the damaging of the common scriptural foundation from which the dialogue sets out; yet there are some doubts whether the Church's case can be made out without an appeal to its own books. On the other hand, the challenge issued by Gnosticism early in the second century and its rejection of the Septuagint (the theological reasons for this need not be entered into) presented a challenge to the Church over its scriptures and their genuine contents. The intention to repulse this can be discerned, for

2.   Wiles 1970: 455-56.
3.   Grant 1970: 284-91.
4.   McKane 1988: 17-19.
5.   Grant 1970: 292-93.

example, in Clement of Alexandria and Dionysius the Areopagite. Clement[6] urges that the Holy Spirit which is active in the Church is the same in substance and energy as the Spirit which informed the Old Covenant (κατὰ τὴν παλαιὰν διαθήκην). This is not a reference to a collection of books; it appears in the context of an affirmation that the Old and New dispensations are not to be severed from each other and that the God of the old is the God of the new. Similarly Dionysius's reference[7] to ἀρχαιότεραν παράδοσιν is part of his counter-blast against the Gnostics. The New Covenant (ἡ καινὴ διαθήκη), along with ἀρχαιότεραν παράδοσιν is a witness to the one God and the moving of one and the same Spirit can be discerned in both of them (ὡς ὑφ' ἑνὸς...πνεύματος κεκινημένην).

Basilides, an Alexandrian Gnostic of the first half of the second century, whose teaching has been preserved by Hippolytus at Rome in the third century, had begun to accord the status of scripture to the Church's books, as is shown in his prefixing of γέγραπται or ὡς γέγραπται to comments on 1–2 Corinthians, Romans and Ephesians[8] or (less certainly) by introducing his exegesis to Matthew, Luke and John with the introductory formula, 'This is what the Gospels mean when they say'.[9] At Rome also, in the first half of the second century, Marcion not only defined a canon of the Church's own books consisting of ten Pauline epistles (minus Hebrews and the Pastorals) and a revised Gospel of Luke, but he engaged in higher literary criticism in order to separate the parts of those books which he deemed genuine from those which he judged spurious. According to his lights, it was a question of separating the wheat from the chaff. Among the orthodox, towards the end of the second century, Theophilus of Antioch approximated one of the Church's books (the Gospel of John) to scripture: John and his book are associated with the holy scriptures and he is described as an 'inspired man'.[10]

The developments within Gnosticism tending towards a canon of the Church's own books were liable to create the impression that they had seized the initiative and that the Church was sitting on its hands. Hence there was pressure from this quarter for it to think more seriously

6. *PG*, IX (1857), 672B.
7. *PG*, III (1889), 432B.
8. Grant 1970: 293.
9. Grant 1970: 292-93.
10. Grant 1970: 294.

about the status of its own books, lest it might appear to be too indifferent or passive in the face of what was becoming a big issue and leave heretics to make all the running in the formulation of a canon. The problem had become one involving textual detail and higher criticism, because it was not just a question of which books should be judged authoritative but what their text should be and so which of their contents were genuine.

A countervailing consideration was the need to keep a level playing-field for dialogue with the Jews and this necessitated a common scriptural basis from which to begin the debate—and so the firm retention of the Septuagint as the Church's scripture. In his second dialogue with Trypho[11] in the fifties of the second century, Justin Martyr, in Rome, illustrates the importance attached to the New Covenant or New Testament in the articulation of his theology. Here, and this obtains often in early Christian literature, ἡ καινὴ διαθήκη is not used of a collection of books and it has no bearing on the definition of a canon. Justin is fully persuaded that ברית חדשה of Jer. 31.31 (καινὴ διαθήκη) is his ace-card and that when he produces it he makes an unbeatable rejoinder to Trypho who is represented as admitting defeat very tamely. It is a victory which is made to appear too utterly comprehensive to be convincing, but the principal interest of the dialogue in the present connection is the context which ἡ καινὴ διαθήκη fills within the polemic. Justin does not appeal to the elaborate priestly exegesis of Jer. 31.31-34 in the epistle to the Hebrews (he may not have had Hebrews). The writer to the Hebrews does not use the term ἡ παλαιὰ διαθήκη, but he refers to the 'first covenant' (ἡ πρώτη διαθήκη) as παλαιά and he asserts that ἡ καινὴ διαθήκη has made the first one obsolescent (πεπαίλωκε τὴν πρώτην). Hence ἡ πρώτη διαθήκη is the equivalent of הברית (Jer. 31.31) which the Israelites are said to have broken or abrogated[12] when Yahweh took them by the hand to lead them out of Egypt, and Justin describes the Law at Horeb as παλαιός. That Justin does not use Hebrews and makes Jer. 31.31-34 the foundation of his case may be accounted for by the exigencies of Jewish–Christian dialogue and may reflect the need to begin the argument from commonly accepted scripture. If Hebrews originated in Alexandria at the beginning of the second century, its use would be a possibility, but Justin provides no evidence that he was

11. *PG*, VI (1884), 498-500; Falls 1948: 164.
12. Cf. Nicholson 1986: 183-84.

acquainted with the Pauline epistles and he may not have had Hebrews to supply him with a full-scale Christian exegesis of Jer. 31.31-34.

Justin's use of ἡ καινὴ διαθήκη is principally related to Jer. 31.31 and there are examples of this phrase in the same context (Heb. 8.8 cited from Jer. 31.31; διαθήκης νέας at Hebrews 12.24; καινήν *sc.* διαθήκην at 8.13) and at 1 Cor. 11.25, in a not dissimilar setting, with reference to the Lord's Supper. καινή is a minus in the shorter Greek text of Matt. 26.28 and Mk 14.24,[13] but it was contained in the text which circulated in the early church.[14] The theological area tenanted by Justin is one that is well represented in early Christian literature and ἡ καινὴ διαθήκη in relation to the institution of the Lord's Supper is a special instance of it. Essentially, he is comparing the New Covenant instituted by Christ and his mediation of it through his death with the Mosaic covenant at Horeb/Sinai. He is setting up an antithesis between Moses and Christ, the Law[15] and the Gospel, and he is identifying the ברית חדשה of Jer. 31.31 with the Gospel. In connection with Christ's death the sense 'testament' for διαθήκη as in 'last will and testament' is emphasized with the intention of establishing that his death was necessary in order to put the covenant into effect.

Justin holds with the writer to the Hebrews that the Sinai covenant is obsolescent (πεπαίλωκε τὴν πρώτην, Heb. 8.13) and his term for Sinai/Horeb is ὁ παλαιὸς νόμος. His exegesis of Jer. 31.31-34 requires a Christian redirection of the sense of the Hebrew passage, where the thought of a covenant which is obsolete and has been transcended is not the main feature. A more positive view of the covenant

13. Aland 1966: 102-103, 184; Metzger 1971: 64.

14. τοῦτο μού ἐστι τὸ αἷμα τὸ τῆς καινῆς διαθήκης. Cf. Lampe 1961: 348, διαθήκη ii.3; cf. Metzger 1971: 173-77.

15. ἐν τῇ παλαιᾷ διαθήκῃ νομοθετεῖ (Clement of Alexandria, *PG*, VIII [1857], 1160a). There was an interest in fixing the end of the old dispensation and the beginning of the new, and the ministry of John the Baptist was thought to mark the end of the old period: ἐπὶ τέλει τῆς παλαιᾶς γενομένης διαθήκης, Origen, *PG*, XIV (1862), 172C. According to Cosmas, a later Alexandrian, John the Baptist was in the middle between the old and new covenants (*PG*, LXXXVIII [1864], 277A). *Disputationes Photini Manichaei cum Paulo Christiani* (*Disp. Phot.*) asserts that Christ existed in the period of the old covenant and practised it until his baptism: μέχρι τοῦ βαπτίσματος ὁ χριστὸς ἐν τῷ τῆς παλαιᾶς διαθήκης καιρῷ ὑπάρχων, τὰ τῆς παλαιᾶς ἔπραττεν (*PG*, LXXXVIII [1864], 549D).

at Sinai/Horeb is taken by Irenaeus[16] and John Chrysostom.[17] It had a beneficial function in disciplining those to whom it was first addressed and it prefigures the Church. John Chrysostom's comment is that the παιδαγωγία (elementary education) of ἡ παλαιὰ δωθήκη is like milk which nourishes infants (γαλακτοτροφία), whereas the philosophy τῆς καινῆς διαθήκης is like strong meat. With this should be compared Origen's juxtaposition[18] of οἱ εἰσαγωγικοί, 'the introductory sayings', which he couples with τὰ παλαιὰ λόγια, and words of an advanced mystical kind or sayings of the new covenant (οἱ τῆς νέας διαθήκης). A breakfast can be made of the former (ἄριστον), but the latter are fare for dinner (δείπνου).

Certainly Jer. 31.31 mentions a new covenant (ברית חדשה) but the antithesis with Sinai/Horeb (some scholars think it is with Deuteronomy, though this is not so *prima facie*) is constructed out of its pure inwardness over against the Law chiselled on tablets of stone. There are those who argue that the Law written on the heart is without detriment to the one incised on stone. Yet there is a profound difficulty, which need not be gone into here, in reconciling the concept of a Law written on the heart with one which is objectively defined and, in the circumstances, seems to be made redundant. The employment of ἡ παλαιὰ διαθήκη or ὁ παλαιὸς νόμος which we have been discussing is a quite distinct context from 2 Cor. 3.14. It has nothing to do with a collection of books, whether the Septuagint or part of it, and it arises secondarily to provide an antithesis for ἡ καινὴ διαθήκη. This kind of triggering or generation of ἡ παλαιὰ διαθήκη or the like is a common *Sitz* of the terminology in early Christian literature.[19] The Mosaic covenant or any covenant preceding ברית חדשה is never termed ברית עתיקה or the like in the Hebrew Bible nor ἡ παλαιὰ διαθήκη in the Septuagint.

Origen in Alexandria, later in the first century, showed the same concern as Justin Martyr for a level playing field, a common basis in scripture, for his dialogue with the Jews. He became acutely aware that after all this was not supplied by the Septuagint, most of whose books had been translated from the Hebrew Bible, knowledge of which was an essential condition of exegetical parity with the Jews. It

16. *PG*, LXXI (1882), 1071B.
17. *PG*, LI (1862), 284.
18. Lampe 1961: 348, διαθήκη 3b.
19. Lampe 1961: 348, διαθήκη ii.3.

was, at least, partly to achieve this end that Origen constructed his Hexapla which was a roundabout way of getting at the Hebrew text through the first-century translations made by Jews (Aquila and Theodotion) which were woodenly literal. The traditional wisdom is that Origen's Hebrew was scrappy and that he supplemented it with Aquila and Theodotion (along with another Greek translation, Symmachus, in his sixth column) to enable him to obtain the knowledge of the Hebrew Bible which he judged necessary for Jewish–Christian dialogue. A French scholar has argued that he did not know any Hebrew and that his use of Aquila and Theodotion was a device for giving him a kind of access to it, a second-best substitute for direct engagement with the Hebrew text.[20] If this were so, the first and second columns of the Hexapla, the Hebrew text and its transcription into Greek letters, do not operate functionally within Origen's design and are a kind of window-dressing, an affectation of erudition.

Origen's work in the Hexapla is interesting because it betrays an awareness that the Septuagint was not an entirely adequate Bible with which to confront the Jews and it is the first, somewhat convoluted, attempt on the part of the Church to appropriate the Hebrew Bible. It may be viewed as the acquisition of a new Greek Bible providing, unlike the Septuagint, a literal translation of the Hebrew, the translation not being newly supplied but extracted from translations done by Jews. Origen was thus enabled to judge more discerningly how Jewish exegesis of the Hebrew Bible was conducted, because these translations were models on which Jewish exegesis was founded. From another angle the Hexapla may be seen as the beginning of the process that culminated in Jerome's translation of the Hebrew Bible into Latin, so that the Vulgate is the terminus. The Church could not forever remain satisfied with a translation of the Hebrew as its Bible. It was essential that is should make direct acquaintance with it and for this Hebrew studies were necessary.

On the narrower terminological front, to which a final return may be made, the questions that were raised concern the use in the early Church's literature, of ἡ παλαιὰ διαθήκη and ἡ καινὴ διαθήκη as nomenclature for collections of books, the Septuagint and the Church's own books respectively. The indications are that this is established for the third century at the latest, though the definition of

20. McKane 1988: 22-31.

the 'New Testament' canon continued to be fluid. Grant[21] remarks that by the end of the second century Christians generally made use of a collection of 'New Testament' books containing most of those in use today, but he notices that Irenaeus gives no evidence of having had James, Jude, 2 Peter and 3 John. With the exception of Jude these books are not attested in the writings of Clement of Alexandria. The use of a collection of books recognized by the Church as authoritative does not determine the constituents of that list and differences remained in the fourth and fifth centuries. Where ἡ παλαιὰ διαθήκη refers to a collection of books, these are the Septuagint or part of it, but the definition of the Hebrew canon, usually connected with the Council of Jamnia towards the end of the first century, had gone ahead and may have exerted some influence on the Church. Yet it is still a far cry to Jerome. The passages that are relevant in these connections are the following: ὡς τῆς τε διαθήκης τῆς παλαιᾶς καὶ τῆς νέας …ὡς τῆς φιλοσοφίας. There is some doubt whether Clement of Alexandria[22] is referring to a collection of books or whether he is juxtaposing Old and New Dispensations, Law and Gospel, Moses and Christ, in the manner already indicated. Another example[23] (ἡ γράφη ἐκ τῆς παλαιᾶς ἤρτηται) is more clear-cut and almost certainly refers to the Septuagint. A similar context is established by Melito of Sardis[24] for ἡ παλαιὰ διαθήκη (τὰ τῆς παλαιᾶς διαθήκης βιβλία) and, in the fourth century, τῆς νέας καὶ καινῆς διαθήκης (Eusebius)[25] falls into the same classification. There is also Origen's πεπιστευμένων…θείων γράφων τῆς τε λεγομένης παλαιᾶς διαθήκης καὶ τῆς καλουμένης καινῆς, which is plain-sailing.[26] The pronouncement of the later Canon of Laodicaea (canon 59) is a more correct canonical definition of authoritative books.[27]

The conclusion is that ἡ παλαιὰ διαθήκη or an equivalence of it (הברית העתיקה) does not occur in the Septuagint or the Hebrew Bible and that the coinage ἡ παλαιὰ διαθήκη, used of the Septuagint or

21. Grant 1970: 295.
22. *PG*, VIII (1857), 717D.
23. *PG*, VIII (1857), 1345A.
24. *PG*, V (1894), 1216A.
25. *PG*, XXIV (1857), 920B.
26. *PG*, XI (1857), 341C.
27. Lampe 1961: 348, διαθήκη, 3: τὰ κανονικὰ τῆς καινῆς καὶ παλαιᾶς διαθήκης.

part of it, can be traced to Paul in the middle of the first century. It is taken up in the literature of the Church and is associated with ἡ καινὴ διαθήκη, this name having been given to the collection of the Church's own books. These had been consolidated into a canon and had been accorded the authority of ἡ καινὴ διαθήκη, but this canon, though its core was firm and well acknowledged, continued to be a source of contention around its edges. The equivalent of ἡ καινὴ διαθήκη appears in the Hebrew Bible (Jer. 31.31), but it is not an allusion to books and the same holds for 1 Cor. 11.25. Hence there is no scriptural prototype for ἡ καινὴ διαθήκη or ἡ νέα διαθήκη, used as nomenclature for a collection of authorized or canonical books, and the coinage, which is that of the Church, emerges secondarily as a supplementation of ἡ παλαιὰ διαθήκη (in the sense of 2 Cor. 3.14) to refer to the books which the Church had generated.

It is a privilege to pay homage to Professor George Anderson and to celebrate the classical and Semitic learning with which he has adorned his *alma mater*.

BIBLIOGRAPHY

Aland, K., *et al.*
1966   *The Greek New Testament* (London: United Bible Societies).
Falls, T.B.
1948   *Saint Justin Martyr* (Washington).
Grant, R.M.
1970   'The New Testament Canon', *CHB*, I, 284-308.
Lampe, G.W.H.
1961   *A Patristic Greek Lexicon* (Oxford).
McKane, W.
1988   *Selected Christian Hebraists* (Cambridge).
Metzger, B.M.
1971   *A Textual Commentary on the Greek New Testament* (London: United Bible Societies).
Migne, J. (ed.)
1857   *Patrologia Graeca*, 9.
Nicholson, E.W.
1986   *God and his People: Covenant and Theology in the Old Testament* (Oxford).
Wiles, M.F.
1970   'Origen as a Biblical Scholar', *CHB*, I, 489-510.

A NEW PROPHETIC MESSAGE FROM ALEPPO
AND ITS BIBLICAL COUNTERPARTS[*]

A. Malamat

J.-M. Durand recently published an intriguing document from Mari (A. 1968), namely, a letter by Nur-Sin, Mari's ambassador to Aleppo, to his lord Zimri-Lim (Durand 1993).[1] The letter contains a relatively lengthy prophecy by Abiya, a prophet, designated the 'respondent' or 'answerer' (*āpilum*) (Malamat 1989: 86-87; Charpin 1992a: 21-22) for the God Adad (or Addu), the great deity of Aleppo (Klengel 1965). Thus we have here a Western prophecy, but what is 'Amorite' about it is difficult to say.

The prophet utters the words of his deity concerning the rulers of Mari, past and present, who were more or less dependent on the kingdom of Aleppo. I shall present here the entire prophecy, and divide it into sections which seem to have no organic connection.

A. First, similar to *ARMT* I 3, in the famous letter of Yasmah-Adad to a deity, the fortunes of the individual Mari rulers are outlined (Charpin and Durand 1985: 297-98, 339-42). There, as in the present prophecy, Yahdun-Lim, the first king of Mari, was granted 'all the countries' by the deity, but was then accused of abandoning the god and consequently was rejected by him. Yahdun-Lim's country was taken away and given to Šamši-Adad, the major king of the rival Amorite dynasty, which established itself in Assyria. But the same harsh fate as Yahdun-Lim's now befell his successor Šamši-Adad. In

[*] This is the sixth instalment on the theme of 'New Mari Prophecies and the Bible'. The previous ones were published in Malamat 1989b, *idem* 1991a, *idem* 1991b. These studies and the present one were prepared within the framework of a grant from the Fund for Basic Research administered by the Israel Academy of Sciences and Humanities.

1. I thank Professor J.-M. Durand for his kindness in supplying me with a galley of his article prior to its publication in *MARI* 7. D. Charpin cites *en passant* this document in a recent paper (Charpin 1992b: 3, 6, 10). Professor P. Artzi kindly read a draft of my paper and commented on it.

the following lacuna in the tablet the name was surely mentioned of King Zimri-Lim, who drove the Šamši-Adad dynasty out of Mari and reigned as the last king of Mari. (For details of the actual expulsion, see Sasson 1972; Charpin and Durand 1985: 319-22; for the further events, cf. Charpin 1992b. 4-5.)

B. Then the text continues: 'I have restored you [= Zimri-Lim] to the throne of your father and the weapons, with which I have beaten the Sea (*ti'amtum, temtum*), I have given you'.

Adad, whose authority lies in the defeat of the Sea, is the patron deity of Zimri-Lim, whom he appointed king of Mari (for a similar prophecy see Malamat 1980; Lafont 1984), thus reflecting the superior status of the land of Yamhad (capital Aleppo) to the kingdom of Mari. The motif of a struggle between the Storm-god and the Sea-god, which is entirely novel to the Mari documents, has already been referred to in some preliminary remarks (Charpin and Durand 1986: 174). The motif is well attested to at Ugarit (Bordreuil and Pardee 1993), as well as in the Bible and even in the talmudic literature. In classical sources may be found sporadic references to a Sea-deity (for the entire subject see Malamat 1989a: 107-12). But nowhere in this context do we hear of any weapons to be delivered by a god to a king. (For an additional instance in the Mari documents [unpublished] where Adad's weapons were sent to Zimri-Lim who deposited them in the temple of Dagan at Terqa, see Durand 1993: 53.)

C. And then: 'I have anointed you with the oil of my luminosity and nobody can withstand you'. The anointment rite, which signifies the divine component of a king's coronation, is known in the ancient Near East, especially in the Bible (see below), but the references to it are relatively rare (Kutsch 1963). In Mari this is the first occurrence of the royal rite, which with due reservation may have been an Amorite custom. Several instances seem to occur in connection with the Hittite kings, in Ugarit as well as in the El-Amarna letters (*EA* 34.47-53; 51.5-9). May we conceive of the cases mentioned above as in some way forerunners of the biblical ceremony?

D. 'Hearken to a single word of mine: When somebody who cries out to you for judgment says: "They wronged me", stand up and let [his case be] judged; render him justice. This is what I desire from you.' The god has the power to make certain demands of the king and singles out his desire for justice. The same motif of rendering justice already occurs in an earlier published prophecy from Aleppo (A. 2731, to be joined to A. 1129; cf. Lafont 1984; Malamat 1980) and thus seems to be characteristic of the god and the prophets (the 'respondents') of his city. Whereas the Mari prophecies generally focus on material demands, here are rare instances of moral, ethical commands particular to Adad of Aleppo (Malamat 1989a: 79 in contrast to p. 83; Anbar 1975). And finally:

E. 'When you participate in a campaign, by no means set out without consulting an oracle. When I, in an oracle of mine, should be favourable, you will set out on a campaign. If it is not so, do not pass the gate [of the city?].'

This procedure, as expected, is widespread, not just at Mari, the deity demanding that a military campaign be determined by mantic means (e.g. Durand 1988: 44-46; 1987: 163-67 [ll. 66-70]). Thus this device (here unusually recommended by a prophet) is mentioned in many Mari letters (e.g. *ARMT* 26/1, nos. 7, 27, 97, 117, 119, 160; see also texts in 26/2).

F. *Epilogue*. The prophecy terminates with a statement found frequently in the prophetic Mari letters: 'This the *āpilum* said to me. Now [a lock of] his hair and the hem of his garment I send them to my lord [i.e. Zimri-Lim].' Various explanations have been put forward for this strange custom (for my own position, regarding these two personal items as a sort of 'identity card' of the prophet, see my most recent statement, Malamat 1989: 95).

*   *   *

Turning now to the Bible, we find counterparts to each of the motifs, although not to a continuous single literary unit as in Mari. Let us outline them according to the sections into which we divided the Mari prophecy:

A. The transfer of a country or kingdom from one ruler to another, because the deity has been neglected, is best expressed in the biblical episode of Saul and David. Here also it is a prophet, Samuel, who acts on behalf of the deity. The two most explicit biblical passages relating to our issue are: 'And Samuel said to him [to Saul], "The Lord has torn the kingdom of Israel from you this day, and has given it to a neighbour of yours, who is better than you"' (i.e. David, 1 Sam. 15.28); '...for the Lord has torn the kingdom out of your hand, and given it to your neighbour David. Because you did not obey the voice of the Lord...' (1 Sam. 28.17-28). In Mari and Israel a similar ideology regarding the behaviour of royalty is manifested.

B. Unlike Mari, in the biblical monotheistic faith there is no place for a separate Sea-deity next to Yahweh. But there are in the Bible certain echoes of the early existence of such a deity, but the latter has already been degraded to a Sea monster (Eissfeldt 1966; Cassuto 1975: 70ff.] who revolts against the God of Israel and is subdued by him. For this motif in the Bible, see, for example, Isa. 51.9-10; Jer. 5.22; Ps. 74.13-14; Job. 7.12, and see above (Bingen 1992; Day 1992).

C. The anointment of a king in Judah and Israel is a significant component of the coronation ceremony (Kutsch 1963; Weisman 1976; de Jonge 1992). In descriptions of six or even seven royal enthronements there is an express reference to this element: Saul (1 Sam. 9.16); David (1 Sam. 16.13 etc.); Absalom, trying to usurp the throne (2 Sam. 19.11); Solomon (1 Kgs 1.34 etc.), Jehu of Israel (1 Kgs 19.16 etc.), Joash (2 Kgs 11.12); and finally Jehoachaz (2 Kgs 23.30). To these cases must be added the anointing of Hazael, king of Damascus, by the prophet Elisha (1 Kgs 19.15). Also indicative here is the term *mašiah*, the anointed one, attributed in the Bible, *inter alia*, to King Cyrus, the Persian.

D. Demanding just and moral behaviour from the king is common to biblical prophecy, whereas in Mari there are only two prophecies on this theme (see above). As for the Bible (see in general Whitelam 1979: 29-37), let us cite Jeremiah's sermon concerning the conduct of the last Judahite rulers: 'Execute justice in the morning and deliver from the hand of the oppressor' (Jer. 21.12); 'Thus says the Lord: "Do justice and righteousness, and deliver from the hand of the oppressor him who has been robbed. And do not wrong or violence to the alien..."' (Jer. 22.3). Concerning King Josiah we have a specific statement made by Jeremiah that this king afforded help to the poor and needy (Jer. 22.15).

It is of interest to note that whereas in Mari the motifs C and D are simply set one after the other, in the Bible they are organically intertwined. See Ps. 45.7 (MT v. 8): 'you love righteousness and hate wickedness. Therefore God, your God, has anointed you with the oil of gladness above your fellows.' The king's anointment is here a consequence of his righteous behaviour towards the people, the logical but reverse sequence of the Mari prophecy. Similarly, it is possible that D and E are intertwined in the demand of the people of Israel for a king (1 Sam. 8.20).

E. Conducting a military campaign or a peaceful march following either an oracle or a prophecy are both attested to in the Bible (Christensen 1975). For the use of an oracle, see the passages in the book of Numbers: 'At the command of the Lord the people of Israel set out, and at the command of the Lord they encamped' (Num. 9.18) and still more expressly, 'And he shall stand before Eleazar the priest, who shall inquire for him by the judgment of the Urim [i.e. the oracle] before the Lord; at his word they shall go out, and at his word they shall come in, both he and all the people of Israel within the whole congregation' (Num. 27.21). See also 1 Sam. 23.35 on a razzia of David during his pre-monarchic days.

For the command of a prophet, let us take one instance out of several, namely, the war of King Ahab against the Arameans of Damascus. There, in contradiction to the 400 prophets who were unanimously in favour of war, the prophet Micaiah alone, upon divine inspiration, opposed the Israelite initiative (1 Kgs 22.6-28; cf. Rofé 1988: 142-52). As for the earlier periods see the biblical motif of the *heilige Krieg* and the use of the Ark of Covenant in warfare.

Our comparison between the Mari prophecy and the Bible has focused only on the major points, nevertheless it has shown a strong affinity between the two corpora—Mari and the Bible. The prophecy from Aleppo, which represents the West, is exceptional in its high standard of theological and moral contemplation, but the real breakthrough in this respect came only with the Bible and especially with the Great Prophets.

BIBLIOGRAPHY

Anbar, M.
1975   'Aspect moral dans un discours "prophetique" de Mari', *UF* 7: 517-18.
Bingen, T.
1992   'Fighting the Dragon', *SJOT* 6: 139ff.
Bordreuil P. and D. Pardee
1993   'Le combat de Ba'alu avec Yammu d'après les textes ougaritiques', *MARI* 7: 63-70.
Cassuto, U.
1975   *Biblical and Oriental Studies*, II (Jerusalem: Magnes).
Charpin, D.
1992a   'Le contexte historique et géographique des prophéties...a Mari', in *Bulletin SCEM* 23: 21-31.
1992b   'Mari entre l'est et l'quest...', *Akkadica* 78 (Mai-Aout): 1-10.

Charpin, D. and J.-M. Durand
1985   'La prise du pouvoir par Zimri-Lim', *MARI* 4: 293-343.
1986   'Fils de Sim'al...', *RA* 80: 141-83.
Christensen, D.L.
1975   *Transformation of the War Oracle in Old Testament Prophecy* (Harvard Dissertations in Religion, 3; Missoula, MO: Scholars Press).
Day, J.
1992   'Dragon and Sea', *The Anchor Bible Dictionary*, II (New York: Doubleday): 228-31.
Durand, J.-M.
1987   'Histoire du royaume de Haute-Mesopotamie', *MARI* 5: 155-98.
1988   *ARMT* 26/1 = *AEM* I/1.
1993   'Le mythologème du combat entre le dieu de l'orage et la mer en Mésopotamie', *MARI* 7: 41-61.
Eissfeldt, O.
1966   'Gott und das Meer in der Bibel', *KS*, III, 256-64.
Jonge, M. de
1992   'Messiah B, C—Anointed King(s)', *The Anchor Bible Dictionary*, IV (New York: Doubleday): 777-80.
Klengel, H.
1965   'Der Wettergott von Halab', *JCS* 19: 87-93.
Kutsch, E.
1963   *Salbung als Rechtsakt im Alten Testament und im alten Orient* (BZAW; Berlin: de Gruyter).
Lafont, B.
1984   'Le roi de Mari et les prophètes du dieu adad', *RA* 78: 7-18.
Malamat, A.
1980   'A Mari Prophecy and Nathan's Dynastic Oracle', in J. Emerton (ed.), *Prophecy: Essays Presented to G. Fohrer* (BZAW, 150; Berlin: de Gruyter): 68-82.
1989a   *Mari and the Early Israelite Experience* (Oxford: Oxford University Press).
1989b   'Parallels between the New Prophecies from Mari and Biblical Prophecy' (I-II), *NABU* 1989/4: 61-63.
1991a   'New Light from Mari on Biblical Prophecy' (III-IV), *Festschrift J.A. Soggin* (Brescia): 185-90.
1991b   'The Secret Council and Prophetic Involvement in Mari and Israel' (V), *FS S. Herrmann* (Stuttgart): 231-36.
Rofé, A.
1988   *The Prophetical Stories* (Jerusalem: Magnes).
Sasson, J.
1972   'Zimri-Lim's March to Victory', *RA* 66: 177-78.
Whitelam, K.W.
1979   *The Just King* (JSOTSup, 12; Sheffield: JSOT Press).
Weisman, Z.
1976   'Anointing as a Motif in the Making of the Charismatic King', *Bib* 57: 378-98.

THE PLACE OF THE OLD TESTAMENT IN UNDERSTANDING ISRAELITE HISTORY AND RELIGION*

A.D.H. Mayes

I

If the Bible is a problem for theology, its role in our understanding of ancient Israelite history and religion is, for very different reasons, equally contentious. The unsystematic and inconsistent presentation of Yahweh in Hebrew narrative may sit uneasily with the systematic formulations of theology (Carroll 1991: 34-36), but it is the highly systematic biblical presentation of Israelite history and religion which has become increasingly and fundamentally suspect in historical study. It is not simply that the Old Testament has harmonized a variety of different and inconsistent traditions into a more or less uniform account, but rather, at a more fundamental level, that it works with presuppositions about the nature of history which no longer command widespread acceptance. Once again, this is not only a matter of the biblical presupposition of the presence of Yahweh in and behind history, but rather, in a much more comprehensive way, it is a problem relating to the effective role of any purpose or intention, divine or human, in the significant aspects of the historical process. So, it is proposed (Brandfon 1981: 108-109) that pre-monarchic Israelite society may have been the unintended consequence of a wide variety of events in the Late Bronze Age, rather than the deliberate and conscious creation of ancient Israelites. But if this is so then indeed the Old Testament sources become more a distraction than a means of access to historical understanding: historical situations, understood as

---

* It is a pleasure to be associated with this tribute to a scholar whose influence has extended into so many areas. Not the least significant of these, in my experience, is his meticulous care in supervising research students, both individually and in memorable Saturday morning seminars.

the unintended result of many causes, are scarcely comprehensible on the basis of the biblical presentation of history. Although the biblical understanding is a synthetic one which not only points to human action as a decisive factor but also includes the forces of nature as an effective cause in historical events, these natural forces are not arbitrary or accidental, but the agents of a divine intention whose purpose is being fulfilled. In some recent study on the other hand, the significance of nature, the environment and climate lies precisely in their character as accidental determinants of history, so that Israel is a human social form that arose as a secondary response to the given conditions of a material context.

The relationship between the history of Israel and the literary record in the Old Testament then seems, in some minds at least, to be in process of radical change: whereas in an earlier phase of historical study, Israel's history was explained from the literature, now the question is one of explaining the literature from the history.[1] The writing of history is no longer to be seen as dependent chiefly on written sources such as the Old Testament with their focus on the unique event as the result of the purposeful actions of the unique individual. Such an approach, and such sources, reflect the belief that 'great men' dictate the course of history. Rather, history's concern should be with the study of the recurrent and the regular, with the aim of developing long term perspectives and showing patterns of change over long periods of time (Whitelam 1986) in which individuals are the reflections, if not the victims, of arbitrary material forces of which they are scarcely conscious and over which they have little control.[2]

The inevitable effect of this change is that historical reconstructions have come increasingly to rely in the first place on non-biblical sources concerned with the material remains and physical environment, and, secondly, on non-biblical disciplines such as sociology and anthropology from which analogies and models are consciously

1.   Cf. Davies in his introduction (1987: 3-4) to the series of papers on Israel's history in *JSOT* 39 (1987): 5-63. The focus of the discussion in this series is the Miller–Hayes volume, *A History of Ancient Israel and Judah*, which, Davies suggests, is the last of this kind of biblical history, based on the Old Testament.

2.   The relationship between the idiographic and the nomothetic interests of history has been widely discussed. See, for example, Mandelbaum 1977, esp. ch. 1; Nagel 1959: 203-15. On the long term perspectives of history see further below on the French *annales* school.

adopted. The archaeologist, geologist and climatologist supply the objectively reliable raw data which may then be organized and comprehended within the framework of chosen models of society and social change. Changes in archaeology, especially, reflect the change in interest and approach. Whereas earlier archaeologists concentrated on the particular sites in isolation, as the loci of the great events of history, the 'new archaeology' shows its awareness of the different aims and presuppositions of historical understanding by attending to surface surveys which reveal patterns of settlement and the relationship between sites, and so to the social and cultural context of archaeological data (see Whitelam 1986: 56-62; de Geus 1982: 50-57; Dever 1990). Models of social development then supply the comprehensive framework within which the concrete information may be systematically presented.[3]

In order to probe further the methodological change implied in these recent approaches to Israelite history and religion, it is helpful to use the distinction, originally developed in linguistic theory but more recently applied in anthropology and then in biblical studies, between emic and etic.[4] These terms have been defined by Harris (1979: 32) as follows:

> Emic operations have as their hallmark the elevation of the native informant to the status of ultimate judge of the adequacy of the observer's descriptions and analyses. The test of the adequacy of emic analyses is their ability to generate statements the native accepts as real, meaningful or appropriate. In carrying out research in the emic mode, the observer attempts to acquire a knowledge of the categories and rules one must know in order to think and act as a native... Etic operations have as their hallmark the elevation of observers to the status of ultimate judges of the categories and concepts used in descriptions and analyses. The test of the adequacy of etic accounts is simply their ability to generate scientifically productive theories about the causes of sociocultural differences and similarities. Rather than employ concepts that are necessarily real, meaningful and appropriate from the native point of view, the observer is free to use

---

3.   A particularly good and fruitful example of this new approach, bringing together the theoretical models and the archaeological data into an effective synthesis, is Frick 1985. See also Mayes 1989: 100-105.

4.   The distinction is discussed particularly by Pike 1967: 37-41; cf. also Headland, Pike and Harris 1990; Brett 1990: 357-65; Brett 1991.

alien categories and rules derived from the language of science. Frequently, etic operations involve the measurement and juxtaposition of activities and events that native informants may find inappropriate or meaningless.

One could, I think, summarize this by saying that emic approaches involve trying to find the meaning of something from a participant's point of view; etic approaches involve trying to find the cause of something from an observer's point of view. Emic involves meaning and description; etic involves cause and explanation.

II

Accounts of the history and religion of Israel have, until fairly recently, been largely unconscious of this distinction between emic and etic approaches, have tended to assume that their reconstructions were of the history of Israel as Israelites consciously lived it and of the religion of Israel as Israelites consciously believed it, and have taken it for granted that these were 'true' reconstructions. They have, evidently, been emic approaches. They have sought out the ancient Israelites' own understandings, and ancient Israelites' own beliefs, and these have been accepted as essentially true accounts. Bright's *History of Israel* is as good an example as any. Like many earlier and some more recent descriptions, it is an account of Israel that is essentially biblical. So, he states: 'although we may be quite sure that the actual happenings were far more complex than a casual reading of the Bible would suggest, enough can be said to justify the assertion that its account is rooted in historical events' (1983: 120).

This, it is fair to say, is the general methodological approach adopted by Bright. The biblical narrative is rooted in historical events we can uncover; it may be embellished and exaggerated here and there, in the interests of making it more effective, but fundamentally it is a reliable account of Israel's history and religion. So:

> There is no reason whatever to doubt that Hebrew slaves had escaped in a remarkable manner from Egypt (and under the leadership of Moses!) and that they interpreted their deliverance as the gracious intervention of Yahweh, the 'new' God in whose name Moses had come to them. There is also no objective reason to doubt that these same people then moved to Sinai, where they entered into covenant with Yahweh to be his people... exodus and Sinai became the normative traditions of all Israel: the

> ancestors of all of us were led by Yahweh through the sea and at Sinai in solemn covenant became his people; in the Promised Land we reaffirmed that covenant, and continually reaffirm it' (1983: 150).

The status of this as an account of the origins and early history of Israel must be made clear. This, for Bright, and others in the emic mode, is more than simply a description of what Israelites happened to believe. This Israelite belief is also the ultimate judge of our understanding; this Israelite belief is also the understanding to which the historian as observer is bound. Israel's understanding, the emic understanding, of its own situation is decisive. So:

> Of the exodus itself we have no extra-Biblical evidence. But the Bible's own witness is so impressive as to leave little doubt that some such remarkable deliverance took place. Israel remembered the exodus for all time to come as the constitutive event that had called her into being as a people... A belief so ancient and so entrenched will admit of no explanation save that Israel actually escaped from Egypt to the accompaniment of events so stupendous that they were impressed for ever on her memory... If Israel saw in this the hand of God, the historian certainly has no evidence to contradict it! (1983: 122).

So the biblical presentation is not simply Israel's rather peculiar story of origins and early history; this is, in principle, the history of Israel.

With this emic approach we can contrast that of Norman Gottwald, which is decidedly etic. Moreover, it is consciously and deliberately etic, holding that while the thoughts and beliefs of the cultural actors may play a role in understanding a culture, they belong within the framework of an analysis achieved by external scientific observation. Such scientific observation cannot be invalidated by the thoughts and beliefs of the actors; rather, the latter form part of the data to be understood and explained by scientific observation (Gottwald 1980: 785 n. 558). So Gottwald refers to

> the wisdom of Marx's insight that no science of society can ever be constructed by naively beginning (or naively ending!) with what people think about themselves as social beings: 'The social structure and the state are continually evolving out of the life-process of definite individuals, but of individuals not as they may appear in their own or other people's imagination, but as they *really* are, i.e. as they operate, produce materially, and hence as they work under definite material limits, presuppositions and conditions independent of their will' (1980: 640).

This dominance of the etic perspective is presupposed throughout Gottwald's presentation, and it leads to conclusions markedly different from those reached by Bright.

In his discussion of the origins of Israel, Gottwald argues that three models of historical reconstruction have been used: conquest, immigration and revolt. The first is the biblical presentation, which is still widely accepted; the second is a model developed in German Old Testament scholarship which presumes that Israel's ancestors were semi-nomads whose form of life involved regular periods of residence in the settled agricultural area; the third presupposes that Canaan was a stress-torn feudal society into which the exodus Israelites introduced a liberation ideology of divine deliverance and so provided the spark that ignited the flame of revolt against centralized political rule by feudal kings. Now, it is very clear that to think in terms of models, and even to examine the biblical conquest presentation as one such model, implies a certain distancing from the text and so from the actors' perceptions—it is now the scientific view of the external observer that counts. That distancing is present in principle from the beginning, but becomes more obvious as we go to the immigration model and then to the revolt model. In all cases, the biblical text is regarded as a reflection of the thinking of the biblical actors which may or may not be an adequate historical representation. Its adequacy is to be judged by reference to criteria introduced by the scientific observer. The text is expressive of the actors' ideas; it is an ideological account and, as such, a symbolic representation which may be more or less distorted in relation to reality. For Gottwald, the biblical account *is* an ideological distortion of reality: on archaeological, anthropological and sociological grounds, it may be determined that Israel's real origins lay in its revolutionary rejection of feudal rule by kings. Israel was a tribal egalitarian society, and its tribalism was 'a self-constructed instrument of resistance and of decentralized self-rule' (Gottwald 1980: 325).

The etic standpoint characterizes also Gottwald's treatment of Israelite religion. Israelite faith is not to be understood in idealist terms as grounded in the revelatory events of the exodus from Egypt and the covenant making at Sinai; rather, it is to be explained as a function of society; that is, it stands in a relationship of dependence on society. Yahwism is a function of Israelite society, and specifically of socio-political egalitarianism in pre-monarchic Israel. This means that any change in Israel's egalitarian social system would lead to a corresponding change in its understanding of Yahweh, in its religion. It is not to be ruled out, of course, that Israel's faith also influenced its society, for it did do so; but this influence was by way of a 'feed-back' from an idea that owes its primary formation to that society. Now, this approach has a very clear pedigree. Gottwald himself bases his work most extensively on Marx, and quotes Marx with approval:

> We do not set out from what men say, imagine, conceive, nor from men as narrated, thought of, imagined, conceived, in order to arrive at men in the flesh. We set out from real, active men, and on the basis of their real life-process we demonstrate the development of the ideological reflexes and echoes of this life process... Morality, religion, metaphysics, all the rest of ideology and their corresponding forms of consciousness, then no longer retain the semblance of independence... Life is not determined by consciousness, but consciousness by life (Gottwald 1980: 633).

It is specifically Marx as understood by Marvin Harris that Gottwald uses as the basis of his method. In this form, Marxism is understood to involve the proposition that all mental ideation, including religion, is rooted in a material infrastructure, and specifically in the environment and the socio-economic conditions determined by the environment. So Israelite religion, like all Israelite thinking, is determined by Israelite society and that in turn is determined by the environment. This 'pyramid of culture' may allow for some influence from the top down, but such influence is secondary and wholly dependent on the primary direction of influence from the bottom up, from the material infrastructure to the mental apex.

We could summarize the contrast between the two approaches in these terms. The emic approach seeks the understanding of the actors in a situation as the key to the *meaning* of that situation; it is thus idealistic and individualistic; it understands history and religion in terms of the conscious and intentional acts and beliefs of individuals; the biblical text, as the record of the conscious acts and beliefs of individuals, is the primary source for our understanding of those acts and beliefs. The etic approach, on the other hand, presupposes that the detached scientific observation of a situation is the key to *explaining* that situation; it brings to bear on that situation conceptions of the nature of the individual, of society and of religion which have been scientifically developed. Durkheim has shown that society has priority over the individual; Marx and Freud have shown how the thinking of the individual is dependent on hidden and unconscious material influences, so the approach must be through the study of society rather than of the individual, it must also be materialistic rather than idealistic; history is not about the conscious actions of great individuals; rather, history is concerned with the basic material economic and social forces that determine individual actions; religion, as all other products of human thinking, is a reflection of the same material, economic and social forces that determine all individuals; the biblical text, as a reflection of individual thinking, is thus a secondary rather than a primary source for our understanding ancient Israelite history and religion. One might reduce the contrast to these terms: the emic approach is concerned with the actor's meaning; the etic approach with the observer's explanation. All other differences depend upon that basic distinction.

III

This formulation of the distinction between emic and etic is one that has been grasped by some as a way out of a dilemma. The emic and etic approaches may then be understood as in fact essentially quite independent, with different concerns; and, consequently, the one does not necessarily invalidate the other. So, the emic approach is essentially descriptive: it is concerned to describe what it was like to be an ancient Israelite in the ancient Israelite situation and historical context; it is concerned with describing the particular thinking of ancient Israelites, the meanings they gave to their existence, the intentions they gave to their actions. The etic approach, on the other hand, is essentially explanatory: it is concerned with why people thought and acted as they did, and in order to answer that question it seeks out general laws, general conditions that can make these particular thoughts and actions explicable to us. In fact, it is argued, so independent is one approach from the other that neither is invalidated by the other. The reality which one represents is not impugned by what the other has to say. And this is the important point: the reality, significance and truth of the religion of ancient Israelites for ancient Israelites is not affected by the explanations put forward by the outside observer. The meaning and reality of a phenomenon is something independent of the explanation of its origin and existence. So, in our present case, we may hold to Bright's emic description of the history and religion of Israel, and at the same time accept Gottwald's etic explanation of that history and religion.

This, however, is a too easy way out. At least it is a way of coping with Bright and Gottwald that neither of them in the end acknowledges and which neither of them would apparently accept. In the case of both Bright and Gottwald there is an intention to present a *true* account of the history and religion of Israel, an account that makes a claim on our understanding and acceptance.[5] This is quite clearly explicit in the case of Gottwald's *explanation* of Israelite history and religion, but it is no less clear in the case of Bright's *description* of Israelite history and religion. So, Bright believes that the modern historian is in no position to deny the essential truth of what the biblical writers have recorded: if Israel saw in the events of the exodus and the crossing of the Red Sea the hand of God, the historian has no reason to contradict it.

It seems that what both Bright and Gottwald are aiming to provide is an account of Israel's history and religion that is both descriptive and explanatory, an account aiming to incorporate the beliefs and actions of ancient Israelites into an explanation that observing historians may accept as true.[6] In other words, insofar as there is a distinction between the accounts provided, it is a distinction that has much to do with presuppositions which determine what each observing historian regards as true. The distinction between emic and etic is not what it at first sight appears to be. It may start off as an objective distinction between native informant and outside observer; it may indeed be developed in terms of a contrast between 'meaning' and 'explanation'. But these distinctions and contrasts are exaggerated and potentially misleading. Both emic and etic are concerned with giving an account of history and religion, an account that is both descriptive and

5.   Cf. also Ricoeur 1965: 29: 'History is animated by a will for *encounter* as much as by a will for *explanation*'.

6.   This is immediately clear with Bright. In the case of Gottwald, his ultimate unwillingness to isolate the conscious beliefs of ancient Israelites from the historian's true explanation of those beliefs is demonstrated by his account of the thinking of Israelites about taking control of the land: 'The loot was appropriated for the needs of the free producers of Israel, who did not think of their action as "stealing", but rather viewed it as the rightful reappropriation of wealth that had been extracted by kings, aristocrats, landowners and merchants from the raw labour of the lower classes. Israel saw itself as legitimately reclaiming what belonged to Yahweh and to the oppressed whom he upheld' (Gottwald 1980: 506; cf. also *ibid.*, 596).

explanatory (cf. Segal 1988: 29-30); the chief difference between them is that the one works in terms of the adequacy of the thoughts and conscious actions of individuals for explanatory purposes (an idealistic approach), the other in terms of the need to uncover the hidden material forces in order to arrive at explanation. But this difference is one that is rooted in the general cultural presuppositions which the observing historian brings to his task. If one's general cultural presuppositions involve attributing a high significance to individual thought and action then one will work in the so-called emic mode, and, in the case of ancient Israel, assign a primary value to the beliefs of ancient Israelites expressed in the Old Testament; if, on the other hand, one's general cultural presuppositions involve attributing a very low significance to individual thought and action then one will work in the etic mode, understanding those beliefs as the distorted expression of hidden material motives and forces. The particular value which the historian may attribute to the Old Testament as an account of Israel's origins may vary from one historian to another, but whether that value be high or low is in large measure finally determined by those presuppositions.[7]

IV

If presuppositions play so significant a role in all historical reconstruction, how do the histories of Bright and Gottwald compare? Surely it is the case that the less baggage we bring into our historical reconstruction the better, and for that reason surely Bright's history, staying as close as it does to the biblical story, is the more reliable piece of work, while Gottwald's is the more hypothetical and speculative. Yet it must be clear that despite appearances Bright's work, no less than that of Gottwald, does bring with it a very definite set of pre-uppositions. We have already seen in a general way that Bright's acceptance of the Old Testament account of Israel's origins presupposes his own general philosophical and religious idealism. Associated with that general presupposition there is also a rather simplistic objectivism and

7.   The problem of discerning the beliefs of ancient Israelites in any given situation, behind the complex process of editing and redaction which the Old Testament records have experienced, constitutes, of course, a further independent difficulty. The present concern, however, is with the principle of using such expressions of belief given that they can be recovered.

realism as far as the meaning of Old Testament statements is concerned. In particular, it is assumed that the meaning, the reality, expressed by any statement stands in direct correlation with that statement's correspondence with the external facts to which it refers. Language is directly and objectively referential: its meaning depends on its correspondence with that to which it refers. That is a presupposition which underpins Bright's whole approach, and it is that understanding which he has also imposed on ancient Israelites. 'The ancestors of all of us [so the ancient Israelites believed] were led by Yahweh through the sea and at Sinai in solemn covenant became his people' (Bright 1983: 150). In fact, one could say that for Bright the meaning of Israel's history is intrinsic in the facts of its historical experience, and that the Old Testament directly and immediately expresses that meaning.

Gottwald, on the other hand, for all the speculation there may be in his work, has a much more subtle approach, and this, despite the conclusions he has drawn, must command respect. In particular, he has made explicit an essential discrimination between language and reality, a discrimination that Bright ignores. Gottwald rightly believes that language functions in a symbolic way in giving meaning to existence. It gives no direct and immediate access to the real, but is an interpretation of the real—that through which the real is mediated and expressed.[8] The recognition that it is through language that reality is mediated, that language constitutes a symbolic system expressive of an interpretation of reality, preserves a discrimination that is vital both for our perception of the nature of religious statements today and for our relating to the religious statements of ancient Israel.

Gottwald's treatment of this topic is illuminating and fundamental. In a discussion of the nature of Israel's historical consciousness, he argues that a distinction must be drawn between the historical awareness of a group with respect to experiences which it has directly undergone, however long ago and however imperfectly the awareness has survived, and the historical awareness of a group that has appropriated another group's remembered experience as a symbolic statement about its own altogether distinct historical experience. So,

---

8. For an even more strongly expressed view of the symbolic nature of historical affirmations, cf. Becker 1959: 120-37. The historian cannot deal with the event. The event is past; the historian can deal only with affirmations about the event. So one must make a basic distinction between the event and the historical fact: the latter is the memory of the event, the image of it in the records or in the mind.

the historical awareness of the Moses group concerning the deliverance from Egypt is of a different order than the historical awareness of 'a deliverance from Egypt' as cultivated by groups of Israelites who did not participate with the Moses group in the events remembered.

At each stage, however, a symbolic element is present.

> In the first stage, a group singles out particular aspects of its past lived experiences as of unusual importance for its present self-understanding and thereby begins the selective symbolization of its past. In the second stage, the already interpreted experience of one group is extended to the experiences of other groups which…are felt to be analogous and capable of illumination when seen through the symbolic categories that first arose in another lived historical context (Gottwald 1980: 83-84).

The distinction between reality, on the one hand, and language as a symbol system that interprets reality, on the other, is of absolutely fundamental significance, and is of particular importance in dealing with texts deriving from times and cultures other than those of the historian. Unless some such distinction is made, the distance between past and present is negated in favour of a fundamentalist type appropriation of texts into the present. With that distinction the way is open towards the adoption of those generalizations which are necessary if history, in the sense of contemporary thought about the past, is to make sense. History cannot be written without presuppositions, for it is these which make the past meaningful for the present. That is to say, a statement about the past is a symbolic affirmation that expresses not a direct and immediate representation of reality but an interpretation of reality based on assumed generalizations, presuppositions that allow a relationship with the past to be established. It is through generalizations, general laws or presuppositions, that it is possible to bridge from the past to the present, while at the same time preserving the past's distinctiveness. If historical study were to be purely idiographic then the past would be a series of discrete events completely inaccessible from the present. Generalizations, expressing how individuals relate to society, how and why people behave in given situations, are the provisional universals constructed in the present which open the way to an understanding of the past.[9]

9.   Cf. also Mandlebaum 1977: 6; Knauf 1991: 34-35; Fischer 1971: 95, who, quoting Tennyson, refers to the past becoming 'a wilderness of single instances'.

V

Gottwald's work represents the major current attempt to approach Israel's history and religion on the basis of an explicitly formulated set of generalizations. The value of his work is to some extent limited because of the particular nature of the presuppositions he has adopted, but in commenting on and criticizing these it must be acknowledged that he has forced Old Testament scholarship into a fundamental examination of the foundations of its activities which is essential for the future development of worthwhile study. Significant perceptions of the past require critical appraisal of the presuppositions and perspectives from which the past is viewed.[10]

In the first place, the view that ideas are dependably related to material conditions, which requires that physical causes must somehow be shown to be open to translation into mental effects, cannot claim Marx as a confirming authority. Marxist materialism is much more dialectical than Gottwald allows for, in that Marx understood human consciousness as that through which people apprehend the world and in terms of which they change it. It is not the physical environment that creates society, but human beings, actively and consciously engaged in production, who create society. Ideas, far from being simply an epiphenomenon of material circumstances, supply the categories and concepts through which those material circumstances are apprehended and changed. Indeed, a basic paradox in Gottwald's work is that he assigns this basic and creative role to ideas by describing Israel's origins in terms of *conscious* social revolution, while he denies that role to ideas in his theoretical discussion of the relationship between religion and society (cf. Brandfon 1981: 101-10; Mayes 1989: 94-96).

This pyramid of culture model finds no support in recent anthropology. In particular, Geertz (1973: 43-51) has demonstrated that culture, understood as a set of control mechanisms or programmes that govern human behavior, is both a human product and also something essential to human evolution given the indeterminate response capacities that characterize human nature. Unlike the lower animals, whose relationship and response to their environment is immediate and direct, human beings have only a very general innate capacity to respond and relate to their environment. Culture is indeed a human

---

10. For a recent treatment see especially Knauf 1991: 26-64.

creation, but it is also an essential condition of human existence.

Secondly, if this is a more appropriate generalization with which to work, then the object of historical study is the integration of particular events and individuals into their comprehensive cultural contexts. This is more than a truism, for it involves not simply the recreation of Israelite social institutions, but the relating of these to long-term movements and patterns of change. In terms of the approach advocated by the French *annales* school (cf. Ricoeur 1980; Brandfon 1987: 30-38; Brandfon 1988: 55-56), there is an interaction of three levels: the *longue durée* level which is that of gradual ecological and environmental change over very extensive periods of time, which influences settlement patterns and agricultural practices; the level of *conjuncture*, that is, the social and economic trends and characteristics that may modify within a single generation, and which likewise influence motivations and ideas of individuals and groups; and the level of the specific event characterized by the meaningful action of individuals. This is not simply a modified form of the pyramid of culture or the mechanistic materialism of Marvin Harris, for it represents an attempt both to incorporate human action at all levels and also to plot its relative significance in relation to the actual course of history.

First steps in tracing long-term movements and patterns of change have been taken, and with some considerable success, in the work of Coote and Whitelam (1986, 1987), who have plotted patterns of expansion and contraction in trade and economy throughout the ancient Near East over very long periods of time. Within this framework the appearance of Israel on the mountains of Palestine has been understood in terms of a response to economic contraction through risk reduction, by opening up alternative sources and forms of living, while the rise of the Israelite monarchy has been set within the framework of an upturn in trade and economy leading to increased urbanization. What still lies ahead is the integration of this with the study of Israelite culture.

Thirdly, the role of the Old Testament in this enterprise cannot be dismissed as secondary. The affirmations about Israel's history and religion which the Old Testament contains are cultural expressions of meaning within an ancient Israelite historical, social and economic context. They cannot simply be translated back into basic economic truths, or read as the ideological distortions of material realities; rather, they form parts of the context within which historical and economic life is led. These are the ideological motivations of ancient Israelite history, not simply the reflections of ancient Israelite history. Yahweh as deliverer of Israel from Egypt provides the ideological motivation of Israelite history to the extent that it is characterized by resistance to centralized monarchic power. That motivation does not disappear behind but stands alongside economic and ecological motivations in the creation of Israelite history and religion.[11]

BIBLIOGRAPHY

Becker, C.A.
1959   'What are Historical Facts?', in Meyerhoff 1959: 120-37.
Brandfon, F.R.
1981   'Norman Gottwald on the Tribes of Yahweh', *JSOT* 21: 101-10.
1987   'Kinship, Culture and Longue Duree', *JSOT* 39: 30-38.
1988   'Archaeology and the Biblical Text', *BARev* 14: 54-59.
Brett, M.G.
1990   'Four or Five Things to Do with Texts: A Taxonomy of Interpretative Interests', in D. Clines, S. Fowl and S. Porter (eds.), *The Bible in Three Dimensions* (JSOTSup, 87; Sheffield: JSOT Press): 357-77.
1991   *Biblical Criticism in Crisis? The Impact of the Canonical Approach on Old Testament Studies* (Cambridge: Cambridge University Press).
Bright, J.
1983   *A History of Israel* (London: SCM Press, 3rd edn).
Carroll, R.P.
1991   *Wolf in the Sheepfold: The Bible as a Problem for Christianity* (London: SPCK).
Coote, R.B. and K. Whitelam
1986   'The Emergence of Israel. Social Transformation and State Formation Following the Decline in Late Bronze Age Trade', *Semeia* 37: 107-47.
1987   *The Emergence of Early Israel in Historical Perspective* (Sheffield: Almond Press).
Davies, P.R.
1987   'The History of Ancient Israel and Judah', *JSOT* 39 (1987): 3-4.
Dever, W.G.
1990   *Recent Archaeological Discoveries and Biblical Research* (Seattle: University of Washington Press).

11. In a recent study Miller (1991) points out how meagre any history of Israel, which relied solely on non-biblical sources, would be. That in itself is not an argument against those who reject the use of the Hebrew Bible, but Miller's further point, viz. that those who adopt this line in fact themselves rely either directly or indirectly on (an often uncritical use of) information provided by the Hebrew Bible, is worth emphasizing.

Edelman, D.V. (ed.)
1991   *The Fabric of History: Text, Artifact and Israel's Past* (JSOTSup, 127; Sheffield: JSOT Press).

Fischer, D.H.
1971   *Historians' Fallacies: Toward a Logic of Historical Thought* (London: Routledge & Kegan Paul).

Frick, F.S.
1985   *The Formation of the State in Ancient Israel* (Sheffield: Almond Press).

Geertz, C.
1973   *The Interpretation of Cultures* (New York: Basic Books).

Geus, J.K. de
1982   'Die Gesellschaftskritik der Propheten und die Archaeologie', *ZDPV* 98: 50-57.

Gottwald, N.K.
1980   *The Tribes of Yahweh: A Sociology of the Religion of Liberated Israel 1250–1050 BCE* (London: SCM Press).

Harris, M.
1979   *Cultural Materialism: The Struggle for a Science of Cultures* (New York: Vintage Books).

Headland, T.N., K.L. Pike and M. Harris (eds.)
1990   *Emics and Etics: The Insider/Outsider Debate* (Frontiers of Anthropology, 7; London: Sage Publications).

Knauf, E.A.
1991   'From History to Interpretation', in Edelman 1991: 26-64.

Mandelbaum, M.
1977   *The Anatomy of Historical Knowledge* (Baltimore: Johns Hopkins University Press).

Mayes, A.D.H.
1989   *The Old Testament in Sociological Perspective* (London: Marshall Pickering).

Meyerhoff, H. (ed).
1959   *The Philosophy of History in our Time* (New York: Doubleday).

Miller, J.M.
1991   'Is it Possible to Write a History of Israel without Relying on the Hebrew Bible?', in Edelman 1991: 93-102.

Nagel, E.
1959   'The Logic of Historical Analysis', in Meyerhoff 1959: 203-15.

Pike, K.L.
1967   *Language in Relation to a Unified Theory of the Structure of Human Behaviour* (The Hague: Mouton).

Ricoeur, P.
1965   *History and Truth* (Evanston, IL: Northwestern University Press).
1980   *The Contribution of French Historiography to the Theory of History* (Oxford: Clarendon Press).

Segal, R.A.
1988   'Interpreting and Explaining Religion', *Soundings* 71: 29-52.

Whitelam, K.
1986   'Recreating the History of Israel', *JSOT* 35: 45-70.

JOHN 5 AND THE LIMITS OF RHETORICAL CRITICISM

D.L. Mealand

I propose to argue, in this piece, that to do justice to John 5, we need to dig deeper than Rhetorical Criticism, and to pay close attention to some more fundamental hermeneutical issues. Many recent analyses of New Testament texts give the impression of finding the question of meaning unproblematic. They focus on the role of the implied author, or of the narrator. They trace ways in which reliable commentary is offered to establish the authority of the narrator, and to elicit or control the responses of the implied reader. There are still, of course, other scholars who continue to offer interpretations that focus on the intentions of an actual author, or which attempt to reconstruct sources, or recover what Ricoeur would call the world before the text. For such people the key to understanding the Fourth Gospel is its use of the Synoptics or of a lost Signs Source. Or else the key is the history of the Johannine community, first reconstructed from the texts, then used to elucidate them. Attempts at a more thoroughly hermeneutical approach to the Fourth Gospel are still relatively rare. Most published work is exegetical or literary. Meaning is discussed, but usually exegetically. Yet one of the most significant hermeneutical commentaries was published some fifty years ago on The Gospel of John by Bultmann. When, in more recent New Testament studies, more fundamental questions are raised about meaning, it is often by scholars such as Crossan or Tolbert in relation to the polysemic character of the parables. But the question of meaning is basic to the study of any text. In the pages that follow I propose to look at this issue in relation to John 5.

Rhetorical criticism has become, in recent years, an increasingly common approach to the New Testament texts. This method sometimes goes under the name of Reader Response Criticism, though that designation may itself contain an ambiguity which is of itself interesting when explored. Is meaning controlled by the text, and are the readers' responses manipulated by the text? Or is it the case that readers are faced with ambiguity or obscurity, with multiple possibilities of meaning and with apparent conflicts within a text and struggle to find patterns of sense in it? Many recent New Testament studies seem to adopt the first of these positions rather than the second (though even more do not express matters in either of these ways). Here I propose to look initially at the first, and currently more popular, of these options, to see first its capabilities, and then its limitations.

John 5 contains several elements. It opens with the healing of the lame man lying by the pool. A controversy over healing on the sabbath follows. This turns into a christological argument, about Jesus' equality with the Father, continued in a discourse. This is then continued in a concluding section about evidence and witness. I propose to offer first what I am tempted to call a 'merely rhetorical' account of how the reader is steered through this material. I will later say why I believe this account to be acceptable but insufficient. I wish to maintain that we require a deeper analysis of a text whose meaning is not simply to be found on its surface.

A First (Rhetorical-Critical) Reading of John 5

The implied first reader approaching John 5 sequentially is pointed to the festival in Jerusalem as the second in a series (2.23; 4.45). The mention, by the narrator, of 'the Jews' and of Jerusalem reminds the reader of the tension and of difficulties that have already been described in earlier chapters (2.20-24; 3.10). The implied reader does indeed seem to need to be told about the topography of Jerusalem and that the name of the pool is Hebrew. But the reader is not ignorant in other respects. The memory of the previously narrated sign at Cana, and of the story of the healing at Capernaum, allow the reader to smile when the sufferer points out that he has no one to help him. The reader knows that Jesus can heal the dullard. In 5.6 the narrator asserts that Jesus knew that the sufferer had been there for a long time. This shallow inside view of Jesus' knowledge also contributes to the reader's sense of superiority. So possibly does a double sense in the question 'Do you wish to be made whole?'

When we come to the decisive command to the man to pick up his bed and walk, the reader is most likely to share the modern scholar's sense that this feature is a Synoptic motif recontextualized. But if the readers or hearers were familiar with Mark's story then the combination of echoes and differences probably would produce a sharp intake of breath. Nor will he or she at once catch the full implications of the mention of the sabbath in 5.9. (Someone familiar with Mark might notice that this story brings together motifs in Mk 2 and Mk 3, found there in separate stories). The reader is assumed to know something about the restrictions on sabbath, but the mention of law and grace in 1.17 is rather too brief and far away to contribute much. Only very careful rereading might suggest a connection. On the other hand, when the sequential reader later arrives at the story of the healing of the blind man in ch. 9 it would be hard to miss the repetition of point after point from ch. 5, and especially of the breach of sabbath law (Culpepper 1983: 139-40). In 5.11 the sufferer offers the somewhat feeble defence that his carrying of the bed was ordered by the itinerant healer.

Staley sees this differently. He argues that the man's reply is essentially that one who can heal can also override the sabbath law (Staley 1991: 61-63). He argues that the healed man can be seen as a bold witness rather than as weak and treacherous. More important is Staley's contention that the narrative has gaps, and that the reader is left to fill in the characterization. But the point here is not so much an insight into the psychology of the former paralytic, whether bold or defensive. There may indeed be an element of characterization here. But much more important for the reader is the reinforcement of the point that it is the healer who is breaking the law (5.11; cf. 5.16). But this point has been delayed. It was first delayed by the withholding until v. 9 of the crucial information that the event happened on Saturday. It was further delayed by focusing first on the former sufferer's offence, and only later and less directly (so far) on that of the healer. Now it is true that the shallow inside view we are offered in v. 13 of the former sufferer's ignorance of the identity of the healer 'fill[s]...[a] gap in the narrative' (Culpepper 1983: 59, following Genette). It also helps the characterization. But as well as noticing the gap which is filled, we should be acutely aware of the much more serious gap which is not filled.

At 5.14 the healed man is found by Jesus and told not to continue in sin. But the reader seems to be left bereft of guidance at this point, and we can certainly detect some actual modern readers straining desperately to make sense of this by linking it to something that is not supplied. Even with the hindsight derived from 9.2-3 and 20.23 much is left unclear. Staley (1991: 62) rightly points to the gap left here, though his speculative fillings of the gap are as problematic as those of most others (we cannot infer from Jesus' negative hints about the Temple that it was sinful for the man to go there). But the presence of narrative gaps is one of the main issues to which we must return in the second section of this paper.

At 5.15 when the man informs against Jesus, the alert reader might be expected to remember that Jesus did not trust himself to those whose belief rested merely (2.23-24) on seeing his signs. On reaching 6.26 (or coming to this chapter on a second reading of the whole) the point is reinforced by the dismissive reference to those who sought Jesus because they had stuffed themselves full of the loaves. In 5.16 the imperfect tenses may well imply that this is but one scene of many, and that provocative acts by Jesus and hostile responses occurred with greater frequency. This story is but one example (20.30). Here in 5.16 the persecution that follows the delation lays down an early marker for the only other use of the verb to persecute, which comes much later at 15.20. If the implied reader finds an 'external prolepse' in which persecution is foretold, does this warrant, or render unnecessary, a trip outside the text on our part to an inference about the sufferings of the Johannine community? It seems arbitrarily prescriptive and restrictive to ban reference to early Christian persecution there. We need to allow for intertextuality. Texts do relate to other texts (Tolbert 1991: 204 citing N. Frye), if not to uninterpreted experiences. More critical is whether we should privilege reference to other 'texts' in which early Christians speak of persecution (or their Jewish contemporaries of due punishment). I am inclined to agree with those who argue that texts relate to other 'texts' and not to uninterpreted experiences. (I am less persuaded that every text is *equally* relevant to every other text, though our capacity to understand word signifiers, as much as we do understand them, does depend on more than the immediate family of texts, and we have texts to refer to only insofar as we have our individual or shared interpretations of those texts.)

The well informed modern reader knows all about the controversies over divine law in early debates between Jews and Christians. The implied reader is assumed to know at least that breaking the sabbath was an offence. The point is not developed at length, though Ashton perhaps goes a shade too far in asserting that the controversy is 'totally remote from his [John's] concern' (Ashton 1991: 139). The shallow inside views of Jewish motivation in 5.16-18 do contribute to the characterization of Jewish concern about the sabbath. But a more interesting literary device is the way that 5.18 ensures that the reader 'does not miss the point' of the words 'My Father' in 5.17. The statement that 'he also called God his own Father' acts as a signpost to steer the reader away from an under-reading of 5.17. The uniqueness, or special character, of Jesus' sonship is signaled by πατέρα ἴδιον. The reader is certainly deterred from seeing him as son in the same way as many others might be sons of God. But should the reader not have spotted this already? Perhaps as far back as 1.14 or 1.18 (depending on how we interpret 'only', and on the text we read in 1.18) the reader might have been pointed in the direction of unique sonship, and certainly in 2.16, 3.18 and 3.35 the special sonship of Jesus is ever more clearly signalled. So something which the reader has been led to accept already by the narrator is now disclosed as highly controversial. Another quite different understanding of this passage takes 5.19 as an indicator that the accusation of claiming equality in 5.18 is a misunderstanding by the opponents. This view is possible, but is criticized by Loader (1989: 162-63).

The quite specific phrase 'broke the sabbath' also serves to prevent an under-reading of another component in 5.17. That Jesus works as his Father does, is now also disclosed to be much more controversial than it appeared to be at first sight. Of course the modern exegete who has troubled to chase up the Jewish debate over how it can be that God does not observe his own sabbath law, is well informed about all this. But an implied reader who has to be told about Jerusalem, and about Hebrew words, is presumably not expected to know all this. It runs through the next few verses, as the traditional exegetes have amply demonstrated. This actual reader will, along with other exegetes, find and claim to recognize in the text a creative use of a rabbinic and Philonic motif. The implied reader is given the somewhat mysterious sequence of a defence against 'doing this' on the sabbath by an appeal to the Father working, a disclosure that this does actually mean that he broke the sabbath, and a further series of statements about the Father raising the dead. The reader is thrown enough to be prevented from under-reading the text. But even then the defence, that Jesus broke the sabbath because his Father does, is not made wholly explicit. There are quite overt signals to the reader in the text, but there are equally clearly things which are not included, and whose absence gives the text something of its mysterious character. A similar situation obtains in the last clause of 5.18 and in 5.19. For someone who knows that claiming equality with God is the mark of godless villains in Jewish literature, the accusation is clear, and so is the rebuttal. Jesus is no rival to the Father. Yet there is complexity here, for anyone who has read and reread the text will have ears ringing with passages implying equality (and some which appear to conflict with it). It is possible to read the text as qualifying, but still endorsing the view initially stated by the opponents. What they say is true, though not in the sense that equality means rivalry. But this is not something immediately evident to a first reader. Is then the ideal narrative audience made up of people who read and re-read the text? Perhaps this is to psychologize too much. We should not personalize the notion of an implied reader. The phrase is a device for discussing the rhetorical structures of the text. Another way to describe the phenomena here would be to ask if the network of response inviting structures in the Fourth Gospel is non-linear. We do need to bear in mind that this text was probably read aloud in sections to people who had heard it before. It is, in this respect, different from the kind of text which is customarily read straight through once only.

The rebuttal in 5.19 insists that Jesus's equality with the Father is not rivalry, as the Son only does what he sees the Father doing. This partially explains the assertion of equality, and also to some extent modifies it. It definitely deters *mis*-reading. In a controversial setting, it rebuts the accusation of an upstart rival claiming equality. But the explanation is very limited. The text minimally explicates and defends equality. It offers the portrait of a docile and obedient Son. In so doing it both asserts and undermines equality. Someone who is able to do what his Father does, is, in that sense, equal. Someone who *only* does what the Father does, seems to be, in that sense, subordinate. The paradoxes of later orthodoxy are not wholly unanticipated here.[1] The

---

1. An alternative view might emphasize not the more ontic character of the language in Jn 5, but that the discourse is about the human son of God, completely dependent upon God and obedient to God—a role exemplified by Jesus. It could be argued that Jesus is depicted as speaking about 'the son' in this sense, and identifying himself and those who believe with that role (cf. 20.17; 21.23). I would, of course, agree that some of the significant christological language of the text develops

text is subtle. Also it may avert misreading but it does not, perhaps cannot, remove the puzzlement of its readers. Its very defence and explanation leave large numbers of things unsaid. By this curiosity is aroused, a sense of mystery deepened, or exasperation created. Perhaps the most sensitive and honest of the interpreters of the text have to admit to being left with elements of all three. Once again we have struck a sudden limit to the perspicuity of the text. This limit may also be a limit which rhetorical criticism has to admit. The text does not just use paradox incidentally. Paradox is deeply embedded in the text. We need a literary theory which is capable of going that deep. The second part of this study will attempt to return to those features with which some versions of New Testament rhetorical criticism seem least successful.

The extent to which the text anticipates the paradoxical character of the more subtle versions of later Christian orthodoxy might also appear in 5.26. The text asserts that the Father has granted the Son 'to have life in himself' (ἔδωκεν ζωὴν ἔχειν ἐν ἑαυτῷ). In context it is clear, with many exegetes, that this includes the power to give life to others. But exegetes are divided over whether that is all that it means. Bultmann argues that it refers to 'the creative power of life'. Brown, more cautiously, argues that 'life' here 'does not refer *primarily* to the internal life of the Trinity, but to a creative life-giving power' exercised towards humanity (Brown 1971: 215; my emphasis). Barrett speaks of the work of the Son, but also says that the giving 'is not a temporal act but describes the eternal relation of the Father and the Son' (Barrett 1978: 262). Lindars says that it refers in the first place to the 'self-subsistent being of God' (Lindars 1972: 225). I believe the last two to be nearer the mark. (For a completely different view see appended n. 1.) The crucial part of the phrase is ἐν ἑαυτῷ. It could be argued that to have life 'in oneself' is surely not to depend on someone else for life. The paradox is ancient, but it could be dragged to the surface and made all too explicit by translating: 'has granted the Son to have ungranted life'. If correct this interpretation would be deeply paradoxical, and it is not impossible that the text could be saying this.

---

out of the Jewish notion of agency. This asserts that the envoy is to be regarded as the one who sends the envoy or agent. But I would agree with Loader that much more is involved. His discussion of this goes into much greater detail than the space allowed to me here (Loader 1989: 12, 154-74).

But such an interpretation could be an overreading of 'in himself'. Bauer's lexicon notes 5.42, 6.53, and 17.13 and also 2 Cor. 1.9 as having a similar idiom. In each of these instances it is people who do not have 'in themselves' the love of God, or life, or do have joy, or the sentence of death. These examples might suggest the slightly weaker sense 'they do not have'. Perhaps we should not press the force of the reflexive here. But on the other hand one could argue that the other passages are speaking about human experience of redemption, whereas this passage is speaking about the relation of Father and Son. Further, one could point to the passages about his doing nothing 'of himself' in the immediate context, where we seem to need a strong reflexive sense. There is a case at least for the stronger more paradoxical interpretation of the passage. The text here is much discussed in Greek patristic writing. In an anti-Arian context there is anxiety to discount the suggestion that the giving is a temporal act. They at least wished to find there the paradox of a non-temporal act of giving. It is when we press such questions of interpretation that we find that historically readers have differed in their interpretations. We do not have an unambiguous text. We have our reading of a text. We try to defend it by appeal to other texts—that is to *our reading* of other texts, for what else do we have? (See Moore 1989: 115-21.) This is not to say that we can never resolve an ambiguity, but rather to argue that we cannot render all the indeterminacies determinate. In reading propositions inscribed in discourses, as in reading narratives, we are confronted with gaps. We try to fill the gaps as best we may.

The rest of the chapter is largely discourse, albeit controversial discourse. In 5.21 the motif of the Son's equality is further explained: just as the Father raises the dead and gives life, so the Son gives life. (We may not find an exact parallel between the clauses here, but we need to read further down the page.) The references here to life and to judgment pick up the references already dropped in earlier chapters (e.g. 3.15, 19), and also give specificity to the defence of the claim to equality. The sabbath theme seems to be subterranean here. Students of Jewish literature know that it is because children are born, and people die, on Saturday, that God is (rabbinically) held to work on his own seventh day (Brown 1971: 217; Barrett 1978: *ad loc.*). But I pass over both this, and the interrelation of texts about judgment, to focus on the ambiguity the text creates as to the life envisaged. It is customary to discuss this in terms of an evangelist who emphasizes the presence of eternal life, and a possible subsequent redactor who (in 5.28-29) reinstates a more traditionally apocalyptic eschatology complete with people emerging from tombs. Another view is that an editor combined later and earlier duplicate forms of this discourse (Brown 1971: 221). But we might at least entertain the possibility of a different perspective on this part of our text.

The reference to those who are in the tombs coming forth (5.28-29) looks very much like an example of *disambiguation*. Until this point the text has left the reader unclear as to whether the life being offered is only present (5.24), but presumably not merely physical, or whether it is also future (as presumably in 5.21). The Fourth Gospel as a whole makes skilful use of a number of literary features: symbolism, irony, and the misunderstanding motif. But what we have here is not quite one of these. We are offered an ambiguity and then a possible resolution. Already we have had references to life, and indications that it is a present reality. In 5.24 this is fairly explicit. In some passages life is further described as eternal life, or the life of the (new) age, and the phrase is used, as here, with a present verb (3.36). It might be argued that the future tense in 3.36b undermines this, but it would be difficult to take the perfect in 5.24 non-temporally. So it is understandable to read 5.21-25 as talking of the giving of new life now to the spiritually dead. Yet 5.21 opens the section by speaking of God's eschatological resurrection of the physically dead. If the Son gives life in a similar way, then is it right to read his work as being (only) the quickening of the spiritually dead? If I have interpreted the text correctly, or rather if my reading is persuasive, then 5.21-25 offers not simply a clear realized eschatology, but something more complex. The text offers ambiguous signals. This is not to say that the different interpretations are incompatible, but they are certainly different. When the reader reaches 5.28, at least in the text as it now stands, the ambiguity is resolved and a reference to future resurrection of the physically dead seems clearly signalled.

To recapitulate: the text has in earlier passages first emphasized realized eschatology against a more apocalyptic pattern, and then, in a sequel which discloses that 5.21-25 was more ambiguous than it first seemed, has pointed forward to future resurrection. In later chapters the complexities do not diminish. In 14.1-3 we also meet with future expectation, but of a much more individualistic character. (On the differing possibilities here see Brown 1971: 626-27; Bultmann 1971: 602 n. 1.) In the story of Lazarus, however, we have a narrative recounting the restoring to physical life of someone 'in the tomb' (11.17), and yet that story is symbolic of the giving of 'life' now (11.25a) but of a life that is not ultimately vulnerable to death (11.25b-26). Once again we could hardly claim that the text as a whole is immediately perspicuous. We have here an ambiguity which is created and resolved, only to be followed later by further complexities. The text is not unsubtle.

The technique used in 5.21-28 of mystification by ambiguity subsequently resolved is used a second time in the next section of the chapter. There the plodding reader is first invited to put weary feet on a rug supported by human testimony, only to have the rug pulled away in 5.34, 'I do not rely on human testimony'. The more subtle notion of the self-authenticating witness of the Father is then offered in 5.37. The effect is achieved by an ambiguity. In 5.32 the reader is told that there is 'another' who bears witness. The mention of John (the Baptist) in 5.33 implies by innuendo that here is the witness. But 5.34 then obliges the readers to retrace their steps by discounting human testimony. It could be argued that this passage in conjunction with 1.6-7 points to John's witness as ultimately being not merely human, but as revelation from God. But 5.36a supports my reading of 5.34; further we might note the tension between 5.35 and 1.8. Here we have not a passage that allows two meanings, and then affirms the second as well as the first, but a passage that hints at one meaning and then almost dismisses that entirely, to replace it with another. In this case the reader has been ambushed as effectively as a reader who has been led down a false trail in a detective novel. Since others have discussed at some length the presence of irony and other features at the close of this chapter I pass over those elements here.

In this section I have tried initially to follow those who locate meaning chiefly in the ways the text guides the reader. I have attempted to avoid the assumption that we can naively appeal to the intention of the actual author. I agree that the text does offer clues which do guide its readers in one direction rather than another. But that guidance is not such as to leave the reader with no further questions to ask. This is far from being the case.

Meta-Reflection on the Interpretation of John 5

The issue which has emerged several times in looking at John 5 sequentially is the extent to which the text guides the reader to a relatively determinate meaning. There is indeed guidance in the text, but we have also been compelled to note that the reader is also confronted with unexpected gaps, with delays in disclosure, and with false trails, and left puzzled in the face of ambiguity, paradox and mystery. To what extent, in this situation, should the reader be satisfied with such illumination as is immediately offered, and to what extent should the reader struggle to extract more? Is the text inviting, even compelling, the reader to puzzle and to make fresh sense of an uncompleted pattern? Or should the reader react by struggling to resist the almost irresistible desire for more certainty than the text affords? Or are there other strategies?

Let us review our findings in the first 'reading' of the text. We need to look at the different kinds of indeterminacies one by one.

1. We have a characterization of (of Jesus, the opponents, the healed man) which is partial but clearly incomplete. Jesus is portrayed both as a human figure and as one whose knowledge is more than ordinary, and we are reminded of his ultimate and mysterious origins. That the result is paradoxical we could see, even if we had never read Ernst Käsemann's *The Testament of Jesus*. The healed man could be craven, or perhaps bold and more subtle than his outwardly dull appearance suggests. Rhetorical criticism does not add much to our understanding here, but does bump against its limits.

2. The text plays on the ambiguity of having now the life of the coming age. It may even disambiguate the future reference of that stranger signifier. Yet the pictorial language of those in the tombs coming forth leaves us with a resolution of ambiguity which is still metaphorical, symbolic or analogical. If we prefer to detect redaction here, we still have unresolved tension.

3. As well as directing the reader towards sense, the text plays with the reader. The release of vital information (that the healing happened on sabbath) is deferred. Worse, the reader is even tricked or ambushed later. Led to believe that the authority of Jesus is underpinned by testimony, the reader is first offered John the Baptist as potential guarantor, only to be told that human testimony is not to be relied upon and that the revelation is its own guarantee. After being treated like this, how

can the reader imagine that the text is unsubtle in its use of this exceedingly tricky concept? Or can we even grasp something so immaterial as a concept here? What is the signified, when the signifier is talk of a self-authenticating revelation? Jn 5.37 offers something either self-evident or inaudible, invisible and unattainable, depending on where the reader stands.

4. We can make much more sense of the text if we allow ourselves to find out about early Christian persecution, by the intertextual consultation of other texts. Similarly, by reading Philo and rabbinic texts we find we can make more sense of a subtle and rewarding argument about God working on his own sabbath. Traditional exegetes will not feel the need to defend this element of intertextuality, but some literary theorists might contest it. We do, however, at least need to maintain that we enhance our understanding of this text by appealing to our understanding of other texts. (It is our understanding of those texts, rather than the texts, we must admit.) But then if we did not understand some things the sceptic's argument would itself be unintelligible to us. We can only point out the limitations of our understanding by assuming that those who read us understand our argument. Sense has its bounds, but so does scepticism.

5. As well as the need to read other texts in order to understand this text the better, we also seem to need to reread this text—that is, the whole of the Fourth Gospel. The response-inviting rhetorical patterns in the text are not all linear. On returning here from rereading John 6 and, above all, John 9 we find our understanding enhanced, as argued above.

6. The text has gaps. The reader seems to be left to struggle to fill the gaps. Notably the text does not explicate why it is that the healed man is told not to continue in sin. The diverse explanations of the classical exegetes speak for themselves. A larger gap opens up when we learn that Jesus is Son in a special sense, and is in some sense equal, yet does what the Father does and has only what the Father grants. This tells us much, but there is even more that it does not clarify. Worse, it is deeply paradoxical, and it is not at all evident how the paradoxes can be shown not to entail contradictions. The rival supplementary explanations which are usually offered at this point are amply documented in the credal and conciliar controversies of the subsequent Christian centuries. Traditional exegetes might well ask whether we need the complexities of rhetorical criticism to arrive at

this well-trodden landmark. Some readers find it quite natural and obvious to supplement the text with credal or conciliar formulae (as for instance with the citation from Lindars above). But one could argue that, while it is possible to find significance in this way, we could usefully sound a note of caution, and invoke the sometimes over-used distinction between significance and meaning. However, we could alternatively argue that these are attempts by readers to give meaning to the text where the text itself leaves off from providing rhetorical guidance. Viewed that way one inference might be to insist that such activities are no longer controlled by the text. That would not worry those who would maintain that with all texts meaning comes from the interpreter rather than the text. But this implication might cause some of those who feel that rhetorical criticism is tame and safe to reflect more carefully on just where close attention to the rhetoric might lead.

7. Confronted by some of these issues, a deeper issue begins to emerge. The text is not wholly determinate; it has gaps and ambiguities, metaphorical and symbolic elements, and it presents us with paradoxes. There are points where the text seems to force the reader to confront the indeterminacies[2] that open up once we have assimilated the initial information which is indeed there. My point is not that the school of rhetorical criticism has discovered this, but rather that it cannot evade it. Is the text then pointing us to something that cannot be asserted in propositions or straightforwardly signified? Some might argue that no signifier straightforwardly signifies. We do not have independent access to what is signified; we have only signifiers. There is another way in which this point is sometimes argued. A signifier means what it does only by being this signifier and not some other. Here we come up against one of the contentions of the deconstructionists. In their works we find polemic directed against concepts, against presence, against logocentrism, against ontotheology. I am not claiming that this text is as amenable to deconstruction as Kelber and Crossan argue. Indeed it may even seem strange to discuss this in connection with a text many regard as a bastion of logocentrism and of ontotheology. Here it is possible only to sketch extremely briefly what

---

2.   If a word as signifier provides no direct access to the concept signified, then the sense of word or sentence is not determinate, or rather is not fully determinate. It is not only Derrida who has pointed to indeterminacy here, as Llewelyn's references to classic philosophical discussions by Goodman and Quine make clear (Llewelyn 1986: 104-11).

would really need to be a much longer story. The text is not simple. When we start to read the Fourth Gospel the text appears logocentric and to offer an ontic Christology. But as we read on we encounter ambiguity, symbol, limits to sense, and more than a hint of paradox. There are those who play with a *via negativa* as an introduction to a more positive theology (onto-theology perhaps, if one must).[3] But what we have here is a text that does the reverse of that. It begins with what look like logocentric and onto-theological assertions and then leads us gently on to a state where we begin to see that everything is far more complex, and where the more carefully we read, the more we find it ever easier to say what that which has been revealed is not, than to say what it is, though clear enough that revelation is central to the text and to its understanding.[4]

3. Derrida certainly specifically rejects any analogy between his philosophy and this kind of use of the *via negativa*. (On this see the careful distinction between different uses of negative theology in Crossan 1982: 38-39.)

4. I am grateful to Kevin Vanhoozer and to Margaret Davies for some comments on earlier oral and written drafts of the first part of this article. I hope that I have correctly represented some points I am grateful to include in the discussion, though not always fully assenting to all of them. The recent book by M. Davies, *Rhetoric and Reference in the Fourth Gospel* (Davies, 1992), contains a significant interpretation of the Christology of the Fourth Gospel which argues that it is too often seen as if it were a fourth century Christological text. Future work on this topic will need to take seriously the arguments that 8.58 asserts superiority rather than priority (p. 86), the discussions of the language of descent (pp. 117, 174), the prologue (p. 122), Jesus As Son of God (p. 136), Jesus as Lord (p. 139), and related passages such as 20.29 (p. 125) and 10.30 (p. 135). On p. 135 there is a fuller statement of the interpretation of 5.18 which does not see it as ironical ('as an accusation within the story, but as a true statement on the narrative level'). The objection is that 5.19-46 refutes the accusation. I see the force of this, though at present I still think that these verses rebut not equality but the inference that equality implies rivalry. This view does involve an admission that Jn 5 contains paradox, but I do not think the text as a whole is free of that. I would also admit that the verses are clearer in asserting an equality of function than an equality of being (he does what the Father does). It is worth nothing that Davies' view of 5.27 (p. 190) is relevant to the interpretation of these verses. While there may be an allusion to the humanity of Jesus here, I do not think I can exclude an echo of the apocalyptic background to some uses of this phrase: the Johannine Christ is seen as a human figure, but one entitled to exercise more than ordinary human power i.e. the power of (final) judgment. I think it is significant that we move here from a Synoptic word about a human figure speaking for or against people at the judgment (Lk. 12.8-9 Q), to the Johannine

I particularly wish to express warm appreciation of the way in which over many years George Anderson brought insight and encouragement from the study of the Hebrew Bible to those working on the neighbouring Testament.

BIBLIOGRAPHY

Ashton, J.
1991   *Understanding the Fourth Gospel* (Oxford: Clarendon).
1992   'Narrative Criticism', unpublished paper shown to me.
Barrett, C.K.
1978   *The Gospel according to St John* (London: SPCK).
Brown, R.E.
1971   *The Gospel according to St John* (London: Chapman).
Bultmann, R.
1971   *The Gospel of John* (Oxford: Basil Blackwell).
Crossan, J.D.
1982   'Difference and Divinity', *Semeia* 23: 29-40.
Culpepper, R.A.
1983   *Anatomy of the Fourth Gospel* (Philadelphia: Fortress).
Davies, M.
1992   *Rhetoric and Reference in the Fourth Gospel* (JSNTSup, 69; Sheffield: JSOT Press).
Haenchen, E.
1984   *The Gospel of John* (Philadelphia: Fortress).
Kelber, W.H.
1990   'Birth of a Beginning: Jn 1.1-18', *Semeia* 52: 121-44.
Lindars, B.
1972   *The Gospel of John* (London: Oliphants).
Llewelyn, J.
1986   *Derrida on the Threshold of Sense* (London: Macmillan).
Loader, W.
1989   *The Christology of the Fourth Gospel* (Frankfurt: Lang).
Moore, S.D.
1989   *Literary Criticism and the Gospels* (London: Yale University Press).
Staley, J.L.
1991   'Stumbling in the Dark, Reaching for the Light: Reading Character in John 5 and 9', *Semeia* 53: 55-80.
Tolbert, M.
1991   'A Response from a Literary Perspective', *Semeia* 53: 203-12.

notion of one allowed to exercise the power of judgment which belongs to God. But Davies quite rightly points out this idea may be anticipated in Dan. 7.

PSALM 73: SCANDINAVIAN CONTRIBUTIONS

E. Nielsen

I

The main problems of Psalm 73 may be summed up in the following way:

1. To which literary category does the Psalm belong, according to form-criticism?
2. To which period of the Israelite-Judaean history should the Psalm be dated?
3. What was the Psalmist's problem?
4. What happened to solve this problem?
5. What is the actual content of the Psalmist's positive confession?
6. Is the present form of the Psalm free of later additions, according to Higher Criticism? and
7. Is there any need for emendations in the Hebrew text of the Psalm?

II

The questions above have been answered in various ways ever since the introduction of historical and philological research within the field of Old Testament literature. Suffice it here to quote two outstanding German scholars, one from the golden age of Higher Criticism (Duhm 1899: 189-93), the other the creator of Old Testament Form Criticism (Gunkel 1926: 311-20).

For historical reasons the first question could not be answered by Duhm; Gunkel understood the Psalm as a didactic poem, and consequently he would answer question 2 by referring the Psalm to later wisdom literature which flourished in the early period of the post-exilic age. Duhm, on the contrary, would date this Psalm to the second century BC and see it as related to the Pharisaic propaganda poems.

As to the third question, Gunkel agrees with Duhm that the main problem is the Divine retaliation, but Gunkel traces in v. 14 the personal misfortune of the Psalmist which so deeply embittered the problem for him. The fourth question concerns the interpretation of vv. 17-20. The admittance to the 'sanctuaries of God'—מִקְדְּשֵׁי אֵל—was, according to Duhm, equal to being introduced to a secret revelation of personal immortality, which became a fundamental principle among the Pharisees as opposed to the conservatism of the Sadducees. Gunkel's answer is quite different: the Psalmist's own reflection on the fate of the unrighteous people convinced him that in the end God would punish them by setting traps for them. By emendation the 'sanctuaries of God' have become 'pitfalls of God'—מוֹקְשֵׁי אֵל.

Since Duhm saw the introduction of the idea of personal immortality as the solution to the Psalmist's problem, his answer to the fifth question—an interpretation of vv. 23-26—was the author's assurance that the Lord will bring him into Paradise in the hereafter. Gunkel, on the contrary, denies the existence of any kind of eschatology within Psalm 73. He finds in vv. 23-26 expressions of confidence similar to those of the Psalms of Lamentation and the Psalms of Confidence; because of his firm conviction that the Lord is his portion for ever, the Psalmist can now forget his own more or less physical pains.

Concerning the sixth question, Duhm is remarkably 'conservative'; according to him none of the verses are secondary and they cannot therefore be omitted. Gunkel, on the other hand, declares v. 1 and v. 12 non-authentic and is tempted to reject also vv. 27-28, thus following C. Briggs (who shortened this Psalm considerably in his commentary in ICC [Briggs 1909: 140-50]). Furthermore Gunkel changes the order of vv. 16-21 (the original order should have been 21, 16, 22, 17-20, he says, but he does not explain *why* this order was changed!). Finally both critics put forward their proposals as to question number 7, but to go into details here would bring us too far away from our theme which concerns the Scandinavian contributions.

III

The Scandinavian contributions to the exegesis of Psalm 73 will be presented in two sections. The first of these deals with regular commentaries on the Psalms, the second is about papers on special problems relating to Psalm 73. Both sections will be arranged in chronological order, regardless of the nationality of the author in question.

Commentaries

The first edition of Frants Buhl's *Salmerne* appeared in 1900; with its 945 pages it was a standard work; the second edition appeared in 1918, revised and with an up-to-date list of literature, but nevertheless shorted to 933 pages. Buhl's commentary on the Psalms is the *opus magnum* in the Danish exegetical literature of this century. In general Buhl regards the OT Psalms as expressions of the rich religious life, typical of post-exilic Judah; Psalm 73 is dated to a fairly late period of Judaism (Buhl 1900: 474), and its author is conceived as an experienced old man. In the first edition Buhl has followed most interpreters by emending לישראל to ליֹשר אל, '[good is] God to the righteous' instead of '[good is God] to Israel' in v. 1, and in a rather diplomatic way he states 'v. 1 puts the result achieved through the scruples of the author at the head of the Psalm'. In the second edition (Buhl 1918: 468) Buhl is inclined to regard the verse as a later addition.

The turning point in vv. 17-18 is interpreted by Buhl as the psalmist's experience which has in a signal way corroborated the expectations of the pious people; v. 17 describes the author's 'introduction to the mysteries of God', for 'coming to the sanctuaries of God' should not be taken literally: that would be too external a mode of expression; this interpretation probably makes the Psalm less valuable as a theodicy; but the loss of value is compensated manifold by v. 23-28a where the psalmist has gained a position independent of incidental experiences (Buhl 1900: 479). As to the contents of vv. 23-28, Buhl remarks (Buhl 1900: 480-82) that

> the profound idea, expressed by the psalmist, is that the consciousness of community with God which in some other Psalms is the departing point for a feeling of being protected against Death, for the author of Psalm 73 to such a degree is the supreme good that any difference between good fortune and distress no longer exists for him.

Thus one understands why Buhl started his exegetical treatment of Psalm 73 by stating that Psalm 73 is probably the deepest and richest in the whole collection of Psalms (Buhl 1900: 474).

Although Sigmund Mowinckel's commentary on the Psalms, found in the annotated Norwegian translation of the Old Testament (*GTMMM*), did not appear until 1955, he may be referred to now, because, during the period from 1917 onwards, he contributed more significantly than any other scholar to a new and—probably—better understanding of the Psalms, with Gunkel's form-critical analyses as the point of departure for his own work on the cultic background of the Psalter. I shall supply his notes from 1955 with his observations, published in *Psalmenstudien I and VI* (1921; 1924) and in *Offersang og Sangoffer* (1951, English translation by D.R. Ap-Thomas: *The Psalms in Israel's Worship*, 1962).

Typical of Mowinckel's attitude to the Psalms are his remarks (1921) that Psalm 73, together with the related Psalms 37 and 49, should not be classified as didactic poems, but rather should be seen as thanksgiving psalms: the author of Psalm 73 has been ill (v. 4; cf. Gunkel above), and he has gone to the sanctuary (v. 17), probably to fulfil the usual purification ritual in order to regain his health. From his experiences at the sanctuary he draws the conclusion that the rich and unjust persons who afflicted him with illness by means of sorcery will be punished by God (Mowinckel 1921: 127-32).

As to the date of the Psalm, Mowinckel concluded from the social conflict attested by the Psalm that it *might* originate in the later period of the kingdoms (Mowinckel 1924: 3); but, more likely, it should be dated to the early post-exilic age (Mowinckel 1924: 42), since the negative judgment of the rich differed too much from that of ancient Israel (Mowinckel 1924: 62).

The problems of the Psalmist are almost the same moral and religious problems as found in the book of Job (Mowinckel 1951: 212).

How these problems were solved for the Psalmist is explained by Mowinckel (1955: 156-57) in the following way: the Psalmist received from the mouth of the priest or the cultic prophet the assurance that God had heard his prayer and would help him. Thereby he became convinced that God was really 'good towards Israel, towards those among his people who were of clean hearts'.

According to Mowinckel (cf. Gunkel above), the author of Psalm 73 does not express any idea of resurrection or eternal life in the hereafter. What he believes is that God will not forsake his devout people, but will save them from sudden or cruel death, so that they may die peacefully, full of days. For the Psalmist the bliss of the communion with God has become the highest value in life (Mowinckel 1951: 242; 569 n. 89).

The Hebrew text of the Psalm is, according to Mowinckel, not only free of later additions, but v. 28 should be added to, partly by means of phrases from the text of LXX, partly by such as Mowinckel himself devised. The text of v. 28 would thus run:

> But I [shall praise the Lord]
> for me it is good to be near to God.
> I made the Lord my refuge
> {have made him the castle of my heart},
> to tell about Thy wonders
> [in the gates of the city of Zion] (Mowinckel 1955: 159 and 456).

It should be added that although Mowinckel understood the Psalmists as temple-poets who wrote the Psalms for cultic/public use, he acknowledged the strongly personal character of Psalm 73: the Psalm contains genuine marks of personal experience which have contributed to the dissolution of the fixed style and created a special form of considerable effect by using elements from the psalms of lamentation, from the thanksgiving psalms and from the proverbial literature (Mowinckel 1924: 65). How such a personal poem came to be included in the psalm-collection is explained by the suggestion (Mowinckel 1962: 114) that Psalm 73, like Psalm 49 and Psalms 34 and 37, may have been deposited as a votive and memorial gift to Yahweh and as a testimony to future generations. On a later occasion these psalms have then been included in the collection of Psalms, the transmission of which was entrusted to the temple bards.

Mowinckel's psalm exegesis had a devotee in one of my OT teachers, Aage Bentzen, who, in 1939, published a commentary on the Psalms of 689 pages. Some years earlier he had written an introduction to the Psalms (Bentzen 1932), and still earlier he had published a study on some temple psalms in which he traced the idea of the sanctuary as a place of refuge, an asylum (Bentzen 1926). In the latter, five pages are devoted to Psalm 73; from this psalm, he says, we learn what the sanctuary meant to pious people. Exactly what the author experienced in the temple Bentzen could not tell us; but basing himself on an idea adopted from the Danish historian of religion Edv. Lehmann (*Stedet og Vejen*, 1918) he distinguished between two types of religion, one tied up with the holy place, the other dissociated from the place on the march, so to say. Psalm 73 belongs to the former type. The author does not say, 'Thou art, O Lord, forever with me', but on the contrary, 'I am forever with Thee' (v. 23). And Bentzen concluded (1926) that the psalmist may have belonged to the levites associated with temple service; these were mostly poor people who may have entertained feelings of enmity against the rich people of society.

In his commentary (1939: 421-30), which unfortunately contains no translation of any of the Psalms, Bentzen started with the question: is Psalm 73 a thanksgiving psalm or a didactical poem? (p. 421), and he ended the commentary (p. 430) by giving the answer: it is a thanksgiving psalm of a special kind, a conclusion drawn from v. 28 which he restored by means of the LXX text (cf. above Mowinckel).

Bentzen would date the psalm to a period of social and religious contrasts, that is, to the period immediately before, or after, the exile, since the temple is depicted as a live institution.

The problem of the psalmist was the contrast between his own unhappy fate (perhaps illness) and the luxurious life of the ungodly rich people which made him doubt God's justice, and this doubt he confesses as his sin (1939: 427). But Bentzen also made the suggestion that the psalm belonged to (his favourite) category of 'prayers applying for asylum' (1939: 430), an idea that is hardly compatible with the conception of the psalm as thanksgiving.

For the psalmist the problem was solved, according to Bentzen, by his experience in the sanctuary, when he perceived God's judgment upon his enemies. Furthermore the psalmist must also, in more than one case, have observed, that the happiness of the ungodly does not last for ever.

As to the content of the psalmist's positive confession in vv. 23-28, the principal idea of v. 25 is this: 'In the whole world nothing whatsoever can replace Thee'. And v. 26 is paraphrased by Bentzen: 'Whatever I have to suffer, God is my portion'. Quite apart from allusions in his commentary to texts from the Book of Job and from the New Testament, Bentzen has, as a matter of fact, offered at least three possible clues to the riddle of Psalm 73: 1. the author was struck by illness and sought the sanctuary; 2. the author applied for asylum in the sanctuary; or 3. the author belonged to the levites, the inferior temple personnel. What makes Bentzen's commentaries so fascinating is the way this author seems to be conversing with preceding interpreters, thus offering the reader a whole range of possibilities.

Finally I would like to refer to Hammershaimb's commentary on 15 OT Psalms, which was published in 1984 and which treats Psalm 73 on pp. 109-21. Hammershaimb presents the Psalm very nicely, translating it and identifying it as an individual psalm of thanksgiving and confidence, the personal character of which indicates a relatively late date of authorship. The problem of the relationship between value and fate, which has been most thoroughly dealt with in the book of Job, has been treated in Psalm 73 in a way which, to quote Buhl (cf. above), has made this psalm the most profound and richest in the entire collection. Hammershaimb refrains from emending the text of v. 1, but finds some kind of disharmony between this verse and the main body of the psalm, which makes it tempting to understand the verse as a later, liturgical, addition. As to the solution of the author's problem (vv. 17ff.) Hammershaimb tends to adopt the cultic interpretation; for the time being he accepts Kraus's idea, that the psalmist, either by divine assertion or by theophany, became aware that the luck of the ungodly will be short-lived and their disaster imminent.

After a thorough treatment of v. 24 Hammershaimb votes for a non-eschatological understanding of the confession; but his closing remark is that the author of Psalm 73 rises to a culmination point which at any rate is close to the idea of the nearness of God as a supreme good lasting beyond death.

Papers on Psalm 73

The Norwegian scholar H. Birkeland, who was, to some extent, a pupil of Mowinckel, has dealt with Psalm 73 on more than one occasion. In his book on the 'enemies' in the individual Psalms of lamentation or of thanksgiving which appeared in 1933, he devoted four pages to Psalm 73 (Birkeland 1933: 270-73). In accordance with his main thesis that 'the enemies' should be understood as foreigners, he rejects any emendation of v. 1; Israel and those of clean heart are identified; consequently the wicked persons, described in vv. 2-12, must be foreign oppressors, a view that Birkeland finds sustained by v. 10, which speaks of 'my nation' or 'his nation'. If the reading, 'my nation' is given priority we may conclude that the psalmist occupied a prominent position among his people, perhaps he was the High Priest. Birkeland rejects Mowinckel's idea of an author describing his own personal fate. The misfortunes depicted in vv. 14 and 21 are of a lasting character and should be understood as expressing national oppression. The רשעים of Psalm 73 'sind somit reichen *Heiden*'.

Verses 25-26 should not be interpreted as a belief in a life after death, but as a confession that the Lord will forever be close to him, the psalmist, and to Israel.

This idea was later revised by Birkeland in a paper on the belief in the resurrection of the dead in the Old Testament (Birkeland 1951: 60-79, esp. p. 70). He maintains that even if the sufferer must die he hopes that Yahweh in a wonderful way will raise him up so that he may stay with him *leʿôlâm* and *tâmîd*. The 'I' of the psalm regarded himself as an exception, Birkeland says: he has had a special revelation, v. 17; we see the belief in the mighty God who is able to perform miracles, and actually does so in some cases.

Birkeland's third contribution to the exegesis of Psalm 73 followed a few years later in a paper entitled 'The chief problems of Ps. 73.17ff.', published in *ZAW* (Birkeland 1955: 99-103). Referring to his book published in 1933, Birkeland regards the enemies as the heathen population. Their religious practice is in v. 27 depicted as a 'whoring away from thee', which is a Hosean expression for idolatry. Most remarkable—or unbelievable, as one prefers—is his interpretation of v. 17: מקדשי אל are taken as the illegitimate places of worship destroyed by the Josian reformation. Seeing them ruined and their idols (v. 20) destroyed, the author became convinced that the idolaters now flourishing would perish just as their sanctuaries of old had fallen into ruins. Birkeland does not ask why the wealthy oppressing class of foreigners are indifferent to what happened to their cherished sanctuaries of old!

The difficult expression אחר כבוד תקחני in v. 24 means, according to Birkeland, that the psalmist can see the glory before his eyes. And this glory does not consist in wealth and richness, but in the communion with God and the restoration of his people.

From a different angle H. Ringgren aimed at throwing light upon Psalm 73 in a paper in *VT* (Ringgren 1953: 265-72). Ringgren went through the psalm from the first to the last verse, stating his observations as remarks to his translation. What is essential to him is to point out the cult-mythological motives of the psalm.

According to Ringgren, the psalm has been written for the temple community, and so there could be no objection against the 'Israel' of v. 1. He rejects the frequent emendation of למותם in v. 4a, which is rendered by him as 'Denn ihr Tod hat keine Fesseln', and 'death', he says, may have been perceived in a personal way, like the Mot of the Ras Shamra texts. To explain v. 9, which he translates 'Sie setzen an den Himmel ihren Mund, und ihre Zunge wandert auf der Erde', Ringgren refers to the Ugaritic I, AB, II where a monster is devouring

Ba'al 'with one lip to the earth, and one to the heaven', and further-more to the text SS, lines 60ff., where a similar expression is used about the spouses of El who swallow the birds of heaven and the fishes of the sea. Thus Ringgren concluded that the ungodly were depicted in mythical colours, and their doings were understood as those of the powers of Chaos. It should be remembered, however, that the surrounding verses do not refer to the voracity of the unrighteous, but to their utterings.

Verses 17-20—the verses which brought the solution to the psalmist's problem—refer, according to Ringgren, to the *ritual combat*, a cultic performance enacted in the sanctuary. The כבוד of v. 24 must have something to do with a cultic appearance of some kind at the New Year festival, and v. 28, finally, which speaks of קרבת אלהים, under-lines the importance of approaching God in the temple.

Three years earlier the Danish minister C.B. Hansen had published a paper in *Dansk Teologisk Tidsskrift* entitled '"Bagefter Herlighed", et Bidrag til Forstaaelse af Psalme 73' ('"Behind glory", a Contribution to the Understanding of Psalm 73', Hansen 1950: 77-87). His paper should be mentioned here, because one of his points is that v. 24, according to the principle of *parallelismus membrorum*, should be rendered 'Thou leadest me by thy counsel and takest me behind glory' and that 'glory' should be understood as a concrete divine revelation, experienced by the psalmist in the temple of Jerusalem. The person who is 'taken behind glory' thereby participates in the divine freedom of borders of space and is initiated in relations and connections hidden to ordinary people (Hansen 1950: 86). But in contrast to Ringgren, Hansen did not point to any particular event at a New Year festival: v. 17 should be interpreted as the outcome of an oracle in connection with a Divine ordeal because of which the psalmist had gone to the sanctuary and possibly passed the night there. Verse 24 contains, according to Hansen, a concise formula of ecstasy in connection with divine revelation and instruction.

The other point worth mentioning is his observation of a corres-pondence between v. 9 and v. 25, both of which speak of 'heaven' and 'earth'. The two verses depict the contrast between the ungodly and the pious (*in casu*: the psalmist). Exercising their magic art, the ungodly associate themselves with various 'powers' on earth and in heaven, whereas the psalmist associates himself with the God of Israel and therefore has no need of any connection with such powers, whatever help they may be able to offer (Hansen 1950: 89).

A paper of a more recent date was published in the Swedish Exegetical Annual, vol. 41–42 (the Ringgren Festschrift), by the Finnish scholar K.-J. Illmann: 'Till tolkningen av Psalm 73' ('Remarks on the Exegesis of Psalm 73') (Illmann 1977: 120-29). In five small chapters he deals with

1.   the question of the type of the psalm: didactic poem or cultic psalm? He quotes various proposals, and in the last section of his paper (5) concurs absolutely with Kellermann: Psalm 73 is a psalm of confidence, bearing the stamp of wisdom.

2.   the question how the text should be divided. His answer comes close to that of Weiser: vv. 1-2; 3-12; 13-17; 18-26; 27-28, but since he speaks of six parts, he may have divided vv. 18-26 in two parts, vv. 18-22 and vv. 23-26.

3.   the question of the significance of the words חלק and, in the related Psalm 16, נחלה. In the Pentateuch we find the idea that the Lord is 'the levite's portion', and in Psalm 16 this levitical prerogative has been applied to the cult, whereas Ps. 73.26 testifies to a more spiritual application of this idea.

4.   the question of the קרבת אלהים, 'to come nearer to God', of v. 28. Most likely the expression points to a levite as the author of the psalm, but this does not prevent the expression from aiming, spiritually, at the role of the sanctuary as an asylum.

Finally I may be allowed to quote myself, at the end of this paper dedicated to a friend and scholar whom I like and admire. It is a very small observation, which has, so far, only been published once before, in *Festskrift til Holm-Nielsen*, which appeared in 1989 (Nielsen 1989: 89-95). The paper dealt with the difficulties connected with the translation of Hebrew play-on-words, and quite especially in the case of onomatopoeias. I happened to find such an onomatopoeia in Ps. 73.10, depicting the result of the seductive activity of the unrighteous. Most scholars in some way or other emend v. 10b, but I would defend the MT of v. 10b against all attacks. The words ומי מלא ימצו למו can be translated 'and abundant waters will be gulped down by them', and, if you read the Hebrew text aloud, you may even hear how they gulp!

What I have offered here are not abundant waters and my intention was not to seduce anybody, least of all George Anderson. I just wanted to hand him a cup of friendship.

BIBLIOGRAPHY

Bentzen, Aa.
    1926   *Jahves gæst* (Copenhagen: Haase).
    1932   *Indledning til de gammeltestamentlige salmer* (Copenhagen: Gad).
    1939   *Salmerne* (Copenhagen: Gad).
Birkeland, H.
    1933   *Die Feinde des Individuums in der israelitischen Psalmenliteratur* (Oslo: Grøndahl).
    1951   'The Belief in the Resurrection of the Dead in the OT', *ST*, III (Lund: Gleerup): 60-78.
    1955   'The Chief Problems of Ps. 73_{17ff}.', *ZAW* 67 (Berlin: Töpelmann): 99-103.
Briggs, C.
    1909   *The Book of Psalms*, II (ICC; Edinburgh: T. & T. Clark).
Buhl, F.
    1900   *Salmerne* (Copenhagen: Gyldendal).
    1918   *Salmerne* (Copenhagen: Gyldendal, 2 udg.).
Duhm, B.
    1899   *Die Psalmen* (KHAT, 14; Tübingen: Mohr).
Gunkel, H.
    1926   *Die Psalmen* (GHKAT, II.2; Göttingen: Vandenhoeck & Ruprecht, 4. Aufl.).
Hammershaimb, E.
    1984   *Femten gammeltestamentlige salmer* (Copenhagen: Gad).
Hansen, C.B.
    1950   ' "Bagefter Herlighed", et Bidrag til Forstaaelsen af Psalme 73', *DTT* 13: 77-87.
Illmann, K.-J.
    1977   'Til tolkningen av Psalm 73', *SEÅ* 41-42: 120-29.
Mowinckel, S.
    1921   *Psalmenstudien. I. Åwän und die individuellen Klagepsalmen* (Kristiania: Dybwad).
    1924   *Psalmenstudien. VI. Die Psalmdichter* (Kristiania: Dybwad).
    1951   *Offersang og sangoffer* (Oslo: Aschehoug).
    1955   'Salmeboken', *GTMMM*, IV (Oslo: Aschehoug): 9-292.
    1962   *The Psalms in Israel's Worship* (Oxford: Basil Blackwell).
Nielsen, E.
    1989   'Om oversættelse af ordspil fra hebraisk til dansk', in *Festskrift til Holm-Nielsen* (Copenhagen: Gad): 89-95.
Ringgren, H.
    1953   'Einige Bemerkungen zum lxxiii Psalm', *VT* 3: 265-72.

THE ENEMY IN THE OLD TESTAMENT[*]

J.W. Rogerson

In an essay entitled 'Segregation and Intolerance' Bernhard Lang asks:

> Is it possible to find in the sacred scripture of Judaism and Christianity an alternative to the religious segregation and intolerance that fills our modern world?[1]

His answer is no. The Jewish community, like other ancient societies, needed to identify itself in opposition to its neighbours, and it therefore instituted laws concerning marriage and religious practices in order to maintain and strengthen the boundaries that separated Jews from non-Jews. In the literature of the Old Testament the Jews were accordingly presented as

> a militarily powerful people who would annihilate polytheistic nations that threatened its unique religion. To the regret of the modern mind, such fantasies became part of the Bible.

Lang allows that this is not the only strand in the Old Testament. At the end of his article he mentions a 'trajectory that, although not opposing separation, was more tolerant'. The examples he gives are the book of Ruth (the possibility of marriage with Moabite women), the book of Judith (conversion to Judaism of an Ammonite) and Esther, where a Jewish girl becomes a Persian queen. However, Lang regards these voices as isolated, and 'not accorded the status of Deuteronomy'. 'In the Old Testament', he concludes, 'the separatist attitude prevails'.

---

[*]   A lecture delivered to a conference organized by the Department of Peace Studies in the University of Bradford, September 1992. Insofar as this paper touches upon the Psalms it gives me the opportunity to record with gratitude the many hours spent translating the Psalms under the chairmanship of Professor G.W. Anderson in the late 1960s and early 1970s as part of the Old Testament Translators' Translation sponsored by the British and Foreign Bible Society.

1.   Lang 1989: 115.

Lang is not writing about the enemy, but about segregation and intolerance; but they amount to the same thing. A society that erects the kinds of barriers described by Lang will not feel kindly towards enemies; and some of the narratives of Deuteronomy seem to bear out his point about the brutal treatments of enemies. Consider the following passage from Deut. 20.10-14:

> When you draw near to a city to fight against it, offer terms of peace to it. And if its answer to you is peace and it opens to you, then all the people who are found in it shall do forced labour for you and shall serve you. But if it makes no peace with you, but makes war against you, then you shall besiege it; and when the LORD your God gives it into your hand you shall put all its males to the sword, but the women and the little ones, the cattle, and everything else in the city, all its spoil you shall take as booty for yourselves...

This injunction applies to cities that are far from Israel. The inhabitants of cities of foreigners in the land of Israel are to be utterly destroyed (Deut. 20.15-18). The fact that, as far as we know, these commandments were never carried out, but were part of a religious object lesson warning readers against worshipping the gods of their neighbours, does not alter their seemingly horrid content. They convey the sense of exclusiveness and intolerance about which Lang writes.[2]

But has Lang said the last word? In two respects, no. First there are several incidents that can be mentioned in the Old Testament that show more generosity towards enemies than the Deuteronomy passage indicates. Second, by far the greatest amount of material on the subject of enemies is in the Psalms.

Among narratives in which enemies are treated generously the following can be mentioned. First, although the Midianites are Israel's enemies in Judges 6–8, it is noteworthy that Moses is portrayed as fleeing to exile in Midian, of marrying a Midianite woman Zipporah (Exod. 2.21), and of being supported by his Midianite father-in-law Jethro when he reaches Mt Sinai after the Exodus (Exod. 19). Second, Elijah went to live with a pagan woman in Zarephath during the drought in the reign of Ahab and brought her son back to life

---

2. For a recent discussion of these passages from Deuteronomy, which, while tracing their literary and social history, does not gloss over their difficulty for modern readers, yet which makes pertinent observations for today's world, see Braulik 1992: 146-51.

(1 Kgs 17). Third, in the midst of the narratives about war between the northern kingdom Israel and Syria, the Syrian commander Naaman was healed from leprosy by the prophet Elisha (2 Kgs 5.1-19a). These two last narratives were given prominence in Jesus' sermon in Nazareth (Lk. 4.20-29) to the distress of his hearers.

However, the bringing of such examples begs the question of how we should use the Old Testament in regard to the matter of enemies. Lang's approach is essentially historical and sociological. He sketches the development of Israelite religion from the perspective of his belief that there was a prophetic 'Yahweh-alone' movement from the ninth–eighth centuries; and he develops a model in which exclusiveness necessarily plays an important part.[3] But this reconstruction (assuming it to be correct—and it is certainly controversial) places the emphasis on Israel's development as apparent to the observer. A quite different approach, by way of the Psalms, opens up what the enemy meant in the religious experience and worship of the Old Testament. From this perspective we are in the realm of theology rather than of history and sociology and more likely to find a way from the Old Testament text to our own situation.[4]

A cursory glance at the Psalms will show how frequently one of the Hebrew words for 'enemy' occurs: twice in Psalm 3, once in Psalms 5 and 6, twice in Psalms 7 and 9, once in Psalm 10 and so on; and where a word for enemy does not occur at all, as in Psalm 2, enemies are nonetheless prominent. In what follows I shall deal with examples of three types of Psalm—Royal Psalms, Psalms of National Lament and Psalms of Individual lament.

Psalm 2 is about the threat to the rule of God's king in Jerusalem on the part of various enemies:

---

3.   See further Lang's stimulating monograph, *Monotheism and the Prophetic Minority* (1983).

4.   For the enemy in the Psalms see especially Keel 1969, and section 5, 'Die feindliche Mächte' in Kraus 1979. An article by Professor G.W. Anderson, 'Enemies and Evildoers in the Book of Psalms' (1965–66) provides a characteristically balanced survey and notes the possibility of a wide range of interpretations. It is in this spirit that I take the approach that I do in this paper. For a different, and in my opinion not wholly successful, attempt to relate the question to modern readers, see T.R. Hobbs and P.K. Jackson, 'The Enemy in the Psalms' (1991).

> The kings of the earth set themselves,
> and the rulers take counsel together,
> against the LORD and his anointed, saying
> 'Let us burst their bonds asunder,
> and cast their cords from us'.

We are not told who these kings and rulers are, nor what is meant by the bonds and cords which they wish to break. I shall return to these in a moment. The Psalm proceeds to point out how futile this opposition is. The Jerusalem king has been enthroned by God, and God has adopted the king as his son, and has promised that he will possess the nations even to the ends of the earth, and will break (or possibly rule, vocalizing *tir'am* for *tero'em*) them with a rod of iron, and dash them in pieces like a potter's vessel.

At first sight this seems no better than Deuteronomy 20; but it has to be read as part of the Zion theology of the Old Testament. This theology is not about Jewish national domination of the world, but about the universal rule of the God of Israel, a rule which, when established, will draw the nations to Jerusalem and give them the desire to

> beat their swords into ploughshares
> and their spears into pruning hooks.

God's rule will put an end to enmity because

> nation shall not lift up sword against nation
> neither shall they learn war any more (Isa. 2.4).

But this will only happen in the latter days. For the moment the hope that the world will be thus transformed is kept alive by the people of God in Jerusalem, for whom the king is the symbol and pledge of God's rule in a hostile world. This is why, in the Psalm, the kings and the rulers are not identified. In actual historical fact, Jerusalem was too insignificant for the kings of the earth to plot against it; nor did Jerusalem control them such that they would conspire together to throw off the bonds and cords by which they had been bound.[5] The language is symbolic; but it is nonetheless real in seeing in the

---

5. Qimhi identifies the problem and seeks to solve it by identifying the kings and rulers as the Philistines and the cords and bonds as those which bound Israel together after David became king over the united kingdom. See R. David Qimhi 1971: 11. Rashi gives the same interpretation in order to oppose the *minim*. See Rashi 1972: 1-2.

Jerusalem king a sign of hope for the ultimate triumph of goodness and justice in the world.[6]

Similar themes are found in Psalm 110, which opens with an explicit reference to enemies:

> The LORD says to my Lord,
> 'Sit at my right hand,
> till I make your enemies your footstool'.

As in Psalm 2, promises are made to the king:

> You are a priest for ever
> after the order of Melchizedek.

There then follow statements about the God-given success of the king against his enemies:

> he [probably God: but there are ambiguities here] will shatter kings on the
> day of his wrath.
> He will execute judgement among the nations,
> he will shatter chiefs over the wide earth.

Again, we see expectations on a world-wide scale which were never true in Israel's experience, and yet which transcend narrow, nationalistic aspirations and look for God's universal rule.

This perspective is seen most clearly in Psalm 97. It begins with the affirmation that the LORD is king, and calls upon the earth and coastlands to rejoice and be glad. His kingship is bad news for his enemies:

> Fire goes before him,
> and burns up his adversaries round about.

But the outcome of this is that 'the heavens proclaim God's righteousness and all the people behold his glory'. Ultimately, all those (including non-Israelites) who hate evil and are upright in heart are vindicated and share in the rejoicing.

If the existence of the people of God and the Jerusalem king are signs of hope for God's future universal rule, then the triumph of Israel's enemies is more than simply a national disaster. Psalm 79, in which a word for enemy does not occur, nevertheless vividly describes a situation in which Israel's foes have triumphed:

6. The same point is true if, with Gerstenberger (1988: 44-50), the Psalm is taken to be post-exilic in its extant form, expressing the hopes of the post-exilic community.

> the heathen have come into your inheritance,
> they have defiled your holy temple;
> they have laid Jerusalem in ruins.

We notice here that the psalmist speaks to God about 'your' not 'our' inheritance, and about 'your' not 'our' temple. What is at issue in the Psalm is not the vindication of Israel as much as the reputation of God himself.

> Why should the nations say, 'Where is their God?'

The Psalmist himself is in no doubt about the lordship of God. It is God's anger against Israel that has led to the defeat, which is why, among other things, the psalmist prays for God to avenge those of his people who have been slain so that this may

> be known among the nations before your eyes!

Part of the prayer for help also appeals to God as the protector of the helpless:

> Let the groans of the prisoners come before you.

Further, the psalmist prays for the punishment of those who have taunted God.

In interpreting this Psalm it must not be denied that there is a nationalistic element in it. The defeat of the nation is an occasion of national shame; reversal will vindicate national honour. But more prominent than the desire for national self-respect is the desire to see God's name vindicated in the world. If the people is restored, it will be so that, for generations to come, they will be able to worship God, give thanks to him and recount his praises.

From the National lament we move to the Individual lament. If defeat for the nation puts into question God's future rule over the world, so the defeat of the individual by his or her enemies questions the place of justice in the world. An excellent example of this point is Psalm 7. It opens with a cry to God for deliverance from the psalmist's enemies:

> O LORD my God, I take refuge in you;
> save me from all my pursuers, and deliver me,
> lest like a lion they rend me,
> dragging me away, with none to rescue.

But the psalmist is not looking for rescue at all costs. He acknowledges that if he has been at fault then his plight is deserved:

> if there is wrong in my hands,
> if I have requited my friend with evil
> or plundered my enemy without cause,
> let the enemy pursue me and overtake me,
> and let him trample my life to the ground...

That the psalmist's prime concern is to see that justice is done is indicated in vv. 6-8:

> Arise, O LORD, in your anger...
> awake, O my God; you have appointed a judgement.
> Let the assembly of the peoples be gathered about you;
> and over it take your seat on high.
> The LORD judges the peoples;
> judge me, O LORD, according to my righteousness
> and according to the integrity that is in me.

A hope for the establishment of God's just rule is expressed in the words of v. 9:

> O let the evil of the wicked come to an end,
> but establish the righteous,
> you who try the minds and heart
> you righteous God.

One of the results of approaching the subject of the enemy in the way suggested here is that, for the individual, the enemy is not necessarily a non-Israelite. In Psalm 35, the psalmist says of those who threaten him,

> I, when they were sick—I wore sackcloth,
> I afflicted myself with fasting.
> I prayed with head bowed on my bosom,
> as though I grieved for my friend or my brother;
> I went about as one who laments his mother,
> bowed down and in mourning.

Now that the psalmist is in some kind of unspecified trouble, these erstwhile friends have become his foes.[7] But again, the psalmist's main desire is that God's justice will be vindicated; for the psalmist's enemies seem to be those who doubt or deny the fact of God's righteous

---

7.   See especially ch. 3, 'Die treulosen Freunde', in Keel 1969.

judgment, and if they triumph it will be a dark day for those who seek to be faithful. This theme is, in fact, common in the Psalms, and there are numerous complaints about those (almost certainly Israelites) who doubt whether God can or will exercise justice and who become active enemies of the faithful accordingly (e.g. Pss. 14, 17, 22, 28, 36 etc.).

In his Commentary on the Epistle to the Romans, Karl Barth marvellously sums up the point I have been trying to make:

> But who is the *enemy*? The Psalmists knew, at any rate. They saw in the *enemy* not merely a rival or an unpleasant person, an opponent or an oppressor but the man who to my horror is engaged before my very eyes in the performance of objective unrighteousness, the man through whom I am enabled to have actual experience of the known man of this world and to perceive him to be evil. The enemy is the man who incites me to render evil for evil... We can now also understand why it is that in the passionate language of the Psalmist the enemy attains before *God* a stature which is almost absolute, and why it is that they cry unto God that they may be avenged of him. The enemy...lets loose in me a tempestuous, yearning cry for a higher—unavailable—compensating, avenging righteousness, and for a higher—absent —judge between me and him.[8]

There is much more in this vein, and the whole passage deserves close study and is important for understanding the enemy in the New Testament. For the present lecture, it leads us back to the Old Testament, because I believe that it helps us to take one final step in the discussion. If, with Barth, we believe that in the Psalms encounter with the enemy 'lets loose...a tempestuous, yearning cry for a higher—unavailable—compensating, avenging righteousness, and for a higher—absent—judge between me and him', how does the Old Testament, at the human level, take the matter into its own hands? It does so in two ways. First, it grants the enemy the temporary status of servant of God to execute his righteous judgment upon the Israelite nation, even if this involves punishing the righteous with the wicked. Isa. 7.18-19 proclaims that

---

8.   Barth 1968: 471-72. I am indebted to Kraus (1979: 166-67) for this reference, the translation of which I have altered at two points with reference to the German. Barth is saying much more than I am attempting here—he is dealing with the whole problem of the temptation in the modern word to overcome evil with evil. Where he is pertinent to the present paper is in linking the theme of the enemy to the wider question of God's justice in the world.

> In that day the LORD will whistle for the fly which is at the sources of the streams of Egypt, and for the bee which is in the land of Assyria. And they will all come and settle in the steep ravines, and in the clefts of the rocks, and on all the thorn bushes, and on all the pastures.

The meaning of the imagery is unmistakable—God will execute judgment on his people by summoning the armies of Egypt and Assyria against them.

At Jer. 25.9, the people are warned that they have not obeyed God, and therefore,

> behold, I will send for all the tribes of the north, says the LORD, and for Nebuchadrezzer the king of Babylon, my servant, and I will bring them against this land and its inhabitants, and against all these nations round about; I will utterly destroy them, and make them a horror, a hissing, and an everlasting reproach.

The status of servant does not last long, for, in v. 12 we are told that

> after seventy years are completed, I will punish the king of Babylon and that nation, the land of the Chaldeans, for their iniquity, says the LORD, making the land an everlasting waste.

But we notice that what is behind this language is the notion of the working out of justice on a universal scale. Babylon will punish Judah for its wickedness; in turn, Babylon will be punished for its wickedness. Thus one way of coping with the problem of evil and the need for justice as it arises in the Psalms is by seeing God at work in the historical process executing the judgment for which prayer is made. Obviously this does not necessarily help the individual's cry for justice nor comfort the psalmist who sees the triumph of the enemy as a setback for God's rule. The Old Testament does not offer a single, consistent answer to these problems.

The second way of coping is through literature such as Deut. 20.10-18. The connection between the prose parts of Jeremiah and the book of Deuteronomy has long been recognized, and the theme of utter destruction was present in the Jeremiah passages quoted a moment ago. If a deuteronomistic school is behind the prose passages of Jeremiah and passages such as Deut. 20.10-18, we have the interesting juxtaposition in which the Israel which is to destroy other peoples utterly, will itself be utterly destroyed by its enemies. Clearly, we are not in the world of reality, but in a world where enemies have become symbols for wickedness, and utter destruction a symbol for the rooting out of evil.

This study of the enemy in the Old Testament has not been

completely exhaustive. It has not dealt, for example, with texts that speak of God as an enemy (e.g. Job 33.10), neither has it dealt with the enmity of personified forces of chaos, illness and death.[9] Its aim has been to argue for a theological approach to the matter via the Psalms. Such an approach defines the enemy not in social terms as the outsider or alien, but in moral terms as those who, even within the community, doubt or seek actively to undermine the justice of God. By transcending the boundaries of the local community or the nation and by placing the problem of enmity in the context of the desire for universal justice, the Old Testament provides us with guidelines for tackling the problem of enmity in our own world.

BIBLIOGRAPHY

Anderson, G.W.
1965–66   'Enemies and Evildoers in the Book of Psalms', *BJRL* 48: 18-29.
Barth, K.
1968   *The Epistle to the Romans* (trans. E.C. Hoskyns; Oxford: Oxford University Press).
Braulik, G.
1992   *Deuteronomium*, II (Die Neue Echter Bibel; Würzburg: Echter Verlag).
Gerstenberger, E.
1988   *The Forms of Old Testament Literature: Psalms Part 1* (Grand Rapids, MI: Eerdmans).
Hobbs, T.R., and P.K. Jackson
1991   'The Enemy in the Psalms', *BTB* 21: 22-29.
Keel, O.
1969   *Feinde und Gottesleugner* (Stuttgarter Biblische Monographien, 7; Stuttgart:Verlag Katholisches Bibelwerk).
Kraus, H.-J.
1979   *Theologie der Psalmen* (Biblischer Kommentar Altes Testament; Neukirchen: Neukirchener Verlag).
Lang, B.
1983   *Monotheism and the Prophetic Minority* (Social World of Biblical Antiquity; Sheffield: Almond Press).
1989   'Segregation and Intolerance' in M. Smith and R.J. Hoffman, (eds.), *What the Bible Really Says* (Buffalo: Prometheus Books): 115-36.
Qimhi
1971   *Haperush Hashalem 'al Tehillim* (Jerusalem: Mossad Harav Kook).
Rashi
1936   *Parshandatha: The Commentary of Rashi on the Prophets and Hagiographs* (ed. I. Maarsen; Jerusalem: Maqor, repr. 1972).

---

9. See Kraus 1979: 168-70.

WHO IS 'THE MAN' IN LAMENTATIONS 3?
A FRESH APPROACH TO THE INTERPRETATION OF THE BOOK OF LAMENTATIONS

M. Saebø

In the perspectives of 'Biblical Interpretation' the book of Lamentations has a most specific position among the Old Testament books. Unlike the Hebrew canon of the Holy Writ the Alexandrian canon attached the book to one of the 'great prophets', to the book of Jeremiah. This well-known placement of the book of Lamentations in the Septuagint was not only an expression of the traditional Jewish claim of a Jeremian authorship of the book (*B. Bat.* 14b/15a), even though the book in the Hebrew canon had an 'independent' position, but it also became indicative for the main Christian understanding of the book, as may be seen in the Vulgate and later Christian Bible translations. Through centuries the book of Lamentations lived its life in the shadow of the book of Jeremiah; and the traditional assumption of its Jeremian authorship was virtually unanimous. When, however, the book's assumed dependence on Jeremiah had become basically weakened in modern biblical scholarship a host of differing opinions of the book arose, as to its time and authorship, style and structure, content and theology. In modern research (cf. Brandscheidt 1983: 1-19; Westermann 1990: 15-81) the book seems to represent an unsolved riddle.

I

As may be indicated by the issues just mentioned, there are *different aspects of the enigmatic character of the book*. Most noteworthy, in the first instance, is its specific stylistic character since all five chapters of the book in one way or another have a form related to the Hebrew alphabet with its 22 letters. Four of five chapters have a firm *acrostic* structure, following the Hebrew alphabet; ch. 5 has 22 verses but not an acrostic form. This stylistic phenomenon provides the book with a literary unity that is unique in the Old Testament; together with the assumption of Jeremian authorship of the book this unitary character may have contributed to the unanimity of the traditional view of the book.

But there are formal differences as well, not only between Lamentations 1–4 and 5, as already mentioned, but also between chs. 1–2 and 4, on the one hand, and ch. 3, on the other. In the first two chapters a stanza has three lines/bicola (except for 1.7 and 2.19 that have four) and in ch. 4 two lines; and in these three chapters, of which the first two seem to constitute the most coherent formal unity, only the first line of each stanza begins with a letter according to the sequence of the Hebrew alphabet; and each chapter has 22 verses. In Lamentations 3, however, each stanza has three lines and every line of the stanza starts with the same Hebrew letter. Here one has counted lines; therefore Lamentations 3 has 66 verses. In other words, the acrostic style seems to be most fully elaborated, being on the highest level of artistry, in Lamentations 3: the middle chapter of the whole. Perhaps this has been done to present the chapter not only as the middle part of the book but even as its central and most important one. Also, Lamentations 3 starts differently from the other chapters: it begins with an emphatic אֲנִי 'I', whereas Lamentations 1–2 and 4 start with אֵיכָה 'how!', which is a standard opening word for a 'dirge' (Isa. 1.21; for קִינָה 'dirge', that does not occur in Lamentations, cf. Amos 5.1; 8.10; Jer. 9.9; 2 Chron. 35.25). In this way there may be some correspondence between the opening words—being like 'titles'—of these chapters and their acrostic differences.

Secondly, modern form criticism has traced the formal differences within the book much further; and the unitary impression that the book may leave at first sight is shown to be only a part of the whole picture. With a starting point in the observation that 'political dirge' seems to be the main *Gattung* of the book (Jahnow 1923: 168-91) one has differentiated in detail between the various forms included, first of all 'communal lament', in Lamentations 1–2 and 4 and mainly in Lamentations 5, and 'individual lament', especially in Lamentations 3 (Gunkel and Begrich 1933: 117, 136; see further section II below). The outcome of this shows that the acrostic units may be covering different and also 'mixed' forms (Gunkel and Begrich 1933: 258, 400-401; cf. 407-15). However, Kraus has strongly questioned the term

'political dirge', maintaining that it is a 'misleading' *Gattung* determination. He has put forward a new cultic and liturgical explanation,
and with reference to some Akkadian texts he has defined the particular genre of the book to be a 'Lament over the Ruined Sanctuary';
thereby he has also tried to explain the difficult question of the book's
Sitz im Leben as a cultic and liturgical one (Kraus 1960: 8-13). But
Kraus, who might be right in some details but not in total, has
received little support for his theory (cf. criticism by scholars like
Rudolph [1962: 9-10], Childs [1979: 592] and Westermann [1990: 22-
31]). As for Lamentations 5, finally, in order to mention but a few
samples of recent scholarly views, Westermann will not simply characterize the concluding chapter of the book as a 'communal lament', but
he has carefully differentiated between framing prayers (5.1, 21) and
a 'we-lament' (5.2-18) as well as other forms (Westermann 1990: 60,
172-80). This procedure of detailed differentiation, here and elsewhere in the book, has been characteristic for much recent study on
the Lamentations and has contributed to a better understanding of it.

Thirdly, the possibility of different 'voices' in different parts of the
book of Lamentations may be regarded as 'a stylistic concern', on a
literary level only (Lanahan 1974: 41). However, the question of
authorship may easily be raised as well, as it also has been done in
different ways, and the more so since the questions of structural unity
and of authorship are closely related to each other. Although many
scholars go for a unity of authorship of the book (recently e.g. Plöger
1969: 129, 163-64; Brandscheidt 1983: 202-203; Johnson 1985: 72),
in current research these questions are more complex and debatable
than ever before, and particularly with reference to Lamentations 3
(see next section). Closely related to this issue is, moreover, the question of historical situation and the 'time' of authorship, whereby an
exilic dating is found to be most likely by the majority of scholars (cf.
e.g. Gottwald 1954: 21; Childs 1979: 593; Hillers 1984: xviii-xix;
Johnson 1985: 72-73); but for some parts much later datings have
been argued for as well (cf. currently Kaiser 1984: 356; 1992: 105-
106). The very differing views in this matter may represent a substantial challenge to future studies in Lamentations.

Lastly, questions of the content and theology of the book of
Lamentations have also been broadly discussed recently, especially
with regard to the problem of what might have been the nearest theological and traditio-historical context for the book. Of special interest

in this respect—apart from a still held relation to the book of Jeremiah (cf. Wiesmann 1936; differently Kaiser 1984: 359)—is the question of a possible Deuteronomistic influence, and if so, the extent of it. This aspect has been discussed by some scholars, notably by Gottwald and Albrektson. Gottwald maintains he has found 'the situational key to the theology of Lamentations in the tension between Deuteronomic faith and historical adversity', particularly so in a time after the Deuteronomic reform, and, more specifically, in the 'terms of the schema of tragic reversal', to which also the 'theme' of Zion belonged (Gottwald 1954: 52-62). Albrektson, in a stimulating discussion with Gottwald (Albrektson 1963: 214-30), has more strongly related the theology of Lamentations to the *Zion tradition* as 'a specific Jerusalem tradition' (p. 219). For him the theological 'key' is to be found 'in the tension between specific religious conceptions and historical realities: between the confident belief of the Zion traditions in the inviolability of the temple and city, and the actual brutal facts' (p. 230). Thereafter, Albrektson also discussed the influence of 'Deuteronomic faith', especially related to Deuteronomy 28 (pp. 231-39). In this way he was able to show that the 'opinions encountered in this book have from a traditio-historical point of view roots in at least two directions', i.e. in the two tradition entities just referred to, and the 'link' between them is the 'concentration on the temple of Jerusalem' (p. 238).

The interpretation of Albrektson may prove to be most fruitful for future scrutiny in the book of Lamentations. Concentrating on Zion, however, Albrektson has first of all brought Lamentations 1–2 and 4–5 into focus; Lamentations 3 is not made a subject for similar or corresponding attention in his *Studies,* nor has the lament as form and phenomenon—*mirabile dictu*—received any proper treatment. Therefore, in the present situation a new concentration on the specific character of Lamentations 3 may be essential and appropriate.

II

There seems to be a growing recognition of *the central position and significance of ch. 3* in the book of Lamentations. Not only did this chapter constitute the main topic of the monograph of Renate Brandscheidt in 1983, but the discussion of problems in Lamentations 3 runs like a scarlet thread also through the most recent research history of Lamentations by Westermann (1990: 32-81, esp. 65-71; cf. 137-60, 187-88). The chapter is not only regarded as 'central' but is also said to be 'the most controversial chapter in the book' (Childs 1979: 592). Especially in view of Lamentations 3 the opinions of scholars have been differing considerably. To take just one example: an impressive bouquet of widely diverging datings of the chapter, reaching from the time soon after 587 BC to the third century BC, has been put nicely together by Kaiser (1992: 104).

There are certainly various reasons for the remarkable plurality of learned views regarding Lamentations 3. To be sure, the varying opinions of scholars may have been dependent on—apart from scholarly subjectivity (cf. Plöger 1969: 163)—changing 'attitudes' in biblical studies and may therefore be regarded as a barometer of altering trends in method. However, the major or really substantial reason is doubtless to be found in the text itself, and then in a double way: the differing views may partly be caused by the very complex structure of the chapter, and partly by the intricate and somewhat confusing question of the identity of 'the man' who is presenting himself at the opening of the chapter: אני הגבר 'I am the man…'.

Much scholarly energy has been used in the identification of this 'man'. As long as the traditional view of the authorship of Lamentations was predominant, it was natural to see the prophet Jeremiah in 'the man' (cf. first of all Wiesmann 1926: 147), and the more so as Jeremiah was a man of suffering (Jer. 8.23), who in his Confessions made many personal complaints (e.g. Jer. 12.7-12; 15.10-18; 20.7-18). With special reference to the word of 2 Chron. 35.25 a relationship between Jeremiah and King Josiah is established: 'Jeremiah also made a lament for Josiah'; from this late notice an identification of 'the man' with King Josiah has been made, although the description in Lamentations 3 is scarcely comparable to his tragic death. Rudolph (1962: 196-99) has shown that neither of these assumptions may be regarded as plausible. But, on the other hand, Rudolph has renewed an identification with Jeremiah, not directly, but in some 'ideal' form, assuming that Jeremiah has become a 'paradigm' (*Vorbild*) of suffering, and in 3.1 he is the 'spokesman' of the author, who is the same in all five chapters of Lamentations (1962: 227-45). In this way, Rudolph may also have intended to include to some extent—without accepting—the older view of a 'collective I', representing the 'congregation' (*Gemeinde*) of the people of Israel, as scholars like

R. Smend and M. Löhr maintained around 1890 (cf. Westermann 1990: 33-34). Differently and yet similarly Kraus has interpreted ch. 3 as a 'paradigmatic demonstration' of suffering (*die Verkündigung des urbildlichen Leidens*, Kraus 1960: 51-70); and 'the man' is anonymous (pp. 54-55). Kaiser, again, will not exclude the possibility that the author of Lamentations 3, from the fourth century, has seen Jeremiah in 'the man', as 'the suffering paradigmatic prayer' (*als den im Leiden vorbildlichen Beter*, Kaiser 1984: 359; cf. 1992: 158). Most elaborate in this respect, however, is the study of Brandscheidt; she relates Lamentations 3 to 'the suffering experiences of the prophet Jeremiah on the level of universal validity (*Allgemeingültigkeit*)' for the people that is still under the wrath of God; and 'the man' is no historical figure but the 'pious one' in general (*der Fromme*), whose faith, after the catastrophe of his people, has deep scruples (Brandscheidt 1983: 350). And, very similar, 'the man' is for Hillers 'not a specific historic figure, but rather the typical sufferer. He is an "Everyman", a figure who represents what any man may feel when it seems that God is against him' (Hillers 1984: 64). More on the 'collective' line is the understanding of Lam. 3.1 by Gordis, who, referring to 'corporate personality', the well-known term of H. Wheeler Robinson, as well as to studies of 'primitive psychology', has characterized 'the man' as a 'fluid personality' (Gordis 1974: 172-74). 'By and large', says Childs finally, summing up, 'the majority opinion favours seeing the figure in ch. 3 as a representative figure without a connection with Jeremiah' (1979: 593).

Many scholars in recent research of Lamentations, then, have favoured interpretations of 'the man' in Lam. 3.1 that either see in him a 'representative figure', an *Urbild* or *Vorbild*, or regard him, in a more general way, as a pious and just 'Everyman'. But I remain reserved with regard to these explanations, because there seem to be adequate grounds for critical questions, as to what sense these notions and terms really might have: whether they are too abstract for the context in Lamentations 3, and whether they are inaccurately neutralizing or suspending the concrete historical aspect of the text. Whatever the sense of these concepts might be, I am inclined to see them as hardly adequate terms for the very concrete descriptions in Lamentations 3. It may, even further, be contended that the special grandeur of the book of Lamentations, in ch. 3 also, is its unique combination of vivid concreteness, extended use of elements from variegated traditions, and of an artistic composition, including the firm form of an acrostic scheme. A proper discussion of the key question, who 'the man' of Lam. 3.1 might be, has to take all three components into balanced consideration.

The very complex composition or structure of Lamentations 3 has been thoroughly analyzed by some scholars; and much scrutiny has been applied to a detailed differentiation of the formal elements of the text; and, again, these efforts have provided rather different results. A prudent and mainly convincing analysis has been presented by Kaiser (1992: 154-60); and significant monographic contributions have been given, among others, by Brandscheidt, who has focused on the wisdom influence, among many other elements, in this chapter (1983: 222-23; cf. 29-50), and by Westermann, who in particular, here as earlier, has paid special attention to the form and content of the lament (e.g. 1990: 66-81, 143-60). It should be unnecessary to rehearse the formal details on this occasion. But, without any possibility of lengthy arguments in this connection, it may be appropriate to reconsider briefly some of the main issues, where it will be crucial to keep the proper balance of elements involved:

a. The complexity of Lamentations 3 is partly grounded in a hermeneutically significant relation of the main form of the book and this chapter, constituted by a strict and advanced acrostic pattern, on the one hand, and the many and variegated tradition fragments used, on the other. That implies that any literary or phraseological differentiation and comparison between individual elements within the chapter itself or between Lamentations 3 and its context (cf. e.g. Brandscheidt 1983: 220) has only limited relevance; for in view of the overarching acrostic form the author has worked rather 'freely' with a rich tradition material (cf. rightly Kaiser 1992: 154).

b. In Lamentations 3 there are units of both an 'I' and a 'we' (in 3.40-47), and they should remain as they are, not being explained, for any reason, by each other, as has been done in some 'collective' theories regarding the 'I'. There is, further, also a difference between the 'I' and his 'people' (cf. 3.14), that may be kept too, although in early Jewish interpretation or *Wirkungsgeschichte* of the text there seems to be a tendency to weaken this aspect, as may be shown by early textual variants to עמי in v. 14 (*BHS*; cf. Albrektson 1963: 137-38; Brandscheidt 1983: 22). A proper definition of the relationship of 'I' and 'we' in this chapter is difficult but challenging.

c. There are clearly relations in Lamentations 3 between various elements of personal experiences, especially in the beginning of the chapter, apparently connected with the historical situation after 587 BC, and elements of a more 'timeless' or instructive and wisdom character (as in v. 27 and some other parts of 3.21-39). Although this relationship also is hard to define properly it is hardly adequate to see a wisdom trait in every personal aspect of description, as Brandscheidt seems to do, at least partly (1983: 222-23).

d. With some connection to the last point a final comment may be made on the relationship of Lamentations 3 to its immediate context. With good reason it is maintained by many that Lamentations 3 is most likely related to the same historical context of early exile as the chapters around. But, more than that, one may even contend that the sequence of chapters in Lamentations seems to be defined not as much on chronological or redaction-historical grounds as for ideological or theological reasons. The relation of Lamentations 3 to chs. 2 and 4, in particular, may be explained anew in a perspective like this, as will be done tentatively in the next section.

III

When, finally, we turn to a positive examination of the puzzling question of *an identification of 'the man' in Lamentations 3*, a fresh approach to the problem will have to take the very complex state of research into due consideration. Even though the number of attempts is most impressive, new insights might still be possible.

Dominantly in the foreground of the book of Lamentations, especially in its first two chapters as well as in the two last ones, stands the figure of *Zion*, being metaphorically and vividly portrayed as a mourning widow. The historical situation described is the catastrophic fall of Jerusalem in 587 BC, followed by miserable conditions for the people who had remained in the ruined city.

The theme of Zion has, as already mentioned, been brought into focus first of all by Albrektson. When introducing the 'new ideas' of the specific 'Jerusalem tradition' he says rightly: 'The leading themes here are the election of David and of his house, and the idea of Zion and its temple as the abode of God' (1963: 219). In the succeeding discussion, however, the latter 'idea' is the only issue, not the theme of 'the election of David and of his house'; and that may be regarded as a serious disadvantage not only for the outstanding *Studies* of Albrektson but for the studies of Lamentations in general, and for the interpretation of Lamentations 3 in particular. For the use of *the twin themes of Zion and the Davidic king* may be regarded as the 'key' to a new solution of the riddle of Lamentations 3, and so also of the book as a whole, especially in view of the sequence of Lamentations 2-3-4.

As for 'the man' in Lam. 3.1 *royal identifications* have also been brought forward: among many others, first of all an identification with King Josiah; but the inadequacy of this identification has already been pointed out by Rudolph, as mentioned above. Further, Porteous has proposed King Jehoiachin to be 'the man' (1961: 244-45), but without being followed by others; and there is really no special evidence for this assumption in the text (cf. Hillers 1984: 63), and even less so since Rudolph's dating of Lamentations 1 to 597 has also proved to be less probable (Kaiser 1992: 104). Even though these identifications may rightly be falsified, the matter of a royal identification as such is by no means disproved.

It may be considered as rather curious that scholars so far—and as far as I know—have not seen what might be the nearest identification and the simplest solution of the problem of Lam. 3.1, namely an identification of 'the man' with the last king of Jerusalem, *King Zedekiah*, whose fall with the temple and the royal city was most dramatic, as it is realistically narrated in 2 Kgs 25.1-21, especially in the vv. 1-7 (REB):

> In the ninth year of [the] reign [of Zedekiah]...King Nebuchadnezzar of Babylon advanced with his whole army against Jerusalem...; the siege lasted till the eleventh year of King Zedekiah. In the fourth month of that year, on the ninth day of the month, when famine was severe in the city and there was no food for the people, the city capitulated. When king Zedekiah of Judah saw this, he and all his armed escort left the city, fleeing by night...The Chaldaean army pursued the king and overtook him in the lowlands of Jericho. His men all forsook him and scattered, and the king was captured and, having been brought before the king of

Babylon at Riblah, he was put on trial and sentenced. Zedekiah's sons
were slain before his eyes; then his eyes were put out, and he was brought
to Babylon bound in bronze fetters.

The text of 2 Kgs 25.1-7, with its parallel in Jer. 52.4-11, seems
nearly to have been overlooked by modern scholars, if compared with
2 Kgs 25.27-30 on the release of King Jehoiachin. But it will be
adequately related to Lamentations 3, since there are some linking
features in 2 Kings 25 and Lamentations 3 that may help to elucidate
the identification of 'the man' in Lam. 3.1.

When, first of all, both 2 Kgs 25.7b and Lam. 3.7b are speaking of
'bronze fetters', there is clearly some conformity between the texts.
The chains are, at the same time, signs of being a prisoner, as it is
directly stated in the interesting addition in Jer. 52.11b ('put in prison
till the day of his death') and is similarly indicated in the description
in Lam. 3.7-9, possibly also in vv. 5-6 and 52-54; and he is treated as
a captive (cf. Lam. 3.15-16). Further, there is a remarkable resem-
blance, if not direct connection, between Lam. 3.2, where 'the man'
complains that 'He has driven me away and made me walk in darkness
rather than light' [NIV], and the narrative of 2 Kgs 25.7b saying, 'his
eyes were put out, and he was brought to Babylon...' Even though the
picture of the deep misery of 'the man' also includes other traditional
elements of individual lament (cf. Lam. 3.10-15), yet it may have
been influenced by the tragic experiences of King Zedekiah in 2 Kings
25, and this point of reference may have constituted some sort of a
'kernel' for the extended and more elaborated lament composition of
Lamentations 3. Also, it is scarcely accidental that there are references
to the *king* of Judah just in the two chapters adjoining Lamentations 3,
namely in Lam. 2.6b ('king and priest alike he spurned') and 2.9b
('Her king and rulers are exiled among the Gentiles') and, notably, in
4.20, which says (REB),

The Lord's anointed (משיח יהוה), the breath of life to us,
was caught in their traps;
although we had thought to live among nations
safe under his protection.

This may contribute to the impression that the chs. 2–3–4 represent a
specific literary sequence in the book of Lamentations. Without a
further discussion here, even the relationship of the individual and the
collective elements of its lament may be more easily explained
through a royal-'messianic' interpretation of Lamentations 3, since the

king in a unique way is the primary representative of the people.

The assumption of an identification of 'the man' with the last *Davidic* king in Jerusalem may, finally, be further substantiated if one refers the picture of 'the man' to the specific Davidic-'messianic' traditions that seem to be rooted in 2 Samuel 7 and are 'developed' in manifold ways in royal Psalms and by some Jerusalem prophets. Remarkably, therefore, the expression of Lam. 3.1b, 'the rod (שֵׁבֶט) of his wrath', may be related to 2 Sam. 7.14b, on the one hand, and to Ps. 89.31-33, on the other; and the complaints of Lam. 3.17-18 (cf. also vv. 14-15 and 59-61) are similar to the lament of Ps. 89.39-46, 51-52, as are also Lam. 3.31-33 in relation to Ps. 89.34. The closeness of Lamentations 3 to Psalm 89 is conspicuous; in general, however, attention has been barely paid to it. Also the well-known reference to the king of Judah, in his unique position, in Lam. 4.20, cited above, comes close to the longer description in Ps. 89.19-38. And, in the end, returning to the book of Jeremiah, it can hardly be overlooked that in the composition of Jer. 22–23.8, after the prophet's complaint about and rebuke of the last kings of Judah, ending with King Jehoiachin, there is a messianic saying in 23.5-6, ending with a most noteworthy name: 'YHWH our Righteousness (צִדְקֵנוּ)', that in some way might be a 'word-play' with the name of King Zedekiah.

In conclusion, it may briefly be stated that the specific form and composition, theology and message of the book of Lamentations, in particular the sequence of Lamentations 2–4 and the interpretation of the complex Lamentations 3, may find an appropriate 'key' in the special Jerusalem traditions of *Zion and David*; it is there that it has its primary traditio-historical context. And the enigmatic 'man' of Lam. 3.1 might be the last king of the House of David in Jerusalem, King Zedekiah.

BIBLIOGRAPHY

Ackroyd, P.R.
1968   *Exile and Restoration: A Study of Hebrew Thought of the Sixth Century BC* (London: SCM Press).
Albrektson, B.
1963   *Studies in the Text and Theology of the book of Lamentations* (Studia Theol. Lundensia, 21; Lund: Gleerup).
Brandscheit, R.
1983   *Gotteszorn und Menschenleid: Die Gerichtsklage des Leidenden Gerechten in Klgl 3* (Trierer Theol. Studien, 41; Trier).

Brunet, G.
1968   *Les lamentations contre Jérémie: Réinterpretation des quatre premières Lamentations* (Bibliothèque de l'école des hautes études: Sciences religieuses, 75; Paris).

Childs, B.S.
1979   *Introduction to the Old Testament as Scripture* (London: SCM Press).

Fuerst, W.J.
1975   *The Books of Ruth, Esther, Ecclesiastes, the Song of Songs, Lamentations* (Cambridge Bible Commentary; Cambridge).

Gordis, R.
1974   *The Song of Songs and Lamentations* (rev. and augmented edn; New York).

Gottlieb, H.
1978   *A Study on the Text of Lamentations* (Acta Jutlandica, XLVIII, Th. Ser. 12; Århus).

Gottwald, N.K.
1954   *Studies in the book of Lamentations* (SBT, I/14; London: SCM Press).

Gunkel, H. and J. Begrich
1933   *Einleitung in die Psalmen* (Göttingen: Vandenhoeck & Ruprecht).

Hillers, D.R.
1984   *Lamentations* (AB, 7A; Garden City, NY: Doubleday [1972]).

Jahnow, H.
1923   *Das hebräische Leichenlied im Rahmen der Völkerdichtung* (BZAW, 36; Giessen: de Gruyter).

Johnson, B.
1985   'Form and Message in Lamentations', *ZAW* 97: 58-73.

Kraus, H.-J.
1960   *Klagelieder (Threni)* (BKAT, 20; Neukirchen–Vluyn: Neukirchener Verlag, 2nd edn).

Kaiser. O.
1984   *Einleitung in das Alte Testament* (Gütersloh: Gütersloher Verlagshaus, 5th rev. edn).
1992   *Klagelieder* (ATD, 16/2; Göttingen: Vandenhoeck & Ruprecht, 4th edn): 91-198.

Lanahan, W.F.
1974   'The Speaking Voice in the book of Lamentations', *JBL* 93: 41-49.

Plöger, O.
1969   *Die Klagelieder* (HAT, I/18; Tübingen: J.C.B. Mohr, 2nd edn): 127-64.

Porteous, N.W.
1961   'Jerusalem—Zion: The Growth of a Symbol', in *Verbannung und Heimkehr* (Festschrift W. Rudolph; Tübingen: J.C.B. Mohr): 235-52.

Provan, I.W.
1991   'Past, Present and Future in Lamentations III 52–66: The Case for a Precative Perfect Re-examined', *VT* 41: 164-75.

Renkema, J.
1988   'The Literary Structure of Lamentations (I–IV)', in W. van der Meer

and J.C. de Moor (eds.), *The Structural Analysis of Biblical and Canaanite Poetry* (JSOTSup 74; Sheffield: JSOT Press): 294-396.

Rudolph, W.
1962   *Das Buch Ruth. Das Hohe Lied. Die Klagelieder* (KAT, XVII,1–3; Gütersloh: Güterslohes Verlagshaus, rev. edn [1939]): 187-263.

Saebø, M.
1986   *Fortolkning til Salomos ordspråk, Forkynneren, Høysangen, Klagesangene* (Oslo: Luther Forlag).

Schmidt, W.H.
1984   *Old Testament Introduction* (trans. M.J. O'Connell; New York: Crossroad).

Westermann, C.
1990   *Die Klagelieder: Forschungsgeschichte und Auslegung* (Neukirchen–Vluyn: Neukirchen Verlag).

Wiesmann, H.
1926   'Das 3. Kap. der Klagelieder', *ZKT* 50: 515-43.
1935   'Der geschichtliche Hintergrund der Klagelieder', *BZ* 23: 20-43.
1936   'Der Verfasser des Büchleins der Klagelieder—Ein Augenzeuge der behandelten Ereignisse?', *Bib* 17: 71-84.
1954   *Die Klagelieder übersetzt und erklärt* (Frankfurt am Main).

J.F.A. Sawyer

There are a good many difficulties in the Hebrew text of Isaiah 24–27, and it is the aim of this short paper, dedicated to a good friend and colleague, who himself 'reconsidered' the passage just 30 years ago (Anderson 1963), to suggest that a solution to some of them can be found in the Book of Daniel.

It is generally agreed that the 'proto-apocalpytic' form and content of these chapters bring them close to Daniel in various respects (Hanson 1975: 313-34; Hanson 1985: 480; Gottwald 1985: 587). At one time it was also widely assumed that the so-called 'Isaiah Apocalypse' was composed last of the many diverse components of what now make up the book of Isaiah, possibly not many years before the earliest parts of the book of Daniel (Wildberger 1974–78: 885-911; Kaiser 1974: 178-79; Vermeylen 1977: 349-81). Michael Fishbane explains the connection between Isaiah 24–27 and Daniel in terms of direct references in Daniel to the earlier prophet (Fishbane 1985: 493). One should not be surprised, then, to find semantic connections between Isaiah and Daniel. Without speculating on the precise socio-political or religious contexts in which Isaiah 24–27 and the Book of Daniel were composed, and there are persuasive arguments for dating the Isaiah passage to a much earlier period than Daniel (Anderson 1963; Miller 1976; Hayes and Irvine 1987: 294-98), it is probable that they belong to the same or a similar universe of discourse.

There is another factor, however, which is to my mind much more important than form, content and supposed date, and one which has not been sufficiently applied to the semantics of biblical Hebrew. This is to do with the nature of the Masoretic Text of the Hebrew Bible as a whole, not just Isaiah 24–27. In an article on Hebrew terms for the resurrection of the dead (Sawyer 1973), I argued that the textual and theological tradition preserved by the Masoretes, and contained in the Leningrad Codex which most modern biblical scholars work from (*BHS* 1967–77), goes back to a variety of ancient Judaism in which an elaborate eschatology, including a belief in the resurrection of the dead, held an important place. This explains why, according to the Masoretic Text, belief in an individual resurrection, the day of judgment and other eschatological doctrines can be found in so many passages of Scripture, though probably in most cases this may not have been the original author's intention (cf. Barr 1992: 43-44). In the context of a community that firmly believed in the resurrection of the dead, including the context in which the Masoretes worked, a substantial set of common Hebrew terms, such as חי 'living' קום 'to arise', הקיץ 'to wake up', ראה 'to see', משפט 'judgment' and עפר 'dust', acquired eschatological associations, which can clearly be recognized in passages like Job 19.25-27, Ps. 1.5 and Isa. 53.11 (Sawyer 1973: 229-34).

The book of Daniel is unique among the books of the Hebrew Bible both in the elaborateness of its apocalyptic and eschatological expression (cf. 12.1-3), and in its historical context within second-century Judaism. It must therefore have a crucial role to play in providing early evidence for the meaning of the MT. Its promotion to the status of Major Prophet, alongside Isaiah, Jeremiah and Ezekiel, in the Greek Bible, which was eventually to form the basis of the Christian canon, confirms its dominant place in at least one of the surviving varieties of Judaism, and further justifies its use as a kind of hermeneutical key to our understanding of MT.

It is significant that Bernhard Duhm noted connections between Isaiah 53 and Daniel: הצדיק in a soteriological sense, for instance, occurs only in Isa. 53.11 and Dan. 12.3 (Duhm 1914: 375). His nineteenth-century preoccupation with historicity, however, led him to the dubious conclusion that the fourth 'Servant Song' (52.13–53.12) must have been written at about the same time as Daniel 12. By contrast, we are not here going to be concerned with questions of dating. Our present contention is that, whatever the original date of Isaiah 24–27, the precise meaning and associations of some of the words and phrases in the Hebrew text in which they have come down to us, can be illuminated by reference to the language of the book of Daniel. Whether it is more correct to take the Masoretic tradition seriously as an important part of our data, or, as most modern commentaries and translations do, prefer 'Sadducean' reconstructions of the original

Hebrew, emending the text and systematically excluding *inter alia* the Masoretes' eschatology, is not a question with which we shall allow ourselves to be detained. I shall simply attempt to describe what is there.

Our first passage is the song of thanksgiving (24.14-16) sung by the righteous after the Day of Judgment (24.1-13). They are like the few olives left on the trees after the beating and shaking have stopped, or the grapes left on the vines for the poor after the vintage (v. 13; cf. Alonso Schökel 1987: 181). An interesting Isaianic parallel to this juxtaposition is the song of individual thanksgiving in praise of God's love, sung immediately after the description of his 'trampling out the vintage where the grapes of wrath are stored' in Isa. 63.1-6. This too must have been sung by the redeemed (63.4; cf. 62.12) after the horrors of 'the day of vengeance' (v. 4).

The passage begins emphatically with the independent personal pronoun 'they', marking a change of subject, from the image of the few grapes and olives clinging to the branches, to the application of this image to the righteous remnant. LXX explains the pronoun as οἱ καταλειφθέντες ἐπὶ τῆς γῆς, 'those who are left behind on the earth'. The last verse of Isaiah 6 makes a similar leap of faith, from the image of a smouldering stump, which is all that remains after a forest fire, to the application of that image to 'the noble stem of Jesse' which survives to produce eventually the royal seed of the Davidic messiah (cf. also 11.1 immediately following 10.33-34).

The language and imagery of the verses describing the celebrations of the righteous remnant is as graphic and colourful as the rest of the chapter. The first Daniel connection is the autobiographical element in v. 16. The appearance of an observer reminds us that this is a vision, like the visions of Daniel, and must be read as such (cf. Chilton 1983: 53). The description of the scene and the reaction of the prophet is in Isaianic language (and I said, '...Woe is me!'), recalling his reaction to the vision of the seraphim in ch. 6, and also perhaps his response to the mysterious voice in ch. 40 ('and I said, What shall I cry?' cf. Whybray 1971: 82). Our interpretation of these verses will be dramatically changed if we consider the possibility that the scene of horrific global destruction is being witnessed by the prophet, in an apocalyptic vision like those of Daniel.

We need not in this context discuss possible historical references such as the identity of the 'city of chaos'. The parallel with Daniel would confirm that there probably are contemporary references in this vision, for example, to the destruction of Jerusalem in 587 or the capture of Babylon by Alexander the Great in 331 or the fall of Carthage in 146, which the first hearers or readers no doubt recognized, whoever they were (cf. Anderson 1963: 118). But such references are inevitably uncertain to us, not least because it is in the nature of apocalyptic texts that they can be, and have been, applied to many different historical events. In any case they do not significantly affect the meaning of the language and imagery of the passage (cf. Miller 1976: 103; Clements 1980: 198-99). We are not concerned with dating the passage, but with trying to understand what it is about.

In the first place the location of the survivors is given in three (possibly four) expressions. Two of these are straightforward: 'from the sea...on islands in the sea'. We must allow ourselves to picture a scene in which the whole earth is 'desolate, twisted (v. 1), utterly broken...rent asunder...violently shaken...'

> The earth staggers like a drunken man
> it sways like a hut...
> it falls and will not rise again (v. 20).

In that context the image of bedraggled survivors washed up on the shores of distant islands, the only dry land left, is most effective. The role of the sea in Daniel's vision of the Last Judgment (Dan. 7) and in that of John of Patmos ('the sea gave up the dead in it...and all were judged...' Rev. 20.13) confirms that this is more convincingly interpreted as a reference to the sea than 'the west' as some, including Kimhi, Kaiser, Hayes and most modern English versions (RSV, NEB, REB, NRSV) would have it.

The third location 'the edge of the earth' also fits well into this scenario. But here again the image may be more subtle than appears in most English versions. The word כנף translated 'edge' here literally means 'wing' or 'skirt', and the latter sense can be beautifully paralleled in another global description of the earth, this time from the Book of Job:

> Have you commanded the morning since your days began,
> and caused the dawn to know its place,
> that it might take hold of the skirts of the earth,
> and the wicked be shaken out of it? (Job 38.18).

The image of the earth as a skirt that can be twisted and shaken so that its inhabitants are scattered far and wide is how Isaiah 24 begins (cf. Rowley 1970: 243).

The fourth term בָּאֻרִים 'in (or with) the fires' (cf. AV) has elicited many suggestions, some more imaginative than others, but none based on totally convincing parallels from other texts. Those who interpret it as a geographical location mostly understand it as 'in the east' (where the 'fires of dawn' first appear), or 'the lands of light', corresponding to 'in the west' (Kaiser 1974: 186; Slotki 1949: 112; RSV, REV; cf. Ps. 113.3). Others, somewhat anachronistically, suggest 'in the tropics'. A seventeenth-century commentator proposes 'when you are in the furnace of affliction' (Poole 1700: 380), a suggestion inspired perhaps by the 'burning fiery furnace' of Daniel 4, although there are no verbal correspondences.

All these suggestions are problematic for one reason or another, and it may be that the expression is not another location at all, but rather one that adds a different kind of detail to the picture of the righteous remnant celebrating their escape. 'With fires' is one possibility proposed already by the fifteenth-century Jewish commentator Isaac Abrabanel. This is what the singular אוּר means in all four of its occurrences elsewhere in Isaiah (31.9; 44.16; 47.14; 50.11; cf. Ezek. 5.2). Perhaps the reference is to 'beacons' passing on the good news from island to island, as in Clytaemnestra's famous speech at the beginning of the *Agamemnon* of Aeschylus (ll. 280-316), although אוּר is not attested elsewhere in this sense and the technical term for 'fire-signal' seems to have been מַשְׂאֵת (cf. Jer. 6.1; Lachish Ostracon 4.10). Another tempting alternative would be to find here a reference to Hanukka, known as חג האורים 'the Feast of Lights' in modern Hebrew (Even-Shoshan 1972: I, 44). Unfortunately no early evidence for this usage has been found either.

Finally, as the only biblical usage of the plural occurs in the phrase 'Urim and Thummim', the name of Israel's mysterious means of divination, it has been suggested that the reference is to the 'Urim' on the high priest's breastplate (Exod. 28.30), and the meaning therefore something like 'for illumination'. Christian commentators for whom Isaiah was the 'Fifth Evangelist' predictably take this to mean 'pointing to Christ' (Poole 1700: 380). Jewish tradition as represented by the Targum, glosses it with the words 'When light comes to the just'.

This is an excellent example of a text declared by some scholars of an older generation to be 'without meaning' (e.g. Mauchline 1962: 186). In fact readers down the centuries have never had that problem with it. The question for them was which of all the numerous meanings, not all of them by any means banal or unconvincing, was to be preferred. The comparison with Daniel's visions encourages us to take a closer look at the details of the language and imagery, even where the result may be inconclusive.

But it is in v. 16b that the link with Daniel seems to me to be especially significant—hence the title of this article. It was suggested to me by an early twelfth-century manuscript of Jerome's Isaiah Commentary in Durham Cathedral Library, where incidentally George and I spent some very enjoyable weeks working on the British and Foreign Bible Society 'Translators' Translation' of Psalms. A miniature at the beginning of Book VIII (on chs. 24–27) shows both the prophet Isaiah and Jerome. Isaiah carries two scrolls, one in each hand. One, predictably, has 7.14 (*Ecce virgo concipiet filium...*) inscribed on it, the verse associated more than any other with Isaiah in the mediaeval Church. The other has on it part of 24.16 (*secretum meum mihi, secretum meum mihi, vae mihi!*). Jerome, who in the preface to his commentary describes Isaiah as 'more evangelist than prophet', is looking up at him and saying (according to the legend on his scroll): '*Dic tu Isaias, dic testimonium Christi* 'Go on, Isaiah, tell them about Christ!'

After his vision of the end of the world, and of the righteous remnant emerging from the chaos to praise the God of Israel, 'the Righteous One' (vv. 15-16b), the prophet comments on what he has seen:

> I said, 'My secret is with me!
> My secret is with me! Woe is me!'

He goes on to condemn the wicked, assuring them of the terrible fate that awaits them (vv. 17-18a), and then his vision of Judgment Day continues to the end of the chapter. In this apocalyptic context the most natural interpretation of these words is the one given above (Kaiser 1974: 189-90). The word רז is taken in its usual sense of 'secret, mystery'. It is an Aramaism in Hebrew. The Aramaic word occurs several times in the Aramaic parts of Daniel, as well as in the Hebrew of Ben Sira 8.18, and we can assume that it was familiar to readers of the Hebrew text of Isaiah from the middle of the Second Temple Period at the latest. The Greek translators of Daniel have μυστήριον for רז in Daniel 2 (8×) and 4.6. In the older Greek versions of Isa. 24.16 the words רזי לי רזי לי are not translated at all, but Theodotion renders it τὸ μυστήριον μου ἐμοί, and the Targum and the Vulgate interpret the text as referring to the secrets revealed in an apocalyptic vision, like Daniel's. The passage is well handled by the Jewish Targum, which, with typical concern for the detail of the text, distinguishes between Isaiah's two secrets: 'the secret of the reward of the righteous and the secret of the punishment of the wicked' (cf. Chilton 1983: 83). Talmudic tradition can be cited in support of this interpretation as well (*Sanh.* 94a: Jastrow 1950: II, 1464; Kaiser 1974: 189). Jerome, as we have seen, representing Christian tradition, interprets the passage as referring to the mysteries of Christ and his church, which no other prophet expounds more eloquently than Isaiah 'the fifth evangelist' (cf. Sawyer 1994).

The notion of keeping the secrets to oneself, only to be revealed (Greek ἀποκαλύπτω) at 'the time of the end' is another obvious link with Daniel (cf. 12.9). It is also familiar from Isa. 8.16 and perhaps also 29.11-12, passages which are also given apocalyptic interpretations in the kind of eschatological context we are considering here.

Without the Daniel connection, most modern commentators and translators, Otto Kaiser being a conspicuous exception, have had to resort to desperate philology. The older view, represented already in the Authorized Version ('My leanness, my leanness!') and in recent translations and commentaries (cf. RSV, NRSV 'I pine away, I pine away'), is that רזי is a noun related to the common Hebrew words רזה 'thin' and רזון 'thinness'. Apart from the fact that the meaning is very strained, the noun רָזִי is otherwise unknown and morphologically anomalous (Gray 1912: 419). The alternative proposed by the NEB translators and perpetuated in the REB, namely, 'depravity, depravity', is also unconvincing. It comes from a comparative philologist's creation, רְזִילִי, morphologically sound but unknown in Hebrew (Brockington 1973: 184). This seems to be a case where the meaning of MT is clear, well documented and convincing. It may not be the original meaning, although what that means is not always obvious (Sawyer 1989), but it is surely preferable to alternatives for which there is absolutely no evidence.

Our other text is perhaps rather better known. Chapters 25 and 26 have always been a particularly rich source for epitaphs and readings for funeral services. St Ambrose, for example, cited 26.18-21 in the funeral oration for his brother Satyrus in 378, speaking of the divine dew that makes our bodies grow again and the hidden chambers where the redeemed can hide safely until the Judgment is past (*FC*, XXII, 226). Luther lists the same passage among his 'biblical texts suitable for epitaphs' (*LW*, LIII, 327-89). Another verse from ch. 26, containing the words 'Peace perfect peace' (v. 3), was the inspiration for at least one hymn popular at funerals, sung, for example, at the funeral of William Robertson Smith at Keig in Aberdeenshire in 1894 (Moffatt 1927: 152).

These uses of our text by Christian communities down the ages are precisely analogous to the way in which some of the earliest Jewish interpreters, in the Maccabean period, for example, and their influential successors, the Masoretes, understood the text. Ancient Aramaic, Greek and Latin versions of 26.19 confirm this. The Targum turns יחיו מתיך 'your dead shall live' into the more personal formula את הוא מחי מתין 'you are he who brings the dead back to life', reminiscent of the second of the Eighteen Benedictions that make up the Amidah, one of the oldest parts of Jewish Daily Prayer (cf. Chilton 1983: 16):

> Thou art faithful to bring the dead to life. Blessed art thou, O Lord, who bringest the dead back to life (Singer 1892: 45).

A modern Jewish commentator declares that Isa. 26.19 is the 'source of the belief in the resurrection of the dead, a fundamental of Jewish dogma...repeated by Daniel (12.2)' (Slotki 1949: 121).

The Septuagint has the following:

> The dead will arise, and those that are in their tombs will awake; and those that are in the earth will rejoice. For the dew that comes from you brings healing to them...

Tertullian's Latin version adds a further detail at the end, making the reference to physical resurrection even more explicit: '...brings healing to their bones'. The Masoretic Text belongs to a similar emotionally and eschatologically charged context.

In the first place, the Hebrew words for 'live', 'arise' and 'awake' carry unmistakable eschatological overtones, especially in a context where terms for 'dead', 'corpse', 'dust' and 'shades' (רפאים) also appear. The closest parallel in biblical Hebrew is Daniel 12.2. The concentration of such vocabulary and imagery in this one verse also separates it from passages about national restoration and revival such as Ezekiel's vision of the dry bones.

The wider context also opposes the fate of the wicked (vv. 11-14, 21) to that of the righteous (vv. 19-20), just as in Dan. 12.1-3, and vv. 20-21 in particular, point to a Day of Judgment outside history, a feature of the passage that predisposed the Targum translators to separate those on whom the dew of light falls (the righteous) from the wicked whose fate is to be sent to Gehenna ('the land of shades') (Stenning 1949: 82).

But there are two other links with Daniel that are even more significant. The two main subjects in the verse, as it stands in MT, have pronominal suffixes: מתיך 'your dead' and נבלתי 'my (dead) body'. The force of the first pronoun is to identify a special relationship between these particular dead people and their God. Jewish and Christian commentators have recognized here a reference to the martyrs, a special group among the dead who died for their faith, and as this is one of the main themes of Daniel, we are entitled to ask whether this is how we are intended to understand Isa. 26.19 as well.

The other word נבלתי again follows Daniel in introducing an autobiographical element into the description of the resurrection of the dead. The grammar is odd but not impossible: 'together with my dead body' (AV). The noun has the same kind of adverbial function as the word ארץ later in the same verse. But once again the meaning is unambiguous: the author, either out of piety or not inconceivably out of fear of imminent martyrdom, wishes to stress that the reference here is to individual resurrection, not national revival, and that he for one believes in it and trusts in God's power to rescue him even in death.

Some of the ancient versions, including the Septuagint quoted above, have the plural 'corpses'. Syriac and Aramaic have 'their corpses'. This provides textual critics with the authority to remove the more difficult singular 'my corpse', explaining the suffix 'my' as the result of a scribal error (dittography). But the Qumran Isaiah scroll, which originated in the context of a variety of ancient Judaism well-known to have had a developed eschatology, has the same first person singular term as the Masoretic Text, and gives all the evidence we need for the view that ancient Hebrew texts from the time of Daniel at the latest, including the received text of Isa. 26.19, contain a highly developed eschatology which the Masoretes painstakingly preserved.

BIBLIOGRAPHY

Adriaen, M. (ed.)
1963   S. *Hieronymi Presbyteri Opera*, LXIII, *Commentariorum in Esaiam Libri I–XI* (Corpus Christianorum, Series Latina).

Alonso Schökel, L.
1987   'Isaiah', in R. Alter and F. Kermode (eds.), *The Literary Guide to the Bible* (London: Collins): 165-83.

Anderson, G.W.
1963   'Isaiah XXIV–XXVII Reconsidered', in G.W. Anderson *et al.* (eds.), *Congress Volume, Bonn 1962* (VTSup, 9; Leiden: Brill): 118-26.

Barr, J.
1992   *The Garden of Eden and the Hope of Immortality* (London: SCM Press).

Weber, R. (ed.)
1975   *Biblia Sacra iuxta Vulgatam Versionem* (2 vols.; Stuttgart, 2nd edn).

Brock, S.
1987   *The Old Testament in Syriac according to the Peshitta Version.* III.1. *Isaiah* (Leiden: Brill).

Brockington, L.H.
1973   *The Hebrew Text of the Old Testament: The Readings Adopted by the Translators of the New English Bible* (London: Oxford University Press).

Burrows, M.
1950   *The Dead Sea Scrolls of St Mark's Monastery.* I. *The Isaiah Manuscript and the Habakkuk Commentary* (New Haven).

Chilton, B.D.
1983   *The Glory of Israel: The Theology and Provenience of the Isaiah Targum* (Sheffield: JSOT Press).

Clements, R.E.
1980   *Isaiah 1–39* (Grand Rapids: Eerdmans; London; Marshall, Morgan & Scott).

Duhm, B.
1914   *Das Buch Jesaia* (Göttingen: Vandenhoeck & Ruprecht, 3rd edn).

Even Shoshan, A.
1972   מלון חדש (Jerusalem).

Fishbane, M.
1985   *Biblical Interpretation in Ancient Israel* (London: Oxford University Press).

Gottwald, N.K.
1985   *The Hebrew Bible: A Socio-Literary Introduction* (Philadelphia: Fortress Press).

Gray, G.B.
1912   *A Critical and Exegetical Commentary on the Book of Isaiah 1–39* (Edinburgh: T. & T. Clark).

Hanson, P.D.
1975 *The Dawn of Apocalyptic* (Philadelphia: Fortress Press).
1985 'Apocalyptic Literature', in *The Hebrew Bible and its Modern Interpreters* (Philadelphia: Fortress Press; Chico, CA: Scholars Press).
Hayes, J.H. and S.A. Irvine
1987 *Isaiah the Eighth-Century Prophet: His Times and his Preaching* (Nashville: Abingdon).
Jastrow, M.
1950 *A Dictionary of the Targumim, the Talmud Babli and Yerushalmi and the Midrashic Literature* (New York).
Kaiser, O.
1974 *Isaiah 13–39: A Commentary* (London: SCM Press).
Mauchline, J.
1962 *Isaiah 1–39: Introduction and Commentary* (London: SCM Press).
Miller, W.R.
1976 *Isaiah 24–27 and the Origin of Apocalyptic* (Missoula, MT: Scholars Press).
Poole, M.
1700 *A Commentary on the Holy Bible* (3 vols.; repr. Edinburgh: Banner of Truth Trust, 1962).
Rowley, H.H.
1976 *Job* (London: Oliphants).
Sawyer, J.F.A.
1973 'Hebrew Words for the Resurrection of the Dead', *VT* 23: 218-34.
1990 'The "Original Meaning of the Text" and Other Legitimate Subjects for Semantic Description', in *Continuing Questions in Old Testament Method and Theology* (Leuven: M. Vervenne, rev. edn).
1994 *The Fifth Gospel: Isaiah in the History of Christianity* (Cambridge: Cambridge University Press).
Segal, M.Z.
1954 ספר בן־סירא השלם (Jerusalem: Bialik).
Singer, S.
1892 *The Authorized Daily Prayer Book* (London).
Slotki, I.W.
1949 *Isaiah. Hebrew Text and English Translation with an Introduction and Commentary* (London & New York: Soncino Press).
Stenning, J.F. (ed. and trans.)
1949 *The Targum of Isaiah* (Oxford: Oxford University Press).
Whybray, R.N.
1971 *The Heavenly Council in Isaiah 40.13-14: A Study of the Sources of the Theology of Deutero-Isaiah* (Cambridge: Cambridge University Press).
Ziegler, J.
1939 *Septuaginta. XIV. Isaias* (Göttingen).

OTTO EISSFELDT 1887–1973

R. Smend

Auf dem fünften Kongreß der International Organization for the Study of the Old Testament, 1965 in Genf, hielt der 78jährige Otto Eißfeldt den einleitenden Vortrag über 'Sechs Jahrzehnte alttestamentlicher Wissenschaft'.[1] Das war exakt der Zeitraum, über den er autobiographisch berichten konnte: 1905 hatte er in Göttingen mit dem Studium der Theologie begonnen und war dabei gleich an das Alte Testament geraten, das ihn zeitlebens festhalten sollte. Er sah seine Arbeit mehr als andere in der Kontinuität der Wissenschaft und ihrem internationalen Zusammenhang. So widmete er die Neubearbeitungen seines Hauptwerkes 'Den Repräsentanten dreier Generationen britischer Alttestamentler', nämlich Theodore H. Robinson, Harold H. Rowley und Aubrey R. Johnson.[2] Die Generationenreihe hätte er aus eigener Erfahrung nach vorn und hinten verlängern können, denn er war noch Wellhausens Hörer gewesen, und in der letzten Phase seines Wirkens unterhielt er zu manchem der damals ganz jungen Alttestamentler die freundlichsten Beziehungen.

Daß er in Göttingen zu studieren anfing, lag buchstäblich nahe. Er war in Northeim geboren, einer zwanzig Kilometer von Göttingen entfernten Kleinstadt, in der sein Vater als Rechtsanwalt arbeitete. Die Heimat der Familie Eißfeldt liegt auf halbem Wege von Northeim oder auch Göttingen nach Halle im östlichen Harz, wo es noch heute eine 'Eisfelder Talmühle' gibt und wo die Eißfeldts Handwerker, Landwirte, Schulzen und Amtleute, aber dann auch studierte Juristen waren.[3] Otto Eißfeldts Vater hieß auch schon Otto; der Name war in

1. VTSup 15 (1966) 1-13.
2. *Einleitung in das Alte Testament* (1956²; 1964³); Robinson war schon die erste Auflage (1934) gewidmet, gemeinsam mit A. Bertholet und E. v. Dobschütz.
3. Vg. G. Wallis in *In memoriam Otto Eißfeldt* (1974) 10-11. Aus Wallis' Gedenkrede auch im Folgenden einiges Biographische, ebenso aus Eißfeldts Genfer

den Kerngebieten des im 10. Jahrhundert regierenden ottonischen Kaiserhauses über die Jahrhunderte hinweg beliebt geblieben. Otto Eißfeldt der jüngere, am 1. September 1887 als ältestes von fünf Kindern geboren, hing an seiner Herkunft. Man meint die praktische Nüchternheit, die zu den Berufen seiner Vorfahren gehörte, bei ihm wiederzuerkennen, auch die Fähigkeit des Juristen, vernünftige Kompromisse zu erzielen, ohne allzutief ins Grundsätzliche zu gehen; Streitlust und rhetorischer Glanz allerdings, wie sie als typische Eigenschaften von Advokaten gelten, lagen ihm fern.

Das Gymnasium besuchte er nacheinander in Northeim, Dortmund und Duisburg. Aufnahmebereit und fleißig, wie er war, erwarb er sich die umfassende humanistische, insbesondere sprachliche und literarische Bildung, wie die Schulen sie damals bieten konnten. Über alle Ortswechsel hinweg behielt er den etwas 'drögen' Dialekt des südlichen Niedersachsen. Ihn aufzufrischen bekam er Gelengenheit, indem er zwei Semester (Sommer 1905 und Winter 1905/6) und dann noch einmal eins (Winter 1907/8) in Göttingen studierte. Dazwischen (Sommer 1906–Sommer 1907) schob er drei Berliner Semester ein.

Wie umfassend er sein Studium anlegte, zeigt ein Blick auf die Veranstaltungen, die er in den ersten beiden Semestern besuchte.[4] Er hörte Theologische Enzyklopädie bei Althaus, Psalmen und Einleitung in das Alte Testament bei Smend, Alttestamentliche Handschriftenkunde bei Rahlfs, Synoptiker, Römerbrief und Johannesoffenbarung bei Bousset, Galater– und 1. Petrusbrief bei Heitmüller, Kirchengeschichte I und II bei Tschackert, Kirchengeschichte des 19. Jahrhunderts bei Bonwetsch, Geschichte des Katholizismus im 19. Jahrhundert sowie 'Der religiöse Determinismus in der Geschichte des Christentums' bei v. Walter. In beiden Semestern nahm er an kirchen– und dogmenhistorischen Übungen teil, zuerst bei Tschackert, dann bei Bonwetsch, und in beiden Semestern überschritt er die Grenze zur philosophischen Fakultät: er hörte über deutsche Ortsnamen bei Edward Schröder, über die Baukunst der Renaissance in Italien bei Robert Vischer, über wissenschaftliche Weltansicht bei Julius

---

Vortrag von 1965, ohne daß jeweils Einzelnachweise gegeben würden. Eine präzise Darstellung und Würdigung bietet H.-J. Zobel, *TRE* 9, 482-86, mancherlei findet sich in G. Wallis (Hg.), *Otto-Eißfeldt-Ehrung 1987* (1988). Die *Kleinen Schriften*, I–VI (1962–1979) werden im Folgenden als I–VI zitiert.

4.   Nach dem Abgangszeugnis im Göttinger Universitätsarchiv (dort 1906 Nr. 985).

Baumann und, last not least, über die semitischen Sprachen und
Völker bei Julius Wellhausen.

Auf Wellhausens Vorlesung wies ihn Smend hin, an den ihn der
gelehrte Dortmunder Pfarrer Friedrich Schnapp empfohlen hatte und
dem er, obwohl ihm seine 'Einleitung in das Alte Testament' nach
eigener Erinnerung 'noch viel zu hoch' war,[5] unter den Göttinger
Lehrern auf die Dauer das meiste verdankte. Mit einem zweiten Rat
hatte Smend weniger Glück. Er empfahl Eißfeldt, der den Studienort
wechseln wollte, Basel und riet ihm vehement von Berlin ab, wo
Baudissin und vollends Gunkel nicht nach seinem Geschmack waren.
Aber eben für Gunkel schwärmte Heitmüller, und dieser erreichte es,
daß Eißfeldt Berlin wählte, wo er mit einer kurzen Göttinger
Unterbrechung anderthalb Jahrzehnte bleiben sollte.

Er wohnte im Johanneum unweit der Spree, das damals unter dem
Ephorat des Praktischen Theologen Paul Kleinert stand, eines
vielseitigen und anregenden Mannes, der, noch Schüler von Heinrich
Ewald und Franz Delitzsch, auch seinerseits in der alttestamentlichen
Wissenschaft Spuren hinterlassen hat. Kleinert holte Eißfeldt, kaum
war dieser zum Abschluß des Studiums noch einmal nach Göttingen
gegangen, ins Amt des Inspektors ('Seniors') des Johanneums wieder
nach Berlin. Als Inhaber dieses Amtes bestand Eißfeldt 1908 in
Hannover das erste, 1912 in Berlin das zweite theologische Examen,
nach dem er zum Frühprediger an der Jerusalems– und Neuen Kirche
gewählt wurde und das Johanneum aufgab.

Natürlich nutzte er, vor allem zu Anfang, die Möglichkeiten aus,
die das akademische Berlin in der theologischen und der philosophischen Fakultät, von Harnack und Wilamowitz abwärts, ihm bot. Als
seine beiden wichtigsten Berliner Lehrer nannte er stets Gunkel und
Baudissin, den einen für 1906/7, den anderen für die Inspektorsjahre
seit 1908, in denen er seine Studien endgültig auf das Alte Testament
und dessen Umwelt konzentrierte. Für das Studium der Umwelt bot
Berlin mit seinen Museen und seiner philosophischen Fakultät, der
Adolf Erman und Eduard Meyer angehörten, ideale Voraussetzungen.
Während Eißfeldt im Ägyptischen bei Erman nicht über die
Anfangsgründe hinauskam, las er bei Friedrich Delitzsch, der ihn
übrigens auch in den Koran einführte, semesterlang assyrische Texte
und verzeichnete neben den sachlichen Kenntnissen als besonderen
Gewinn die Fähigkeit, 'Texte, über die es noch keine Kommentar-

5. VTSup 15, 2.

Tradition gibt, ganz aus sich selbst heraus zu verstehen, was die Hörer vielfach zu besserem Verständnis mancher mit Kommentar-Überlieferung überlasteter Abschnitte des Alten Testaments geführt hat'.[6] Nach Gunkels Fortgang 1907 übernahm Hugo Greßmann sein Extraordinariat und später auch seine Rolle für Eißfeldt: die eines vielfältigen Anregers, vor allem die Umwelt des Alten Testaments betreffend, bei bleibender Distanz in der Einschätzung der Literarkritik. Die wichtigste unter den Freundschaften, die in jenen Jahren entstanden, war die mit Enno Littmann, der während des Weltkrieges als Orient-Experte einen Gastrolle im Berliner Generalstab spielte; bei keinem dürfte Eißfeldt über das Morgenland mehr gelernt haben als bei ihm; 1958 hielt er ihm die Gedenkrede.[7]

Seine literarische Produktion begann er als 23jähriger mit einem Vorschlag, die Rätsel in Richter 14 erotisch zu verstehen.[8] 1913 folgte die Berliner theologische Dissertation über den Maschal im Alten Testament,[9] ein ihm nach seiner eigenen Angabe[10] durch Gunkels Gattungsforschung und Kleinerts Interesse an der Weisheit nahegelegtes Thema. 1916 erwarb er in Göttingen auch den philosophischen Doktorgrad mit Littmann als Referenten. Diesmal hatte das Thema sozusagen noch Wellhausen gestellt, mit dem Satz in den *Prolegomena*: 'Das Verhältnis von מעשר, ראשית, בכורים יד, תרומה zu einander bedürfte einer genauen Untersuchung, mit sorgsamer Unterscheidung der verschiedenen Quellen und Zeiten, bis zur Mischna herunter'.[11] Eißfeldt untersuchte also 'Erstlinge und Zehnten im Alten Testament', wobei er sich 'bis zu einem gewissen Grade Baudissins *Geschichte des alttestamentlichen Priesterthumes* von 1889 zum Vorbild nahm'.[12]

Nach seinen eigenen 'Erstlingen' floß der Strom seiner Produktion kontinuierlich und gewann allmählich eine kaum noch überschaubare Breite. Man hat 55 selbständige Veröffentlichungen gezählt, dazu 282 Aufsätze, 107 Lexikonartikel, 863 Rezensionen, 31 Nachrufe und Würdigungen, 116 Nennungen als Herausgeber—und in dieser

6.   VTSup 15, 6.
7.   Erschienen als Heft 5 der *Tübinger Universitätsreden*.
8.   *ZAW* 30 (1910) 132-35.
9.   BZAW 24.
10. VTSup 15, 6.
11. J. Wellhausen, *Prolegomena zur Geschichte Israels* (1905[6]) 152[2].
12. VTSup 15, 7.

Aufzählung ist noch nicht alles berücksichtigt.[13] Hinter der immensen Menge von Gedrucktem stand kein wilder Geltungstrieb, sondern das Bedürfnis nach regelmäßiger Bewältigung und Mitteilung eines mit unablässigem Fleiß verarbeiteten Stoffes. Vieles, nicht nur in den Rezensionen, ist nicht ins letzte durchdrungen und ausgeformt, bleibt zu großen Teilen klassifizierende Bibliographie, Zitatenkette oder einfach Wiedergabe von Inhaltsverzeichnissen, oft eingeschachtelt in Sätze, die nicht für Hörer, sondern nur für Leser gedacht sind. Aber auch für Leser ist es nicht immer leicht, den langen Atem dieses Autors zu haben. Dieser Autor hat sichtlich keine Schwierigkeiten mit dem Ausdruck gehabt, alles scheint ihm leicht und schnell aus der Feder geflossen zu sein, ohne daß es darum jemals unbedacht und unsorgfältig wirkte—dafür war Eißfeldt viel zu gewissenhaft.

Weil in der Masse dieser Produktion das wirklich wichtige in der Gefahr steht unterzugehen, war es eine sinnvolle, wenngleich keineswegs unproblematische Aufgabe, sechs Bände *Kleine Schriften* (1962–1979) und aus diesen noch einmal einen einzigen, für den Gebrauch in der DDR bestimmten Band *Kleine Schriften zum Alten Testament* (1971) herauszudestillieren. Im Nachwort der großen Sammlung bescheinigen die Herausgeber ihrem Lehrer einen 'geraden Weg' und fügen hinzu: 'Die Sicherheit seines Urteils in allen anstehenden Fragen hat nie getrogen; sie war um so überzeugender, als sie ohne jede Spur von Eigensinnigkeit und Rechthaberei war, sich vielmehr mit weitherziger Toleranz paarte. Seine Kritik war stets positiv und aufbauend, niemals negativ und zerstörend. Er gab nie vor, die Lösung eines Problems zur Hand zu haben, aber er hat Fragen gestellt, sie mit Intensität zu beantworten versucht, und er war niemals gezwungen, seine Ergebnisse zurückzunehmen'.[14] Nun, wenn er auch nicht geradezu gezwungen war, hätten sich doch da und dort stärkere Modifikationen, vielleicht auch ein Abstandnehmen und Neueinsetzen infolge von geäußerter Kritik und gewandelten Fragestellungen erwarten lassen, wo stattdessen doch nicht ganz 'jede Spur von Eigensinnigkeit' fehlt. Hatte Eißfeldt für ein Problem eine Lösung, dann neigte er fortan, von Ausnahmen abgesehen, nicht zur Revision, allenfalls zur Variation.

Das Hauptbeispiel dafür ist das magnum opus der Berliner Jahre, 1922 zum Abschied von dort 'den Stätten meines Lernens und Lebens

13. VI, VIII, vgl. V, 222¹.
14. VI, VI.

in Berlin und allen dort gewonnenen Förderern und Freunden als Zeichen des Dankes dargebracht'.[15] Der Ursprung dieses Werkes lag in Göttingen, bei Eißfeldts erstem Lehrer Smend. Er hatte sich in den Jahren, seit Eißfeldt in Göttingen studierte, der riesigen Aufgabe einer neuen Analyse der Erzählung des Hexateuchs unterzogen und war zu einem Ergebnis gekommen, das Eißfeldt später 'die neueste Urkundenhypothese' nannte: eine fast vollständige Aufteilung des gesamten Stoffes auf vier Quellenschriften, J^1, J^2, E und P.[16] Dem Erfolg seines Buches hatte Smend, dem man 'Eigensinnigkeit und Rechthaberei' weniger leicht absprechen kann als Eißfeldt, selbst im Wege gestanden, indem er die Vertreter anderer Meinungen schroff zurechtwies oder überhaupt nicht beachtete und indem er es nicht verstand, die meist sehr komplizierten Tatbestände faßlich und übersichtlich darzustellen. So gewann er nur wenige Anhänger, darunter den jungen Eißfeldt, den er tief beeindruckte: 'Gleicht die unmittelbar vor ihm gegebene Lösung der Hexateuchfrage einem durch allerlei Anbauten und Überbauten bis zur Unübersehbarkeit entstellten Grundbau, so mutet Smends Buch wie ein in seiner Gliederung klar erkennbarer gotischer Dom an, von strengen Formen und von herber Schönheit'.[17] Dies allgemein 'klar erkennbar' zu machen, ist das Ziel, das sich Eißfeldts 1922 erschienene *Hexateuch-Synopse* setzt, ein Abdruck jener Quellenschriften in vier Kolumnen nebeneinander. Als ich Eißfeldt einmal berichtete, ich hätte das Buch meines Großvaters erst anhand seiner Synopse verstanden, sagte er lachend, er sei meinem Großvater immer sehr dankbar dafür gewesen, daß er so schwer lesbar geschrieben habe, denn dadurch habe er selbst die Chance bekommen, die These von den zwei Jahwisten noch einmal und nun wirkungsvoller zu vertreten.

Die Hexateuch-Synopse ist noch bis in unsere Tage hinein mehrfach nachgedruckt worden (zuletzt 1987), nicht um der ihr zugrundeliegenden Smend-Eißfeldtschen Spezialthese willen, sondern weil sie auf eine bisher unübertroffene Weise die literarische Zusammengesetztheit des Hexateuchs veranschaulicht und noch immer ein nützliches Hilfsmittel zur ersten Orientierung über einzelne Stellen und Texte ist. Albrecht Alt pflegte im Kolleg mit ihr einen etwas billigen Spott zu

15. *Hexateuch-Synopse* V, vgl. die vorangestellte Widmung.
16. R. Smend, *Die Erzählung des Hexateuch auf ihre Quellen untersucht* (1912).
17. *Hexateuch-Synopse* 4.

treiben, indem er sie bei Gen. 18, 6 aufschlug, wo Eißfeldt die beiden
unverbunden nebeneinanderstehenden Wörter 'Mehl' und 'Feinmehl'
auf seine beiden Jahwisten verteilt, und man wird wohl annehmen
dürfen, daß Eißfeldt in Wellhausens Augen zu den Vertretern der
'mechanischen Mosaikhypothese' gehört hätte, die er 'verrückt'
nannte.[18] In der Tat hat Eißfeldts Verfahren etwas Mechanisches. In
'vorläufiger Vernachlässigung der anderen Argumente' ist seine
Vorüberlegung: 'Lassen sich im Hexateuch [...] etwa fünfzig Stellen
aufzeigen, an denen vierfache Elemente auftauchen; gelingt es, diese
fünfzigmal vier Punkte zu vier Punktreihen zu ordnen, oder vielmehr,
[hier erschrickt Eißfeldt selbst ein wenig vor der Gefahr und dem
Verdacht des 'Mechanischen']: nötigt eindringende Beobachtung des
Tatbestandes zu dieser Ordnung; und wird dabei der ganze Stoff des
Hexateuch so gut wie restlos aufgebraucht: so darf die Annahme eines
vierfachen Erzählungs-Fadens als erwiesen betrachtet werden.' Das
Vorhaben gelingt aufs beste, die 'in die zweite Linie gestellten
Argumente brauchen nur gelegentlich herangezogen zu werden, um
das auf dem Hauptwege gefundene Ergebnis zu bestätigen'.[19] Dieses
Ergebnis soll kein Selbstzweck sein, sondern dem Ziel dienen, 'Die
Schichten des Hexateuch als vornehmste Quelle für den Aufriß einer
israelitisch-jüdischen Kulturgeschichte' zu nutzen und dabei über
Wellhausen hinauszukommen, wie Eißfeldt 1919, noch vor der
Hexateuch-Synopse, programmatisch ausführte.[20] Auf dieser Linie lag
es, wenn er in der Synopse den Smendschen J[1] in L = 'Laienquelle'
umbenannte, womit er außer der Eigenständigkeit dieser Quelle den
Gegensatz der Frühzeit zum 'Klerikalismus' der jüngsten Quelle, der
Priesterschrift, ausdrücken wollte—was ein eher vergröberter
Wellhausen war.

In eine Landschaft, die fortschreitend von der Stoff– und
Gattungsforschung Gunkelscher Provenienz geprägt wurde, drohte
dergleichen immer weniger zu passen. Um so wichtiger war es, daß
Eißfeldt sich dem, was um ihn herum geschah, nicht verschloß. Und
es geschah wirklich in seiner nächsten Nähe. Denn 1922 wurde er
nach Halle berufen, wo Gunkel auf dem anderen alttestamentlichen
Lehrstuhl saß. Beide kannten sich ja seit Eißfeldts Berliner
Studentenzeit, und es war vor anderen auf Gunkel gemünzt und wohl

---

18. Vgl. R. Smend, *Epochen der Bibelkritik* (1991) 180.
19. *Hexateuch-Synopse* 6, Durchführung, 6-84.
20. I, 33-43.

auch ein wenig an ihn adressiert, wenn Eißfeldt eben 1922 im Vorwort der Hexateuch-Synopse von sich selber schrieb: 'indem er hier in Berlin in eine Betrachtungsweise des Alten Testaments eingeführt wurde, die von der in Göttingen vertretenen in vieler Hinsicht abwich, gewann er der Forschungsart und den Forschungsergebnissen seiner ersten Lehrer gegenüber eine gewisse Selbständigkeit und damit die Fähigkeit zu eigener Arbeit'. In Halle stand er mit Gunkel und seit 1927 mit dessen Schüler und Nachfolger Hans Schmidt auf gutem Fuß. Gunkel, wie Eißfeldt des Gesprächs fähig und bedürftig, tauschte sich mit ihm ständig aus über die zweite Auflage der *Religion in Geschichte und Gegenwart*, die er damals herausgab, und über seinen seit langem in Arbeit befindlichen Psalmenkommentar.

Eißfeldt blieb nicht bei allgemeinen Respektsbezeugungen, sondern ließ sich ein Stück weit auch seinerseits auf Gunkelsche Themen und Fragestellungen ein, wofür hier einige Aufsatztitel stehen mögen: *Die Bedeutung der Märchenforschung für die Religionswissenschaft, besonders für die Wissenschaft vom Alten Testament* (1918),[21] *Stammessage und Novelle in den Geschichten von Jakob und von seinen Söhnen* (1923),[22] *Die kleinste literarische Einheit in den Erzählungsbüchern des Alten Testaments* (1927).[23] Hatte Smend das Verhältnis der literarischen Werke zu einer (von ihm nicht geleugneten) 'älteren schriftlichen und zur mündlichen Überlieferung' außerhalb seiner Untersuchung gelassen,[24] so hielt es Eißfeldt wenigstens der Absicht nach anders. Aber ein Grundton von Skepsis blieb und verstärkte sich eher. 1918 schrieb er fast beschwichtigend, seine kritischen Bemerkungen zu Gunkels Märchenbuch 'sollten nicht im geringsten Buch und Methode herabsetzen', sondern 'womöglich dazu helfen, daß die von ihm eingeschlagene Methode ohne Irrungen und Wirrungen das Verständnis des Alten Testaments fördere'.[25] Noch etwas offener ist das Resümee von 1927, nach dem hinsichtlich der kleinsten literarischen Einheiten in den alttestamentlichen Erzählungsbüchern 'die letzten Jahre nicht nur Fortschritte der Erkenntnis zu verzeichnen haben, sondern auch Rückschritte'.[26] In

21. I, 23-32.
22. I, 84-104.
23. I, 143-49.
24. R. Smend, a.a.O. 347.
25. I, 32.
26. I, 143.

Wahrheit seien die meisten Erzählungen, 'wie sie uns vorliegen, von vornherein als Teile größerer Zusammenhänge konzipiert', und 'kleinste Einheit' sei dann nicht die Einzelerzählung, 'sondern der jeweilige größere Zusammenhang, dessen Ausdehnung durch Untersuchung des Horizontes der einzelnen Erzählungen festgestellt werden' müsse, Analogie seien weniger Grimms Märchen oder 1001 Nacht, sondern (natürlich mit Vorbehalt) 'zusammenhängende Darstellungen der Geschichte eines Volkes oder auch historische Romane'. Nachdem 'in den letzten 30 Jahren', also seit Gunkels *Genesis*, 'das von den Früheren erarbeitete Verständnis der größeren Zusammenhänge [...] vielfach abhanden gekommen' ist, wird es 'Zeit, höchste Zeit, daß hier ein Wandel eintritt'.[27] Bis zu diesem Wandel brauchte es allerdings noch mindestens 30 weitere Jahre der 'Irrungen und Wirrungen'.

Eißfeldt, wie kein zweiter zum ehrlichen Makler geboren, hat 1934 in seiner *Einleitung in das Alte Testament* die beiden großen Forschungsrichtungen unter einen Hut oder wenigstens zwischen zwei Buchdeckel zu bringen versucht. Er bestimmte als 'Aufgabe der Einleitungswissenschaft [...] die Darstellung der Entstehungsgeschichte des AT von seinen ersten Anfängen bis zu seinem völligen Abschluß'[28] und löste diese Aufgabe in drei Schritten. Zunächst besprach er in Gunkels Sinn auf weit mehr als 100 Seiten übersichtlich und lehrreich die 'kleinsten Redeformen und ihren Sitz im Leben'. Auf diese 'vorliterarische Stufe' ließ er, kaum ein Viertel so lang, die 'literarische Vorgeschichte der Bücher des Alten Testaments' folgen, wobei eigentlich nur ein etwas künstlich vorausgenommener Ableger des mit rund 450 Seiten bei weitem ausführlichsten dritten Teils, der 'Analyse der Bücher des Alten Testaments', zustandekam. Am Schluß stehen mit reichlich 100 Seiten die Geschichte des Kanons (mit einer Besprechung der Apokryphen und Pseudepigraphen) und die des Textes. Eißfeldts *Einleitung* ist vielleicht sogar über den deutschsprachigen Bereich hinaus das klassische Buch dieser Disziplin im 20. Jahrhundert gewesen, obwohl sie sich wegen ihrer etwas umständlichen Ausführlichkeit nicht besonders gut als Nachschlagewerk eignet und eben darum auch kein eigentliches Studentenbuch werden konnte. Das erreichten andere, die sich Eißfeldts Arbeit in mehr oder weniger großem Umfang ad usum Delphini zunutze machten.

27. I, 148-49.
28. *Einleitung in das Alte Testament* (1934) 6.

Unter den vielen Anerkennungen, die Eißfeldt im Lauf seines Lebens widerfuhren, erfreute ihn besonders die Widmung, die der berühmte Amerikaner William F. Albright seinem Buch *Yahweh and the Gods of Canaan* (1968) voransetzte: 'In Honour of the Eightieth Birthday 1 September 1967 of Otto Eißfeldt Whose Scholarly Exploration Has Made This Volume Possible'. Im Vorwort nannte Albright den Jubilar 'my old friend [...] whose indomitable spirit and acuteness in exploring *terra incognita* have so often opened new paths for me'. Das gingbeileibe nicht auf Hexateuch und Literarkritik, sondern auf das durch Albrights Buchtitel bezeichnete Gebiet: die israelitische Religion im Verhältnis zu ihren Nachbarreligionen, besonders der kanaanäischen. Hier brachte es Eißfeldt zu seiner eigentlichen Meisterschaft. 'Israels Religion ist synkretistische Religion', heißt, 1914 geschrieben, der erste Satz im ersten Band der *Kleinen Schriften*, in unausgesprochener Anknüpfung an Gunkels berühmten Satz: 'Das Christentum ist eine synkretistische Religion'.[29] Bei aller Anregung, die er ihm gab, war aber nicht Gunkel der Lehrer Eißfeldts auf diesem Gebiet, sondern der Graf Baudissin. Eißfeldt trat ihm erst nach seinem Ersten Theologischen Examen näher, empfing dann aber 'starke Anregungen': 'Von ihm habe ich gelernt, was behutsame Exegese ist, nämlich unabläßliche, von vorschnellen Textänderungen absehende Bemühung um das Verständnis des überlieferten Textes, und weiter bin ich durch ihn erst so recht in die Erforschung der kanaanäisch-phönizischen Religion und der Religionen der semitischen Völker überhaupt eingeführt worden, und zwar sowohl um ihrer selbst willen als auch im Hinblick auf ihr positives oder negatives Verhältnis zur israelitischen Religion'.[30] Eißfeldts ausführlicher Nekrolog auf Baudissin[31] läßt einiges von Wahlverwandtschaft zwischen diesen beiden frommen, vornehmen und gelehrten Männern ahnen.

Das wichtigste Denkmal dieser Beziehung ist indessen nicht der Nekrolog, sondern sind die vier umfangreichen Bände *Kyrios als Gottesname im Judentum und seine Stelle in der Religionsgeschichte*, das Monumentalwerk Baudissins, dessen Vollendung und Herausgabe Eißfeldt dem Lehrer 1924, zwei Jahre vor dessen Tod, versprochen

---

29. H. Gunkel, *Zum religionsgeschichtlichen Verständnis des Neuen Testaments* (1903) 95.
30. VTSup 15, 6-7.
31. I, 115-42.

hatte. Er unterzog sich dieser entsagungsvollen Aufgabe und legte 1929 das Ganze vor. Bei aller Mühe brachte diese Arbeit ihm und der Wissenschaft einen größeren Nutzen, als man damals wissen konnte. Denn im gleichen Jahr 1929 begann die Ausgrabung des antiken Ugarit auf dem Ras esch-schamra an der phönikisch-syrischen Küste und damit die Entdeckung einer Vielzahl von Texten, die die Kenntnis der Kultur und Religion jenes Bereichs in vorisraelitischer Zeit auf eine ganz neue Grundlage gestellt haben. In dem, was man bis dahin davon wußte, war Eißfeldt durch seine Arbeit an Baudissins *Kyrios* so bewandert wie kaum ein zweiter. Das prädestinierte ihn, bei der Auswertung der neuen Funde alsbald eine führende Rolle zu spielen. Hinzu kam, daß er in dem Hallenser Semitisten Hans Bauer (1878–1937) den Mann am Ort hatte, dem schon 1930 der entscheidende Schritt zur Entzifferung der alphabetischen Keilschrift von Ugarit gelang. Eißfeldt beteiligte sich von da an nicht nur an der in internationaler Zusammenarbeit schnell aufblühenden Ugaritologie im engeren Sinn, sondern setzte die dort gewonnenen Erkenntnisse in Beziehung zu dem, was aus anderen Quellen schon bekannt war und worin er sich so gut auskannte. Die wichtigste unter ihnen war und blieb das Alte Testament, so wie er selbst Alttestamentler war und blieb—aber als einer der nicht allzu vielen in diesem Jahrhundert, die auch auf Nachbargebieten mehr als nur Sporadisches oder Dilettantisches geleistet haben und damit außerhalb ihrer angestammten Zunft ernstgenommen werden konnten.

Hier ist nicht Raum, diese Arbeit auch nur im Überblick darzustellen.[32] Ich muß mich damit begnügen, einige Aufsätze und Monographien in der Reihenfolge ihres Erscheinens aufzuzählen, ohne sie danach zu ordnen, ob jeweils das Schwergewicht beim Alten Testament oder bei Ugarit oder bei Quellen aus der griechisch-römischen Antike oder solchen aus dem alten Orient liegt. Die Titel, dem Kenner geläufig, können auch dem Laien ein gewisses Bild geben:[33] *Der Gott Bethel* (1930),[34] *Baal Zaphon, Zeus Kasios und der Durchzug der Israeliten durchs Meer* (1932), *Der Gott des Tabor und*

---

32. Vgl. dazu R. Hillmann in: *Otto-Eißfeldt-Ehrung* 67-98.

33. Bedauerlicherweise fehlen einige der wichtigsten unter diesen Arbeiten in den *Kleinen Schriften*, weil selbständig erschienene Schriften nicht in sie aufgenommen wurden.

34. I, 206-33.

seine Verbreitung (1934),[35] *Die Wanderung palästinisch-syrischer
Götter nach Ost und West im zweiten vorchristlichen Jahrtausend*
(1934),[36] *Molk als Opferbegriff im Punischen und Hebräischen und
das Ende des Gottes Moloch* (1935), *Philister und Phönizier* (1936),
Ras Schamra und Sanchunjaton (1937), *Ba'alšamem und Jahwe*
(1939),[37] *Tempel und Kulte syrischer Städte in hellenistisch-römischer
Zeit* (1941), *El im ugaritischen Pantheon* (1951), *Sanchunjaton von
Berut und Ilumilku von Ugarit* (1952), *Taautos und Sanchunjaton*
(1952), *Der Gott Karmel* (1953), *El und Jahwe* (1956),[38] *Phönikische
und griechische Kosmogonie* (1960),[39] *Der kanaanäische El als Geber
der den israelitischen Erzvätern geltenden Nachkommenschafts- und
Landbesitzverheißungen* (1968),[40] *Adonis und Adonaj* (1970).

Die Liste ist bei weitem nicht vollständig, und sie betrifft nur eins
von Eißfeldts Arbeitsgebieten. Das imponiert um so mehr, als die
Zeiten alles andere als ruhig waren. Das Jahr 1929 hatte für Eißfeldt
nicht nur als Kyrios- und Ugarit-Jahr Bedeutung, sondern auch durch
zwei miteinander zusammenhängende akademische Entscheidungen.
Zunächst lehnte er einen ihn sehr verlockenden Ruf nach Gießen ab.
'Je länger ich', schrieb er dem dortigen Dekan, 'die Dinge mit mir
herumgetragen habe, um so klarer ist mirs geworden, daß ich nach
Gießen gehen möchte, aber in Halle bleiben muß.'[41] Gleich danach trat
er in Halle das Amt des Rektors an, das in jenen Jahren besonders
verantwortungsvoll war und das er mit Geschick und Charakter
verwaltete. Auf das zweijährige Rektorat seines Nachfolgers, des
Wirtschaftswissenschaftlers Gustav Aubin, fiel schon der Schatten des
Dritten Reiches. Angesichts des studentischen Terrors gegen den
neuberufenen Praktischen Theologen Günther Dehn bewies Aubin
Zivilcourage und bezahlte dafür mit dem Verlust des Lehrstuhls.
Eißfeldt, der ihm als Prorektor zur Seite stand, blieb die Probe
erspart. An seiner Gesinnung konnte kein Zweifel sein. Er war 1923
der Deutschnationalen Volkspartei beigetreten, hatte sie aber 1928 wie
viele seiner Standesgenossen wieder verlassen, als Alfred Hugenberg,

---

35. II, 29-54.
36. II, 55-60.
37. II, 171-98.
38. III, 386-97.
39. III, 501-12.
40. V, 50-62.
41. Bei Wallis a.a.O. 15.

der Führer ihres schroff antirepublikanischen Flügels, den Vorsitz übernahm. In der braunen Zeit hielt er sich abseits.

Aber er engagierte sich in der Kirche. 1936 berief ihn der Oberkirchenrat der Evangelischen Kirche der altpreußischen Union zum nebenamtlichen Konsistorialrat im Magdeburger Konsistorium. Als solcher verbrachte er einen Tag jeder Woche in Magdeburg. Im besonderen war er 'theologischer Dezernent' für die kirchenkreise Mühlhausen, Bleicherode und das Eichsfeld. 1949 wechselte er in die Zuständigkeit für das Erste Theologische Examen. Erst gleichzeitig mit seiner Emeritierung als Professor im Jahre 1957 entließ ihn die Kirche aus dem Amt des Konsistorialrats. Eine derartige Mitarbeit in der Kirche war ihm wie vielen anderen liberalen Theologen selbstverständlich, und zweifellos wurde sie geschätzt und brachte Nutzen. Man hat nicht den Eindruck, daß ihm das Verhältnis von Theologie und Kirche oder auch das von Glauben und Bibelkritik jemals ernstliche Kopfschmerzen bereitet hätte, zu schweigen von den wahrhaft fundamentalen Fragen, die die ihm gleichaltrigen Begründer der Dialektischen Theologie bewegten. Dabei war ihm immer bewußt, daß die meisten seiner Studenten Pfarrer werden wollten, und er trug dem Rechnung, soweit es in seinen Möglichkeiten stand. Über die theologische Dimension seiner Aufgabe hat er sich hin und wieder geäußert, zuerst 1926 unter der durchaus programmatischen Überschrift: *Israelitisch-jüdische Religionsgeschichte und alttestamentliche Theologie.*[42] Er sah einen Fehler der Dialektischen Theologie darin, daß dort 'die beiden verschiedenen Betrachtungsweisen, die von außen her (die historische) und die von innen (vom Glauben) her, nicht reinlich auseinandergehalten' würden.[43] Die erste verlange eine historische, die zweite eine systematische Darstellung, 'wobei systematisch nicht in dem Sinne einer alles aus einem Prinzip methodisch entwickelnden Behandlung zu verstehen ist, sondern eher als eine loci-artige Aneinanderreihung der Aussagen'. Historisch kann sie nicht vorgehen, weil der Glaube 'es nicht mit Vergangenem zu tun' hat, 'sondern mit Gegenwärtig-Zeitlosem; und die Offenbarung ist über die Kategorie der Zeit erhaben'.[44] Nach dem, was aufmerksame Hörer

42. I, 105-14.
43. 106[1].
44. 113.

aus Eißfeldts Vorlesungen festgehalten haben,[45] ist er in der Praxis
(zum Glück) nicht so alternativ verfahren, wie man nach der Theorie
meinen könnte. Seine einschlägige Vorlesung hieß 'Alttestamentliche
Theologie', zeitweise mit dem eingeklammerten Zusatz 'Israelitisch-
jüdische Religionsgeschichte'. In ihr sprach ein Religionshistoriker
von hohen Graden, der das Interesse angehender Theologen zu
befriedigen suchte, der aber auch seinerseits offenkundig nicht ohne
theologisches Temperament war. Seine grundsätzlichen Äußerungen
späterer Jahre variieren die These von 1926; es muß hier genügen,
den wiederum programmatischen Titel einer kleinen Sammlung von
Vorträgen aus dem Jahre 1947 zu nennen: *Geschichtliches und
Übergeschichtliches im Alten Testament.*

Eben fiel das Wort Temperament. Ich gestehe, daß ich bei der
ersten Begegnung mit Eißfeldt, im Sommer 1954, aufs höchste
überrascht war. Nach seinen Schriften hatte ich einen behäbigen,
umständlichen, etwas langweiligen Mann erwartet. Aber er war
lebendig und beweglich, lief beim Reden hin und her, unterbrach sich
selbst häufig durch Zwischenfragen und kam schnell von einem
Thema zum anderen. Er war zwar kein begnadeter, aber ein
begeisterter Anekdotenerzähler; man konnte mit ihm viel Vergnügen
haben und manchmal lachte er buchstäblich Tränen. Seine unpräten-
tiöse und unkomplizierte, dabei grundgütige Art überwand mit
Leichtigkeit Distanzen, wobei er allerdings auch einmal über das Ziel
hinausschießen konnte: nach zehn Jahren der Bekanntschaft schrieb er
mir, ich solle ihn fortan nicht mehr als 'hochverehrten Herrn
Professor' und überhaupt nicht als 'Herrn' anreden, sondern mit
'Lieber Eißfeldt'—das ging mir dann gegenüber einer Respektsperson
wie ihm nur schwer über die Lippen und in die Feder.

Daß er eine Respektsperson war, hatte ihm 1945 die schwerste Last
seines akademischen Lebens aufgelegt. Nach der Eroberung Halles
durch die Amerikaner im April wurde er zum Dekan der
Theologischen Fakultät, Ende Juni, kurz vor der Übernahme der
Besatzungsmacht durch die Sowjetunion, zum Rektor der Universität
gewählt. Am 12. Juli trat er dieses Amt an und hielt sogar eine
Rektoratsrede über 'Prophetie und Politik'. Es war eine Zeit, in der
sich manche auf eine würdige Wiederherstellung der Universität
Hoffnungen machten, die sich je länger desto mehr als Illusionen

---

45. Vgl. H.-J. Zobel in: *Otto-Eißfeldt-Ehrung* 35-40. Er verwendet dort auch eine
Nachschrift von K.-M. Beyse.

erwiesen. Als der Pragmatiker, der er war, wird Eißfeldt die Lage einigermaßen realistisch eingeschätzt und unermüdlich versucht haben, das Bestmögliche zu erreichen. Näheres darüber zu sagen, fehlen mir die Kenntnisse, und es bedarf dazu wohl auch einer Erschließung der Quellen, die jetzt erst am Anfang steht. Keinem Zweifel unterliegt, daß der Respekt, der Eißfeldt in das Amt des Rektors gebracht hatte, in diesen Jahren auf allen Seiten nicht kleiner, sondern noch größer geworden ist. Die Besatzungsmacht und später die DDR war klug genug, ihn für sich in Anspruch zu nehmen und ihn mit einem 'Vaterländischen Verdienstorden' und einem 'Banner der Arbeit' zu dekorieren. Eißfeldt trug die Last drei volle Jahre. Er warf sie ab, als 1948 'Übergangsbestimmungen für die Verwaltung der Martin-Luther-Universität' oktroyiert wurden, die 'der demokratischen Mitverantwortung neuartige Dimensionen' erschlossen, und er war klug genug, sich danach unter noch verschärften Bedingungen auch nicht, wie 1930–32, als Prorektor verpflichten zu lassen.[46]

Um so lieber kehrte er in die volle wissenschaftliche Tätigkeit zurück, und alsbald strömte der—ja schon vor dem Rektorat durch die Begleiterscheinungen des Krieges gehemmte—Fluß seiner Produktion wieder in gewohnter Breite. Zu den bisher bearbeiteten Stoffen war unverhofft ein ganz neuer gekommen: wie in die Zeit von Eißfeldts erstem Rektorat die Entdeckung von Ugarit fiel, so in die Zeit des zweiten die der Qumran-Texte. Er erfaßte deren Bedeutung sofort, berichtete seit 1949 laufend in mehreren Organen über ihre Erschließung, zu der er auch eigenständige Beiträge lieferte, und machte die Varianten der beiden Jesajarollen und des Habakuk-kommentars leicht nutzbar, indem er sie 1951 als dritten Apparat unter den Text der Bücher Jesaja und Habakuk in Kittels Biblia Hebraica einrückte. Der Biblia Hebraica hatte seine Arbeit schon vorher jahrelang gegolten: nach Rudolf Kittels Tod (1929) hatte die Württembergische Bibelanstalt ihn und Albrecht Alt mit der dritten Auflage betraut, und beide teilten sich so in die Aufgabe, daß Alt den Pentateuch und die Prophetae priores, Eißfeldt die Prophetae posteriores und die Hagiographen übernahm. Das Gesamtwerk war 1937 abgeschlossen und blieb in Gebrauch, bis 1968–77 die Biblia Hebraica Stuttgartensia erschienen, bei denen Karl Elliger und Wilhelm Rudolph an Alts und Eißfeldts Stelle traten; diesmal beteiligte sich Eißfeldt durch die Bearbeitung der Genesis (1969).

46. Vgl. E. Poppe–H. Schwabe in *Otto-Eißfeldt-Ehrung* 61-62.

Er war auch sonst ein idealer Herausgeber, und zwar ein solcher,
der die eigentliche Arbeit nicht auf andere abwälzte, sondern selbst
besorgte: man konnte ihm in den fünfziger Jahren kaum irgendwo
begegnen, ohne daß er einen Stapel Korrekturen der ZAW mit sich
führte. Dabei war er hier nicht einmal der eigentliche Herausgeber,
sondern hatte 1948 'nur' seinen Namen für das Titelblatt hergegeben,
wo er vor dem Johannes Hempels stand, des Herausgebers seit 1927,
der sich und die Zeitschrift durch seine Haltung im Dritten Reich
einigermaßen kompromittiert hatte; Eißfeldts Beteiligung machte
manchem Kollegen im In- und Ausland die Mitarbeit wieder möglich.
Sein Name als Herausgeber ist vor allem mit dem *Handbuch zum
Alten Testament* verbunden, 'Eißfeldts Handbuch', das sich wie sein
Vorgänger im Verlag J.C.B. Mohr (Paul Siebeck), Martis *Kurzer
Hand-Commentar zum Alten Testament*, und wie Lietzmanns
Handbuch zum Neuen Testament von anderen Kommentaren durch
gehaltvolle Kürze und schnelles Erscheinen unterscheiden sollte.
Mindestens das zweite verhinderten die Zeitläufte. Von Eißfeldts
übrigen Herausgeberschaften sei nur auf seine Mitwirkung bei der
Orientalischen Literaturzeitung (seit 1953) hingewiesen. Er war dort
auch einer der fleißigsten Rezensenten, so wie überhaupt die Zahl
seiner Rezensionen in der Nachkriegszeit schwindelerregende Höhen
erreichte. Ein Motiv dabei war die Nötigung, auf solche Weise
Literatur in das vom Westen abgeschnittene Ostdeutschland zu
schaffen. Aber der Nötigung kam Eißfeldts große Begabung entgegen,
schnell aufzufassen und kaum weniger schnell zu schreiben—und das
nicht nur mit der Schreibmaschine, sondern sehr oft auch in seiner
erstaunlich ruhigen und harmonischen Handschrift. Seine Gelassenheit
verlor er nämlich nicht.

In seinen letzten Jahrzehnten glich er immer mehr dem 'Hausvater,
der aus seinem Schatz Neues und Altes hervorholt'. Von beidem hatte
er viel zu bieten, en detail, aber doch auch en gros. Denn außer
zahlreichen (um nicht zu sagen: zahllosen) Aufsätzen zu Einzelfragen
lieferte er auch kurz hintereinander einige Synthesen größeren Stils:
1964 *Kanaanäisch-ugaritische Religion* im *Handbuch der Orienta-
listik*,[47] 1965 *The Exodus and the Wanderings* und *The Hebrew
Kingdom* in der erneuerten *Cambridge Ancient History*[48] und 1967
Syrien und Palästina vom Ausgang des 11. bis zum Ausgang des 6.

---

47. I, 8, 1, 76-91.
48. II, XXVIb, XXXIV.

Jahrhunderts v. Chr. in der *Fischer Weltgeschichte.*[49] Diese Überblicke wurden nicht nur darum weniger beachtet, als sie es verdienten, weil sie in Handbüchern ein etwas beengtes und verstecktes Dasein führen, sondern mehr noch weil das Publikum, wenigstens das deutsche, noch unter dem Bann der Synthesen stand, die die beiden großen Schüler Albrecht Alts, Martin Noth und Gerhard v. Rad, geschaffen hatten. Eißfeldt begegnete ihnen mit nüchterner Skepsis und wiederholte damit die Haltung, die er Gunkel gegenüber eingenommen hatte—kein Wunder, da sie ihre Argumente ja zu einem guten Teil aus der Formgeschichte bezogen. Um die Jahrhundertmitte und noch darüber hinaus, als in den Augen mancher die alttestamentliche Wissenschaft erst mit Gunkel begann, konnte Eißfeldt als arg rückständig erscheinen. Heute, wiederum im Selbstgefühl einer neuen Zeit, werden da nicht mehr so große Unterschiede gemacht. Wenn man Eißfeldt noch läse, würde man ihn wohl ebenso wie seine Antipoden am ehesten mit dem Etikett 'konservativ' versehen. Übrigens, bei aller Problematik solcher Etiketten im allgemeinen und in diesem Fall, nicht ganz zu Unrecht: Eißfeldt jagte nicht nach Unechtheiten, sondern freute sich, wenn er in alten Zeiten Boden unter die Füße bekam oder zu bekommen glaubte, mochte es sich um die Historizität des bei Euseb von Caesarea bzw. Philo von Byblos zitierten Sanchunjaton von Berut handeln oder um die Möglichkeit, einzelnen Psalmen einen Platz in der Geschichte anzuweisen, ja bei zweien von ihnen sogar die Angabe der Überschrift über ihre Situation in Davids Leben für historisch zu verlässig zu halten.[50] Hierher kann man auch seine späten Arbeiten zum Gottesnamen Adonaj rechnen, besonders den zusammenfassenden Artikel Adon im ersten Band des *Theologischen Wörterbuchs zum Alten Testament*, der in seinem letzten Lebensjahr erschien.[51] Nach ihm ist das *aj* am Ende von *Adonaj* nicht als Personalsuffix ('meine Herren' bzw. 'mein Herr'), sondern vom Ugaritischen her als verstärkende Nominalendung ('der Allherr') zu verstehen und das Wort in diesem Sinn bereits im 10. Jahrhundert v. Chr. gebraucht (Ex. 15, 17); seine Verwendung bei der Aussprache des Namens Jahwe geht (gegen eine der Hauptthesen Baudissins) nicht auf das *Kyrios* der Septuaginta zurück.

49. IV, 135-219.
50. Zu letzterem vgl. V, 192-93.
51. Die erste Lieferung mit diesem Artikel wurde allerdings schon 1970 ausgegeben.

Leider hat ihn die Fülle der kleineren Arbeiten gehindert, rechtzeitig das Buch in Angriff zu nehmen, das sein Lebenswerk krönen sollte: den Genesiskommentar in seinem *Handbuch*. Er hätte dort am klassischen Gegenstand noch einmal die Ergebnisse seiner literarischen und seiner religionsgeschichtlichen Arbeit bewähren und weiterführen können. Als die Kräfte nachließen, erwog er, zum Ersatz sein Kollegmanuskript über die Genesis drucken zu lassen, doch mußte er auch diesen Plan aufgeben. So ist der einzige Kommentar, den wir von ihm, einem, wie man meinen möchte, geborenen Kommentator, besitzen, die Übersetzung und Erläuterung der Königsbücher in Bertholets Neuausgabe von Kautzschs *Heiliger Schrift des Alten Testaments* (1922).

Von dem, was er sonst noch vorhatte, nenne ich einen etwas kuriosen, auch von ihm nicht ganz ernstgemeinten Plan. Er meinte, es sei sinnvoll, einmal diejenigen Forschungsergebnisse zusammenzustellen, die in der Wissenschaft auf völligen Konsens rechnen könnten, also die Verbindung des Deuteronomiums mit der Reform des Josia, die Zuschreibung von Jes. 40–55 an einen Propheten im babylonischen Exil, Umfang und Alter der Priesterschrift und ähnliches mehr. Von diesen sicheren Punkten hätte die Forschung immer wieder auszugehen, sie werde dann nie den festen Grund verlieren. Welch hübscher Gedanke und wie beneidenswert der, der ihn hatte! Vielleicht liegt hier das Geheimnis nicht nur seiner gelehrten Arbeit, sondern seines Lebens überhaupt. Es gab für ihn einige Konstanten, die unverrückbar feststanden, und das befähigte ihn zu dem vielen, was er geleistet hat und gewesen ist.

Am Ende seines Lebens mußte Otto Eißfeldt erleiden, was für jemanden wie ihn fast das Schlimmste war: die Unfähigkeit zur Arbeit. Aber er blieb teilnehmend und liebenswürdig, wie er es immer gewesen war.[52] Der Tod erlöste ihn am 23. April 1973, in der Frühe des Ostermontags. Auf dem St. Laurentius-Friedhof liegt er begraben.

---

52. Vgl. R. Sellheims Bericht in *Otto-Eißfeldt-Ehrung* 117.

NOTES ON THE JOSEPH STORY

J.A. Soggin

I

The Joseph story has been called 'At once the most artistic and the most fascinating of OT biographies' (Skinner 1930: 438) and 'One of the most beautiful tales of the whole Bible' (F.-W. Busch, Preface to Golka 1991: 3). Little wonder therefore that it has become a subject for writers and playwrights alike and that even a film has been made about it. It also explains why so many oriental and biblical scholars have devoted to the story a considerable degree of interest.

Before tackling its contents proper, allow me to signal a few false cues which ought to be discarded in its interpretation.

Source Division
A first one is the division into the sources 'J' and 'E' of the Pentateuch, as it was maintained not without a polemical undertone by Wellhausen almost one century ago (1899: 52). His statement is interesting because he seems to have realized that the story was fundamentally unitary; but he nevertheless chose to argue that 'the main source is, also for this last section of Genesis, "JE"...; our previous results require this assumption and would be shattered, if it were not provable'. But the problem is that this assumption is not required, nor can it be proved; not only so, it seems also extremely improbable, as has been rightly seen already by Gunkel in 1922 and Gressmann in 1923. Both authors came to the conclusion that the Joseph Story has a unitary and coherent plot, an element that would be lost by dividing it along source lines. But having realized this, they did not draw the obvious consequence: that the Documentary Hypothesis is not applicable to the Story; and the same charge can be made against von Rad's treatment (1953) many decades afterwards and in his masterly

commentary (1949–72); and also against the entry by Schmidt (1988). The general trend nowadays is, rightly I think, to consider the story as unitary (cf. the latest treatment by Becking [1991]).

The only Pentateuchal source that may be identified with a reasonable probability is 'P': it appears in 37.2; 41.42a; 42.5-6a; 46.6 (8–27); 47.5a, 6a, 7–11, 27b–28; 48.3-6; 49.1a, 33aαb; 50.12-13. Therefore there cannot be any doubt: applying the Documentary Hypothesis is using a false cue; the story cannot be fragmented.

This does not mean that there are no irregularities; they are mostly concentrated in ch. 37: the mention of the Ishmaelites and the Midianites (37.25, 27, 28, 36, compare 39.1) as the caravans to whom Joseph was sold, paradoxically an almost classic example for introducing the beginner to the Documentary Hypothesis; there are, further, the speeches of Reuben (37.21-22, cp. 42.22) and of Judah (37.26-27, cf. 44.18-34), where a duplicate might be detected; further the alternation of Jacob—Israel, an element which could be explained as a parallel. But they will have to be accounted for in a different way, as shown by Rudolph (1933); von Rad (1953); Winnett (1965); de Vaux (1971—he formerly, in the BJ, accepted a division into sources); Whybray (1974); Donner (1977); Otto (1977); Crüsemann (1978) and, of course, the recent works by Blum (1985) and Becking (1991). Dietrich (1989) tries to distinguish between an original story (featuring Reuben, Jacob and Midianites) and a later addition (featuring Judah, Israel and Ishmaelites. Whybray shows rightly the contradiction existing in those who wish at the same time to stress the unity of the narration and to maintain the Documentary Hypothesis.

Another false cue is looking for ancient tribal elements in the story. I hope to be able to show in this paper that the issue is at the same time different and much more complex. This point has been particularly made by Galling in 1959 and Kaiser in 1960 among others.

The story has been connected by Gunkel (1922) and Gressmann (1923), followed by Meinhold (1975–76), with those of Esther, Judith and Tobit. This seems to me another false cue: these late stories are too different as far as their plots and their various heroes are concerned, although one can detect considerable affinities of style between them.

Another false cue is to connect Joseph as a dreamer with Joseph as an interpreter of dreams, as is often done. The dreams of the former are perfectly clear to those concerned and need therefore no interpretation; they would be interesting also to a modern psychologist, who could interpret them not necessarily as an indication of future events but as signs of boundless ambition. The latter dreams need, on the contrary, to be interpreted, something which in the ancient Near East was usually performed by means of certain techniques, officially prohibited in Israel (cf. Deut. 13.2 and 18.10, 12).

Literary Genre

A problem which has not been, as yet, solved in a satisfactory manner is the one of the literary genre of the story. What are its aims, why was it composed, and where did it originate? One is reminded of the answer that von Rad gave in 1953: he called the story 'Wisdom Teaching', born within the context of what he called the 'Solomonic Enlightenment', and was followed by Otto (1977), Crüsemann (1978) and Boecker (1992). Can this definition be maintained even though, on the historical level, the concept of a Solomonic Enlightenment must be dropped, as is generally accepted nowadays? I notice only one exception, Williams (1975).

In an important essay, Müller (1977–78) answered the question in the affirmative: in the 'Didactic Wisdom Narrative', as he calls the Story, the hero incarnates in his own life a virtue or a complex of virtues, as happens e.g. in the 'framework' of the book of Job, in the story of 'Aḥîqār, in parts of the Book of Daniel and in the books of Esther and Tobit. Typical of the Didactic Wisdom Narrative is the character of the wise man, counsellor of kings and eventually saviour of nations. But is it possible to apply this category to the Joseph story? I do not think so: it has been rightly stressed by Westermann (1982: 282-83) that the stories of Joseph and of Daniel do not present the image of wise men in the way this is done in the ancient Near East. In the biblical stories wisdom and the connected skills are not the product of learning, self-discipline and personal application to a subject, but something which is mainly the product of divine inspiration, being therefore a divine gift to the hero.

Will Gressmann (1923) be proved right in calling it a story of adventures, combined with a royal fairy tale (*Königsmärchen*)? This is a description of the plot of the story that has many advantages, not the least of being pertinent, and which I would therefore endorse. To it also Redford rallied in 1970. Interesting is a further proposal by Gressmann: the narrative is the product of a combination of a 'Family Story' (of Joseph and his brethren) with a 'Political Narrative'

(*Staatserzählung*): in the latter, the former becomes the narrative about a high official at the Pharaoh's court, about his agricultural and economic policies and their consequences.

All these proposals help to clarify the issue, as long as one bears in mind that we are dealing not with history or with ancient, traditional legendary material, but with a story, with a novel, as I hope soon to make evident.

Still, the tale's plot is not wholly coherent, despite what a first reading may lead us to presume. As from ch. 46 the family story of Joseph and his brethren debouches again into the more general patriarchal narrative. The aim of all this is to relate the latter to the Exodus stories. Or, in other words, while the so-called Confessions of Faith in Deut. 26.5b-9 and Josh. 24.2b-13 simply state that 'My father' or 'Your ancestors' went to Egypt, our story explains why and how this happened.

One last word in this section: Westermann does not like the story being called a novel. He stresses, rightly, the differences existing between a modern novel (especially the 'short story' of Anglo-American literature) and our narrative; he maintains on the contrary that the persons described did exist, are therefore real. These elements, however, he does not prove, but only assumes and I hope to be able to contribute to a more viable solution of this problem.

II

In the story there are a few more or less objective cues, that have been often overlooked and which I wish to examine now.

A first cue, hinted at, as seen, by Westermann and observed only, as far as I know, independently from myself by Golka (1991: 25), is the obvious analogy existing between Joseph and Daniel in their interpretation of dreams (Gen. 41.1-36, cf. 40.1-23; Dan. 2.1-49 and 4.1-27). In both cases it is a foreign king whose dreams the local magicians or wise men are unable to interpret; in both cases the dreams are interpreted by a Jew who has been taken to the king's country against his will. But, as stressed before, he does not do this by means of learned and therefore acquired skills, but by divine inspiration, thus complying at the same time with the strict laws against the techniques of interpreting dreams and other signs in the skies and on the earth.

A second cue is the charge Joseph makes against his brethren of being spies, Gen. 42.8-17, 30-34; it can of course be taken just as an act of revenge against his brethren who had treated him so badly; but it has an interesting counterpart in the fears of the Pharaoh before the Exodus who did not know Joseph, Exod. 1.9-12, that the now numerous 'Israelites' could eventually become something like a fifth column, in case of enemy aggression. All this cannot refer to any situation of the second millennium BCE, when the whole of Palestine and the southern part of Syria were under Egyptian sovereignty; it hardly fits into the first half of the first millennium BCE, when Israel and Judah relied heavily on Egyptian help against Assyria first and Babylon afterwards; it can refer only to much later times, when the region was politically independent from Egypt which had become an enemy power. There is only one period in which such a situation is clearly known: the beginning of the second century BCE, when Syria and Palestine had been incorporated into the Seleucid empire; another one could perhaps be identified a few centuries earlier, when Egypt was in a frequent state of rebellion against its Persian overlord.

Another cue, although this time a controversial one, appears in one of the Egyptian words which are quoted in the story: *'abrēk* in 41.43, and maybe in the various but relatively few indigenous names quoted in 37.36, 39.1 and 41.45. For the proper names various proposals have been made in order to identify them with Egyptian words and meanings (a list in Skinner 1930: 470; Vergote 1959: 141ff. and Ellenbogen 1965; cf. Westermann 1982: 99); but for *'abrēk*, a word which cannot be reasonably explained in Egyptian nor in Hebrew (cf. the various attempts already in the ancient translations, listed *apud* Skinner and Westermann), it seems more and more probable that the model is Akkadian *abarakku* (*AHw* 1, 3) and Phœnician *hbrk* (KAI 26, 1, where, in the Karatepé inscription, the king is the *hbrk* of *ba'al*); this points to the title of a high official: *vizier* or something of this kind, a title quite fitting for Joseph (against Westermann 1982: 99); the proposal was first made by Delitzsch (1881: 225), was quoted by the dictionaries of BDB and Zorrell and was adopted by Croatto (1966), Lipiński (1974) and Zurro (1991); it is mentioned with approval in the new edition of Gesenius's Dictionary (*GesHW*, 18th edn).

Another, notable cue appears in what Skinner (1930: 82), following Gunkel (1910), has called '...an interesting glimpse of Egyptian manners': 43.32; here it is stated that the Egyptians do not eat with foreigners. Skinner (1930) explains this as 'perhaps due to his (Joseph's) having been admitted a member of the priestly caste (41.45)', but, as he goes on, was also something 'which would have been perfectly intelligible to the later Jews, [but] evidently struck the ancient Israelite as peculiar'. By his reference to later Israelite custom, Skinner is on the right path, although he does not follow it to its logical end.

In any case, as far as I can see, nothing of the kind appears in ancient Egyptian sources, while it is attested by later Greek authors. Therefore one is at least entitled to ask the question whether the whole reasoning should not be reversed, in the sense that the reference is to the later Israelite custom, with its severe dietary laws that made it practically impossible to share meals with foreigners.

In this case the author seems to be aiming at imparting a lesson to his countrymen: if the Egyptians were that strict, why cannot also you be at least as zealous? This seems to be a much better explanation, as it is stated nowhere that Joseph had been admitted to the Egyptian priesthood (41.45 does not say this) and had therefore to submit to special dietary and eventually other norms.

In this context the contention by Westermann (1982: 136) does not appear pertinent, 'that such an amazement...is possible only in the early times of Israel' (a similar point has been made recently by Boecker [1992]), although even he admits that the custom is known through Greek authors from Herodotus onward, i.e. the reference to Egypt is again one attested only in later times.

Another interesting cue is the notice about the birth and the blessing of Ephraim and Manasseh (41.20-22). It is obvious that, according to Jewish law and custom, the two sons were considered to be *mamzērîm*, something like 'bastards' from a religious point of view, not having been born by a Jewish mother. Could this have been, originally, a polemical pun directed against the North? But the matter must have worried the author(s), especially in view of the later prevailing Twelve-Tribes ideology—so at the end of the story the two sons are, as it seems, 'adopted' (or just legitimated: see Donner 1969) by their grandfather, 48.1-20, thus providing them with a status which formerly they did not enjoy. The trend is strengthened in later Judaism: the story of *Joseph and Asenath* (first half of the first century CE) makes Joseph's Egyptian wife pass through a complete ritual of conversion to Judaism, thus fully legitimizing the children. The original circumstances of the children's birth must therefore have been eventually considered as something scandalous, so that remedies had to be found.

III

The Joseph story has often been quoted as a relevant source of information about Egyptian law, administration and custom, in whatever time it is dated. But can such a proposition be maintained? Again the approach of Skinner (1930: 440) and Rowley (1948: *passim*) is cautious: the former speaks of 'the comparatively faint traces of local colour'; the latter maintains a general historicity, which, however, cannot be verified in detail; and one later author (Redford 1970—but cf. the very critical review by Kitchen [1973]) dates the story in much later times. For a traditional assessment implying a relatively early redaction, see Ringgren (1989 and 1991).

So what does the story yield about Egyptian customs?

Embalming

The practice of embalming, sometimes mentioned in favour of the substantial historicity of the story and its wisdom interests, is referred to only twice and at its end: 50.2, 26; it was probably generally known also outside the country, but is hardly an important subject; the story shows no particular interest in the custom itself, except for the fact that it made the preservation of the bodies of the deceased possible in view of their transport. Nothing is said about the ideological and theological elements which were at the base of the rites of embalming. It seems therefore impossible to detect wisdom or similar interests in this element of the story, against the proposals by von Rad in 1953 and 1949–72, followed by Boecker (1992).

Administration

As far as the descriptions of the Egyptian administration are concerned, there is strong evidence that the reader is dealing here more with what the Germans call *Lust zum Fabulieren* than with factual, historically verifiable information. Some examples may suffice.

What the reader is told about Joseph's advice to the king that the crown should buy wheat when the harvest had been good, the product abundant and therefore cheap, in order to establish reserves for the case of famine would not be *per se* impossible or improbable: common sense and economical planning existed also in ancient times. But when one gets to the septennial cycles, one of rich harvests, followed by one of dearth, one is again confronted with a fairy tale motif, used here as a narrative element. Similar considerations can be seen to apply in the case of the 'plagues' in the Exodus stories.

In the ancient Egyptian sources there is nothing which suggests that at a certain time the crown should have been able to to get hold of all privately owned fields and cattle and that this happened through the clever manoeuvring and policies of a foreign *vizier*. What is known is that the crown and the priesthood owned all the arable land from time immemorial (cf. Grottanelli and Zaccagnini 1991).

The story seems to take a certain interest in the organization of the Egyptian state and of the court; but again, the information remains vague and generic, so that it cannot be conveniently checked. The same applies to agriculture, commerce and economy in general: what is reported can be related to any time in the history of the country. The fundamental element of the Egyptian economy until this day, the yearly floods of the Nile, are only marginally alluded to and do not play any role in the story.

On the other hand the story and the Exodus texts show no interest at all in those monumental buildings which have made Egypt famous in antiquity and until this day. Exod. 1.11 does not speak of monumental constructions, but only of two 'store cities' or whatever the expression means. It is therefore understandable that Williams (1975) does not, as far as I can see, refer to the Joseph Story, but concentrates his analysis mostly on Wisdom.

IV

It seems, therefore, that from the Joseph story only very little first-hand information, if any at all, can be gathered about Egypt: its history, its institutions, its economy. It is very doubtful, further, that the author had such an aim in mind. The only element which the story seems to have borrowed from Egyptian folklore is one motif of the 'Tale of the Two Brethren' (*ANET*, 23–25), but not without consider-able variants. The reader is therefore confronted with a situation similar to the one of the patriarchs and of the Exodus.

V

If this is the way things are, a further question now seems appropriate: What then were the aims of the story? Is there any message it wants to convey?

Most authors agree on the importance of the phrases 45.4-8 and 50.19-21. Their content is, further, confirmed by the addresses given by Joseph to the two officials in prison, 40.8, and later to the Pharaoh, 41.16: it is the God of Israel who grants wisdom to the faithful and who directs human acts, even wicked ones, in order that good should finally come out of them as a result. All this seems to have been accepted by Joseph's brethren (42.28, and especially 42.21 and 44.16) and also by the Egyptians (Westermann 1982: 285ff.). So one could summarize the main thesis of the story with the words of the Nicene fathers: things happened '*hominum confusione, sed Dei providentiā*', a rather unusual thesis, by the way, in the Hebrew Bible.

On this basis I would like to argue now that the story has been constructed sometime in late post-exilic Judaism to reassure its readers about the truth of its two leading phrases. Things were not going well for Judah: political independence seemed for ever lost (the century of Hasmonean rule had never been accepted as something equivalent); the re-establishment of the Davidic dynasty had been put off to the end of time (and the Hasmonean dynasty was generally rejected); the rule of the priesthood must at times have been hard to endure, also considering the readiness of so many priests to compromise with the occupying powers. Confronted with such problems, the author of the story confesses his faith: what is happening at present is bad, but it is in God's power and it is his will to direct everything to a good end; and he will actually do so, as he did with Joseph and with Egypt, a country abundantly blessed through the divine blessing to Joseph. At the end, therefore, everything will turn out well for the people of God and for those on good terms with it.

This must not have been an easy thing to confess, against so many odds; but the author(s) managed it well and gave the world a literary masterpiece which modern human beings are still capable of enjoying.

BIBLIOGRAPHY

1. *Commentaries*

Gunkel, H.
1910   *Genesis* (Göttingen: Vandenhoeck & Ruprecht, 3rd edn, and repr. [1901]).

Rad, G. von
1972   *Das erste Buch Moses—Genesis* (Göttingen: Vandenhoeck &

Ruprecht, 9th edn [1949] [ET London: SCM Press; Philadelphia: Westminster Press, 1972]).

Skinner, J.
1930   *A Critical and Exegetical Commentary on the Book of Genesis* (Edinburgh: T. & T. Clark, 2nd edn [1910]).

Vaux, R. de
1962   *La Genèse* (Paris: Les Editions du Cerf [1951]).

Westermann, C.
1982   *Genesis*, I.3 (Neukirchen–Vluyn: Neukirchener Verlag [ET Philadelphia: Fortress Press, 1985]).

2. *Monographs*

Albright, W.F.
1918   'Historical and Mythological Elements in the Story of Joseph', *JBL* 37: 111-43.

Becking, B.
1991   ' "They Hated him even More'. Literary Techniques in Genesis 37.1-11', *BN* 60: 40-47.

Blum, E.
1985   *Die Komposition der Vätergeschichte* (Neukirchen–Vluyn: Neukirchener Verlag): 229-57.

Boecker, H.J.
1992   'Überlegungen zur Josephsgeschichte', in J. Hausmann and H.-J. Zobel (eds.), *Alttestamentlicher Glaube und biblische Theologie—Festschrift für H.D. Preuss zum 65. Geburtstag* (Stuttgart: W. Kohlhammer): 35-45.

Coats, G.W.
1974   'Redactional Unity in Genesis 37–50', *JBL* 93: 15-21.
1975   'The Joseph Story and Ancient Wisdom', *CBQ* 35: 285-87.
1976   *From Canaan to Egypt...*(CBQMS; Washington, DC).

Crenshaw, J.L.
1969   'Method in Determining Wisdom Influence upon "Historical" Literature', *JBL* 88: 129-42, esp. 135ff.

Croatto, J.S.
1966   '*Abrek*, "Intendant" dans Genèse XLI 43', *VT* 16: 113-15.

Crüsemann, F.
1978   *Der Widerstand gegen das Königtum* (Neukirchen–Vluyn: Neukirchener Verlag): 143-55.

Delitzsch, F.
1881   *Wo lag das Paradies? Eine biblisch-assyriologische Studie* (Leipzig).

Dietrich, W.
1989   *Die Josepherzählung als Novelle und Geschichtsschreibung: Zugleich ein Beitrag zur Pentateuchfrage* (Neukirchen–Vluyn: Neukirchener Verlag).

Dolce, R. and C. Zaccagnini (eds.)
1989   *Il pane del re* (Bologna: CLUEB).

Donner, H.
1969   'Adoption oder Legitimation?...' *OA* 8: 87-119.
1976   *Die literarische Gestalt der alttestamentlichen Josephgeschichte* (Heidelberg: Heidelberger Akademie der Wissenschaften).
Ehrlich, E.L.
1953   *Der Traum im Alten Testament* (Berlin: W. de Gruyter).
Eissfeld, O.
1923   'Stammessage und Novelle in den Geschichten von Jakob und seinen Söhnen', in *EYXAPIΣTHPION...Hermann Gunkel...* (Göttingen: Vandenhoeck & Ruprecht): 56-77 (= *Kl. Schr.* I: 84-104).
Ellenbogen, M.
1965   *Foreign Words in the Old Testament* (London: Luzac & Co.).
Engel, H.
1979   *Die Vorfahren Israels in Ägypten* (Frankfurt: J. Knecht).
Fritsch, C.T.
1955   ' "God was with him"—A Theological Study of the Joseph Narrative', *Int* 9: 21-34.
Galling, K.
1959   'Joseph I', in *RGG*, III (3rd edn): 859-61.
Gan, M.
1961-62   'The Book of Esther in the Light of the Story of Joseph in Egypt', *Tarbiz* 31: 144-49 (Heb., Eng. summ.).
Gevirtz, S.
1971   'The Reprimand of Reuben', *JNES* 30: 87-98.
Golka, F.W.
1991   *Die biblische Josefsgeschichte und Thomas Manns Roman* (Oldenburger Universitätsreden, Nr. 45; Oldenburg).
Görg, M.
1990   'Die Amtstitel des Potifar', *BN* 53: 14-20.
Gressmann, H.
1923   *Ursprung und Entwicklung der Joseph Sage* (Göttingen: Vandenhoeck & Ruprecht).
Grottanelli, C.
1976   'Spunti comparativi nella storia di Giuseppe', *OA* 15: 115-50.
1978   'Giuseppe nel pozzo', *OA* 17: 107-22.
1989   'Dal re al profeta—Distribuzione di cereali e ideale religioso nella Bibbia ebraica', in Dolce and Zaccagnini 1989: 117-35.
Gunkel, H.
1922   'Die Komposition der Josephgeschichte', *ZDMG* 76: 55-71.
Heaton, E.W.
1947-48   'The Joseph Saga', *ExpTim* 59: 134-36.
Herrmann, J.
1950   'Zu Genesis 41, 43', *ZAW* 62: 321-22.
Herrmann, S.
1953-54   'Die Königsnovelle in Ägypten und Israel', *WZ* 3: 51-62.
1960   'Joseph in Ägypten', *TLZ* 85: 827-30.
Honeyman, A.M.
1952   'The Occasion of Joseph's Temptation', *VT* 2: 85-87.

Kaiser, O.
1960 'Stammesgeschichtliche Hintergründe der Josephgeschichte', *VT* 10: 1-15.
King, J.R.
1987 'The Joseph Story and Divine Politics...', *JBL* 106: 577-94.
Kingsbury, E.C.
1967 ' "He Set Ephraim before Manasse" ', *HUCA* 38: 129-36.
Kitchen, K.A.
1973 Review of Redford 1970, *OA* 12: 233-42.
*Knipping, B.R.
1992 'Textwahrnehmung "häppchenweise" ', *BN* 62: 61-95.
Layton, S.C.
1990 'The Steward in Ancient Israel', *JBL* 109: 633-49.
Lipiński, E.
1974 'From Karatepe to Pyrgi', *RSE* 2: 45-61.
1976 'L'esclave hébreu', *VT* 26: 120-23.
Luther, B.
1906 'Die Josephgeschichte', in Meyer and Luther 1906.
May, H.G.
1930-31 'The Evolution of the Joseph Story', *AJSLL* 47: 83-93.
Meinhold, A.
1975-76 'Die Gattung der Josephgeschichte und des Estherbuches— Diasporanovelle', *ZAW* 87: 306-23; *ZAW* 88: 72-93.
Meyer, E. and B. Luther
1906 *Die Israeliten und ihre Nachbarstämme* (Halle: Niemeyer, and repr.).
Meyer, R. and H. Donner (eds.)
1987 *Wilhelm Gesenius Hebräisches und Aramäisches Wörterbuch über das Alte Testament...* (Berlin: Springer-Verlag, 18th edn).
Morenz, S.
1959 'Joseph in Ägypten', Review of Vergote 1959, *TLZ* 84: 401-16.
Müller, H.-P.
1977-78 'Die weisheitliche Lehrerzählung im Alten Testament und seiner Umwelt', *WO* 9: 77-98.
Niditch, S. and R. Doran
1977 'The Success Story of the Wise Courtier...', *JBL* 96: 179-93.
Noth, M.
1948 *Überlieferungsgeschichte des Pentateuch* (Stuttgart: Kohlhammer [ET *History of the Pentateuchal Traditions* (Englewood Cliffs, NJ: Prentice–Hall, 1972)]): 226-32.
Oppenheim, A.L.
1956 *The Interpretation of Dreams in the Ancient Near East* (AOS; New Haven: Yale University Press).
Otto, E.
1977 'Die "Synthetische Lebensauffassung" in der frühköniglichen Novellistik Israels', *ZTK*, 74: 371-400.
Rad, G. von
1953 'Josephgeschichte und ältere Chokma', in J.A. Emerton *et al.* (eds.),

Congress Volume, Copenhagen 1953 (VTSup, 1; Leiden: Brill): 120-27 (*Ges. St.*, I: 272-88).

Redford, D.B.
1970   *A Study of the Biblical Story of Joseph (Genesis 37–50)* (Leiden: Brill).

Richter, W.
1963   'Traum und Traumdeutung im Alten Testament', *BZ* NS 7: 202-20.

Ringgren, H.
1989   'Die Versuchung Josefs (Gen. 39)', in A.R. Müller and M. Görg (eds.), *Die Väter Israels—Beiträge zur Theologie der Patriarchenüberlieferungen...* (Festschrift J. Scharbert; Stuttgart: Katholisches Bibelwerk): 267-70.
1991   'Early Israel', in D. Garrone and F. Israel (eds.), *Storia e tradizioni di Israele, scritti in onore di J.A. Soggin* (Brescia: Paideia): 217-20.

Rowley, H.H.
1948   *From Joseph to Joshua* (London: Oxford University Press, and repr.).

Rudolph, W.
1933   'Die Josephgeschichte', in Volz and Rudolph 1933.

Ruppert, L.
1965   *Die Josepherzählung der Genesis* (Munich: Kösel).
1989   'Zur neuen Diskussion im die Josephgeschichte der Genesis', *BZ* NS 33: 92-97.

Scharbert, J.
1987   'Joseph als Sklave', *BN* 37: 104-28.

Schmidt, L.
1986   *Literarische Studien zur Josephgeschichte* (Berlin: de Gruyter).
1988   'Josephnovelle', *TRE* 17: 255-58.

Schmitt, H.C.
1980   *Die Nichtpriesterliche Josephgeschichte* (Berlin: de Gruyter).
1985   'Hintergründe der neuen Pentateuchkritik und der literarkritische Befund der Josephgeschichte', *ZAW* 97: 161-79.

*Schweizer, H.
1991   *Die Josephgeschichte—Konstituierung des Textes* (Tübingen).

Seebass, H.
1978   *Geschichtliche Zeit und theonome Tradition in der Joseph-Erzählung* (Gütersloh: Gerd Mohn).
1986   'The Joseph Story, Genesis 48 and the Canonical Process', *JSOT* 35: 29-53.

Thompson, T.O. and D. Irvin
1977   'The Joseph and Moses Narratives', in J.H. Hayes and J.M. Miller (eds.), *Israelite and Judaean History* (London: SCM Press; Philadelphia: Westminster Press): 149-203.

Vaux, R. de
1971   *Histoire ancienne d'Israël* (Paris: Gabalda).

Vergote, J.
1959   *Joseph en Egypte* (Louvain: Publications Universitaires).

Volz, P. and W. Rudolph
1933   *Der Elohist als Erzähler...* (Giessen: Töpelmann).

Ward, W.A.
1960 'The Egyptian Office of Joseph', *JSS* 5: 144-50.

Wellhausen, J.
1893 *Die Composition des Hexateuch* (Berlin: de Gruyter, and repr.).

Whybray, R.N.
1968 'The Joseph Story and Patriarchal Criticism', *VT* 18: 522-28.
1974 *The Intellectual Tradition in the Old Testament* (Berlin: de Gruyter).

Williams, R.J.
1975 ' "A People Come out of Egypt". An Egyptologist Looks at the Old Testament', in J.A. Emerton *et al.* (eds.), *Congress Volume, Edinburgh 1974* (VTSup, 28; Leiden: Brill): 231-52.

Willi-Plein, I.
1979 'Historische Aspekte der Josephgeschichte', *Hen* 1: 305-31.

Winckler, H.
1903 *Abraham als Babylonier—Joseph als Ägypter* (Leipzig).

Winnett, F.V.
1965 'Re-Examining the Foundations', *JBL* 84: 1-19.

Zaccagnini, C.
1989 'Nota sulla distribuzione di cereali nel vicino oriente del II-I millennio', in Dolce and Zaccagnini 1989.

Zeitlin, S.
1975–76 'Dreams and their Interpretation from the Biblical Period to the Tannaitic Times', *JQR* 66: 1-18.

Zurro, R.E.
1991 'El Hapax *'abrek* (Gn 41.43)', *EstBíb* 49: 266-69.

* The essays so marked could not be used.

D. TEMPLETONI MORONIS

GEORGICON*

Scripta virumque cano carmenque georgicon uror 1
E corde eructans, salit et fons laeta canendi.
Felix qui potuit verbi cognoscere formas
Materiamque dei divinam inflataque fata.
Laudabunt alios alii bene dicta probantes 5
Doctaque clarorum. Stat praeclarissimus iste,
Soracte niveo stat non nive candidus exstans
Superior. Floruit sapiens sapiensque florebit.
O fortunatos nimium sua si bona nossent
Emeritos; ficus sub tegmine quisque, sub umbra 10
Quisque sedet vitis. Ridet rubicunda senectus,
Ridet amans conjunx, sub eodem tegmine tecta;
Dum balant olim comites, dum tota facultas
Mugitus circum mensam dat; vana vacat vox.
At nunc laudantes, at tu laudate, canorae 15
Suspensam citharae deferte salice rapinam:
Primum hominem vacuum ipse pater jactavit in orbem,
Ultimus advenit jactatus filius ipse—
Christi grande meo canto tibi carmine carmen.

 * I am very grateful to Ms K. Moir for corrections, help and advice for these *vv*. To put it another way, apotropaic of *Robigus* (the god of rust), she en*gender*ed help in *quantities*: *laeta* will have to do what it can with *canendi*, not with *fons*, and *Soracte*, whatever else it can be, *cannot* be *nivea* (found in the autograph). *Facultas*, if it is to mean here what it must, is first (Murray thinks) found in this sense in 1255 (in the *Chartularium* of the University of Paris). But this is a little late. The best defence of what remains may be found in Ps. 45.2 (*Nova Vulgata* MCMLXXXVI): *Lingua mea calamus scribae velociter scribentis* (if *velociter* is allowed sufficient force). A translation is appended to the Bibliography, together with a copy of Paul's song.

THE PAULINE EPISTLES AS BORDER BALLADS
TRUTH AND FICTION IN THE *CARMEN CHRISTI*

D.A. Templeton

In Genesis 2–3, George, Farmer George Adam (for smiths are not invented till Gen. 4), in dire circumstances (he is married), eats an apple. In Philippians 2, George Adam eats no apple. He is, in a word, amelophagous. He is George Adam (Mk 2)—and flying, on one reading (what may be called 'the catabatic-anabatic'), at high Mach numbers. In Philippians 2, Paul sings a song (*carmen canit*) and, in singing a song, rewrites a story. He rewrites a piece of narrative fiction, by writing out, erasing, an apple. In addition, he re-sings a song: Isaiah's dumb lamb is a re-sung lamb, glossed (they say) by Paul, as a slaughtered lamb (...*mortem autem crucis*!). If a 'Hebrew of the Hebrews' is thus parasitic on Hebrew song and story, if Paul is imagining among imaginers, literary criticism *s'impose*.

The *Carmen Christi* looks unlike 'The Economic Influence of the Developments in Shipbuilding Techniques, 1450 to 1485' (Amis 1961: 15). What we require here, desiderate, perhaps, is not the historical method, but an ontology of fiction. In *Hamlet and the Philosophy of Literary Criticism*, Weitz (1965) first recommends to the critic 'non-trivial description'. I attempt to offer here only some ante-prole-gomena to trivial description.

All run the race and all win prizes. Philippians 2 cannot be said to suffer from a paucity either of attention or of readings of what has been attended to. The Adamic line, following Grotius's *tanquam Adam*[1] (1646 Phil. 2.7 *ad loc.*, *cit.* Henry 1950: 43, *cit.* Martin 1967:

---

1. Grotius (1646 Phil. 2.7 *ad loc.*): 'ὡς ἄνθρωπος *kᵉādām, tanquam Adam, qui* πρῶτος ἄνθρωπος. *Dignitate talis apparuit qualis Adam, id est, dominio in omnes creaturas, in mare, ventos, panes, aquam. ob quam causam id quod de Adamo dictum fuerat in* Ps. VIII *Christo* μυστικῶς *applicatur.*' Grotius's Ps. VIII also produces (*v.* 7) *tᵉaṭṭᵉrēhû* (MT), ἐστεφάνωσας (LXX), *coronasti* (*nov. vg.*), which accord well with Käsemann's form-critical remarks, based on Peterson (1926), on *Akklamation* (*re* Phil. 2.11). (Another Acknowledgement is due to the stirling efforts of Dr Simpson and the New College Library Staff, the *norma normans* by which other libraries are *normatae* (Jdt 2, Paul *passim*)—the 17th cent. accent of the widow of I. Pelé [see Bibliography] offers acute difficulties to the uninitiated. And yet another to Drs Provan & Wyatt for the conventional Scottishing of Hebrew.)

161), will be followed here: Adam made a pretty kettle of fish, Jesus not; or Adam erred, Jesus not. And an appropriate debt will be paid to Herrick ('Gather ye rosebuds...') and Murphy-O'Connor (1976), who with a well-armed missile from the Ecole Biblique holes pre-existence below the water-line, when it had already anyway, since Reimarus, been sailing in the wrong direction. For Herrick and Murphy-O'Connor concentrate also on the fate, or destiny, of the good man in Wisdom, who is compassed about by a cloud of perfumes and bad men wreathed in roses:

> Let us take our fill of costly wine and perfumes,
>   and let no flower of spring pass by us.
> Let us crown ourselves with rosebuds before they wither...
>
> Let us lie in wait for the righteous man...
>   (Wisd. 2.7-8, 12)

Adam in the Genesis story, we are sometimes told, was in the 'image' or 'form' of God. And we need not be surprised that according to this early story an anthropomorphic god should have fashioned a theomorphic man. Everything in the garden was lovely —lots of fruit, no death, no thistles (though the Scot may be permitted the question whether Paradise can be complete without them). Everything in the garden was lovely, except for one real snake. And though, according to the myth, there were no signs with the legend, *Das Betreten ist verboten*, 'Do Not Walk on the Grass', there was one tree and one prohibition promulgated by the anthropomorphic pedestrian (it was, we remember, the 'cool of the day').

In some of the best stories animals talk. And this one is no exception. And the talking snake very soon makes clear what is in the wind: 'Here's a pretty kettle of fruit' (Joyce), he says, 'and if you eat it you will be like God. You too will be pedestrians on an equal footing with Capability Jehovah.' Then, without so much as a 'by your leave', Adam's early feminist hinder-meet 'took of its fruit'.

Like θανάτου δὲ σταυροῦ ('even death on a cross') *HARPAGMOS* ('robbery': Phil. 2.6) is a crux, that, taken by Grotius, remains, it seems, a prize for the taking. There are many more positive and more negative ways of tying, re-tying and severing the Gordian nots (*sic*) here (for example O'Neill 1988 [one of our negatives is missing]: '...thought it not robbery *not* to be equal with God').

Let us drink and be merry, dance, joke, and rejoice,
With claret and sherry, theorbo and voice...

(Thomas Jordan)

Coronemus nos rosis antequam marcescant, 'let us crown ourselves with roses, before they fade'. A man who is going to crown himself with what Mimnermus (fr. 1.4, *cit.* Burton, 1962: 12) calls ἥβης ἄνθεα...ἁρπαλέα, 'flowers of youth for the picking', must pick them first (Mimnermus, we may be relieved to hear [Bowra 1949 *s.v.*], also 'tempers his hedonism with a respect for truth [fr. 8]'—it is, he says there, if not quite in these words, a *sine qua non* of the interpersonal). If Hedea at Isthmia is to win the race for war-chariots (she won [Dittenberger no. 802, *cit.* Murphy-O'Connor 1983: 16]), she must get it straight (if a woman of that sort [four victories], with those sisters [two sisters, four victories], needs the telling) that the gift of athletic success is ἁρπαλέα δόσις (Pindar P.8.65, *cit.* Burton *ibid.*), 'a gift to be snatched eagerly'. The word, 'take', has some force in the context of flowers, but still more elsewhere, as we see from 2 Cor. 11.20, where RSV translates with 'takes advantage of', NEB with 'gets...in his clutches' and Lorimer with 'taks ye in his girns (*sc.* 'noose', 'snares'). Nor is there more rapacity and rapine in the Greek than in the Hebrew *lāqaḥ* (BDB *s.v* 9: 'take = carry off: a. as booty... b. as prisoners'), while the cognate noun, *malqôaḥ* can mean, indifferently, the 'booty' taken and the 'jaw' that takes it. Nor is the violence diminished by either the English or the German of Bonhoeffer's ex-, or eisegesis, of Adam's 'Nazi' *Apfelergreifung* ('apple-seizure'—Bonhoeffer gave these lectures in Berlin, in the Winter Semester 1932 and wrote the introduction to their publication when 1933 was sufficiently well advanced to draw the exegete's attention to the more sinister aspects of the semantic range of this one Hebrew word [Bethge 1967: 161-64])—'snatch', 'violate', *rauben*, 'rob', *an sich reissen*, 'wrest to oneself' (Bonhoeffer 1955 and 1959 *ad loc.*). The apple, the *res rapienda*, 'the thing to be snatched', rapidly became a *res rapta*, 'a thing snatched'. And then not a *res retinenda*, 'a thing to be retained', for the forbidden fruit, understood by Eve as a *res donanda*, 'a thing to be given', rapidly (again) became *donata*, 'given' (Adam an early Donatist?). There is good and there is evil and there is knowing and there is mis-knowing. Only recently introduced to one another, Adam and Eve knew evil. And we know the result: thistles (in the English sense) and labour-pains.

Suppose you do retell the story, with Jesus taking the place of Adam, with Jesus taking the place of Man, with a man, the man Jesus, taking the place of Man, with Adam (Mark II) taking the place of Adam (Mark I), then you do not aim upwards at the knowledge of good and evil, you do not aim to know too much, or at 'equality with God', at *sicut deus*, τὸ εἶναι ἴσα θεῷ, but downwards at the knowledge of the good, the knowledge of one thing only, for the gravest problems are only to be dealt with by a 'deeper immersion in existence' (Kierkegaard [no ref.], *cit.* Robinson 1963: 47). While the sluggard must go to the ant and the Samaritan to the ditch, the good man must go early to his long home. You aim at obedience to the prohibition, you aim to respond to God and man. You are an earthen pot full of coins and you pour out your treasure. You are a pitcher and you pour out water, not onto the thirsty ground, but into thirsty mouths, to slake the heart: ἑαυτὸν ἐκένωσεν (Phil. 2.7: he 'emptied himself').

'What is man?' you might ask. Supremely memorable? Master of fish and fowl? Lord of creation? What do you make of this one, the one of whom I sing? Supremely forgettable. Contemptible, a mere nothing—and 'contempt is the imagination of anything which touches the mind so little that the mind is moved by the presence of that thing to think rather of things which are not contained in the thing than those which are contained in it' (Spinoza 1843 III: 318 [= *Ethics*, III, def. V[2]]). When a man is born, something is born; when this man was born, nothing was born. A silhouette without substance. Form without content:

> his appearance was so marred,
> beyond human semblance,
> and his form beyond that of the sons of men.
> (Isa. 52.14)

Crowned less with honour than with the absence of honour. Born like others, become less than others. 'Jesus of Nazareth? I don't seem to remember the name' (France 1891 '*Jésus de Nazareth? Je ne me rappelle pas*'). But his distinctness from those who did not honour him both brings to light and by bringing to light brings about the discomfort of those who are now conscious of *their* distinctness from *him*:

---

2.   Contemtus est rei alicuius imaginatio, quae mentem adeo parum tangit, ut ipsa mens ex rei praesentia magis moveatur ad ea imaginandum, quae in ipsa re non sunt, quam quae in ipsa sunt.

the very sight of him is a burden to us,
because his manner of life is unlike that of others,
and his ways are strange.

(Wisd. 2.15)

Lest his name should be only too well remembered, erase the written discomfort and liquidate the man.

Once this biography, compressed into these three verbs, 'emptied... humbled...became obedient', has been thrown as a supposititious sop to the historian, less substantial, less extended, less discursive, than one day in Dublin for Joyce's Bloom, this poem, this social lyric, introduces, with 'Therefore...' a caesura. Isaiah's dumb dulocrat, Genesis's theomorphic master of fish, fowl and fauna, the Genesis might-have-been, finds himself the occasion of the 'acclamation' (Peterson 1926: 317, *cit.* Käsemann 1960: 87): 'Jesus Christ is Lord', from the lips of multiple (and beyond necessity multiplied) entities, astral, terrestrial and chthonic, with whom Jesus joins in genuflection. As tongue acknowledges a coronation, the coronation of a regent (Jesus), so knee acknowledges the hand (God's) that bestows the crown. When what has been named has been named, but Jesus remains un-named, you have not named the highest under the Most High.

Subordinationist texts invite subordinationist reading.

It is unlikely that 'the handling of a medium' (*sc.* words) 'that facilitates the simultaneous achievement of numerous effects' (Hepburn 1984: 4) can be exhausted by one brief reading. Nor is it exhaustive to claim that the poem, as a whole, is refracted through Genesis, Isaiah and Wisdom as the leading texts of the linguistic universe in which this poet has his being.

For some aesthetic theorists,

> the more aesthetically valuable is to be distinguished from the less valuable by reference to the concept of form. They argue that both mimetic and creative activity may result in ill-formed objects which offer no reward to contemplation; but it is by reason of their form that other objects do reward and inexhaustibly sustain contemplation (Hepburn 1984: 4).

Critics, at least since Lohmeyer (1928), have been easily persuaded that we have to do here with formal excellence, but have not been able so easily to persuade one another to agree on what that form precisely is: three four-line strophes? Six two-line strophes? Six three-line strophes? This last version (Lohmeyer's [1928: 5-6]) has much to be said for it. It requires only the omission of 'even death on a cross' as metrically redundant and a Pauline cliché, or rather *theologoumenon* (Paul never has clichés). Now the song, the poem (what is the right word here?), is very widely thought to be of non-Pauline authorship, but it may surely be asked whether the man who was capable of the rhythmic, artistic prose (*Kunstprosa*) of 1 Corinthians 13 could not also have been capable of creating this *carmen* himself. But whether Paul is providing a gloss to what someone else wrote, or to what he wrote himself (the word is in process for Paul, too), these words of the gloss are, if any words are, the words most likely to 'speak themselves', to have spoken themselves, in Paul's own mind.

The triple division, then, of reality, of 'that which is', into astral, terrestrial and chthonic is replicated in two groups of six three-line stanzas, many of them of triple ictus, or 'three-beat tristichs', a form which Burney (1925: 30) finds, for example, in Ps. 24.7-10. And nine of the eighteen lines of Levertoff and Martin's retro-translation of Phil. 2 into Aramaic (Levertoff [no ref.], in Clarke 1929: 148, *cit.* Martin 1967: 40) consist of no more than three Aramaic words (with the wrong word for 'robbery' [*šālālā*]).

'The peculiarity of this psalm', writes Lohmeyer (1928: 10), 'consists in this, that it narrates, as it were, in ballad-like tones (...*dass er wie in balladenartigem Tone erzählt*...), that it, so to say, crystallizes around verbs'. But Lohmeyer's comparison with the ballad has wider relevance. There is the same conciseness, concision even (κατατομή (!) Phil. 3.2). We may compare:

> She sought to bind his many wounds,
> But he lay dead on Yarrow...

with:

> ...and became obedient unto death...

And compare:

> And he's stayed for seven lang years and a day,
> And the birk and broom blooms bonnie:

> Seven lang years by land and sea...

Here in neighbouring stanzas (7-8) of 'Hynd Horn' (Allingham 1865: 6-7) 'seven lang years' is resumed, much as 'in human likeness', the last line of stanza 2, is resumed by 'in human shape', the first line of stanza 3 (NEB, which here more accurately replicates the form of the

Greek). Or compare how 'the name which is above every name' (the last line of stanza 4) is picked up by 'that at the name of Jesus...' (the first line of stanza 5). 'Form of God', moreover, clashes antithetically and anaphorically with 'form of a servant', while the 'humbled himself' of stanza 3 and the 'highly exalted' of stanza 4 form a closely conjoined contrast within the overall architectonic contrast between 'servant', or 'slave' (stanza 2) and 'master' or 'lord' (stanza 6). And add to all this the list of bewildering near-synonyms: 'form', 'likeness' and 'shape' (stanza 3 for this last, where RSV translates [again] by 'form').

Matthew 23.12 summarizes well: 'whoever humbles himself will be exalted'.

So much for some observations on the song's artistic form. But what of the *content* thus formed? What can the literary critic say of this, without turning like Strauss (or George Eliot) to Hegel, or like Bultmann to Heidegger? The epic sweep of *Paradise Lost* and *Regained* is here contracted into a lyrical encomium of eighteen lines. And to contract is not to narrate, is to abbreviate, is to allude to. Milton was a long-distance runner, but what we have here is something more like the valetudinarian primary school twenty-yard dash. Our author's breath is briefer. 'An apple a day', he says, 'keeps the doctor on the way; but doctors should keep off apples and this doctor did.'

There is a double allusion here (to leave Isaiah and Wisdom out of account for the moment), (1) a literary and (2) a historical, to the life of Adam and the life of Jesus, neither of these being narrated, though both narratives are presupposed. And these presuppositions, the literary and the historical, make a double appeal to the imagination, the literary imagination and the historical. A story (Gen. 2–3) is alluded to; it is not narrated. A history (the history of Jesus) is alluded to; it is presupposed.

But this word, 'historical', does not tell the whole truth, because the history of Jesus, that is alluded to and that we find in the Synoptics, is rather more like the 'history' of Tom Jones and rather less like 'Developments in Shipbuilding'. It is storied history, history and story fused; historical sense combined with historical nonsense. It is fictionalized history, or 'faction'; not the facts of the matter, but, to put it that way, the 'ficts'. It is a character assessment ('he humbled himself'), but without the facts on which such an assessment should be based. We are offered the banality that Jesus did not know everything and did not try to know more than human beings can. He knew his limits and he knew his limits, as Adam in the story did not know his. And 'hybris breeds the tyrant' (Sophocles OT 873 ὕβρις φυτεύει τύραννον), for aiming at too much makes too much of man and woman alike. Adam's trouble was 'titanism' (von Rad 1949: 72), Jesus's trouble was humanism.

Paul of Tarsus, to judge by his non-practice, malpractice even, cannot tell a story for a sweetmeat from the suq. *Ab abesse ad non posse consequentia valet*, from the absence of something to the impossibility of something the conclusion is valid enough for my purposes: Paul does not tell stories, so he cannot. But he stands to the biblical tradition, the one, that is, that was written, not the one he was writing, much as Mark, in Augustine's view, stands to Matthew: *tanquam pedisequus et breviator*, as following in the footsteps of the tradition and abbreviating it. 'Jesus ate no apple', he tells us. By contrast with Jesus, Adam, lord of hens and hamsters, did eat the apple and, doubtless to the playing of the first trump, is rapidly sent out of the park.

Paul's song now turns from paradise-park to Isaiah's famous image (52–53) of the pariah and to 'the righteous man' of Wisdom (2): ἑαυτὸν ἐκένωσεν...ἐταπείνωσεν ἑαυτόν (chiasmus[!]: 'himself he emptied ...he humbled himself'). To turn aside Spinoza's critique of 'humility' as the tactic of self-destruction, or, at any rate, as giving rise to self-despising (1843 I: 323 [= *Ethica* III, *def.* XXVIII, *explic.*: *abjectio*]), humility and self-emptying in Philippians 2 are to be understood not as under-estimation, but as adequate, not exaggerated, estimation, and as the kind of generosity (*generositas*) towards others which does not preclude 'animosity' (*animositas*) or 'spiritedness towards oneself'. Christ acts in a societal context where virtue, or manliness, is not prized highly by the vicious. It is not Jesus's fault, if the endeavours wherewith he endeavoured, combining *generositas* and *animositas*, to persist in his own being were annihilated, deed and doer, by the pride and contempt to which risible man is prone. It was by external causes that he was overcome and those contrary to his nature (*cf.* Spinoza 1843: I, 345 [= *Ethica* IV, Prop. XX *schol.*]). Spinoza's hilarity, his *hilaritas*, Nietsche's *fröhliche Wissenschaft*, his 'gay science', are banished by loathèd melancholy to Erebus; the happy by the unhappy, the just by the unjust.

But 'But...', or 'Therefore...', for διό, 'Therefore', (Phil. 2.9) inserts a caesura into the song. For 'Then they blew the trumpet; and the people said, "Long live King Jesus!" And all the people went up after him, playing on pipes, and rejoicing with great joy, so that the earth was split by their noise' (1 Kgs 1.39-40 [my emendation]). These verses belong, of course, not to the song in Philippians 2, but to the narrative of Zadok and Nathan and the anointing of Solomon as king. The 'account', in Philippians, of Jesus's coronation is Scottish and spare. Thus subject becomes monarch and high is related to low by what we might call 'executive antithesis', the antithesis being 'executive', God being God (to use a 'significant tautology' [Ramsey 1967: 40]). When God is in question, 'low' is made 'high'. The making is by the kind of executive *fiat* that makes, if two nouns may be juxtaposed, for quality assurance.

One of the constituents, or apanages, of this poem is a historical fact, namely, that there was once a man, Jesus. And he died—perhaps, was executed. We could not be sure from the poem alone that this was a historical fact, but we can be pretty sure, when we correlate with this poem written evidence that we find elsewhere. We are, moreover, offered a character assessment, a 'mere how' added to a 'mere that': Jesus's actions warrant the judgment that he was humble and prepared to expend himself, that indeed he expended himself. But much the larger part of the poem is concerned with the explanation and understanding of the fact, implicating the warp of fact in the woof of story and song.

Jesus is understood in terms of a story, a piece of narrative fiction about hanky-panky in the rose garden. Further, Jesus is understood in terms of two poems about recurrent features of human behaviour (Aristotle's τὰ καθόλου [1925: 1451b 7: 'the universal']), on how the pariah is cast out, or how the gadfly comes to hemlock (Isa. 53, Wis. 2). And finally he is understood in terms of imagery that Feuerbach would derive from the Hebrew monarchy, the *vivat rex* motif, which calls into question the evaluations of the despisers.

Paul's readers, then and now, are invited to rehearse this movement in themselves, for 'each of us has been the Adam of his own soul' (2 Bar. 54.19). And each of us can be the second Adam of his own soul. Though each can fall like that Adam, each too can fail to fall, can rise like this one. Particularity and generality are paradoxically combined by the artists here: garden and snake, leaves and thistles, dumb sheep and rose-garland. But *their* stories, *their* songs and stories, of Adam, of the Servant, of the Righteous One, is *our* story, is our song. Hepburn (1984: 128) thus puts Baruch's point: 'In watching a drama we are often—even typically—aware both of a character in his particularity and of the general insights he yields about humanity-at-large (Hamlet the man, for instance, and the Hamlet in men).' Humanity-at-large is offered possibilities by the particularities of Paul's poem. The poem is formally a wrought gem, a miniature of major content, an intaglio, a seal that stamps, that impresses the impressionable reader. It is a classic.

But what of the ontology of the poem? Shall we say that we have here *tout court* the ontology of fiction, a poetic ontology? Shall we say that what we have here is the product of an *ars adulterina*, an adulterous art, a mixed form, a fusion of history and fiction? Or a fusion of time and eternity fictionally expressed? Is the poem autonomous? Does the history belong to the poem as Lady Macbeth's children to the play? Is the history extra-textual? Not quite, surely. The aorists, not in themselves decisive, have a historical smell and so strike the sense. It is the Jesus who was (*der Dagewesene*, 'the one who was there') who has taught the poet to sing, though it is the Jesus, no less certainly, of the poet's experience. Most men, like most women, can wear different hats. The combined office of poet and historian belongs to man as such. And yet the question remains here: What hat was the poet wearing? For the Iliad does not make Homer a historian of the Trojan War. Or if the *Carmen Christi* is not the Iliad, and if the author was wearing two hats, which hat is the top hat?

The question arises whether, rather, the hats are collateral, whether the ontology of fiction and the ontology of history have here equivalent weighting, whether each is making an equally substantial contribution, whether the truth of the one is not less true than the truth of the other, or whether poetry is substituting the vacuous for the substantial, the would-be real for the really real.

Not so, at least Aristotle. Fact cannot thus be contrasted with fiction, for 'poetry is more philosophical than history' (1925: 1451b 5-6). And, it may be contended (against Spinoza), no less philosophical than philosophy. For what is more philosophical than history and no less philosophical than philosophy can be set by the poet 'before the eyes' (Aristotle Rh. 1405b 12), '[i]n this way, seeing everything with the utmost vividness, as if he were a spectator of the action' (Aristotle Po. 1455a 23-24: οὕτω γὰρ ἂν ἐναργέστατα [ὁ] ὁρῶν ὥσπερ παρ' αὐτοῖς γιγνόμενος τοῖς πραττομένοις), in such a way that it commands our assent. The rhythm of the poem itself convinces, sets its truth within the ear. And the textual background (Genesis, Isaiah, Wisdom) supplies density of meaning. 'Knee' and 'tongue', for instance, the tree of knowledge, provide concretion. And 'God', the presiding term, the term that presides over the whole, begins to provide an ontological argument and supply a reference for the sense.

To turn from the Peloponnesian War, the history of the Papacy, 'The Economic Influence of Developments in Shipbuilding Techniques 1450–1485' is to turn from history. It is not to turn from reality. To touch on these and turn to other things and grasp them is not to turn from history, but to do other things as well and more importantly. To touch on the Jesus of history and turn to Hebrew song and story on the one hand and the God and the Christ of the poet's experience on the other is to turn not from the real to the imaginary, but to the imagined.

In this ballad-like lyric, in this ballad-like ballad, the historical Jesus plays the part that Moscow plays in *War and Peace*. Had Moscow, however, been different, *War and Peace* would have been otherwise. In this lyric, in that novel, the sentences do not have the assertorial quality of a historical narrative. They are, Ingarden (1985: 133) tells us, 'quasi-assertive': Jesus is Adam, Jesus is a lamb, Jesus is a king and wears a crown. It is only by delicate inference from such plainly metaphorical predications that we arrive at the history that Paul's song plainly presupposes and which is plainly present, though not as incision, but as striation. But behind these quasi-assertive lie non-quasi-assertive sentences, such as (1) that Jesus was a man, was a good man; and as good men go, he went; and (2) that *sub specie aeternitatis* Jesus *is* a man and a good one; and (3) that the reader may be so also, in Paul's antinomian sense.

This is a *mode* of saying it (in Eliot's and Spinoza's sense), but not, George, very satisfactory, not to be preferred before Paul's, or A.N. Thropostis's, George Adam. The song is better than what is said about it. It might be regretted that it is not Alcaics that we have here, not Sapphics, not Glyconics, nor even the iambic tetrameter catalectic (Hammond and Griffith 1979: 605). For what Spinoza says is true of John is no less true of Paul's *carmen grande*: *quamvis... Graece scripserit, hebraizat tamen* ('though he has written...in Greek, he hebraizes nonetheless' 1843: II, 200 [*Epistola* XXIII]). But that for a Hebraist is all to the good.

BIBLIOGRAPHY

Allingham, W.
1865   *The Ballad Book* (London: Macmillan).
Amis, K.
1961   *Lucky Jim* (Harmondsworth: Penguin Books).
Aristotle
1924   'Rhetorica', ed. W.R. Roberts in W.D. Ross, *The Works of Aristotle*, XI
            (Oxford: Oxford University Press).
1925   *The Poetics of Aristotle* (ed. S.H. Butcher; London: Macmillan).
Bethge, E.
1967   *Dietrich Bonhoeffer* (Munich: Kaiser Verlag).
Bonhoeffer, D.
1955   *Schöpfung und Fall* (Munich: Kaiser Verlag) (ET *Creation and Fall*
            [London: SCM Press, 1959]).
Bowra, M.
1938   *Early Greek Elegists* (London: Oxford University Press).
1949   'Mimnermus', in *The Oxford Classical Dictionary* (Oxford: Oxford
            University Press).
Buchan, D.
1985   *A Book of Scottish Ballads* (London: Routledge & Kegan Paul).
Burney, C.F.
1925   *The Poetry of our Lord* (Oxford: Oxford University Press).
Burton, R.W.B.
1962   *Pindar's Pythian Odes* (Oxford: Oxford University Press).
Campbell, D.A.
1967   *Greek Lyric Poetry* (London: Macmillan).
Clarke, W.K.L.
1929   *New Testament Problems* (London: SPCK; New York: Macmillan).
Diehl E.
1925   *Anthologia Lyrica Graeca*, I (Leipzig: Teubner).
Dittenberger, W.
1915–24   *Sylloge Inscriptionum Graecarum* (Leipzig: Hirzel, 3rd edn).
France, A.
1891   'Le Procurateur de Judée', *Le Temps*, 25 December 1891 (also in
            L'etui de nacre [Paris: Calmann–Levy, 1892]) (ET n.d. [repr. 1947]
            The World's Greatest Short Stories [London: Odhams Press]).
Grotius, H.
1646   *Annotationum in Novum Testamentum Tomus Secundus* (Paris: Pelé &
            Duval).
Hammond, N.G.L. and G.T. Griffith
1979   *A History of Macedonia*, II (Oxford: Oxford University Press).
Heidegger, M.
1927   'Sein und Zeit', in E. Husserl (ed.), *Jahrbuch für Phänomenologie
            und phänomenologische Forschung*, VIII (ET *Being and Time* [trans.
            J. Macquarrie and E. Robinson; London: SCM Press, 1962]).

Henry, P.
1950   'Kénose', *DBSup*, XXIV (Paris: Letouzey & Ané): 7-161.
Hepburn, R.W.
1984   *Wonder and Other Essays* (Edinburgh: Edinburgh University Press).
Ingarden, R.
1985   'Uwagi na marginesie *Poetyki* Arystotelesa' and 'O tak zwanej
            "prawdzie" w literaturze', in *Studia z Estetyki*, I (Warsaw: Panstwowe
            Wydawn. Naukowe [ET: 'A Marginal Commentary on Aristotle's
            Poetics', and 'On So-called "Truth" in Literature', in *Selected
            Papers in Aesthetics* [Washington: The Catholic University of America
            Press; Vienna: Philosophia Verlag]).
Käsemann, E.
1960   'Kritische Analyse von Phil. 2, 5-11', in *idem, Exegetische Versuche
            und Besinnungen* (Göttingen: Vandenhoeck & Ruprecht): 51-95.
Lohmeyer, E.
1928   *Kyrios Jesus* (Heidelberg: Carl Winters)
Martin, R.P.
1967   *Carmen Christi* (Cambridge: Cambridge University Press).
Murphy-O'Connor, J.
1976   'Christological Anthropology in Phil. II, 6-11', in *RB* 83: 25-50.
O'Neill, J.C.
1988   'Hoover on *Harpagmos* Reviewed, with a Modest Proposal concerning
            Philippians 2.6', *HTR* 81: 445-49.
Peterson, E.
1926   *ΕΙΣ ΘΕΟΣ* (Göttingen: Vandenhoeck & Ruprecht).
Rad, G.von
1949   *Das erste Buch Mose: Genesis Kapitel 1–12, 9* (Göttingen: Vanden-
            hoeck & Ruprecht) (ET *Genesis* [trans. J.H. Marks; London: SCM
            Press, 3rd edn, 1972]).
Ramsey, I.T.
1967   *Religious Language* (London: SCM Press).
Robinson, J.A.T.
1963   *Honest to God* (London: SCM Press).
Spinoza, B. de
1843   *Opera*, I–III (ed. C.H. Bruder; Leipzig: Tauchnitz).
Strauss, D.F.
1840   *Das Leben Jesu* (Tübingen: Osiander, 4th edn) (ET: *The Life of Jesus*
            [trans. M. Evans (George Eliot); Michigan: Scholarly Press, 1970]).
Weitz M.
1965   *Hamlet and the Philosophy of Literary Criticism* (London: Faber &
            Faber).
Wordsworth J. and H.J. White
1911   *Novum Testamentum Latine* (Oxford: Oxford University Press).

[Translation: 'Writings and the man I sing and I am consumed with
passion as I bubble forth from the heart a song for George, and there
leaps up a fountain of singing joyful things. Happy is he who is able to

know the forms of the word and the divine content of God and the sayings he has in(suf)flated. Let others praise others, (testing and) approving what they have said well and the learned (utterances) of famous men. But that man stands supremely famous, stands, white not with snow, standing out higher than snowy Soracte. He has flourished a wise man and a wise man he will flourish. O happy, more than happy are the Emeriti, were they but knowing it; each one under the covering of his fig-tree, each one under the shadow of his vine. Ruddy old-age smiles, there smiles the loving wife, protected under the same covering, †while the former colleagues bleat, while the whole Faculty (Ability?) moos around the table; their vain voice is vacant (*sc.* of sense)†. But now you, who praise, but now you, who are praised, take down from the willow-tree the suspended robbery of your canorous harp: the first man the father himself threw into the empty world, the last man, thrown, the son himself, has arrived—Christ's great song in my song I sing to you'.]

THE SONG (Phil. 2)

1

ὃς ἐν μορφῇ Θεοῦ ὑπάρχων
who, though he was in the form of God,
    οὐχ ἁρπαγμὸν ἡγήσατο
    did not count a thing to be grasped
        τὸ εἶναι ἴσα Θεῷ,
        equality with God,

2

ἀλλὰ ἑαυτὸν ἐκένωσεν
but emptied himself
    μορφὴν δούλου λαβών,
    taking the form of a servant,
        ἐν ὁμοιώματι ἀνθρώπων γενόμενος·
        being born in the likeness of men.

3

καὶ σχήματι εὑρεθεὶς ὡς ἄνθρωπος
and being found in human form
    ἐταπείνωσεν ἑαυτόν
    he humbled himself
        γενόμενος ὑπήκοος μέχρι θανάτου...
        and became obedient unto death.

4

διὸ καὶ ὁ θεὸς αὐτὸν ὑπερύψωσεν
Therefore God has highly exalted him
    καὶ ἐχαρίσατο αὐτῷ
    and bestowed on him
        τὸ ὄνομα τὸ ὑπὲρ πᾶν ὄνομα,
        the name which is above every name,

5

ἵνα ἐν τῷ ὀνόματι 'Ιησοῦ
that at the name of Jesus
    πᾶν γόνυ κάμψῃ
    every knee should bow,
        ἐπουρανίων καὶ ἐπιγείων καὶ καταχθονίων,
        in heaven and on earth and under the earth,

6

καὶ πᾶσα γλῶσσα ἐξομολογήσηται
and every tongue confess
    ὅτι κύριος 'Ιησοῦς Χριστὸς
    that Jesus Christ is lord,
        εἰς δόξαν θεοῦ πατρός.
        to the glory of God the father.

'THE HERMENEUTICS OF I-WITNESS TESTIMONY:
JOHN 21.20-24 AND THE "DEATH" OF THE "AUTHOR"'

K.J. Vanhoozer

> These are not memoirs about myself. These are memoirs about other
> people. Others will write about us…One must speak the truth about the
> past or not at all. It's very hard to reminisce and it's worth doing only in
> the name of truth…I was an eyewitness to many events and they were
> important events…This will be the testimony of an eyewitness.
>
> (*Testimony: The Memoirs of Dimitri Shostakovich*, p. 11)

Introduction

John 21.20-24 calls not only for interpretation but for reflection on
the interpretative process itself. Its subject, the Beloved Disciple, is
presented as at once an interpreter *par excellence* and the victim of a
misinterpretation, namely, the rumor that he would not die. The
attempt to understand this text thus leads us to think about the aims
and methods of textual understanding in general. Exegesis passes naturally into hermeneutics. For Jn 21.20-24 raises several crucial and
absorbing hermeneutical issues concerning the author, text and reader.
These issues all centre on the figure of the Beloved Disciple, who is
mentioned six times in the Fourth Gospel (13.23-30; 19.25-27; 20.2-
10; 21.7; 21.21-23; 21.24), usually in passages emphasizing eyewitness
testimony. Jn 21.24, the last of these references, serves as touchstone
and structuring principle for our enquiry with its threefold reference
to the Beloved Disciple: he is (1) the author 'who has written these
things', (2) the witness 'who is bearing witness to these things', and
(3) the model disciple for the reader, for 'his testimony is true'.

The Beloved Disciple is a controversial figure in Johannine scholarship. Not only his identity, but his very existence and historicity, is the
subject of some dispute. While some commentators find the disclosure
of the author's identity as that of the Beloved Disciple to be the climax

of the Gospel, others maintain that 21.24 is a later editorial addition. In this essay I wish to explore the extent to which the question of authorship becomes a properly hermeneutical as opposed to historical problem. To what extent does the question of authorship affect the interpretation of text and the activity of interpretation? And to what extent ought it to do so?

If such a question holds centre stage, it is because the rumour of the 'death of the author' is being spread not only in the wings and on the margins of biblical scholarship but increasingly 'among the brethren'. I intend to show that this latter rumour, distinctly lacking in dominical authority, has serious implications for the way we interpret biblical testimony. Just as the death, actual or contemplated, of the Beloved Disciple raised the problem of a continuing authoritative witness in the original believing community, so the death of the Author raises for us the problem of how to preserve and do justice to the authoritative textual witness of the Other.

Though Jesus never promised immortality to the Beloved Disciple, he probably did not envisage the way that the Beloved Disciple would be killed off, at least as an author, in modern and postmodern biblical scholarship. Much historical-critical work on the Fourth Gospel has taken the form of a quest for the historical author. But all too often the question of historical authorship has shaded into a discussion of the historical reliability of the Johannine tradition. The result: conservative and liberal commentators alike have treated authorship as a matter of apologetics rather than interpretation. With some exceptions, most historical critics have concluded that the Fourth Gospel in its present form could not have been written by the Beloved Disciple. Why? Because 21.23, together with a complicated theory concerning the composition of the Gospel, implies that he had probably died before the Gospel was published.

Of late, however, scholars have begun to read the Fourth Gospel with literary-critical aims and interests. A recent book-length review of Johannine scholarship between 1970 and 1990 concludes with this thought: 'The most contemporary development, perhaps, is the reading of John as the kind of literary product it is, a narrative or story, independently of historical consideration such as authorship and time, or circumstances of composition' (Sloyan 1991: 948). Such approaches have convincingly demonstrated the Evangelist's literary artistry and rhetorical strategies while neatly sidestepping the vexed question of historical authorship. While agreeing that the 'how' and the 'what' of discourse are legitimate objects of textual study, one may nevertheless wonder what has happened to the 'about what' of discourse, that is, to the question of reference to historical reality.

Deconstruction takes the literary approach to an extreme, not only killing but burying the author, effectively extinguishing all signs of his presence. The idea of the author is ultimately, as Roland Barthes correctly observes, a theological notion (1986: 54). The Author is the origin of meaning, the place where words and world come together, the guarantee that talk corresponds to reality. The presence of the Author thus assures the objectivity of meaning. 'Logocentrism' is Derrida's term for the confidence that language refers to the real. For Derrida, however, logocentrism is a myth; the author is absent, not present. Signs refer not to reality but only to other signs. Of the writing which is Text there is no end: 'The necessity of commentary ...is the very form of exiled speech. In the beginning is hermeneutics' (Derrida 1978: 67). Perhaps no text is more conspicuously logocentric than the Fourth Gospel, the Book of Signs and testimonies which point to an incarnate Logos who is Truth. And of the many logocentric texts in the Fourth Gospel, 21.24 is doubtless one of the more offensive to deconstructionist sensibilities. 'We know that his testimony is true' is the supreme manifesto for logocentric hermeneutics.

To what extent is authorship of hermeneutical importance? Should biblical interpreters resist or celebrate the death of the author? The purpose of this essay is not to answer that general query, but rather to examine the consequences of the death of the author for the interpretation of one kind of text in particular, namely, 'I-witness' testimony (I use the pronoun rather than the name of the bodily part in order to stress the fact that the witness is a human person). I shall argue that testimony, of all literary forms, is least welcoming to deconstruction and radical reader-response criticism. For the reader either to impose his own meaning or to affirm indeterminate multiple meanings is to deny the very nature of testimony; it is to subject testimony to interpretative violence. Deconstruction castrates the text; bereft of its true voice, must not the text necessarily speak falsetto? Radical reader-response criticism therefore risks excluding the very idea of testimony, the voice of the 'Other'. Rightly to receive testimony, I shall argue, means to attend to and respect the voice of the author. Testimony may indeed lead to the death of the author, but not in the way suggested by deconstruction. It is precisely because the witness articulates the voice of an unwanted 'Other' that the author is killed. Testimony challenges us to respect the alterity of the other and to resist the temptation to reduce the voice of the Other to our own.

The Voice of the 'Other' and Authorial Rights

'who wrote these things' (Jn 21.24)

Who—and What—is the Author?

'The question of the authorship of the book is tantalizing' and confronts us 'with the problem of interpretation' (Barrett 1978: 3-4). Indeed, and not only so for historical-critical scholarship, as a riddle to be solved, but also for hermeneutics—as a problem with which to reckon. But what exactly is the question of authorship? For historical criticism, the question is 'Who?'; for hermeneutics, the question is 'What?'

The salient facts with regard to the question of the identity of the author of the Fourth Gospel are quickly summarized; not so the multifarious theories which they have spawned. The earliest external evidence is virtually unanimous in attributing the Fourth Gospel to John the son of Zebedee, though much of this evidence can be traced back to the testimony of Irenaeus: 'Afterwards John, the disciple of the Lord, who also reclined on his bosom, published his gospel, while staying at Ephesus in Asia' (*adv. Haer.* III, i, 1). The earliest known manuscripts are headed *kata Ioannēn* and, significantly, they all include 21.24, which identifies the author as an 'I-witness'.

Of course, the text itself constitutes the bulk of the relevant data, and the internal evidence is the subject of wildly divergent assessments. What does 21.24 say and when did it say it? First, when was 21.24 added to the Fourth Gospel? Bultmann believes that the evangelist used four sources to compose the bulk of the narrative which was reshaped by a later editor who also added ch. 21, and he is largely followed by Brown, who agrees that the evangelist cannot be the Beloved Disciple (Brown 1970: 1078-82).

But what exactly does 21.24 say? 'This is the disciple...who has written these things'. Does this verse make the claim that the Beloved Disciple is the author of the Fourth Gospel? There are two parts to this question. First, what is the scope of 'these things'? Is this a reference to the anecdote immediately preceding about the rumour concerning the Beloved Disciple (Dodd 1953; Davies 1992), or a reference to the whole of ch. 21, or is it a reference to the entire Gospel (Minear 1983)? Again, the case must rest entirely on internal evidence, that is, upon interpretation. But second, and more importantly for our purposes, what is the meaning of 'who has written' (*grapsas*)? At one extreme is the suggestion that the author wrote in his own hand. Others take the term in a causative sense: 'had these things written' (e.g. by dictating or supervising the account). At the other extreme, G. Schrenk suggests that *grapsas* indicates a much more remote conception of authorship: the Beloved Disciple's recollections were only the basis or the occasion for the composition of the Fourth Gospel (Schrenk 1964: 743). D. Moody Smith gives a succinct picture of the critical consensus, such as it is:

> The Johannine community conceived of itself as linked directly to Jesus and the original circle of disciples through the Beloved Disciple, however that linkage may have been understood and whatever may be its validity as a historical claim. One finds a wide consensus on this point, a narrower one on whether the Beloved Disciple was an eyewitness, and a small but articulate minority willing to identify him with John the Son of Zebedee in accord with the ancient church tradition (Smith 1989: 285).

Can we say anything more about the nature of this 'link' between the Beloved Disciple and the Fourth Gospel? Barrett thinks that *grapsas* 'means no more than that the disciple was the ultimate and responsible authority for "these things"'. Similarly, Smalley believes that the Beloved Disciple handed on to a disciple or a group of disciples an oral account of the deeds and sayings of Jesus. The disciples then wrote a first draft and after the death of the Beloved Disciple the church published an edited version. Brown locates the Beloved Disciple's involvement in the first stage alone of the five stages of the Gospel's composition. The question 'Who?' leads therefore to the more fundamental query: '*What* is an author?' There is little evidence in ancient literature of *grapsas* referring to such a notion of remote authorship, to authorship at a distance of four compositional stages (Hitchcock 1930: 271-75). What is at stake here is not merely the fact, but the very meaning, of authorship.

Smalley concludes that the Beloved Disciple's witness lies behind the Gospel though others were responsible for its composition and writing (Smalley 1978: 121). But on such a reconstruction, does the Beloved Disciple meet Barrett's definition of an author: 'the man (or group) who would accept responsibility for the book as we read it in the ancient MSS' (Barrett 1978: 5)? Does it make sense to say that it is the Beloved Disciple 'who has written' or even 'had these things written' if he is only a source? And even if he were the prime or only source, can we really say, with Schrenk, that the Beloved Disciple is 'spiritually responsible' for the contents of the Gospel? Is this not a bit like saying that Paganini was 'responsible' for Rachmaninov's variations and modifications of his theme? Surely the mind and spirit behind 'Rhapsody on a Theme of Paganini' is distinctly Rachmaninov's? Paganini did not author or compose the 'Rhapsody', nor could he have. Historical critics, in their zeal to solve one riddle about authorship, have created a new one: how can a distant source be responsible for a text over which he had no final control? Nineham insists that eye-witness testimony had little impact on the process of Gospel composition (Nineham 1958: 13). The Fourth Gospel, however, is a finely tuned work, dependent on the subtleties of structure, irony, and so forth to achieve its effect. It is difficult to see how the substance of the witness could be preserved if the Beloved Disciple were not also responsible for its form. But if he is responsible for its form and substance, would he then not be the sole author?

Literary critics, as one might expect, take a different approach to the question of the meaning of authorship. Culpepper is more interested in the author as an implication of the text than he is in a historical figure. The 'implied author' is the presence whose values and vision shape the work and response of the reader. As such, the implied author is 'an ideal, literary, created version of the real man; he is the sum of his own choices' (Booth 1961: 74-75). 'The Beloved Disciple may be just another character through whom the author's point of view is communicated, or he may be an idealized representation of the author (hence a dramatic approximation of the implied author)' (Culpepper 1983: 44). In an ironic reversal, the 'author' moves from being the cause of the text to being one of its rhetorical effects.

One of the great services of rhetorical criticism has been to call to our attention the vast array of techniques an author employs to inform, engage and guide the reader. Now one of the principal means of persuading the reader to accept the world of the text is to create a sense of the author's presence, intelligence and moral sensibility. Aristotle, in his *Rhetoric*, recognized that this sense of the personal character or 'ethos' of the speaker itself functions as a means of persuasion. The equivalent of ethos in a narrative is the voice of the implied author.

The ethos of the Fourth Gospel largely depends on the identification of the author with the Beloved Disciple. The Beloved Disciple enjoys, says Brown, the 'authority of a witness' (Brown 1970: 1121). According to Calvin, the author reveals his identity as the Beloved Disciple in 21.24 'so that the greater weight may be attached to an eye-witness who had fully known all that he writes about' (Calvin 1961: 226). 'A witness is someone who has seen and/or heard something and then testifies to others in order to persuade them of its truth' (Ashton 1991: 523). Bearing witness is thus the evangelist's function and peculiar authority. The Beloved Disciple is depicted in each of his appearances as having either privileged access to the meaning of Jesus' ministry and death (e.g., in 13.23-26 he enjoys the intimacy of Jesus' bosom; in 19.25-27 he stands at the foot of the cross; in 20.2-5 he is the first to the empty tomb) or privileged insight into the identity of Jesus (in 20.8 he believes in the risen Jesus; in 21.7 he recognizes the risen Jesus; in 24.21 he bears true testimony to Jesus). Evidently, the Beloved Disciple was hermeneutically gifted: 'He has no misunderstandings' (Culpepper 1983: 121).

Authorship is a hermeneutical as well as historical category insofar as it relates to the ethos of the work, particularly a work of 'I-witness' testimony. In testimony, the questions 'Who?' and 'What?' converge, for if the text is 'I-witness' testimony then the integrity of the 'I' makes all the difference. For the authority of testimony depends not only on the correctness of the reports but on the competence or ethos of the witness. As Martin Warner observes, rhetorical criticism here subverts the historical-critical tendency to focus on the history of the text's composition and the history of the community that composed it. To say that the narrative is an invention is to destroy the ethos of the work and 'to evacuate the rhetoric of its persuasive power' (Warner 1990: 176). To the author(s) of 21.24, if different from the Beloved Disciple, we must say—'The Beloved Disciple we know, but who are you?'

The 'Death of the Author'

It is well-known that the Fourth Gospel uses its characters' misunderstandings as a foil to clarify important points. The rumour concerning the Beloved Disciple, later identified as the author, is one such case in point. It is the climax of a series of gentle contrasts between Peter and the Beloved Disciple, who, according to Augustine, represent two states of the Christian life: active faith (Peter) and eternal contemplation (the Beloved Disciple) (Augustine 1956: 450-1). More recent scholarship correlates the contrast between the two disciples with the historical situation of the Johannine community: Peter stands for a pastoral, John for a prophetic ministry (Barrett 1978: 583; Talbert 1992: 262-63).

According to Bultmann, however, the purpose of 21.15-23 is to show that Peter's ecclesiastical authority has been transferred after his death to the Beloved Disciple, and thus to the Gospel (Bultmann 1971: 717). Bultmann finds it incredible that an author could pass himself off as the Beloved Disciple and at the same time attest to his own death. Here Bultmann displays a surprising lack of sensitivity: one would have expected a former student of Heidegger's to be open to the possibility that it is not his actual death but his being-towards-death, his mortality, that is here acknowledged. For Bultmann, however, the story of the fates of Peter and the Beloved Disciple is just a prop for the claim that the Fourth Gospel enjoys apostolic authority. Similarly, Brown suggests that the saying about Peter's death was merely a means of getting to the real point—the death of the Beloved Disciple. For Brown, the rumour about the Beloved Disciple not dying was false because he had in all probability already died. The episode is included because the community 'was disturbed by the death of their great master since they had expected him not to die' (Brown 1970: 1119). The anecdote about his respective task and fate is intended to reassure the Johannine community that his testimony would survive in the Gospel. Ashton suggests that the Farewell Discourse as well was intended to help the community confront not only the departure of Jesus but that of the Beloved Disciple too (Ashton 1991: 444, 478).

These interpretations make the figure of the Beloved Disciple a 'device' in an ideological struggle. The Johannine community claims apostolic authority for its Gospel even though the apostle (whoever he was) stands at a distance from the finished product. If the Beloved Disciple has died, then it is certainly not his voice we hear in the text. Whose voice, then, is it? This literal deconstruction of the author plays into the hands of the literary deconstructionists who contend that the very idea of an 'author' is an ideological construct.

'The anonymity of the biblical writers chimes in nicely with the "death of the author" approach to literature of certain post-war French writers...For Barthes "writing is the destruction of every voice, of every point of origin"' (Carroll 1990: 74). The anonymity of biblical writings wonderfully facilitates post-structuralist readings. The death of the author liberates the reader from the bondage of having to discover authorial intentions and from having to decipher the text. For Foucault, the idea of the author serves to give a false sense of textual unity and coherence: 'The author is therefore the ideological figure by which one masks the manner in which we fear the proliferation of meaning' (Foucault 1979: 159).

What is at stake in the death of the author, and the death of this author, the Beloved Disciple, in particular, is the integrity and authority of the text. Is there an independent voice or source of knowledge in this text or are all voices merely pretenders, ideological constructs and rhetorical effects? Such a question strikes at the very heart of the nature of discourse that claims to be true testimony.

Authorial Rights

Is the figure of the Beloved Disciple merely a rhetorical or ideological product of an anonymous later redactor, or is it possible that the Beloved Disciple is in some real sense the author? Barrett says that 'the balance of probability is that a man would not so refer to himself' (Barrett 1978: 117). What other explanation is there for this curious epithet? Augustine attributes it to authorial modesty: 'For it was a custom with those who have supplied us with the sacred writings, that when any of them was relating the divine history, and come to something affecting himself, he spoke as if it were about another' (Augustine 1956: 311). Westcott proposes a similar explanation: 'it is quite intelligible that an Apostle...should separate himself as the witness from his immediate position as the writer' (Westcott 1980: lv). It is worth noting that these hypotheses are not incommensurable with what we established earlier with regard to the ethos of the implied author. The Beloved Disciple indeed functions as a rhetorical device, but rhetoric may be enlisted to serve the interests of truth as well as power (Warner 1990: 8).

In 20.2 the Beloved Disciple is referred to as 'the other disciple'. Brown believes that this was perhaps a self-designation whereas 'Beloved Disciple' was the title given him by his disciples to indicate his elevated status. What is intriguing, however, is the restraint with which this figure is depicted. There is no hint that he is superior to Peter, just different. Moreover, it has been widely noticed that, though the Beloved Disciple has inside knowledge, he does not share it: 'He understands but does not bear witness until later' (Culpepper 1983: 44). Of course, the modesty of the laconic 'other disciple' who figures in the narrative is more than compensated for by the profound witness of the loquacious Beloved Disciple in his capacity as writer of the Fourth Gospel.

What we appear to have in the Fourth Gospel is the voice of the 'other disciple'. The hermeneutic question with regard to authorship is simply this: should interpreters seek to recover the voice of the author, the voice of the 'Other'? Robert Morgan and John Barton have recently suggested that 'Texts, like dead men and women, have no rights, no aims, no interests' (Morgan 1988: 7). Writers, they go on to say, have some short-term moral right to be understood as they intended, but 'that right dies with them or with the occasions for which the utterance was intended' (Morgan 1988: 270). Not only has the author died; he has died intestate. Such a condition is especially troubling when the text in question is testimony. Indeed, one of the main points of ch. 21 is to provide (possibly in advance) for the departure of the I-witness. The testament is precisely that which survives its author.

In an era where not only animals and plants (not to mention bacteria) are increasingly accorded certain rights (at least the right to survive), it strikes even the politically incorrect interpreter as a bit odd that Barton and Morgan deny to texts and authors the same courtesy. Do we not owe a debt to the past, an obligation never to forget, say, the Shoah testimony of those who endured the Holocaust, as well as the unspoken testimony of those who did not? In an age where minorities and other marginal groups are being granted a hearing, it remains something of a scandal that the author's voice remains on the margins of biblical scholarship. The Other's testimony to Christ has been displaced by theories about the Gospel's composition that make the Fourth Gospel answer questions about the history of the Johannine community. Is it not time to campaign for the rights of the author—for the author's right to be heard and understood?

To return to the definition of the author: I shall understand by 'author' the person(s) responsible for the final form of the text. The author of the Fourth Gospel, as Other, is an I-witness. Attending to the ethos of his testimony may persuade us that he is an eyewitness as well. I-witness testimony insists that it be taken for what it is: the voice of the Other. Of all literary forms, testimony most vigorously resists an interpreter's reading something into it. Indeed, radical reader-response excludes the very possibility of true testimony, the voice of the 'Other'. As a significant and signifying Other, the author has an initial right (it may be forfeited; one could be a compulsive liar) to have his or her primary communicative intent attended to and respected. As I hope now to show, authors have a right to be considered innocent (truthful) until proven guilty.

Testimony: Trying the Text

'He is bearing witness to these things...'

With regard to the author we asked: are there any rights? Turning to the text, we now ask, are there any wrongs? that is, are false interpretations possible? Jn 21.23 treats one instance of misinterpretation in an interesting manner. It is but one of several instances in the Fourth Gospel in which the logos is fulfilled unexpectedly. In the case of 21.23, however, we are not given the correct interpretation. Rather, we are redirected to Jesus' words. The disciples had failed to give sufficient attention to Jesus' words. Readers of the Fourth Gospel would do well to take this cautionary example to heart. The words matter. Logos is a form of rhetoric too, a means of persuading by means of the apparent proof of the speech itself. Testimony has to do not only with the ethos of the one who bears witness but with the content or logos of the witness too. But why should we trust the witness's testimony? If we must believe in order to understand, are we not caught in a vicious variation of the hermeneutical circle? For if we deem a witness trustworthy, is it not because we trust the testimony; and do we not often trust one's testimony because we trust the one giving it?

Hermeneutics of Suspicion

In light of the above dilemma, modern critics have opted out of the hermeneutical circle all together. A hermeneutics of suspicion casts its pall over the history of much modern biblical criticism. Josipovici, commenting on Jn 21.24, defines the trial of testimony: 'Unfortunately such assertions remain nothing but words, and the rule of the game seems to be that the more an author asserts the truth of what he is saying the less likely we are to believe him' (Josipovici 1988: 213).

Multiplying the number of witnesses, as the Fourth Gospel does, 'will only reinforce our sense of the author behind the scenes, manipulating things' (Josipovici 1988: 216).

A distrust of appearances is the reflex of biblical critics who profess the new morality of historical knowledge. According to D.E. Nineham, whereas ancient historians regarded testimony as 'the bed-rock truth below which he cannot dig', their modern counterparts question testimony: 'His very integrity and autonomy as an historian prevent his taking his "sources" at face value' (Nineham 1960: 258). Nineham approves of Collingwood's reluctance to accept eyewitness testimony, for doing so implies that the historian is 'allowing someone else to do for him what, if he is a scientific thinker, he can only do for himself' (Nineham 1960: 258). Justification by one's own (academic) works is apparently the only way to achieve epistemological virtue. For Locke, faith is the assent to propositions made on the basis not of sufficient reason but upon the credit of the proposer—which is as much to say, upon no basis at all. Or as W.K. Clifford put it in his celebrated essay, 'The Ethics of Belief': 'it is wrong always, everywhere, and for anyone, to believe anything upon insufficient evidence' (Clifford 1886: 346).

The hermeneutics of suspicion is taken to the limit in deconstruction, which denies the very possibility of knowledge as justified true belief. For deconstruction, justification is always rationalization. Judgment is never impartial or even-handed; we might as well speak of the amorality of literary knowledge. For deconstruction, the author's voice is both undecidable and indecipherable. Texts have no determinate meaning, and texts with no determinate meaning can neither witness, report nor confess. Honest readers must resist the seduction of the text: like Venus fly-traps, texts lure the unsuspecting readers with the promise of representation and the scent of reality, only to close their jaws, entrapping them in an unending, self-referring labyrinth of language and textuality. Shed of its naiveté, interpretation becomes 'a *hostile* act in which interpreter victimises the text' (Taylor 1982: 65). Because there is no text-in-itself that subsists apart from interpretation, the text only exists as victim. To be a text is to submit to interpretative violence. After the indignities of being prodded and examined by historical critics, the deconstructed text now suffers the ultimate humiliation—interpretative rape.

Hermeneutics of Belief

'Beyond the wastelands of critical thought, we wish to be challenged anew' (Ricoeur 1974: 28). Is there any way to recover the voice of the Other, and once it has been recovered, can we again heed its call and believe?

Authorship has largely been treated by scholars of the left and right as an apologetical or historical rather than a hermeneutical or theological problem. Most scholars today consider the evidence with regard to the Fourth Gospel to be inconclusive. Does this legitimate our withholding belief? For Brevard Childs, historical-critical theories about origin and purpose try to give to the text 'an historical concreteness which it simply does not have' (Childs 1984: 124). Childs says that the witness of the Beloved Disciple (21.24) is not historically verified but is rather taken up into the living voice of the believing community. 'The crucial methodological issue at stake is doing justice to the theological function of the book's witness to authorship without converting the question immediately into one of historicity' (Childs 1984: 130). Thanks to the ending (21.24), the text is capable of addressing future generations of readers.

Childs is right, I think, to remind us that the problems of meaning cannot be reduced to the domain of historical reference. But it is also possible that Childs exaggerates the canonical function. Where the historical critics immediately convert the question of meaning into questions concerning the original situation, Childs converts the question into one that addresses the Church's future situation. Texts have an interest in being recognized for what they are, rather than for what they were or might become. Childs moves to canon too fast. Before proceeding to canonical function, one must take the necessary detour of analyzing the various literary genres, in this case, testimony.

A number of recent approaches to the Fourth Gospel agree with Childs that historical-critical readings which look for some data behind the testimonies are misguided. 'It is inappropriate to focus on anything other than the final form of the text of John' (Talbert 1992: 63-64). But neither is it appropriate to assign to the Fourth Gospel the same canonical function as texts of very different genres may perform. No, the canonical role of the Fourth Gospel must be a function of the kind of thing, the kind of logos, it is. What is the Fourth Gospel? It is I-witness testimony that claims to be eyewitness testimony as well: 'The witness...makes a report of the event...This first trait anchors all the other meanings in a quasi-empirical sphere. It consequently transfers things seen to the level of things said' (Ricoeur 1980: 123). Testimony is neither simply rhetorical nor simply rational, but both together; it is 'caught in the network of proof and persuasion' (Ricoeur 1980: 127). Testimony is a literary form that aims to persuade rationally through reliable reportage (both investigative and interpretative) and through the quality of the character of the witness.

Because literary form and content are inseparable, the attempt to verify the witness by going beyond or behind it is doomed to failure. This is especially the case with testimony, a genre which attempts to convey the fact and meaning of singular events of absolute significance. Testimony is a speech act in which the witness's very act of stating *p* is offered as evidence 'that *p*', it being assumed that the witness has the relevant competence or credentials to state truly 'that *p*' (Coady 1992: ch. 2). With many if not most cases in the Fourth Gospel, the testimony is the only access we have to the events in question. Fiorenza draws the obvious implication: 'The attempt to get behind these testimonies does not enable us to say more but to say less than they do' (Fiorenza 1986: 41).

For too long now, a picture of responsible scholarship has held us captive. The hermeneutics of suspicion is not misguided, only misplaced. Distrust should never be the first hermeneutical reflex, especially not with testimony. It is time to unmask the historical critic's vaunted autonomy for what it is: a species of ethical individualism and intellectual pride. Much of the suspicion and skepticism surrounding the interpretation of Jn 21.20-24 is unwarranted. The epistemological foundationalism grounding the historical-critical enterprise has itself been severely shaken of late. In a recent philosophical monograph, C.A.J. Coady argues 'that our trust in the word of others is fundamental to the very idea of serious cognitive activity' (Coady 1992: vii). Trusting the word of others in a necessary and inescapable dimension of human intellectual activity: what passes for autonomous knowledge is actually underpinned by a covert reliance on what others tell us.

For Nineham and Clifford, on the other hand, eyewitness testimony is only reliable if it is *mine*. Testimony is trustworthy only if I have confirmed the account, or at least the character of the witness. Anything less is an abdication of cognitive autonomy. This means, however, that the autonomous scholar will not believe anything that he or she does not observe first-hand. If this is the sole criterion for reliable knowledge, then historical-critics are skating on thin ice in a very small pond indeed. Coady offers a caustic verdict: the tendency to privilege perception over testimony is really 'a hankering after a primacy for my perception' (Coady 1992: 148). But it should be evident that, by the very nature of the case, modern critics are at a distinct disadvantage when it comes to the subject matter of the Fourth Gospel.

Testimony is as basic a means of knowledge as are perception and memory. Just as we do not infer that an object is blue from our perception of it, so we believe someone's testimony that the object is blue. We do not have to infer it. A person's stating it is, under normal circumstances, reason enough. We have little choice but to believe what we are told unless there is good reason for doubting it. The witness is thus considered epistemically innocent until proven guilty. This principle is, I believe, of the utmost importance for the interpretation of the Fourth Gospel. Testimony is a legitimate mechanism for producing beliefs. There need be no contradiction between the rhetoric and the rationality of the Fourth Gospel, nor is there need to make some further inference about the reliability (or identity?) of the Beloved Disciple before taking his word for it. To repeat: testimony is as reliable a means of knowing as perception and memory. Indeed, testimony makes the past and present perceptions of others available to those who could or did not perceive for themselves.

None of this, of course, means that the witness of the Fourth Gospel is true. As the writers of the Scriptures well knew, false testimony unfortunately abounds. But which attitude—suspicion or belief—is hermeneutically more fruitful when it comes to interpreting testimony? The skeptic, at best, enjoys greater safety from error, but runs the risk of ignoring a narrative framework with greater explanatory power than the alternatives and of losing a number of beliefs that may be true. The believer runs the risk of acquiring false beliefs, but is open to receiving a greater number of true beliefs and an interpretative framework for understanding the life and fate of Jesus. The 'believer' is not necessarily a fideist, however: 'We may have "no reason to doubt" another's communication even where there is no question of our being gullible; we may simply recognize that the standard warning signs of deceit, confusion, or mistake are not present' (Coady

1992: 47). With the notion of the reader as a believer we now move from the morality of knowledge to the ethics of interpretation.

Reader-Response and Reader-Responsibility: The Trial of Reading

'His testimony is true'

To this point we have assessed the Beloved Disciple's role as author and witness. But the Beloved Disciple plays yet another role in the Fourth Gospel: that of model disciple. By the end of the Fourth Gospel, the disciple who has witnessed the significance of Jesus' life and fate begins to give testimony. Indeed, the whole point in contrasting the fates of the Beloved Disciple and Peter is to show that the ministry of the Beloved Disciple will take the form of a 'martyrdom of life' (Westcott 1980: 374) rather than death. The Beloved Disciple follows Jesus by 'remaining', remaining that is, to give constant witness.

Accordingly, the Beloved Disciple prefigures the role of the ideal reader, the role of one who receives testimony and believes it. The Beloved Disciple shows how the reader should be affected by the narrative testimony of the Fourth Gospel. As ideal reader, the Beloved Disciple now stands under Aristotle's third rhetorical sign, that of pathos. Pathos has to do with the way in which readers respond to or appropriate discourse. Interpretations that fall short of this moment of appropriation remain incomplete, short-circuited. If discourse is someone's saying something to someone, then discourse is unfulfilled until the addressee receives the message. The Beloved Disciple is a model reader who not only follows testimony in the sense of understanding it, but follows out its implications to the point where his or her own life becomes a life of testimony. The aim of the author is to make the reader a disciple. This is perhaps the deepest irony of the Fourth Gospel: ostensibly an account of Jesus' trial, the narrative ends up trying the reader.

Responsibility to the Other

What obligation, if any, does the reader have vis-à-vis the text? Barton and Morgan imply that, just as authors have no rights, so readers have no universal responsibilities. What a reader does with a text is a function of the reader's aims and interests (Morgan 1988: 270). As a description of what readers actually do with texts, it is hard to fault this statement. But is there nothing else to be said? Is every reader lord of his or her own hermeneutic fiefdom? Or, following

Lévinas rather than Clifford, does the individual's uniqueness lie not in autonomy but rather in responsibility to the Other (Levinas 1989: 202)?

Ricoeur has argued repeatedly that humans are not self-constituting but rather progressively appropriate a self through interpreting texts that mediate traditions, cultures and worlds (Vanhoozer 1990: 249-66). The self is summoned to responsibility by the Other, particularly by the suffering Other. By 'suffering', Ricoeur means 'the reduction, even the destruction, of the capacity for acting, of being-able-to-act, experienced as a violation of self-integrity' (Ricoeur 1990: 190). On the basis of this definition, we can speak of the text suffering too, and of the witness as a suffering servant. The text 'suffers' in the sense that it is unable to take the initiative in interpretation; that privilege belongs to the reader. The witness is a suffering servant in the sense that he or she labours to repay an obligation to the past and to Others not to forget. The witness is under obligation to the Other to testify. One must read Shostakovich's *Testimony*, not to mention those of Solzhenitsyn, bearing this in mind. The witness becomes a martyr because his or her testimony is a dangerous memory. Shostakovich's testimony was a condemnation of Soviet society that was smuggled out of the country and published only after his death. But the memories embodied in the Fourth Gospel are no less dangers to the powers of this world—especially to the world of the reader.

If the text is indeed at the mercy of the reader, what should the reader do? The answer is *to let it be*—not in the sense of leaving it alone but in the sense of letting it fulfil its aim as a work of written discourse. If the initiative belongs to the reader, the reader should lend an ear and receive this discourse of the Other with courtesy and respect. What the ethical reader gives to the text is, in the first place, attention. The text, thus restored to life, is able to give something back in turn. Indeed, in testimony the text gives something to the reader that the reader is capable only of receiving, not achieving: the narrative confession of the ministry and fate of Jesus Christ. 'In true sympathy, the self, whose power of acting is at the start greater than that of its other, finds itself affected by all that the suffering other offers to it in return' (Ricoeur 1990: 191).

Anselmian Hermeneutics

What does it mean to give respect and attention to a text? What is the appropriate way for the reader to approach testimony? The ideal reader knows how to respond to the rhetorical strategies of the text. 'The implied reader of the Fourth Gospel is encouraged by its rhetoric to accept its view of Jesus' significance and to lead a life characterized by a love like Jesus' (Davies 1992: 367). Readers can only come to a correct understanding 'by accepting the role of the narratees, by understanding Jesus from the perspective of belief' (p. 368).

For the ideal reader, therefore, the moment of understanding is also the moment of belief. We here encounter Anselm's famous *credo ut intelligam*: I believe in order to understand. Barth read Anselm as saying that the truly scientific or critical approach to an object lets the object dictate the manner in which it is known or appropriated. Such an approach might be called, when applied to literary objects, 'Anselmian hermeneutics'. Hans Frei has shown how this hermeneutics works when applied to the Synoptic Gospels. As realistic narratives, they literally mean what they say (cf. 21.23). There is no way to get at their subject matter without going through the story. To read those narratives correctly, says Frei, is to see that they identify Jesus as the one who now lives. Their rhetoric escapes the level of textuality and makes an extratextual reference, namely, to the risen Lord. Frei observes, 'To know who he is in connection with what took place is to know that he is' (Frei 1974: 145).

Something similarly Anselmian happens when we interpret the Fourth Gospel as testimony. To understand this text—testimony-narration to the life and fate of Jesus—is to receive and believe it. To understand this testimony is to believe that it is true. The hermeneutics of I-witness testimony is twice Anselmian: first, it recognizes that testimony can only be received on its own terms. Testimony may not be reduced to metaphysical symbols of the human condition nor to moral examples. Testimony is an irreducible, unsubstitutable form of knowledge. Second, the testimony of the Fourth Gospel is such that it is not understood if it is not believed. If you are not reading with belief, then you must not be reading with understanding. As with Anselm's God, which must exist if one correctly thinks it (as the being than which nothing greater can be conceived), so with the Beloved Disciple's testimony: if one is reading it properly one will see that it is trustworthy and true. 'Those who cannot play this role, even for the duration of their reading, are unlikely to continue the task the text sets them' (Davies 1992: 373).

Discipl(in)ing the Reader

Ideal readers, however, will continue the task the text sets them. This may well involve a certain degree of self-discipline. For though the text calls the reader to respond, some responses are less helpful than others. Some readers may wish to play with texts in order to experience an auto-erotic pleasure, but such self-centred indulgences are unlikely to advance the cause of textual understanding. Wilfully to go one's own way as a reader is to abdicate the responsibility to attend to and understand the Other.

Testimony calls us, as it did the one who wrote it, to bear witness. Testimony calls us to trust the voice of the Other, to follow its call. This is what we find the Beloved Disciple doing at the conclusion of the Fourth Gospel. Jesus' last words, after his cryptic remarks about the Beloved Disciple's remaining, are 'Follow me'. But the Beloved Disciple was already following (21.20). Moreover, he had been following Jesus' story from the moment he was introduced. And 21.24, which identifies the Beloved Disciple with the author of the Fourth Gospel, shows what form his following now takes. He has taken Jesus' story up; he is bearing it by bearing witness to it. As the Father sends the Son, so the Son sends his disciples. Why? To bear witness.

For the reader to respond as does the Beloved Disciple, he or she must accept the truth of his testimony. Accepting the truth of his testimony means becoming a witness oneself. Such is the 'martyrdom of life'. 'The Gospel's rhetoric encourages fidelity but supposes that only the Paraclete can create it' (Davies 1992: 367). Jesus prayed not only for those who have seen and bear witness but for those who believe in him through their word (Jn 17.20). Thanks to the ministry of the Paraclete, the reader is assured of being able to respond—of being able to be responsible—to the call of the text.

As we have seen, it is part of the logic of testimony that the witness himself or herself becomes a premise for the truth of the testimony. The I-witness testimony of the Beloved Disciple is prima facie evidence for his claim concerning God's presence in Christ. If the Beloved Disciple is indeed the model reader, can the good reader today likewise become a witness? Jesus' words to Peter could well be redirected to historical and literary critics who become preoccupied with the identity of the witness to the point of losing its content. They too must desist from wild speculation about the fate of the Beloved Disciple and get on with attending to the words and following the Word:

For indeed that is John's object in creating this character in the first place... It is his hope that each reader will be so drawn by the Gospel to believe in Jesus and to follow him, that he will discover himself in the true discipleship of the Beloved Disciple (Lindars 1972: 640).

A witness's stating 'that *p*' is itself a reason for believing it. How much more so a witness's living 'that *p*', dying 'that *p*', testifying in every possible way, 'that you may believe that Jesus is the Christ' (20.30).

BIBLIOGRAPHY

Ashton, J.
1991   *Understanding the Fourth* Gospel (Oxford: Clarendon).
Augustine
1956   'Homilies on the Gospel of John', in P. Schaff (ed.), *Nicene and Post-Nicene Fathers of the Christian Church*, VII (Grand Rapids: Eerdmans): 7-452.
Barrett, C.K.
1978   *The Gospel according to St John* (London: SPCK, 2nd edn).
Barthes, R.
1986   'The Death of the Author', in *The Rustle of Language* (New York: Hill & Wang): 50-54.
Booth, W.C.
1961   *The Rhetoric of Fiction* (Chicago: University Press).
Brown, R.E.
1970   *The Gospel according to John XIII–XXI* (AB, 29; New York: Doubleday).
Bultmann, R.
1971   *The Gospel of John: A Commentary* (trans. G.R. Beasley-Murray; Oxford: Basil Blackwell).
Calvin, J.
1961   *Calvin's Commentaries: The Gospel according to St John 11–21* (trans. T.H.L. Parker; Edinburgh: Oliver & Boyd).
Carroll, R.P.
1990   'Authorship', in R.J. Coggins and J.L. Houlden (eds.), *A Dictionary of Biblical Interpretation* (London: SCM Press): 72-74.
Chapman, J.
1930   ' "We Know That his Testimony is True"', *JTS* 31: 379-87.
Childs, B.S.
1984   *The New Testament as Canon: An Introduction* (London: SCM Press).
Clifford, W.K.
1886   'The Ethics of Belief', in *Lectures and Essays* (London: Macmillan): 339-63.
Coady, C.A.J.
1992   *Testimony: A Philosophical Study* (Oxford: Clarendon).

Culpepper, R.A.
1983 *Anatomy of the Fourth Gospel: A Study in Literary Design* (Philadelphia: Fortress Press).

Davies, M.
1992 *Rhetoric and Reference in the Fourth Gospel* (JSNTSup, 69; Sheffield: JSOT Press).

Derrida, J.
1978 *Writing and Difference* (trans. A. Bass; Chicago: Chicago University Press).

Dodd, C.H.
1953 'Note on John 21, 24', *JTS* 4: 212-13.

Fiorenza, F.S.
1986 *Foundational Theology: Jesus and the Church* (New York: Crossroad).

Foucault, M.
1979 'What is an Author', in J.V. Harari (ed.), *Textual Strategies: Perspectives in Post-Structuralist Criticism* (Ithaca, NY: Cornell University Press): 141-60.

Frei, H.
1974 *The Identity of Jesus Christ: The Hermeneutical Bases of Dogmatic Theology* (Philadelphia: Fortress Press).

Hitchcock, F.R.M.
1930 'The Use of *graphein*', *JTS* 31: 271-75.

Jonge, M. de
1979 'The Beloved Disciple and the Date of the Gospel of John', in E. Best and R. McL. Wilson (eds.), *Text and Interpretation: Studies in the New Testament Presented to Matthew Black* (Cambridge: Cambridge University Press): 99-114.

Josipovici, G.
1988 *The Book of God: A Response to the Bible* (New Haven: Yale University Press).

Lévinas, E.
1989 *The Lévinas Reader* (ed. S. Hand; Oxford: Basil Blackwell).

Lindars, B.
1972 *The Gospel of John* (AB; London: Oliphants).

Minear, P.S.
1983 'The Original Functions of John 21', *JBL* 102/1: 85-98.

Morgan, R. and J. Barton
1988 *Biblical Interpretation* (The Oxford Bible Series; Oxford: Oxford University Press).

Moore, S.D.
1989 *Literary Criticism and the Gospels: The Theoretical Challenge* (New Haven: Yale University Press).

Nineham, D.E.
1958 'Eye-Witness Testimony and the Gospel Tradition. I', *JTS* 9: 13-25.
1960 'Eye-Witness Testimony and the Gospel Tradition. III', *JTS* 11: 253-64.

Ricoeur, P.

1974   *The Conflict of Interpretations* (Evanston, IL: Northwestern University Press).

1980   'The Hermeneutics of Testimony', in L. Mudge (ed.), *Essays on Biblical Interpretation* (Philadelphia: Fortress Press): 119-54.

1990   *Oneself as Another* (trans. K. Blamey; Chicago: Chicago University Press).

Schrenk, G.

1964   'γράφω', *TDNT*, I, 742-46.

Shostakovich, D.

1981   *Testimony: The Memoirs of Dimitri Shostakovich* (London: Faber & Faber).

Sloyan, G.S.

1991   *What are they Saying about John?* (New York: Paulist Press).

Smalley, S.

1978   John—Evangelist and Interpreter (Exeter: Paternoster Press).

Smith, D.M.

1989   'Johannine Studies', in E.J. Epp and G.W. McRae (eds.), *The New Testament and its Modern Interpreters* (Atlanta: Scholars Press): 271-96.

Talbert, C.

1992   *Reading John: A Literary and Theological Commentary on the Fourth Gospel and the Johannine Epistles* (London: SPCK).

Taylor, M.C.

1982   'Text as Victim', in T.J.J. Altizer *et al.* (eds.), *Deconstruction and Theology* (New York: Crossroad): 58-78.

Vanhoozer, K.J.

1990   *Biblical Narrative in the Philosophy of Paul Ricoeur: A Study in Hermeneutics and Theology* (Cambridge: Cambridge University Press).

Warner, M.

1990   'The Fourth Gospel's Art of Rational Persuasion', in M. Warner (ed.), *The Bible as Rhetoric: Studies in Biblical Persuasion and Credibility* (Warwick Studies in Philosophy and Literature; London: Routledge & Kegan Paul): 153-77.

Westcott, B.F.

1980   *The Gospel according to St John* (Grand Rapids: Baker).

JUDGES 1.1–2:5: THE CONQUEST UNDER THE
LEADERSHIP OF THE HOUSE OF JUDAH

M. Weinfeld

The introductory paragraph to Judg. 1.1-4 excluding the initial clause
'After the death of Joshua', which belongs to a later author and which
already presupposes the existence of the book of Joshua according to
the received division of the books[1] (cf. 'After the death of Moses' at
the beginning of the book of Joshua), serves as a heading for the conquest enterprise at the front of which the tribe of Judah marched. We
learn in these verses that an ancient oracle of God commissioned this
tribe with the task of initiating the war against the Canaanites: 'The
Israelites inquired of YHWH, saying: "Who will go up for us first
against the Canaanites to fight them?" YHWH said: "Judah shall go up"'
(vv. 1-2). This contradicts the traditions in the book of Joshua and
those in the books of Numbers (27.15-23) and Deuteronomy (chs. 1–
3; 31.1-8). According to these traditions, Joshua initiated the war of
conquest at God's command. Moreover, similar to what is said about

---

1. In the original edition of the Deuteronomistic history, the period of the conquest ends with Joshua's farewell speech (Josh. 23), whereas the period of the
Judges begins with the discourse in Judges 2.11–3.4. The later writers, however,
who divided the material into books (Joshua and Judges) found a place to insert
between Josh. 23 and Judg. 2.11 the ancient tradition known to them regarding
Joshua and the period of the judges. Josh. 24.1-28 and Judg. 1.1–2.5 are appendices
of sorts that were added after the Deuteronomistic historiography had already been
formed and in a period when the material was separated into books as we presently
find them. Actually, these appendices contain glaring contradictions to the viewpoint
of the Deuteronomistic editor: According to Josh. 24 Israel served foreign gods in
the days of Joshua (v. 23). This contradicts the Deuteronomistic view (Judg. 2.7).
Moreover, Judg. 1 presupposes Canaanite enclaves within the territory of the
apportioned land of Israel. This contradicts the Deuteronomistic viewpoint about a
total conquest in the days of Joshua.

inquiring of YHWH before Judah goes forth to war,[2] the Priestly tradition informs us in Num. 27.15-23 that after Joshua is appointed leader of the community, he will need to inquire of God through the decision of the Urim before God by means of Eleazar the priest, his 'going out' and 'coming in', that is, respecting the wars he will fight (cf. Josh. 14.11: 'As my strength was then, so it is now, to undertake battle and *to go out and come in*').[3] According to this tradition, whose basis is in northern Israel (see below), the conquest of the land began by a leader belonging to the house of Joseph who inquired of God through a priest who was tied to Shiloh in the hill country of Ephraim. In contrast to this, in Judges 1 the tribe of Judah begins the conquest, not a leader from the tribe of Ephraim.

A similar inclination to show the prominence of the tribe of Judah over the other tribes is found in Judg. 20.18 in connection with the war against the Benjaminites: 'They inquired of God... "Who will go up for us first in battle against the Benjaminites". YHWH said: "Judah first"'. This language is identical to that in Judg. 1.1. Scholars have already dealt with the fact[4] that Judg. 20.18 reflects the anti-Saul attitude of its Judaean writer who wanted to thrust his tribe into prominence in the war against the Benjaminites at Gibeah, the city of Saul. It seems, furthermore, that the passage in Judges 1 has been written with the desire to glorify the tribe of Judah against a background of

2. Inquiring of God before going forth to establish new settlements is found in the context of the settlement of the tribe of Dan (Judg. 1.8). This is a basic phenomenon found in the Greek colonization. See my article: Weinfeld 1988.

3. Y. Kaufmann in his commentary (Kaufmann 1962) to Judg. 1.1 claims that 'we do not find in the time of Joshua or in the days of a judge that God was inquired of through a priest about going forth to war', He adds: 'despite Num. 27.21'. It seems to me, rather, than Num. 27.21 is an exemplary case for this matter. In ancient periods the kings and leaders inquired of YHWH before going out to war (see 1 Sam. 14.18, 36-38; 23.2-12; 2 Sam. 2.1; etc.). Num. 27.21 thus can constitute an ancient testimony for the matter of inquiring of YHWH by a leader. If we do not find this practice in the book of Joshua in regard to Joshua, this is apparently because it has been omitted by the Deuteronomistic editor, who had no need for the Urim and Thummim and inquiring of God by technical means. See what I have written in my book, *Deuteronomy* (Weinfeld 1972), pp. 233-36. For the change that occurred in the tradition of the book of Deuteronomy concerning the appointment of Joshua (in comparison to the Priestly tradition in Num. 27.15-23), see my book *From Joshua to Josiah* (Weinfeld 1992: 198-99).

4. See in particular Güdemann (1869: 357-68) and recently the entry '*Šōpᵉṭîm*' in Zakowitz and Loewenstamm (1976: 594).

disgrace that the other tribes suffer, especially the tribe of Benjamin (the tribe of Saul), which did not succeed in driving out the foreign inhabitants of Jerusalem which was conquered for Benjamin by the Judahites (see below).

According to the description in Judges 1, Judah went up together with Simeon his brother,[5] whose inheritance was integrated into the inheritance of Judah (cf. Josh. 19.1), against the Canaanites for battle, and smote them: 'And YHWH delivered the Canaanites and Perizzites into their power' (Judg. 1.4). The 'Canaanites and Perizzites' indicate in the ancient biblical sources the early inhabitants of the land (see Gen. 13.7; 34.30; and the LXX of Josh. 16.10). There is a tendency to generalize by means of this expression and say that Judah in fact smote all the inhabitants of the land of Canaan (cf. Gen. 34.30). The place of the battle, Bezek, perhaps reflects the Judaean editor's tendentiousness in locating the struggle in the same place from which Saul went out to fight his first war against the Ammonites (1 Sam. 11.8). Against Bezek as the starting point for the first war of Saul, the Benjaminite, king of Israel, the editor of our chapter sets Bezek as the starting point for the wars of Judah against the Canaanites when the tribe began to undertake settlement. It seems to me that all the attempts to determine the site of Bezek are pursuits after wind. The writer has used here a well known geographical fact in order to advance his tendentious goal which is an attack on Benjamin and the praise of Judah. One cannot identify Bezek here with Khirbet Ibziq which is by Beth-Shean and hypothesize that Judah went up into the passes of the hill country of Ephraim, because Judg. 1.1–2.5 is based on a tradition of the Israelite tribes' ascending from across the Jordan around the area of Gilgal (2.1). In Judges 1 we are dealing with the use of literary motifs, which is proved further by the anecdote that follows about the seventy kings whose thumbs and big toes were cut off and who gather crumbs under Adoni-Bezek's table (in vv. 6-7). This little story serves the author in order to show that Adoni-Bezek, king of Jerusalem (see below), was punished measure for measure with the same cruelty he dealt out to the kings in subjugation to him. One wonders if there is perhaps in this story some connection to what is said about the Ammonite king Nahash before Saul went to war with him. This king was about to put out the right eye of all the peoples of Jabesh-Gilead

---

5.   The cooperation between Judah and Simeon appears also in v. 17, and there is no justification in seeing this as a late motif, in contrast to Rösel (1982: 19).

(1 Sam. 11.2),[6] for breach of treaty.[7] As a consequence Saul went forth to war with him. Adoni-Bezek acted in a similar way toward his vassal kings.[8] But while no act to avenge the cruelty of Nahash the Ammonite is reported, the author in Judges 1 was interested in emphasizing the act of recompense that the Judahites meted out to him.

According to all indications, Adoni-Bezek is a king of Jerusalem, and is to be identified with Adoni-Zedek, king of Jerusalem (Josh. 10.1-5).[9] It appears that the story about the war with Adoni-Bezek in Judges 1 and his being brought to Jerusalem depends on an ancient tradition of a battle that the Israelite tribes fought with a king of Jerusalem at the time of the conquest, a war that also stands behind the story in Joshua 10.[10] But the two stories contrast in this way. The tradition in Joshua 10 is anchored in the cycle of stories that were creations of the tribe of Benjamin (Saul's tribe) and whose scenes of battle are Gilgal, Jericho, Ai and Gibeon—all in the inheritance of Benjamin. Thus Jerusalem was found outside the area of war and attempts were not made to capture it.[11] The editor of Judges 1, in contrast, transferred the scene of battle to Jerusalem and even told of its capture.[12]

Actually there is no hint of a capture of Jerusalem before the days

6. According to the reading of the Qumran scroll, Nahash actually put out the right eye of each of them. See the text and the analysis in Cross (1983: 148-58).

7. In light of the fact that the version from Qumran says that Nahash gouged out the eyes of the Gadites and Reubenites before deliberations with him, it is reasonable to posit that we have here a punishment for breaking a pact (see Cross 1983: 157, and n. 23 there). On piercing out the eyes of Zedekiah in connection with breaking his treaty with Nebuchadnezzar (2 Kgs 25.7), see Weinfeld and Meridor 1984: I, 223-29.

8. Regarding cutting off hands and feet as a punishment for breach of covenant, see my article in the foregoing note. See also the Greek traditions on this matter in Gaster 1969: II, 416-17.

9. See Auld 1975: 268-69.

10. The description of this war seems to be a faithful representation of a real historical event in light of the condition of the Jerusalem kingdom just prior to the conquest. See Kallai and Tadmor 1969–70: 138-47.

11. In the battles after the war at Aijalon presented by the Deuteronomistic editor, the cities Makkedah, Libnah, Eglon, Hebron and Debir were captured. Jerusalem was not captured. It is to be noted that even the Deuteronomistic editor, who passed these stories on to us, did not add Jerusalem to the list.

12. The idea that the Jebusites arrived at Jerusalem after the Canaanite city was destroyed by Judah (see Aharoni 1979: 214) has no support and is pure conjecture.

of David. This notice about such a capture in Judges 1, whose reliability is doubtful, has the goal of attributing to the tribe of Judah not
only the conquest of the land, but also the capture of the first capital
of the Israelite kingdom. As we will see later on, the editor knew that
the Jebusites lived in Jerusalem at that time, but he blames the
Benjaminites for that (v. 21). Judah is therefore credited with the
conquest of Jerusalem, while Benjamin is faulted for failing to expel
the Jebusites. This stands in explicit contradiction to Josh. 15.63 where
the *Judahites* were the ones who were not able to drive out the
Jebusites of Jerusalem.

From a perspective of historical trustworthiness, there is no difference between the events of conquest enumerated in the pre-
Deuteronomistic portion of the book of Joshua (see below) and the
events enumerated in Judges 1. The two sources use popular folk-
loristic traditions and historical lists available to them in order to exalt
their respective 'house' in whose name they speak. The narrator in
Joshua 2–10 is interested in crediting the house of Joseph with the
conquest, while the author of Judges 1 wants to bestow the title on
Judah. The editor of the traditions in the (pre-Deuteronomistic) book
of Joshua praises the parts played by *Joseph* and *Benjamin* in the conquest: Joshua, from the posterity of Ephraim, is the actor in the area
of Benjamin, from Gilgal to Gibeon (Josh. 2–9), and in the Aijalon
area he is the one who subjugates the five Amorite kings (10.1-15).
Thus he became indeed the conqueror of Canaan. In contrast the author
of Judges 1 praises the part of Judah in the conquest of Jerusalem and
the entire southern district (Hebron and Debir, Arad and Hormah;
Gaza, Ashkelon and Ekron). By this he turns Judah into the one who
took possession of the 'Canaanites and Perizzites' on behalf of all the
Israelites. Therefore, the chapter begins with inquiring of YHWH
regarding going up to battle against the Canaanites and finishes by
marking off the southern boundary of the conquered land ('the
territory...from the Scorpion Descent', v. 36; cf. Josh. 15.3 where
this appears as the southern boundary of Judah's inheritance; see also
Num. 34.4). To be sure, the chapter leaves room for the activity of
the house of Joseph in seizing Bethel (Judg. 1.22-26). But apart from
this achievement, which is actually accomplished by deceit and not by
direct military confrontation like that which the Judahites used in
taking Jerusalem, the chapter does not ascribe anything to the merit of
the house of Joseph but speaks disparagingly of him and the tribes

associated with him, who did not drive out the Canaanites and the inhabitants of their various cities and the cities' dependencies (vv. 27-35).

The Conquest of Hebron and Debir (vv. 9-15)

After the conquest of Jerusalem the editor of Judges 1 describes Judah's success in war in the south: the Judahites fought there against the Canaanites dwelling in 'the mountain country, in the Negev, and the lowland' (v. 9), an all-inclusive expression which we find also in the context of the conquests of Joshua in Josh. 10.40 (cf. Deut. 1.7: in the mountain country, the lowland and the Negev). In the list of Judah's conquests Hebron and Debir are mentioned: Judah came to Hebron and smote the three kings of the Anakim there: Sheshai, Ahiman and Talmai (Judg. 1.10).

This notice stands in contradiction to what is reported in Josh. 14.6-15 and 15.13-17 where Caleb is the one who conquered Hebron and expelled the Anakim from there. It also contradicts what follows in Judges 1 itself (see below). There is no doubt that the tradition about Caleb's conquest is ancient and more reliable, because the area of Hebron belonged to Caleb, a matter reflected also in the tradition of Numbers 13–14. Indeed, only when the tribe of Judah became established in the south were the inheritances of Caleb and the Kenizzites swallowed up in the area of the tribe of Judah (as was the case with Simeon). At the end of the description of Judah's conquests in Judges 1 we actually find a mention, as already hinted, of the ancient tradition that Caleb expelled the 'three Anakites' (v. 20). It is difficult to decide if the editor of the chapter himself had reason to introduce this correction or if this actually is a corrective addition from a later writer. At any rate it is clear that, at the beginning of his words about the conquest of the south, the writer was interested in showing that the Anakim were driven out by 'Judah'; he used the ancient tradition that appears in Josh. 15.13-17, but changed the subject: *Caleb* did not 'go up' or 'go',[13] as appears in Josh. 15.15; rather, Judah did. In regard to Debir the author leaves the episode as it is found in Josh. 15.15-17.

In the Deuteronomistic description of the national conquest under

---

13. In Josh. 15.15 we find 'he went up' (*wayya'al*), whereas in Judg. 1.11 we find 'he went' (*wayyēlek*). The LXX text A has 'they went' (*wayyel^ekû'*); text B has 'they went up' (*wayya'^alû*).

the leadership of Joshua, the conquest of Hebron and Debir, as is known, is attributed to Joshua in a campaign with all of Israel (Josh. 10.29-37). With regard to Hebron we find then three traditions which reflect three different periods. The most ancient and reliable is that which attributes the conquest of Hebron to Caleb (Josh. 14.6-15; 15.14). A later tradition is that in Judges 1 which attributes the conquest of the city to the Judahites (v. 10) with a description of giving the city to Caleb (v. 20). The latest tradition is the Deuteronomist's, who relates the conquest of Hebron to Joshua in his campaign with all the Israelites (Josh. 10.36-37).

Arad and Hormah (vv. 16-17)

After the traditions of settling Hebron and Debir in Judges 1, the text presents traditions about settling the area of Arad and Hormah, south of the mountain country of Hebron. Just as the traditions about settling Hebron and Debir are tied originally to autochthonous clans—that is, the Calebites and Kenizzites—so here the tradition of settling in Arad and Hormah is connected originally to the Kenites and Jerahmeelites who lived in the south.[14] According to what we know from archaeological excavations, there were no Canaanite cities in the area of these cities at the time of the conquest and settlement (the thirteenth cent. BCE),[15] and the tradition about a war by a Canaanite king of Arad with Israel, adduced in Num. 21.1, and also the tradition about the defeat of the Israelites in war with the Canaanites–Amorites at Hormah (Num. 14.44-45; 33.40; Deut. 1.44) are to be considered anachronistic.[16] Actually, the settlement of the Kenites and Jerahmeelites began there at the end of the thirteenth century BCE,[17] parallel to the settlement of the Calebites and Kenizzites in the area of the hill country of Hebron. Only at a later stage were the Judahites and Simeonites joined to them. As for Arad, Judg. 1.16 testifies that the

14. On this matter see Mazar 1991: 67-77.

15. See recently Kempinsky *et al.* 1980–81: 154-80.

16. It seems that the fortified cities of the Canaanites from the Middle Bronze Age that served as an obstacle before the nomads, remembered for many years by those dwelling in the area, are those that stand behind the tradition about the wars with the Canaanites in this area. See Aharoni 1975: 114-24.

17. In the topographical list of Shishak, king of Egypt, we find *'rd bt yrḥm*, a phrase that shows the connection between Arad and the Jerahmeelite families. See Mazar 1991: 71.

Kenites went up to settle there with the Judahites, and as for Hormah, Judah again took upon himself the conqueror's crown telling us that he went with Simeon his brother and smote the Canaanites dwelling in the place (v. 17). As we have already said, there were no Canaanite cities in this area at this period, but only nomad settlements: Simeonites, Kenites and Jerahmeelites (1 Sam. 30.29-30). If so, this description is also anachronistic. Actually we find here a phenomenon similar to what we find in the case of Hebron: just as the author of Judges 1 attributed the conquest of Hebron to Judah, which was actually accomplished by the Calebites, so he attributed the capture of Hormah to Judah, which actually was captured first by nomads in the area. In regard to Arad and Hormah we find then a development in a redactional direction similar to that found with Hebron and Debir: just as the conquest of Hebron and Debir was attributed in the later stages of tradition to all the Israelites on a campaign led by Joshua (Josh. 10.36-37), so also the conquest of Arad and Hormah was attributed in the end to all the Israelites under the leadership of Moses (Num. 21.1-3).[18] As with Hebron, the author here too with Arad and Hormah represents Judah as the tribe that stood at the head of the conquests in this area. In order to glorify the conquests of Judah the author used ancient traditions about the settlement of the Calebites, Kenizzites and Kenites, and attributed them to Judah and Simeon.

The Conquest of Gaza, Ashkelon, and Ekron (vv. 18-19)

As a conclusion to the conquests of the south we find a notice about the conquest of southern coastal cities: Gaza, Ashkelon and Ekron (v. 18). This event has no historical basis.[19] The LXX reads: 'And Judah did not capture Gaza...' instead of 'And Judah captured Gaza...', which is in the MT. It seems that the following phrase 'because the inhabitants of the valley were not expelled' (v. 19) was understood to be in contradiction to v. 18 and led to the correction in the LXX.[20]

---

18. The fact that the national tradition is found in the book of Numbers does not mean it precedes the tradition in Judges. On this principle, see recently Auld 1980.

19. See Aharoni 1979: 218. It seems that this piece of information is influenced by Judah's claim of dominion over the Philistine area. See Josh. 15.45-47; but there the cities are Ekron, Ashdod and Gaza. The source of the existence of these cities in this list (in Joshua) is, it seems, in the period when Judah expanded in the days of Hezekiah (cf. 2 Kgs 18.8) or Josiah. On this matter, see Kallai 1986: 372-77.

20. See Kallai 1986: 109.

Nevertheless, according to what appears in the MT, Judah did succeed in capturing the coastal cities but was not able to expel their inhabitants as was the case in Jerusalem. One must note that the verse does not say directly that Judah 'did not expel' (*wᵉlô hôriš*), as we find with the other tribes in what follows, but says rather, *kî lô lᵉhôrîš*. This formulation uses an infinitive without specifying the verbal agent of the verb because it was impossible to relate failure and lack of success explicitly to Judah (see the concluding remarks in the discussion of vv. 22-26, below).

Caleb Expels the Three Anakites (v. 20)

Verse 20 is a sort of corrective footnote that somewhat darkens the brightness of the success of Judah's conquest dealt with at the beginning of Judges 1. Caleb not Judah, according to this verse, is the one that expels the three Anakites (see the remarks above on vv. 9-15). As we have noted, the notice in this verse represents a well known fact that could not be contradicted. Therefore it was brought at the end as a miscellaneous note. The verse may be an addition in the original text.

The Benjaminites and the Jebusites who Dwelt at Jerusalem (v. 21)

The Benjaminites did not expel the Jebusites that dwelt at Jerusalem and the mention of Benjamin thereby calls to mind other northern tribes that did not drive out the Canaanites from their cities (vv. 27-33). As I remarked earlier, this verse contradicts what is said in Josh. 15.63, which says that the Judahites were not able to expel the Jebusites dwelling at Jerusalem. If so, there is no escape from seeing in Judg. 1.21 a tendentiousness that seeks to glorify Judah at the cost of Benjamin.[21]

It is difficult to determine if this verse constitutes the conclusion of the preceding section about Judah's achievements or if it is attached to the following list of failures of the house of Joseph to drive out the people of the land in the second half of the chapter.[22] It must be

21. According to Auld (1975: 274-75), Josh. 15.63 is the original verse, and Judg. 1.21 is a tendentious reworking of the verse in Joshua.

22. It is possible to explain the unique expression *yšb 't* (*bny bnymyn*) instead of *yšb bqrb* found in what follows (vv. 29, 30, 32, 33) by saying the verse's language

admitted that the episode in vv. 22-26 interrupts the report of Benjamin's failure and that of the other northern tribes. But if the author followed a geographical order in his presentation,[23] it would make sense to discuss Benjamin immediately after Judah. It is possible, too, that the author was interested in beginning with the most important failure: not driving the Jebusites out of Jerusalem, which in the future would become 'the chosen city'.

The House of Joseph and its Conquests (vv. 22-26)

Verses 22-26, which tell about the conquest of Bethel by the house of Joseph and which reflect undoubtedly an ancient tradition, may be considered an introduction to the settlement of the northern tribes. The house of Joseph indeed conquered Bethel, but not by methods of warfare, as Judah did in its conquests, but by deceit. They penetrated the city through a secret entrance and then smote all the inhabitants. But the tribes of the house of Joseph did not succeed in driving out the inhabitants of the other large cities that were Joseph's lot, such as Beth-Shean, Taanach, Megiddo and Gezer (vv. 27-29). And even when the house of Joseph grew strong, they did not drive them out but put the inhabitants of the cities under forced labor (v. 28).

The editor drew these details about the tribes' failures to dispossess the people of the land from sources available to him.[24] We find the same details in the lists of inheritances in Joshua 14–19 (15.63; 16.10; 17.12-13). But the editor of Judges 1 gathered these together in order to impress the reader with the failures of the northern tribes vis-à-vis the achievements of the Judahites. Just as he gathered data regarding the failure of the house of Joseph, so he adduced a list of failures related to the Galilaean tribes: Zebulon did not drive out the inhabitants of Kitron and Nahalol (v. 30), and Asher not only did not succeed in driving out 'the inhabitants of Akko, the inhabitants of Sidon, and Ahlab, Achzib, Helbah, Aphek and Rehob', but even *dwelt in the midst of the Canaanites* (v. 32) who apparently prevailed over Asher in this region of strong Phoenician cities.[25] Naphtali as well did not succeed in driving out the inhabitants of Beth-Shemesh and those

was derived from an ancient tradition (Josh. 15.63). See the preceding note.

23. Kallai 1978: 254-55 n. 13.
24. But these lists too do not precede the unified kingdom. See Kallai 1986.
25. Aharoni 1971.

of Beth-Anath (v. 33). And Issachar is not mentioned at all, since, we learn from Gen. 49.14-15, he was himself enslaved by Canaanites in the area whence, it seems, comes the name Issachar: *'yš śkr*: 'and he bent his shoulder to bear and became a slave laborer'.[26]

The Danites were also pressed into the hill country by the Amorites (v. 34) and, as we know from Josh. 19.47 and Judges 18, they were finally forced to seek an inheritance in the north. Hence they appear in Judges 1 next to Naphtali in the north, which indicates that the editor knew that Dan was now living in the north.

In comparison to the achievements of Judah in the south, the tribes of Israel in the north did not succeed in driving out the Canaanites, and when they had the power to do so, they did not expel them but put the Canaanites under forced labor (v. 28). As shown elsewhere,[27] they were considered as having sinned by doing this.

There is no doubt that the document in Judges 1 tendentiously serves to glorify the tribe of Judah and to lessen the stature of 'Israel' in the north. This tendency, which is interlocked with a criticism of Benjamin, derives, it seems, from circles from the house of David who sought to show that Judah, David's tribe, was that which stood behind the conquest of the land and not the tribes of the North. These other tribes did not drive out the Canaanites from their cities, and only in the days of David did they prevail over them. Moreover, when the tribes of the north had it in their power to drive out the Canaanites from their cities they did not do this (v. 28). This is considered a sin as is said in the rebuke of the angel in Judg. 2.1-5. It was because of this sin that the troubles of the period of the judges came about.

BIBLIOGRAPHY

Aharoni, Y.
1971   'The Settlement in Canaan', *The World History of the Jewish People*.
          III. *Judges* (Tel Aviv: Massada): 115-16.
1975   'Tel-Masos—Historical Considerations', *Tel Aviv* 2: 114-24.

26. On 'people put to forced labor' (LÚ. MEŠ *massa*), who were accustomed to work in the Jezreel Valley in the period before the Israelite conquest, see the letter of Biridya, king of Megiddo, to the king of Egypt: 'I am he who plows in the city of Shunem, and I am he who transports the men put under forced labor (to work)' (Tel el-Amarna letter §365); see Alt 1969: 169-70.

27. Cf. my article: Weinfeld 1967.

1979   *The Land of the Bible: A Historical Geography* (trans. and ed.
              A.F. Rainey; London: Burns & Oates, 2nd rev. edn).

Alt, A.
1959   'Neues über Palastina aus dem Archiv Amenophis IV', *Kleine
              Schriften*, III (Munich: C.H. Beck): 158-75.

Auld, A.G.
1975   'Judges 1 and History: A Reconsideration', *VT* 25: 261-85.
1980   *Joshua, Moses and the Land* (Edinburgh: T. & T. Clark).

Cross, F.M.
1983   'The Ammonite Oppression of the Tribes of Gad and Reuben:
              Missing Verses from 1 Samuel 11 Found in 4QSamuel', in H. Tadmor
              and M. Weinfeld (eds.), *History, Historiography, and Interpretation:
              Studies in Biblical and Cuneiform Literatures* (Jerusalem: Magnes):
              148-58.

Gaster, T.H.
1969   *Myth, Legend, and Custom in the Old Testament* (New York: Harper &
              Row).

Güdemann, M.
1869   'Tendenz und Abfassungszeit der letzten Kapitel des Buches der
              Richter', *Monatschrift fur die Geschichte und Wissenschaft des
              Judentums*: 357-68.

Kallai, Z. and H. Tadmor
1969–70   'Bit Ninurta = Beth Horon—On the History of the Kingdom of
              Jerusalem in the Amarna Period', *Eretz Israel* 9 (Albright Volume;
              Jerusalem: The Israel Exploration Society): 138-47.

Kallai, Z.
1978   'Judah and Israel—A Study in Israelite Historiography', *IEJ* 28: 251-
              61.
1986   *Historical Geography of the Bible* (Jerusalem: Magnes; Leiden: Brill).

Kaufmann, Y.
1962   *The Book of Judges* (Jerusalem: Kiriat Sepher) (Hebrew).

Kempinsky, A. *et al.*
1980–81   'Excavations at Tel Masos', *Eretz Israel* 15 (Aharoni Volume;
              Jerusalem: The Israel Exploration Society): 154-80 (Hebrew).

Mazar, B.
1991   'The Sanctuary at Arad and the Family of Hobab the Kenite', in
              S. Ahituv (ed.), *Biblical Israel—State and People* (Jerusalem:
              Magnes): 67-77.

Rösel, H.N.
1982   'Judges I and the Settlement of the "Leah Tribes"', *Proceedings of
              the Eighth World Congress of Jewish Studies* (Division A, The World
              of the Bible; Jerusalem: World Union of Jewish Students): 17-24.

Weinfeld, M.
1967   'The Period of the Conquest and the Judges as Seen by the Earlier and
              the Later Sources', *VT* 17: 93-113.
1972   *Deuteronomy and the Deuteronomic School* (Oxford: Clarendon
              Press).

Weinfeld, M. and R. Meridor
    1984   'The Punishment of Zedekiah and the Punishment of Polymestor',
                I.L. Seeligmann Volume, I (Jerusalem: E. Rubinstein's Publishing
                House): 223-29.
    1988   'The Pattern of the Israelite Settlement in Canaan', in J.A. Emerton
                (ed.), *Congress Volume, Jerusalem 1988* (VTSup, 40; Leiden: Brill):
                270-83.
    1992   *From Joshua to Josiah* (Jerusalem: Magnes).
Zakowitz, Y. and E. Loewenstamm
    1976   'Šôpᵉtîm', *Encyclopedia Miqra'it*, VII: cols. 583-98 (Jerusalem: The
                Bialik Institute) (Hebrew).

ISAIAH 1.11 AND THE SEPTUAGINT OF ISAIAH

H.G.M. Williamson

> He is Translation's thief that addeth more,
> As much as he that taketh from the store
> Of the first author. (Andrew Marvell)

It is an old adage that 'translation inevitably involves interpretation'. As has recently been illustrated with characteristic elegance by Brock (1988), this was as well known to scholars in antiquity as it is today. It remains the case, however, that the implications of this are not always given sufficient consideration when the evidence of the ancient versions is adduced in critical work on the text of the Hebrew Bible. Despite repeated recognition of the necessity first to study the translation technique of the rendering of any given book in, say, the Septuagint, examples continue to multiply of instances where its rendering is cited piecemeal and in isolation in support of emendation. The following remarks will therefore seek to re-emphasize the point by setting the translation of Isaiah 1.11 in the context of the LXX of Isaiah as a whole.[1]

It is widely recognized that the Greek translator of Isaiah exercised a considerable degree of freedom in his task. Not only did he introduce interpretative elements into his work,[2] but he also seems to have been less than precise over some of the more mechanical aspects of translation. As Ziegler (1934: 51-52 and 56) has observed, the LXX not infrequently omits a synonym occurring either in parallelism or in

---

1. It is now generally agreed that the LXX of Isaiah is essentially the work of a single translator; cf. Ziegler 1934: 31-46; Seeligmann 1948: 39-42; van der Kooij 1981: 31-32 (all responding to Gray 1911 and Baumgärtel 1923: 20-31). Continuing uncertainty about chs. 36–39 in this regard is not relevant for the present study; cf. Hurwitz 1957, but contrast the implications of the study by Fritsch (1960).

2. In addition to the works cited in the previous note, see also Koenig 1982: 1-198.

an adjacent position. It does not, however, appear to have been noted that an extension of this feature results in what we might be inclined to regard as a somewhat cavalier treatment of lists. Almost inevitably, lists are likely to include a number of rare words, and it would not be surprising if these sometimes posed particular problems for the translator. Whether or not this is the explanation, it is certainly the case that he sometimes seems to have been content to represent the general impression of a list as such rather than attempting a one-for-one equivalent for each individual item.

At 41.19, for instance, seven trees are mentioned, four in the first half of the verse, and three in the second. Although there are some uncertainties over identification, the verse may tentatively be rendered:

> I will plant in the wilderness cedar, acacia, myrtle and oleaster;
> I will set in the desert juniper, pine (?) and cypress together.

In its translation, the LXX ignores the obvious parallelism by supplying only one verb and then listing a total of five trees: 'I will plant in the waterless land cedar and box, and myrtle and cypress, and white poplar'.[3] Elliger (1978: 158) suggests that the end of each line in the *Vorlage* of the LXX may have been damaged, but this fails to account for the omission of אשים בערבה at the start of the second line, which in principle need have caused the translator no difficulty.[4] It looks rather as though the translator, faced with a list of trees, some of which may have been unfamiliar to him, has merely rendered loosely *ad sensum*.

Support for this conclusion comes from 60.13, where the last three trees mentioned in 41.19 are listed in the same order: ברוש תדהר ותאשור. This is translated (ἐν) κυπαρίσσῳ καὶ πεύκῃ καὶ κέδρῳ, the last of which undoubtedly rendered ארז when it appeared as the first word in the list at 41.19. Perhaps the translator thought that a reference to the cedar would be appropriate in view of the mention of Lebanon in the first part of the verse ('The glory of Lebanon shall come unto thee') and so substituted it for the unfamiliar תאשור, one of the words which he seems not to have translated at 41.19. (The other was most probably עץ שמן, a tree whose meaning is transparent, and which is familiar

---

3.   Cf. Ottley 1904: I, 227. It is possible that λεύκην is an inner-Greek corruption for πεύκην, as comparison with 60.13 suggests (so three manuscripts and the Sahidic, according to Ziegler [1983: 275]; note that this edition is used for the text of the LXX throughout this article).

4.   The lack of a translation of יחדו at the end of the second line may be accounted for by its repetition at the end of the first line of v. 20 immediately following.

besides from 1 Kgs 6.23, 31, 32, 33, and Neh. 8.15.). If, on the other hand, he thought that האשור was itself a cedar, then we can understand that he will have been stymied when he reached it in 41.19, having already used κέδρος earlier in the verse. Either way, he was clearly not concerned to supply an equivalent for every word in his *Vorlage*, a conclusion borne out, as we have seen, by his treatment of עץ שמן and of אשים בערבה.[5]

Another list in Isaiah is the well-known description of the finery of the 'daughters of Jerusalem' which the Lord will remove 'in that day' (Isa. 3.18-23). Many items in this list are of uncertain meaning,[6] and must have been equally obscure to the Greek translator. His rendering has been the subject of a particularly detailed study by Ziegler (1934: 203-11), who has shown both that the translator drew on contemporary Alexandrian terminology in order to give what might be called a 'dynamic equivalent' and that in the process of doing so he did not concern himself with necessarily producing a rendering of each individual word in his *Vorlage*. Amidst much that is uncertain, some matters stand out with reasonable clarity, and a few examples will suffice for our present purposes.

First, v. 18 concludes in the MT with השהרנים 'crescents', which is familiar from Judg. 8.21 and 26 where it is rendered by μηνίσκος. At the end of Isa. 3.18 in the Ziegler edition we also find τοὺς μηνίσκους, so that we may reasonably conclude that for this word, at least, we have an equivalent. Before it, however, come just two items in the Hebrew text, but four in the Greek, a clear indication of free expansion at this point. Ziegler is probably right to suggest that the single Hebrew word תפארת, which is in any case in the construct state, has been taken on its own and expanded into a generalizing introduction: 'the glory of their apparel and their ornaments'.

Secondly, v. 19 moves in the opposite direction—three specific items in the MT but only two in the Greek, of which the second is again more general: καὶ τὸν κόσμον τοῦ προσώπου αὐτῶν.

Thirdly, v. 20 has a further general expression to start with, καὶ τὴν σύνθεσιν τοῦ κόσμου τῆς δόξης, which Ziegler suggests may

5. 44.14 might at first sight appear to be a far more radical example with regard to trees, the list in the first half of the verse being summarized simply as ξύλον ἐκ τοῦ δρυμοῦ. More probably, however, the translator (or his *Vorlage*) skipped straight from לכרת to בעצי־יער.

6. For the fullest recent attempt at identifications, cf. Wildberger 1980: 140-45.

have arisen from reflection on the root פאר in פארים, the first word in v. 20, but even so κόσμος has been somewhat overexploited by this stage (three times in as many verses, and none with specific warrant in the *Vorlage*).

Fourthly, since on the basis of regular equivalents elsewhere we may conclude that (האף) הטבעות ונזמי (v. 21) is represented by τοὺς δακτυλίους καὶ τὰ ἐνώτια (v. 20), it is possible that the remainder of v. 20 is intended to follow the Hebrew more closely.[7] Thereafter to the end of the list, however, not only do equivalents peter out but in places the Greek includes some compound expressions that contrast with its *Vorlage*'s simple string of nouns.

All in all, therefore, it can be clearly seen that in its rendering of this list the LXX has not even attempted a one-for-one translation. Had that been the intention, we should not have been surprised to find many guesses and false etymologies to help render the obscure vocabulary, but we should have expected that the general shape of the list would have remained clear. Instead, however, we are confronted with a mixture of material in which some recognizable translation equivalents are combined with other items that by no stretch of the imagination could ever have been derived directly from the Hebrew text as we know it. The result is that the two lists do not even have the same number of items, the Greek exceeding the Hebrew on this occasion by two or three elements.

Lists of place names occur from time to time in Isaiah, and on several occasions the Greek translator has exercised freedom in his choice of equivalents with the intention, no doubt, of modernizing the terminology for the benefit of his later readers. Seeligmann (1948: 76-81) and van der Kooij (1981: e.g. 34-39), in particular, have exploited this tendency in their attempts to specify his setting and date. At 9.1 (MT 8.23*b*), however, this freedom goes beyond merely the substitution of modern equivalents. Simplest to observe is that at the end of the verse τὰ μέρη τῆς Ιουδαίας has been added without any warrant from the Hebrew. In addition, however, the parallelism earlier in the verse has been ignored (rather as in the case of 41.19) and והאחרון הכביד may have become another geographical designation: καὶ οἱ λοιποὶ οἱ τὴν παραλίαν κατοικοῦντες. Seeligmann (1948: 74 and 80) finds here the influence of Ezek. 25.16 and suggests that it

---

7.   τοὺς χλιδῶνας, for instance, fits well with הצעדות, since at Num. 31.50 and 2 Sam. 1.10 it renders אצעדה.

may have been a 'probably more original' rendering of דרך הים, a more accurate translation of which (ὁδὸν θαλάσσης) now precedes it in the present form of the text. It is tempting to suppose, however, that there may also have been influence from the Hebrew *Vorlage*: והאחרון could well have been (mis)read as והאחרים (hence καὶ οἱ λοιποί), and הכביד may have been read as הככר, which, under the influence of the following דרך הים, might have given rise to τὴν παραλίαν. If this speculation be accepted, the translator will have inverted the order of phrases in the line; if not, he will have omitted one phrase from his *Vorlage* and added another on his own account. Either way, and together with the further addition at the end of the list, he has clearly not felt himself too closely tied in his rendering of this list.

Of course, not every list is treated in this way, and on at least one occasion the LXX's greater literalness in rendering most items leads to uncertainty in deciding whether its two apparent departures from its *Vorlage* are the result of more mechanical textual factors. Isa. 3.2-3 comprises a lengthy list of the leaders of society, and most of these occur in the same order in the LXX. There are two exceptions, however. The first noun in the list, גבור, has two equivalents in the Greek: γίγαντα καὶ ἰσχύοντα. Both words are used elsewhere in Isaiah to render גבור (cf. 13.3; 49.24, 25 on the one hand, and 5.22; 10.21 on the other), so that the possibility of the later preservation of earlier variant translations cannot be ruled out. Alternatively, it is possible that Ziegler (1934: 60-61) and others are right to see in the second word an exegetical comment by the translator himself who wished to link γίγαντα with the ἰσχύοντα which he had introduced into the previous verse. In v. 3, two types of leader, נשׂוא פנים and יועץ, are represented by only one in the LXX: θαυμαστὸν σύμβουλον. Gray (1912: 67) suggests that יועץ did not stand in the LXX's *Vorlage*, but this seems an improbable solution. As has frequently been observed, the rendering here is identical with 9.6(5), where it represents פלא יועץ. At the same time, we should note that at 9.14 נשׂוא־פנים is rendered τοὺς τὰ πρόσωπα θαυμάζοντας. Ziegler is therefore surely right to conclude that 'The translator linked together both the elements of his *Vorlage* ("respected person and counsellor") into a single idea under the influence of 9.6(5)'.[8] We may thus claim 3.2-3 as a further, if less

8. 'Der Übers. faßte die beiden Begriffe seiner Vorlage: "Angesehener (Respektsperson) und Rat" zu einem Begriffe zusammen unter dem Einfluß von 9,6(5)' (1934: 136).

striking, example of the characteristic under consideration.

There are examples too of lists of roughly synonymous verbs which the LXX has on occasion chosen to modify.[9] This seems to be a feature of the composition of the so-called 'Isaiah Apocalypse' (chs. 24–27) in particular, so that we should be more hesitant than *BHS* in rushing to eliminate elements of these lists on the basis of the LXX. At 24.4, for instance, the first line clearly piles up comparable verbs for alliterative and rhetorical effect: אבלה נבלה הארץ אמללה נבלה תבל ('the earth mourns, withers; the world languishes, withers').[10] The LXX, however, represents only one verb in each half of the line; the sense is hardly affected, though of course the specific effect of the Hebrew style is inevitably lost in translation.

Similarly, at 25.12 three verbs describe the destruction of a wall: השח השפיל הגיע (לארץ), but the Greek contents itself with two. Gray and Wildberger again both defend the integrity of the MT, whereas Ziegler (1934: 54) suggests that השפיל may have entered the text secondarily from v. 11. Against this, however, it should be noted that the LXX equally has only one phrase for the synonymous expressions at the end of the verse: לארץ עד־עפר (ἕως τοῦ ἐδάφους), and that the same group of verbs occurs in the same order in 26.5.[11]

A short list of related verbs occurs in the last line of 1.6. The Hebrew text poses some problems; the root of זרו is not certain, and in particular it is curious that the third verb, רככה, appears to switch to the third person feminine singular after the plurals of the previous two verbs.[12] Despite this, the general sense is clear, and there is no

---

9. For a recent discussion of 52.12 in this regard, cf. Hofius 1992.

10. The text is defended by, for instance, Gray (1912: 414) and Wildberger (1978: 914); cf. Clines 1992.

11. Indeed, 26.5 may furnish a further example of the translation characteristic under consideration. In this verse, the verb השפיל is repeated (ישפילנה ישפילה), but this is represented only once in the LXX. On this occasion, some commentators have argued that the Hebrew text has arisen as the result of dittography, for 1QIsa[a] and Pesh. also have the verb only once. Nonetheless, Wildberger (following several others) maintains on metrical grounds that the *athnaḥ* should be moved to include the first occurrence of the verb in the first line and that the versions have not surprisingly abbreviated at this point. Clearly, the evidence is too finely balanced for certainty.

12. None of the proposed explanations is entirely satisfying. Unless it is a simple error for רככו, the possibility might be considered that it is a rare example of the third person feminine plural, used for euphonic reasons. This suggestion would require fuller exploration than can be offered here.

reason to suppose that the Greek translator was confused. Nonetheless, his rendering is interesting in two respects: οὐκ ἔστι μάλαγμα ἐπιθεῖναι οὔτε ἔλαιον οὔτε καταδέσμους ('there is no means to apply a balm, or oil, or bandages'). First, of course, the construction of the line has been changed so that the verbs are represented as nouns. More significant for our purpose, however, is that he has changed the order of the items, with the result that bandaging now follows balm and oil, as is logical. The MT has bandaging in the second position, before the application of oil; the reason for this is probably related to the author's concern for poetic balance: the longer phrase ולא רככה בשמן could hardly come comfortably between the two shorter phrases לא חבשו and לאזרו. Be that as it may, the fact remains that once again the Greek translator has demonstrated his freedom to alter the order of items in a list when he so desired.

Though other examples of this phenomenon could be added, these are perhaps sufficient to establish the case that the Greek translator of Isaiah was especially prone to free renderings of lists in his *Vorlage*. Sometimes he abbreviated, sometimes he expanded, sometimes he altered the order and sometimes he gave comparable rather than exact equivalents; his concern was more to convey the general impression of a list than to follow the Hebrew slavishly in every particular.

In the light of this conclusion, we may turn finally to Isa. 1.11, where many commentators have adduced the evidence of the LXX in an attempt to improve the text. The Masoretic text (from which 1QIsa[a] differs only with regard to orthography) reads

למה־לי רב־זבחיכם יאמר יהוה
שׂבעתי עלות אילים וחלב מריאים
ודם פרים וכבשׂים ועתודים לא חפצתי

which the RV renders

To what purpose is the multitude of your sacrifices unto me?
    saith the Lord:
I am full of the burnt offerings of rams, and the fat of fed beasts;
    and I delight not in the blood of bullocks, or of lambs, or of he-goats.

The Septuagint has rendered this verse in a straightforward manner for the most part with the exception of its apparent failure to supply a translation of וכבשׂים in the last line. Because of this, it has been proposed that the word should be deleted as a later addition.[13]

---

13. See, for instance, Marti 1900: 10; Condamin 1905: 4; Fullerton 1919: 56;

It should be clear from the preceding discussion that, since the word forms part of a list of sacrificial animals, this argument is open to question. And indeed, further inspection reveals that there is evidence to support the conclusion that this is another case where the translator has treated his *Vorlage* in a manner similar to those already examined.

First, in the second line of the verse, he has rendered the phrase וחלב מריאים with the words καὶ στέαρ ἀρνῶν 'and the fat of lambs'. ἀρνός is used occasionally elsewhere to translate מריא (e.g. at 2 Sam. 6.13; 1 Kgs 1.9, 19 and 25), but not in Isaiah, where it is used rather for such words as גדי (5.17),[14] כבש (11.6) and טלאים/טלה (40.11; 65.25). מריא occurs in only one other place in Isaiah, at 11.6, but there are difficulties with the text;[15] if the LXX's *Vorlage* was identical with the MT, he must have rendered it ταῦρος, an equivalent not found anywhere else and involving also a change in the order of this short list of animals. It is thus clear that he was far from being consistent in his rendering of such terms, so that his choice at 1.11*b* causes no immediate difficulty. However, having thus introduced ἀρνός into his list, it would not be at all surprising if he had then not bothered to reproduce it when he came to וכבשים in the following line. The situation is comparable with 41.19 where, as we saw above, having used κέδρος at the start of the list for ארז, he then did not repeat it again at the end of the list for תאשור, which 60.13 suggests he also identified with a cedar.

Secondly, a comparison with the text of 34.6-7 is instructive. There too we have a list of sacrificial animals, albeit in a metaphorical context. In the Hebrew text, the list overlaps only partially with that in 1.11—אילים, פרים and עתודים appear in both, but מריאים and כבשים are

Gray 1912: 19; Feldmann 1925: 12; Begrich 1933–34: 205; Eichrodt 1960: 29; Fey 1963: 69; Fohrer 1966: 31; Wildberger 1980: 33; Kaiser 1981: 38; Deck 1991: 137. *BHS* is more cautious than *BHK* in this regard; although it notes the omission in the Septuagint at this point, it does not, unlike its predecessor, recommend a change to the MT.

14. This assumes the widely adopted emendation of גרים, at least as far as the LXX's *Vorlage* is concerned. The situation in the MT is far more complicated than this, however; if the first two words of the phrase are vocalised וְחָרְבוֹת מְחִים (cf. Wildberger 1980: 178, partly following Driver 1937: 38-39), then גרים could conceivably be retained as a later, historicizing gloss on the metaphorical מחים.

15. If the LXX is cited to support an emendation of ומריא to ימראו (so, for instance, Wildberger 1980: 438), then it should be noted that the LXX will have added one animal to the list, so that the main point made above still stands.

found only at 1.11 and כרים, ראמים and אבירים only at 34.6-7. In the Septuagint, however, the two lists overlap completely, something which at 34.6-7 involves (i) the addition of ἀρνῶν after στέατος (so giving the same phrase as at 1.11) where the MT has only חלב, (ii) the repetition of κριός (once for איל, its standard equivalent, and once for פר, which in about 175 uses in the LXX is only found once elsewhere as an equivalent—at Ezek. 46.7), and (iii) some free rewriting at the beginning of 34.6*b*.[16] It thus looks very much as though the five animals listed in the Greek in the two passages are those which the translator took to be standard sacrificial animals and that he merely listed them accordingly when his *Vorlage* seemed to call for it. The two passages may thus again be seen to fit very much into the pattern outlined in the first part of this article.

It may therefore be concluded that the Greek translator of Isaiah has rendered 1.11 in a manner characteristic of his treatment of comparable lists elsewhere in the book where there is no good reason to suppose that his *Vorlage* differed substantially from the MT. In the light of this characteristic, it is clearly illegitimate to appeal to his testimony in support of the deletion of כבשים from the third line of the verse.

Without that support, the subsidiary argument of those cited in note 13 above, namely that the line is metrically overloaded, has to carry the full weight of the case, and we may question whether it is strong enough to do so unaided. Our continuing uncertainty about the mechanics of Hebrew metre is in evidence at this point, for arguments from it have been advanced to support both sides of the argument.[17] Those who favour the counting of syllables or even letters[18] will observe that the third line is longer than its predecessors, while those who work rather from the general balance of phrases can reply that there is symmetry between the two lines (verbal element—שבעתי and

16. The only difference as regards the animals in these verses is the use of ἁδροί (for ראמים) at 34.7. Even here, however, it should be noted that the translator has chosen a vague, descriptive word for the more specific Hebrew noun, thus producing an equivalence which is attested nowhere else.

17. The metre is claimed to support the retention of כבשים by, for instance, Procksch (1930: 38), who is followed by Watts (1985: 14); the opposite point of view is maintained by both Gray (1912: 19) and Wildberger (1980: 33).

18. For the latter, cf. Loretz 1984. Loretz seems to be unclear on our particular matter, however, for on p. 29 he implies that ועתודים is the later addition but on p. 145 וכבשים.

לא חפצתי—together with two nominal phrases comprising two words each), and that the slight rallentando, caused by the fact that the last of the nominal phrases is made up of two independent nouns rather than the construct relationship of the preceding three phrases, is appropriate at the end of a minor poetic unit. In the present state of our knowledge, it would clearly be unwise to base a case solely on this argument.

The interpretation of the Hebrew Bible began early, and the ancient versions already testify to the directions it took. The fact that it is embedded in translation sometimes makes it more difficult to discern, but as research continues on the versions in their own right, we may hope that textual critics too will benefit by a more accurate understanding of the nature of the evidence at their disposal.

I am delighted to have the opportunity of contributing to this volume in honour of Professor Anderson, who has shown me much kindness on numerous occasions since 1975.

BIBLIOGRAPHY

Baumgärtel, F.
1923   'Die Septuaginta zu Jesaja das Werk zweier Übersetzer', in J. Hermann and F. Baumgärtel, *Beiträge zur Entstehungsgeschichte der Septuaginta* (BWAT, NF 5; Berlin: Kohlhammer): 20-31.

Begrich, J.
1933–34   'Der Satzstil im Fünfer', *Zeitschrift für Semitistik* 9: 169-209.

Brock, S.P.
1988   'Translating the Old Testament', in D.A. Carson and H.G.M. Williamson (eds.), *It is Written: Scripture Citing Scripture. Essays in Honour of Barnabas Lindars, SSF* (Cambridge: Cambridge University Press): 87-98.

Clines, D.J.A.
1992   'Was There an '*bl* II "be dry" in Classical Hebrew?', *VT* 42: 1-10.

Condamin, A.
1905   *Le livre d'Isaïe* (EtBib; Paris: Librairie Victor Lecoffre).

Deck, S.
1991   *Die Gerichtsbotschaft Jesajas: Charakter und Begründung* (Forschung zur Bibel, 67; Würzburg: Echter Verlag).

Driver, G.R.
1937   'Linguistic and Textual Problems: Isaiah i–xxxix', *JTS* 38: 36-50.

Eichrodt, W.
1960   *Der Heilige in Israel: Jesaja 1–12* (Die Botschaft des Alten Testaments; Stuttgart: Calwer Verlag).

Elliger, K.
1978   *Deuterojesaja*. 1. Teilband: *Jesaja 40,1–45,7* (BKAT; Neukirchen–
               Vluyn: Neukirchener Verlag).
Feldmann, F.
1925   *Das Buch Isaias: Erster Teil (Kap. 1–39)* (Exegetisches Handbuch
               zum Alten Testament; Münster: Aschendorff).
Fey, R.
1963   *Amos und Jesaja: Abhängigkeit und Eigenständigkeit des Jesaja*
               (WMANT, 12; Neukirchen–Vluyn: Neukirchener Verlag).
Fohrer, G.
1966   *Das Buch Jesaja*. 1. Band: *Kapitel 1–23* (Zürich: Zwingli-Verlag, 2nd
               edn).
Fritsch, C.T.
1960   'The Concept of God in the Greek Translation of Isaiah', in
               J.M. Myers, O. Reimherr and H.N. Bream (eds.), *Biblical Studies in
               Memory of H.C. Allemann* (Locust Valley: J.J. Augustin): 155-69.
Fullerton, K.
1919   'The Rhythmical Analysis of Is. 1:10-20', *JBL* 38: 53-63.
Gray, G.B.
1911   'The Greek Version of Isaiah: Is it the Work of a Single Translator?',
               JTS 12: 286-93.
1912   *A Critical and Exegetical Commentary on the Book of Isaiah i–xxvii*
               (ICC; Edinburgh: T. & T. Clark).
Hofius, O.
1992   'Zur Septuaginta-Übersetzung von Jes 52, 13b', *ZAW* 104: 107-10.
Hurwitz, M.S.
1957   'The Septuagint of Isaiah 36–39 in Relation to that of 1–35, 40–66',
               HUCA 28: 75-83.
Kaiser, O.
1981   *Das Buch des Propheten Jesaja: Kapitel 1–12* (ATD; Göttingen:
               Vandenhoeck & Ruprecht, 5th edn).
Koenig, J.
1982   *L'herméneutique analogique du judaïsme antique d'après les témoins
               textuels d'Isaïe* (VTSup, 33; Leiden: Brill).
Kooij, A. van der
1981   *Die alten Textzeugen des Jesajabuches: Ein Beitrag zur Textgeschichte
               des Alten Testaments* (OBO, 35; Freiburg: Universitätsverlag;
               Göttingen: Vandenhoeck & Ruprecht).
Loretz, O.
1984   *Der Prolog des Jesaja Buches (1,1–2,5). Ugaritologische und Rolome-
               trische Studien zum Jesaja-Buch* (Ugaritisch-Biblische Literatur, 1;
               Altenberge: CIS-Verlag).
Marti, K.
1900   *Das Buch Jesaja* (KHAT; Tübingen: Mohr [Paul Siebeck]).
Ottley, R.R.
1904   *The Book of Isaiah according to the Septuagint* (London: Cambridge
               University Press).

Procksch, O.
 1930   *Jesaia I* (KAT; Leipzig: Deichert).
Seeligmann, I.L.
 1948   *The Septuagint Version of Isaiah: A Discussion of its Problems* (Leiden: Brill).
Watts, J.D.W.
 1985   *Isaiah 1–33* (WBC; Waco, TX: Word Books).
Wildberger, H.
 1978   *Jesaja. 2. Teilband: Jesaja 13–27* (BKAT; Neukirchen–Vluyn: Neukirchener Verlag).
 1980   *Jesaja. 1. Teilband: Jesaja 1–12* (BKAT; Neukirchen–Vluyn: Neukirchener Verlag, 2nd edn).
Ziegler, J.
 1934   *Untersuchungen zur Septuaginta des Buches Isaias* (Alttestamentliche Abhandlungen, xii.3; Münster: Aschendorff).
 1983   *Septuaginta. XIV. Isaias* (Göttingen: Vandenhoeck & Ruprecht, 3rd edn).

ACCOMMODATION AND BARBARITY IN JOHN CALVIN'S
OLD TESTAMENT COMMENTARIES

D.F. Wright

What difference does it make to profess the study of the Old
Testament in a distinctively Reformed context—compared with, say,
an Anglican or a Lutheran or a Baptist one? This is a question on
which the views of the distinguished *honorandus* of this volume would
be at least doubly valuable. Not only did George Anderson teach for
many years in New College, which is both the Divinity Faculty of the
University of Edinburgh and, in an important if at times somewhat
elusive sense, a Church of Scotland theological college, but also his
own belonging to the people called Methodists will be certain to have
sharpened his apprehension of the distinctives of the Reformed tradition. Perhaps in an era in which Old Testament studies, like nearly all
the theological disciplines, have become irreversibly ecumenical and
international—a development in which George Anderson has long
been conspicuously active—the distinguishing features of a Reformed
approach to the Hebrew Bible have ceased to be recognizable.

It was not always thus. All the leading sixteenth-century architects
of Reformed Protestantism, whether Zwingli in Zürich, Martin Bucer
in Strasbourg and Cambridge, Calvin in Geneva or Scotland's own
John Knox (who conceived of his calling as that of a non-writing
prophet), possessed a strong sense of the continuity of the people and
promises of God between the two Testaments, and of the abiding value
of the earlier one within the Christian order. Of no one was this more
true than John Calvin. He made the principal 'use of the law', by
which he understood not only the Decalogue but 'the form of religion
handed down by Moses' (*Institutes* 2.7.1), its role in teaching and
exhorting 'believers in whose hearts the Spirit of God already lives
and reigns. For even though they have the law written and engraved
upon their hearts by the finger of God,…they still profit by the

(written) law' in these two ways (*ibid.* 2.7.12). Calvin spelt out at length this evaluation of the Mosaic law—so starkly contrasting with Luther's—both in his expansive exposition of the Decalogue in the *Institutes* (2.8) and in his commentary on Exodus–Deuteronomy, for which he constructed his own masterly and intriguing harmony of the whole corpus of Pentateuchal legislation (Wright 1986; Parker 1986: ch. 4).

The prominence of the Psalter in the worship and piety of Reformed churches, even when it has not been the exclusive form of hymnody, is another measure of the tradition's identification with the church of Israel. It has been suggested that the Psalter's dominance derives in part 'from the underlying assumption that [the Psalms] are Christological in a thoroughgoing respect' (McKane 1984: 258), but Calvin in particular stands out among Reformation expositors of the Old Testament in the restraint of his Christocentric interpretation.[1] Indeed, it would not be difficult to heap up citations attesting the merits of Calvin's commitment to the historical sense of Scripture and the abiding usefulness of his biblical commentaries.[2] He certainly devoted an enormous amount of time and energy, especially in the last decade and a half of his life, to lecturing, preaching and commentating on the books of the Old Testament (Parker 1986, 1992). Not only did he lecture but also, it seems, preach (Parker 1992: 172-78) with nothing but the Hebrew text in front of him.

An illuminating recent essay finds Calvin in a decided minority— 'perhaps, even, a minority of one'—when his treatment of the immoralities of the Hebrew patriarchs is compared with some twenty Fathers and other Reformers (Thompson 1991: 45; cf. Wright 1983: 465-67). He is almost alone in the relentless consistency with which he dismisses virtually all of the excusatory arguments advanced by other interpreters, and often with some contempt. 'To excuse such misconduct, Calvin asserts, is somehow to impugn "the clear authority of Scripture"…it dishonors Scripture to read its silence as excusing the very sins which it elsewhere so loudly condemns' (Thompson 1991: 44). And as Calvin himself put it, generalizing as a pastor from these

---

1.   Kraeling (1955: 23ff.) gives a travestied account, as well as discovering a still lost work by Calvin, *Central Doctrines of St Paul* (1539).

2.   Cf. Kraus 1982: 15, 'Dass Calvin in dieser unerbittlichen Consequenz dem sensus historicus alle Aufmerksamkeit zuwandte, hat für die Geschichte der Bibelforschung eine ausserordentlich grosse Bedeutung gehabt'.

particular cases, 'whenever the faithful fall into sin, they do not desire to be lifted out of it by false defences, for their justification consists in a simple and free demand of pardon for their sin' (on Exod. 1.18; *CO* 24.19 = CTS I: 35; cited Thompson 1991: 43). 'What the patriarchs require is far less a rationalization than simple forgiveness' (*ibid.*; cf. the related discussion of Calvin in Zagorin 1990).

Calvin's position here invites extended discussion, but a few comments must suffice. His rigorous biblicism forbids him invoking special divine dispensation for the patriarchs to lie or deceive when the text provides no evidence for it, or resorting to other devices for getting them off the hook that fly in the face of the simple clarity of Scripture. He thus displays a remarkable readiness to read the narratives just as they stand, while agreeing with most earlier and contemporary commentators that the patriarchal misdeeds set no precedent. It is particularly interesting that he seems to make little or no use in this context of any of the forms of accommodation which elsewhere assist him in coming to terms with unpalatable features of the Old Testament.

The recognition of the importance of accommodation in Calvin's theology as well as exegesis goes back less than half a century (Dowey 1952). Its full ramifications and roots still require extensive investigation.[3] Scholars have been too ready to speak of 'the principle of accommodation' (*ibid.* 18; Battles 1977: 19; even Wright 1986: 36), whereas in reality, once we venture beyond the placid waters of the *Institutes* into the vast choppy sea of the commentaries on Scripture, what confronts us is more a handful of practices, whereby Calvin steers perhaps a not always wholly consistent course through the reefs and shallows of the Old Testament in particular. Or it may be, to risk a provisional judgment in advance of further published studies, that we should think in terms of a single hermeneutical tendency that finds expression in different, and at first sight not always compatible, ways.[4]

3. The basic essay is Battles 1977 (which fails to mention Dowey 1952), which is based too exclusively on the *Institutes* and is mistaken in arguing for its roots in classical rhetoric. The forthcoming monograph by S.D. Benin, *The Footprints of God* (New York: SUNY Press, 1993) will throw much light on antecedents. Meanwhile see Benin 1983 and 1984 for some orientation to the literature, and on Calvin see Wright 1986; Parker 1986: 98-101; Baxter 1988; Frye 1990; and Jellema 1980 for examples.

4. Dowey (1952: 3) refers to accommodation as 'the process by which God

In the *Institutes*, Calvin lists five differences between the Old and New Testament, relating not to substance but to mode or form of administration (2.10.1). The second of these depicts the Old Testament era as the childhood of the church. Calvin takes his cue from Paul in Galatians 3.24, 4.1-2, and explains as follows:

> It was fitting that, before the sun of righteousness had arisen, there should be no great and shining revelation, no clear understanding. The Lord, therefore, so meted out the light of his Word to them that they still saw it afar off and darkly. Hence Paul expresses this slenderness of understanding by the word 'childhood'. It was the Lord's will that this childhood be trained in the elements of this world and in little external observances, as rules for children's instruction, until Christ should shine forth, through whom the knowledge of believers was to mature (*Institutes* 2.11.5; McNeill and Battles 1960: I, 455).

The same image, likening the span from Abraham to Christ to a human life, even allows Calvin, prompted this time by Hab. 3.2, to speak of God's people at that time being in mid-life, still to attain to adult maturity (*CO* 43: 566 = CTS IV: 137). The perspective is basic to one of the important contexts for divine accommodation: 'he accommodated diverse forms to diverse ages' (*Institutes* 2.11.13).[5]

Yet little in the *Institutes* prepares the student of Calvin for the not unrelated yet significantly different developmental scale that he frequently uses in the Old Testament commentaries. The dominant metaphor is not childlikeness or childishness, but rawness, primitiveness, crudity, even barbarity, not infancy but hardness of heart. Calvin acknowledges the presence in the Old Testament, especially in the Pentateuch and Joshua (he produced no commentaries on Judges to Job; sermons survive on 1 and 2 Samuel and Job but those on Judges and 1 Kings are lost), of not a little that his contemporaries would call barbaric and that he does not appear to hesitate so to call himself. We are reminded that his first publication was a commentary on Seneca's *De Clementia*, and that he was profoundly shaped by his humanist

---

reduces or adjusts to human capacities what he wills to reveal of the infinite mysteries of his being, which by their very nature are beyond the power of the mind of man to grasp' (cited also by Baxter 1988: 20). I doubt if this is adequate even for Dowey's own further exposition. Battles (1977) avoids a formal definition. Willis (1974: 58) formulates the principle for Calvin, *Humanitas capax divinitatis per accommodationem*.

5. See Parker 1986: 83-90; Battles 1977: 27-29.

education. In Calvin we meet a cultivated son of the renaissance who knew uncivilized rawness when he saw it, even in Scripture. He has different ways of coping with it, not all of which invoke a form of accommodation.

First and foremost, God was personally responsible for barbaric behaviour by his people on some occasions. When the Israelites, on capturing Jericho, destroyed every living thing in it, humans and animals alike (Jos. 6.20), the indiscriminate (*promiscue*) slaughter without distinction of age or sex would have been savagery (*immanis*) had not God instructed it. Although Canaan's putrid obscenities merited purging, if the Israelites had on their own initiative slain tender babies (*foetus*) with their mothers, it would have been a deed of atrocious and barbaric ferocity (*quod atrociter et barbara saevitia factum esset, CO* 25: 469 = CTS: 97). The similar treatment meted out to Achan and all his family and possessions (Josh. 7.24-26) provokes a similar comment from Calvin. It seems harsh, savage and barbaric (*durum, immane, barbarum*) that innocent infants should be thus cruelly executed. 'God even publicly inflicts punishment on children for their parents' offences, contrary to what he declares through Ezekiel'. Although Calvin cannot, of course, accept that any who were innocent were killed, we can but submit in our ignorance to God's incomprehensible wisdom (*CO* 25: 479-80 = CTS: 117).[6]

The ignominious execution of the five Amorite kings (Josh. 10.16-26) evokes parallel comments from Calvin in the light of their royal status. Because they had been elevated *in sacram dignitatem* by God (*divinitus*), it would have been *barbara atrocitas* and monstrous arrogance to trample on their necks and hang them from gibbets without divine command. Again, like the young and old, women and babies massacred in the two earlier incidents, no doubt these kings deserved to die, but on a scale of justice that resided in God's inscrutable counsel and took no need of the humane conventions of warfare (*CO* 25: 502 = CTS: 158).

Calvin expresses himself even more vehemently on Josh. 10.40, 'So Joshua subdued the whole region... He left no survivors. He totally

---

6. Cf. also the discussion of the vengeance threatened on animals, birds and fishes in Zeph. 1.3 at *CO* 44.5-6 = CTS IV: 188-89. The reason why God's impenetrable judgment to extend destruction to them is disclosed to Judah lies in Judah's numbness (*torpeant...vel stupeant potius in sua socordia*) which called for violent disturbance.

destroyed all who breathed, just as the Lord, the God of Israel, had commanded':

> Had Joshua of his own accord raged with indiscriminate fury (*promiscue saeviisset*) against women and children, no excuse could have freed him of execrable savagery (*detestabilis immanitas*), the equal of which we do not read of even among wild tribes living almost like beasts. But what otherwise would horrify everyone they must reverently accept as issuing from God (*CO* 25: 505 = CTS: 163).

And if we judge at least the bairns and most of the womenfolk to be guiltless, 'let us remember that the court of heaven is not one whit subject to our laws'.

The examples we have cited have so far all been taken from the Joshua commentary, which Calvin worked on to the very last days of his life.[7] But we should not imagine that we have encountered only an untypical Calvin, soured by advancing pain and incapacity. In his lectures on Ezekiel, he explains that 'our prophet was not a barbarian (*homo barbarus*), driven by indignation to vomit out coarse reproaches (*atrociter evomeret convicia*) against his people; the Spirit of God dictated what might seem too harsh for tender and sensitive ears'. Though often savage and fierce (*saevi et atroces*) of speech, the prophets breathed pure *humanitatem* at heart (*CO* 40: 71 = CTS I: 122). Or again, in the extermination of the peoples of Palestine decreed in Deut. 20.16-18, 'an exception is made to prevent the Jews applying the common laws of war to the Canaanite nations. God not only armed the Jews to wage war on them but appointed them the agents and executors of his retribution' (*CO* 24: 632 = CTS III: 53-54).

What is remarkable about this last citation is that it follows immediately on an endorsement of the received terms of the 'just war' (with a reference to Cicero), which justifies Calvin in criticizing the 'concession' given to the Israelites in Deut. 20.12-15—to kill all the males without exception in other cities—as 'conferring too great a license'. The passage is worth quoting at length, because it takes us on to the next stage in our argument, in which, far from God shouldering the responsibility for his servants' barbaric actions or words, Calvin

---

7.   French and Latin versions were published—in that order, it seems—soon after Calvin's death by Beza, with his first sketch of Calvin's life. I have used the Latin version, since this is the one included in the *Corpus Reformatorum*. See *CO* 21:5-10; Parker 1986: 32-33.

finds fault with what God commands or allows the Israelites as excessively barbaric.

> Since pagan writers order even the conquered to be spared and teach that those who lay down their arms...should be accepted,...how does God, the Father of mercies, sanction indiscriminate (*promiscuis*) carnage?... More was conceded to the Jews in regard for their hardheartedness than was justly lawful for them. Certainly by the rule of love, even armed men should have been spared if they threw down their swords and craved mercy; at any rate, it was not lawful to kill other than those captured armed with a sword. This authorization to kill extended to all males thus falls far short of perfection. But since in their *ferocia* the Jews would scarcely have tolerated a prescription of unqualified justice, God at least determined to curb their indiscipline from descending to the extremes of cruelty... This much savagery was checked, that they should slay neither women nor children (*CO* 24: 632 = CTS III: 53).

We will return to the question why Calvin differentiated so sharply between parallel commands of God within this single passage in Deuteronomy 20. Meanwhile, further illustration is needed of God's excessive accommodation, in Calvin's judgment, to human barbarity.

After Ai was taken, Joshua hanged the king's body on a tree for a day before casting it down before the city gate (Josh. 8.29). Calvin thinks that Joshua faithfully observed the Mosaic regulation of Deut. 21.23, on which he comments: 'Lest the people become accustomed *ad barbariem*, God allowed criminals to be hanged, provided they did not hang unburied for more than one day'. Nor does Calvin so interpret the verse that Joshua was guilty of savagely (*immane*) exposing the body to be torn by animals and birds (*CO* 25: 487 = CTS: 130). On the other hand, the provision in Num. 35.19, 21, 27 for 'the avenger of blood'—normally a close relative—to execute the murderer outside the cities of refuge 'smacks of barbarity (*barbariem sapere*)'. Indeed, so 'absurd' was this relaxing of the reins for the satisfaction of bloodlust that Calvin doubts if it ever had divine approval. The apparent authorization should really be read as a warning, that unless the innocent are protected, the anger of the relatives of murder victims will be uncontrollable. Calvin wriggles uncomfortably to evacuate this concession to barbarity of its offensiveness (*CO* 24: 639 = CTS III: 64-65).

Calvin took a close interest in the Mosaic legislation concerning slavery. The stipulation in Exod. 21.1-6 (which is separated from its sequel in Calvin's harmony), that, if a Hebrew slave had married and had children during his six years' service, they could not accompany him on his release, revealed the intractability of the Israelites' 'servile condition' (cf. Gal. 4). It could not be regulated *sine prodigio*, 'without this monstrosity'—a word which the next sentence shows that Calvin meant strictly:

> For nothing was more contrary to nature than for a husband to forsake his wife and abandon his children and move elsewhere. But the bond of slavery could be dissolved in no other way than by divorce, that is, by this godless violation of marriage. There was then in this tearing asunder truly gross barbarity.

This perversion has to be counted with the others which God tolerated 'because of the people's callousness, which was almost incorrigible' (*CO* 24: 700-701 = CTS III: 160). When he deals elsewhere with Exod. 21.7-11, Calvin is again reminded 'how many depravities had to be permitted in that people'. For fathers to sell their children to relieve their own poverty was 'utterly barbaric' (*CO* 24: 650 = CTS III: 80-81).

We move on to note more briefly a third category of material, in which Calvin discerns God setting bounds or restraints on Israelite rawness or barbarity. This is how the Joshua commentary views the renewed instruction to appoint cities of refuge (Josh. 20). Unless this remedy had been provided, the kindred of those who were murdered would have doubled the evil by proceeding without discrimination (*promiscue*) to avenge their death (*CO* 25: 545 = CTS: 239). In rather starker terms, Calvin asserts that for the drinking of the blood of a brute beast to be atoned for by the death of a human being was quite incongruous, but such a form of *paedagogiam* (cf. Gal. 3.24) was essential for this *rudi populo*, to prevent them descending *ad barbariem* (Lev. 17.10-14; *CO* 24: 619 = CTS III: 31). And we have already cited Calvin's comment on the law that allows victims of execution to hang unburied until sunset.

Calvin interprets the legislation in Exod. 21.10-21, on a master's violence against slaves, with considerable subtlety. On the one hand, he applauds the absence of discrimination between the penalties for murdering a slave and for murdering a free person. It was savage barbarism (*immanis barbaries*) among the Romans and other nations to grant a slave-owner the power of life and death over slaves. But on the other hand he is troubled by the apparent serious injustice that the master goes unpunished if the slave survives injury for a couple of days; Calvin's Latin translation of the beginning of v. 21 is: ...*si per diem vel duos dies steterit*, literally, 'if he stands for one day or two'. Eventually Calvin satisfies himself that this clause means that the slave was sound and whole in every limb, and that no yawning license for murder with impunity has been opened up (*CO* 24: 624-25 = CTS III: 40-41).

This is not by any means the only place in the commentary on the Mosaic harmony where Calvin's exegesis, normally so respectful of what the text does or does not say, reaches a strained conclusion because to do otherwise would countenance something patently unacceptable. A good example is Exod. 21.22-25, concerning a premature birth resulting from accidental injury to the mother. Calvin's translation, it must be noted, makes death the outcome that may or may not ensue. His problem is that the passage appears to punish only the mother's death, and not that of the *foetus*, 'which would be a great absurdity. For the *foetus* enclosed in its mother's womb is already a human being, and it is quite monstrous (*prodigiosum*) for it to be deprived of the life it has not yet begun to enjoy.' He cannot avoid concluding that the proviso 'if death ensues' must extend to the *foetus* no less than to the mother.

Calvin's dilemma here is not untypical of his response to numerous aspects of the early books of the Old Testament. Too often what he finds is inconsistent with an external objective standard of measurement which he calls 'equity' (*aequitas*), a compound of natural law, the law engraved on the human conscience and 'the law of the nations' (*lex gentium*). The Decalogue is its perfect expression—hence Calvin's embarrassment at discovering features of the 'political laws' of Moses which fall short of 'equity' and even of the law codes of pagan peoples such as Rome. It is in such a context that he repeatedly brings into play the device of God's accommodation to an intractable people. God was unable to enact ceremonial, political and judicial legislation that in every case embodied the perfection of the Decalogue itself. And the reason was the resistance offered by the obstinacy or torpor or blindness of the chosen people (Wright 1986). The *Institutes* censured the 'barbaric and wild laws' of other nations that failed to conform to the perpetual principle of love and were abhorrent to all justice, humanity and peaceableness (*Institutes* 4.20.15). What is missing in the *Institutes*, in its recognition that every nation was free to frame its own 'judicial laws' to give expression to the perfect moral law, is any hint that not all of Israel's laws come up to this standard. For this one needs to turn to the commentaries of Calvin.

Sometimes what is there condemned is unwarrantable leniency, as in Calvin's amusing verdict on Exod. 21.18-19 (*CO* 24: 622-23 = CTS III: 39-40). But normally the concession is in the direction of a materialism or crassness or superstition that respected the limited capacity (*captus*) of Israel to receive the Lord's full demand. As we have seen, Calvin from time to time depicts this interaction as one between God and *barbaries*. (Calvin seems to have no single word to represent the opposite of *barbaries* in his thinking, unless it is *humanitas*.) Sometimes the Mosaic law restricts the scope for barbaric behaviour. On other occasions, as we have seen, God commands or allows something barbaric which Calvin disapproves of. Probably in a majority of cases, often without the language of barbarity being present, a mixture of these last two motifs is at issue. That is to say, God reins in his people's indiscipline or license, but imperfectly, leaving in Calvin's eyes some undesirable concession. A notable instance is his sharp critique of the provision for divorce in Deut. 24.1-4 (*CO* 24: 657-58 = CTS III: 93-94).

At this point we must ask how we should view the vocabulary of barbarity. In particular, is it more than a metaphor? After all, the pope is condemned for *barbaries* in allowing children to marry without parental consent (on Gen. 24.3; *CO* 23: 331 = CTS II: 14), and 'to feel no sadness at the sight of death is more *barbaries* and *stupor* than bravery of spirit' (on Gen. 23.2; *CO* 23: 322 = CTS I: 578). A rhetorical usage is certainly present in Calvin's writings, and the current fashion that fastens on rhetoric as the hermeneutical key to unlock the Calvinian treasure-chest, enabling his theology to be described as 'rhetorical theology' (Bouwsma 1986), may yet cast light on it. Yet it must be *a priori* highly improbable that the humanist education that made Calvin such a consummate scholar left him with a solely metaphorical notion of barbarity.[8]

In any case, internal considerations make it inescapably clear that Calvin was thinking of the *mores* of an uncivilized, primitive people. The Latin term *barbaries* belongs to a group of words that he uses to characterize the religious and moral crudity of Israel. The most

---

8.   In the 1559 *Institutes* alone, the usage of the *barbar-* word-group (now easily surveyed using Wevers 1992) ranges from the polemical (e.g. 4.10.1, 16.10, 20.1) to the strictly historical (4.4.13, 11.16) to what might be called the socio-cultural (e.g. 2.10.11, 3.4.24, 4.20.15).

prominent is *rudis* (and *rudimenta*) and *crassus* is also common, while the comment of Jesus on divorce provides *durities*, 'hardness', and cognates. We have noted some other terms earlier in this chapter. Without attempting to be exhaustive, I should mention Calvin's fondness for words that express insensitivity, unresponsiveness, thickness, such as *stupor, torpor, socordia, hebetudo,* and the related emphasis on obstinacy and contumacy.

There is, of course, some overlap with the language of infancy, through *puerilitas* in particular, but also inevitably with *rudimenta* and *elementa*. But it is unmistakable that Calvin's language in portraying the intractability, recalcitrance and sheer rawness of Israel goes well beyond what 'the infancy of the church' would lead us to expect. The human condition to which divine limitation corresponds quite often in the Old Testament commentaries is worse than restricted capacity (for milk only, not meat; cf. 1 Cor. 3.2), elementary mentality, ignorance, fickleness, even stubbornness—which are all predicable of the child. To the images of the human being highlighted by Battles—child, schoolboy, invalid, frail creature (Battles 1977: 20, 27-32)—we must add the brute, the primitive, the savage. This will correct the imbalance in the direction of recipient passivity that has tended to distort presentations of God's '...Accommodating Himself to Human Capacity' (Battles 1977). Above all we must avoid any cross-contamination of the concept of the church's Israelite infancy by the language of the nurse's baby-talk (*balbutio*) used by Calvin and others before him in this context (*Institutes* 1.13.1; *OS* III: 109).[9]

What a concentration on depictions of human grossness and barbarity brings into sharp focus is the resistant nature of the human material God had to work with. To the fore here is not the finite creature but the perverse sinner—variously pig-headed, leadenly sluggish, aggressive, rapacious, pertinaciously obtuse, almost unmanageable. Thompson concludes his survey with the verdict that 'Calvin's judgments of all the patriarchal misdeeds studied are significantly harsher than those of his predecessors and contemporaries' (Thompson 1991: 40). When the revealing and teaching God tempers (*attempero*) himself to this humanity, the result, as we have seen, is sometimes a wrong, rather than a partial or imperfect, portrayal of his will.

9.   Cf. Erasmus, *Enchiridion militis christiani: Balbutit nobis divina sapientia et veluti mater quaepiam officiosa ad nostram infantiam voces accommodat. Lac porrigit infantulis in Christo, holus infirmis* (ed. Holborn 1933: 34).

There remains the question we deferred earlier: how did Calvin discriminate between the barbarity decreed by God of which he approved (e.g. the extermination of the Palestinian tribes) and the barbarity likewise decreed by God of which he disapproved? We saw above that the distinction is neatly encapsulated in his contrasting treatment of Deut. 20.12-15 and 16-17. The subject here is the application or suspension of the standard rules for the just war, in which Calvin showed repeated interest. Certainly the answer is not to be found in the presence or absence of explicit textual indications of the divine will; Calvin makes no attempt to fudge the issue that in Deut. 20.12-15 it is 'God, the Father of mercies' who 'gives his sanction to indiscriminate slaughter'. The application of the scriptural criterion so evident in his assessments of the patriarchs' misdemeanours will not suffice here (Thompson 1991: 44-45). The one qualification that might be made to this is the manner in which Calvin generalizes from Mt. 19.8, 'Jesus replied, "Moses permitted you to divorce your wives because your hearts were hard"'. Since nothing in Deut. 24.1-4 itself tells Calvin that 'divorce was never lawful' but only the words of the Gospel (*CO* 24: 657 = CTS III: 93), what was to prevent him citing 'hardness of heart' elsewhere as a divining rod to detect a hidden will of God? In his comment on Deuteronomy 24 he cites the legal tag, 'nature's bonds are indissoluble (*iura naturae insolubilia*)', which reminds us also of the influential role played by his concept of equity in identifying actions or legislation that fell short of God's perfection. But Calvin apparently never asked how God's people were to escape from barbarity when God himself directly ordered 'deeds of atrocious and barbaric ferocity'.[10]

The eighth edition of the *Encyclopaedia Britannica* contains a warm appreciation of Calvin's corpus of biblical exposition:

> In the estimation of many, these constitute the most valuable of his works. His candour and sincerity as an inquirer into the meaning of Scripture—his judiciousness, penetration, and tact in eliciting his author's meaning—his precision, condensation and concinnity as an expositor—the accuracy of his learning, the closeness of his reasoning, and the

---

10. There appear to be greater formal similarities on accommodation between Calvin and later Genevan theologians than Klauber and Sunshine (1990) allow, whatever may be said of actual influence.

elegance of his style, all conspire to confer a high value on his exegetical works, and to make them at once rich sources of biblical knowledge and admirable models of biblical exposition (*EB* [1853–60], VI, 111).

This came from the pen of the versatile William Lindsay Alexander (1808–84), for over forty years the learned and eloquent pastor of the congregation that from 1861 met in Augustine Church, Edinburgh (which got its name from his frequent quotations of St Augustine and where he introduced an organ as early as 1863), tutor in the Scottish Congregational theological hall from 1856 and its principal 1877–82, and in his day 'perhaps the most prominent figure in the Scottish ministry...outside Presbyterianism' (Escott 1960: 136). It may have been during his labours as one of the Revisers of the Old Testament of the English Bible that he conceived such a high estimate of Calvin's exegesis.

But his article did not please everyone,[11] although the passage survived intact (through the ninth edition co-edited by William Robertson Smith)[12] until the eleventh edition, when it was revised by Alexander James Grieve (1874–1952), also destined to be an eminent Congregationalist. He was A.S. Peake's assistant on his famous Bible commentary, and, like Alexander, Principal of the Scottish Congregational College (1917–21; for his last two years he also taught church history in Edinburgh University). Grieve's revision topped and tailed Alexander's eulogy given above, cooling its ardour (but retaining 'concinnity'!), and added at the outset, 'Though naturally knowing nothing of the modern idea of a progressive revelation...' (*EB* [1910–11], V, 75).[13]

Pity Calvin, to live in such a benighted era! Yet in view of the fresh

---

11. The Unitarian John Gordon circularized *A Letter to the Subscribers to the Eighth Edition...* (London: E.T. Whitfield, 1854), criticizing it and another article by Alexander. Alexander was the occasion of another open letter, *...on the Question of Cooperation with Dissenters...*, addressed in 1843 to Thomas Chalmers and Thomas Guthrie by Peter Hateley Waddell, translator of *The Psalms: frae Hebrew intil Scottis* (Edinburgh: J. Menzies, 1871, repr. Aberdeen University Press in 1987), editor of the Waverley novels, ecclesiastical gipsy and founder of 'the Church of the Future' at Girvan. The biography of Alexander by James Ross (London: James Nisbet, 1877) mentions neither of these letters.

12. Worth noting in this context is McKane's suggestion that the title of Smith's *The Old Testament in the Jewish Church* reflects the influence of Calvin's common practice of calling God's people in Israel 'the church' (McKane 1984: 254).

13. I owe my knowledge of this to Woudstra (1986: 153-54 n. 8).

light that has since shone on his writings, he deserves greater credit than Grieve implies, both for historical perspectives that, long before post-Darwinian notions of 'progressive revelation', gave remarkable weight to cultural, social and religious development in Israel, and for theological perspectives that did not discriminate against earlier ages as the recipients of only a partial self-disclosure by God. Calvin's flexible, self-adapting God did not reveal himself in escalating stages, but was ever giving himself wholly as far as the people could bear.

BIBLIOGRAPHY

Battles, F.L.
    1977   'God was Accommodating Himself to Human Capacity', *Int* 31: 19-38.
Baxter, A.G.
    1988   'What did Calvin Teach about Accommodation?', *Evangel* 6.1: 20-22.
Benin, S.D.
    1983   'Sacrifice as Education in Augustine and Chrysostom', *CH* 52: 7-20.
    1984   'The "Cunning of God" and Divine Accommodation', *Journal of the History of Ideas* 45: 179-91.
Bouwsma, W.J. *et al.*
    1986   *Calvinism as Theologia Rhetorica* (Protocol of the Fifty-Fourth Colloquy, Center for Hermeneutical Studies, University of California at Berkeley, CA).
Dowey, E.A.
    1952   *The Knowledge of God in Calvin's Theology* (New York: Columbia University Press).
Escott, H.
    1960   *A History of Scottish Congregationalism* (Glasgow: Congregational Union of Scotland).
Frye, R.M.
    1990   'Calvin's Theological Use of Figurative Language', in T. George (ed.), *John Calvin and the Church* (Louisville, KY: Westminster–John Knox Press): 172-94.
Holborn, H. (ed.)
    1933   *Desiderius Erasmus Ausgewählte Werke* (Munich: Beck).
Jellema, D.W.
    1980   'God's "Baby-talk": Calvin and the "Errors" in the Bible', *Reformed Journal* 30.4: 25-27.
Klauber, M.I. and G.S. Sunshine
    1990   'Jean-Alphonse Turrettini on Biblical Accommodation: Calvinist or Socinian?', *CTJ* 25: 7-27.
Kraeling, E.G.
    1955   *The Old Testament since the Reformation* (London: Lutterworth).

Kraus, H.-J.
1982   *Geschichte der historisch-kritischen Erforschung der Alten
            Testaments* (Neukirchen–Vluyn: Neukirchener Verlag, 3rd edn).
McKane, W.
1984   'Calvin as an Old Testament Commentator', *Ned Geref Teologiese
            Tydskrif* 25: 250-59.
McNeill, J.T. (ed.) and F.L. Battles (trans.)
1960   *Calvin: Institutes of the Christian Religion* (2 vols.; LCC, 20–21;
            London: SCM Press; Philadelphia: Westminster Press).
Parker, T.H.L.
1986   *Calvin's Old Testament Commentaries* (Edinburgh: T. & T. Clark).
1992   *Calvin's Preaching* (Edinburgh: T. & T. Clark).
Thompson, J.L.
1991   'The Immoralities of the Patriarchs in the History of Exegesis: A
            Reappraisal of Calvin's Position', *CTJ* 26: 9-46.
Wevers, R.F.
1992   *A Concordance to Calvin's Institutio 1559* (6 vols.; Grand Rapids:
            Digamma Publishers).
Willis, E.D.
1974   'Rhetoric and Responsibility in Calvin's Theology', in A.J. McKelway
            and E.D. Willis (eds.), *The Context of Contemporary Theology: Essays
            in Honor of Paul Lehmann* (Atlanta: John Knox): 43-63.
Woudstra, M.H.
1986   'Calvin Interprets What "Moses Reports": Observations on Calvin's
            Commentary on Exodus 1–19', *CTJ* 21: 151-74.
Wright, D.F.
1983   'The Ethical Use of the Old Testament in Luther and Calvin: A
            Comparison', *SJT* 36: 463-85.
1986   'Calvin's Pentateuchal Criticism: Equity, Hardness of Heart, and
            Divine Accommodation in the Mosaic Harmony Commentary', *CTJ*
            21: 33-50.
Zagorin, P.
1990   *Ways of Lying: Dissimulation, Persecution and Conformity in Early
            Modern Europe* (Cambridge, MA: Harvard University Press).

INDEXES

INDEX OF REFERENCES

OLD TESTAMENT

40.22	201	52.5	117	3.15-18	97, 109
40.23	201	52.12	406	4.3–6.30	97
40.26	200	52.13–53.12	119, 308	4.3	97
40.28	200	52.14	354	4.5	97
40.30	200	53	359	4.11	97
40.31	200	53.6	146	5.1	97
41.19	402-404,	53.11	308	5.18-19	93
	408	54.1	117	5.20	97
41.20	202, 402	54.16	199, 202,	5.22	239
41.21	202		207	6.1	311
41.29	201	57.18-19	204	6.30	97
42.5	200	57.18	204	7.1–10.25	98
42.6	200	57.19	204	7.1–10.16	98, 99
42.8	200, 202	57.21	204	7.1-15	98, 109
42.9	200	60.13	402, 408	7.1	93
42.10	200	62.12	309	7.4	99
42.24	202	63.1-6	309	7.8-11	99
43.1-7	201	63.4	309	7.14	99
43.7	202	65	119	7.16-26	98
43.14	202	65.1-3	119	7.30-34	98, 99
43.15	202	65.17	203, 206	8.23	298
44.6	202	65.17-18	203	9.9	295
44.9	201	65.18	203	9.12-16	93
44.13	201	65.19-25	203	10.10-16	98
44.14	403	65.25	408	10.12-16	98
44.16	311	66.24	117	10.13	143
44.20	404			10.17-25	99
44.21	404	*Jeremiah*		11–20	99, 101-103
45.6-8	201	1–25	94-96, 101,	11.1-8	99, 102, 109
45.7	201, 202		103, 106-11	11.1	93
45.12	202	1–52	111	11.10	100
45.18-19	200	1.1-19	95	11.14-15	100
45.18	201	1.1-3	93	11.18-20	100
45.19	201	1.14-19	96	11.21-23	100
45.23	119	1.17-19	96	12.7-12	298
47.14	201, 311	2.1	93, 97	14.3	128
48.3	203	2.1–4.2	97	14.12	177
48.6-7	203	2.1–3.5	96	15.1	101
48.11	202	2.2	96	15.1-4	100
49.4	201	3.1-40	121	15.10-18	298
49.24	405	3.1	93, 298	15.15-21	100
49.25	405	3.6-12	109	17.14-18	100
50	119	3.6-11	96	18.19-23	100
50.11	311	3.6	96	20.7-18	298
51.2	143	3.10-11	97	20.7-12	101
51.9	206, 239	3.10	96	20.14-18	101
52–53	358	3.11	96	21.1–24.10	103, 105
52.2	118	3.12–4.2	96	21.1-10	103, 104, 109

NEW TESTAMENT

JOURNAL FOR THE STUDY OF THE OLD TESTAMENT

Supplement Series